THE LIBRARY OF THE JEWISH PEOPLE

AMY LEVY

COLLECTED WRITINGS

EDITOR, LUKE DEVINE

Amy Levy
Collected Writings

First Edition, 2023

The Library of the Jewish People

POB 8531, New Milford, CT 06776-8531, USA
& POB 4044, Jerusalem 9104001, Israel
www.ljp.pub

ISBN 978-1-61329-212-9, *hardcover*

Printed and bound in the PRC

Contents

Publisher's Preface

Our death is in the cool of night, our life is in the pool of day.
The darkness glows, I'm drowning, the day has tired me with light.

Over my head in leaves grown deep, sings the young nightingale.
It only sings of love there, I hear it in my sleep.
Heinrich Heine

As an accomplished novelist, poet, essayist, and translator, Amy Levy was a remarkable person. A New Woman of the Victorian period, she was steeped in and struggled with her Jewish tradition, rejected and reclaimed it, the first Jewess to study at Newnham College, Cambridge University. In putting to paper the tensions she experienced, Levy not only enriched us with the genius of her literature but also foreshadowed those of our own day, and while she left this world all too young – depriving us of much more she had to say – her voice should continue to reverberate. Her remaining writings fill this volume, offering us the opportunity to appreciate what she has given us.

A first and monumental collection, edited by Professor Melvyn New, was published almost thirty years ago. Since then, major research has uncovered many additional works and added new perspectives. We thank the editor of this volume, Dr. Luke Devine of the University of Worcester, for his research and introduction, and the new and sensitive insights he brings to *Amy Levy: Collected Writings*, which is among the first volumes in the new *Library of the Jewish People*.

We also thank Uri Bollag, our Managing Editor; Tani Bayer for designing the covers; Tomi Mager for creating the typography; and Rachel Bernstein for editing the works. Furthermore, we appreciate the kind cooperation of Kayla Beth Moore at the University Press of Florida in the matter of rights.

We hope that this volume will awaken new interest and appreciation of this remarkable and overlooked British Jewish writer.

Matthew Miller, Publisher
Library of the Jewish People
2023

Timeline

	Amy Levy	Jewish Context	Global Context
1861	Amy Judith Levy is born in Clapham, London, on 10 November.		Death of Prince Albert, husband of Queen Victoria, who reigned from 1837–1901.
1862			
1863		Avraham Dov Ber Lebensohn publishes second edition of poetry collection, *Shiray Sefat Kodesh*, which is seminal in the context of Hebrew revivalism.	Abraham Lincoln, President of the United States, issues proclamation of emancipation leading to Thirteenth Amendment (1865) and abolition of slavery.
1864		Birth of Anglo-Jewish author, Israel Zangwill. Mendele Moykher Seforim, pseudonym of bilingual (Hebrew/Yiddish) Shalom Ya'akov Abramovitsch, publishes *Dos Kleyne Mentshele*, or *The Little Man*, establishing influential tradition of Yiddish literature.	
1865		Birth of Abraham Isaac Kook, who would later become the first Chief Rabbi (Ashkenazi) for the British Mandate in Palestine.	End of American Civil War (began 1861). Assassination of Abraham Lincoln.
1866			Austro-Prussian War. Algernon Charles Swinburne publishes *Poems and Ballads*.
1867			Publication of Karl Marx's *Das Kapital*.
1868			Benjamin Disraeli, baptised in his youth, begins his first term as Prime Minister. First Trades Union Congress.
1869			Opening of the Suez Canal. Matthew Arnold publishes *Culture and Anarchy*. John Stuart Mill publishes *The Subjection of Women*.

	Amy Levy	Jewish Context	Global Context
1870		Establishment of the United Synagogue. Establishment of West London Reform Synagogue in Upper Berkeley Street.	Franco-Prussian War (to early 1871).
1871		Constitution of the German Empire enshrines legal and political emancipation of German-Jews. In the United Kingdom, political emancipation was granted with the Jews Relief Act of 1858, allowing the already elected Lionel de Rothschild to legally take his seat in Parliament. University Tests Act allows Anglo-Jews admission to universities.	Unification of Germany. Publication of Charles Darwin's *The Descent of Man* (follow up to *Origin of Species*, published in 1857). Paris Commune. Founding of Newnham College at Cambridge University.
1873		Birth of Hayim Nahman Bialik, architect of modern Hebrew poetry and posthumously the national poet of Israel. Stock market crash impels periodic rise of antisemitism in Vienna.	
1874		Death of Abraham Geiger, pioneer of Reform Judaism in Germany. Birth of Chaim Weizmann, later president of the Zionist Organisation and of Israel (1949–1952).	Benjamin Disraeli, Prime Minister, 1874–1880 (second term). James Thomson publishes "The City of Dreadful Night."
1875	Levy's first publication, "The Ballad of Ida Grey." Levy wins the "Junior Prize" for her short essay on *Aurora Leigh* by Elizabeth Barrett Browning.		
1876	Levy publishes a short essay on biblical David. Levy begins at Brighton High School for Girls.		George Eliot publishes *Daniel Deronda.*
1877			Queen Victoria assumes the title, Empress of India.
1878		Adolf Stoecker establishes antisemitic Christian Social Workers' Party in Germany. Richard Wagner publishes completed version of the antisemitic essay, "What is German?"	Congress of Berlin.
1879	Levy becomes a student (until 1881) at Newnham College, Cambridge University. Two of Levy's letters, titled "Jewish Women and 'Women's Rights,'" are published in *The Jewish Chronicle.*	Wilhelm Marr, founder of the League of Antisemites, publishes *The Victory of Judaism over Germanism.* German historian, Heinrich von Treitschke, states: "The Jews are our misfortune!"	Anglo-Zulu War.

	Amy Levy	Jewish Context	Global Context
1880	Levy travels between her family's London home and Europe, in particular Germany, Italy, and Switzerland, throughout the 1880s.		First Boer War (to 1881).
1881	*Xantippe and Other Verse* is published, including Levy's poem "A Prayer," which reappropriates Jesus in his Jewish context.	Theodor Herzl, architect of political Zionism and founder of the Zionist Organisation, becomes correspondent for the *Neue Freie Presse* in Paris, where he will later cover the infamous Dreyfus Affair. Following the assassination of Alexander II, antisemitic pogroms in Russian Empire lead to migration of Russian-Jews to Western Europe and the United States. Beginning of First Aliyah.	
1882	Levy's first published translation of Heinrich Heine's poetry, "From Heine."	Antisemitic May Laws enacted in Russian Empire by Alexander III.	Establishment of Triple Alliance. Friedrich Nietzsche proclaims "God is dead" in *The Gay Science.*
1883	Levy's letter on "Paul Heyse" is published in *The Jewish Chronicle.*	Establishment of Hovevei Zion.	Social Darwinist, Francis Galton, coins the term, "eugenics."
1884	*A Minor Poet and Other Verse* is published, including Levy's poem "Magdalen," which deconstructs Jesus' appropriation for Christian tradition through Mary Magdalene's avowal of Judaism and rejection of Christian supersessionism.		Berlin Conference (to 1885).
1885	Levy's poem "Captivity," which draws on themes associated with diasporic medieval Hebrew poetry, is published in *The Cambridge Review.*		
1886	Five of Levy's essays are published in *The Jewish Chronicle*: "The Ghetto at Florence," "The Jew in Fiction," "Jewish Humour," "Middle-Class Jewish Women of To-Day," and "Jewish Children."	Naftali Imber's "Hatikvah," which would later become the national anthem of Israel, is published. Birth of David Ben-Gurion, who would later become the first Prime Minister of Israel.	Eleanor Marx and Edward Aveling publish *The Woman Question.* Sigmund Freud, pioneer of psychoanalysis, establishes private practice in Vienna.

	Amy Levy	Jewish Context	Global Context
1888	*The Romance of a Shop* and *Reuben Sachs: A Sketch* are published. Katie Magnus' *Jewish Portraits* is published, including Levy's translations of Yehuda Halevi (from Abraham Geiger's German versions).		Murders attributed to "Jack the Ripper" in Whitechapel, London.
1889	*A London Plane-Tree and Other Verse* is published, including the poem "Borderland," which draws on Heinrich Heine to rethink the symbolism and allegorical implications of the biblical Song of Songs.		
	Miss Meredith is published.		
	Levy commits suicide on 10 September; she is cremated and her ashes are buried at Balls Pond Road Cemetery (West London Synagogue).		

Chronology of Writings by Amy Levy

Texts included in this collection; * indicates text not included in Melvyn New's *The Complete Novels*

1875

"The Ballad of Ida Grey (A Story of Woman's Sacrifice): Part I." *The Pelican: A Quarterly Magazine Advocating the Social and Educational Progress of Woman* 2, no. 5 (January-April 1875): 20–1; "Part II." Reprinted with permission of The Camellia Collections.*

"Junior Prize Review: Aurora Leigh." *Kind Words for Boys and Girls*, October 1, 1875, 318.*

"Original Definitions: Heroism." *Kind Words for Boys and Girls*, December 1, 1875, 27.*

1876

"Junior Prize Essay." *Kind Words for Boys and Girls*, October 1, 1876, 292.*

"Definitions." *Kind Words for Boys and Girls*, December 1, 1876, 51.*

1879

"Jewish Women and 'Women's Rights.'" *The Jewish Chronicle*, February 7, 1879, 5; February 28, 1879, 5.*

"Run to Death." *The Victoria Magazine* 33 (May-October 1879): 248–50.

1880

"Xantippe: A Fragment." *The University Magazine* 5, no. 29 (May 1880): 592–7.

"Mrs. Pierrepoint: A Sketch in Two Parts." *Temple Bar: A London Magazine for Town and Country Readers* 59 (June 1880): 226–36.*

"The Shepherd (From Goethe)." *The Cambridge Review: A Journal of University Life and Thought* 1, no. 26 (June 9, 1880): 158.*

"Euphemia: A Sketch." *The Victoria Magazine* 36 (August-September 1880): 129–41, 199–203.*

1881

Xantippe and Other Verse. Cambridge: E. Johnson, 1881.[1]

"Newnham College." Reprinted with permission of The Camellia Collections.*

1882

"From Grillparzer's Sappho." *The Cambridge Review: A Journal of University Life and Thought* 3, no. 59 (February 1, 1882): 141.*

"From Heine." *The Cambridge Review: A Journal of University Life and Thought* 3, no. 67 (April 26, 1882): 270.*

1883

"James Thomson: A Minor Poet." *The Cambridge Review: A Journal of University Life and Thought* 4, no. 89 (February 21, 1883): 240–1; 4, no. 90 (February 28, 1883): 257–8.

---

1. Includes the following additions since New's *The Complete Novels*: "Ralph to Mary" and "Translated from Geibel."

"A Ballad of Last Seeing." *The Cambridge Review: A Journal of University Life and Thought* 4, no. 95 (May 2, 1883): 337.*

"The Diary of a Plain Girl." *London Society: An Illustrated Magazine of Light and Amusing Literature for the Hours of Relaxation* 44, no. 261 (September 1883): 295–304.*

"Paul Heyse." *The Jewish Chronicle*, October 12, 1883, 4.*

"Between Two Stools." *Temple Bar: A London Magazine for Town and Country Readers* 69 (November 1883): 337–50.

1884

A Minor Poet and Other Verse. 1884; rpt. London: T. Fisher Unwin, 1891.[2]

"Olga's Valentine." *London Society: An Illustrated Magazine of Light and Amusing Literature for the Hours of Relaxation* 45, no. 266 (February 1884): 152–7.*

"Sokratics in the Strand." *The Cambridge Review: A Journal of University Life and Thought* 5, no. 113 (February 6, 1884): 163–4.

"The New School of American Fiction." *Temple Bar: A London Magazine for Town and Country Readers* 70 (March 1884): 383–9.

"Mariana in the Ballroom." *London Society: An Illustrated Magazine of Light and Amusing Literature for the Hours of Relaxation* 45, "The Holiday Number for 1884" (1884): 76.*

"In Switzerland." *London Society: An Illustrated Magazine of Light and Amusing Literature for the Hours of Relaxation* 46, no. 271 (July 1884): 120.*

"In Holiday Humour." *London Society: An Illustrated Magazine of Light and Amusing Literature for the Hours of Relaxation* 46, no. 272 (August 1884): 177–84.*

"In Retreat." *London Society: An Illustrated Magazine of Light and Amusing Literature for the Hours of Relaxation* 46, no. 273 (September 1884): 332–5.*

2. Includes the following additions since New's *The Complete Novels*: "Medea," "To Sylvia," "A Greek Girl," "Christopher Found," "A Dirge," "A June Tide Echo," "In a Minor Key," "A Cross Road Epitaph."

"In the Black Forest." *London Society: An Illustrated Magazine of Light and Amusing Literature for the Hours of Relaxation* 46, no. 274 (October 1884): 392–4.*

1885

"Revenge." *London Society: An Illustrated Magazine of Light and Amusing Literature for the Hours of Relaxation* 47, no. 280 (April 1885): 389–99.*

"Easter-Tide at Tunbridge Wells." *London Society: An Illustrated Magazine of Light and Amusing Literature for the Hours of Relaxation* 47, no. 281 (May 1885): 481–3.*

1886

"Out of the World." *London Society: An Illustrated Magazine of Light and Amusing Literature for the Hours of Relaxation* 49, no. 289 (January 1886): 53–6.*

"After Heine." *The Cambridge Review: A Journal of University Life and Thought* 7, no. 169 (February 24, 1886): 237–8.*

"The Ghetto at Florence." *The Jewish Chronicle*, March 26, 1886, 9.

"Another Morning in Florence." *London Society: An Illustrated Magazine of Light and Amusing Literature for the Hours of Relaxation* 49, no. 292 (April 1886): 386–90.*

"The Jew in Fiction." *The Jewish Chronicle*, June 4, 1886, 13.*

"Lost and Won." *Lawn-Tennis* (August 4, 1886): 152–3. Reprinted with permission of The Camellia Collections.*

"Jewish Humour." *The Jewish Chronicle*, August 20, 1886, 9–10.

"A Meadowshire Romance: In Five Chapters." *Lawn-Tennis* (August 18; August 25; September 1; September 8, 1886): 176–7; 186–8; 202–3; 214–5. Reprinted with permission of The Camellia Collections.*

"Middle-Class Jewish Women of Today." *The Jewish Chronicle*, September 17, 1886, 7.

"Jewish Children." *The Jewish Chronicle*, November 5, 1886, 8.

1888

Reuben Sachs: A Sketch. London: Macmillan and Co., 1888.

The Romance of a Shop. 1888; rpt. Boston: Cupples and Hurd, 1889.

Translations of Jehudah Halevi in Katie Magnus, *Jewish Portraits*. London: T. Fisher Unwin, 1888, 15–6, 24–5, 30.[3]

Translation of Heinrich Heine in Katie Magnus, *Jewish Portraits*. London: T. Fisher Unwin, 1888, 73.*

"Rondel." *Pall Mall Gazette*, February 24, 1888, 13.*

"At Prato." *Time* 19, no. 43 (July 1888): 68–74.*

"Griselda." *Temple Bar: A London Magazine for Town and Country Readers* 84, no. 334 (September 1888): 65–6.

"The Recent Telepathic Occurrence at the British Museum." *The Woman's World* 1 (1888): 31–2.

"The Poetry of Christina Rossetti." *The Woman's World* 1 (1888): 178–80.*

"Women and Club Life." *The Woman's World* 1 (1888): 364–7.

1889

A London Plane-Tree and Other Verse. London: T. Fisher Unwin, 1889.[4]

Miss Meredith. London: Hodder and Stoughton, 1889.

"Addenbrooke." *Belgravia: A London Magazine* 68, no. 269 (March 1889): 24–34.*

"Readers at the British Museum." *Atalanta* 2, no. 7 (April 1, 1889): 449–54.*

"Cohen of Trinity." *The Gentleman's Magazine* 266, no. 1901 (May 1889): 417–24.

---

3. Includes an additional three new translations since New's *The Complete Novels*.
4. Includes the following additions since New's *The Complete Novels*: "To Clementina Black," "A March Day in London," "Straw in the Street," "Between the Showers," "The Village Garden," "New Love, New Life," "Impotens," "Youth and Love," "The Dream," "In the Night," "Last Words," "June," "Contradictions," "Twilight," "Captivity," "The Two Terrors," "The Promise of Sleep," "The Lost Friend," "The Old Poet," "On the Wye in May," "The End of the Day."

"A Slip of the Pen." *Temple Bar: A London Magazine for Town and Country Readers* 86, no. 344 (July 1889): 371–7.

"Eldorado at Islington." *The Woman's World* 2 (1889): 488–9.*

1890

"Wise in Her Generation." *The Woman's World* 3 (1890): 20–3.

1915

"A Ballad of Religion and Marriage" (1915). Circulated privately by Clement Shorter.

Introduction

Amy Levy and the "Jewish Literary Complex"

Dr. Luke Devine

Since the publication of Melvyn New's *Complete Novels and Selected Writings of Amy Levy* in 1993, Amy Levy (1861–1889) scholarship has flourished, although outside academia Levy will still be unfamiliar to most readers.[1] New introduced scholars to a diverse range of texts, including novels, short fiction, poetry, and essays that had not yet been subjected to scholarly analysis or made accessible to the wider public. For many years, New's collection, as well as Linda Hunt Beckman's pathbreaking biography, *Amy Levy: Her Life and Letters*, 2000, were the standard texts for scholars interested in Levy. Beyond scholarly research, however, little has really changed since Beth Zion Lask in the

1. Melvyn New, ed., "Introduction," in *The Complete Novels and Selected Writings of Amy Levy, 1861–1889* (Gainesville: University Press of Florida, 1993), 2; Linda Hunt Beckman, *Amy Levy: Her Life and Letters* (Athens: Ohio University Press, 2000), xi.

late 1920s pointed to "a much-neglected Jewess."[2] In fact, even with the weight of scholarship that has come since these groundbreaking texts, Levy's life and works, and in particular her Jewish identity and place in what Dan Miron has called a "Jewish literary complex," still remain obscure.[3] Moreover, readers might justifiably question what makes Levy's writing characteristically *Jewish* when so many of her texts are seemingly unrelated to Jewish history, tradition, and the Anglo-Jewish communities of the *fin de siècle*? And when Levy's own Jewish identity and the extent of her engagement with the communal, religious, and spiritual aspects of Anglo-Jewish life are still contested? These are not easy questions to answer. However, as this introduction makes clear, Levy might have written in English and mostly for English (Christian) audiences, and on seemingly non-Jewish themes more than she did directly on Anglo-Jewish communal politics. Nevertheless, the Levy corpus speaks to a complex and hybrid tradition of *Jewish* literature. It is a literature characteristic of modernity, expressed in national languages beyond Hebrew and Yiddish, written from a minoritized perspective confronting the challenges brought into being by the *Haskalah*, legal and political emancipation, the rise of romantic and political Zionisms, reform and liberal Judaisms, and the nineteenth-century context of nationalism and imperialism, Darwinism and social Darwinism (eugenics), and pervasive antisemitism.[4] Levy's place in a diverse "Jewish literary complex" is a reflection of how, to use Miron's words again, she experienced "*Judesein*" (Jewishness) and "being Jewish."[5] Accordingly, this new collection, which includes over sixty new texts, continues the process of piecing together and further understanding Levy's biography, corpus, and intricate relationship with Jewish history, tradition, and communal politics. In doing so,

2. Beth Zion Lask, "Amy Levy," *Transactions of the Jewish Historical Society of England* 11 (1928): 168.
3. Dan Miron, *From Continuity to Contiguity: Toward a New Jewish Literary Thinking* (Stanford: Stanford University Press, 2010), 8.
4. See Miron, *From Continuity to Contiguity*, 6–8, 10, 39, 58, 133, 188, 206, 247, 270.
5. Miron, *From Continuity to Contiguity*, 9, 88, 270, 275, 404–5, 474.

this new edition of Levy's *Collected Writings* places her biography and corpus firmly within the "Jewish literary complex," analysing her writing in the context of its inflection by her own sense of *Judesein* and what this meant navigating hegemonic Christian and nationalistic social, political, and literary cultures.

When writing the introduction to the 1993 collection, New was mostly reliant on Zion Lask's 1928 paper, identifying it as the most comprehensive account of Levy's life currently available.[6] More recent scholarship has proffered a rich and diverse range of readings on Levy's life and writings.[7] What is clear in these interpretations is that Levy was a complex, unconventional intellectual and, for Cynthia Scheinberg, "a true child of Anglo-Jewish emancipation."[8] Levy's biography has been read as embodying multiple identity positions that resist any single account of her life.[9] Readers of Levy's texts and associated scholarship will have come across an author who at one time or another has been identified in a diverse array of religious, secular, political, feminist, literary, and cultural contexts.[10] The one

6. New, "Introduction," 4.
7. See Naomi Hetherington and Nadia Valman, eds., *Amy Levy: Critical Essays* (Athens: Ohio University Press, 2010).
8. Cynthia Scheinberg, "'And We Are Not What They Have Been': Anglo-Jewish Women Poets, 1839–1923," in *Jewish Women Writers in Britain*, ed. Nadia Valman (Detroit: Wayne State University Press, 2014), 44.
9. Naomi Hetherington and Nadia Valman, eds., "Introduction," in *Amy Levy*, 2–3.
10. On Levy as "postreligious" see Hetherington and Valman, "Introduction," 18; on Levy in different political contexts see Hunt Beckman, *Amy Levy*, 5; for Levy's feminist/New Woman politics see Ana Parejo Vadillo, "New Woman Poets and the Culture of the *Salon* at the *Fin de Siècle*," *Women: A Cultural Review* 10, no. 1 (1999): 28; on Levy's sexuality see Hetherington and Valman, "Introduction," 2; Hunt Beckman, *Amy Levy*, 87–91; Kate Thomas, "Lesbian Postmortem at the Fin de Siècle," in *The Cambridge Companion to Lesbian Literature*, ed. Jodie Medd (Cambridge: Cambridge University Press, 2015), 122; Alex Goody, "Passing in the City: The Liminal Spaces of Amy Levy's Late Work," in *Amy Levy*, eds. Hetherington and Valman, 168–9; Christine Pullen, *The Woman Who Dared: A Biography of Amy Levy* (Kingston Upon Thames: Kingston University Press, 2010), 91. On Levy as a marginalised and excluded literary figure, see Joseph Bristow, "'All Out of Tune in This World's Instrument': the 'Minor' Poetry of

constant for Levy, however, was her awareness that as a *Jewish* author, criticism would always be contextualised according to racialising and antisemitic constructions of Jewishness prevalent in the late-Victorian period.[11] Defining the latter, Levy's Jewish identity, and the extent of Levy's engagement with Jewish texts, traditions, and religion, has been the subject of considerable and diverse debate among scholars. Scholarly literature puts Levy in an existential struggle between the conflicting identity categories of Anglo-Jewish identity, feminist politics, and hegemonic Christian literary culture. However, as several scholars have pointed out, Levy's biography is much more complex.[12] Levy was born in 1861 in Clapham, London, to an assimilated middle-class Anglo-Jewish family. As was often the norm for acculturated middle-class Anglo-Jewish families, Levy's education was secular. Levy attended Brighton's Highschool for Girls and spent two years at Newnham College, Cambridge (1879–1881), in both cases being the first Jewish woman to enrol.[13] Levy's life passion was writing, and she began publishing poetry and short essays as a teenager. Aside from numerous publications in periodicals, magazines, and newspapers, Levy published three poetry collections: *Xantippe and Other Verse* (1881), *A Minor Poet and Other Verse* (1884), and *A London*

Amy Levy," *Journal of Victorian Culture* 4, no. 1 (Spring 1999): 76, 89; Deborah Epstein Nord, *Walking the Victorian Streets: Women, Representation, and the City* (Ithaca: Cornell University Press, 1995), 197; Deborah Parsons, *Streetwalking the Metropolis: Women, the City and Modernity* (Oxford: Oxford University Press, 2003), 105; on Levy as the focal point of avant-garde culture see Pullen, *The Woman Who Dared*, 203.

11. Cynthia Scheinberg, "Canonizing the Jew: Amy Levy's Challenge to Victorian Poetic Identity," *Victorian Studies* 39, no. 2 (Winter 1996): 195.
12. Hetherington and Valman, "Introduction," 2–3; Pullen, *The Woman Who Dared*, 203.
13. Hunt Beckman, *Amy Levy*, 1, 9, 29; New, "Introduction," 1; Susan David Bernstein, ed., "Introduction," in *The Romance of a Shop*, by Amy Levy (Peterborough: Broadview Editions, 2006), 15. According to Ellen Umansky, secular education signified "Jewish adaptability" (*Lily Montagu and the Advancement of Liberal Judaism: From Vision to Vocation* (New York: Edwin Mellen Press, 1983), 27).

Plane-Tree and Other Verse (1889), and three novels: *The Romance of a Shop* (1888), *Reuben Sachs* (1888), and *Miss Meredith* (1889). Residing mostly in London, Levy travelled throughout Europe in the 1880s, particularly in Switzerland, Germany, and Italy. Levy was also active in London's political, literary, and avant-garde circles, and regularly visited the British Museum's Reading Room (see her fictional "The Recent Telepathic Occurrence at the British Museum," published in 1888 (pp. 774–7), and essay (1889) on "Readers at the British Museum," pp. 954–61), developing correspondence, friendships, and socialising with luminaries such as Olive Schreiner, Eleanor Marx, Clementina Black, Vernon Lee (Violet Paget), Constance and Richard Garnett, Mary Robinson, Ernest and Dollie Radford (née Maitland), Margaret Harkness, George Bernard Shaw, Karl Pearson, Beatrice Webb (née Potter), Bella Duffy, Havelock Ellis, Ellen Darwin, Oscar Wilde, etc. (this list is by no means exhaustive).[14] Following Levy's suicide in 1889, Wilde wrote that "the world must forego the full fruition of her power. The loss is the world's, but perhaps not hers."[15] Indeed, throughout her life, Levy struggled with depression and a personal sense that her Jewishness was a source of stigmatisation.[16]

Any biographical account of Levy's life has to take stock of the late-Victorian context of antisemitism, secularism, and an Anglo-Jewish community understood through her fiction, poetry, and essays as underpinned by traditions and a patriarchal culture at odds with modernity.[17] Thus, Levy's corpus can only be understood in the way that it is inflected

14. Pullen, *The Woman Who Dared*, 13; Bernstein, "Introduction," in *The Romance of a Shop*, 20; idem, ed., "Introduction" and "A Brief Chronology" in *Reuben Sachs*, by Amy Levy (Peterborough: Broadview Editions, 2006), 43, 45; Hunt Beckman, *Amy Levy*, 76, 79, 210. See also Deborah Epstein Nord, "'Neither Pairs nor Odd': Female Community in Late Nineteenth-Century London," *Signs* 15, no. 4 (Summer, 1990): 733–54.
15. Oscar Wilde, "Amy Levy," *Woman's World* 3 (1890): 52. Levy's suicide was by "charcoal gas inhalation" (New, "Introduction," 1).
16. Hunt Beckman, *Amy Levy*, 7.
17. Nadia Valman, *The Jewess in Nineteenth-Century British Literary Culture* (Cambridge: Cambridge University Press, 2010), 176–7.

by historical and cultural constructions of the Jewish Diaspora and its emancipatory and Zionist responses, the othering of Jewishness in English (Christian) literary traditions, and pervasive racialising tropes associating assimilated Anglo-Jewish middle-class families and culture with excessive materialism and lack of spirituality.[18] If these factors compromise any reconstruction of Levy's biography and assimilated, middle-class, London background, the available source material further compounds the issue. Private archival material is available, including correspondence, manuscripts, and personal notes, but there is actually very little to draw on in terms of Levy's personal life, possibly because a number of her papers were either redacted or disposed of following her suicide in 1889.[19] Hunt Beckman's biography points to the difficulties in establishing "the truth about who she was," particularly in relation to Levy's Jewish identity.[20] Hunt Beckman does, however, provide some tentative evidence of potential engagement with Jewish tradition, including a childhood examination of King David in the magazine, *Kind Words*, and therefore probable familiarity with some of the biblical texts, possible tuition in Hebrew, and attendance at the Upper Berkeley Street Reform Synagogue in London (the Levy family being members).[21] Levy's essay on King David (pp. 873–5) is very short

18. Cynthia Scheinberg, *Women's Poetry and Religion in Victorian England: Jewish Identity and Christian Culture* (Cambridge: Cambridge University Press, 2008), 190–1; idem, "'And We Are Not What They Have Been,'" 44–5; Valman, *The Jewess*, 178.
19. Pullen, *The Woman Who Dared*, 10–1, 142; Hunt Beckman, *Amy Levy*, 285 n. 15.
20. Hunt Beckman, *Amy Levy*, 7, 15; Scheinberg, "'And We Are Not What They Have Been,'" 44.
21. Hunt Beckman, *Amy Levy*, 17; see also Pullen, *The Woman Who Dared*, 207 n. 24; Bernstein, "Introduction," in *Reuben Sachs*, 14. For Levy's juvenilia see Naomi Hetherington, "New Woman, 'New Boots': Amy Levy as Child Journalist," in *The Child Writer from Austen to Woolf*, eds. Christine Alexander and Juliet McMaster (Cambridge: Cambridge University Press, 2009), 254–68; additionally, for Levy's play, *The Unhappy Princess*, which was performed by the family and close friends in 1880 and in 1883 and then published in 1888 (Hunt Beckman, *Amy Levy*, 14–5), see "The Unhappy Princess: An Extravaganza for Little People (1888)," in *Thousands of Noras: Short Plays by Women, 1875–1920*, eds. Sherry

and concludes: "whilst we unquestioningly reverence Abraham and Moses, it is with David alone that we sympathise. The whole tenor of his somewhat romantic life is of itself calculated to awaken our interest."[22] The essay is confident and knowledgeable in its style but is too succinct to draw any conclusions about Levy's familiarity with biblical texts. Also potentially revealing is the surviving correspondence, included in Hunt Beckman's biography, which shows Levy asking her sister, Katie, "'how did everybody fast?'" in relation to Yom Kippur, saying, "'being Friday, you can't go,'" probably because of Shabbat, and advising: "'please tell Mama that I went to Synagogue yesterday.'"[23] So, even before accounting for her writing, there is enough evidence to suggest that Levy did at least have some understanding of Jewish history and tradition, even if only rudimentary.[24]

Scholars have endeavoured to further understand Levy's biography by analysing the limited evidence available in correspondence alongside the novels, poetry, and essays, the former being less fraught with problems than trying to read autobiographical components into fiction and poetic musings, even if they do construct and interpret Jewish historical, traditional, diasporic, and biblical themes.[25] Undoubtedly, Levy's novel, *Reuben Sachs,* has received the most attention from scholars trying to make sense of Levy's Jewish identity. Historian Geoffrey Alderman describes *Reuben Sachs* as "conceptually and stylistically brilliant" and "the best and most realistic

Engle and Susan Croft (Bloomington: iUniverse, 2015), 28–43. For the original publication, see Amy Levy, *The Unhappy Princess: An Extravaganza for Little People* (London: Samuel French, 1888).

22. The young Levy did also write a short poem (unpublished) on the "Wisdom of Solomon."

23. Levy quoted in Hunt Beckman, *Amy Levy,* 17, 225, 236.

24. Pullen, *The Woman Who Dared,* 16; Bernstein, "Introduction," in *The Romance of a Shop,* 14.

25. Bristow, "'All Out of Tune,'" 100 n. 16. See Richa Dwor's point that it is "in literary form … that Levy's dialogue with Judaism can be detected" (*Jewish Feeling: Difference and Affect in Nineteenth-Century Jewish Women's Writing* (London: Bloomsbury, 2017), 119).

account we have of the undisguised nepotism and the deep, irreverent materialism of the Jewish middle classes in London."[26] Alternatively, historian Todd Endelman analyses *Reuben Sachs* in the context of "Jewish self-hatred" and as part of a literary genre bent on producing "crude, antisemitic representations of Jews and Judaism."[27] The reality is that there is merit in both interpretations of *Reuben Sachs*, even if they seem polarised. No one was more desperate than Levy to provide a critical, even grotesque, account of middle-class Anglo-Jewry, given it fitted her logic that earlier novels written by Anglo-Jewish authors had been unrealistic in their descriptions of Anglo-Jews as deserving of political emancipation and equation with Englishness.[28] Moreover, Levy's account served the dual purpose of highlighting the limited opportunities for agency and intellectual fulfilment afforded to Anglo-Jewish women as well as establishing a racialised dichotomy between a supposedly degenerate community and a heroine offering potential renewal.[29]

The novel is a story of unrealised love. The beautiful Judith Quixano, a possible rereading of biblical Judith, has value because of her Sephardic ancestry and family who once belonged to "the *vieille noblesse* of the Jewish community" (p. 198):[30]

26. Geoffrey Alderman, *Modern British Jewry* (Oxford: Clarendon Press, 1992), 72.
27. Todd Endelman, *The Jews of Britain 1656 to 2000* (Berkeley: University of California Press, 2002), 170.
28. Michael Galchinsky, *The Origins of the Modern Jewish Woman Writer: Romance and Reform in Victorian England* (Detroit: Wayne State University Press, 1996), 15, 37; Valman, *The Jewess*, 175–6.
29. Richa Dwor, "The Racial Romance of Amy Levy's *Reuben Sachs*," *English Literature in Transition, 1880–1920* 55, no. 4 (2012): 466, 474; Nadia Valman, "'Barbarous and Medieval': Jewish Marriage in Fin de Siècle English Fiction," in *The Image of the Jew in European Liberal Culture, 1789–1914*, eds. Bryan Cheyette and Nadia Valman (London: Vallentine Mitchell, 2004), 113–5; idem, *The Jewess*, 183–7; idem, "Amy Levy and the Literary Representation of the Jewess," in *Amy Levy*, eds. Hetherington and Valman, 92–3.
30. On the possibility that Levy's character invokes the iconography of the biblical figure of Judith, see chapter five of Luke Devine's *From Anglo-First-Wave towards American Second-Wave Jewish Feminism: Negotiating with Jewish Feminist*

> She was twenty-two years of age, in the very prime of her youth and beauty; a tall, regal-looking creature, with an exquisite dark head, features like those of a face cut on gem or cameo, and wonderful, lustrous, mournful eyes, entirely out of keeping with the accepted characteristics of their owner.
>
> Her smooth, oval cheek glowed with a rich, yet subdued, hue of perfect health; and her tight-fitting fashionable white evening dress showed to advantage the generous lines of a figure which was distinguished for stateliness rather than grace. (p. 192)

Alternatively, Reuben Sachs is a career politician and figured as Ashkenazi in heritage. In stark contrast to Judith, Reuben is paradigmatic of devolution, degeneration, and the decaying of race symbolic of *fin de siècle* pessimism:[31]

> He was, as I have said, of middle height and slender build. He wore good clothes, but they could not disguise the fact that his figure was bad, and his movements awkward; unmistakably the figure and movements of a Jew.
>
> And his features, without presenting any marked national trait, bespoke no less clearly his Semitic origin.
>
> His complexion was of a dark pallor; the hair, small moustache and eyes, dark, with red lights in them; over these last the lids were drooping, and the whole face wore for the moment a relaxed, dreamy, impassive air, curiously Eastern, and not wholly free from melancholy. (pp. 186–7)

Several scholars have analysed *Reuben Sachs*'s invoking of prevailing late-Victorian social Darwinist eugenical themes and notions

---

Theology in the Writing of Amy Levy (Piscataway: Gorgias Press, 2010), 171–93, and Dwor's *Jewish Feeling*, 165, 167–71, 174–6. In the Book of Judith, the heroine saves Bethulia (and Israel) from invasion by decapitating the enemy general, Holofernes. In the biblical text, not included in the Tanakh or King James Bible, Judith is renowned for her piety, asceticism, and beauty.

31. Emma Francis, "Socialist Feminism and Sexual Instinct: Eleanor Marx and Amy Levy," in *Eleanor Marx (1855–1898): Life, Work, Contacts*, ed. John Stokes (Aldershot: Ashgate, 2000), 118–9; Valman, *The Jewess*, 184; Hetherington and Valman, "Introduction," 8.

of race degeneration.[32] In one of the novel's most poignant scenes, Reuben and Judith share an intimate moment at a party. However, the encounter is abruptly ended when Reuben must fulfil his career ambition of becoming a member of Parliament (given the announcement of a local member of Parliament's death):

> "Judith!"
>
> She turned her face, with its almost ecstatic look, towards him, letting fall the curtain.
>
> There were some chrysanthemums like snowflakes in her bodice, scarcely showing against the white, and as she turned, Reuben bent towards her and laid his hand on them.
>
> "I am going to commit a theft," he said, and his low voice shook a little. Judith yielded, passive, rapt, as his fingers fumbled with the gold pin. It was like a dream to her, a wonderful dream, with which the whirling maze of dancers, the heavy scents, the delicious music were inextricably mingled. And mingling with it also was a strange, harsh sound in the street outside, which, faint and muffled at first, was growing every moment louder and more distinct.
>
> Reuben had just succeeded in releasing the flowers from their fastening; but he held them loosely, with doubtful fingers, realizing suddenly what he had done.
>
> Judith shivered, vaguely conscious of a change in the moral atmosphere. (pp. 262–3)

The announcement shatters the connection between Reuben and Judith. The failure of their romance signals a missed opportunity for race regeneration and as Richa Dwor has rightly noted, effective Darwinist "sexual selection."[33] This failure is seemingly compounded with Judith's marriage to the convert, the satirical character, Bertie Lee-Harrison, and with the news of Reuben's death because of a

32. Francis, "Socialist Feminism," 122; Dwor, "The Racial Romance," 460–1; see also Lyssa Randolph, "Verse or Vitality? Biological Economies and the New Woman Poet," in *Amy Levy*, eds. Hetherington and Valman, 198–220.

33. Dwor, *Jewish Feeling*, 147; Francis, "Socialist feminism," 122; Valman, "'Barbarous and Medieval,'" 114.

heart attack.[34] There is, however, hope at the close of the novel with Judith's pregnancy and the possibility that she might yet raise a child imbued with her noble ancestry.[35]

In *The Complete Novels and Selected Writings of Amy Levy,* New suggested that Levy was hoping to put in place a credible account of modern Anglo-Jewry.[36] New based this claim on Levy's 1886 article for the *Jewish Chronicle,* "The Jew in Fiction" (pp. 918–20), and its position that George Eliot's (Mary Ann Evans) *Daniel Deronda* and its portrayal "of Jewish contemporary life, that of a little group of enthusiasts, with their yearnings after the Holy Land and dreams of a separate nation," was unrealistic and not an accurate depiction of "Jewish life and Jewish character."[37] Indeed, Levy claimed in the article that in English literature there had been little or no realistic portrayals of Anglo-Jewry:

> It is curious, that, while the prominent position of the Jew is recognised as one of the characteristic features of English social life of the present day, so small a place should be allotted him in contemporary fiction.
>
> In finance, in politics, in society; in every branch of art and science, the English Jew is to be found in a position of more or less distinction. It is only in the novel … that his claims to consideration have been almost entirely overlooked.

It is in this context that *Reuben Sachs* has often been interpreted as indicative of "revolt," or as Nadia Valman has argued, as an "audacious challenge … to an Anglo-Jewish literary tradition of representing Jews as contented, pious, and obedient citizens."[38] Levy made a similar

34. Hunt Beckman, *Amy Levy,* 160.
35. Dwor, "The Racial Romance," 476.
36. New, "introduction," 17.
37. New, "Introduction," 17; Dwor, *Jewish Feeling,* 121–2. See also Iveta Jusova and Dan Reyes, "Edward Said, Reuben Sachs, and Victorian Zionism," *Social Text* 24, no. 2 (2006): 35–46, and George Eliot, *Daniel Deronda* (Ware: Wordsworth Classics, 1996).
38. On *Reuben Sachs* as a "revolt" see Bryan Cheyette, "From Apology to Revolt: Benjamin Farjeon, Amy Levy and the Post-Emancipation Anglo-Jewish Novel, 1880–1900," *Transactions of the Jewish Historical Society of England* 24 (1982–1986): 253–65; Valman, "Amy Levy," 91.

point in her article, "Jewish Children," suggesting that Eliot might be able to replicate "the humours," but not "the charms" of Jewish life (p. 930). Even in the context of a "revolt," Levy's lurid account of acculturated Anglo-Jewry's supposed unabashed materialism and spiritual emptiness, whatever its intention, certainly went too far for some contemporary readers. In a review entitled, "The Deterioration of the Jewess," one critic stated:

> [Levy] apparently delights in the task of persuading the general public that her own kith and kin are the most hideous types of vulgarity; she revels in misrepresentations of their customs and modes of thought and she is proud of being able to offer her testimony in support of the antisemitic theories of the clannishness of her people and the tribalism of their religion. At least, so we gather from the fact that her peculiarly Hebraic name appears in prominent capitals on both the title page and cover of her very infelicitous romance.[39]

For Hunt Beckman, *Reuben Sachs* is overloaded with "too many generalizations about Jews," in the process caricaturing antisemitic literary themes.[40] Hunt Beckman, like several other scholars, has looked at themes of "Jewish self-hatred" in the novel, analysing *Reuben Sachs* in the context of Levy's other stories, "Leopold Leuniger: A Study" (unpublished) and "Cohen of Trinity" (pp. 832–40), using Sander Gilman's classic text, *Jewish Self-Hatred*. Hunt Beckman has also led on suggesting the importance of accounting for the ways in which Levy's writing engages in experimentation, satirising processes, and the deployment of a diversity of narrating voices that defy consistency.[41]

39. Anon., "The Deterioration of the Jewess," *Jewish World*, February 22, 1889, 5, quoted in Bernstein, ed., *Reuben Sachs*, 165.
40. Hunt Beckman, *Amy Levy*, 169.
41. Linda Hunt Beckman, "Leaving 'the Tribal Duckpond': Amy Levy, Jewish Self-Hatred, and Jewish Identity," *Victorian Literature and Culture* (1999): 186, 190, 195–6; see Sander Gilman, *Jewish Self-Hatred and the Hidden Language of the Jews* (Baltimore: John Hopkins University Press, 1986).

"Leopold Leuniger" is a short story about two friends who have met at Cambridge: Leo, who is Jewish, and Gerald, who is from a prestigious aristocratic background. When Leo visits Gerald's home, he overhears him stating to his friends: "'I think it is a disgrace to society that such people should be received. The whole race is a low-born, underbred [illegible] of moneyed intruigers [*sic*]'"[42] (the latter presumably a misspelling of "intriguers"). It is then, alone in his room, that Leo notices "'a well-worn copy of [Heinrich] Heine; Heine the Jew-poet; Heine is best-beloved of singers.'"[43] For Hunt Beckman, the moment symbolises how Leo's Jewishness excludes him from English high culture.[44] "Cohen of Trinity" similarly focuses on Cambridge, potentially pointing to Levy's own experiences of university life.[45] The story, coming after *Reuben Sachs*, again focuses on stereotypical representations of Anglo-Jews, but is clear in delineating between how Alfred Lazarus Cohen comes to be racialised by the non-Jewish narrator and his own agency and hopes for recognition.[46] Despite expulsion from Cambridge, Cohen goes on to achieve fame by publishing a popular book, *Gubernator*, but it is actually acceptance that he had desired all along as opposed to prestige.[47] Indeed, "Cohen of Trinity" shows how Anglo-Jews are racially and stereotypically constructed in the same way as the narrating voice in *Reuben Sachs* makes assumptions about the Jewish characters described in the novel.[48] Before hearing from Cohen, the narrator, in the absence of facts, visualises Cohen's home and family:[49]

---

42. Amy Levy, "Leopold Leuniger: A Study," quoted in Hunt Beckman, *Amy Levy*, 70–1.
43. Levy, "Leopold Leuniger," 71.
44. Hunt Beckman, *Amy Levy*, 71; idem, "Leaving 'the Tribal Duckpond,'" 187.
45. Pullen, *The Woman Who Dared*, 146.
46. Pullen, *The Woman Who Dared*, 147; Hunt Beckman, *Amy Levy*, 186–7; idem, "Leaving 'the Tribal Duckpond,'" 197.
47. Hunt Beckman, *Amy Levy*, 189; Pullen, *The Woman Who Dared*, 148.
48. Hunt Beckman, *Amy Levy*, 188–9.
49. Hunt Beckman, *Amy Levy*, 188–9; idem, "Leaving 'the Tribal Duckpond,'" 198.

> On the subject of his family, Cohen himself, at times savagely reserved, at others appallingly frank, volunteered little information, though on one occasion he had touched in with a few vivid strokes the background of his life.
>
> I seemed to see it all before me: the little new house in Maida Vale; a crowd of children, clamorous, unkempt; a sallow shrew in a torn dressing-gown, who alternately scolded, bewailed herself, and sank into moody silence; a fitful paternal figure coming and going, depressed, exhilarated, according to the fluctuations of his mysterious financial affairs; and over everything the fumes of smoke, the glare of gas, the smell of food in preparation. (pp. 835–6)

Leopold Leuniger is given another role, this time as "Little Leuniger, who played the fiddle, a Jew," who, according to the narrator, is unwilling to engage with Cohen (p. 835). Leopold, or Leo, also appears in *Reuben Sachs* as an "idealist" studying at Cambridge who reads Heine and has come to the conclusion that Anglo-Jewry has irrevocably succumbed to materialism, to his lament: "'ours is the religion of materialism. The corn and the wine and the oil; the multiplication of the seed; the conquest of the hostile tribes – these have always had more attraction for us than the harp and crown of a spiritualized existence'" (pp. 238, 275). Not only do these interrelated texts demonstrate how representations of Anglo-Jews in the period are inflected through Christian and antisemitic perspectives, but Levy's own anxieties about being seen as a "Jew" and interacting with other Jews in public.[50]

Using Gilman's definition of the term, Hunt Beckman suggests that self-hatred is a process of internalising hegemonic antisemitic discourses. However, where Hunt Beckman differs from Gilman is in seeing Levy's self-hatred and its deployment as a literary device evolving in conjunction with her ability to portray fictional Anglo-Jews. In this way, the antisemitic tropes in *Reuben Sachs* that paint a

50. Hunt Beckman, "Leaving 'the Tribal Duckpond,'" 193; Linda Hunt, "Amy Levy and the 'Jewish Novel': Representing Jewish Life in the Victorian Period," *Studies in the Novel* 26, no. 3 (Fall 1994): 14–5 n. 33.

picture of acculturated Anglo-Jewish materialism do so in the same way that other novels of the period envisaged high society in general, including *Daniel Deronda*.[51] Indeed, as a number of scholars have noted, it is problematic to assume that the voices narrating *Reuben Sachs* are Levy speaking and therefore the novel should not be read as autobiographical.[52] Thus, the novel is now generally read by scholars as a feminist account of the limited agency afforded to wealthy Anglo-Jewish women in the 1880s.[53] Aside from Judith, this is most starkly exhibited in the character, Esther Kohnthal, who bemoans her existence as an unmarried woman devoid of opportunity. The novel links Esther's cynicism with a rewording of one of the traditional morning blessings: "'When I was a little girl,' cried Esther, still looking at her [Judith], 'a little girl of eight years old, I wrote in my prayer-book: "Cursed art Thou, O Lord my God, Who hast had the cruelty to make me a woman." And I have gone on saying that prayer all my life – the only one'" (p. 272).[54] Dwor points out that the feminist underpinnings of the novel do not necessarily reflect self-hatred, but the voicing of an "anger" that its heroine, Judith, is never able to iterate because of the communal limitations imposed on her, but also given she is subject to the account delivered by the narrator(s). In this context, Dwor reads *Reuben Sachs* as an examination of the possibilities that Judith and Reuben's romance can offer for Judaism and Jewish survival in general, if only they could resist the materialist impulse that haunts the novel's construction of middle-class Anglo-Jewish life

---

51. Hunt Beckman, "Leaving 'the Tribal Duckpond,'" 186, 196.
52. Susan David Bernstein, "'Mongrel Words': Amy Levy's Jewish Vulgarity," in *Amy Levy*, eds. Hetherington and Valman, 151; Hunt Beckman, *Amy Levy*, 171–3; Dwor, "The Racial Romance," 476.
53. Meri-Jane Rochelson, "Jews, Gender, and Genre in Late-Victorian England: Amy Levy's *Reuben Sachs*," *Women's Studies* 25 (1996): 311; Valman, "Amy Levy," 91; Pullen, *The Woman Who Dared*, 128; Emma Francis, "Amy Levy: Contradictions? – Feminism and Semitic Discourse," in *Women Poetry, Late Romantic to Late Victorian: Gender and Genre, 1830–1900*, eds. Isobel Armstrong and Virginia Blain (Basingstoke: Macmillan Press Ltd, 1999), 186.
54. Valman, "Amy Levy," 90.

in the 1880s. Dwor further points to the close relationship between Judith and Joshua Quixano, her father, who is a scholar working on a Jewish history of the Iberian Peninsula.[55] In considering her engagement to Lee-Harrison, Judith, upset, is embraced by her father, and in the process questions the all-encompassing materialism that has so far in her life seemed important:

> Material advantage; things that you could touch and see and talk about; that these were the only things which really mattered, had been the unspoken gospel of her life.
>
> Now and then you allowed yourself the luxury of a fine sentiment in speech, but when it came to the point, to take the best that you could get for yourself was the only course open to a person of sense.
>
> The push, the struggle, the hunger and greed of her world rose vividly before her. Wealth, power, success – a flaunting success for all men to see; had she not believed in these things as the most desirable on earth? Had she not always wished them to fall to the lot of the person dearest to her? Did she not believe in them still? Was she not doing her best to secure them for herself?
>
> But she was Joshua Quixano's daughter – was it possible that she cared for none of these things? (p. 291)

Scholars have looked to Levy's essays, such as "Middle-Class Jewish Women of Today" (1886), to help contextualise the account of Judith's subjection. The article, written anonymously for the *Jewish Chronicle*, condemns the absence of opportunities available to middle-class Anglo-Jewish women beyond marriage:

> What, in fact, is the ordinary life of a Jewish middle-class woman? Carefully excluded, with almost Eastern jealousy, from everyday intercourse with men and youths of her own age, she is plunged all at once – a half-fledged, often half-chaperoned creature – into the "vortex" of a middle-class ballroom, and is there expected to find her own level. In the very face of statistics, of the unanswerable logic of facts, she is taught to look upon marriage as the only satisfactory termination to her career. (p. 925)

---

55. Dwor, "The Racial Romance," 461, 476; idem, *Jewish Feeling*, 144, 163–4, 178.

As early as 1879, Levy submitted two letters to the *Jewish Chronicle* on "Jewish Women and 'Women's Rights'" (pp. 876–80). The letters were part of an exchange with a correspondent identifying as "ש" who had commented on "Women's Rights." In the first letter, Levy castigates "ש" for assuming forced marriage is the singular issue confronting Anglo-Jewish women:

> Thus, he is mistaken in thinking that "coercion into marriage" (as he expresses it) is the great ground of complaint among women; it is rather the obstacles which are placed to hinder "from attaining higher culture," and "sharing in the sterner struggles of life," those women, who, from circumstance or temperament, do not marry. (p. 876)

Susan David Bernstein argues that Levy's letters to the *Jewish Chronicle* in 1879 foreshadow the versions of "Jewish vulgarity" constructed in *Reuben Sachs,* which are deployed as a critical literary mechanism to signal materialist and sexist privilege through the lens of race and to deconstruct stereotypical portrayals of Anglo-Jews in the period.[56] The second letter is similar in tone to the first, lamenting the limited conception of agency identified by "ש" in relation to Jewish women:

> It is a great fact that there has sprung up a large class of intelligent, capable women who are willing and able to perform work from which they find themselves shut out by the tradition of ages – women, who are destitute of their "natural protectors," or whose aims lie outside the circle which convention has marked out for them. The growth of such a class seems to point to the higher development of woman, to the fact that she is beginning to wake up to the sense of her own responsibility as a human being. All that she claims is freedom of competition. (p. 879)

Reuben Sachs accordingly employs diverse and complex strategies to highlight the different ways in which representations of Anglo-Jewry are inflected by antisemitic, Christian, and literary constructions, but in the process, uses these genres to demonstrate the limited agency

56. Bernstein, "'Mongrel Words,'" 136, 151–2; Dwor, *Jewish Feeling*, 121.

afforded to Anglo-Jewish women and the perils alleged traditional conservatism can bring in terms of racial degeneration.[57] *Reuben Sachs* is therefore difficult to interpret given multiple narratives are at work that employ antisemitic tropes and terms that had currency with the general reading public outside of the Anglo-Jewish communities in Levy's time.[58] Even so, it is easy to see why accounts of Levy's biography following her suicide assumed she was in some shape or form akin to Judith Quixano.[59]

The opening line of the novel (p. 181), "This is my beloved Son," taken from Matthew 3:17, 17:5, Mark 9:7, Luke 9:35, 2 Peter 1:17, hints that the narrator is Christian, not Jewish.[60] Bernstein contends that the line demonstrates the ways in which Anglo-Jewry and Judaism in general are conveyed through the lens of, and as being superseded by, Christian biblical and literary traditions.[61] In this way, the novel can be read as comprising different and competing voices, what Hunt Beckman has called a "polyphonic" format, and as invoking already extant antisemitic tropes to highlight their insidiousness.[62] Scholars have, however, had to grapple with the fact that Levy's own private correspondence includes comments that point to the potential internalisation of antisemitic tropes and to an ambivalent and even racist attitude towards the Jews she encountered when travelling in Europe.[63] In a letter to her sister from Germany, Levy asks that Katie tell their mother that she has attended synagogue, but that the experience was unbearable:

> Please tell Mama that I went to Synagogue yesterday – & a beastly place it was. Zion unventilated and unrefreshed sent forth an odour

57. Hetherington and Valman, "Introduction," 8–9; Valman, "Amy Levy," 91.
58. Hunt Beckman, *Amy Levy*, 173; Dwor, *Jewish Feeling*, 121–2, 141.
59. Valman, "Amy Levy," 107.
60. Bernstein, "Introduction," in *Reuben Sachs*, 34; Scheinberg, "Canonizing the Jew," 181.
61. Bernstein, "Introduction," in *Reuben Sachs*, 34; see also p. 55 n. 1.
62. Hunt, "Amy Levy and the 'Jewish Novel,'" 9–10.
63. Hunt Beckman, *Amy Levy*, 110; T.D. Olverson, "'Such Are Not Woman's Thoughts': Amy Levy's 'Xantippe' and 'Medea,'" in *Amy Levy*, eds. Hetherington and Valman, 125.

> wh. made me feel [illegible] for the rest of the day. The place was crammed with evil-looking Hebrews. Lots of the shops were shut yesterday. When you write do you mind sending me some English stamps – I want them for literary purposes. This afternoon we call on the Sulzburgers – some wealthy Hebrews of our "acquaintance" who, for Js [Jews], don't seem half bad. I say, "for Js" because the German Hebrew makes me feel, as a rule, that the antisemitic movement is a most just & virtuous one.[64]

Ana Parejo Vadillo has identified the ways in which the letter shows Levy's awareness of political antisemitism in imperial Germany. For Vadillo, Levy's criticism is targeted at an Orthodox German-Jewish community identified as backward, unchanged by the Enlightenment (or more specifically its Jewish component, the *Haskalah*), and still pinning itself to nationalistic principles.[65] Thus, Levy's comments can be read as Anglophile or in the same context as West End assimilated communities in London being critical of East End migrants.[66] Additionally, the letter could reflect Levy's interest in German Reform Judaism, which several scholars have detected in *Reuben Sachs* and in some of Levy's essays and poems.[67] The German Reformers, particularly Abraham Geiger, offered a vision of Judaism liberated from its supposed "Orientalism" and traditional legalistic elements and focused on modernisation, universalism,

64. Levy quoted in Hunt Beckman, *Amy Levy*, 110, 236.
65. Ana Parejo Vadillo, "Cosmopolitan Disturbances: Amy Levy in Dresden," *Forum for Modern Language Studies* 53, no. 3 (July 2017): 330.
66. Vadillo, "Cosmopolitan Disturbances," 330; Bernstein, "Introduction," in *Reuben Sachs*, 25; Hunt Beckman, "Leaving the 'Tribal Duck Pond,'" 193.
67. See Luke Devine, "'I Sleep but My Heart Waketh': Contiguity between Heinrich Heine's Imago of the Shulamite and Amy Levy's 'Borderland,'" *Association for Jewish Studies Review* 40, no. 2 (November 2016): 222; idem, *From Anglo-First-Wave*, 76; Pullen, *The Woman Who Dared*, 9, 130; Naomi Hetherington, "'A Jewish Robert Elsmere?': Amy Levy, Israel Zangwill and the Post-Emancipation Jewish Novel," in *Amy Levy*, eds. Hetherington and Valman, 190.

and notions of gender parity.[68] In "Middle-Class Jewish Women of Today," Levy stated:

> Conservative in politics; conservative in religion; the Jew is no less conservative as regards his social life; and while in most cases outwardly conforming to the usages of Western civilisation, he is, in fact, more Oriental at heart than a casual observer might infer. For a long time, it may be said, the shadow of the harem has rested on our womankind; and if today we see it lifting, it is only in reluctant obedience to the force of circumstances, the complex conditions of our modern civilisation.... As a matter of fact, so many of our men are absorbed in money-making, and are moreover such genuine Orientals at heart, that they scarcely feel the need of feminine society in its higher forms. (pp. 925–6)

Hunt Beckman has also examined how Levy's correspondence indicates her own sense of not being accepted as "English," pointing to a letter to Katie identifying Jews as "'yr. co-religionists'" in contradistinction to "'English people.'"[69] This however can in no way excuse Levy's use of racist language and ignorance in relation to Germany's Jewish communities and naivety about the steady creep of political and cultural antisemitisms in the period. As Zion Lask points out, Levy "did not know" about those Jewish communities (or their experiences of antisemitism) beyond her own immediacy.[70] Moreover, for Vadillo, Levy could only account for her experience of the synagogue in the context of her assumption about a supposedly "closed" and "conservative community" at odds with modernity.[71] Levy's comments could have been satirical, but as Vadillo notes, there is too

68. Riv-Ellen Prell, "The Dilemma of Women's Equality in the History of Reform Judaism," *Judaism* 30, no. 4 (Fall 1981): 418–9; idem, "The Vision of Woman in Classical Reform Judaism," *Journal of the American Academy of Religion* 50, no. 4 (Dec. 1982): 576–7, 579.
69. Levy quoted in Hunt Beckman, *Amy Levy*, 110–1, 241.
70. Zion Lask, "Amy Levy," 180.
71. Vadillo, "Cosmopolitan Disturbances," 330.

much "closeness" in the letter to the pervasive antisemitic discourses at work in Dresden at the time.[72]

In the introduction to the 1993 collection, *The Complete Novels*, New identified "The Ghetto at Florence," an 1886 article for the *Jewish Chronicle* (pp. 914–7), as signalling an "awakening to her Jewish heritage."[73] Similarly, Hunt Beckman identifies 1886 as a "major turning point in Levy's relationship to her cultural and religious background" and the moment at which she became a specifically "Jewish poet and fiction writer" and "voice within the Jewish community" (given her publication of several articles with the *Jewish Chronicle* that year).[74] In the article, Levy makes a connection between her own sense of regret and the long since gone Florentine-Jews who suffered the hardships of the ghetto:[75]

> It is only sentimentalists, like ourselves, that trouble themselves in this unnecessary fashion. There are a great many Jews here tonight, evidently quite undisturbed by "inherited memory." A sprightly, if unhandsome, son of Shem urges us, in correct cockney, to take shares in a lottery; another, with his wife on his arm, trips gaily from booth to booth; the repressed energy, the stored exuberance of centuries is venting itself with its wonted force. We ourselves, it is to be feared, are not very good Jews; is it by way of "judgment" that the throng of tribal ghosts haunts us so persistently tonight? That white-bearded old man peering round the corner, surely it was he that Mantegna chose for the model for his famous Circumcision? (p. 916)

72. Vadillo, "Cosmopolitan Disturbances," 330.
73. New, "Introduction," 1, 17.
74. Hunt Beckman, "Leaving 'the Tribal Duckpond,'" 194; Richa Dwor, "'Poor Old Palace Prison!': Jewish Urban Memory in Amy Levy's 'The Ghetto at Florence' (1886)," *Partial Answers* 13, no. 1 (2015): 155. New suggests that an anonymous article in the *Jewish Chronicle*, "Some Aspects of Our Social Life," September 3, 1886, 9, was *possibly* written by Levy ("Introduction," 46 n. 38); The Camellia Collections have however confirmed that the text does not match anything in their archive.
75. Luke Devine, "'The Ghetto at Florence': Reading Jewish Identity in Amy Levy's Early Poetry, 1880–86," *Prooftexts* 31, no. 1–2 (Winter/Spring 2011): 6; Hunt Beckman, *Amy Levy*, 118–9; Pullen, *The Woman Who Dared*, 129.

Levy's account, for Dwor, while reading as a simplistic history, provides an understanding of the ghetto as a place in which the "experiences of modernity and emancipation" come to be understood through its symbolism as a means of "confinement" and "urban existence."[76] Levy might also have been interested in Florence given it was "once a hub of Sephardic scholarship,"[77] in the same way as Judith is framed in *Reuben Sachs* as a paragon of Sephardic racial elitism. Moreover, Italy provides the backdrop for Levy's serialised novel, *Miss Meredith* (pp. 309–89), likely commissioned, which tells the story of an English governess who marries above her station.[78] In this context, far from experiencing some kind of (re)connection with her Jewish heritage, Levy had long been influenced by the broad foundational tenets of classical German Reform Judaism.[79] This is possibly reflected in *Reuben Sachs*' description of the "Fast Day, or Day of Atonement" at the Upper Berkeley Street Reform Synagogue (pp. 222–6), which is described through a series of ironic binaries: "lax Jews" are compared to the "'Samuel Sachses,'" who are described by Reuben as a "'remarkable survival'" given their "observation of the Mosaic and Rabbinical laws in various minute points"; the Leuniger family have "all breakfasted," yet the one convert present, Bertie, will wait until the evening, as appropriate; Ernest Leuniger, who is described as "nervous, delicate," and an "idiot" (p. 191), is "devout," wears "talith," "an embroidered cap," and prays in Hebrew, is contrasted with Leo Leuniger, who is only present "under protest"; children squabble "for possession of a prayer-book" while

76. Dwor, "'Poor Old Palace Prison,'" 156, 158–9, 164, 167.
77. Devine, "'The Ghetto at Florence,'" 8.
78. Pullen, *The Woman Who Dared*, 146. According to Hunt Beckman (*Amy Levy*, 184), *Miss Meredith* "has nothing much to say"; more generally, Hunt Beckman suggests that "A good many of Levy's short stories were written for the market" (212). Indeed, in correspondence Levy referred to some of her short stories for *London Society* as "pot-boilers" (quoted in Pullen, *The Woman Who Dared*, 85; Hunt Beckman, *Amy Levy*, 250). Hunt Beckman speculates that this is why some of Levy's publications, the "hackwork," are anonymous (*Amy Levy*, 299 n. 60).
79. Devine, "'The Ghetto at Florence,'" 1. Pullen goes as far as to say Levy was influenced by the "asceticism of rabbinical tradition" (*The Woman Who Dared*, 130).

Israel Leuniger prays in "the corrupt German-Hebrew [Yiddish] of his youth – a jargon not recognized by the modern culture of Upper Berkeley Street" and its innovations, such as the introduction of an "organ" and "glorious music"; Reuben, "bored," and Bertie, engrossed "with all the zeal of a convert," command "a good view of the ladies," who in turn all wear the "latest fashion" and "perfume" and prefer to gossip, the most important point being the maintenance of "decorum." The account is also significant given the description of Judith's rigid observance:[80]

> Judith Quixano went through her devotions upheld by that sense of fitness, of obedience to law and order, which characterized her every action.
>
> But it cannot be said that her religion had any strong hold over her; she accepted it unthinkingly.
>
> These prayers, read so diligently, in a language of which her knowledge was exceedingly imperfect, these reiterated praises of an austere tribal deity, these expressions of a hope whose consummation was neither desired nor expected, what connection could they have with the personal needs, the human longings of this touchingly ignorant and limited creature?

Reuben Sachs's account of Yom Kippur has been read by several scholars as characteristic of the late-nineteenth-century critique of Reform Judaism as being too conservative in relation to the ideals outlined by Geiger and other Reform rabbis in Germany.[81] Levy's article, "Jewish Children" (pp. 929–934), displays a similar tendency to frame

80. Nadia Valman, "From Domestic Paragon to Rebellious Daughter: Victorian Jewish Women Novelists," in *Amy Levy*, eds. Hetherington and Valman, 25. See Iveta Jusova, *The New Woman and the Empire* (Columbus: Ohio State University Press, 2005), in particular the section, "Irony in *Reuben Sachs*," 153–60.

81. Luke Devine, "Imagining Fin-de-Siècle Anglo-Jewish Minority Sub-Genres: Proto-Feminist Visions of Religious Reform in 'West End' London in Amy Levy's *Reuben Sachs* and Lily Montagu's *Naomi's Exodus*," *Melilah: Manchester Journal of Jewish Studies* 8, no. 1 (2013): 75; idem, "'I Sleep but My Heart Waketh,'" 222; Valman, "Amy Levy," 90; idem, "'Barbarous and Medieval,'" 113; idem, *The Jewess*, 99, 165; Scheinberg, "'And We Are Not What They Have Been,'" 45.

analysis of the Anglo-Jewish community through ironic binary opposites: "love of children" is instinctual and "the most touching and characteristic stories of the Hebrew Scriptures are those which turn on the affection of parents for their children." However, "the Jewish child, in point of fact, runs great danger, metaphorically speaking, of being killed with kindness." Levy uses the article to make a wider point about "Jewish parents" taking responsibility, in line with the latest "teachings of psychology and physiology," for "the most careful training, mental, moral, and physical" of Anglo-Jewish children. This will combat, Levy posits, "the rate of mental and nervous diseases among Jews." Even so, Levy's analysis, while laying the blame squarely with "past existence" and a "deep-seated Oriental love of splendour," equally points to inherent "intelligence" and "abnormal toughness and vitality". These binaries deploy antisemitic tropes to carefully undo them, instead pointing to future potential for Anglo-Jewry if only it will heed "scientific teachings."[82]

In conjunction with Levy's correspondence, Hunt Beckman has analysed some of Levy's personal sketches of caricatured Jews, which invoke antisemitic stereotyping in the form of overstated noses, materialist finery, and excessive ugliness. A drawing of her sister and an imagined partner includes the caption: "Katie: Now d'out zer Isaac. I've got to fry the fish. / Isaac Harris: Oh one more for the sake of Shabbos and Pesach!"[83] For Hunt Beckman, the images convey Levy's obsession with race and the stigmatisation of Jewish identity, particularly if examined alongside another drawing that depicts a "blond woman" with the caption, "The Fair One with Gold Locks (A Child's Ideal)."[84] In this context, scholars have drawn attention to Levy's poem, "Medea" (pp. 432–47). In the poem, Medea of ancient Hellenistic mythology and Euripides's play (Franz Grillparzer's own version

82. Dwor, "The Racial Romance," 462.

83. Hunt Beckman, "Leaving the 'Tribal Duck Pond,'" 190–2; idem, *Amy Levy*, 111–2.

84. Hunt Beckman, *Amy Levy*, 112.

of the tragedy, "Medea," may have impacted Levy's portrayal), hailing from Colchis, is an obvious foreigner living among the Corinthians:[85]

> When all around the air is charged and chill,
> And all the place is drear and dark with hate?
> Alas, alas, this people loves me not!
> This strong, fair people, marble-cold and smooth
> As modelled marble. I, an alien here,
> That well can speak the language of their lips,
> The language of their souls may never learn.
> And in their hands, I, that did know myself
> Ere now, a creature in whose veins ran blood
> Redder, more rapid, than flows round most hearts,
> Do seem a creature reft of life and soul.
> If they would only teach the subtle trick
> By which their hearts are melted into love,
> I'd strive to learn it. I am very meek.
> They think me proud, but I am very meek,
> Ready to do their bidding. Hear me, friends!
> Friends, I am very hungry, give me love!
> 'Tis all I ask! Is it so hard to give?
> You stand and front me with your hostile eyes;
> You only give me hatred? (pp. 433–4)

A number of scholars have gone so far as to say that in the poem, Levy is speaking through Medea, who, racialised and stereotyped according to antisemitic imagery, is condemned because of her "swart skins and purple hair" and "black, fierce eyes"(p. 435).[86] For Hunt Beckman,

85. Hunt Beckman, *Amy Levy*, 112; Nord, "'Neither Pairs nor Odd,'" 749; Olverson, "'Such Are Not Woman's Thoughts,'" 122. Levy translated some of Grillparzer's play, "Sappho," for the *Cambridge Review* (1882); see pp. 556–7.

86. Nord, "'Neither Pairs nor Odd,'" 749; Olverson, "'Such Are Not Woman's Thoughts,'" 122, 125–7; Pullen, *The Woman Who Dared*, 54. See Marta Villalba-Lázaro's analysis of "Medea" and claim that the poem exhibits "the full acknowledgment of" Levy's "Jewish consciousness" ("Radicalizing the Myth: Amy Levy's Medea, the (Un)Assimilated Jewish Victorian Woman," *Women in Judaism: A Multidisciplinary Journal* 15, no. 2 (2018): 2).

however, Medea speaks as if one of Levy's Jewish caricatures.[87] Either way, the point is that Medea can speak the language of acculturation, though is unable or possibly reluctant to adopt its spirit.[88] A similar theme arises in "A Greek Girl" (pp. 452–4), where the speaker, ignored, acknowledges that a potential lover, now dead, instead chose a Christian woman, identified in conjunction with the Holy Trinity:[89]

> Thrice-blest, thrice-crowned, of gods thrice-loved she –
> That other, fairer maid, who tombward brings
> Her gold, shorn locks and piled-up offerings
> Of fragrant fruits, rich wines, and spices rare,
> And cakes with honey sweet, with saffron fair;
> And who, unchecked by any thought of shame,
> May weep her tears, and call upon his name,
> With burning bosom prest to the cold ground,
> Knowing, indeed, that all her life is crown'd,
> Thrice-crowned, thrice honoured, with that love of his; –
> No dearer crown on earth is there, I wis. (p. 453)

This is perhaps the key point in *Reuben Sachs*. The novel highlights already extant antisemitic discourses and anxieties that can be interpreted as forms of self-hatred, but its underlying premise, as Iveta Jusova has shown, is to call into a question a literal reading of the text. The characters throughout are framed in exaggerated and ironic ways, while the narrating voices are inconsistent, confusing, and make it difficult to understand whether the story is being told by a Christian "gentile" or a "Jewish" narrator.[90] Thus, while the story was to some extent written for a wider audience outside of the Jewish community,

---

87. Hunt Beckman, *Amy Levy*, 113.
88. Olverson, "'Such Are Not Woman's Thoughts,'" 128.
89. Devine, *From Anglo-First-Wave*, 111–2; see the third chapter, "Amy Levy's Midrashic Poetry: 'A Greek Girl' and 'Magdalen,'" *passim*.
90. Jusova, *The New Woman*, 156–7; Hunt Beckman, *Amy Levy*, 162; idem, "Leaving 'the Tribal Duckpond,'" 196–7, 199; Cynthia Scheinberg, "Recasting 'Sympathy and Judgement': Amy Levy, Women Poets, and the Victorian Dramatic Monologue," *Victorian Poetry* 35, no. 2 (Summer, 1997): 179.

as well as to call into question earlier romantic and idealised accounts of Anglo-Jewry, *Reuben Sachs* is still there to be read for Anglo-Jews able to fathom its complex format and underlying thematic that Judith is paradigmatic of racial and spiritual redemption, just like poems such as "Medea" and "A Greek Girl" highlight themes of exclusion and othering in English high culture. Much of Levy's poetry operates in this way and should not be read as literal in meaning.[91]

"Xantippe," the opening poem of Levy's *Xantippe and Other Verse* short collection (pp. 399–408), has also been interpreted as indicative of Levy's sense of marginalisation and of her awareness that in attending Cambridge, she could take the Tripos, but would not be awarded the degree itself.[92] "Xantippe" is an account of Socrates's wife, who angrily responds to his description of Aspasia, the mistress of Pericles:[93]

> "This fair Aspasia, which our Perikles
> Hath brought from realms afar, and set on high
> In our Athenian city, hath a mind,
> I doubt not, of a strength beyond her race;
> And makes employ of it, beyond the way
> Of women nobly gifted: woman's frail –
> Her body rarely stands the test of soul;
> She grows intoxicate with knowledge; throws
> The laws of custom, order, 'neath her feet,
> Feasting at life's great banquet with wide throat." (p. 404)

Xantippe's response is triggered by Socrates's intolerance. Lonely and denied intellectual agency, Xantippe takes Socrates to task.[94] According to Karen Weisman, Levy makes "female intelligence" synonymous with Xantippe and, in doing so, possibly makes a point about pervasive *fin de siècle* medical discourses disproportionately

91. See Jusova, *The New Woman*, 157.
92. Karen Weisman, "Playing with Figures: Amy Levy and the Forms of Cancellation," *Criticism* 43, no. 1 (Winter 2001): 77; Bristow, "'All Out of Tune,'" 84.
93. Jusova, *The New Woman*, 135.
94. Olverson, "'Such Are Not Woman's Thoughts,'" 113–4.

associating Jews with a host of nervous conditions and her own sense of marginalisation:[95]

> "By all great powers around us! Can it be
> That we poor women are empirical?
> That gods who fashioned us did strive to make
> Beings too fine, too subtly delicate,
> With sense that thrilled response to ev'ry touch
> Of nature's, and their task is not complete?
> That they have sent their half-completed work
> To bleed and quiver here upon the earth?
> To bleed and quiver, and to weep and weep,
> To beat its soul against the marble walls
> Of men's cold hearts, and then at last to sin!" (pp. 404–5)

In *The Complete Novels,* New rightly pointed to the feminist underpinnings of the monologue.[96] Since then, several scholars have taken this premise further to analyse how "Xantippe" invokes notions of race exclusion in Socrates's description of Aspasia, how the monologue adds Xantippe's personal voice to the original Platonic dialogues, how Xantippe stands as a solitary figure at the expense of her maids (and in doing so signals the need for unity and cooperation beyond class stratification), and how the framing of the story makes the case for the "learned woman."[97] Weisman goes as far as to say that Levy's Xantippe is actually an "image of the Jew" and speaks to her own

95. Weisman, "Playing with Figures," 76–7; see Sander Gilman, *The Jew's Body* (New York: Routledge, 1991), for an analysis of *fin de siècle* pseudo-science and the supposed association between Jews and "disease." Additionally, see Levy, "Jewish Children," pp. 929–34.
96. New, "Introduction," 5–6; see also Zion Lask's analysis of "Xantippe" ("Amy Levy," 170–2).
97. Olverson, "'Such Are Not Woman's Thoughts,'" 119–20; Jusova, *The New Woman,* 135–6; Emily Harrison, "'A Merciful Fury Sent to Save Me': Amy Levy's 'Xantippe' and Women's Conversations," *Victorian Studies* 62, no. 2 (2020): 191–2; Linda Hughes, "Discoursing of Xantippe: Amy Levy, Classical Scholarship, and Print Culture," *Philological Quarterly* 88, no. 3 (2009): 260.

sense of isolation.[98] Indeed, the best way to approach Levy's poetry is to understand that it is multi-layered and similar to *Reuben Sachs*, adopts complex identity positions and voices to speak to different audiences, often, as Christine Pullen has posited, from "behind the mask."[99] Certainly, in the period Levy was active, such an approach was not unusual. On the one hand, women poets were expected to be appropriately "feminine." But on the other, even if authoritative theological dogma was considered inappropriate, poets such as Levy still critically engaged with scriptural, religious, and theological questions. This is often missed given such poetry, at least superficially, conforms to typical Victorian expectations that it should be altruistic, sentimental, and spiritual (as opposed to doctrinal).[100]

In particular, the framing of *Reuben Sachs* and much of Levy's poetry points to the influence of the German poet, Heinrich Heine, identified in her youth as a "favourite."[101] Levy makes this clear in "Jewish Humour," written for the *Jewish Chronicle* in 1886 (pp. 921–4). In the article, Levy argues that Heine's poetry represents the apotheosis of "Jewish Humour" and perfectly captures "the spirit of the nation." For Levy, this has immediate implications in that where there is growing secularism, acculturation, and the fading of tradition, there is something that still operates as a binding force for Anglo-Jews:

> Only a Jew perceives to the full the humour of another; but it is a humour so fine, so peculiar, so distinct in flavour, that we believe it impossible to impart its perception to anyone not born a Jew. The most hardened

98. Weisman, "Playing with Figures," 76–7.
99. Pullen, *The Woman Who Dared*, 130; Nord, "'Neither Pairs nor Odd,'" 748.
100. Rebecca Styler, *Literary Theology by Women Writers of the Nineteenth Century* (Farnham: Ashgate, 2010), 13–5; Julie Melnyk, ed., "Introduction," in *Women's Theology in Nineteenth-Century Britain: Transfiguring the Faith of Their Fathers* (New York: Garland Publishing, 1998), xii; Susan Brown, "The Victorian Poetess," in *The Cambridge Companion to Victorian Poetry*, ed. Joseph Bristow (Cambridge: Cambridge University Press, 2000), 188.
101. Pullen, *The Woman Who Dared*, 51; "Amy Levy's Confessions Book entry," quoted in Hunt Beckman, *Amy Levy*, 16.

> Agnostic deserter from the synagogue enjoys its pungency, where the zealous alien convert to Judaism tastes nothing but a little bitterness. In these days, indeed, of slackening bonds, of growing carelessness as to long-cherished traditions; when the old order is changing and giving place to new with startling rapidity it is, perhaps, our sense of humour as much as anything else, which keeps alive the family feeling of the Jewish race. The old words, the old customs, are disappearing, soon to be forgotten by all save the student of such matters. There is no shutting our eyes to this fact. The trappings and the suits of our humour must vanish with the rest; but that is no reason why what is essential of it should not remain to us a heritage of the ages too precious to be lightly lost; a defence and a weapon wrought for us long ago by hands that ceased not from their labour. If we leave off saying Shibboleth, let us, at least, employ its equivalent in the purest University English. Not for all Aristophanes can we yield up our national free-masonry of wit; our family joke, our Jewish Humour. (p. 924)

The article highlights what New refers to as the "enormous influence of Heinrich Heine" on Levy, as well as her hopes for some form of identifying language and a means of articulation that signals something peculiarly Jewish based on the biblical meaning of Shibboleth as a password, or in the form of what Miron has called a "defining shibboleth."[102] Shibboleth, for Levy, is a buffer against encroaching acculturation and a means of identifying Jewish specificity.[103] In the article Levy suggests that Heine "has cracked the communal joke ... for all to enjoy and understand," but being "born a Jew" is essential in "that only a Jew perceives to the full the humour of another." This means that however universalising, Heine's "tribal humour," just like the "Jewish Family Joke," "the subtle words *'hine* and *chutzpah*," and the "apt saying[s] in Jüdisch-Deutsch," will never be understood even by the most devoted "alien convert" to Judaism.[104] This avowal

102. New, "Introduction," 36; Scheinberg, "Canonizing the Jew," 189–90; idem, *Women's Poetry*, 210–2; Miron, *From Continuity to Contiguity*, 8.
103. Bristow, "'All Out of Tune,'" 95; Dwor, "'Poor Old Palace Prison,'" 164; Bernstein, "'Mongrel Words,'" 142.
104. See Scheinberg, *Women's Poetry*, 209–10; Bernstein, "'Mongrel Words,'" 141.

denotes something that all readers of Heine can attest to, particularly Eliot, that "His sarcasms are so subtly prepared and so slily allusive, that they may often escape readers whose sense of wit is not very acute."[105] Accordingly, even though much of Levy's poetry belies any connection to Jewish tradition, this does not mean it cannot be made to speak with deciphering.[106]

Heine's influence on Levy can be seen throughout her corpus.[107] This is not to say that Levy did not draw on a wide range of literary influences, either to venerate or subject them to parody:[108] Johann Wolfgang von Goethe (see Levy's translation of "The Shepherd (From Goethe)," p. 555), Algernon Charles Swinburne, Robert Browning, Elizabeth Barrett Browning (see Levy's 1875 "Junior Prize Review" of *Aurora Leigh*, pp. 871–2), and Christina Rossetti (see Levy's article on "The Poetry of Christina Rossetti," pp. 935–44) are to name but a few of the writers that Levy regularly drew on and that crop up frequently in her corpus. However, in Heine Levy had someone who had experienced identity crises akin to her own, and someone who could speak to, and help her understand and engage with her Jewish identity. Indeed, Zion Lask points to one of Levy's childhood publications, "The Ballad of Ida Grey" (pp. 549–52), which she identifies as using a "running metre distinctly that of Heine's 'Donna Clara.'"[109] *Xantippe* begins with an extract taken from Heine's "*Lyrisches Intermezzo*" ("Lyrical Interludes"): "*Aus meinen grossen Schmerzen Mach' ich die kleinen Lieder*" ("From the great pain of my spirit / Come the little

105. Georg Eliot, "German Wit: Heinrich Heine," *The Westminster Review* 137 (January 1856): 17–8.
106. Scheinberg, "'And We Are Not What They Have Been,'" 44; Weisman, "Playing with Figures," 69.
107. Pullen, *The Woman Who Dared*, 51, 53–4; Devine, "'I Sleep but My Heart Waketh,'" 223.
108. Hunt Beckman, *Amy Levy*, 56.
109. Zion Lask, "Amy Levy," 169; for Heine's "Donna Clara" see *The Complete Poems of Heinrich Heine: A Modern English Version*, ed. and trans. Hal Draper (Boston: Suhrkamp/Insel, 1982), 115–7.

songs").[110] In 1882, Levy translated Heine for the *Cambridge Review* (pp. 558–9); in *A Minor Poet,* the poem of the same title says "farewell" to "Heine that stings and smiles" (p. 427), "A Cross-Road Epitaph" (p. 475) and "A Dirge" (pp. 462–3) both begin with extracts from Heine, and "A Farewell" is "After Heine" (p. 474), although was originally published under the title "Imitation of Heine";[111] in 1886, Levy wrote the poem, "After Heine," for the *Cambridge Review* (p. 565); in "Jewish Humour," Levy quotes and translates two lines from Heine's "The Homecoming", having already identified the popularity of his *Buch der Lieder* in her time at Cambridge in the article, "Newnham College" (pp. 881–90): "Sun and moon and stars are laughing; / I am laughing, too – and dying" (p. 922).[112] In "The Ghetto at Florence" (pp. 914–7), readers might detect echoes of Heine's *Der Rabbi von Bacherach* and its romanticised portrayal of the medieval Frankfurt ghetto.[113] Similarly, *The Romance of a Shop* includes a quotation from Heine at the beginning of chapter eighteen (p. 141): "*Die aeltre*

110. Quoted in New, "Introduction," 44 n. 18. For Heine's "Lyrisches Intermezzo" see *The Complete Poems*, ed. and trans. Draper, 51–75.
111. Bristow, "'All Out of Tune,'" 103 n. 57; New, "Introduction," 9, 36, 552 n. 15; Hunt Beckman, *Amy Levy*, 100, 291 n. 10, 299–300 n. 63; Vadillo, "Cosmopolitan Disturbances," 331. For the "Imitation of Heine" version see *The Cambridge Review: A Journal of University Life and Thought* 3, no. 58 (December 7, 1881): 127. In her private correspondence, Levy produced another poem entitled "Imitation of Heine"; for a copy, see Hunt Beckman, *Amy Levy*, 274.
112. Devine, "'I Sleep, but My Heart Waketh,'" 224. For Heine's "The Homecoming," see *The Complete Poems*, ed. and trans. Draper, 76–122; for the lines in Levy's quotation, see p. 61.
113. George Peters, "'Jeder Reiche ist ein Judas Ischariot': Heinrich Heine and the Emancipation of the Jews," *Monatshefte* 104, no. 2 (2012): 210–1; Cecile Schroder Simonsen, "A Spatial Expansion of a Pocket-Size Homeland: Heinrich Heine's Construction of Jewish Space," *Partial Answers* 14, no. 2 (2016): 311; see also Christhard Hoffman, "From Heinrich Heine to Isidore Kracauer: The Frankfurt Ghetto in German-Jewish Historical Culture and Historiography," *Jewish Culture and History* 10, no. 2–3 (2008): 45–64. Additionally, see Heinrich Heine, "The Rabbi of Bacherach: A Fragment," in *The Rabbi of Bacherach and Other Stories*, ed. Elizabeth Petuchowski (Princeton: Markus Wiener Publishers, 2014), 19–80.

Tochter gaehnet / 'Ich will nicht verhungern bei euch, / Ich gehe morgen zum Grafen, / Und der ist verliebt und reich.'" The translation reads: "Then yawns the eldest daughter, / 'I will starve no longer here; / I will go to the Count tomorrow, / He is rich, and he loves me dear.'"[114] In *Reuben Sachs,* Leo hums "*Ich grolle nicht*" (p. 210) from Heine's *Lyrisches Intermezzo* (put to song in Robert Schumann's *Dichterliebe*), and his own book collection includes (p. 275) "volumes of Heine."[115] In fact, even Judith's Sephardic ancestry and its potential for Anglo-Jewish renewal is possibly a product of Levy's reading of *Der Rabbi von Bacherach* or *Hebrew Melodies* and the complex ways in which Heine responded to German-Jewish scholars' attempts to reconstruct Sephardic histories of medieval Andalusia.[116] Heine was keen to disrupt utopian or revisionist portrayals of Jewish life in Al-Andalus and to offer a more nuanced account, as well to destabilise any notion of Sephardic hegemony and suitability for assimilation over and above stereotypes of Ashkenazi Jews as being culturally retrograde.[117] In "Donna Clara," for example, Heine has Clara employ antisemitic discourses in courting the knight: "'Gnats were stinging me, beloved, / Gnats are worst of all in Summer, / And I passionately hate them / Like a bunch of long-nosed Jew-boys.'" The knight demonstrates his love by avowing "'the Saviour / Whom that God-accursed Jewry / Murdered out of wicked malice,'" only to reveal in the last verse: "'I, Senora, your beloved, / Am the son of the distinguished, / Eminent and learned Rabbi / Israel of Saragossa.'"[118] In the poem, Heine's

114. Emma Lazarus' translation, quoted by Bernstein, ed., *The Romance of a Shop,* 164 n. 1.

115. Devine, "'I Sleep but My Heart Waketh,'" 223–4; Vadillo, "Cosmopolitan Disturbances," 331.

116. Gabriel Cooper, "Facing the East: Orientalism and Anti-Semitism in Heine's *Hebräische Melodien,*" *Seminar: A Journal of Germanic Studies* 56, no. 1 (2020): 71; Simonsen, "A Spatial Expansion," 313–4. See Heinrich Heine, *Hebrew Melodies,* trans. Stephen Mitchell and Jack Prelutsky (University Park: Pennsylvania State University Press, 2019).

117. Cooper, "Facing the East," 55–9, 67, 71–2.

118. Heine, "Donna Clara," 116–7.

converso knight is dignified and proud of his heritage in surprising the antisemitic Clara.[119] A similar twist takes place in *Der Rabbi von Bacherach* when the "Spanish cavalier" reveals to "Beautiful Sara" that he too is "'sprung from the House of Israel.'"[120] The latter, "Beautiful Sara," might even be the inspiration for Judith and her experience of the synagogue in *Reuben Sachs* (pp. 222–6). In *Der Rabbi von Bacherach*, "Beautiful Sara" visits the synagogue in Frankfurt. "Beautiful Sara" wears "white linen," possesses a "slender form and good and gentle face," is "touchingly beautiful," with "lovely features" that indicate "a sorrowful intensity."[121] In Heine's satiric account of the synagogue and construction of what S.S. Prawer called his "Jewish portraits," just as Judith is confronted by women in the gallery wearing the "very latest fashion," the "sickly … smell of stale perfume," fainting, and an overplus of gossip, so too, Sara's experience:[122]

> Several times she [Schnapper-Elle] glanced aside with contemptuous looks, apparently directed at some sneering young women who were apparently sizing up her clothes. Truly this dress was remarkable enough – a very puffed skirt of white satin, on which all the animals of Noah's Ark were embroidered in gaudy colours; a jacket of cloth of gold like a cuirass, the sleeves of red velvet slashed with yellow; on her head, a superhumanly tall cap; round her neck, a mighty ruff of stiff white linen; furthermore a silver chain, hung with all kinds of coins, cameos, and curiosities, chief among which was a great image of the city of Amsterdam, which rested on her bosom.
>
> But the dresses of the other women were not less remarkable. They consisted of a medley of fashions of different ages, and many a little woman there was so covered with gold and diamonds as to look like a walking jeweller's shop.… the women competed in coming up with

119. John Efron, *German Jewry and the Allure of the Sephardic* (Princeton: Princeton University Press, 2016), 170.
120. Heine, "The Rabbi of Bacherach," 70, 73; Efron, *German Jewry*, 175.
121. Heine, "The Rabbi of Bacherach," 26, 28.
122. S. S. Prawer, *Heine's Jewish Comedy: A Study of His Portraits of Jews and Judaism* (Oxford: Clarendon Press, 1983), 381; Jeffrey Sammons, "Heine's *Rabbi von Bacherach*: The Unresolved Tensions," *The German Quarterly* 37, no. 1 (January 1964): 29.

> as much finery as they could – partly to arouse envy in the others, and partly to advertise the wealth and credit rating of their husbands.
>
> While downstairs in the synagogue, passages from the Books of Moses are being read, the devotion is apt to relax somewhat. Many make themselves comfortable and sit down, whispering with a friend about mundane affairs, or one might go out into the courtyard to get a little fresh air. Small boys take the liberty of visiting their mothers in the women's gallery where the worshipful mood has suffered an even greater decline. There's chatting, gossiping, laughing, and, as will always happen, the younger women make fun of the elder, while the latter complain of youth and the general degeneracy of the times. And just as there was a cantor downstairs in the synagogue of Frankfurt, so there was a head-cackler and gossip in the second floor, above. This was Puppy Reiss, a flat, greenish woman who had a nose for every bit of trouble and always some scandal on her tongue.[123]

More generally, Heine's "On Poland" (1823) can possibly indicate what Levy was trying to achieve in *Reuben Sachs*. "Über Polen," when it appeared in *Der Gesellschafter*, was anonymous.[124] The account begins with Heine's speaker claiming to be someone who "moved in the higher spheres of society" and for the first time is visiting a *shtetl*. His immediate reaction is to exclaim that "The external experience of the Polish Jew is terrible. A shudder runs down my spine when I remember my first experience ... of a Polish village inhabited mainly by Jews."[125] For Prawer, Heine's account is meant to be read as how a well-educated, liberal German would understand the socio-economically deprived *shtetl* community. In the process, Prawer argues, Heine sought to undermine several antisemitic suppositions to demonstrate that "Jews are what the stereotypes in the heads of German writers and readers make them out to be."[126] The text, like *Reuben Sachs*, has been interpreted as activating antisemitic tropes and

123. Heine, "The Rabbi of Bacherach," 64–5.
124. Jeffrey Sammons, *Heinrich Heine: A Modern Biography* (Princeton: Princeton University Press, 1979), 87.
125. Heine, "On Poland," quoted in Prawer, *Heine's Jewish Comedy*, 59, 61.
126. Prawer, *Heine's Jewish Comedy*, 63.

as indicative of Jewish self-hatred.[127] However, scholars acknowledge that Heine was actually critiquing assimilationist and emancipatory rhetoric that assumed such communities had no intrinsic cultural value beyond Enlightenment or romantic nationalist discourses.[128] Thus, the antisemitic caricatures in *Reuben Sachs* might reflect the ways in which Heine used characters, real and fictional, as signifiers of particular issues and how they are interpreted from different perspectives.[129] In Levy's novel, the materialism and degeneracy of the characters points to a range of ills. However, just like with Heine, it is probable that Levy hoped her Jewish surname would work in a way that indicated the satiric nature of the novel, if the Gospel reference to "my beloved son" that begins the story was not enough in itself.[130]

Levy was, however, naive to think that readers would understand the complex narrative voices and satirising processes at work in the novel. Understandably, whether taken as satiric or not, Levy's deployment of antisemitic tropes was a cause of indignation in Anglo-Jewish communal politics, particularly against a backdrop of growing antisemitism, national questions about migration and assimilation, and alongside a number of similar texts accused of being, according to a contributor

127. Jeffrey Grossman, "Heine and Jewish Culture: The Poetics of Appropriation," in *A Companion to the Works of Heinrich Heine*, ed. Roger Cook (Woodbridge: Camden House, 2002), 258; see, for example, Gilman, *Jewish Self-Hatred*, 173–5, in particular on Heine and the "image of the bad Jew." Gilman did however acknowledge his later indebtedness (see 416 n. 51) to Prawer's *Heine's Jewish Comedy*.

128. Prawer, *Heine's Jewish Comedy*, 63–4; Grossman, "Heine and Jewish Culture," 260; Ritchie Robertson, "Enlightened and Romantic Views of the Ghetto: David Friedlander versus Heinrich Heine," in *Ghetto Writing: Traditional and Eastern Jewry in German-Jewish Literature from Heine to Hilsenrath*, eds. Anne Fuchs and Florian Krobb (Drawer: Camden House, 1999), 35–7.

129. Prawer, *Heine's Jewish Comedy*, 4–6; Dwor, *Jewish Feeling*, 127–8.

130. Ari Joskowicz, "Heinrich Heine's Transparent Masks: Denominational Politics and the Poetics of Emancipation in Nineteenth-Century Germany and France," *German Studies Review* 34, no. 1 (2011): 77. See also Scheinberg's point that some readers may have ignored Levy's "formal experiments" and the "literary contexts" underpinning *Reuben Sachs* ("Canonizing the Jew," 181).

to *Jewish World*, "malicious and nasty" and providing ammunition "in support of … antisemitic theories."[131] So, while in *Reuben Sachs* it is in the fullness of time possible to identify the influence of what Ari Joskowicz has referred to as Heine's deployment of "identity games" and a "transparent mask,"[132] contemporaneous readers of the novel were not privy to its overly-complex and "experimental" insights or its appropriation of a literary Shibboleth that is consistently employed in Levy's poetry and short stories to indicate subversive components and sub and counter-narratives.[133] The same can be said of Levy's articles for the *Jewish Chronicle*. In particular, Levy's discussion of William Shakespeare's *Merchant of Venice* and the character, Shylock, who has figured extensively in antisemitic imagery, is a case in point. In "The Jew in Fiction," Levy lists Shylock as one of many unrealistic "Jewish" fictional characters and concludes: "there has been no serious attempt at serious treatment of the subject; at grappling in its entirety with the complex problem of Jewish life and Jewish character" (p. 920). Likewise, in "Jewish Children" Levy states that "Even Shylock can divert some of his attention from his ducats to his daughter" when making the point: "Love of offspring might, indeed, be described as our master-passion, stronger than our love of money, than our love of success" (p. 930). Just like in *Reuben Sachs* Levy deploys antisemitic archetypes to frame contemporary social issues and to develop critique, but was certainly naive in assuming readers would understand her wider point about how an antisemitic discursive framework informs literary, mediatised, and socio-cultural representations of "Jews." In its literal form and interpretation, *Reuben Sachs* is an antisemitic novel. Levy expected her readers to understand that the characters are framed by a narrative voice through

131. Anon., "The Deterioration of the Jewess," 5. The contributor to *Jewish World* had in mind Julia Frankau's novel, *Dr. Phillips: A Maida Vale Idyll* (London: Vizetelly, 1887); Frankau wrote using the pseudonym, Frank Danby.

132. Joskowicz, "Heinrich Heine's Transparent Masks," 74–5.

133. See Hunt Beckman's suggestion that *Reuben Sachs*' "narrative strategy" is "experimental" (*Amy Levy*, 212); similarly, see Scheinberg's point about Levy's deployment of a "narrative persona" that was neither "Jewish or Christian" in the novel ("Canonizing the Jew," 181).

pervasive antisemitic literary tropes and stereotypes. Moreover, Levy tried to make an overly complex sociological point about how assimilated Anglo-Jewish middle-class identity is constructed and constrained according to prevalent capitalist notions of bourgeois material success. Indeed, the stereotypes and tropes deployed in the novel and that are used in Levy's polemical articles on the Jewish community are there to convey complex discourses, but there is little or no direct repudiation.[134] In fact, much of Levy's writing is framed in ways that are excessively complex, overloaded with cryptic, satirical, and obscure references, and allusions that in some cases will remain forever known only to her. This literary strategy, if it can even be called that, is at the root of the entire Levy corpus. Indeed, in her "Junior Prize Review" short essay on Elizabeth Barrett Browning's *Aurora Leigh*, Levy complained that Browning was too fond of "introducing too many learned allusions" and that "her writings" can only be understood by those willing to take "the trouble to understand them" (p. 872). Interestingly, in writing about Christina Rossetti years later, Levy described her as "a poetic personality difficult to grasp, difficult to classify": "she is at one moment intensely human, intensely personal; at another, she paddles away in her rainbow shell, and is lost to sight as she dips over the horizon-line of her halcyon sea" (pp. 943–4). These comments can help to explain the complexities of Levy's corpus and the potential underpinnings of her over-compensatory writing style. Levy adopted such stratagems, particularly through her reading of Heine, to compensate for her own sense of exclusion, insecurity, and "minority."[135] Thus, Hunt Beckman has a point in stating that when it was published, "*Reuben Sachs* was mistakenly perceived … as an attack on Jewish life," but whatever her intention, Levy put in to print a range of antisemitic tropes.[136]

---

134. Francis, "Amy Levy," 201; idem, "Socialist Feminism," 117-23; Peters, "'Jeder Reiche ist ein Judas Ischariot,'" 219.

135. Scheinberg, *Women's Poetry*, 191.

136. Linda Hunt Beckman, "Amy Levy," The Shalvi/Hyman Encyclopedia of Jewish Women (2021), accessed August 27, 2021, https://jwa.org/encyclopedia/article/levy-amy.

That Levy used different narrators, satirising discourses, and binaries or dichotomies in the same way that Heine adopted stereotypes and cliches only for them to be disassembled, the most obvious being the avowal in *Ludwig Börne: A Memorial* (1840) that "all men are either Jews or Hellenes,"[137] would have been lost on most readers of *Reuben Sachs*. In fact, even Levy's critique of materialism is characteristic of Heine's linking of assimilation to capitalism and the entry of acculturated German-Jews into high society.[138] Katie Magnus's *Jewish Portraits* (1888) includes one of Levy's translations of Heine (p. 569), as well as translations of Jehudah Halevi's poetry (pp. 566–8).[139] The Halevi translations, taken from Geiger's German versions, possibly say more about Levy's fascination with Heine's "Jehuda ben Halevy" than they do about her interest in the medieval poet.[140] Indeed, Eleanor Marx, who met Levy at the British Museum, claimed that "her affinity was with Heine, the sublimated essence of Jewish genius."[141] Levy's poem, "Borderland" (p. 503), is perhaps typical of her debt to Heine's "*Das*

137. Heine quoted in Alan Levenson, "Invidious Distinctions: Hebraism and Hellenism in Heinrich Heine and Matthew Arnold," *Jewish Quarterly Review* 110, no. 1 (Winter 2020): 106; on Heine's use of "dichotomy" see Levenson, *passim*. See also Heine's *Ludwig Börne: A Memorial*, ed. and trans. Jeffrey Sammons (Woodbridge: Camden House, 2006).

138. Peters, "'Jeder Reiche ist ein Judas Ischariot,'" 217, 221, 225.

139. See also Levy's translation (not included in this volume) of J.B. Peres, *Historic and Other Doubts; or the Non-Existence of Napoleon Proved*, ed. Lily (London: E. W. Allen, 1885).

140. Zion Lask, "Amy Levy," 183; Hunt Beckman, *Amy Levy*, 77, 295 n. 6; New, "Introduction," 45 n. 26; Devine, "'I Sleep but My Heart Waketh,'" 224–5; idem, "Exile and Redemption: Amy Levy's Association with Yehuda Halevi and the Transmission of the Sephardic Tradition of Hebrew Poetry," *Literature & Theology* 26, no. 2 (June 2012): 126. See Abraham Geiger, *Divan des Castiliers Abu'l-Hassan Juda ha-Levi* (Breslau: Kern, 1851). For Heine's "Jehuda ben Halevy," see *Hebrew Melodies*, 19–66.

141. Eleanor Marx quoted in Francis, "Socialist Feminism," 117; Hunt Beckman, *Amy Levy*, 82. Marx translated *Reuben Sachs* into German; see Susan David Bernstein, "Radical Readers at the British Museum: Eleanor Marx, Clementina Black, Amy Levy," *Nineteenth Century Gender Studies* 3, no. 2 (Summer 2007): no page number.

Hohelied" ("The Song of Songs") and "*Lyrisches Intermezzo*."[142] "*Das Hohelied*" and its account of the love between Solomon and the Shulamite encourages Christian readers to assume they are reading a symbolic account of the relationship between God and Church, just as Jewish readers are expected to read in a symbiosis between God and Israel.[143] Heine's actual emphasis however is on the erotic elements of Song of Songs and the beauty of the Shulamite: "A woman's body truly is / The Song of Songs."[144] Levy's "Borderland" tries to do something very similar by offering a complex intertextual reading that draws on Heine's interpretation of the biblical text:[145]

> Am I waking, am I sleeping?
> As the first faint dawn comes creeping
> Thro' the pane, I am aware
> Of an unseen presence hovering,
> Round, above, in the dusky air:
> A downy bird, with an odorous wing,
> That fans my forehead, and sheds perfume,
> As sweet as love, as soft as death,
> Drowsy-slow through the summer-gloom.
> My heart in some dream-rapture saith,
> *It is she*. Half in a swoon,
> I spread my arms in slow delight. –
> O prolong, prolong the night,
> For the nights are short in June!

The poet's dream-like state might also indicate Levy's reading of Heine's "Seraphine," particularly its opening verses that describe "the

142. For Heine's "*Das Hohelied*" (in German) see Paul Peters, "A Walk on the Wild Side: Heine's Eroticism," in *A Companion to the Works*, ed. Cook, 86–7; for "*Das Hohelied*" in English see Draper's version in *The Complete Poems*, 743–4.
143. Beate Perrey, *Schumann's Dichterliebe and Early Romantic Poetics: Fragmentation of Desire* (Cambridge: Cambridge University Press, 2002), 93–4; Devine, "'I Sleep but My Heart Waketh,'" 219, 235.
144. Perrey, *Schumann's Dichterliebe*, 93–4; Peters, "A Walk on the Wild Side," 86–8; *The Complete Poems*, ed. and trans. Draper, 743.
145. Devine, "'I Sleep but My Heart Waketh,'" 230, 240.

dusky wood of dream" and the presence "hovering."[146] Much like Heine's *imago*, Levy's poem, or its subtext, focuses on Song of Songs, in particular 5:2–6, and seeks to offer a new reading. Unlike the biblical version, in "Borderland" the Shulamite is active in initiating the romantic encounter, while the male lover is passive. The ambiguity is established from the outset: instead of the line, "I sleep, but my heart waketh" (5:2), "Am I waking, am I sleeping?" sets up the dream-like sequence. In this retelling, the romance, as in the biblical text, is feminised (according to nineteenth-century notions of femininity) and "soft as death," a play on 8:6 where "love is strong as death." Likewise, the "unseen presence hovering," symbolising Israel, and the male speaker, Solomon or God, captures the essence of the traditional rabbinic allegory. However, the focus is clearly on the Shulamite woman, just as in Heine's "*Das Hohelied*."[147] Indeed, Heine constructed complex and opposing identity positions and distinctions, "Hellene" in opposition to the "Hebraic" or "Nazarene," Christian/Jewish, German/Jewish, "'good' Jew" in contradistinction to "'bad' Jew," only to show the fragility of each label in satirical, comical and ironic ways that suggest none of them have any intrinsic value.[148] Hunt Beckman has pointed to Heine's influence on Levy's poem, "In the Mile End Road" (p. 510). For Hunt Beckman, the poem deploys an unexpected "reversal" characteristic of Heine in suddenly revealing that an encounter with a past romantic interest is impossible given the realisation: "For one strange moment I forgot / My only love was dead."[149] Such

146. For Heine's "Seraphine" see *The Complete Poems*, ed. and trans. Draper, 330–5.

147. Devine, "'I Sleep but My Heart Waketh,'" 230–6, 238; Perrey, *Schumann's Dichterliebe*, 92, 95.

148. Willi Goetschel, *The Discipline of Philosophy and the Invention of Modern Jewish Thought* (New York: Fordham University Press, 2015), 25, 27, 33–6; Noam Pines, "Life in the Valley: Figures of Dehumanization in Heinrich Heine's 'Prinzessin Sabbat,'" *Prooftexts* 33, no. 1 (2013): 26–7; Levenson, "Invidious Distinctions," 105, 108, 110; Richard Whittington-Egan, "Amy Levy: A Tragic Victorian Novelist," *Contemporary Review* 280, no. 1632 (Jan. 2002): 44; Sander Gilman, *Jewish Self-Hatred*, 170, 172.

149. Hunt Beckman, *Amy Levy*, 196.

reversals or twists are evident in "Euphemia: A Sketch" (1880), where it is revealed that Euphemia will marry Dr. Frank Thorpleigh (p. 605); in "The Diary of a Plain Girl" (1883), when Ralston reveals his love for Milly rather than Dahlia (p. 639); in "Olga's Valentine" (1884) when the "old maid," Olga, realises that Jack wanted to marry her seven years earlier, but had been duped by the "shifty" Humphrey in to wrongly believing that he had already secured her agreement to marry (p. 656); in "In Holiday Humour" (1884), when Olivia reveals to Sydney that marriage is impossible given when they were on a boat earlier in the day and it had stormed, she was actually thinking about another person (pp. 668–9); in "A Meadowshire Romance" (1886), when Agnes assumes Kitty will be marrying Claude, but it is instead Gilbert (p. 763); in "At Prato" (1888) when Elinor suddenly disappears (p. 772); and in "Eldorado at Islington" (1889) when the poverty stricken Lloyd family cannot accept inheritance given "it was wrung from the starving poor" (p. 852).

Ada Wallas, writing ten years after Levy's death, described her poetry as engaging in "open imitation" of Heine.[150] It is perhaps helpful to see Levy's short stories and novels in a similar light. Levy's corpus exhibits a similar desire to construct, sometimes occupy, and then deconstruct various identity positions. Scholars have identified Levy's employment of "subversive identities,"[151] "fictive selves,"[152] and "'minority' voices,"[153] as well as her penchant to "play with figures."[154] In playing with the genders of her speakers, exploiting and then disassembling stereotypes, relying on complex symbolism, and in repeating insidious antisemitic discourses only to undermine them,[155]

150. Ada Wallas, "The Poetry of Amy Levy," *The Academy*, August 12, 1899, 162; see Bristow, "'All Out of Tune,'" 95.

151. Alex Goody, "Murder in Mile End: Amy Levy, Jewishness, and the City," *Victorian Literature and Culture* 34 (2006): 461.

152. Hunt Beckman, *Amy Levy*, 58–74, 193.

153. Scheinberg, *Women's Poetry*, 191.

154. Weisman, "Playing with Figures," 59.

155. Goody, "Murder in Mile End," 467–8; Scheinberg, "Recasting 'Sympathy and Judgement,'" 180; Nord, "'Neither Pairs nor Odd,'" 748; Jusova, *The New Woman*,

Levy clearly adopted a discursive strategy comparable to Heine, who utilised different personas as well as discourses associated with antisemitism, self-hatred, and discriminatory constructions of Jewishness to develop critique.[156] Despite writing in different contexts, both were aware, whether Heine through religious conversion or Levy through attending Cambridge or engaging in literary, political, and avant-garde circles, that through an antisemitic lens, and even in the context of philosemitism, constructions of "'Juden, Judentum, jüdisch'" or "Jews, Judaism, Jewish" could never have value or be assigned any form of genuine acceptance.[157] Heine, having been baptised and being one of the first European-Jews to publicly use the term, "emancipation," lamented that he would never find acceptance in Christian or Jewish culture, and gradually found that despite once identifying as a "Hellene," he was unable to move beyond the racial constraints of his own "Jewishness."[158] Heine finally conceded in 1849 that he was "no longer … a well-fleshed Hellene who enjoys his life and smiles down on melancholy Nazarenes – all I am now is a poor Jew sick unto death, an emaciated image of wretchedness, an unhappy man!"[159] Scheinberg argues that Levy did not formally posit a specific "Jewish poetic identity," but that her surname did mark her out as Jewish.[160] Levy was plagued by anxiety driven by a racialised understanding of her Jewishness and concerns about how others would perceive her.[161] Comments by the poet, Katharine Tynan, recalling meeting Levy, despite

---

177; Dwor, "The Racial Romance," 462, 464. On Levy's symbolism see Linda Hunt Beckman, "Amy Levy: Urban Poetry, Poetic Innovation, and the Fin-de-Siecle Woman Poet," in *The Fin-de-Siecle Poem: English Literary Culture and the 1890s,* ed. Joseph Bristow (Athens: Ohio University Press, 2005), 207–30.

156. Levenson, "Invidious Distinctions," 110–1; Gilman, *Jewish Self-Hatred,* 187.
157. Levenson, "Invidious Distinctions," 110–1.
158. Peters, "'Jeder Reiche ist ein Judas Ischariot,'" 209; Pines, "Life in the Valley," 26; Levenson, "Invidious Distinctions," 105, 108.
159. Heine quoted in Pines, "Life in the Valley," 26.
160. Scheinberg, "'And We Are Not What They Have Been,'" 45; idem, "Canonizing the Jew," 95.
161. Hunt Beckman, *Amy Levy,* 112; Pullen, *The Woman Who Dared,* 26–7.

being well-meaning, reveal the extent to which Anglo-Jews could be subject to processes of racialization characteristic of the period and its fixation on race:[162] "I remember Amy Levy, that tragic personality, who had so short a time to live, sitting opposite to me, her charming little Eastern face dreamy in a cloud of tobacco-smoke."[163] Miron thus poses the question, directed at Heine but equally applicable to Levy: "was not Heine labelled by his antisemitic detractors the representative of 'Young Judea' rather than of *Jung Deutschland*?"[164]

Levy's "A Minor Poet" (pp. 424–31) is the monologue that established her status as a "minor" poet in relation to the canon, universalising hegemonic Christian discourses, and Matthew Arnold's claim that: "'[t]o ascertain the master-current in the literature of an epoch, and to distinguish this from all minor currents, is one of the critic's highest functions."[165] For Joseph Bristow, Levy's poem and identification as "A Minor Poet" was a direct challenge to Arnold.[166] Similarly, Scheinberg has analysed how Arnold's criticism of Heine is couched in tropes of Christian hegemony, subtle forms of antisemitism, and appropriation of the "Hebraic" beyond its Jewish context.[167] In particular, Scheinberg points to how Arnold's critique of Heine is framed according to the Gospels and Christian supersessionism, specifically Matthew 22:14,[168] evident in the following passages:

162. Jusova, *The New Woman*, 133.
163. Katharine Tynan, *Twenty-Five Years: Reminisces* (London: John Murray, 1913), 290.
164. Miron, *From Continuity to Contiguity*, 133.
165. Bristow, "'All Out of Tune,'" 76, 81; Scheinberg, *Women's Poetry*, 213; idem, "Canonizing the Jew," 173; Arnold's point (quoted by Bristow, "'All Out of Tune,'" 80) is from the essay, "Heinrich Heine," in *Lectures and Essays in Criticism*, ed. R. H. Super (Ann Arbor: The University of Michigan Press, 1962), 107–32; see also Arnold's *Culture and Anarchy: An Essay in Social and Political Criticism* (London: Smith, Elder and Co., 1869).
166. Bristow, "'All Out of Tune,'" 80; see also Scheinberg, *Women's Poetry*, 54–8, 210–2; idem, "Canonizing the Jew," *passim*.
167. Scheinberg, *Women's Poetry*, 56–7. On the "Hebraic-Hellenic dichotomy" see Levenson, "Invidious Distinctions," 105 and *passim*.
168. Scheinberg, *Women's Poetry*, 57.

> He died, and has left a blemished name; with his crying faults, – his intemperate susceptibility, his unscrupulous in passion, his inconceivable attacks on his enemies, his still more inconceivable attacks on his friends, his want of generosity, his sensuality, his incessant mocking, – how could it be otherwise? ... To his intellectual deliverance there was ... something else wanting, and that something else was something immense; the old-fashioned, laborious, eternally needful moral deliverance. Goethe says that he was deficient in *love*; to me his weakness seems to be not so much a deficiency in love as a deficiency in self-respect, in true dignity of character.... And what have we got from Heine? A half-result, for want of moral balance, and of nobleness of soul and character. That is what I say: there is so much power, so many seem able to run well, so many give promise of running well; – so few reach the goal, so few are chosen. *Many are called, few chosen* [Matthew 22:14].[169]

Scheinberg has further identified Levy's rejection of Arnold's claim that "'Hebraism for our race [is] an eternal possession.'"[170] For Arnold:

> Heinrich Heine, and other writers of his sort, give us the spectacle of the tables completely turned, an of Hebraism brought in just as a foil and contrast to Hellenism, and to make the superiority of Hellenism more manifest. In both these cases there is injustice and misrepresentation. The aim and end of both Hebraism and Hellenism is ... one and the same ... But while Hebraism seizes upon certain plain, capital limitations of the universal order, ... the bent of Hellenism is to follow, with flexible activity, the whole play of the universal order.[171]

Arnold concluded that while "it is a time to Hellenise," Hebraism could continue to provide "discipline" and inspiration for the "great Christian virtue, Faith."[172] However, as Scheinberg has pointed out, Levy avowed in "Jewish Humour" (pp. 921–4) that "not for all Aristophanes" could Jewish social-cultural and linguistic identity be

169. Arnold, "Heinrich Heine," 131–2.
170. Scheinberg, *Women's Poetry*, 57.
171. Arnold, *Culture and Anarchy*, 145–6.
172. Arnold, *Culture and Anarchy*, lviii-lix.

subsumed and extinguished by Arnold's "'master-current'" of Christian tradition, literature, and theology.[173] Accordingly, Scheinberg posits, Levy's "Jewish signature" made her a minoritized "Jewish voice" in Christian cultural and literary contexts and a corrective to Arnold's analysis of Heine.[174] Levy, as a "minor poet," could therefore use her poetry to signify how Christian tradition informs and underpins literary culture.[175]

Levy did this, like Heine, by appropriating Greek classical, romantic, modernist, Christian, and Jewish biblical, secular, cultural, and literary perspectives, what has been identified as a literary "cosmopolitanism."[176] And akin to Heine, it can be difficult to identify whether Levy is identifying with a particular tradition or critiquing it.[177] Heine's "*Gedächtnisfeier*" is a case in point: "No mass will be chanted / no Kaddish will be recited, / nothing said and nothing chanted."[178] The lines symbolise Heine's exclusion from both Christian and Jewish traditions.[179] Levy too adopts a similar tone in "A Ballad of Religion and Marriage," which was not actually circulated until 1915 (pp. 571–2). The poem's lines, "The Father, Son, and Holy Ghost, / Pale and defeated, rise and go. / The great Jehovah is laid low, / Vanished his burning bush and rod," signal a future in which Christianity and Judaism, like the "Domestic round

173. Scheinberg, *Women's Poetry*, 209–12; idem, "Canonizing the Jew," 176–8.
174. Scheinberg, "Canonizing the Jew," 178, 183, 185–7; Bristow, "'All Out of Tune,'" 98.
175. Scheinberg, "Canonizing the Jew," 173; idem, *Women's Poetry*, 191; Bristow, "'All Out of Tune,'" 76, 81.
176. See Mordecai Roshwald, "Heinrich Heine: The Predicament of a Cultural Pluralist," *Modern Age* 53, no. 1 (Winter/Spring 2011): 33–8; see also Dwor's point about Levy's exploitation of "popular and Christian biblical materials" (*Jewish Feeling*, 178).
177. Roshwald, "Heinrich Heine," 33, 38–9; Peters, "'Jeder Reiche ist ein Judas Ischariot,'" 219.
178. Heine, "*Gedächtnisfeier*," quoted in Roshwald, "Heinrich Heine," 38.
179. Roshwald, "Heinrich Heine," 38.

of boiled and roast" (marriage), will no longer exist.[180] Like for Heine, both faiths were sources of anxiety and exclusion for Levy. Levy's poem, "Lohengrin" (p. 515), referring to the Wagnerian opera of the same name, makes a similar point in commenting on secularisation.[181] Scheinberg sees the knight, Lohengrin, as symbolic of the "'new'" Christian faith, and Elsa's brother, Gottfried, who reappears when Lohengrin is forced to leave following Elsa's questioning of his background, as signifying the "'old' Jewish order." In Scheinberg's interpretation Elsa's romance with Lohengrin is superseded by recommitment to her "Brother" and a "return rather than conversion":[182]

> Back to the mystic shore beyond the main
> The mystic craft has sped, and left no trace.
> Ah, nevermore may she behold his face,
> Nor touch his hand, nor hear his voice again!
> With hidden front she crouches; all in vain
> The proffered balm. A vessel nears the place;
> They bring her young, lost brother; see her strain
> The new-found nursling in a close embrace.
>
> God, we have lost Thee with much questioning.
> In vain we seek Thy trace by sea and land,
> And in Thine empty fanes where no men sing.
> What shall we do through all the weary days?
> Thus wail we and lament. Our eyes we raise,
> And, lo, our Brother with an outstretched hand!

180. Hunt Beckman, *Amy Levy*, 140–1; Nord, "'Neither Pairs Nor Odd,'" 740; Vadillo, "New Woman Poets," 30. See also Carolyn Lake's point that the poem seeks to create a "utopic otherworld" in "'All the World is Blind': Unveiling Same-Sex Desire in the Poetry of Amy Levy," in *Changing the Victorian Subject*, eds. Maggie Tonkin *et al.* (Adelaide: University of Adelaide Press, 2014), 249. On Levy's conclusion that "Folks shall be neither pairs nor odd" (p. 572) see Goody, "Passing in the City," 168, and Hunt Beckman, *Amy Levy*, 141. See also Pullen's extensive analysis of the poem and why it was addressed to Grant Allen in *The Woman Who Dared*, 182–91.
181. Hunt Beckman, *Amy Levy*, 262 n. 5; Scheinberg, *Women's Poetry*, 229.
182. Scheinberg, *Women's Poetry*, 228–30.

"Lohengrin," in indicating a re-engagement with Jewish origins, might also relate to Levy's reading of Heine and his own return to the ancestral faith, "Holy city Yerushalayim," even if he continued to be enthralled by many different cultures and philosophies.[183] Thus, it is not surprising to find poems in the Levy corpus that utilise Christian biblical tradition only to unearth its Jewish underpinnings.[184] This is particularly the case in "A Prayer" (pp. 409–10). Scheinberg claims that in the poem "the speaker figures herself as Christ before Resurrection," reinterpreting Christian tradition and symbology, with the "key" signifying that God has sought to exclude the speaker from the traditions arising from the Gospel accounts:[185]

> To live – it is my doom –
> Lonely as in a tomb,
> This cross on me was laid;
> My God, I know not why;
> Here in the dark I lie, Lonely, yet not afraid.
> It has seemed good to Thee
> Still to withhold the key
> Which opes the way to men;
> I am shut in alone,
> I make not any moan,
> Thy ways are past my ken. (p. 409)

The poem, in reappropriating Jesus and signifying his Jewishness, potentially experiments with the "midrashic imagination" and the historicity of the Jesus movement in the same way that the *Wissenschaft des Judentums* movement tried to locate the historical Jesus.[186] Indeed, the

---

183. Roshwald, "Heinrich Heine," 38–9. Roshwald's quotation is taken from an *Atta Troll* manuscript quoted in Prawer, *Heine's Jewish Comedy*, 447–8.
184. Scheinberg, *Women's Poetry*, 229; idem, "Canonizing the Jew," 194.
185. Scheinberg, *Women's Poetry*, 223, 226–7.
186. Devine, "'The Ghetto at Florence,'" 11; see the analysis of "A Prayer" as midrash in Devine, *From Anglo-First-Wave*, 63, 71–95. Additionally, see Dwor's appropriation of "midrash" as a means of reading and interpreting texts, including Levy's, in *Jewish Feeling, passim.*

poem identifies the point at which Jesus is appropriated by Christian biblical tradition and the New Covenant over the Mosaic Law.[187] Levy addresses similar themes in "Magdalen" (pp. 455–7), which again looks to the Gospels, in this instance focusing on Mary Magdalene. The poem reappropriates biblical symbology in describing a liaison between Magdalene and Jesus.[188] In this way, Scheinberg suggests, the poem works as an avowal of "Jewish identity" given the speaker, Magdalene, in conversation with Jesus following the Resurrection, castigates his refusal to countenance their earlier "Jewish" love having instead chosen the path of "Christian" tradition:[189]

> You were so tender with me, too!
> One summer's night a cold blast blew,
> Closer about my throat you drew
> The half-slipt shawl of dusky blue.
> And once my hand, on a summer's morn,
> I stretched to pluck a rose, a thorn
> Struck through the flesh and made it bleed
> (A little drop of blood indeed!)
> Pale grew your cheek; you stoopt and bound
> Your handkerchief around the wound;
> Your voice came with a broken sound;
> With the deep breath your breast was riven;
> I wonder, did God laugh in Heaven? (pp. 455–6)

Magdalene's painful recollection, Scheinberg suggests, as well as the symbology of the "thorn" and its piercing the "flesh," reveals that what matters in this instance is Jesus's struggle and attunement to Christian

187. Devine, *From Anglo-First-Wave*, 78–9.
188. Scheinberg, *Women's Poetry*, 221–3; Devine, *From Anglo-First-Wave*, 126.
189. Scheinberg, *Women's Poetry*, 222–3; idem, "Canonizing the Jew," 191–2. The "stone" symbol appears in the poems, "To a Dead Poet" and "Epitaph" (pp. 423 and 476), and possibly signifies in these instances the limited options for intellectual fulfilment available to educated women; see Karen Alkalay-Gut, "Aesthetic and Decadent Poetry," in *The Cambridge Companion to Victorian Poetry*, ed. Bristow, 244.

eschatology that she, as a Jewish woman, does not understand.[190] For Scheinberg, the poem says "Shibboleth" to those able to identify its incorporation of "Jewish identity," signified most prominently in its "stone" metaphor:[191] "All night I lie and think and think; / If my heart were not made of stone, / But flesh and blood, it needs must shrink / Before such thoughts. Was ever known / A woman with a heart of stone?" (p. 457). Scholars have read the poem as an account of the Magdalen institutions for reforming so called "fallen women," identifying a speaker prostrate with anguish at the prospect of dying in a Magdalen asylum.[192] Scheinberg, however, argues that the line, "Was ever known / A woman with a heart of stone," points to Magdalene's "unconverted" Jewishness given the "heart of stone" metaphor symbolises Jewish covenantal claims against Christian supersessionism.[193] The poem might also reflect Levy's reading of Heine's "Katharina," in particular verses seven and eight, when "Walking through the realm of heaven," the speaker reveals jealous pangs that "Jesus Christ, our Holy Saviour," who at one time had cast romantic eyes on "Magdalen," so too had turned them to *his* muse: "So he looked upon you also. / Ah, I know he meant well – / No one is so pure and noble – / Yet I could not keep from feeling / Pangs of jealousy shoot through me – / ... I was vexed at / Jesus Christ." Consequently, the poet concedes, "I pluck a rose, I pluck it sighing / With mind distraught, with aching rue; / I don't know whom I'll give it to."[194]

---

190. Scheinberg, *Women's Poetry*, 222–3; idem, "Canonizing the Jew," 193–4; Sarah Minsloff, "Amy Levy and Identity Criticism: A Review of Recent Work," *Literary Compass* 4, no. 4 (2007): 1323.
191. Scheinberg, "Canonizing the Jew," 195; idem, *Women's Poetry*, 211–2.
192. Scheinberg, "Canonizing the Jew," 191; see Angela Leighton, "'Because Men Made the Laws': The Fallen Woman and the Woman Poet," *Victorian Poetry* 27, no. 2 (Summer 1989): 123; Pullen, *The Woman Who Dared*, 72; Francis, "Amy Levy," 183–204.
193. Scheinberg, *Women's Poetry*, 223; idem, "Canonizing the Jew," 194–5.
194. Heine, "Katharina," in *The Complete Poems*, ed. and trans. Draper, 360–1; Prawer, *Heine's Jewish Comedy*, 381–2.

"Captivity," published in the *Cambridge Review* in 1885 and later included in *A London Plane-Tree* (pp. 519–20), can be read as a comment on Jewish exilic experience and classical Hebrew poetry. The poem shows the contradictions of envisaging a romantic notion of Zion amid a context of forced acculturation:[195]

> I cannot remember my country,
> The land whence I came;
> Whence they brought me and chained me and made me
> Nor wild thing nor tame.
>
> This only I know of my country
> This only repeat:–
> It was free as the forest, and sweeter
> Than woodland retreat. (p. 520)

Alex Goody argues that the poem is symbolic of Levy's "in-betweenness."[196] Thus, Levy's (p. 519) "lion in chains" and imprisoned "bird" are doomed to retrospectively search for the "jungle in vain" or to return to the "cage."[197] Dwor argues that Levy's poem is symbolic of the "ghetto" and its restrictions.[198] "Captivity" also potentially reflects Levy's reading of Heine's "Jehuda ben Halevy" and her identification with his sense of exile and the fact that he could never square the German and Jewish components of his identity, nor could he fully bridge the perceived gap between Jewish tradition and emancipation, assimilation, and modernity, the latter inevitably bringing with it the withering of communal and religious continuities.[199] In this context, Levy's social Darwinist response to Anglo-Jewish assimilation and its supposed association with materialism and loss of tradition in *Reuben Sachs* can perhaps be read through Heine's critique of acculturation and

195. Scheinberg, *Women's Poetry*, 231.
196. Goody, "Passing in the City," 163.
197. Devine, "Exile and Redemption," 125.
198. Dwor, "'Poor Old Palace Prison,'" 157.
199. Simonsen, "A Spatial Expansion," 305–6, 311, 314; Peters, "'Jeder Reiche ist ein Judas Ischariot,'" 221, 224–5.

its supposed conjunction with capitalism.[200] Heine's "Jehuda ben Halevy" does not ask for renewed interest in the Hebrew poets of the Golden Age. Instead, in its yearning for Zion, Heine could empathise with the sense of exile, even if his was that of a poet living in Paris.[201] In "Captivity" too, Levy adopts themes resonant of exilic poetry, but makes no direct references to Halevi or to Zion-Jerusalem; instead, readers must interpret the latter elements through the poem's biblical symbology:[202]

The lion remembers the forest,
    The lion in chains;
To the bird that is captive a vision
    Of woodland remains.

One strains with his strength at the fetter,
    In impotent rage;
One flutters in flights of a moment,
    And beats at the cage.

If the lion were loosed from the fetter,
    To wander again;
He would seek the wide silence and shadow
    Of his jungle in vain.

He would rage in his fury, destroying;
    Let him rage, let him roam!
Shall he traverse the pitiless mountain,
    Or swim through the foam?

If they opened the cage and the casement,
    And the bird flew away;
He would come back at evening, heartbroken,
    A captive for aye. (p. 519)

---

200. Peters, "'Jeder Reiche ist ein Judas Ischariot,'" 214, 225.
201. Roger Cook, *By the Rivers of Babylon: Heinrich Heine's Late Songs and Reflections* (Detroit: Wayne State University Press, 1998), 322.
202. Devine, "Exile and Redemption," 126, 132–3; Scheinberg, *Women's Poetry*, 231.

The speaker, therefore, suffers as does the raging lion, reminiscent of Judah as a lion in Genesis 49:9 and the symbolism of an imprisoned bird yearning for "wings" in Psalms 55:7,[203] in that the "largeness and freedom" and search "for my county" described in the concluding stanzas (p. 520) is futile, hence the admission: "I cannot remember my country, / The land whence I came."[204] This line might have a precursor in Heine's short poem, "Abroad," where the poet bewails, "Oh, once I had a lovely fatherland."[205] Moreover, "Captivity" and its unfulfilled hopes for return and redemption, conjuring images of Halevi's own legend, possibly indicate Levy's own feeling of impotence in confronting assimilationist and antisemitic culture,[206] and for Scheinberg, her sense of "being at home nowhere."[207]

The discourses of urban modernity characteristic of *A London Plane-Tree* and the novel, *The Romance of a Shop*, even accounting for Levy's drawing on a range of literary sources, can be read through the Jewish encounter with urbanism and the city in line with the *Haskalah*, the rise of Reform and Liberal Judaisms, and growing assimilation.[208] In her "Jewish Humour" article (pp. 921–4), Levy suggests that the defining element of such humour is its "distinctly urban quality," the product of "prolonged life in cities" and that "the Jew" is devoid of "bucolic blood." Levy saw in Heine, "The Poet stretched on his couch of pain; the nation whose shoulders are sore with the yoke of oppression," potential for a "minority" (Jewish) literary discourse in contradistinction to "majority" culture and language.[209] As Jefferson Chase has pointed out, the Jewish joke, or *Judenwitz*, was of course

203. In the King James Bible 55:6.
204. Scheinberg, *Women's Poetry*, 230–1.
205. Heine, "Abroad," in *The Complete Poems*, ed. and trans. Draper, 363.
206. Devine, "Exile and redemption," 137.
207. Scheinberg, *Women's Poetry*, 232.
208. Miron, *From Continuity to Contiguity*, 327; Stephen Sharot, "Reform and Liberal Judaism in London," *Jewish Social Studies* 41, no. 3/4 (Summer/Fall 1979): 211.
209. Jefferson Chase, *Inciting Laughter: The Development of Jewish Humor in 19th Century German Culture* (Berlin: De Gruyter, 1999), 1, 3, 5–6, 9.

a "stereotype," but it could also work as an "authorial strategy."[210] In particular, Heine's Jewish humour, his satire, parody, wit, and exploitation of clichés, was a product of his own "outsider" position as a Jewish convert to Christianity, something he regretted and that could only be elucidated through the "majority" German language.[211] Heine rejected the assumption that poetry or fiction could indicate an author's identity, biography, and politics.[212] For Jeffrey Grossman, Heine's writings utilise components of hegemonic discourses to create "alternative discourse."[213] This is evident in Levy's saying "Shibboleth… in the purest University English" (p. 924).[214] Indeed, several scholars have identified in *A London Plane-Tree* and *The Romance of a Shop* Levy's utilisation of discourses associating Jewish modernity with urban life and the city.[215] Levy was of course drawing on prevalent medical and antisemitic discourses linking assimilated urban Jews with a host of mental health conditions.[216] Moreover, like Heine, Levy conflated urban existence with the history of the ghetto, which continues to signify, even after legal and political emancipation, the endurance of "centuries of city life" (p. 934).[217] But Levy also found

210. Chase, *Inciting Laughter*, 3, 9.
211. Chase, *Inciting Laughter*, 4, 149–51; Pines, "Life in the Valley," 26; Arie Sover, *Jewish Humor: An Outcome of Historical Experience, Survival and Wisdom* (Newcastle: Cambridge Scholars Publishing, 2021), 102. On Heine's exploitation of both "insider" and "outsider" discourses see Joskowicz, "Heinrich Heine's Transparent Masks," 70.
212. Grossman, "Heine and Jewish Culture," 252; Prawer, *Heine's Jewish Comedy*, 1.
213. Grossman, "Heine and Jewish Culture," 253; Grossman points to Heine's poem, "*Deutschland. Ein Wintermärchen*," as a key example of his strategy in that it draws on "politically charged symbols of German culture and national identity" only to "satire … nationalist discourses" (254).
214. See Goody's claim that Levy identified with "a Jewishness that can be articulated from *within* the dominant culture" ("Passing in the City," 162).
215. Dwor, "'Poor Old Palace Prison,'" 164; Goody, "Murder in Mile End," 466–8; Hunt Beckman, "Amy Levy," 211; Parsons, *Streetwalking the Metropolis*, 104.
216. Gilman, *The Jew's Body*, 63; see Parsons, *Streetwalking the Metropolis*, particularly the chapter: "The New Woman and the Wandering Jew," 82–122.
217. Dwor, "'Poor Old Palace Prison,'" 156, 158, 167; Jonathan Skolnik, *Jewish Pasts, German Fictions: History, Memory, and Minority Culture in Germany, 1824–1955* (Stanford: Stanford University Press, 2014), 66.

in Heine a precedent for positive urban discourse, particularly in *Ludwig Börne: A Memorial* and its description of Paris at night.[218] As it did for Heine, the city, for Levy, while dangerous, equally signalled liberation, particularly in the New Woman's shared marginalisation with the figure of the "Jew."[219] Moreover, urban life could work, as Heine found out, as a means for understanding identity and its dialectics.[220] The opening section of *A London Plane-Tree* indicates Levy's "urban persona" and association with urban poetry.[221] In particular, the collection points to Levy's reverence for James Thomson (see her essay, "James Thomson: A Minor Poet," pp. 891–901), who she identified as a fellow "minor poet" in tune with "his spiritual kinsmen," one of them being "Heine," who like Levy, he translated (pp. 897, 900).[222] The opening poem, "A London Plane-Tree" (p. 480), places the urban poet in an attic staring through a "garret-pane" at a "plane-tree" which "loves the town" and the "city breezes."[223] "London Poets: In Memoriam" (p. 492) connects Levy to a poetic tradition of "melancholy," "woe," and "sorrow," and to the "Weltschmerz" and "Pessimism" described in her essay on Thomson. "The Village Garden" (pp. 493–4) signals the calling of "The city" and "her old persistence" given the "burden / Of individual life" is less painful

218. Willi Goetschel, "Street, Life, and Other Signs: Heine in the Rue Laffitte," *City & Society* 21, no. 2 (2009): 230, 233, 235.
219. Goetschel, "Street, Life, and Other Signs," 241; Goody, "Murder in Mile End," 468, 475; idem, "Passing in the City," 164. See also Parsons' claim that "the figure of the cosmopolitan Jew in London is a recurring motif at the turn of the century for women urban artists such as Amy Levy" (*Streetwalking the Metropolis*, 86).
220. See Hinrich Seeba, "'Keine Systematie': Heine in Berlin and the Origin of the Urban Gaze," in *Heinrich Heine's Contested Identities: Politics, Religion, and Nationalism in Nineteenth-Century Germany*, eds. Jost Hermand and Robert Holub (New York: Peter Lang, 1999), 89.
221. Hunt Beckman, "Amy Levy," 217.
222. Goody, "Murder in Mile End," 461; Bristow, "'All Out of Tune,'" 103 n. 57; see James Thomson, *The City of Dreadful Night and Other Poems* (London: Reeves and Turner, 1880).
223. Goody, "Passing in the City," 164.

in the "roar and hurry of the town."[224] The poems, "London in July" (p. 481), "Between the Showers" (p. 489), "Out of Town" (p. 490), and "In the Mile End Road" (p. 510) reveal Levy's use of a male speaker searching for their "only love," a "woman's face."[225] For Goody, these poems, as well as "Ballade of an Omnibus" (pp. 484–5) and "Straw in the Street" (p. 488), point to Levy's utilisation of a male voice as a means of travelling across the city without being identified as a "transgressive woman" and of achieving "loss of self."[226] Similarly, Vadillo describes these poems as signifying Levy's development of "a mobile lyric self."[227] Levy's urban poetry and fiction suggest that the city can provide some sense of belonging or at least the chance to be anonymous.[228] However, as Levy's described in her discussion of Thomson's *City of Dreadful Night,* danger is still omnipresent in the city amid the "brooding shadow of nameless horror" and even "hell" is preferable to "the void agony of the city" (p. 894). Equally, at the close of Levy's short story, "Wise in Her Generation" (pp. 854–66), published after her suicide, the perils of social Darwinism and capitalist materialism, and disillusionment with the city, are laid bare (p. 866): "Black, black in its heart the City; the blackness of man's heart is revealed in its huge, hideous struggle for existence. Better be unfit and perish, than survive at such a cost."[229]

---

224. Hunt Beckman, *Amy Levy,* 193.
225. Hunt Beckman, "Amy Levy," 212–3; Goody, "Passing in the city," 165; Elizabeth Ludlow, "Christina Rossetti, Amy Levy, and the Composition of Roundels in Late-Victorian Bloomsbury: Poetic Snapshots of Urban Subjects," *English Literature in Transition* 56, no. 1 (2013): 85–6. Parsons suggests that in "London in July" Levy "confronts the figure of the male flaneur in the persona of a man wandering the city" (*Streetwalking the Metropolis,* 97).
226. Goody, "Passing in the City," 166–7; see Nord, "'Neither Pairs Nor Odd,'" 748, 753. On the "submergence of self" in "The Village Garden" see Hunt Beckman, *Amy Levy,* 193; idem, "Amy Levy," 218–9.
227. Ana Parejo Vadillo, *Women Poets and Urban Aestheticism: Passengers of Modernity* (Basingstoke: Palgrave Macmillan, 2005), 41.
228. Bristow, "'All Out of Tune,'" 97.
229. Pullen, *The Woman Who Dared,* 135; Hunt Beckman, *Amy Levy,* 200.

The Romance of a Shop has by no means captured the attention of readers, either historical or contemporary, in the same way that *Reuben Sachs* continues to fascinate. Levy herself claimed in correspondence that the novel "aims for the young person" and was written only "for sale purposes."[230] *The Romance of a Shop* however can be read as an example of Levy's adeptness at developing diverse personas, in this case, the four Lorimer sisters, who open their own photography business.[231] Gertrude, as a "poet" and feminist with a "rebellious heart," has been identified as the sister most like Levy (p. 29).[232] Levy has also been associated with "industrious" Lucy (p. 90) and a friend of the sisters, Conny, "at heart a shrewd, far-seeing daughter of the City" (p. 26).[233] Bernstein suggests that *The Romance of a Shop* works as a "guide to the modern city" given its detailed account of London.[234] Likewise, Elizabeth Evans has convincingly shown that while the novel utilises clichéd tropes, its deployment of the "shopgirl" shows how "femininity, respectability, and business acumen can coexist" in the city, in the process challenging conventional literature on the topic and expectations that stigmatised women's urban mobility and the prevalence of the New Woman.[235] *The Romance of a Shop* has also been interpreted

230. Levy quoted in Hunt Beckman, *Amy Levy*, 155, 268, 270.

231. Jusova, *The New Woman*, 142–3. See David Wanczyk's argument that *The Romance of a Shop* "parodies the novels of William Dean Howells and others" in "Framing Gertrude: Photographic Narration and the Subjectivity of the Artist-Observer in Levy's *The Romance of a Shop*," *Victorian Literature and Culture* 43, no. 1 (2015): 131.

232. Parsons, *Streetwalking the Metropolis*, 93; Pullen, *The Woman Who Dared*, 137; Elizabeth Evans, "'We are Photographers, Not Mountebanks!' Spectacle, Commercial Space, and the New Public Woman," in *Amy Levy*, eds. Hetherington and Valman, 34.

233. Parsons, *Streetwalking the Metropolis*, 93.

234. Bernstein, "Introduction," in *The Romance of a Shop*, 22–3; see also Evans, "'We are Photographers, Not Mountebanks,'" 32.

235. Evans, "'We are Photographers, Not Mountebanks,'" 35–7, 41; see also, Emma Francis, "Why Wasn't Amy Levy More of a Socialist? Levy, Clementina Black, and Liza of Lambeth," in *Amy Levy*, eds. Hetherington and Valman, 56, 58. For

as a parody and satire that includes caricatures and comedy specific to the author.[236] Indeed, when Lucy's partner, Frank, is presumed dead, Fanny interjects that "People always come back in books," only for him to return later in the novel (pp. 140, 165).[237] Such humour, clearly picked up from Heine, pervades Levy's "In Retreat" (pp. 670–6), "The Black Forest" (pp. 677–82), "Easter-Tide at Tunbridge Wells" (pp. 698–702), and "Out of the World" (pp. 703–8), all presented as correspondence from "Melissa," and "Another Morning in Florence" (pp. 709–15). In these texts, it is possible to see the influence of Heine's travel writing and his melding of accounts of romantic scenery and nature with the quirks of the narrator.[238] For instance, in the latter account of a trip to Florence, Melissa is guided by John Ruskin's *Mornings in Florence,* only to be sealed in "the main square of the cloisters" amid torrential rain. When the ordeal is over, Melissa ironically concludes: "'It was all Ruskin's fault'" (pp. 712, 715).[239] Similarly, *Miss Meredith,* which has received little scholarly attention compared to *Reuben Sachs* and *The Romance of a Shop,* possibly exhibits, Iveta Jusova speculates, comparable parody and playing with clichés.[240] In the novel, the governess, Elsie, comes

a reading of *The Romance of a Shop* from the perspective of "literary naturalism," see Jessica Murphy, "'"[T]he World's a Beast, and I Hate It!"': *Naturalism in Amy Levy's* The Romance of a Shop," *Studies in American Naturalism* 15, no. 1 (Summer 2020): 75–91.

236. Parsons, *Streetwalking the Metropolis,* 92; Hunt Beckman, *Amy Levy,* 156–8; Nord, *Walking the Victorian Streets,* 202; Jusova, *The New Woman,* 143, 145; Stephanie Russo and Lee O'Brien, "Sex, Sisters and Work: Mary Robinson's The Natural Daughter and Amy Levy's Romance of a Shop," *Women's Writing* 28, no. 1 (2021): 47; see Russo and O'Brien's point that "In Levy's hands, literary devices facilitate critique" (47).
237. Hunt Beckman, *Amy Levy,* 157.
238. Ritchie Robertson, ed. and trans., "Introduction," in *The Harz Journey and Selected Prose,* by Heinrich Heine (London: Penguin Books, 2006), 13. See Pullen on the biographical elements of Levy's travel writing (*The Woman Who Dared,* 80–1).
239. See John Ruskin, *Mornings in Florence: Being Simple Studies of Christian Art, for English Travellers,* 6 Vols (Orpington: Grant Allen, 1875–1877).
240. Jusova, *The New Woman,* 148.

across an English married couple examining Andrea del Sarto's painting of St. Catherine in the cathedral at Pisa. Having listened to their crass conversation, Elsie concludes, "They were Philistines, no doubt; but I was in no mood to be critical, and must confess that the sound of their English voices was almost too much for my self-control" (p. 333).[241] For Jusova, the moment can possibly be read as "Elsie actually laughing at the English Philistine couple and, by extension, perhaps some portions of her readership as well," and in the process signalling that the text should not be taken literally.[242] In New's introduction to *The Complete Novels* he described the ending of *Miss Meredith* as "rushed," possibly indicating that "Levy lost interest in her subject."[243] However, Jusova points to the possibility that Levy used the Brogi family's initial reluctance to sanction marriage between Elsie and Andrea to make a comparison between the story's Italian family and the stereotypes and misconceptions directed at Anglo-Jews in English Christian culture. This is reflected in the Marchesa's statement: "there are traditions, feelings, sacred customs, and emotions belonging to the family where you have been received of which you can have no knowledge. That is not required, nor expected of you. What is expected of you, as of every right-minded person, is that you should at least respect what is of such importance to others" (pp. 378–9).[244] The growing sense of closeness as the novel comes to a close, Jusova argues, can be linked back to Levy's "The Ghetto at Florence" article and its making a connection between "Jew and Florentine": "Who knows but that, long ago, those old and mystic races, the Etrurians and Semites, were kinsfolk, pasturing their flocks together in Asia Minor?" (pp. 916–7).[245]

241. In Heine's "The Town of Lucca," the "Wedding of Cana, by a pupil of Andrea del Sarto," is described in a visit to the Cathedral of Lucca; see Heine, *The Harz Journey*, ed. and trans. Robertson, 165.
242. Jusova, *The New Woman*, 149.
243. New, "Introduction," 28.
244. Jusova, *The New Woman*, 152–3.
245. Jusova, *The New Woman*, 153.

Following her suicide in 1889, as per her own wish, Levy became the first Anglo-Jewish woman to opt for cremation. Her ashes were laid to rest in the Reform cemetery on Balls Pond Road.[246] For someone identified as "the first modern Jewish women poet,"[247] it is perhaps difficult to speculate about the extent of potential output lost given the cutting short of Levy's life at a time when her texts were being regularly published. However, this volume is an opportunity to renew interest in Levy's life and works and to provide something that Levy perhaps never enjoyed in her own lifetime: a sense of belonging to a "Jewish literary complex" (qua Miron).[248] Indeed, Levy produced a diversity of texts, including polemical essays, novels, short stories, and poetry, exploring a diverse array of topics ranging from insidious and pervasive antisemitism to etiquette in the ballroom. The biggest mistake any reader of Levy's texts can make, however, is to assign value to one item over another; not one, but all of Levy's texts are inflected by her own experience and "sense of *Judesein*, being Jewish."[249] This means that the most polemical to the seemingly inane texts can say something intrinsic, whether it be personal to Levy, humorous, or a comment on the social, cultural, and political crises of the 1870s and 1880s. On this note, it seems apt to set the tone of Levy's *Collected Writings* with an example that signifies her ability, like Heine, to speak to identity, minority, and humour in ways that will pass the casual reader by. The extract (p. 762) is from Levy's short story, "A Meadowshire Romance" (pp. 723–64):

246. Bernstein, "Introduction," in *Reuben Sachs*, 14; Thomas, "Lesbian Postmortem," 127. See Holly Laird, "The Death of the Author by Suicide," in *The Fin-de-Siecle Poem*, ed. Bristow, 69–100.

247. Elaine Feinstein cited in Hetherington and Valman, "Introduction," 2.

248. New too did express hope in *The Complete Novels* that a "complete edition of her [Levy's] poetry and prose" would one day be published ("Introduction," 14).

249. Miron, *From Continuity to Contiguity*, 405.

"Agnes, Agnes, open the door, dear."

"In a minute, Kitty."

I get up from the chair by the open window, where I seated myself mechanically when I came in half an hour ago, and, going over to the door, admit my cousin in silence.

"In the dark, Aggie! and still in your flannel gown!"

"Never mind about that, Kitty. Wait a moment; I want to look at you."

I light a candle, and hold it up to my cousin's face, who blinks her bright eyes in sweet protest.

"You look like Moses, Kitty, when he came down from the Mount."

Kitty laughs softly.

"I didn't know you were present on that occasion, Agnes."

Novels

The Romance of a Shop (1888)

Chapter 1
In the Beginning

Turn, Fortune, turn thy wheel and lower the proud;
Turn thy wild wheel through sunshine, storm, and cloud;
Thy wheel and thee we neither love nor hate.

TENNYSON[1]

There stood on Campden Hill a large, dun-coloured house, enclosed by a walled-in garden of several acres in extent. It belonged to no particular order of architecture, and was more suggestive of comfort than of splendour, with its great windows, and rambling, nondescript proportions. On one side, built out from the house itself, was a big glass structure, originally designed for a conservatory. On the April morning of which I write, the whole place wore a dejected and dismantled appearance; while in the windows and on the outer wall of the garden were fixed black and white posters, announcing a sale of effects to take place on that day week.

1. From Alfred, Lord Tennyson's (1809–1892) poem, "The Marriage of Geraint." For other annotated versions of *The Romance of a Shop* see *The Complete Novels and Selected Writings of Amy Levy 1861–1889*, ed. Melvyn New (Gainesville: University Press of Florida, 1993), 59–196, 539–43, and Susan David Bernstein's (ed.) *The Romance of a Shop*, by Amy Levy (Peterborough: Broadview Editions, 2006), 51–194.

The air of desolation which hung about the house had communicated itself in some vague manner to the garden, where the trees were bright with blossom, or misty with the tender green of the young leaves. Perhaps the effect of sadness was produced, or at least heightened, by the pathetic figure that paced slowly up and down the gravel path immediately before the house; the figure of a young woman, slight, not tall, bare-headed, and clothed in deep mourning.

She paused at last in her walk, and stood a moment in a listening attitude, her face uplifted to the sky.

Gertrude Lorimer was not a beautiful woman, and such good looks as she possessed varied from day to day, almost from hour to hour; but a certain air of character and distinction clung to her through all her varying moods, and redeemed her from a possible charge of plainness.

She had an arching, unfashionable forehead, like those of Leonardo da Vinci's women, short-sighted eyes, and an expressive mouth and chin. As she stood in the full light of the spring sunshine, her face pale and worn with recent sorrow, she looked, perhaps, older than her twenty-three years.

Pushing back from her forehead the hair, which, though not cut into a "fringe," had a tendency to stray about her face, and passing her hand across her eyes, with a movement expressive of mingled anxiety and resolve, she walked quickly to the door of the conservatory, opened it, and went inside.

The interior of the great glass structure would have presented a surprise to the stranger expectant of palms and orchids. It was fitted up as a photographer's studio.

Several cameras, each of a different size, stood about the room. In one corner was a great screen of white-painted canvas; there were blinds to the roof adapted for admitting or excluding the light; and paste-pots, bottles, printing-frames, photographs in various stages of finish – a nondescript heap of professional litter – were scattered about the place from end to end.

Standing among these properties was a young girl of about twenty years of age; fair, slight, upright as a dart, with a glance at once alert and serene.

The two young creatures in their black dresses advanced to each other, then stood a moment, clinging to one another in silence.

It was the first time that either had been in the studio since the day when their unforeseen calamity had overtaken them; a calamity which seemed to them so mysterious, so unnatural, so past all belief, and yet which was common-place enough – a sudden loss of fortune, immediately followed by the sudden death of the father, crushed by the cruel blow which had fallen on him.

"Lucy," said the elder girl at last, "is it only a fortnight ago?"

"I don't know," answered Lucy, looking round the room, whose familiar details stared at her with a hideous unfamiliarity; "I don't know if it is a hundred years or yesterday since I put that portrait of Phyllis in the printing-frame! Have you told Phyllis?"

"No, but I wish to do so at once; and Fanny. But here they come."

Two other black-gowned figures entered by the door which led from the house, and helped to form a sad little group in the middle of the room.

Frances Lorimer, the eldest of them all, and half-sister to the other three, was a stout, fair woman of thirty, presenting somewhat the appearance of a large and superannuated baby. She had a big face, with small, meaningless features, and faint, surprised-looking eyebrows. Her complexion had once been charmingly pink and white, but the tints had hardened, and a coarse red colour clung to the wide cheeks. At the present moment, her little, light eyes red with weeping, her eyebrows arched higher than ever, she looked the picture of impotent distress. She had come in, hand in hand with Phyllis, the youngest, tallest, and prettiest of the sisters; a slender, delicate-looking creature of seventeen, who had outgrown her strength; the spoiled child of the family by virtue of her youth, her weakness, and her personal charms.

Gertrude was the first to speak.

"Now that we are all together," she said, "it is a good opportunity for talking over our plans. There are a great many things to be considered, as you know. Phyllis, you had better not stand."

Phyllis cast her long, supple frame into the lounge which was regarded as her special property, and Fanny sat down on a chair, wiping her eyes with her black-bordered pocket-handkerchief Gertrude put her hands behind her and leaned her head against the wall.

Phyllis's wide, grey eyes, with their half-wistful, half-humorous expression, glanced slowly from one to the other.

"Now that we are all grouped," she said, "there is nothing left but for Lucy to focus us."

It was a very small joke indeed, but they all laughed, even Fanny. No one had laughed for a fortnight, and at this reassertion of youth and health their spirits rose with unexpected rapidity.

"Now, Gertrude, unfold your plans," said Lucy, in her clear tones and with her air of calm resolve.

Gertrude played nervously with a copy of *The British Journal of Photography* which she held, and began to speak with hesitation, almost with apology, as one who deprecates any undue assumption of authority.

"You know that Mr. Grimshaw, our father's lawyer, was here last night," she said; "and that he and I had a long talk together about business. (He was sorry you were too ill to come down, Fanny.) He told me all about our affairs. We are quite, quite poor. When everything is settled, when the furniture is sold, he thinks there will be about £500 among us, perhaps more, perhaps less."

Fanny's thin, feminine tones broke in on her sister's words –

"There is my £50 a-year that my Mamma left me; I am sure you are all welcome to that."

"Yes, dear, yes," said Lucy, patting her shoulder; while Gertrude bit her lip and went on –

"We cannot live for long on £500, as you must know. We must work. People have been very kind. Uncle Sebastian has telegraphed for two of us to go out to India; Mrs. Devonshire offers another two of us a home for as long as we like. But I think we would all rather not accept these kind offers?"

"Of course not!" cried Lucy and Phyllis in chorus, while Fanny maintained a meek, consenting silence.

"The question remains," continued the speaker; "what can we do? There is teaching, of course. We might find places as governesses; but we should be at a great disadvantage without certificates or training of any sort. And we should be separated."

"Oh, Gertrude," cried Fanny, "you might write! You write so beautifully! I am sure you could make your fortune at it."

Gertrude's face flushed, but she controlled all other signs of the irritation which poor hapless Fan was so wont to excite in her.

"I have thought about that, Fanny," she said; "but I cannot afford to wait and hammer away at the publishers' doors with a crowd of people more experienced and better trained than myself. No, I have another plan to propose to you all. There is one thing, at least, that we can all do."

"We can all make photographs, except Fan," said Phyllis, in a doubtful voice.

"Exactly!" cried Gertrude, growing excited, and walking across to the middle of the room; "we can make photographs! We have had this studio, with every proper arrangement for light and other things, so that we are not mere amateurs. Why not turn to account the only thing we can do, and start as professional photographers? We should all keep together. It would be a risk, but if we failed we should be very little worse off than before. I know what Lucy thinks of it, already. What have you others to say to it?"

"Oh, Gertrude, need it come to that – to open a shop?" cried Fanny, aghast.

"Fanny, you are behind the age," said Lucy, hastily. "Don't you know that it is quite distinguished to keep a shop? That poets sell wallpapers,[2] and first-class honour men sell lamps? That Girton

2. Refers to the socialist artist William Morris (1834–1896), a figure in the Arts and Crafts movement and associated with the Pre-Raphaelites; see New, ed., *The Complete Novels*, 539 n. 2; Bernstein, ed., *The Romance of a Shop*, 55 n. 1.

students make bonnets, and are thought none the worse of for doing so?"

"*I* think it a perfectly splendid idea," cried Phyllis, sitting up; "we shall be like that good young man in *Le Nabab*."[3]

"Indeed, I hope we shall not be like Andre," said Gertrude, sitting down by Phyllis on the couch and putting her arm round her, "especially as none of us are likely to write successful tragedies by way of compensation."

"You two people are getting frivolous," remarked Lucy, severely, "and there are so many things to consider."

"First of all," answered Gertrude, "I want to convince Fanny. Think of all the dull little ways by which women, ladies, are generally reduced to earning their living! But a business – that is so different. It is progressive; a creature capable of growth; the very qualities in which women's work is dreadfully lacking."

"We have thought out a good many of the details," went on Lucy, who was possessed of less imagination than her sister, but had a clearer perception of what arguments would best appeal to Fanny's understanding. "It would not absorb all our capital, we have so many properties already. We thought of buying some nice little business, such as are advertised every week in *The British Journal*. But of course we should do nothing rashly, nor without consulting Mr. Grimshaw."

"Not for his advice," put in Gertrude, "but to arrange any transaction for us."

"Gertrude and I," went on Lucy, "would do the work, and you, Fanny, if you would, should be our housekeeper."

"And I," cried Phyllis, her great eyes shining, "I would walk up and down outside, like that man in the High Street, who tells me every day what a beautiful picture I should make!"

"Our photographs would be so good and our manners so charming that our fame would travel from one end of the earth to the other!"

---

3. Alphonse Daudet's (1840–1897) *Le Nabab* (1877).

added Lucy, with a sudden abandonment of her grave and didactic manner.

"We would have afternoon tea in the studio on Sunday, to which everybody should flock; duchesses, cabinet ministers, and Mr. Irving.[4] We should become the fashion, make colossal fortunes, and ultimately marry dukes!" finished off Gertrude.

Fanny looked up, helpless but unconvinced. The enthusiasm of these young creatures had failed to communicate itself to her. Their outburst of spirits at such a time seemed to her simply shocking.

As Lucy had said, Frances Lorimer was behind the age. She was an anachronism, belonging by rights to the period when young ladies played the harp, wore ringlets, and went into hysterics.

Living, moving, and having her being well within the vision of three pairs of searching and intensely modern young eyes, poor Fan could permit herself neither these nor any kindred indulgences; but went her way with a vague, inarticulate sense of injury – a round, sentimental peg in the square, scientific hole of the latter half of the nineteenth century.

Now, when the little tumult had in some degree subsided, she ventured once more to address the meeting.

That was the worst of Fan; there was no standing up in fair fight and having it out with her; you might as soon fight a feather-bed. Convinced, to all appearances, one moment; the next, she would go back to the very point from which she had started, with that mild but terrible obstinacy of the weak.

"I suppose you know," she said, having once more recourse to the black-bordered pocket-handkerchief, "what everyone will think?"

"Everyone will be dead against it. We know that, of course," said Lucy, with the calm confidence of untried strength.

Fortunately, the discussion was interrupted at this juncture, by the loud voice of the gong announcing luncheon.

---

4. The actor, Henry Irving (1838–1905).

Fanny rushed off to bathe her eyes. Gertrude ran upstairs to wash her hands, and the two younger girls lingered together a few moments in the studio.

"I wonder," said Phyllis, with the complete and unconscious cynicism of youth, "why Fan has never married; she has just the sort of qualities that men seem to think desirable in a wife and a mother!"

"Poor Fanny, don't you know?" answered Lucy. "There was a person once, ages ago, but he was poor and had to go away, and Fan would have no one else."

This was Lucy's version of that far away, uninteresting little romance; Fanny's "disappointment," to which the heroine of it was fond of making vaguely pathetic allusion. Fan would have no one else, her sister had said; but perhaps another cause lay at the root of her constancy (and of much feminine constancy besides); but if Lucy did not say no one else would have Fan, Phyllis, who was younger and more merciless, chose to accept the statement in its inverted form; which, by the by, neither she, nor I, nor you, reader, have authentic grounds for doing.

"Oh, I had heard about that before, naturally," she answered; but further conversation on the subject was cut short by the appearance of Fanny herself, come to summon them to the dining room, where lunch was set out on the great table.

Old Kettle, the butler, waited on them as usual, and there was nothing in the nature of the viands to bring home to them the fact of their altered circumstances; but it was a dismal meal, crowned with a sorrow's crown of sorrow, the remembrance of happier things. In the vacant place they all seemed to see the dead father, as he had been wont to sit among them; charming, gay, *debonnair*, the life of the party; delighting no less in the light-hearted sallies of his daughters, than in his own neatly-polished epigrams; a man as brilliant as he had been unsatisfactory; as little able to cope with the hard facts of existence as he had been reckless in attacking them.

"Oh, girls," said Fanny, when the door had finally closed upon Kettle; "Oh, girls, I have been thinking. If only circumstances had been otherwise, if only – things had happened a little differently, I might have had a home to offer you, a home to which you might all have come!"

Overcome by this vision of possibilities, this resuscitation of her dead and buried might-have-been, Miss Lorimer began to sob quietly; and the poor eyes, which she had been at such pains to bathe, overflowed, deluging the streaky expanses of newly-washed cheeks.

"Oh, I can't help it, I can't help it," moaned this shuttlecock of fate, appealing to the stern young judges who sat silent around her; an appeal which, if duly considered, will seem to be even more piteous than the outbreak of emotion of which it was the cause.

Gertrude got up from her chair and went from the room; Phyllis sat staring, with beautiful, unmoved, accustomed eyes; only Lucy, laying a cool hand on her half-sister's burning fingers, spoke words of comfort and of common sense.

Chapter 2
Friends In Need

And never say "no," when the world says "ay,"
For that is fatal.
E. B. BROWNING[5]

When Gertrude reached her room, she flung herself on the bed, and lay there passive, with face buried from the light.

She was worn out, poor girl, with the strain of the recent weeks; a period into which a lifetime of events, thoughts, and experience seemed to have crowded themselves.

Action, or thoughts concerned with plans of action, had become for the moment impossible to her.

She realised, with a secret thrill of horror, that the moment had at length come when she must look full in the face the lurking anguish of which none but herself knew the existence; and which, in the press of more immediate miseries, she had hitherto contrived to keep well in the background of her thoughts. Only, she had known dimly throughout, that face it she must, sooner or later; and now her hour had come.

5. The quotation is from Elizabeth Barrett Browning's (1806–1861) *Aurora Leigh* (1857); see also Levy's analysis of *Aurora Leigh* for *Kind Words* (1875) on pp. 871–2.

There was someone, bound to her by every tie but the tie of words, who had let the days of her trouble go by and had made no sign; a fair-weather friend, who had fled before the storm.

In these few words are summed up the whole of Gertrude's commonplace story.

Only to natures as proud and as passionate as hers, can the words convey their full meaning.

She was not a woman easily won; not till after long siege had come surrender; but surrender, complete, unquestioning, as only such a woman can give.

Now, her being seemed shaken at the foundations, hurt at the vital roots. As a passionate woman will, she thought: "If it had been his misfortune, not mine!"

In the hall lay a bit of pasteboard with "sincere condolence" inscribed on it; and Gertrude had not failed to learn, from various sources, of the presence at half a dozen balls of the owner of the card, and his projected visit to India.

Gertrude rose from the bed with a choked sound, which was scarcely a cry, in her throat. She had looked her trouble fairly in the eyes; had not, as some women would have done, attempted to save her pride by refusing to acknowledge its existence; but from the depths of her humiliation, had called upon it by its name. Now forever and ever she turned from it, cast it forth from her; cast forth other things, perhaps, round which it had twined itself; but stood there, at least, a free woman, ready for action.

Thank God for action; for the decree which made her to some extent the arbiter of other destinies, the prop and stay of other lives. For the moment, she caught to her breast and held as a friend that weight of responsibility which before had seemed –and how often afterwards was to seem – too heavy and too cruel a burden for her young strength.

"And now," she said, setting her lips, "for a clearance."

Soon the floor was strewn with a heap of papers, chiefly manuscripts, whose dusty and battered air would have suggested to an experienced eye frequent and fruitless visits to the region of Paternoster Row.

Gertrude, kneeling on the floor, bent over them with anxious face, setting some aside, consigning others ruthlessly to the waste-paper basket. One, larger and more travel-worn than the rest, she held some time in her hand, as though weighing it in the balance. It was labelled: *Charlotte Corday; a tragedy in five acts*;[6] and for a time its fate seemed uncertain; but it found its way ultimately to the basket.

A smart tap at the door roused Gertrude from her somewhat melancholy occupation.

"Come in!" she cried, pushing back the straying locks from the ample arch of her forehead, but retaining her seat among the manuscripts.

The handle turned briskly, and a blooming young woman, dressed in the height of fashion, entered the room.

"My dear Gertrude, what's this? Rachel weeping among her children?"[7]

She spoke in high tones, but with an exaggeration of buoyancy which bespoke nervousness. When last these friends had met, it had been in the chamber of death itself; it was a little difficult, after that solemn moment, to renew the every-day relations of life without shock or jar.

"Come in, Conny, and if you must quote the Bible, don't misquote it."

Constance Devonshire, heedless of her magnificent attire, cast herself down by the side of her friend, and put her arms caressingly round her. Her quick blue eye fell upon the basket with its overflowing papers.

---

6. Amos C. Morey's *Charlotte Corday: a Tragedy in Five Acts* (1844). Corday was executed during the French Revolution for the murder of Jean-Paul Marat.
7. Refers to Jeremiah 31:15 and Matthew 2:18; it is important to note that Levy's biblical references, the New Testament aside, would not have come from the Tanakh, but the standard King James Bible.

"Gerty, what is the meaning of this massacre of the innocents?"[8]

"'Vanity of vanities, saith the preacher,'[9] since you seem bent on Scriptural allusion, Conny."

"But, Gerty, all your tales and things! I should have thought" – she blushed as she made the suggestion – "that you might have sold them. And *Charlotte Corday*, too!"

"Poor Charlotte, she has been to market so often that I cannot bear the sight of her; and now I have given her her quietus as the Republic gave it to her original. As for the other victims, they are not worth a tear, and we will not discuss them."

She gathered up the remaining manuscripts, and put them in a drawer; then, turning to her friend with a smile, demanded from her an account of herself.

Miss Devonshire's presence, alien as it was to her present mood, acted with a stimulating effect on Gertrude. To Conny she knew herself to be a very tower of strength; and such knowledge is apt to make us strong, at least for the time being.

"Oh, there's nothing new about me!" answered Conny, wrinkling her handsome, discontented face. "Gerty, why won't you come to us, you and Lucy, and let the others go to India?"

Gertrude laughed at this summary disposal of the family.

"Of course I knew you wouldn't come," said Conny, in an injured voice; "but, seriously, Gerty, what are you going to do?"

In a few words Gertrude sketched the plan which she had propounded to her sisters that morning.

"I don't believe it is possible," said Miss Devonshire, with great promptness; "but it sounds very nice," she added with a sigh, and thought, perhaps, of her own prosperous boredom.

The bell rang for tea, and Gertrude began brushing her hair. Constance endeavoured to seize the brush from her hands.

8. Matthew 2:16–18.
9. Ecclesiastes 1:2.

"You are not coming down, my dear, indeed you are not! You are going to lie down, while I go and fetch your tea."

"I had much rather not, Conny. I am quite well."

"You look as pale as a ghost. But you always have your own way. By the by, Fred is downstairs; he walked over with me from Queen's Gate. He's the only person who is decently civil in the house, just at present."

Tea had been carried into the studio, where the two girls found the rest of the party assembled. Fan, with an air of elegance, as though conscious of performing an essentially womanly function, and with much action of the little finger, was engaged in pouring out tea. In the middle of the room stood a group of three people: Lucy, Phyllis, and Fred Devonshire, a tall, heavy young man, elaborately and correctly dressed, with a fatuous, good-natured, pink and white face.

"Oh, come now, Miss Lucy," he was heard to say, as Gertrude entered with his sister; "that really is too much for one to swallow!"

"He won't believe it!" cried Phyllis, clasping her hands, and turning her charming face to the newcomers; "it's quite true, isn't it, Gerty?"

"Have you been telling tales out of school?"

"Lucy and I have been explaining *the plan* to Fred, and he won't believe it."

Gertrude felt a little vexed at this lack of reticence on their part; but then, she reflected, if the plan was to be carried out, it could remain no secret, especially to the Devonshires. Assured that there really was some truth in what he had been told, Fred relapsed into an amazed silence, broken by an occasional chuckle, which he hastened, each time, to subdue, considering it out of place in a house of mourning.

He had long regarded the Lorimer girls as quite the most astonishing productions of the age, but this last freak of theirs, as he called it, fairly took away his breath. He was a soft-hearted youth, moreover, and the pathetic aspect of the case presented itself to him with great force in the intervals of his amusement.

Constance had brought a note from her mother, and having delivered it, and had tea, she rose to go. Fred remained lost in abstraction, muttering, "By Jove!" below his breath at intervals, the chuckling having subsided.

"Come on, Fred!" cried his sister.

He sprang to his feet.

"Are you slowly recovering from the shock we have given you?" asked Lucy, demurely, as she held out her hand.

"Miss Lucy," he said, solemnly, looking at her with all his foolish eyes, "I'll come every day of the week to be photographed, if I may, and so shall all the fellows at our office!"

He was a little hurt and disconcerted, though he joined in the laugh himself, when everyone burst out laughing; even Lucy, to whom he had addressed himself as the least puzzling and most reliable of the Miss Lorimers.

Gertrude walked down the drive with the brother and sister, a colourless, dusky, wind-blown figure beside their radiant smartness, and let them out herself at the big gate. Here she lingered a moment, while the wind lifted her hair, and fanned her face, bringing a faint tinge of red to its paleness.

Phyllis and Lucy opened the door of the studio which led to the garden, and stood there arm-in-arm, soothed no less than Gertrude by the chill sweetness of the April afternoon. The sound of carriage wheels roused them from the reverie into which both of them had fallen, and in another moment a brougham, drawn by two horses, was seen to round the curve of the drive and make its way to the house.

The two girls retreated rapidly, shutting the door behind them.

"Great heavens, Aunt Caroline!" said Lucy, in dismay.

"She must have passed Gertrude at the gate; Fanny, do you hear who has come?"

"Kettle must take the tea into the drawing room," said Fanny, in some agitation. "You know Mrs. Pratt does not like the studio."

Phyllis was peeping through the panes of the door, which afforded a view of the entrance of the house.

"She is getting out now; the footman has opened the carriage door, and Kettle is on the steps. Oh, Lucy, if Aunt Caroline had been a horse, what a hard mouth she would have had!"

In another moment, a great swish of garments and the sound of a metallic voice were heard in the drawing room, which adjoined the conservatory; and Kettle, appearing at the entrance which divided the two rooms, announced lugubriously: "Mrs. Septimus Pratt!"

A tall, angular woman, heavily draped in the crispest, most aggressive of mourning garments, was sitting upright on a sofa when the girls entered the drawing room. She was a handsome person of her age, notwithstanding a slightly equine cast of countenance, and the absence of anything worthy the adjectives graceful or *sympathique* from her individuality.

Mrs. Septimus Pratt belonged to that mischievous class of the community whose will and energy are very far ahead of their intellect and perceptions. She had a vulgar soul and a narrow mind, and unbounded confidence in her own judgments; but she was not bad-hearted, and was animated, at the present moment, by a sincere desire to benefit her nieces.

"How do you do, girls?" she said, speaking in that loud, authoritative key which many benevolent persons of her sex think right to employ when visiting their poorer neighbours. "Yes, please, Fanny, a cup of tea and some bread-and-butter. Cake? No, thank you. I didn't expect to find cake!"

This last sentence, uttered with a sort of ponderous archness, as though to take off the edge of the implied rebuke, was received in unsmiling silence; even Fanny choking down in time a protest which rose to her lips.

With a sinking of the heart, Lucy heard the handle of the door turn, and saw Gertrude enter, pale, severe, and distant.

"How do you do, Gerty?" cried Aunt Caroline, "though this is not our first meeting. How came you to be standing at the gate, without your hat, and in that shabby gown?"

For Gertrude happened to be wearing an old black dress, having taken off the new mourning garment before clearing out the dusty papers.

"I beg your pardon, Aunt Caroline?"

The opposition between these two women may be said to have dated from the cradle of one of them.

"You ought to know at your age, Gertrude," went on Mrs. Pratt, "that now, of all times, you must be careful in your conduct; and among other things, you can none of you afford to be seen looking shabby."

Mrs. Septimus spoke, it must be owned, with considerable unction. She really meant well by her nieces, as I have said before, but at the same time she was very human; and that circumstances should, as she imagined, have restored to her the right of speaking authoritatively to those independent maidens, was a chance not to be despised. Gertrude, once discussing her, had said that she was a person without respect, and, indeed, a reverence for humanity, as such, could not be reckoned among her virtues.

There was a pause after her last remark, and then, to the surprise and consternation of everyone, Fanny flung herself into the breach.

"Mrs. Pratt," she said, vehemently, "we are poor, and we are not ashamed that anyone should know it. It is nothing to be ashamed of; and Gertrude is the last person to do anything wrong; and I believe you know that as well as I do!"

Poor Fan's heroics broke off suddenly, as she encountered the steel-grey eye of Mrs. Pratt fixed upon her in astonishment.

Opposition in any form always shocked her inexpressibly; she really felt it to be a sort of sacrilege; but Frances Lorimer was such a poor creature, that one could do nothing but pity her, trampled upon as she was by her younger sisters.

"Fanny is right," said Gertrude, trusting herself to speak, "we are very poor."

"Now do you know exactly how you stand?" went on Aunt Caroline, who allowed herself all the privileges of a near relation in the matter of questions.

"It is not known yet, exactly," answered Lucy, hastily, "but Mr. Devonshire and our father's lawyer, and, I thought, Uncle Septimus, are going into the matter after the sale."

"So your uncle tells me. He tells me also that there will be next to nothing for you girls. Have you made up your minds what you are going to do? Which of you goes out to the Sebastian Lorimers? I hear they have telegraphed for two. I should say Fanny and Phyllis had better go; the others are better able to look after themselves."

Silence; but not in the least disconcerted, Aunt Caroline went on.

"It is a pity that none of you has married; girls don't seem to marry in these days!" (with some complacency, the well-disciplined, well-dowered daughters of the house of Pratt being in the habit of "going off" in due order and season) "but India works wonders sometimes in that respect."

"Oh, let me go to India, Gerty!" cried Phyllis, in a very audible aside, while Gertrude bent her head and bit her lip, controlling the desire to laugh hysterically, which the naive character of her aunt's last remark had excited.

"Now, Gertrude and Lucy," continued the speaker, "I am empowered by your uncle" (poor Septimus!) "to offer you a home for as long as you like. Either as a permanency, or until you have found suitable occupations."

"*We* are in India, Fan, that's why there is no mention of us," whispered naughty Phyllis.

"Aunt Caroline," broke in Gertrude, suddenly, lifting her head and speaking with great decision. "You are very kind, and we thank you. But we contemplate other arrangements."

"My dear Gertrude, other arrangements! And what 'arrangements,' pray, do you 'contemplate'?"

"Fanny, Lucy, Phyllis, shall I tell Aunt Caroline?"

They all consented; Fanny, whose willingness to join them had seemed before a doubtful matter, with the greatest promptness of them all.

"We think of going into business as photographers."

Gertrude dropped her bomb without delight. For a moment she saw herself and her sisters as they were reflected in the mind of Mrs. Septimus Pratt: naughty children, idle dreamers.

Aunt Caroline refused to be shocked, and Gertrude felt that her bomb had turned into a pea from a pea-shooter.

"Nonsense!" said Mrs. Pratt. "Gertrude, I wonder that you haven't more common sense. And before your younger sisters, too. But common sense," with unpleasant emphasis, "was never a family characteristic."

Lucy, who had remained silent and watchful throughout the last part of the discussion, if discussion it could be called, now rose to her feet.

"Aunt Caroline," she said in her clear young voice; "will you excuse us if we refuse to discuss this matter with you at present? We have decided nothing; indeed, how could we decide? Gertrude wrote yesterday to an old friend of our father's, who has the knowledge and experience we want; and we are waiting now for his advice."

"I think you are a set of wilful, foolish girls," cried Mrs. Pratt, losing her temper at last; "and heaven knows what will become of you! You are my dead sister's children, and I have my duties towards you, or I would wash my hands of you all from this hour. But your uncle shall talk to you; perhaps you will listen to *him*; though there's no saying."

She rose from her seat, with a purple flush on her habitually pale face, and without deigning to go through the formalities of farewell, swept from the room, followed by Lucy.

"A good riddance!" cried Fan. She too was flushed and excited, poor soul, with defiance.

Lucy, coming back from leading her aunt to the carriage, found Gertrude silent, pale, and trembling with rage. "How dare she!" she said below her breath.

"She is only very silly," answered Lucy; "I confess I began to wonder if I was an ill-conducted pauper, or a lunatic, or something of the sort, from the tone of her voice."

"She spoke so loud," said Gertrude, pressing her hand to her head.

"I never felt so labelled and docketed in my life," cried Phyllis; "*This is a poor person*, seemed to be written all over my clothes. Poor Fred's chuckles and 'By Joves' were much more comfortable."

Kettle came into the room with a letter addressed to Miss G. Lorimer.

"It is from Mr. Russel," she said, examining the postmark, and broke the seal with anxious fingers.

Mr. Russel was the friend of their father to whom she had applied for advice the day before. He carried on a large and world-famed business as a photographer in the north of England; to the disgust of a family that had starved respectably on scholarship for several generations.

Gertrude's mobile face brightened as she read the letter. "Mr. Russel is most encouraging," she said; "and very kind. He is actually coming to London to talk it over with us, and examine our work. And he even hints that one of us should go back with him to learn about things; but perhaps that will not be necessary."

Everyone seized on the kind letter, and the air was filled with the praises of its writer, Fanny even going so far as to call him a darling.

Gertrude, walking up and down the room, stopped suddenly and said: "Let us make some good resolutions!"

"Yes," cried Phyllis, with her usual frankness; "let us pave the way to hell a little!"

"Firstly, we won't be cynical."

The motion was carried unanimously.

"Secondly, we will be happy."

This motion was carried, with even greater enthusiasm than the preceding one.

"Thirdly," put in Phyllis, coming up behind her sister, laying her nut-brown head on her shoulder, and speaking in tones of mock pathos: "Thirdly, we will never, never mention that we have seen better days!"

Thus, with laughing faces, they stood up and defied the Fates.

Chapter 3
Ways and Means

O 'tis not joy and 'tis not bliss,
Only it is precisely this
That keeps us all alive.

A. H. CLOUGH[10]

"So you are really, really going to do it, Gerty?"

"Yes, really, Con."

It was the day before the sale, and the two girls, Gertrude Lorimer and Constance Devonshire, were walking round the garden together for the last time. It had been a day of farewells. Only an hour ago the unfortunate Fan had rolled off to Lancaster Gate in a brougham belonging to the house of Pratt. Lucy was now steaming on her way to the north with Mr. Russel; and upstairs Phyllis was packing her boxes before setting out for Queen's Gate with Constance and her sister.

"If it hadn't been for Mr. Russel," went on Gertrude, with enthusiasm, "the whole thing would have fallen through. Of course, all the kind, common-sense people opposed the scheme tooth and nail; Mr. Russel told me in confidence that he had no belief in common

10. Arthur Hugh Clough's (1819–1861) poem, "Life is Struggle."

sense; that I was to remember that, before trusting myself to him in any respect."

"Well, I don't think that particularly reassuring myself."

Gertrude laughed.

"At least, he has justified it in his own case. Delightful person! He actually appeared here in the flesh, the very day after he wrote. Common sense would never have done such a thing as that."

"You are very intolerant, Gertrude."

"Oh, I hope not! Well, Mr. Russel insisted on going straight to the studio, and examining our apparatus and our work. He turned over everything, remained immersed, as it were, in photographs for such a long time, and was throughout so silent and so serious, that I grew frightened. At last, looking up, he said brusquely: 'This is good work.' He talked to us very seriously after that. Pointed out to us the inevitable risks, the chances of failure which would attend such an undertaking as ours; but wound up by saying that it was by no means a preposterous one, and that for his part, his motto through life had always been, 'nothing venture, nothing have.'"

"Evidently a person after your own heart, Gerty."

"He added, that our best plan would be, if possible, to buy the good-will of some small business; but, as we could not afford to wait, and as our apparatus was very good as far as it went, we must not be discouraged if no opportunity of doing so presented itself, but had better start in business on our own account. Moreover, he says, if the worst comes to the worst, we should always be able to get employment as assistant photographers."

"But, Gerty, why not do that at first? You would be so much more likely to succeed in business afterwards," said Conny, for her part no opponent of common sense; and who, despite much superficial frivolity, was at heart a shrewd, far-seeing daughter of the City.

"If I said that one was life and the other death," answered Gertrude, with her charming smile, "you would perhaps consider the remark unworthy a woman of business. And yet I am not sure that it does not state my case as well as any other. We want a home and an occupation, Conny; a real, living occupation. Think of little Phyllis, for instance, trudging by herself to some great shop in all weathers and seasons!"

"Little Phyllis! She is bigger than any of you, and quite able to take care of herself."

"I wish – it sounds unsisterly – that she were not so very good-looking."

"It's a good thing there's no person of the other sex to hear you, Gerty. You would be made a text for a sermon at once."

"'Felines and Feminines,' or something of the sort? But here is Phyllis herself."

Cool, careless, and debonair, the youngest Miss Lorimer advanced towards them; the April sunshine reflected in her eyes; the tints of the blossoms outrivalled in her cheeks.

"My dear Gertrude," she said, patronisingly, "do you know that it is twelve o'clock, that my boxes are packed and locked, and that not a rag of your own is put away?"

Gertrude explained that she did not intend leaving the house till the afternoon, but that the other two were to go on at once to Queen's Gate, and not keep Mrs. Devonshire waiting for lunch. This, after some protest, they consented to do; and in a few moments Gertrude Lorimer was standing alone in the familiar garden, from which she was soon to be shut out forever.

Pacing slowly up and down the oft-trodden path, she strove to collect her thoughts; to review, at leisure, the events of the last few days. Her avowed contempt of the popular idol Common Sense notwithstanding, her mind teemed with practical details, with importunate questionings as to ways and means.

These matters seemed more perplexing without the calm and soothing influence of Lucy's presence; for Lucy had been borne off by the benevolent and eccentric Mr. Russel for a three-months' apprenticeship in his own flourishing establishment.

"I will see that your sister learns something of the management of a business, besides improving herself in those technical points which we have already discussed," had been his parting assurance. "While, as for you, Miss Lorimer, I depend on you to look round, and be on a fair way to settling down by the time the three months are up. Perhaps, one of these days, we shall prevail on you to pay us a visit yourself."

It had been decided that for the immediate present Gertrude and Phyllis should avail themselves of the Devonshires' invitation; while Fan, borne down by the force of a superior will, had been prevailed upon to seek a temporary refuge at the house of Mrs. Septimus Pratt.

Poor Aunt Caroline had been really shocked and pained by the firm, though polite, refusal of her nieces to accept her hospitality. Their differences of opinion notwithstanding, she could see no adequate cause for it. If her skin was thick, her heart was not of stone; and it chagrined her to think that her dead sister's children should, at such a time, prefer the house of strangers to her own.

But the young people were obdurate; and she had had at last to content herself with Fan, who was a poor creature, and only a spurious sort of relation after all.

Reviewing one by one all those facts which bore upon her present case; setting in order her thoughts; and gathering up her energies for the fight to come; Gertrude felt her pulses throb, and her bosom glow with resolve.

Of the darker possibilities of human nature and of life, this girl – who believed herself old, and experienced – had no knowledge, save such as had come to her in brief flashes of insight, in passing glimpses scarcely realised or remembered. Even had circumstances given her leisure, she was not a woman to have brooded over the one personal injury which had been dealt her; her pride was too deep and too delicate for this; rather she recoiled from the thought of it, as from an unclean contact.

If the arching forehead and mobile face bespoke imagination and keen sensibilities, the square jaw and resolute mouth gave token, no less, of strength and self-control.

> "And all her sorrow shall be turned to labour,"[11]

said Gertrude to herself, half-unconsciously. Then something within her laughed in scornful protest. Sorrow? on this spring day, with the young life coursing in her veins, with all the world before her, an undiscovered country of purple mists and boundless possibilities.

There were hints of a vague delight in the sweet, keen air; whisperings, promises, that had nothing to do with pyrogallic acid and acetate of soda; with the processes of developing, fixing, or intensifying.

A great laburnum tree stood at one end of the lawn, half-flowered and faintly golden; a blossoming almond neighboured it, and beyond, rose a gnarled old apple tree, pink with buds. Birds were piping and calling to one another from all the branches; the leaves of the trees, the lawn, the shrubs, and bushes, wore the vivid and delicate verdure of early spring; life throbbed, and pulsed, and thrust itself forth in every available spot.

Gertrude, as we know, was by way of being a poet. She had a rebellious heart that cried out, sometimes very inopportunely, for happiness.

And now, as she drank in the wonders of that April morning, she found herself suddenly assailed and overwhelmed by a nameless rapture, an extreme longing, half-hopeful, half-despairing.

Sorrow, labour; what had she to do with these?

> "I love all things that thou lovest
> Spirit of delight!"[12]

cried the voices within her, with one accord.

"Please, Miss," said Kettle, suddenly appearing, and scattering the thronging visions rather rudely; "the people have come from the Pantechnicon about those cameras, and the other things you said was to go."

---

11. From James Thomson's (1834–1882) *The City of Dreadful Night and Other Poems* (1880); see Levy's "James Thomson: A Minor Poet," (pp. 891–901).
12. From Percy Bysshe Shelley's (1792–1822) "Rarely, Rarely Comest Thou."

"Yes, yes," answered Gertrude, rubbing her eyes and wrinkling her brows – curious, characteristic brows they were; straight and thick, and converging slightly upwards – "everything that is to go is ready packed in the studio."

They had decided on retaining a little furniture, besides the photographic apparatus and studio fittings, for the establishment of the new home, wherever and whatever it should be.

"Very well, Miss Gertrude. And shall I bring you up a little luncheon?"

"No, thank you, Kettle. And I must say goodbye, and thank you for all your kindness to us."

"God bless you, Miss Gertrude, every one of you! I have made so bold as to give my address-card to Miss Phyllis; and if there's anything in which I can ever be of service, don't you think twice about it, but write off at once to Jonah Kettle."

Overcome by his own eloquence, and without waiting for a reply, the old man shuffled off down the path, leaving Gertrude strangely touched by this unexpected demonstration.

"We resolved not to be cynical," she thought. "Cynical! What is the meaning of the current commonplaces as to loss of friends with loss of fortune? How did they arise? What perverseness of vision could have led to the creation of such a person as Timon of Athens,[13] for instance? If misery parts the flux of company,[14] surely it is the miserable people's own fault."

Balancing the mass of friends in need against one who was only a fair-weather friend, Gertrude refused to allow her faith in humanity to be shaken.

Ah, Gertrude, but it is early days!

---

13. See William Shakespeare's (1564–1616) *The Life of Timon of Athens* (Bernstein, ed., *The Romance of a Shop*, 72 n. 1).
14. Line taken, albeit slightly reworded, from Shakespeare's *As You Like It* (Bernstein, ed., *The Romance of a Shop*, 72 n. 2).

Chapter 4

Number Twenty B

Bravant le monde et les sots et les sages,
Sans avenir, riche de mon printemps,
L'este et joyeux je montais six étages,
Dans un grenier qu'on est bien a vingt ans!

BÉRANGER[15]

The Lorimers' tenacity of purpose, backed by Mr. Russel's support and countenance, at last succeeded in procuring them a respectful hearing from the few friends and relatives who had a right to be interested in their affairs.

Aunt Caroline, shifting her ground, ceased to talk of the scheme as beneath contempt, but denounced it as dangerous and unwomanly. She spoke freely of loss of caste; damage to prospects – vague and delicate possession of the female sex – and of the complicated evils which must necessarily arise from an undertaking so completely devoid of chaperons.

Uncle Septimus said little, but managed to convey to his nieces quiet marks of support and sympathy; while the Devonshires, after

15. From Pierre-Jean de Béranger's (1780–1857) "Le Grenier," or "The Garret" (Bernstein, ed., *The Romance of a Shop*, 72 n. 3; New, ed., *The Complete Novels*, 540 n. 15).

much preliminary opposition, had ended by throwing themselves, like the excellent people they were, heart and soul into the scheme.

To Constance, indeed, the change in her friends' affairs may be said to have come, like the Waverley pen, as a boon and a blessing. She was the somebody to whom their ill wind, though she knew it not, was blowing good.

Like many girls of her class, she had good faculties, abundant vitality, and no interests but frivolous ones. And with the wealthy middle-classes, even the social business is apt to be less unintermittent, less absorbing, than with the better born seekers after pleasure.

Her friendship with the Lorimers, with Gertrude especially, may be said to have represented the one serious element in Constance Devonshire's life. And now she threw herself with immense zeal and devotion into the absorbing business of house-hunting, on which, for the time being, all Gertrude's thoughts were centred.

After the sale, and the winding up (mysterious process) of poor Mr. Lorimer's affairs, it was intimated to the girls that they were the joint possessors of £600; not a large sum, when regarded as almost the entire fortune of four people, but slightly in excess of that which they had been led to expect. I said almost, for it must not be forgotten that Fanny had a modest income of £50 coming to her from her mother, of which the principal was tied up from her reach.

There was nothing now to do but to choose their quarters, settle down in them, and begin the enterprise on which they were bent.

For many weary days, Gertrude and Conny, sometimes accompanied by Fred or Mr. Devonshire, paced the town from end to end, laden with sheaves of "orders to view" from innumerable house-agents.

Phyllis was too delicate for such expeditions, and sat at home with Mrs. Devonshire, or drove out shopping; amiable but ironical; buoyant but never exuberant; the charming child that everybody conspired to spoil, that everybody instinctively screened from all unpleasantness.

One day, the two girls came back to Queen's Gate in a state of considerable excitement.

"It certainly is the most likely place we have seen," said Gertrude, as she sipped her tea, and blinked at the fire with dazzled, short-sighted eyes.

"But such miles away from South Kensington," grumbled Conny, unfastening her rich cloak, and falling upon the cake with all the appetite born of honest labour.

"And the rent is a little high; but Mr. Russel says it would be bad economy to start in some cheap, obscure place."

"So we are to flaunt expensively," said Phyllis, lightly; "but all this is very vague, is it not Mrs. Devonshire? Please be more definite, Gerty dear."

"We have been looking at some rooms in Upper Baker Street," explained Gertrude, addressing her hostess; "there are two floors to be let unfurnished, above a chemist's shop."

"Two floors, and what else?" cried Conny; "you will never guess! Actually a photographer's studio built out from the house."

Mrs. Devonshire disapproved secretly of their scheme, and had only been won over to countenance it after days of persuasion.

"Someone has been failing in business there," she said, "or why should the studio stand empty?"

The girls felt this to be a little unreasonable, but Gertrude only laughed, and said: "No, but somebody has been dying. Our predecessor in business died last year."

"At least we should be provided with a ghost at once," said Phyllis; "I suppose if we go there we shall be 'Lorimer, late so-and so'?"

"What ghouls you two are!" objected Conny, with a shudder; then resumed the more practical part of the conversation. "The studio is in rather a dilapidated condition; but if it were not it would only count for more in the rent; it has to be paid for one way or another."

"There are a great many photographers in Baker Street already," demurred Mrs. Devonshire.

She liked the Lorimers, but feared them as companions for her daughter; there was no knowing on what wild freak they might lead Constance to embark.

"But, Mrs. Devonshire," protested Gertrude, with great eagerness, "I am told that it is the right thing for people of the same trade to congregate together; they combine, as it were, to make a centre, which comes to be regarded as the emporium of their particular wares."

Gertrude laughed at her own phrases, and Phyllis said:

"Don't look so poetical over it all, Gerty! Your hat has found its way to the back of your head, and there is a general look of inspiration about you."

She straightened the hat as she spoke, and put back the straggling wisps of hair.

"There is no bathroom!" went on Conny, sternly. She had a love of practical details and small opportunity for indulging it, except with regard to her own costume; and now she proceeded to plunge into elaborate statements on the subject of hot water, and the practicability of having it brought up in cans.

The end of it was that an expedition to Baker Street was organised for the next day; when the whole party drove across the park to that pleasant, if unfashionable, region, for the purpose of inspecting the hopeful premises.

It was a chill, bright afternoon, and notwithstanding that it was the end of May, the girls wore their winter cloaks, and Mrs. Devonshire her furs.

"What number did you say, Gertrude?" asked Phyllis, as the carriage turned into New Street, from Gloucester Place.

"Twenty B."

As they came into Baker Street, a young man, slim, high-coloured, dark-haired, darted out, with some impetuosity, from the post-office at the corner, and raised his hat as his eye fell on the approaching carriage.

Constance bowed, colouring slightly.

"Who is your friend, Conny?" said her mother.

"Oh, a man I meet sometimes at dances. I believe his name is Jermyn. He dances rather well."

Conny spoke with somewhat exaggerated indifference, and the colour on her cheek deepened perceptibly.

"Here we are!" cried Phyllis.

The carriage had drawn up before a small, but flourishing-looking shop, above which was painted in gold letters; *Maryon; Pharmaceutical Chemist.*

"This is it."

Gertrude spoke with curious intensity, and her heart beat fast as they dismounted and rang the bell.

Mrs. Maryon, the chemist's wife, a thin, thoughtful-looking woman of middle-age, with a face at once melancholy and benevolent, opened the door to them herself, and conducted them over the apartments.

They went up a short flight of stairs, then stopped before the opening of a narrow passage, adorned with Virginia cork and coloured glass.

"We will look at the studio first, please," said Gertrude, and they all trooped down the little, sloping passage.

"Reminds one forcibly of a summer house at a tea garden, doesn't it?" said Phyllis, turning her pretty head from side to side. They laughed, and the melancholy woman was seen to smile.

Beyond the passage was a little room, designed, no doubt, for a waiting or dressing room; and beyond this, divided by an aperture, evidently intended for curtains, came the studio itself, a fair-sized glass structure, in some need of repair.

"You will have to make this place as pretty as possible," said Conny; "you will be nothing if not aesthetic. And now for the rooms."

The floor immediately above the shop had been let to a dressmaker, and it was the two upper floors which stood vacant.

On the first of these was a fair-sized room with two windows, looking out on the street, divided by folding doors from a smaller room with a corner fireplace.

"This would make a capital sitting room," said Conny, marching up and down the larger apartment.

"And this," cried Gertrude, from behind the folding doors, which stood ajar, "could be fitted up beautifully as a kitchen."

"You will have to have a kitchen range, my dears," remarked Mrs. Devonshire, who was becoming deeply interested, and whose spirits, moreover, were rising under the sense that here, at least, she could speak to the young people from the heights of knowledge and experience; "and water will have to be laid on; and you will certainly need a sink."

"This grey wallpaper," went on Conny, "is not pretty, but at least it is inoffensive."

"And the possibilities for evil of wallpapers being practically infinite, I suppose we must be thankful for small mercies in that respect," answered Gertrude, emerging from her projected kitchen, and beginning to examine the uninteresting decoration in her short-sighted fashion.

Upstairs were three rooms, capable of accommodating four people as bedrooms, and which bounded the little domain.

Mr. and Mrs. Maryon and their servant inhabited the basement and the parlour behind the shop; and it was suggested by the chemist's wife that, for the present at least, the ladies might like to enter on some arrangement for sharing Matilda's services; the duties of that maiden, as matters now stood, not being nearly enough to fill up her time.

"That would suit us admirably," answered Gertrude; "for we intend to do a great deal of the work ourselves."

They drove away in hopeful mood; Mrs. Devonshire as much interested as any of them. It took, of course, some days before they were able to come to a final decision on the subject of the rooms. Various persons had to be consulted, and various matters inquired into. Mr. Russel came flying down from the north directly when Gertrude's letter reached him. He surveyed the premises in his rapid, accurate fashion; entered into details with immense seriousness; pronounced in favour of taking the apartments; gave a glowing account of Lucy; and rushed off to catch his train.

A few days afterwards the Lorimers found themselves the holders of a lease, terminable at one, three, or seven years, for a studio and upper part of the house, known as 20B, Upper Baker Street.

Then followed a period of absorbing and unremitting toil. All through the sweet June month, the girls laboured at setting things in order in the new home. Expense being a matter of vital consequence, they endeavoured to do everything, within the limits of possibility, themselves. Workmen were of course needed for repairing the studio and fitting the kitchen fireplace, but their services were dispensed with in almost every other case. The furniture stored at the Pantechnicon proved more than enough for their present needs; Gertrude and Conny between them laid down the carpets and hung up the curtains; and Fred, revealing an unsuspected talent for carpentering, occupied his leisure moments in providing the household with an unlimited quantity of shelves.

Indeed, the spectacle of that gorgeous youth hammering away in his shirt sleeves on a pair of steps, his immaculate hat and coat laid by, his gardenia languishing in some forgotten nook, was one not easily to be overlooked or forgotten. It was necessary, of course, to buy some additional stock-in-trade, and this Mr. Russel undertook to procure for them at the lowest possible rates; adding, on his own behalf, a large burnishing machine. The girls had hitherto been accustomed to have their prints rolled for them by the Stereoscopic Company.

In their own rooms everything was of the simplest, but a more ambitious style of decoration was attempted in the studio.

The objectionable Virginia cork and coloured glass of the little passage were disguised by various aesthetic devices; lanterns swung from the roof, and a framed photograph or two from Dürer and Botticelli, Watts and Burne-Jones,[16] was mingled artfully with the specimens of their own work, which adorned it as a matter of course.

A little cheap Japanese china, and a few red-legged tables and chairs converted the waiting room, as Phyllis said, into a perfect bower of

16. The line refers to the Renaissance German painter, Albrecht Dürer (1471–1528), the Renaissance Florentine painter, Sandro Botticelli (1445–1510), the Symbolist painter, George Frederic Watts (1817–1904), and the Pre-Raphaelite artist, Edward Burne-Jones (1833–1898); see Bernstein, ed., *The Romance of a Shop*, 78 n. 3; New, ed., *The Complete Novels*, 540–1 n. 18–9.

art and culture; while Fred contributed so many rustic windows, stiles, and canvas backgrounds to the studio, that his bankruptcy was declared on all sides to be imminent.

Over the street door was fixed a large black board, on which was painted in gold letters:

G. & L. LORIMER: THE PHOTOGRAPHIC STUDIO

and in the doorway was displayed a showcase, whose most conspicuous feature was a cabinet portrait of Fred Devonshire, looking, with an air of mingled archness and shamefacedness, through one of his own elaborate lattices in Virginia cork.

The Maryons surveyed these preparations from afar with a certain amused compassion, an incredulous kindliness, which were rather exasperating.

Like most people of their class, they had seen too much of the ups and downs of life to be astonished at anything; and the sight of these ladies playing at photographers and house decorators, was only one more scene in the varied and curious drama of life which it was their lot to witness.

"I wish," said Gertrude, one day, "that Mrs. Maryon were not such a pessimist."

"She is rather like Gilbert's patent hag who comes out and prophesies disaster," answered Phyllis. "She always thinks it is going to rain, and nothing surprises her so much as when a parcel arrives in time."[17]

"And she is so very kind with it all."

The sisters had been alone in Baker Street that morning; Constance being engaged in having a ball dress tried on at Russell and Allen's; and now Gertrude was about to set out for the British Museum, where she was going through a course of photographic reading, under the direction of Mr. Russel.

---

17. Taken from W.S. Gilbert (1836–1911) and Arthur Sullivan's (1842–1900) *Ruddigore; or, the Witch's Curse* (Bernstein, ed., *The Romance of a Shop*, 79 n. 3; New, ed., *The Complete Novels*, 541 n. 20).

"Look," cried Phyllis, as they emerged from the house; "there goes Conny's impetuous friend. I have found out that he lodges just opposite us, over the auctioneer's."

"What busybodies you long-sighted people always are, Phyllis!"

At Baker Street Station they parted; Phyllis disappearing to the underground railway; Gertrude mounting boldly to the top of an Atlas omnibus.

"Because one cannot afford a carriage or even a hansom cab," she argued to herself, "is one to be shut up away from the sunlight and the streets?"

Indeed, for Gertrude, the humours of the town had always possessed a curious fascination. She contemplated the familiar London pageant with an interest that had something of passion in it; and, for her part, was never inclined to quarrel with the fate which had transported her from the comparative tameness of Campden Hill to regions where the pulses of the great city could be felt distinctly as they beat and throbbed.

By the end of June, the premises in Upper Baker Street were quite ready for occupation; but Gertrude and Phyllis decided to avail themselves of some of their numerous invitations, and strengthen themselves for the coming tussle with fortune with three or four weeks of country air.

At last there came a memorable evening, late in July, when the four sisters met for the first time under the roof which they hoped was to shelter them for many years to come.

Gertrude and Phyllis arrived early in the day from Scarborough, where they had been staying with the Devonshires, and at about six o'clock Fanny appeared in a four-wheel cab; she had been borne off to Tunbridge Wells by the Pratts, some six weeks before.

When she had given vent to her delight at rejoining her sisters, and had inspected the new home, Phyllis led her upstairs to the bedroom, Gertrude remaining below in the sitting room, which she paced with a curious excitement, an irrepressible restlessness.

"Poor old Fan!" said Phyllis, reappearing; "I don't think she was ever so pleased at seeing anyone before."

"Fancy, all these months with Aunt Caroline!"

"She says little," went on Phyllis; "but from the few remarks dropped, I should say that her sufferings had been pretty severe."

"Yes," answered Gertrude, absently. The last remark had fallen on unheeding ears; her attention was entirely absorbed by a cab which had stopped before the door. One moment, and she was on the stairs; the next, she and Lucy were in one another's arms.

"Oh, Gerty, is it a hundred years?"

"Thousands, Lucy. How well you look, and I believe you have grown."

Up and down, hand in hand, went the sisters, into every nook and corner of the small domain, exclaiming, explaining, asking and answering a hundred questions.

"Oh, Lucy," cried Gertrude, in a burst of enthusiasm, as they stood together in the studio, "this is work, this is life. I think we have never worked or lived before."

Fan and Phyllis came rustling between the curtains to join them.

"Here we all are," went on Gertrude. "I hope nobody is afraid, but that everyone understands that this is no bed of roses we have prepared for ourselves."

"We shall have to work like niggers,[18] and not have very much to eat. I think we all realise that," said Lucy, with an encouraging smile.

"Plain living and high thinking," ventured Fanny; then grew overwhelmed with confusion at her own unwonted brilliancy.

"At least," said Phyllis, "we can all of us manage the plain living. And as a beginning, I vote we go upstairs to supper."

18. Outdated racist term in regular usage in Levy's time.

Chapter 5

This Working Day World

O the pity of it.

OTHELLO[19]

If a sudden reverse of fortune need not make us cynical, there is perhaps no other experience which brings us face to face so quickly and so closely with the realities of life.

The Lorimers, indeed, had no great cause for complaint; and perhaps, in condemning the Timons of this world, forgot that, as interesting young women, embarked moreover on an interesting enterprise, they were not themselves in a position to gauge the full depths of mundane perfidy.

Of course, after a time, they dropped off from the old set, from the people with whom their intercourse had been a mere matter of social commerce; but, as Phyllis justly observed, when you have no time to pay calls, no clothes to your back, no money for cabs, and very little for omnibuses, you can hardly expect your career to be an unbroken course of festivities.

On the other hand, many of their friends drew closer to them in the hour of need, and a great many good-natured acquaintances

19. From Shakespeare's *Othello*.

amused themselves by patronising the studio in Upper Baker Street, and recommending other people to go and do likewise.

Certainly, these latter exacted a good deal for their money; were restive when posed, expected the utmost excellence of work and punctuality of delivery, and, like most of the Lorimers' customers, seemed to think the sex of the photographers a ground for greater cheapness in the photographs.

One evening, towards the middle of October, the girls had assembled for the evening meal – it could not, strictly speaking, be called dinner – in the little sitting room above the shop.

They were all tired, for the moment discouraged, and had much ado to maintain that cheerfulness which they held it a point of honour never to abandon.

"How the evenings do draw in!" observed Fan, who sat near the window, engaged in fancywork.

Fanny's housekeeping, by the way, had been tried, and found wanting; and the poor lady had, with great delicacy, been relegated to the vague duty of creating an atmosphere of home for her more strong-minded sisters. Fortunately, she believed in the necessity of a thoroughly womanly presence among them, womanliness being apparently represented to her mind by any number of riband bows on the curtains, antimacassars on the chairs, and strips of embroidered plush on every available article of furniture; and accepted the situation without misgiving.

"Yes," answered Lucy, rather dismally; "we shall soon have the winter in full swing, fogs and all."

She had been up to the studio of an artist at St. John's Wood that morning, making photographs of various studies of drapery for a big picture, and the results, when examined in the darkroom later on, had not been satisfactory; hence her unusual depression of spirits.

"For goodness' sake, Lucy, don't speak in that tone!" cried Phyllis, who was standing idly by the window. "What does it matter about Mr. Lawrence's draperies? Nobody ever buys his pokey pictures.

You've not been the same person ever since you developed those plates this afternoon."

"Don't you see, Phyllis, Mr. Russel introduced us to him; and besides, though he is obscure himself, he might recommend us to other artists if the work was well done."

"Oh, bother! Come over here, Lucy. Do you see that lighted window opposite? It is Conny's Mr. Jermyn's."

"What an interesting fact!"

"Conny said he danced well. I wish he would come and dance with us sometimes. It is ages and ages since I had a really good waltz."

"Phyllis! do you forget that you are in mourning?" cried Fanny, shocked, as she moved towards the table, where Lucy had lit the lamp.

Gertrude came through the folding doors bearing a covered dish. Her aspect also was undeniably dejected. Business had been slacker, if possible, than usual, during the past week; regarded from no point of view could their prospects be considered brilliant; and, to crown all, Aunt Caroline had paid them a visit in the course of the day, in which she had propounded some very direct questions as to the state of their finances, questions which it had been both difficult to answer and difficult to evade.

Phyllis ceased her chatter, which she saw at once to be out of harmony with the prevailing mood, and took her place in silence at the table.

At the same moment the studio bell echoed with considerable violence throughout the house.

"What can anyone want this time of night?" cried Fan, in some agitation.

"They must have pulled the wrong bell," said Lucy; "but one of us had better go down and see."

Gertrude lighted a candle, and went downstairs, and the rest proceeded rather silently with their meal.

In about five minutes Gertrude reappeared with a grave face.

"Well?"

They all questioned her, with lips and eyes.

"Someone has been here about work," she said, slowly; "but it's rather a dismal sort of job. It is to photograph a dead person."

"Gerty, what *do* you mean?"

"Oh, I believe it is quite usual. A lady – Lady Watergate – died today, and her husband wishes the body to be photographed tomorrow morning."

"It is very strange," said Fanny, "that he should select ladies, young girls, for such a piece of work!"

"Oh, it was a mere chance. It was the housekeeper who came, and we happened to be the first photographer's shop she passed. She seemed to think I might not like it, but we cannot afford to refuse work."

"But, Gertrude," cried Fan, "do you know what Lady Watergate died of? Perhaps scarlet fever, or smallpox, or something of the sort."

"She died of consumption," said Gertrude shortly, and put her arm round Phyllis, who was listening with a curious look in her great, dilated eyes.

"I wonder," put in Lucy, "if this poor lady can be the wife of *the* Lord Watergate?"

"I rather fancy so; I know he lives in Regent's Park, and the address for tomorrow is Sussex Place."[20]

A name so well known in the scientific and literary world was of course familiar to the Lorimers. They had, however, little personal acquaintance with distinguished people, and had never come across the learned and courteous peer in his social capacity, his frequent presence in certain middle-class circles notwithstanding.

Mrs. Maryon, coming up later on for a chat, under pretext of discussing the unsatisfactory Matilda, was informed of the new commission.

"Ah," she said, shaking her head, "it was a sad story that of the Watergates." So passionately fond of her as he had been, and then for

20. The Levy family lived at Sussex Place 1872–1885 (Bernstein, ed., *The Romance of a Shop*, 85 n. 1).

her to treat him like that! But he took her back at the last and forgave her everything, like the great-hearted gentleman that he was. "And do you mean," she added, fixing her melancholy, humorous eyes on them, "that you young ladies are actually going by yourselves to the house to make a picture of the body?"

"I am going – no one else," answered Gertrude calmly, passing over Phyllis's avowed intention of accompanying her.

"She always has some dreadful tale about everybody you mention," cried Lucy, indignantly, when Mrs. Maryon had gone. "She will never rest content until there is something dreadful to tell of us."

"Yes, I'm sure she regards us as so many future additions to her Chamber of Horrors," said Phyllis, reflectively, with a smile.

"And oh," added Fan, "if she would only not compare us so constantly with that poor man who had the studio last year! It makes one positively creep."

"Nonsense," said Gertrude; "she is quite as fond of pleasant events as sad ones. Weddings, for instance, she describes with as much unction as funerals."

"We will certainly do our best to add to her stock of tales in that respect," cried Phyllis, with an odd burst of high spirits. "Who votes for getting married? I do. So do you, don't you, Fan? It must be such fun to have one's favourite man dropping in on one every evening."

* * * * *

At an early hour the next morning, Gertrude Lorimer started on her errand. She went alone; Lucy of course must remain in the studio; Phyllis was in bed with a headache, and Fan was ministering to her numerous wants. As she passed out, laden with her apparatus, Mdlle. Stéphanie, the big, sallow Frenchwoman who occupied the first floor, entered the house and grinned a vivacious "*Bonjour!*"

"A fine, bright morning for your work, miss!" cried the chemist from his doorstep; while his wife stood at his side, smiling curiously.

Gertrude went on her way with a considerable sinking of the heart. She had no difficulty in finding Sussex Place; indeed, she had often remarked it; the white curve of houses with the columns, the cupolas, and the railed-in space of garden which fronted the Park.

Lord Watergate's house was situated about midway in the terrace. Gertrude, on arriving, was shown into a large dining room, darkened by blinds, and decorated in each gloomy corner by greenish figures of a pseudo-classical nature, which served the purpose of supports to the gas-globes.

At least a quarter of an hour elapsed before the appearance of the housekeeper, who ushered her up the darkened stairs to a large room on the second storey.

Here the blinds had been raised, and for a moment Gertrude was too dazzled to be aware with any clearness of her surroundings.

As her eyes grew accustomed to the light, she perceived herself to be standing in a daintily-furnished sleeping apartment, whose open windows afforded glimpses of an unbroken prospect of wood, and lawn, and water.

Drawn forward to the middle of the room, well within the light from the windows, was a small, open bedstead of wrought brass. A woman lay, to all appearance, sleeping there, the bright October sunlight falling full on the upturned face, on the spread and shining masses of matchless golden hair. A woman no longer in her first youth; haggard with sickness, pale with the last strange pallor, but beautiful withal, exquisitely, astonishingly beautiful.

Another figure, that of a man, was seated by the window, in a pose as fixed, as motionless, as that of the dead woman herself.

Gertrude, as she silently made preparations for her strange task, instinctively refrained from glancing in the direction of this second figure; and had only the vaguest impression of a dark, bowed head, and a bearded, averted face.

She delivered a few necessary directions to the housekeeper, in the lowest audible voice, then, her faculties stimulated to curious accuracy, set to work with camera and slides.

As she stood, her apparatus gathered up, on the point of departure, the man by the window rose suddenly, and for the first time seemed aware of her presence.

For one brief but vivid moment, her eyes encountered the glance of two miserable grey eyes, looking out with a sort of dazed wonder from a pale and sunken face. The broad forehead, projecting over the eyes; the fine, but rough-hewn features; the brown hair and beard; the tall, stooping, sinewy figure: these together formed a picture which imprinted itself as by a flash on Gertrude's overwrought consciousness, and was destined not to fade for many days to come.

* * * * *

"They are some of the best work you have ever done, Gerty," cried Phyllis, peering over her sister's shoulder. The habits of this young person, as we know, resembled those of the lilies of the field;[21] but she chose to pervade the studio when nothing better offered itself, and in moments of boredom even to occupy herself with some of the more pleasant work.

Gertrude looked thoughtfully at the prints in her hand. They represented a woman lying dead or asleep, with her hair spread out on the pillow.

"Yes," she said, slowly, "they have succeeded better than I expected. Of course the light was not all that could be wished."

"Poor thing," said Phyllis; "what perfect features she has. Mrs. Maryon told us she was wicked, didn't she? But I don't know that it matters about being good when you are as beautiful as all that."

21. Matthew 6:28.

Chapter 6
To the Rescue

We studied hard in our styles,
Chipped each at a crust like Hindoos,
For air, looked out on the tiles,
For fun, watched each other's windows.
R. BROWNING[22]

"Mr. Frederick Devonshire, I positively refuse to minister any longer to such gross egotism! You've been cabinetted, vignetted, and carte de visited. You've been taken in a snowstorm; you've been taken looking out of the window, drinking afternoon tea, and doing I don't know what else. If your vanity still remains unsatisfied, you must get another firm to gorge it for you."

"You're a nice woman of business, you are! Turning money away from the doors like this," chuckled Fred. Lucy's simple badinage appealed to him as the raciest witticisms would probably have failed to do; it seemed to him almost on a par with the brilliant verbal coruscations of his cherished *Sporting Times*.

"Our business," answered Lucy demurely, "is conducted on the strictest principles. We always let a gentleman know when he has had as much as is good for him."

22. Robert Browning's (1812–1889) poem, "Youth and Art."

"Oh, I say!" Fred appeared to be completely bowled over by what he would have denominated as this "side-splitter," and gave vent to an unearthly howl of merriment.

"Whatever is the matter?" cried his sister, entering the sitting room. She and Gertrude had just come up together from the studio, where Conny had been pouring out her soul as to the hollowness of the world, a fact she was in the habit periodically of discovering. "Fred, what a shocking noise!"

"Oh, shut up, Con, and let a fellow alone," grumbled Fred, subsiding into a chair. "Conny's been dancing every night this week – making me take her, too, by Jove! – and now, if you please, she's got hot coppers."

Miss Devonshire deigned no reply to these remarks, and Phyllis, who, like all of them, was accustomed to occasional sparring between the brother and sister, threw herself into the breach.

"You're the very creature I want, Conny," she cried. "Come over here; perhaps you can enlighten me about the person who interests me more than anyone in the world."

"Phyllis!" protested Fan, who understood the allusion.

"It's your man opposite," went on Phyllis, unabashed; "Lucy and I are longing to know all about him. There he is on the doorstep; why, he only went out half an hour ago!"

"That fellow," said Fred, with unutterable contempt; "that foreign-looking chap whom Conny dances half the night with?"

"Foreign looking," said Phyllis, "I should just think he was! Why, he might have stepped straight out of a Venetian portrait; a Tintoretto,[23] a Bordone,[24] any one of those *mellow* people."

"Only as regards colouring," put in Lucy, whose interest in the subject appeared to be comparatively mild. "I don't believe those old Venetian nobles dashed about in that headlong fashion. I often wonder what his business can be that keeps him running in and out all day."

---

23. (Jacopo Robusti) Tintoretto (1518–1594), Venetian Renaissance painter.
24. Paris Bordone (1500–1571), Venetian Renaissance painter.

Fortunately for Constance, the fading light of the December afternoon concealed the fact that she was blushing furiously, as she replied coolly enough, "Oh, Frank Jermyn? he's an artist; works chiefly in black and white for the illustrated papers, I think. He and another man have a studio in York Place together."

"Is he an Englishman?"

"Yes; his people are Cornish clergymen."

"All of them? 'What, all his pretty ones?'"[25] cried Phyllis; "but you are very interesting, Conny, today. Poor fellow, he looks a little lonely sometimes; although he has a great many oddly-assorted pals."

"By the by," went on Conny, still maintaining her severely neutral tone, "he mentioned the photographic studio, and wanted to know all about 'G. and L. Lorimer.'"

"Did you tell him," answered Phyllis, "that if you lived opposite four beautiful, fallen princesses, who kept a photographer's shop, you would at least call and be photographed."

"It is so much nicer of him that he does not," said Lucy, with decision.

Phyllis struck an attitude:

> "It might have been, once only,
> We lodged in a street together ..."[26]

she began, then stopped short suddenly.

"What a thundering row!" said Fred.

A curious, scuffling sound, coming from the room below, was distinctly audible.

"Mdlle. Stéphanie appears to be giving an afternoon dance," said Lucy. "I will go and see if anything is the matter," remarked Gertrude, rising. As a matter of fact, she snatched eagerly at this opportunity for separating herself from this group of idle chatterers. She was tired,

25. From Shakespeare's *Macbeth* (Bernstein, ed., *The Romance of a Shop*, 89 n. 3; New, ed., *The Complete Novels*, 541 n. 28).
26. From Browning's "Youth and Art" again.

dispirited, beset with a hundred anxieties; weighed down by a cruel sense of responsibility.

How was it all to end? she asked herself, as, oblivious of Mdlle. Stéphanie's performance, she lingered on the little dusky landing. That first wave of business, born of the good-natured impulse of their friends and acquaintance, had spent itself, and matters were looking very serious indeed for the firm of G. and L. Lorimer.

"We couldn't go on taking Fred's guineas forever," she thought, a strange laugh rising in her throat. "Perhaps, though, it was wrong of me to refuse to be interviewed by *The Waterloo Place Gazette*. But we are photographers, not mountebanks!" she added, in self-justification.

In a few minutes she had succeeded in suppressing all outward marks of her troubles, and had rejoined the people in the sitting room.

"Mrs. Maryon says there is nothing the matter," she cried, with her delightful smile, "and that there is no accounting for these foreigners."

Laughter greeted her words, then Conny, rising and shaking out her splendid skirts, declared that it was time to go.

"Aren't you ever coming to see us?" she said, giving Gertrude a great hug. "Mama is positively offended, and as for Papa – disconsolate is not the word."

"You must make them understand how really difficult it is for any of us to come," answered Gertrude, who had a natural dislike to entering on explanations in which such sordid matters as shabby clothes and the comparative dearness of railway tickets would have had to figure largely. "But we are coming one day, of course."

"I'll tell you what it is," cried Fred, as they emerged into the street, and stood looking round for a hansom; "Gertrude may be the cleverest, and Phyllis the prettiest, but Lucy is far and away the nicest of the Lorimer girls."

"Gerty is worth ten of her, *I* think," answered Conny, crossly. She was absorbed in furtive contemplation of a light that glimmered in a window above the auctioneer's shop opposite.

As the girls were sitting at supper, later on, they were startled by the renewal of those sounds below which had disturbed them in the afternoon.

They waited a few minutes, attentive; but this time, instead of dying away, the noise rapidly gathered volume, and in addition to the scuffling, their ears were assailed by the sound of shrill cries, and what appeared to be a perfect volley of objurgations. Evidently a contest was going on in which other weapons than vocal or verbal ones were employed, for the floor and windows of the little sitting room shook and rattled in a most alarming manner.

Suddenly, to the general horror, Fanny burst into tears.

"Girls," she cried, rushing wildly to the window, "you may say what you like; but I am not going to stay and see us all murdered without lifting a hand. Help! Murder!" she shrieked, leaning half her body over the windowsill.

"For goodness' sake, Fanny, stop that!" cried Lucy, in dismay, trying to draw her back into the room. But her protest was drowned by a series of ear-piercing yells issuing from the room below.

"I will go and see what is the matter," said Gertrude, pale herself to the lips; for the whole thing was sufficiently blood-curdling.

"You'd better stay where you are," answered Lucy, in her most matter-of-fact tones, as she led the terrified Fan to an armchair.

Phyllis stood among them silent, gazing from one to the other, with that strange, bright look in her eyes, which with her betokened excitement; the unimpassioned, impersonal excitement of a spectator at a thrilling play.

"Certainly I shall go," said Gertrude, as a door banged violently below, to the accompaniment of a volley of polyglot curses.

"I will not stay in this awful house another hour," panted Fanny, from her armchair. "Gertrude, Gertrude, if you leave this room I shall die!"

With a sickening of the heart, for she knew not what horror she was about to encounter, Gertrude made her way downstairs, the cries and sounds of struggling growing louder at each step. At the bottom of the first flight, she paused.

"Go back, Phyllis."

"It's no good, Gerty, I'm not going back."

"I am going to the shop; and if the Maryons are not there we must call a policeman."

Swiftly they went down the next flight, past the horrible doors, on the other side of which the battle was raging, still downwards, till they reached the little narrow hall. Here they drew up suddenly before a figure which barred the way.

Long afterwards Gertrude could recall the moment when she first saw Frank Jermyn under their roof; could remember distinctly – though all at the time seemed chaos – the sudden sensation of security that came over her at the sight of the kind, eager young face, the brilliant, steadfast eyes; at the sound of the manly, cheery voice.

There were no explanations; no apologies.

"There seems to be a shocking row going on," he said, lifting his hat; "I only hope that it does not concern any of you ladies."

In a few hurried words, Gertrude told him what she knew of the state of affairs. Meanwhile, the noise had in some degree subsided.

"Great heavens!" cried Frank; "there may be murder going on at this instant." And in less time than it takes to tell he had sprung past her, and was hammering with all his might at the closed door.

The girls followed timidly, and were in time to see the door fly open in response to the well-directed blows, and Mrs. Maryon herself come forward, pale but calm. Within the room all was now dark and silent.

Mrs. Maryon and the newcomer exchanged a few hurried words, and the latter turned to the girls, who clung together a few paces off.

"There is no cause for alarm," he said. "Pray do not wait here. I will explain everything in a few minutes, if I may."

"Now please, Miss Lorimer, go back upstairs; there's nothing to be frightened at," chimed in Mrs. Maryon, with some asperity.

A few minutes afterwards Frank Jermyn knocked at the door of the Lorimers' sitting room, and on being admitted, found himself well within the fire of four questioning pairs of feminine eyes.

"Pray sit down, sir," said Fan, who had been prepared for his arrival. "How are we ever to thank you?"

"There is nothing to thank me for, as your sisters can tell you," he said, bluntly. He looked a modest, pleasant little person enough as he sat there in his light overcoat and dress clothes, all the fierceness gone out of him. "I have merely come to tell you that nothing terrible has happened. It seems that the poor Frenchwoman below has been in money difficulties, and has been trying to put an end to herself. The Maryons discovered this in time, and it has been as much as they could do to prevent her from carrying out her plan. Hence these tears," he added, with a smile.

When once you had seen Frank Jermyn smile, you believed in him from that moment.

The girls were full of horror and pity at the tale.

"We have had a great shock," said Fan, wiping her eyes, with dignity. "Such a terrible noise. But you heard it for yourself."

A pause; the young fellow looked round rather wistfully, as though doubtful of what footing he stood on among them.

"We must not keep you," went on Fan, whose tongue was loosened by excitement; "no doubt (glancing at his clothes) you are going out to dinner."

She spoke in the manner of a fallen queen who alludes to the ceremony of coronation.

Frank rose.

"By the by," he said, looking down, "I have often wished – I have never ventured" – then looking up and smiling brightly, "I have often wondered if you included photographing at artists' studios in your work."

Lucy assured him that they did, and the young man asked permission to call on them the next day at the studio. Then he added –

"My name is Jermyn, and I live at Number 19, opposite."

"I think," said Lucy, in the candid, friendly fashion which always set people at their ease, "that we have an acquaintance in common, Miss Devonshire."

Jermyn acknowledged that such was the case; a few remarks on the subject were exchanged, then Frank went off to his dinner party, having first shaken hands with each of the girls in all cordiality and frankness.

Mrs. Maryon came up in the course of the evening, to express her regret that the ladies had been frightened and disturbed; setting aside with cynical good humour their anxious expressions of pity and sympathy for the heroine of the affair.

"It isn't for such as you to trouble yourselves about such as her," she said, "although I'm sorry enough for Steffany myself – and never a penny of last quarter's rent paid!"

"Poor woman," answered Lucy, "she must have been in a desperate condition."

"You see, miss," said Mrs. Maryon circumstantially, "she had been going on owing money forever so long, though *we* knew nothing about it; and at last she was threatened with the bailiffs. Then what must she do but go down to the shop and make off with some of Maryon's bottles while we were at dinner. He found it out, and took one away from her this afternoon when you complained of the noise. Later he missed the second bottle, and went up to Steffany, who was uncorking it and sniffing it, and making believe she wanted to do away with herself."

"How unutterably horrible!" Gertrude shuddered.

"You heard how she went on when he tried to take it from her. Such strength as she has, too –it was as much as me and Maryon and the girl could do between us to hold her down."

"Where has she gone to now?" said Lucy.

"Oh, she don't sleep here, you know, miss. She's gone home with Maryon as meek as a lamb; took her bit of supper with us, quite cheerfully."

"What will she do, I wonder?"

"Ah," said Mrs. Maryon, thoughtfully; "there's no saying what she and many other poor creatures like her have to do. There'd be no rest for any of us if we was to think of that."

Gertrude lay awake that night for many hours; the events of the day had curiously shaken her. The story of the miserable Frenchwoman, with its element of grim humour, made her sick at heart.

Fenced in as she had hitherto been from the grosser realities of life, she was only beginning to realise the meaning of life. Only a plank – a plank between them and the pitiless, fathomless ocean[27] on which they had set out with such unknowing fearlessness; into whose boiling depths hundreds sank daily and disappeared, never to rise again.

*****

Mademoiselle Stéphanie actually put in an appearance the next morning, and made quite a cheerful bustle over the business of setting her house in order, preparatory to the final flitting.

Gertrude passed her on the stairs on her way to the studio, but feigned not to notice the other's morning greeting, delivered with its usual crispness. The woman's mincing, sallow face, with its unabashed smiles, sickened her.

Phyllis, who was with her, laughed softly.

"She does not seem in the least put out by the little affair of yesterday," she said.

"Hush, Phyllis. Ah, there is the studio bell already. No doubt it is Mr. Jermyn," and she unconsciously assumed her most business-like air.

A day or two later, Mademoiselle Stéphanie vanished forever; and not long afterwards her place was occupied by a serious-looking umbrella-maker, who displayed no hankering for Mr. Maryon's bottles.

27. From William McGonagall's (1825–1902) "The Wreck of the Whaler 'Oscar'" (Bernstein, ed., *The Romance of a Shop*, 95 n. 1).

Chapter 7
A New Customer

Stately is service accepted, but lovelier service rendered,
Interchange of service the law and condition of Beauty.

A. H. CLOUGH[28]

Frank Jermyn, whom we have left ringing at the bell, followed Gertrude down the Virginia cork passage into the waiting room.

The curtains between this apartment and the studio were drawn aside, displaying a charming picture – Lucy, in her black gown and holland pinafore, her fair, smooth head bent over the retouching frame; Phyllis, at an ornamental table, engaged in trimming prints, with great deftness and grace of manipulation.

Neither of the girls looked up from her work, and Frank took possession of one of the red-legged chairs, duly impressed with the business-like nature of the occasion; although, indeed, it must be confessed that his glance strayed furtively now and then in the direction of the studio and its pleasant prospect.

Gertrude explained that they were quite prepared to undertake studio work. Frank briefly stated the precise nature of the work he had ready for them, and then ensued a pause.

---

28. From Clough's "The Bothie of Tober-Na-Vuolich: A Long-Vacation Pastoral."

It was humiliating, it was ridiculous, but it was none the less true, that neither of these business-like young people liked first to make a definite suggestion for the inevitable visit to Frank's studio.

At last Gertrude said, "You would wish it done today?"

"Yes, please; if it be possible."

She reflected a moment. "It must be this morning. There is no relying on the afternoon light. I cannot arrange to go myself, but my sister can, I think. Lucy!"

Lucy came across to them, alert and serene.

"Lucy, would you take number three camera to Mr. Jermyn's studio in York Place?"

"Yes, certainly."

"I have some studies of drapery I should wish to be photographed," added Frank, with his air of steadfast modesty.

"I will come at once, if you like," answered Lucy, calmly.

"You will, of course, allow me to carry the apparatus, Miss Lorimer."

"Thank you," said Lucy, after the least possible hesitation.

Everyone was immensely serious; and a few minutes afterwards Mrs. Maryon, looking out from the dressmaker's window, saw a solemn young man and a sober young woman emerge together from the house, laden with tripod-stand and camera, and a box of slides, respectively.

"I wish I could have gone myself," said Gertrude, in a worried tone; "but I promised Mrs. Staines to be in for her."

"Yes, he is a nice young man," answered Phyllis, unblushingly, looking up from her prints.

"Oh Phyllis, Phyllis, don't talk like a housemaid."

"I say, Gerty, all this is delightfully unchaperoned, isn't it?"

"Phyllis, how can you?" cried Gertrude, vexed.

The question of propriety was one which she always thought best left to itself, which she hated, above all things, to discuss. Yet even her own unconventional sense of fitness was a little shocked at seeing her sister walk out of the house with an unknown young man, both of them being bound for the studio of the latter.

She was quite relieved when, an hour later, Lucy appeared in the waiting room, fresh and radiant from her little walk.

"Mrs. Staines has been and gone," said Gertrude. "She worried dreadfully. But what have you done with 'number three?'"

"Oh, I left the camera at York Place. I am going again tomorrow to do some work for Mr. Oakley, who shares Mr. Jermyn's studio."

"Grist for our mill with a vengeance. But come here and talk seriously, Lucy."

Phyllis, be it observed, who never remained long in the workshop, had gone out for a walk with Fan.

"Well?" said Lucy, balancing herself against a five-barred gate, Fred Devonshire's latest gift, aptly christened by Phyllis the White Elephant. "Well, Miss Lorimer?"

"I'm going to say something unpleasant. Do you realise that this latest development of our business is likely to excite remark?"

"'That people will talk,' as Fan says? Oh, yes, I realise that."

"Don't look so contemptuous, Lucy. It is unconventional, you know."

"Of course it is; and so are we. It is a little late in the day to quarrel with our bread-and-butter on that ground."

"It is a mere matter of convention, is it not?" cried Gertrude, more anxious to persuade herself than her sister. "Whether a man walks into your studio and introduces himself, or whether your hostess introduces him at a party, it comes to much the same thing. In both cases you must use your judgment about him."

"And whether he walks down the street with you, or puts his arm round your waist, and waltzes off with you to some distant conservatory, makes very little difference. In either case, the chances are one knows nothing about him. I am sure half the men one met at dances might have been haberdashers or professional thieves for all their hostesses knew. And, as a matter of fact, we happen to know something about Mr. Jermyn."

"Oh, I have nothing to say against Mr. Jermyn, personally. I am sure he is nice. It was rather that my vivid imagination saw vistas of studio-work looming in the distance. It was quite different with Mr. Lawrence, you know," said Gertrude, whom her own arguments struck as plausible rather than sound. "One thing may lead to another."

"Yes, it is sure to," cried Lucy, who saw an opportunity for escaping from the detested propriety topic. "Today, for instance, with Mr. Oakley. He is middle-aged, by the bye, Gerty, and married, for I saw his wife."

They both laughed; they could, indeed, afford to laugh, for, regarded from a financial point of view, the morning had been an unusually satisfactory one.

Gertrude's prophetic vision of vistas of studio work proved, for the next few days at least, to have been no baseless fabric of the fancy. The two artists at York Place kept them so busy over models, sketches, and arrangements of drapery, that the girls' hands were full from morning till night. Of course, this did not last, but Frank was so full of suggestions for them, so genuinely struck with the quality of their work, so anxious to recommend them to his comrades in art, that their spirits rose high, and hope, which for a time had almost failed them, arose, like a giant refreshed,[29] in their breasts.

In all simplicity and respect, the young Cornishman took a deep and unconcealed interest in the photographic firm, and expected, on his part, a certain amount of interest to be taken in his own work.

Frank, as Conny had said, worked chiefly in black and white. He was engaged, at present, in illustrating a serial story for *The Woodcut* but he had time on his hands for a great deal more work, time which he employed in painting pictures which the public refused to buy, although the committees were often willing to exhibit them.

"If they would only send me out to that wretched little war," he said. "There is nothing like having been a special artist for getting a man on with the pictorial editors."

29. Psalm 78:66 (Bernstein, ed., *The Romance of a Shop*, 95 n. 1).

There is nothing like the salt of healthy objective interests for keeping the moral nature sound. Before the sense of mutual honesty, the little barriers of prudishness which both sides had thought fit in the first instance to raise, fell silently between the young people, never again to be lifted up.

For good or evil, these waifs on the great stream of London life had drifted together; how long the current should continue thus to bear them side by side – how long, indeed, they should float on the surface of the stream at all, was a question with which, for the time being, they did not very much trouble themselves.

No one quite knew how it came about, but before a month had gone by, it became the most natural thing in the world for Frank to drop in upon them at unexpected hours, to share their simple meals, to ask and give advice about their respective work.

Fanny had accepted the situation with astonishing calmness. Prudish to the verge of insanity with regard to herself, she had grown to look upon her strong-minded sisters as creatures emancipated from the ordinary conventions of their sex, as far removed from the advantages and disadvantages of gallantry as the withered hag who swept the crossing near Baker Street Station.

Perhaps, too, she found life at this period a little dull, and welcomed, on her own account, a new and pleasant social element in the person of Frank Jermyn; however it may be, Fanny gave no trouble, and Gertrude's lurking scruples slept in peace.

One bright morning towards the end of January, Gertrude came careering up the street on the summit of a tall, green omnibus, her hair blowing gaily in the breeze, her ill-gloved hands clasped about a bulky notebook. Frank, passing by in painting coat and sombrero, plucked the latter from his head and waved it in exaggerated salute, an action which evoked a responsive smile from the person for whom it was intended, but acted with quite a different effect on another person who chanced to witness it, and for whom it was certainly not intended. This was no other than Aunt Caroline Pratt, who, to Gertrude's dismay, came dashing past in an open carriage, a look of speechless horror on her handsome, horselike countenance.

Now it is impossible to be dignified on the top of an omnibus, and Gertrude received her aunt's frozen stare of non-recognition with a humiliating consciousness of the disadvantages of her own position.

With a sinking heart she crept down from her elevation, when the omnibus stopped at the corner, and walked in a crestfallen manner to Number 20B, before the door of which the carriage, emptied of its freight, was standing.

Aunt Caroline did not trouble them much in these days, and rather wondering what had brought her, Gertrude made her way to the sitting room, where the visitor was already established.

"How do you do. Aunt Caroline?"

"How do you do, Gertrude? And where have you been this morning?"

"To the British Museum."

Gertrude felt all the old opposition rising within her, in the jarring presence; an opposition which she assured herself was unreasonable. What did it matter what Aunt Caroline said, at this time of day? It had been different when they had been little girls; different, too, in that first moment of sorrow and anxiety, when she had laid her coarse touch on their quivering sensibilities.

Yet, when all was said, Mrs. Pratt's was not a presence to be in any way passed over.

"It is half-past one," said Aunt Caroline, consulting her watch; "are you not going to have your luncheon?"

"It is laid in the kitchen," explained Lucy; "but if you will stay we can have it in here."

"In the kitchen! Is it necessary to give up the habits of ladies because you are poor?"

"A kitchen without a cook," put in Phyllis, "is the most ladylike place in the world."

Mrs. Pratt vouchsafed no answer to this exclamation, but turned to Lucy.

"No luncheon, thank you. I may as well say at once that I have come here with a purpose; solely, in fact, from motives of duty. Gertrude, perhaps your conscience can tell you what brings me."

"Indeed, Aunt Caroline, I am at a loss – "

"I have come," continued Mrs. Pratt, "prepared to put up with anything you may say. Gertrude, it is to you I address myself, although, from Fanny's age, she is the one to have prevented this scandal."

"I do not in the least understand you," said Gertrude, with self-restraint.

Mrs. Pratt elevated her gloved forefinger, with the air of a well-seasoned counsel.

"Is it, or is it not true, that you have scraped acquaintance with a young man who lodges opposite you; that he is in and out of your rooms at all hours; that you follow him about to his studio?"

"Yes," said Gertrude, slowly, flushing deeply, "if you choose to put it that way; it is true."

"That you go about to public places with him," continued Aunt Caroline; "that you have been seen, two of you and this person, in the upper boxes of a theatre?"

"Yes, it is true," answered Gertrude; and Lucy, mindful of a coming storm, would have taken up the word, but Gertrude interrupted her.

"Let me speak, Lucy; perhaps, after all, we do owe Aunt Caroline some explanation. Aunt, how shall I say it for you to understand? We have taken life up from a different standpoint, begun it on different bases. We are poor people, and we are learning to find out the pleasures of the poor, to approach happiness from another side. We have none of the conventional social opportunities for instance, but are we therefore to sacrifice all social enjoyment? You say we 'follow Mr. Jermyn to his studio'; we have our living to earn, no less than our lives to live, and in neither case can we afford to be the slaves of custom. Our friends must trust us or leave us; must rely on our self-respect and our judgment. Convention apart, are not judgment and self-respect what we most of us do rely on in our relations with people, under any circumstances whatever?"

It was only the fact that Aunt Caroline was speechless with rage that prevented her from breaking in at an earlier stage on poor Gertrude's heroics; but at this point she found her voice. Sitting very still, and looking hard at her niece with a remarkably unpleasant expression in her cold eye, she said in tones of concentrated fury:

"Fanny is a fool, and the others are children; but don't *you*, Gertrude, know what is meant by a lost reputation?"

This was too much for Gertrude; she sprang to her feet.

"Aunt Caroline," she cried, "you are right; Lucy and Phyllis are very young. It is not fit that they should hear such conversation. If you wish to continue it, I will ask them to go away."

A pause; the two combatants standing pale and breathless, facing one another. Then Lucy went over to her sister and took her hand; Fanny sobbed; Phyllis glanced from one to the other with her bright eyes.

Now, Gertrude's conduct had been distinctly injudicious; open defiance, no less than servile acquiescence, was understood and appreciated by Mrs. Pratt; but Gertrude, as Lucy, who secretly admired her sister's eloquence, at once perceived, had spoken a tongue not understanded of Aunt Caroline.

As soon, in these non-miraculous days, strike the rock for water, as appeal to Aunt Caroline's finer feelings or imaginative perceptions.

"If you will not listen to me," she said, suddenly assuming an air of weariness and physical delicacy, "it must be seen whether your uncle can influence you. I am not equal to prolonging the discussion."

Pointedly ignoring Gertrude, she shook hands with the other girls; angry as she was, their shabby clothes and shabby furniture smote her for the moment with compassion. Poverty seemed to her the greatest of human calamities; she pitied even more than she despised it.

To Lucy, indeed, who escorted her downstairs, she assumed quite a gay and benevolent manner; only pausing to ask on the threshold, with a good deal of fine, healthy curiosity underlying the elaborate archness of her tones:

"Now, how much money have you naughty girls been making lately?"

Lucy stoutly and laughingly evaded the question, and Aunt Caroline drove off smiling, refusing, like the stalwart warrior that she was, to acknowledge herself defeated. But it was many a long day before she attempted again to interfere in the affairs of the Lorimers.

Perhaps she would have been more ready to renew the attack, had she known how really distressed and disturbed Gertrude had been by her words.

Chapter 8

A Distinguished Person

... I can give no reason, nor I will not;
More than have a lodged hate and a certain loathing
I bear Antonio."

MERCHANT OF VENICE[30]

One morning, towards the middle of March, the sisters were much excited at receiving a letter containing an order to photograph a picture in a studio at St. John's Wood.

It was written in a small legible handwriting, was dated from The Sycamores, and signed, Sidney Darrell.

"I wonder how he came to hear of us?" said Lucy, who cherished a particular admiration for the works of this artist.

"Perhaps Mr. Jermyn knows him," answered Gertrude.

"He would probably have spoken of him to us, if he did."

"Here," said Gertrude, "is Mr. Jermyn to answer for himself."

Frank, who had been admitted by Matilda, came into the waiting room, where the sisters stood, a look as of the dawning spring-time in his vivid face and shining eyes.

30. From Shakespeare's *The Merchant of Venice*. See Levy's discussion of the latter on p. 918.

"I have brought the proofs from *The Woodcut*," he said, drawing a damp bundle from his painting coat. The Lorimers always read the slips of the story he was illustrating, and then a general council was held to decide on the best incident for illustration.

Lucy took the bundle and handed him the letter.

"Aren't you tremendously pleased?" he said.

"Do you know anything about this?" asked Lucy.

"How?"

"I mean, did you recommend us to him?"

"Not I. This letter is simply the reward of well-earned fame."

"Thank you, Mr. Jermyn; I really think you must be right. Do you know Sidney Darrell?"

"I have met him. But he is a great swell, you know, Miss Lucy, and he is almost always abroad."

"Yes," put in Gertrude; "his exquisite Venetian pictures!"

"Oh, Darrell is a clever fellow. Too fond of the French school, perhaps, for my taste. And the curious thing is, that, though his work is every bit as solid as it is brilliant, there is something rather sensational about his reputation."

"All this," cried Gertrude, "sounds exciting."

"I think that must be owing to the man himself," went on Frank. "Oakley knows him fairly well; says you may meet him one night at dinner, and he will ask you up to his studio. The first thing next morning you get a note putting you off; he is very sorry, but he is starting that day for India."

"Does he paint Indian pictures?"

"No, but is bitten at times with the 'big game' craze; shoots tigers and sticks pigs, and so on. I believe his studio is quite a museum of trophies of the chase."

"By the by, Lucy, which of us is to go to The Sycamores tomorrow morning?"

"You must go, Gerty; I can't trust anyone else to finish off those prints of little Jack Oakley, and they have been promised so long."

Gertrude consulted the letter.

"I shall have to take the big camera, which involves a cab."

"I wish I could have walked up with you," said Frank; "but, strange to say, I am very busy this week."

"I wish we were busy," answered Gertrude; "things are a little better, but it is slow work."

"I consider this letter of Darrell's a distinct move forward," cried hopeful Frank; "*he* will be able to recommend you to artists who are not a lot of out-at-elbow fellows," he added, holding out his hand in farewell, with a bright smile that belied the rueful words. "Now, please don't forget you are all coming to tea with Oakley and me on Sunday afternoon. And Miss Devonshire – you gave her my invitation?"

"Yes," said Lucy promptly; then added after a pause: "May her brother come too; he says he would like to?"

Frank scanned her quickly with his bright eyes.

"Certainly, if you like; he is not a bad sort of cub."

And then he departed abruptly.

"That was quite rude, for Mr. Jermyn," said Gertrude.

Lucy turned away with a slight flush on her fair face.

"It would be quite rude for anybody," she said, and went over to the studio.

Phyllis was spending the day at the Devonshires, but came back for the evening meal, by which time her sisters' excitement on the subject of Darrell's letter had subsided; and no mention was made of it while they were at table.

After the meal, Phyllis went over to the window, drew up the blind, and amused herself, as was her frequent custom, by looking into the street.

"I wish you wouldn't do that," said Lucy; "anyone can see right into the room."

"Why do you waste your breath, Lucy? You know it is never any good telling me not to do things, when I want to."

Gertrude, who had herself a secret, childish love for the gas-lit street, for the sight of the hurrying people, the lamps, the hansom cabs, flickering in and out the yellow haze, like so many fireflies, took no part in the dispute, but set to work at repairing an old skirt of Phyllis's, which was sadly torn.

Meanwhile the spoilt child at the window continued her observations, which seemed to afford her considerable amusement.

"There is a light in Frank Jermyn's window – the top one," she cried; "I suppose he is dressing. He told me he had an early dance in Harley Street. I wish *I* were going to a dance."

There was a look of mischief in Phyllis's eyes as she looked round at Lucy, who was buried in the proofsheets from *The Woodcut.*

"Phyllis, you are coughing terribly. Do come away from that draughty place," cried Gertrude, with real anxiety.

"Oh, I'm all right, Gerty. Ah, there goes Master Frank. It is wet underfoot, and he has turned up his trousers, and his pumps are bulging from his coat pocket. I wonder how many miles a week he walks on his way to dances?"

"It is quite delightful to see a person with such an enjoyment of every phase of existence," said Gertrude, half to herself.

"You poor, dear *blasée* thing. It is a pretty sight to see the young people enjoying themselves, as the little boy said in *Punch,*[31] is it not? I wonder if Mr. Jermyn is going to walk all the way? Perhaps he will take the omnibus at the corner. He never 'soars higher than a 'bus,' as he expresses it."

Wearying suddenly of the sport, Phyllis dropped the blind, and, coming over to Gertrude, knelt on the floor at her feet.

"It is a little dull, ain't it, Gerty, to look at life from a top-floor window?"

A curious pang went through Gertrude, as she tenderly stroked the nut-brown head.

"You haven't heard our news," she said, irrelevantly. "There, read that." And taking Mr. Darrell's note from her pocket, she handed it to Phyllis.

The latter read it through rather languidly.

"Yes, I suppose it is a good thing to be employed by such a person," she remarked. "Sidney Darrell? – Didn't I tell you I met him last week at the Oakleys, the day I went to tea?"

31. The magazine, *Punch.*

*****

The Sycamores was divided from the road by a high grey wall, beyond which stretched a neglected-looking garden of some size, and, on the March morning of which I write, this latter presented a singularly melancholy appearance.

The house itself looked melancholy also, as houses will which are very little lived in, and appeared to consist almost entirely of a large studio, built out like a disproportionate wing from the main structure.

Gertrude was led at once to the studio by a serious-looking manservant, who announced that his master would join her in a few minutes.

The apartment in which Gertrude found herself was of vast size, and bore none of the signs of neglect and disuse which marked the house and garden.

It was fitted up with all the chaotic splendour which distinguishes the studio of the modern fashionable artist; the spoils of many climes, fruits of many wanderings, being heaped, with more regard to picturesqueness than fitness, in every available nook.

Going up to the carved fireplace, Gertrude proceeded to warm her hands at the comfortable wood-fire, a position badly adapted for taking stock of the great man's possessions, of which, as she afterwards confessed, she only carried away a prevailing impression of tiger-skins and Venetian lanterns.

The fire-light played about her slim figure and about the faded richness of a big screen of old Spanish leather, which fenced in the little bit of territory in the immediate neighbourhood of the fireplace; a spot in which had been gathered the most luxurious lounges and the choicest ornaments of the whole collection; and where, at the present moment, the air was heavy with the scent of tuberose, several sprays of which stood on a small table in a costly jar of Venetian glass.

In a few minutes the sound of footsteps outside, and of the rich, deep notes of a man's voice were audible.

> "Et non, non, non,
> Vous n'êtes plus Lisette,
> Ne portez plus ce nom."[32]

As the footsteps drew nearer the words of the song could be clearly distinguished.

Gertrude turned towards the door, which fronted the fireplace, and as she did so the song ceased, the curtain was pushed aside, and a person, presumably the singer, came into the room.

He was a man of middle height, and middle age, with light brown hair, parted in the centre, and a moustache and Vandyke beard of the same colour. He was not, strictly speaking, handsome, but he wore that air of distinction which power and the assurance of power alone can confer. His whole appearance was a masterly combination of the correct and the picturesque.

He advanced deliberately towards Gertrude.

"Allow me, Miss Lorimer, to introduce myself."

He spoke carelessly, yet with a note of disappointment in his voice, and a shade of moodiness in his heavy-lidded eyes.

Gertrude, looking up and meeting the cold, grey glance, became suddenly conscious that her hat was shabby, that her boots were patched and clumsy, that the wind had blown the wisps of hair about her face. What was there in this man's gaze that made her, all at once, feel old and awkward, ridiculous and dowdy; that made her long to snatch up her heavy camera and flee from his presence, never to return?

What, indeed? Gertrude, we know, had a vivid imagination, and that perhaps was responsible for the sense of oppression, defiance, and self-distrust with which she followed Mr. Darrell across the room to one of the easels, on which was displayed a remarkable study in oils of a winter aspect of the Grand Canal at Venice.

---

32. From Béranger's "Ce n'est plus Lisette" (Bernstein, ed., *The Romance of a Shop*, 107 n. 2).

There was certainly, superficially speaking, no ground for her feeling in the artist's conduct. With his own hands he set up and fixed the heavy camera on the tripod stand, questioned her, in his low, listless tones, as to her convenience, and observed, by way of polite conversation, that he had had the pleasure of meeting her sister the week before at the Oakleys.

To her own unutterable vexation, Gertrude found herself rather cowed by the man and his indifferent politeness, through which she seemed to detect the lurking contempt; and as his glance of cold irony fell upon her from time to time, from beneath the heavy lids, she found herself beginning to take part not only against herself but also against the type of woman to which she belonged.

Having made the necessary adjustments, and given the necessary directions, Darrell went over to the fireplace, and cast himself into a lounge, where the leather screen shut out his well-appointed person from Gertrude's sight. She, on her part, set about her task without enjoyment, and was glad when it was over and she could pack up the darkslides. As she was unscrewing the camera from the stand, the curtain before the doorway was pushed aside for the second time, and a man entered unannounced. At the same moment Darrell advanced from behind his screen, and the two men met in the middle of the room.

"Delighted to see you back, my dear fellow."

It seemed to Gertrude that a shade of deference had infused itself into the artist's manner, as he cordially clasped hands with the newcomer.

This person was a tall, sinewy man of from thirty-five to forty years of age, with stooping shoulders and a brown beard. From her corner by the easel, Miss Lorimer could see his face, and her casual glance falling upon it was arrested by a sudden sense of recognition.

Where had she seen them before; the ample forehead, the clear, grey eyes, the rough yet generous lines of the features?

This man's face was sunburnt, cheery, smiling; the face which it recalled had been pale, haggard, worn with watching and sorrow.

Then, as by a flash, she saw it all again before her eyes; the dainty room flooded with October sunlight; the dead woman lying there with her golden hair spread on the pillow; the bearded, averted face, and stooping form of the figure that crouched by the window.

"I only hope," she reflected, "that he will not recognise me. The recollections that the sight of me would summon up could scarcely be pleasant. I have no wish to enact the part of skeleton at the feast."[33]

With a desponding sense that she had no right to her existence, Gertrude gathered up her possessions and made her way across the room.

Darrell came forward slowly. "Oh, put down those heavy things," he said.

Lord Watergate, for it was he, went over to the fireplace and stood there warming his hands.

"May I trouble you to have a cab called?"

Gertrude spoke in her most dignified manner.

"Certainly. But won't you come to the fire?"

Darrell rang a bell which stood on the mantelshelf, and indicated to Gertrude a chair by the screen.

Gertrude, however, preferred to stand, and for some moments the three people on the tiger-skin hearthrug stared into the fire in silence.

Then Darrell said in an offhand manner: "Miss Lorimer has been kind enough to photograph my 'Grand Canal' for me."

Lord Watergate, looking up suddenly, met Gertrude's glance. For a moment, a puzzled expression came into his eyes, then changed to one of recognition and recollection. After some hesitation, he said:

"It must be difficult to do justice in a photograph to such a picture."

She threw him back his commonplace:

"Oh, the gradations of tone often come out surprisingly well."

Inwardly she was saying, "How he must hate the sight of me."

33. Refers to James Jeffrey Roche's (1847–1908) poem, "The Skeleton at the Feast" (Bernstein, ed., *The Romance of a Shop*, 109 n. 1).

Darrell looked from one to the other, dimly suspicious of their mutual consciousness, then rejected the suspicion as an absurd one.

"I will write to you about those sketches," he said, as the cab was announced.

Lucy and Phyllis were frisking about the studio, as young creatures will do in the spring, when Gertrude entered, weary and dispirited, from her expedition to The Sycamores.

The girls fell upon her at once for news.

She flung herself into the sitter's chair, which half revolved with the violence of the action.

"Say something nice to me," she cried. "Compliment me on my beauty, my talents, my virtues. There is no flattery so gross that I could not swallow it."

Phyllis looked from her to Lucy and tapped her forehead in significant pantomime.

"You are everything that is most delightful," said Lucy; "only do tell us about the great man."

"He was odious," cried Gertrude.

"She has never been quarrelling, I will not say with her own, but with *our* bread-and-butter," said Phyllis, in affected dismay.

"I will never go there again, if that's what you mean."

"But what is the matter, Gerty? I found him quite polite."

"Polite? It is worse than rudeness, a politeness which says so plainly: 'This is for my own sake, not for yours.'"

"You are really cross, Gerty; what has the illustrious Sidney been doing to you?" said Lucy, who did not suffer from violent likes and dislikes.

"Oh," cried Gertrude, laughing ruefully; "how shall I explain? He is this sort of man; – if a woman were talking to him of – of the motions of the heavenly bodies, he would be thinking all the time of the shape of her ankles."

"Great heavens, Gerty, did you make the experiment?"

Phyllis opened her pretty eyes their widest as she spoke.

"We all know," remarked Lucy, with a twinkle in her eye, "that it is best to begin with a little aversion."

Phyllis struck an attitude:

"'Friends meet to part, but foes once joined – '"[34]

"Girls, what has come over you?" exclaimed Gertrude, dismayed.

"Gerty is shocked," said Lucy; "one is always stumbling unawares on her sense of propriety."

"She is like the Bishop of Rumtyfoo,"[35] added Phyllis; "she does draw the line at such unexpected places."

34. Refers to Lord (George Gordon) Byron's (1788–1824) "The Giaour" (Bernstein, ed., *The Romance of a Shop*, 110 n. 1).

35. From Gilbert's poem "The Bishop of Rum-Ti-Foo" in *The Bab Ballads* (Bernstein, ed., *The Romance of a Shop*, 110 n. 2; New, ed., *The Complete Novels*, 541 n. 34).

Chapter 9
Show Sunday

La science l'avait gardé naïf.

ALPHONSE DAUDET[36]

The last Sunday in March was Show Sunday; and Frank, who was of a festive disposition, had invited all the people he knew in London to inspect his pictures and Mr. Oakley's before they were sent in to the Royal Academy.

Mr. Oakley was a middle-aged Bohemian, who had made a small success in his youth and never got beyond it. It had been enough, however, to launch him into the artistic world, and it was probably only owing to the countenance of his brothers of the brush that he was able to sell his pictures at all. Oakley was an accepted fact, if nothing more; the critics treated him with respect if without enthusiasm; the exhibition committees hung him, though not indeed on the line, and the public bought his pictures, which had the advantage of being moderate in price and signed with a name that everybody knew.

Of course, this indifferent child of the earth had a wife and family; and he had been only too glad to share his studio expenses with young Jermyn, whose father, the Cornish clergyman, had been a friend of his own youth.

36. From Daudet's *Jack* (1876).

"I wonder," said Gertrude, as the Lorimers dressed for Frank's party, "if there will be a lot of gorgeous people this afternoon?" And she looked ruefully at the patch on her boot, with a humiliating reminiscence of Darrell's watchful eye.

"I don't expect so," answered Phyllis, whose pretty feet were appropriately shod. "You know what dowdy people one meets at the Oakleys. Oh, of course they know others, but they don't turn up, somehow."

"Then there will be Mr. Jermyn's people," said Lucy, inspecting her gloves with a frown.

"A lot of pretty, well-dressed girls, no doubt," answered Phyllis; "I expect that well-beloved youth has a wife in every port, or at least a young woman in every suburb."

"*Apropos*," said Gertrude, "I wonder if the Devonshires will be there. We never seem to see Conny in these days."

"Isn't it rather a strain on friendship," answered Phyllis, shrewdly, "when two sets of our friends become acquainted, and seem to prefer one another to *us*, the old and tried and trusty friend of each?"

"What horrid things you say sometimes, Phyllis," objected Lucy, as the three sisters trooped downstairs.

Fanny was not with them; she was spending the day with some relations of her mother's.

A curious, dreamlike sensation stole over Gertrude at finding herself once again in a roomful of people; and as an old war-horse is said to become excited at the sound of battle, so she felt the social instincts rise strongly within her as the familiar, forgotten pageant of nods and becks and wreathed smiles burst anew upon her.

Frank shot across the room, like an arrow from the bow, as the Lorimers entered.

"How late you are," he said; "I was beginning to have a horrible fear that you were not coming at all."

"How pretty it all is," said Lucy, sweetly. "Those great brass jars with the daffodils are charming; and what an overwhelming number of people."

Conny came up to them, splendid as ever, but with a restless light in her eyes, an unnatural flush on her cheek.

"How do you do, girls?" she said, abruptly. "You look seedy, Gerty." Then, as Frank moved off to fetch them some tea: "I do so hate afternoon affairs, don't you?"

"How pretty Frank looks," whispered Phyllis to Lucy; "I like to see him flying in and out among the people, as though his life depended on it, don't you? And the daffodil in his coat just suits his complexion."

"Phyllis, don't be so silly!"

Lucy refrained from smiling, but her eyes followed, with some amusement, the picturesque and active figure of her host, as he went about his duties with his usual air of earnestness and candour.

"Come and look at the pictures, Lucy. That's what you're here for, you know," remarked Fred, who had joined their group, and was looking the very embodiment of Philistine comeliness. "I haven't seen you for an age," he added, as they made their way to one of the easels.

"That is your own fault, isn't it?" said Lucy, lightly.

"Conny has got it into her head that you don't care to see us."

"How can Conny be so silly?"

"Don't tell her I told you. She would be in no end of a wax," he added, as Phyllis and Constance pressed by them in the crush.

Gertrude was still standing near the doorway, sipping her tea, and looking about her with a rather wistful interest. She had caught here and there glimpses of familiar faces, faces from her own old world – that world which, taken *en masse,* she had so fervently disliked; but no one had taken any notice of the young woman by the doorway, with her pale face and suit of rusty black.

"I feel like a ghost," she said to Frank, as she handed him her empty cup.

"You do look horribly white," he answered, with genuine concern; "I wish you were looking as well as your sisters – Miss Phyllis for instance."

He glanced across as he spoke with undisguised admiration at the slim young figure, and blooming face of the girl, who stood smiling down with amiable indifference at one of his own canvasses.

Phyllis Lorimer belonged to that rare order of women who are absolutely independent of their clothes.

By the side of her old black gown and well-worn hat, Constance Devonshire's elaborate spring costume looked vulgar and obtrusive; and Constance herself, in the light of her friend's more delicate beauty, seemed *bourgeoise* and overblown.

The effect of this contrast was not lost on two men who, at this point of the proceedings, strolled into the room, and whom the Oakleys came forward with some *empressement* to receive.

"I have brought you Lord Watergate," Gertrude heard one of them say, in a voice which she recognised at once, the sound of which filled her with a vague sense of discomfort.

"Darrell, by all that's wonderful!" said Frank, *sotto voce,* his eyes shining with enthusiasm; "there, with the light Vandyke beard – but you know him already."

"Hasn't he a Show Sunday of his own?" replied Gertrude, in a voice that implied that the wish was father to the thought.

"He has a gallery all to himself in Bond Street this season. I wonder if he will sing this afternoon."

"Mr. Darrell is a person of many accomplishments it seems."

"Oh, rather!" and Frank went off to offer a pleased and modest welcome to the illustrious guest.

Sidney Darrell, having succeeded in escaping from the Oakleys and their tea-table, made his way across the room, stopping here and there to exchange greetings with the people that he knew, and moving with that ostentatious air of lack of purpose which is so often assumed in society to mask a set and deliberate plan.

"How do you do, Miss Lorimer?" He stopped in front of Phyllis and held out his hand.

Phyllis's flower-face brightened at this recognition from the great man.

"Now, don't you think this is the most ridiculous institution on the face of the earth?" said Darrell, as he took his place beside her, for Conny had moved off discreetly at his approach.

"Which institution? Tea, pictures, people?"

"Their incongruous combination under the name of Show Sunday."

"Oh, I think it's fun. But then I have never seen the sort of thing before."

"You are greatly to be envied, Miss Lorimer."

"How lovely Phyllis is looking," cried Conny, who had joined Gertrude near the doorway; "she grows prettier every day."

"Do you think so?" answered Gertrude. "She looks to me more delicate than ever, with that flush on her cheek, and that shining in her eyes."

"Nonsense, Gerty; you are quite ridiculous about Phyllis. She appears to be amusing Mr. Darrell, at any rate. She says just the sort of things Mr. Lorimer used to. She is more like him than any of you."

"Yes." Gertrude winced; then, looking up, saw Mr. Oakley and a tall man standing before her.

"Lord Watergate, Miss Lorimer."

The grey eyes looked straight into hers, and a deep voice said –

"We have met before. But I scarcely ventured to regard myself as introduced to you."

Lord Watergate smiled as he spoke, and, with a sense of relief, Gertrude felt that here, at least, was a friendly presence.

"I met you at The Sycamores on Wednesday."

"If it could be called a meeting. That's a wonderful picture of Darrell's."

"Yes."

"Oakley has been telling me about the great success in photography of you and your sisters."

"I don't know about success!" Gertrude laughed.

"You look so tired, Miss Lorimer; let me find you a seat."

"No, thank you; I prefer to stand. One sees the world so much better."

"Ah, you like to see the world?"

"Yes; it is always interesting."

"It is to be assumed that you are fond of society?"

"Does one follow from the other?"

"No; I merely hazarded the question."

"One demands so much more of a game in which one is taking part," said Gertrude; "and with social intercourse, one is always thinking how much better managed it might be."

They both laughed.

"Now what is your ideal society, Miss Lorimer?"

"A society not of class, caste, or family – but of picked individuals."

"I think we tend more and more towards such a society, at least in London," said Lord Watergate; then added, "You are a democrat, Miss Lorimer."

"And you are an optimist, Lord Watergate."

"Oh, I'm quite unformulated. But let us leave off this mutual recrimination for the present; and perhaps you can tell me who is the lady talking to Sidney Darrell."

Lord Watergate's attention had been suddenly caught by Phyllis; Gertrude noted that he was looking at her with all his eyes.

"That is one of my sisters," she said.

He turned towards her with a start; there was a note of constraint in his tones as he said –

"She is very beautiful."

What was there is his voice, in his face, that suddenly brought before Gertrude's vision the image of the dead woman, her golden hair, and haggard beauty?

Phyllis, on her part, had been aware of the brief but intense gaze which the grey eyes had cast upon her from the other side of the room.

"Who is that person talking to my sister?" she said.

Darrell looked across coldly, and answered: "Oh, that's Lord Watergate, the great physiologist."

"I have never met a lord before."

"And, after all, this isn't much of a lord, because the peer is quite swallowed up in the man of science."

Oakley came up, entreating Darrell to sing.

"But isn't it quite irregular, today?"

"Oh, we don't pretend to be fashionable. This isn't 'Show Sunday,' pure and simple, but just a pretext for seeing one's friends."

"By the by," said the artist, as Oakley went off to open the little piano, "is it any good my sending the sketches this week? though it's horribly bad form to talk shop."

"You must ask my sister about those things."

"Oh, your sister is far and away too clever for me."

"Gertrude is clever, but not in the way you mean."

"Nevertheless, I am horribly afraid of her."

Darrell went over to the piano and sang a little French song, with perfect art, in his rich baritone. Gertrude watched him, as he sat there playing his own accompaniment, and a vague terror stole over her of this irreproachable-looking person, who did everything so well; whose quiet presence was redolent of an immeasurable, because an unknown strength; and who, she felt (indignantly remembering the cold irony of his glance) could never, under any circumstances, be made to appear ridiculous.

At the end of the song, Phyllis came over to Gertrude.

"Aren't we going, Gerty?" she said; "It is quite unfashionable to 'make a night of it' like this. One is just supposed to look round and sail off to half-a-dozen other studios."

Lord Watergate, who stood near, caught the half-whispered words, and smiled, as one smiles at the nonsense of a pretty child. Gertrude saw the expression of his face as she answered –

"Yes, it is time we went. Tell Lucy; there she is with Mr. Jermyn."

Darrell came over to them as they were going, and shook hands, first with Gertrude, and then with Phyllis.

"Thank you," he said to the latter, "for a very pleasant afternoon."

Both he and Lord Watergate lingered in York Place till the other guests had departed, when they fell upon Frank for further information respecting the photographic studio.

"It doesn't look as if it paid them," remarked Darrell, by way of administering a damper to loyal Frank's enthusiasm.

"I wonder," said Lord Watergate, "if they would think it worthwhile to prepare some slides for me?"

"For the Royal Institution lectures?" Darrell sat down to the piano as he spoke, and ran his hands over the keys. "She is a charming creature – Phyllis."

"Charming!" cried Frank; "and so is Miss Lucy. And Gertrude is charming, too; she is the clever one."

"Oh, yes, Gertrude is the clever one; you can see that by her boots."

Meanwhile the Lorimers and the Devonshires were walking up Baker Street together, engaged, on their part also, in discussing the people from whom they had just parted.

"You are quite wrong, Gerty, about Mr. Darrell," cried Phyllis; "he is very nice, and great fun."

"What, the fellow with the goatee?" said Fred.

"Oh, Fred, his beautiful Vandyke beard!"

"I don't care, I don't like him."

"Nor do I, Fred," said Gertrude, with decision, as the whole party turned into Number 20B, and went up to the sitting room.

"I think really you are a little unreasonable," said Lucy, putting her arm round her sister's waist; "he seemed quite a nice person."

"He looks," put in Conny, speaking for the first time, "as though he meant to have the best of everything. But so do a great many of us mean that."

"But not," cried Gertrude, "by trampling over the bodies of other people. Ah, you are all laughing at me. But can one be expected to think well of a person who makes one feel like a strong-minded clown?"

They laughed more than ever at the curious image summoned up by her words; then Phyllis remarked, critically –

"There is one thing I don't like about him, and that is his eye. I particularly detest that sort of eye; prominent, with heavy lids, and those little puffy bags underneath."

"Phyllis, spare us these realistic descriptions," protested Lucy, "and let us dismiss Mr. Darrell, for the present at least. Perhaps our revered chaperon will tell us something of her experiences with a certain noble lord," she added, placing in her dress, with a smile of thanks, the gardenia of which Fred had divested himself in her favour.

"It was very nice of him," said Gertrude, gravely, "to get Mr. Oakley to introduce him to me, if only to show me that the sight of me did not make him sick."

"I like his face," added Lucy; "there is something almost boyish about it. Do you remember what Daudet says of the old doctor in *Jack*, 'La science l'avait gardé naïf.'"[37]

"What a set of gossips we are," cried Conny, who had taken little part in the conversation. "Come along, Fred; you know we are dining at the Greys tonight."

"Botheration! They are certain to give me Nelly to take in," grumbled Fred, who, like many of his sex, was extremely modest where his feelings were concerned, but cherished a belief that the mass of womankind had designs upon him; "and we never know what on earth to say to one another."

"There goes Mr. Jermyn," observed Phyllis, as the door closed on the brother and sister; "he said something about coming in here tonight."

Lucy, who was seated at some distance from the window, allowed herself to look up, and smiled as she remarked–

"What ages ago it seems since we used to wonder about him and call him 'Conny's man.'"

"'Conny's man'" added Phyllis, with a curl of her pretty lips, "who does not care two straws for Conny."

37. Quotation used at the beginning of this chapter.

Chapter 10

Summing Up

J'ai peur d'Avril, peur de l'emoi
Qu'éveille sa douceur touchante.
SULLY PRUDHOMME[38]

April had come round again; and, like M. Sully-Prudhomme, Gertrude was afraid of April.

As Fanny had remarked to Frank, the month had very painful associations for them all; but Gertrude's terror was older than their troubles, and was founded, not on the recollection of past sorrow, so much as on the cruel hunger for a present joy. And now again, after all her struggles, her passionate care for others, her resolute putting away of all thoughts of personal happiness, now again the Spring was stirring in her veins, and voices which she had believed silenced forever arose once more in her heart and clamoured for a hearing.

Often, before business hours, Gertrude might be seen walking round Regent's Park at a swinging pace, exorcising her demons; she was obliged, as she said, to ride her soul on the curb, and be very careful that it did not take the bit between its teeth – this poor, weak

38. Taken from René François Armand Prudhomme's (1839–1907) "Douceur d'Avril" (1875); see Bernstein, ed., *The Romance of a Shop*, 119 n. 1.

Gertrude, who seemed such a fountainhead of wisdom, such a tower of strength to the people among whom she dwelt.

At this period, also, she had had recourse, in the pauses of professional work, to her old consolation of literary effort, and had even sent some of her productions to Paternoster Row, with the same unsatisfactory results as of yore, she and Frank uniting their voices in that bitter cry of the rejected contributor, which in these days is heard through the breadth and length of the land.

One morning, she came into the studio after her walk, to find Lucy engaged in focussing Frank, who was seated, wearing an air of immense solemnity, in the sitter's chair. Phyllis, meanwhile, hovered about, bestowing hints and suggestions on them both, secretly enjoying the quiet humour of the scene.

"It is Mr. Jermyn's birthday present," she announced, as Gertrude entered. "He is going to send it to Cornwall, which will be a nice advertisement for us."

Frank blushed slightly; and Lucy cried from beneath her black cloth, "Don't get up, Mr. Jermyn; Gertrude will excuse you, I am sure."

Gertrude, laughing, retreated to the waiting room; where, throwing herself into a chair, and leaning both her elbows on a rickety scarlet table, she stared vaguely at the little picture of youth and grace, which the parted curtains revealed to her.

How could they be so cheerful, so heedless? cried her heart, with a sudden impatience. Was this life, this ceaseless messing about in a pokey glass outhouse, this eating and drinking and sleeping in the shabby London rooms?

Was any human creature to be blamed who rebelled against it? Did not flesh and blood cry out against such sordidness, with all the revel of the springtime going on in the world beyond?

It is base and ignoble perhaps to scorn the common round, the trivial task, but is it not also ignoble and base to become so immersed in them as to desire nothing beyond?

"What mean thoughts I am thinking," cried Gertrude to herself, shocked at her own mood; then, gazing mechanically in front of her, saw Lucy disappear into the darkroom, and Frank come forward with outstretched hand.

"At last I can say 'good morning,' Miss Lorimer."

Gertrude gave him her hand with a smile; Jermyn's was a presence that somehow always cleared the moral atmosphere.

"You will never guess," said Frank, "what I have brought you."

As he spoke, he drew from his pocket a number of *The Woodcut*, damp from the press, and opening it at a particular page, spread it on the table before her.

Phyllis, becoming aware of these proceedings, came across to the waiting room and leaned over her sister's shoulder.

"Oh, Gerty, what fun."

On one side of the page was a large wood engraving representing four people on a lawn tennis court. Three of them were girls, in whom could be traced distinct resemblance to the three Lorimers; while the fourth, a man, had about him an unmistakable suggestion of Jermyn himself. The initials "F. J." were writ large in a corner of the picture, and on the opposite page were the following verses:

What wonder that I should be dreaming*
    Out here in the garden today?
The light through the leaves is streaming;
    Paulina cries, "Play!"

The birds to each other are calling;
The freshly-cut grasses smell sweet –
To Teddy's dismay comes falling
    The ball at my feet!

"Your stroke should be over, not under."
"But that's such a difficult way!"
The place is a spring-tide wonder
    Of lilac and may.

Of lilac and may and laburnum;
Of blossom – *"we're losing the set!*

Those volleys of Jenny's, return them,
Stand close to the net!"

ENVOI.

You are so fond of the may-time,
My friend far away,
Small wonder that I should be dreaming
Of you in the garden today.

* From *Lawn Tennis.*[39]

The verses were signed "G. Lorimer"; and Gertrude's eyes rested on them with the peculiar tenderness with which we all of us regard our efforts the first time that we see ourselves in print.

"How nice they look, Gerty," cried Phyllis. "And Mr. Jermyn's picture. But I think they have spoilt it a little in the engraving."

"It is rather a come down after *Charlotte Corday*, isn't it?" said Gertrude, pleased yet rueful.

Frank, who had been told the history of that unfortunate tragedy, answered rather wistfully –

"We have all to get off our high horse, Miss Lorimer, if we want to live. I had ten guineas this morning for that thing; and there is the *Death of Oedipus*[40] with its face to the wall in the studio – and likely to remain there, unless we run short of firewood one of these days."

"Do you remember," said Gertrude, "how Warrington threw cold water on Pendennis by telling him to stick to poems like the *Church Porch* and abandon his beloved *Ariadne in Naxos*?"[41]

"Yes," answered Frank, "and I never could share Warrington's – and presumably Thackeray's – admiration for those verses."

39. Levy's own poem, "A Game of Lawn Tennis"; see p. 541.
40. Henry Fuseli's (1741–1825) painting, "The Death of Oedipus."
41. From William Makepeace Thackeray's (1811–1863) *The History of Pendennis* (Bernstein, ed., *The Romance of a Shop*, 122 n. 1; New, ed., *The Complete Novels*, 542 n. 40).

"Nor I," said Gertrude, as Lucy emerged triumphantly from the darkroom and announced the startling success of her negatives.

She was shown the wonderful poem, and the no less wonderful picture, and then Phyllis said –

"Don't gloat so over it, Gerty." For Gertrude was still sitting at the table absorbed in contemplation of the printed sheet spread out before her.

Gertrude laughed and pushed the paper away; and Lucy quoted gravely –

> "'We all, the foolish and the wise,
> Regard our verse with fascination,
> Through asinine-paternal eyes,
> And hues of fancy's own creation!'"[42]

A vociferous little clock on the mantelpiece struck ten.

"I must be off," said Frank; "there will be my model waiting for me. I am afraid I have wasted a great deal of your time this morning."

"No, indeed," said Lucy, as Gertrude rose and folded the seductive *Woodcut*, with a get-thee-behind-me-Satan air;[43] "though I am glad to say we are quite busy."

"There are Lord Watergate's slides," added Phyllis; "and Mr. Darrell's sketches to finish off; not to speak of possible chance-comers."

"How do you get on with Darrell?" said Frank, who seemed to have forgotten his model, and made no movement to go.

"He has only been here once," answered Lucy, promptly; "but I like what I have seen of him."

"So do I," cried Phyllis.

"And I," added Frank.

In the face of this unanimity Gertrude wisely held her peace.

"Well then, goodbye," said Frank, reluctantly holding out his hand to each in turn – to Lucy, last. "I am dining out tonight and tomorrow, so shall not see you for an age, I suppose."

---

42. From Frederick Locker-Lampson's (1821–1895) "Advice to a Poet."
43. See specifically Matthew 4:10, but also Matthew 16:23, Mark 8:33, Luke 4:8.

"Gay person," said Lucy, whose hand lingered in his; held there firmly, and without resistance on her part.

"It's a bore," cried Frank, making wistful eyebrows, and looking at her very hard.

Gertrude started, struck for the first time by something in the tone and attitude of them both. With a shock that bewildered her, she realised the secret of their mutual content; and, stirred up by this unconscious revelation, a conflicting throng of thoughts, images, and emotions arose within her.

Gertrude worked like a nigger that day, which, fortunately for her state of mind, turned out an unusually busy one. Lucy was industrious too, but went about her work humming little tunes, with a serenity that contrasted with her sister's rather feverish laboriousness. Even Phyllis condescended to lend a hand to the finishing off of the prints of Sidney Darrell's sketches.

All three were rather tired by the time they joined Fanny round the supper table, who, herself, presented a pathetic picture of lady-like boredom.

The meal proceeded for some time in silence, broken occasionally by a professional remark from one or other of them; then Lucy said –

"You're not eating, Fanny."

"I'm not hungry," answered Fan, with an injured air.

She looked more like a superannuated baby than ever, with her pale eyebrows arched to her hair, and the corners of her small thin mouth drooped peevishly.

"This pudding isn't half bad, really, Fan," said Phyllis, good-naturedly, as she helped herself to a second portion. "I should advise you to try it."

Fanny's underlip quivered in a touchingly infantile manner, and, in another moment, splash! fell a great tear on the tablecloth.

"It's all very well to talk about pudding," she cried, struggling helplessly with the gurgling sobs. "To leave one alone all the blessed day, and not a word to throw at one when you do come upstairs, unless, if you please, it's 'pudding'! Pudding!" went on Fan, with contemptuous emphasis, and abandoning herself completely to her rising emotions. "You seem to take me for an idiot, all of you, who think yourselves so clever. What do you care how dull it is for me up here all day, alone from morning till night, while you are amusing yourselves below, or gadding about at gentlemen's studios."

"That sounds just like Aunt Caroline," said Phyllis, in a stage-whisper; but Lucy, rising, went round to her weeping sister, and, gathering the big, silly head, and wide moist face to her bosom, proceeded to administer comfort after the usual inarticulate, feminine fashion.

"Fanny is right," cried Gertrude, smitten with sudden remorse. "It is horribly dull for her, and we are very thoughtless."

"I am sorry I said anything about it," sobbed Fanny; "but flesh and blood couldn't stand it any longer."

"You were quite right to tell us, Fan. We have been horrid," cried Lucy, as she gently led her from the room. "Come upstairs with me, and lie down. You have not been looking well all the week."

In about ten minutes Lucy reappeared alone, to find the table cleared, and her sisters sewing by the lamplight.

"Fan has gone to bed," she announced; "she was a little hysterical, and I persuaded her to undress."

"It is dull for her, I know," said Gertrude, really distressed; "but what is to be done?"

"And she has been so good all these months," answered Lucy. "She has had none of the fun, and all the anxiety and pinching, and this is the first complaint we have heard from her."

"Yes, she has come out surprisingly well through it all."

Gertrude sighed as she spoke, secretly reproaching herself that there was not more love in her heart for poor Fanny.

Mrs. Maryon appeared at this point to offer the young ladies her own copy of the *Waterloo Place Gazette,* a little bit of neighbourly courtesy in which she often indulged, and which tonight was especially appreciated, as creating a diversion from an unpleasant topic.

"'A woman shot at Turnham Green,'" cried Phyllis, glancing down a column of miscellaneous items, while the lamplight fell on her bent brown head. "'More fighting in Africa.' Ah, here's something interesting at last. – 'We understand that the exhibition of Mr. Sidney Darrell, A.R.A.'s pictures, to be held in the Berkeley Galleries, New Bond Street, will be opened to the public on the first of next month. The event is looked forward to with great interest in artistic circles, as the collection is said to include many works never before exhibited in London.' I shall go like a shot; shan't you, Gerty?"

"Yes, and slip little dynamite machines behind the pictures. Let me look at that paper, Phyllis."

Phyllis pushed it towards her, and, as she took it up, her eye fell on the date of the month printed at the top of the page.

"Do you know," she said, "that it is a year today that we finally decided on starting our business?"

"Is it?" said Lucy. "Do you mean from that day when Aunt Caroline came and pitched into us all?"

"Yes; and when Mr. Russel's letter appeared on the scene, just as we were thinking of rushing in a body to the nearest chemist's for laudanum."

"And when we made a lot of good resolutions; do you remember?" cried Phyllis.

"What were they?" said Gertrude. "One was, that we would be happy."

"Well, I think we have kept that one at least," observed Lucy, with decision.

Gertrude looked across at her sister rather wistfully, as she answered, "Yes, on the whole. What was the other resolution? That we would not be cynical, was it not?"

"There hasn't been the slightest ground for cynicism; quite the other way," said Lucy. "It is not much credit to us to have kept that resolution."

"Oh, I don't know," observed Phyllis, lightly; "some people have been rather horrid; have forgotten all about us, or not been nice. Don't you remember, Gerty, how Gerald St. Aubyn dodged round the corner at Baker Street the other day because he didn't care to be seen bowing to two shabby young women with heavy parcels? And, Lucy, have you forgotten what you told us about Jack Sinclair, when you met him, travelling from the north? How he never took any notice of you, because you happened to be riding third class, and had your old gown on? Jack, who used to make such a fuss about picking up one's pocket-handkerchief and opening the door for one."

"It seems to me," said Gertrude, "that to think about those sort of things makes one almost as mean as the people who do them."

"And directly a person shows himself capable of doing them, why, it ceases to matter about him in the least," added Lucy, with youthful magnificence.

Gertrude was silent a moment, then said, with something of an effort: "Let us direct our attention to the charming new people we have got to know. One gets to know them in such a much more pleasant way, somehow."

Lucy bent her head over her work, hiding her flushed face as she answered, "That is the best of being poor; one's chances of artificial acquaintanceships are so much lessened. One gains in quality what one loses in quantity."

"How moral we are growing," cried Phyllis. "We shall be quoting Scripture next, and saying it is harder for the camel to get through the needle's eye, etc., etc."[44]

Gertrude laughed.

"There is another point to consider," she said. "I suppose you both know that we are not making our fortunes?"

"Yes," answered Lucy; "but, at the same time, the business has almost doubled itself in the course of the last three months."

"That sounds more prosperous than it really is, Lucy. If it hadn't done so, we should have had to think seriously of giving it up. And, as it is, we cannot be sure, till the end of the year, that we shall be able to hold on."

"You mean the end of the business year; next June?"

---

44. Matthew 19:24.

"Yes; Mr. Russel is coming, and there is to be a great overhauling of accounts."

Gertrude lay awake that night long after her sisters were asleep. Her brief rebellious mood of the morning had passed away, and, looking back on the year behind her, she experienced a measure of the content which we all feel after something attempted, something done. That she had been brought face to face with the sterner side of life, had lost some illusions, suffered some pain, she did not regret. It seemed to her that she had not paid too great a price for the increased reality of her present existence.

She fell asleep, then woke at dawn with a low cry. She had been dreaming of Lucy and Frank; had seen their faces, as she had seen them the day before, bright with the glow of the light which never was on sea and land. Oh, she had always known, nay, hoped, that this, or rather something akin to this, would come; yet sharp was the pang that ran through her at the recollection.

It had always seemed to her highly improbable that her sisters, portionless as they were, should remain unmarried. One day, she had always told herself, they would go away, and she and Fanny would be left alone. She did not wish it otherwise. She had a feminine belief in love as the crown and flower of life; yet, as the shadow of the coming separation fell upon her, her spirit grew desolate and afraid; and, lying there in the chill grey morning, she wept very bitterly.

Chapter 11

A Confidence

It may be one will dance today,
And dance no more tomorrow;
It may be one will steal away,
And nurse a lifelong sorrow;
What then? The rest advance, evade,
Unite, disport, and dally,
Reset, coquet, and gallopade,
Not less – in "Cupid's Alley."

AUSTIN DOBSON[45]

"Mr. Darrell has sent us a card for his Private View," announced Gertrude, as they sat at tea one Saturday afternoon in the sitting room.

"Oh, let me look, Gerty," cried Phyllis, taking possession of the bit of pasteboard. "'The Misses Lorimer and friends.' Why Conny might go with us."

Constance Devonshire had dropped in upon them unexpectedly that afternoon, after an absence of several weeks. She was looking wretchedly ill. Her usually blooming complexion had changed to

45. From Henry Austin Dobson's (1840–1921) poem, "Cupid's Alley."

a curious waxen colour; her round face had fallen away; there were dark hollows under the unnaturally brilliant eyes.

"I should rather like to go, if you think you may take me," she said; then added, with an air of not very spontaneous gaiety; "I suppose it will be what the society papers call a 'smart function.'"

Stoicism, it has been observed, is a savage virtue. There was something of savagery in Conny's fierce reserve; in the way in which she resolutely refused to acknowledge, what was evident to the most casual observer, that there was something seriously amiss with her health and spirits.

"Is it not fortunate," said Lucy, "that Uncle Sebastian should have sent us that cheque? Now we shall be able to get ourselves some decent clothes."

"I mean to have a grey cachemire walking-dress, and my evening dress shall be grey too," announced Phyllis, who was one of the rare people who can wear that colour to advantage. Fanny, who had rigid ideas about mourning, declared with an air of severity that her own new outfit should be black, then sighed, as though to call attention to the fact of her constancy to the memory of the dead, in the face of the general heedlessness.

"Gerty is thinking of rose-colour, is she not?" asked Phyllis, innocently, as she marked Gertrude's rapidly-suppressed movement of irritation.

"As regards a gown for this precious Private View – I am not going to it."

"The head of the firm ought to show up on such an occasion, as a mere matter of business," observed Lucy, smiling amiably at everyone in general.

"Yes, really, Gerty," added Phyllis, "you are the person to inspire confidence as to the quality of our work. No one would suspect *us*" – indicating herself and her two other sisters – "of being clever. It would be considered unlikely that nature should heap up *all* her benefits on the same individuals."

"Am I such a fright?" asked Gertrude, a little wistfully.

"No, darling; but there could be no doubt about your brains with that face."

"Wait a few years," said Conny; "she will be the best looking of you all."

"We will 'wait till she is eighty in the shade,'"[46] quoted Phyllis; "but when one comes to think of it, what a well-endowed family we are. Not only is our genius good-looking; that is a comparatively common case; but our beauties are so exceedingly intelligent; aren't they, Lucy?"

Constance Devonshire was right. Sidney Darrell's Private View at the Berkeley Galleries, held on the last day of April, was a very smart function indeed. There were duchesses, beauties, statesmen, and clever people of every description galore. In the midst of them all Darrell himself shone resplendent; gracious, urbane, polished; infusing just the right amount of cordiality into his many greetings, according to the deserts of the person greeted.

"I never saw anyone who possessed to greater perfection the art of impressing his importance on other people," whispered Conny to Gertrude, as the two girls strolled off together into one of the smaller rooms. Lucy had been led off by Frank and one of his friends. That young woman was never long in any mixed assembly without attracting persons of the male sex to her side.

As for Phyllis, radiant in the new grey costume, its soft tints set off by a knot of Parma violets at the throat, she was making the round of the pictures under the escort of no less a person than Lord Watergate, who had come up to the Lorimers at the moment of their entrance; and Fanny, in a jetted mantle and bonnet, clanked about with Mr. Oakley, happy in the consciousness of being for once in the best society.

"What a dreary thing a London crowd is," grumbled Conny, who was not accustomed, in her own set, to being left squire-less.

46. From the opera, *The Mikado,* by Gilbert and Sullivan (Bernstein, ed., *The Romance of a Shop,* 129 n. 1).

"Oh, but this is fun. So different from the parties one used to go to," said Gertrude, smiling, as Lord Watergate and her sister came up to them, to direct their attention to a particular canvas in the other room.

As they sauntered, in a body, to the entrance, Darrell came up with a young man of the masher type in his wake, whom he introduced to Phyllis as Lord Malplaquet.

"Lord Malplaquet is dying to hear your theories of life," he said playfully, bestowing a beaming and confidential smile upon her.

"Mr. Darrell, you shall not amuse yourself at my expense," she responded gaily, as she plunged into the crowd under the wing of her new escort, who was staring at her with the languid yet undisguised admiration of his class.

"Now this is the real thing," said Lord Watergate to Gertrude, as they stopped before the canvas they had come to seek.

"Yes," said Gertrude, in mechanical acquiescence.

She was thinking: "What a mean soul I must have. Everyone seems to like and admire this Sidney Darrell: and I suspect everything about him – even his art. For the sake of a prejudice; of a little hurt vanity, perhaps, as well."

"That, 'yes,' hasn't the ring of the true coin, Miss Lorimer."

"This is scarcely the time and place for criticism, Lord Watergate," laughed Gertrude.

"For hostile criticism, you mean. You are a terrible person to please, are you not?"

As the room began to clear, Darrell took Frank aside, and glancing in the direction of the sisters, who had reunited their forces, said: "You know those girls, intimately, I believe."

"Yes." (Very promptly.)

"I wonder if that beautiful Phyllis would sit for me?"

"She would probably be immensely honoured."

"Well, you see, it's this: I want her for Cressida."[47]

47. From Shakespeare's *Troilus and Cressida* (New, ed., *The Complete Novels*, 542 n. 44).

"Rather a disagreeable sort of subject, isn't it?" said Frank, doubtfully; then added, with professional interest: "I didn't know you had such a picture on hand, Mr. Darrell."

"The idea occurred to me this very afternoon. It was the sight of the fair Phyllis, in fact, which suggested it."

"Were you thinking of the scene in the orchard, or in the Greek camp?"

"Neither; one could hardly ask a lady to sit for such a picture. No, it is Cressida, before her fall, I want; as she stands at the street corner with Pandarus, waiting for the Trojan heroes to pass, don't you know? Half ironical, half wistful; with the light of that little *tendre* for Troilus just beginning to dawn in her eyes.[48] She would be the very thing for it."

"Are you going to propose it to her?" said Frank, who looked as if he did not much relish the idea.

"I shall ask her to sit for me, at any rate. There's the dragon-sister to be got round first."

"Indeed you are mistaken about Miss Lorimer."

Darrell gave a short laugh. "I beg your pardon, my dear fellow!"

Frank frowned, and Darrell, going forward to the Lorimers, preferred his request.

Phyllis looked pleased; and Gertrude, suppressing the signs of her secret dislike to the scheme, said, quietly:

"Phyllis must refer you to her sister Fanny. It depends on whether she can spare the time to bring her to your studio."

She glanced up as she spoke, and met, almost with open defiance, the heavy grey eyes of the man opposite. From these she perceived the irony to have faded; she read nothing there but a cold dislike.

It was an old, old story the fierce yet silent opposition between these two people; an inevitable antipathy; a strife of type and type, of class and class, rather than of individuals: the strife of the woman who demands respect, with the man who refuses to grant it.

* * * * *

48. See the above footnote.

Phyllis was in high feather at her successful afternoon, at the compliment paid her by the great Sidney in particular; and Fanny rather brightened at the prospect of what bore even so distant a resemblance to an occupation, as chaperoning her sister to a studio.

Only Conny was silent and depressed, and when they reached Baker Street, followed Gertrude to her room. Here she flung herself on the bed, regardless of her new transparent black hat, and its daffodil trimmings.

"Gerty, 'the world's a beast, and I hate it!'"[49]

"You are not well, Conny. If you would only acknowledge the fact, and see a doctor."

"Gerty, come here."

Gertrude went over to the bed, secretly alarmed; something in her friend's tones frightened her.

Conny crushed her face against the pillows, then said in smothered tones:

"I can't bear it any longer. I must tell someone or it will kill me."

Gertrude grew pale; instinctively she felt what was coming; instinctively she desired to ward it off.

"Can't you guess? Oh, you may say it is humiliating, unworthy; I know that." She raised her face suddenly: "Oh, Gerty, how can I help it? He is so different from them all; from the sneaks who want one's money; from the bad imitations of fashionable young men, who snub, and patronise, and sneer at us all. Who could help it? Frank – "

"Conny, Conny, you mustn't tell me this."

Gertrude caught her friend in her arms, so as to shield her face. She disapproved, generally speaking, of confidences of this kind, considering them bad for both giver and receiver; but this particular confidence she felt to be simply intolerable.

"Gerty, what have I done, what have I said?"

---

49. From Gilbert's *Tom Cobb; or Fortune's Toy* (Bernstein, ed., *The Romance of a Shop*, 131 n. 1). See also New, ed., *The Complete Novels*, 542 n. 45; as New points out, Levy uses *Tom Cobb* again in "Sokratics in the Strand" (pp. 640–8) and "Cohen of Trinity" (pp. 832–40).

"Nothing, really nothing, Con, dear old girl. You have told me nothing."

A pause; then Conny said, between the sobs which at last had broken forth: "How can I bear my life? How can I bear it?"

Gertrude was very pale.

"We all have to bear things, Conny; often this kind of thing, we women."

"I don't think I can."

"Yes, you will. You have no end of pluck. One day you are going to be very happy."

"Never, Gerty. We rich girls always end up with sneaks – no decent person comes near us."

"There are other things which make happiness besides – pleasant things happening to one."

"What sort of things?"

Gertrude paused a minute, then said bravely. "Our own self-respect, and the integrity of the people we care for."

"That sounds very nice," replied Conny, without enthusiasm, "but I should like a little of the more obvious sorts of happiness as well."

Gertrude gave a laugh, which was also a sob.

"So should I, Conny, so should I."

Chapter 12
Gertrude Is Anxious

Lady, do you know the tune?
Ah, we all of us have hummed it!
I've an old guitar has thrummed it
Under many a changing moon.
THACKERAY[50]

When Frank next saw Sidney Darrell, the latter told him that he had abandoned the idea of the "Cressida," and was painting Phyllis Lorimer in her own character.

"Grey gown; Parma violets; grey and purplish background. Shall let Sir Coutts have it, I think," he added; "it will show up better at his place than amid the *profanum vulgus* of Burlington House."

"Mr. Darrell doesn't often paint portraits, does he?" Lucy said, when Jermyn was discussing the matter one evening in Baker Street.

"Not often; but those that he has done are among his finest work. That one of poor Lady Watergate for instance – it is Carolus Duran[51] at his very best."

"By the bye, what an incongruous friendship it always seems to me – Lord Watergate and Mr. Darrell," said Lucy.

50. From Thackeray's poem, "Mrs. Katherine's Lantern."
51. French artist, Charles Auguste Émile Carolus-Duran (1837–1917).

"Oh, I don't know that it's much of a friendship," answered Frank.

"Lord Watergate often drops in at The Sycamores," put in Phyllis, helping herself from a smart *bonbonnière* from Charbonnel and Walker's; for Sidney found many indirect means of paying his pretty model; "I think he is such a nice old person."

"Old," cried Fanny; "he is not old at all. I looked him out in Mr. Darrell's Peerage. He is thirty-seven, and his name is Ralph."

"'I love my love with an R.' You said it just in that way, Fan," laughed Phyllis. "Yes, it is an odd friendship, if one comes to think of it – that big, kind, simple, Lord Watergate, and my elaborate friend, Sidney."

"Mr. Darrell is a perfect gentleman," interposed Fan, with dignity.

The occasional mornings at The Sycamores, afforded a pleasant break in the monotony of her existence. Darrell treated her with a careful, if ironical politeness, which she accepted in all good faith.

"Fan, as they call her, is a fool, but none the worse for that," had been his brief summing up of the poor lady, whom, indeed, he rather liked than otherwise.

It was the end of May, and the sittings had been going on in a spasmodic, irregular fashion, throughout the month. Both the girls enjoyed them. Darrell, like the rest of the world, treated Phyllis as a spoilt child; gave her sweets and flowers galore; and what was better, tickets for concerts, galleries, and theatres, of which her sisters also reaped the benefit.

Gertrude secretly disliked the whole proceeding, but, aware that she had no reasonable objection to offer, wisely held her peace; telling herself that if one person did not turn her little sister's head, another was sure to do so; and perhaps the sooner she was accustomed to the process the better.

"Why won't you come up and see my portrait?" Phyllis had pleaded; "I am going next Sunday, so you can have no excuse."

"I shall see it when it is finished," Gertrude had answered.

"Oh, but you can get a good idea of what it will look like, already. It is a great thing, life-size, and ends at about the knees. I am standing up and looking over my shoulder, so. I suppose Mr. Darrell has found out how nicely my head turns round on my neck."

Gertrude had laughed, and even attempted a pun in her reply, but she did not accompany her sister to The Sycamores. Indeed, more subtle reasons apart, she had little time to spare for unnecessary outings.

The business, as businesses will, had taken a turn for the better, and the two members of the partnership had their hands full. Rumours of the Photographic Studio had somehow got abroad, and various branches of the public were waking up to an interest in it.

People who had theories about woman's work; people whose friends had theories; people who were curious and fond of novelty; individuals from each of these sections began to find their way to Upper Baker Street. Gertrude, as we know, had refused at an early stage of their career to be interviewed by *The Waterloo Place Gazette*; but, later on, some unauthorised person wrote a little account of the Lorimers' studio in one of the society papers, of which, if the taste was questionable, the results were not to be questioned at all.

Moreover, it had got about in certain sets that all the sisters were extremely beautiful, and that Sidney Darrell was painting them in a group for next year's Academy, a *canard* certainly not to be deprecated from a business point of view.

Such things as these, do not, of course, make the solid basis of success, but in a very overcrowded world, they are apt to be the most frequent openings to it. In these days, the aspirant to fame is inclined to over-value them, forgetting that there is after all something to be said for making one's performance such as will stand the test of so much publicity.

The Lorimers knew little of the world, and of the workings of the complicated machinery necessary for getting on in it; and while chance favoured them in the matter of gratuitous advertisement, devoted their energies to keeping up their work to as high a standard as possible.

Life, indeed, was opening up for them in more ways than one. The calling which they pursued brought them into contact with all sorts and conditions of men, among them, people in many ways more congenial to them than the mass of their former acquaintance; intercourse with the latter having come about in most cases through "juxtaposition" rather than "affinity."

They began to get glimpses of a world more varied and interesting than their own, of that world of cultivated, middle-class London, which approached more nearly, perhaps, than any other to Gertrude's ideal society of picked individuals.

And it was Gertrude, more than any of them, who appreciated the new state of things. She was beginning, for the first time, to find her own level; to taste the sweets of genuine work and genuine social intercourse. Fastidious and sensitive as she was, she had yet a great fund of enjoyment of life within her; of that impersonal, objective enjoyment which is so often denied to her sex. Relieved of the pressing anxieties which had attended the beginning of their enterprise, the natural elasticity of her spirits asserted itself. A common atmosphere of hope and cheerfulness pervaded the little household at Upper Baker Street.

The evening of which I write was one of the last of May, and Frank had come in to bid them farewell, before setting out the next morning for a short holiday in Cornwall; "the old folks," as he called his parents, growing impatient of their only son's prolonged absence.

"The country will be looking its very best," cried Frank, who loved his beautiful home; "the sea a mass of sapphire with the great downs rolling towards it. I mean to have a big swim the very first thing. No one knows what the sea is like, till they have been to Cornwall. And St. Colomb – I wish you could see St. Colomb! Why, the whole place is smaller than Baker Street. The little bleak, grey street, with the sou'wester blowing through it at all times and seasons – there are scarcely two houses on the same level. And then –

"'The little grey church on the windy hill,'[52]

and beyond, the great green vicarage garden, and the vicarage, and the dear old folks looking out at the gate."

He rose reluctantly to go. "One day I hope you will see it for yourselves – all of you."

With which impersonal statement, delivered in a voice which rather belied its impersonal nature, Frank dropped Lucy's hand, which he had been holding with unnecessary firmness, and departed abruptly from the room.

Gertrude looked rather anxiously towards her sister, who sat quietly sewing, with a little smile on her lips. How far, she wondered, had matters gone between Lucy and Frank? Was the happiness of either or both irrevocably engaged in the pretty game which they were playing? Heaven forbid that her sisterly solicitude should lead her to question the "intentions" of every man who came near them; a hideous feminine practice abhorrent to her very soul. Yet, their own position, Gertrude felt, was a peculiar one, and she could not but be aware of the dangers inseparable from the freedom which they enjoyed; dangers which are the price to be paid for all close intimacy between young men and women.

After all, what do women know about a man, even when they live opposite him? And do not men, the very best of them, allow themselves immense license in the matter of loving and riding away?

As for Frank, he never made the slightest pretence that the Lorimers enjoyed a monopoly of his regard. He talked freely of the charms of Nellie and Carry and Emily; there was a certain Ethel, of South Kensington, whose praises he was never weary of sounding. Moreover, there could be no doubt that at one time or other he had displayed a good deal of interest in Constance Devonshire; dancing with her half the night, as Fred had expressed it; a mutual fitness in waltz-steps scarcely being enough to account for his attentions. And even supposing a more serious element to have entered into his regard

52. From Matthew Arnold's (1822–1888) poem, "The Forsaken Merman."

for Lucy, was he not as poor as themselves, and was it not the last contingency for a prudent sister to desire?

"What a calculating crone I am growing," thought Gertrude; then observing the tranquil and busy object of her fears, laughed at herself, half ashamed.

The next day, Mr. Russel came to see them, and entered on a careful examination of their accounts: compared the business of the last three months with that of the first; praised the improved quality of their work, and strongly advised them, if it were possible, to hold on for another year. This they were able to do. Although, of course, the money invested in the business had returned anything but a high rate of interest, their economy had been so strict that there would be enough of their original funds to enable them to carry on the struggle for the next twelve months, by which time, if matters progressed at their present rate, they might consider themselves permanently established in business.

Before he went Mr. Russel said something to Lucy which disturbed her considerably, though it made her smile. He had been for many years a widower, living with his mother, but the old lady had died in the course of the year, and now he suggested, modestly enough, that Lucy should return as mistress to the home where she had once been a welcome guest.

The girl found it difficult to put her refusal into words; this kind friend had hitherto given everything and asked nothing; but there was a delicate soul under the brusque exterior, and directly he divined how matters stood, he did his best to save her compunction.

"It really doesn't matter, you know. Please don't give it another thought," he had observed in an offhand manner, which had amused while it touched her.

Lucy was magnanimous enough to keep this little episode to herself, though Gertrude had her suspicions as to what had occurred.

Chapter 13
A Romance

When strawberry pottles are common and cheap
Ere elms be black or limes be sere,
When midnight dances are murdering sleep,
Then comes in the sweet o' the year!

ANDREW LANG[53]

The second week in June saw Frank back in his old quarters above the auctioneer's. He had arrived late in the evening, and put off going to see the Lorimers till the first thing the next day. It was some time before business hours when he rang at Number 20B, and was ushered by Matilda into the studio, where he found Phyllis engaged in a rather perfunctory wielding of a feather duster.

She was looking distractingly pretty, as he perceived when she turned to greet him. Her close-fitting black dress, with the spray of tuberose at the throat, and the great holland apron with its braided bib suited her to perfection; the sober tints setting off to advantage the delicate tones of her complexion, which in these days was more wonderfully pink and white than ever.

53. From Andrew Lang's (1844–1912) "Ballade of Summer." Lang also figures in Levy's poems, "Ballade of an Omnibus" (pp. 484–5) and "Alma Mater" (pp. 516–7), and possibly in "Between Two Stools" (pp. 607–24).

"And how are your sisters? I needn't ask how you are?" cried Frank, who, in the earlier stages of their acquaintance, had been rather surprised at himself for not falling desperately in love with Phyllis Lorimer.

"Everybody is flourishing," she answered, leaning against the little mantelshelf in the waiting room, and looking down upon Frank's sunburnt, uplifted face.

A look of mischief flashed into her eyes as she added, "There is a great piece of news."

Frank grasped the back of the frail red chair on which he sat astride in a manner rather dangerous to its wellbeing, and said abruptly, "Well, what is it?"

"One of us is going to be married."

"Oh!" said Frank, with a sort of gasp, which was not lost on his interlocutor.

"I am not going to tell you which it is. You must guess," went on Phyllis, looking down upon him demurely from under her drooped lids, while a fine smile played about her lips.

"Oh, I'll begin at the beginning," said poor Frank, with rather strained cheerfulness. "Is it Miss Gertrude?"

Phyllis played a moment with the feather duster, then answered slowly, "You must guess again."

"Is it Miss Lucy?" (with a jerk).

A pause. "No," said Phyllis, at last.

Frank sprang to his feet with a beaming countenance and caught both her hands with unfeigned cordiality. "Then it is you, Miss Phyllis, that I have to congratulate."

Her eyes twinkled with suppressed mirth as she answered ruefully, "No, indeed, Mr. Jermyn!"

Frank dropped her hands, wrinkling his brows in perplexity, then a light dawned on him suddenly, and was reflected in his expressive countenance.

"It must be Fan!" He forgot the prefix in his astonishment.

Phyllis nodded. "But you mustn't look so surprised," she said, taking a chair beside him. "Why shouldn't poor old Fan be married as well as other people?"

"Of course; how stupid of me not to think of it before," said Frank, vaguely.

"It is quite a romance," went on Phyllis; "she and Mr. Marsh wanted to be married ages and ages ago. But he was too poor, and went to Australia. Now he is well off, and has come back to marry Fan, like a person in a book. A touching tale of young love, is it not?"

"Yes; I think it a very touching and pretty story," said Frank, severely ignoring the note of irony in her voice.

He had all a man's dislike to hearing a woman talk cynically of sentiment; that should be exclusively a masculine privilege.

"Perhaps," said Phyllis, "it takes the bloom off it a little, that Edward Marsh married on the way out. But his wife died last year, so it is all right."

Frank burst out laughing, Phyllis joining him. A minute later Gertrude and Lucy came in and confirmed the wonderful news; and the four young people stood gossiping, till the sound of the studio bell reminded them that the day's work had begun.

Jermyn came in, by invitation, to supper that night, and was introduced to the new arrival, a big, burly man of middle age, whose forest of black beard afforded only very occasional glimpses of his face.

As for Fanny, it was touching to see how this faded flower had revived in the sunshine. The little superannuated airs and graces had come boldly into play; and Edward Marsh, who was a simple soul, accepted them as the proper expression of feminine sweetness.

So she curled her little finger and put her head on one side with all the vigour that assurance of success will give to any performance; gave vent to her most illogical statements in her most mincing tones, uncontradicted and undisturbed; in short, took advantage to the full of her sojourn (to quote George Eliot) in "the woman's paradise where all her nonsense is adorable."[54]

54. The quotation is from George Eliot's (1819–1880) *Daniel Deronda* (1876).

"I don't know what those girls will do without me," Fanny said to her lover, who took the remark in such good faith as to make her believe in it herself; "we must see that we do not settle too far away from them."

And she delicately set a stitch in the bead-work slipper which she was engaged in "grounding" for the simple-hearted Edward.

Fanny patronised her sisters a good deal in these days; and it must be owned – such is the nature of woman – that her importance had gone up considerably in their estimation.

As for Mr. Marsh, he regarded his future relatives with a mixture of alarm and perplexity that secretly delighted them. Never for a moment did his allegiance to Fanny falter before their superior charms; never for a moment did the fear of such a contingency disturb poor Fanny's peace of mind.

Only the girls themselves, in the depths of their hearts, wondered a little at finding themselves regarded with about the same amount of personal interest as was accorded to Matilda, by no means a specimen of the sparkling soubrette.

Gertrude, who had rather feared the effect of the contrast of Fanny's faded charms with the youthful prettiness of the two younger girls, was relieved, and at the same time a little indignant, to perceive that, as far as Edward Marsh was concerned, Phyllis's hair might be red and Lucy's eyes a brilliant green.

For once, indeed, Fan's tactlessness had succeeded where the finest tact might have failed. In dropping at once into position as the Fanny of ten years ago; as the incarnation of all that is sweetest and most essentially feminine in woman; in making of herself an accepted and indisputable fact, she had unconsciously done the very best to secure her own happiness.

"There really is something about Fanny that pleases men. I have always said so," Phyllis remarked, as she watched the lovers sailing blissfully down Baker Street, on one of their many house-hunting expeditions.

"You know," added Lucy, "she always dislikes walking about alone, because people speak to her. No one ever speaks to us, do they, Gerty?"

"Nor to me – at least, not often," said Phyllis, ruefully.

"Phyllis, will you never learn where to draw the line?" cried Gertrude; "but it is quite true about Fan. She must be that mysterious creature, a man's woman."

"Mr. Darrell likes her," broke forth Phyllis, after a pause; "he laughs at her in that quiet way of his, but I am quite sure that he likes her. I hope," she added, "that she won't get married before my portrait is finished. But it wouldn't matter, I could go without a chaperon."

"No, you couldn't," said Gertrude, shortly.

"Why are you seized with such notions of propriety all of a sudden?"

"I have no wish to put us to a disadvantage by ignoring the ordinary practices of life."

"Then put up the shutters and get rid of the lease. But, Gerty, we needn't discuss this unpleasant matter yet awhile. By the by, Mr. Darrell is going to ask me to sit for him in a picture, after the portrait. He has made sketches for it already – something out of one of Shakespeare's plays."

"Oh, I am tired of Mr. Darrell's name. Go and see that your dress is in order for the Devonshires' dance tonight."

"*Apropos*," said Lucy, as Phyllis flitted off on the congenial errand, "why is it that we never see anything of Conny in these days?"

"She is going out immensely this season," answered Gertrude, dropping her eyelids; "but, at any rate, we get a double allowance of Fred to compensate."

"Silly boy," cried Lucy, flushing slightly, "he has actually made me promise to sit out two dances with him. Such waste, when one is dying for a waltz."

"Oh, there will be plenty of waltzing. I wish you could have my share," sighed Gertrude, who had been won over by Conny's entreaties to promise attendance at the dance that night.

"It is time you left off these patriarchal airs, Gerty. You are as fond of dancing as any of us; and I mean you to spin round all night like a teetotum."

"What a charming picture you conjure up, Lucy."

"You people with imaginations are always finding fault. Fortunately for me, I have no imagination, and very little humour," said Lucy, with an air of genuine thankfulness that delighted her sister.

Thus, with work and play, and very much gossip, the summer days went by. The three girls found life full and pleasant, and Fanny had her little hour.

Chapter 14
Lucy

Who is Silvia? What is she,
That all our swains commend her?

TWO GENTLEMEN OF VERONA[55]

There was no mistaking the situation. At one of the red-legged tables sat Fred, his arms spread out before him, his face hidden in his arms; while Lucy, with a troubled face, stood near, struggling between her genuine compunction and an irrepressible desire to laugh.

It was Sunday morning; the rest of the household were at church, and the two young people had had the studio to themselves without fear of disturbance; a circumstance of which the unfortunate Fred had hastened to avail himself, thereby rushing on his fate.

They had now reached that stage of the proceedings when the rejected suitor, finding entreaty of no avail, has recourse to manifestations of despair and reproach.

"You shouldn't have encouraged a fellow all these years," came hoarsely from between the arms and face of the prostrate swain.

"'All these years!' how can you be so silly, Fred?" cried Lucy, with some asperity. "Why, I shall be accused next of encouraging little

55. From Shakespeare's *The Two Gentlemen of Verona.*

Jack Oakley, because I bowled his hoop round Regent's Park for him last week."

Lucy did not mean to be unkind; but the really unexpected avowal from her old playmate had made her nervous; a refusal to treat it seriously seemed to her the best course to pursue. But her last words, as might have been supposed, were too much for poor Fred. Up he sprang, "a wounded thing with a rancorous cry" –[56]

"There is another fellow!"

Back started Lucy, as if she had been shot. The hot blood surged up into her face, the tears rose to her eyes.

"What has that to do with it?" she cried, stung suddenly to cruelty; "what has that to do with it, when, if you were the only man in the world, I would not marry you?"

Fred, hurt and shocked by this unexpected attack from gentle Lucy, gathered himself up with something more like dignity than he had displayed in the course of the interview.

"Oh, very well," he said, taking up his hat; "perhaps one of these days you will be sorry for what you have done. I'm not much, I know, but you won't find many people to care for you as I would have cared." His voice broke suddenly, and he made his way rather blindly to the door.

Lucy was trembling all over, and as pale as, a moment ago, she had been red. She wanted to say something, as she watched him fumbling unsteadily with the doorhandle; but her lips refused to frame the words.

Without lifting his head, he passed into the little passage. Lucy heard his retreating footsteps, then her eye fell on a roll of newspapers at her feet. She picked them up hastily.

"Fred," she cried, "you have forgotten these."

But he vouchsafed no answer, and in another moment she heard the outer door shut.

---

56. A line from Tennyson's "Maud" (Bernstein, ed., *The Romance of a Shop*, 143 n. 1); the poem also figures in "Out of the World," (pp. 703–8), and "A Meadowshire Romance" (pp. 723–64).

She stood a moment with the ridiculous bundle in her hand – *Tit-Bits*[57] and a pink, crushed copy of *The Sporting Times* – then something between a laugh and a sob rose in her throat, the papers fell to the ground, and sinking on her knees by the table, she buried her face in her hands and burst into bitter weeping.

Gertrude, coming in from church some ten minutes later, found her sister thus prostrate.

The sight unnerved her from its very unusualness; bending over Lucy she whispered, "Am I to go away?"

"No, stop here."

Gertrude locked the door, then came and knelt by her sister.

"Oh, poor Fred, and I was so horrid to him," wept the penitent.

"Ah, I was afraid it would come."

Gertrude stroked the prone, smooth head; she feared that the thought of someone else besides Fred lay at the bottom of all this disturbance. She was very anxious for Lucy in these days; very anxious and very helpless. There was only one person, she knew too well, who could restore to Lucy her old sweet serenity, and he, alas, made no sign.

What was she to think? One thing was clear enough; the old pleasant relationship between themselves and Frank was at an end; if renewed at all, it must be renewed on a different basis. A disturbing element, an element of self-consciousness had crept into it; the delicate charm, the first bloom of simplicity, had departed forever.

It was now the middle of July, and for the last week or two they had seen scarcely anything of Jermyn, beyond the glimpses of him as he lounged up the street, with his sombrero crushed over his eyes, all the impetuosity gone from his gait.

That he distinctly avoided them, there could be little doubt. Though he was to be seen looking across at the house wistfully enough, he made no attempt to see them, and his greetings when they chanced to meet were of the most formal nature.

57. A newspaper.

The change in his conduct had been so marked and sudden, that it was impossible that it should escape observation. Fanny, with an air of superior knowledge, gave it out as her belief that Mr. Jermyn was in love; Phyllis held to the opinion that he had been fired with the idea of a big picture, and was undergoing the throes of artistic conception; Gertrude said lightly, that she supposed he was out of sorts and disinclined for society; while Lucy held her peace, and indulged in many inward sophistries to convince herself that her own unusual restlessness and languor had nothing to do with their neighbour's disaffection.

It was these carefully woven self-deceptions that had been so rudely scattered by Fred's words; and Lucy, kneeling by the scarlet table, had for the first time looked her fate in the face, and diagnosed her own complaint.

"Lucy," said Gertrude, after a pause, "bathe your eyes and come for a walk in the Park; there is time before lunch."

Lucy rose, drying her wet face with her handkerchief.

"Let me look at you," cried Gertrude. "What is the charm? Where does it lie? Why are these sort of things always happening to you?"

"Oh," answered Lucy, with an attempt at a smile, "I am a convenient, middling sort of person, that is all. Not uncomfortably clever like you, or uncomfortably pretty like Phyllis."

The two girls set off up the hot dusty street, with its Sunday odour of bad tobacco. Regent's Park wore its most unattractive garb; a dead monotony of July verdure assailed the eye; a verdure, moreover, impregnated and coated with the dust and soot of the city. The girls felt listless and dispirited, and conscious that their walk was turning out a failure.

As they passed through Clarence Gate, on their way back, Frank darted past them with something of his normal activity, lifting his hat with something like the old smile.

"He might have stopped," said Lucy, pale to the lips, and suddenly abandoning all pretence of concealment of her feelings.

"No doubt he is in a hurry," answered Gertrude, lamely. "I daresay he is going to lunch in Sussex Place. Lord Watergate's Sunday luncheon parties are quite celebrated."

The day dragged on. The weather was sultry and everyone felt depressed. Fanny was spending the day with relations of her future husband's; but the three girls had no engagements and lounged away the afternoon rather dismally at home.

All were relieved when Fanny and Mr. Marsh came in at suppertime, and they seated themselves at the table with alacrity. They had not proceeded far with the meal, when footsteps, unexpected but familiar, were heard ascending the staircase; then someone knocked, and before there was time to reply, the door was thrown open to admit Frank Jermyn.

He looked curiously unlike himself as he advanced and shook hands amid an uncomfortable silence that everybody desired to break. His face was pale, and no longer moody, but tense and eager, with shining eyes and dilated nostrils.

"You will stay to supper, Mr. Jermyn?" said Gertrude, at last, in her most neutral tones.

"Yes, please." Frank drew a chair to the table like a person in a dream.

"You are quite a stranger," cried arch, unconscious Fan, indicating with head and spoon the dish from which she proposed to serve him.

Frank nodded acceptance of the proffered fare, but ignored her remark.

Silence fell again upon the party, broken by murmurs from the enamoured Edward, and the ostentatious clatter of knives and forks on the part of people who were not eating. Everyone, except the plighted lovers, felt that there was electricity in the air.

At last Frank dropped his fork, abandoning, once for all, the pretence of supper.

"Miss Lucy," he cried across the table to her, "I have a piece of news."

She looked up, pale, with steady eyes, questioning him.

"I am going abroad tomorrow."

"Oh, where are you going?" cried Fanny, vaguely mystified.

"I am going to Africa."

He did not move his eyes from Lucy as he spoke; her head had drooped over her plate. "They are sending me out as special from *The Woodcut,* in the place of poor Leadpoint, who has died of fever. I heard the first of it last night, and this morning it was finally settled. It makes," cried Frank, "an immense difference in my prospects."

Edward Marsh, who objected to Frank as a spoilt puppy, always expecting other people to be interested in his affairs, asked the young man bluntly the value of his appointment. But he met with no reply; for Frank, his face alight, had sprung to his feet, pushing back his chair.

"Lucy, Lucy," he cried in a low voice, "won't you come and speak to me?"

Lucy rose like one mesmerised; took, with a presence of mind at which she afterwards laughed, the key of the studio from its nail, and followed Frank from the room, amidst the stupefaction of the rest of the party.

It was a sufficiently simple explanation which took place, some minutes later, in the very room where, a few hours before, poor Fred had received his dismissal.

"But why," said Lucy, presently, "have you been so unkind for the last fortnight?"

"Ah, Lucy," answered Frank; "you women so often misjudge us, and think that it is you alone who suffer, when the pain is on both sides. When it dawned upon me how things stood with you and me – dear girl, you told me more than you knew yourself – I reflected what a poor devil I was, with not the ghost of a prospect. (I have been down on my luck lately, Lucy.) And I saw, at the same time, how it was with Devonshire; I thought, he is a good fellow, let him have his chance, it may be best in the end – "

"Oh, Frank, Frank, what did you think of me? If these are men's arguments I am glad that I am a woman," cried Lucy, clinging to the strong young hand.

"Well, so am I, for that matter," answered Frank; and then, of course, though I do not uphold her conduct in this respect, Lucy told him briefly of Fred Devonshire's offer and her own refusal.

It was late before these two happy people returned to the sitting room, to receive congratulations on the event, which, by this time, it was unnecessary to impart.

Fanny wondered aloud why she had not thought of such a thing before; and felt, perhaps, that her own *rechauffé* love affair was quite thrown into the shade. Phyllis smiled and made airy jests, submitting her soft cheek gracefully to a brotherly kiss.

Edward Marsh looked on mystified and rather shocked, and Gertrude remained in the background, with a heart too full for speech, till the lovers made their way to her, demanding her congratulations.

"Don't think me too unworthy," said Frank, in all humility.

"I am glad," she said.

Glancing up and seeing the two young faces, aglow with the light of their happiness, she looked back with a wistful amusement on her own doubts and fears of the past weeks.

As she did so, the beautiful, familiar words flashed across her consciousness –

"Blessed are the pure in heart, for they shall see God."[58]

* * * * *

Late that night, when the guests had departed and the rest of the household was asleep, Gertrude heard Lucy moving about in the room below, and, throwing on her dressing gown, went downstairs. She found her sister risen from the table, where she had been writing a letter by the lamplight.

"Aren't you coming to bed, Lucy? Remember, you have to be up very early."

---

58. Matthew 5:8.

The shadow of the coming separation, which at first had only seemed to give a more exquisite quality to her happiness, lay on Lucy. She was pale, and her steadfast eyes looked out with the old calm, but with a new intensity, from her face.

"Read this," she said, "it seemed only fair."

Stooping over the table, Gertrude read –

"DEAR FRED, – I am engaged to Frank Jermyn, who goes abroad tomorrow. I am sorry if I seemed unkind, but I was grieved and shocked by what you said to me. Very soon, when you have quite forgiven me, you will come and see us all, will you not? Acknowledge that you made a mistake, and never cease to regard me as your friend. – L.L."

Gertrude thought: "Then I shall not have to tell Conny, after all."

Chapter 15
Cressida

Beauty like hers is genius.

D. G. ROSSETTI[59]

Lucy slept little that night. At the first flush of the magnificent summer dawn she was astir, making her preparations for the traveller's breakfast.

She had changed suddenly, from a demure and rather frigid maiden to a loving and anxious woman. Perhaps the signet-ring on her middle finger was a magic ring, and had wrought the charm.

Frank's notice to quit had been so short, that he had been obliged to apply for various necessaries to Darrell, who, with Lord Watergate, had supplied him with the main features of a tropical outfit. His ship sailed that day, at noon, so there was little time to be lost. He came over at an unconscionably early hour to Number 20B, for there was much to be said and little opportunity for saying it.

Lucy, displaying a truly feminine mixture of the tender and the practical, packed his bag, strapped his rugs, and put searching questions as to his preparations for travel. Already, womanlike, she had taken him under her wing, and henceforward the minutest detail of his existence would be more precious to her than anything on earth.

59. From Dante Gabriel Rossetti's (1828–1882) "Genius in Beauty."

Gertrude, when she had kissed the vivid young face in sisterly farewell, saw the lovers drive off to the station and wondered inwardly at their calmness.

Later in the day, coming into the studio, she found Lucy quietly engaged in putting a negative into the printing-frame.

"It is his," she said, looking up with a smile; "I never felt that I had a right to do it before."

At luncheon, Phyllis reminded her that tonight was the night of Mr. Darrell's *conversazione* at the Berkeley Galleries, for which he had sent them two tickets.

"It's no good expecting Lucy to go; you will have to take me, Gerty," she announced.

Gertrude had a great dislike to going, and she said – "Can't Fanny take you?"

"Edward and I are dining at the Septimus Pratts'," replied Fanny.

After much hesitation, she and her betrothed had had to resign themselves to the inevitable, and dispense with the services of a chaperon; a breach of decorum which Mr. Marsh, in particular, deplored.

"Are you very anxious about this party?" pleaded Gertrude.

"Oh Gerty, of course. And if you won't take me, I'll go alone," cried Phyllis, with unusual vehemence.

Gertrude was indignant at her sister's tone; then reflected that it was, perhaps, hard on Phyllis, to cut off one of her few festivities.

Phyllis, indeed, had not been very well of late, and demanded more spoiling than ever. She coughed constantly, and her eyes were unnaturally bright.

Gertrude ended by submitting to the sacrifice, and at ten o'clock, she and Phyllis found themselves in Bond Street, where the rooms were already thronged with people.

Phyllis had blazed into a degree of beauty that startled even her sister, and made her the frequent mark for observation in that brilliant gathering.

Her grey dress was cut low, displaying the white and rounded slenderness of her shoulders and arms; the soft brown hair was coiled about the perfect head in a manner that afforded a view of the neck and its graceful action; her eyes shone like stars; her cheeks glowed exquisitely pink. Wherever she went, went forth a sweet strong fragrance, the breath of a great spray of tuberose which was fastened in her bodice, and which had arrived for her that day from an unnamed donor.

Darrell's greeting to both the sisters had been of the briefest. He had shaken hands unsmilingly with Phyllis; he and Gertrude had brought their fingertips into chill and momentary contact, without so much as lifting their eyes, and Gertrude had felt humiliated at her presence there.

She had not seen Darrell since his Private View, more than six weeks ago; and now, as she stood talking to Lord Watergate, her eye, guided by a nameless curiosity, an unaccountable fascination, sought him out. He was looking ill, she thought, as she watched him standing in his host's place, near the doorway, chatting to an ugly old woman, whom she knew to be the Duchess of Kilburne; ill, and very unhappy. Happiness indeed, as she instinctively felt, is not for such as he – for the egotist and the sensualist.

Her acute feminine sense, sharpened perhaps by personal soreness, had pierced to the second-rateness of the man and his art. Beneath his arrogance and air of assured success, she read the signs of an almost craven hunger for pre-eminence; of a morbid self-consciousness; an insatiable vanity. And for all the stupendous cleverness of his workmanship, she failed to detect in his work the traces of those qualities which, combined with far less skill than his, can make greatness.

As for her own relations to Darrell, the positions of the two had shifted a little since the first. In the brief flashes of intercourse which they had known, a drama had silently enacted itself; a war without words or weapons, in which, so far, she had come off victor. For Sidney had ceased to regard her as merely ridiculous; and she, on her part, was no longer cowed by his aggressive personality, by the all-seeing, languid glance, the arrogant, indifferent manner. They stood on a level platform of unspoken, yet open distaste; which, should occasion arise, might blaze into actual defiance.

Lord Watergate, as I have said, was talking to Gertrude; but his glance, as she was quick to observe, strayed constantly toward Phyllis. She had wondered before this, as to the measure of his admiration for her sister; it seemed to her that he paid her the tribute of a deeper interest than that which her beauty and her brightness would, in the natural course of things, exact.

As for Phyllis, she was enjoying a triumph which many a professional beauty might have envied. People flocked around her, scheming for introductions, staring at her in open admiration, laughing at her whimsical sallies.

"That young person has a career before her."

"Who is she?"

"Oh, one of Darrell's discoveries. Works at a photographer's, they say."

"Darrell is painting her portrait."

"No, not her portrait; but a study of 'Cressida.'"

"Cressida!"

> "'There's language in her eye, her cheek, her lip;
> Nay, her foot speaks – '"[60]

"Hush, hush!"

Such floating spars of talk had drifted past Gertrude's corner, and had been caught, not by her, but by her companion.

Lord Watergate frowned, as he mentally finished the quotation, which struck him as being in shocking taste. He had adopted, unconsciously, a protective attitude towards the Lorimers; their courage, their fearlessness, their immense ignorance, appealed to his generous and chivalrous nature. He made up his mind to speak to Darrell about that baseless rumour of the Cressida.

---

60. From Shakespeare's *Troilus and Cressida*.

Gertrude, on her part, was not too absorbed in conversation to notice what her sister was doing. She saw at once that, in spite of some thrills of satisfied vanity, Phyllis was not enjoying herself. There was a restless, discontented light in her eyes, a half-weary recklessness in her pose, as she leant against the edge of a tall screen, which filled Gertrude with wonder and anxiety. She felt, as she had felt so often lately, that Phyllis, her little Phyllis, whom she had scolded and petted and yearned over for eighteen years, was passing beyond her ken, into regions where she could never follow.

The evening wore itself away as such evenings do, in aimless drifting to and fro, half-hearted attempts at conversation, much mutual staring, and a determined raid on the refreshment buffet, on the part of people who have dined sumptuously an hour ago.

"Our English social institutions," Darrell said aside to Lord Watergate; "the private view, where everyone goes; the *conversazione*, where no one talks."

Lord Watergate laughed, and went back to Gertrude, to propose an attack on the buffet, by way of diversion; and Sidney, with his inscrutable air of utter purposelessness, made his way through the crowd to where Phyllis stood in conversation with two young men.

Some paces off from her he paused, and stood in silence, looking at her.

Phyllis shot her glance to his, half-petulant, half-supplicating, like that of a child.

It was late in the evening, and this was the first attempt he had made to approach her. Darrell advanced a step or two, and Phyllis lowered her eyes, with a sudden and vivid blush.

"At last," said Darrell, in a low voice, as the two young men instinctively moved off before him.

"You are just in time to say 'goodnight' to me, Mr. Darrell."

Darrell smiled, with his face close to hers. His smile was considered attractive –

"Seeming more generous for the coldness gone."[61]

"It is not 'goodnight,' but 'goodbye,' that I have come to say."

The brilliant and rapid smile had passed across his face, leaving no trace.

"What do you mean, Mr. Darrell?"

"I mean that I am going away tomorrow."

"Forever and ever?" Phyllis laughed, as she spoke, turning pale.

"For several months. I have important business in Paris."

"But you haven't finished my portrait, Mr. Darrell."

Sidney looked down, biting his lip.

"Shall you be able to finish it in time for the Grosvenor?"

"Possibly not."

"Now you are disagreeable," cried Phyllis, in a high voice; "and ungrateful, too, after all those long sittings."

"Not ungrateful. Thank you, thank you, thank you!" Under cover of the crowd, he had taken both her hands, and was pressing them fiercely at each repetition, while his miserable eyes looked imploringly into hers.

"You are hurting me." Her voice was low and broken. She shrank back afraid.

"Goodbye – Phyllis."

Gertrude, coming back from the refreshment room a minute later, found Phyllis standing by herself, in an angle formed by one of the screens, pale to the lips, with brilliant, meaningless eyes.

"We are going home," said Gertrude, walking up to her.

"Oh, very well," she answered, rousing herself; "the sooner the better. I am not well." She put her hand to her side. "I had that pain again that I used to have."

Lord Watergate, who stood a little apart, watching her, came forward and gave her his arm, and they all three went from the room.

In the cab, Phyllis recovered something of her wonted vivacity.

61. From Eliot's *The Spanish Gypsy* (1868); see Bernstein, ed., *The Romance of a Shop*, 152 n. 1.

"Isn't it a nuisance," she said, "Mr. Darrell is going away for a long time, and doesn't know when he will be able to finish my portrait."

Gertrude started.

"Well, I suppose you always knew that he was an erratic person."

"You speak as if you were pleased, Gerty. I am very disappointed."

"Put not your trust in princes, Phyllis, nor in fashionable artists, who are rather more important than princes, in these days," answered Gertrude, secretly hoping that their relations with Darrell would never be renewed. "He has tired of his whim," she thought, indignant, yet relieved.

Mrs. Maryon opened the door to them herself.

Phyllis shuddered as they went upstairs.

"That bird of ill-omen!" she cried, beneath her breath.

"Poor Mrs. Maryon. How can you be so silly?" said Gertrude, who herself had noted the long and earnest glance which the woman had cast on her sister.

In the sitting room they found Lucy sewing peacefully by the lamplight.

"You hardly went to bed at all last night; you shouldn't be sitting up," said Gertrude, throwing off her cloak; while Phyllis carefully detached the knot of tuberose from her bodice, as she delivered herself for the second time of her grievance.

Afterwards, going up to the mantelpiece, she placed the flowers in a slender Venetian vase, its crystal flecked with flakes of gold, which Darrell had given her; took the vase in her hand, and swept upstairs without a word.

"I do not know what to think about Phyllis," said Gertrude.

"You are afraid that she is too much interested in Mr. Darrell?"

"Yes."

"She does not care two straws for him," said Lucy, with the conviction of one who knows; "her vanity is hurt, but I am not sure that that will be bad for her."

"He is the sort of person to attract – " began Gertrude; but Lucy struck in –

"Why, Gerty, what are you thinking of? he must be forty at least; and Phyllis is a child."

Something in her tones recalled to Gertrude that clarion-blast of triumph, in the wonderful lyric –

> "Oh, my love, my love is young!"[62]

"At any rate," she said, as they prepared to retire, "I am thankful that the sittings are at an end. Phyllis was getting her head turned. She is looking shockingly unwell, moreover, and I shall persuade her to accept the Devonshires' invitation for next month."

---

62. From "Crabbed Age and Youth" in *The Passionate Pilgrim,* an anthology often wrongly assumed to have been written entirely by Shakespeare, though only some of its poems are likely to have been authored by the latter (Bernstein, ed., *The Romance of a Shop,* 154 no. 1; New, ed., *The Complete Novels,* 542 n. 56).

Chapter 16
A Wedding

A human heart should beat for two,
Whate'er may say your single scorners;
And all the hearths I ever knew
Had got a pair of chimney-corners.

F. LOCKER: London Lyrics[63]

The next day, at about six o'clock, just as they had gone upstairs from the studio, Constance Devonshire was announced, and came sailing in, in her smartest attire, and with her most gracious smile on her face.

"I have come to offer my congratulations," she cried, going up to Lucy; "you know, I have always thought little Mr. Jermyn a nice person."

Lucy laughed quietly.

"I am glad you have brought your congratulations in person, Conny. I rather expected you would tell your coachman to leave cards at the door."

Conny turned away her face abruptly.

"What is the good of coming to see such busy people as you have been lately? ... And with so much lovemaking going on at the same time! What does Mrs. Maryon think of it all?"

63. From Locker-Lampson's poem, "Old Letters."

"Oh, she finds it very tame and hackneyed, I am afraid."

"You see," added Phyllis, who lounged idly in an armchair by the window, pale but sprightly, "the course of true love runs so monotonously smooth in this household. And Mrs. Maryon has a taste for the dramatic."

Conny laughed; and at this point the door was thrown open to admit Aunt Caroline, whose fixed and rigid smile was intended to show that she was in a gracious mood, and was accepted by the girls as a signal of truce.

"What is this a little bird tells me, Lucy?" she cried archly, for Mrs. Pratt shared the liking of her sex for matters matrimonial.

Fanny, who was, in fact, none other than the little bird who had broken the news, put her head on one side in unconsciously avine fashion, and smiled benevolently at her sister.

"I am engaged to Mr. Jermyn," said Lucy, her clear voice lingering proudly over the words.

Conny winced suddenly; then turned to gaze through the window at the blank casements above the auctioneer's shop.

"Then you have found out who Mr. Jermyn *is*?" went on Aunt Caroline, still in her most conciliatory tones.

"We never wanted to know," said Lucy, unexpectedly showing fight.

Aunt Caroline flushed, but she had come resolved against hostile encounter, in which, hitherto, she had found herself overpowered by force of numbers; so she contented herself with saying –

"And have you any prospect of getting married?"

"Frank has gone to Africa for the present," said Lucy.

Aunt Caroline looked significant.

"I only hope," she said afterwards to Fanny, who let her out at the street door, "that your sister has not fallen into the hands of an unscrupulous adventurer. It will be time when the young man comes home, if he ever does, for Mr. Pratt to make the proper inquiries."

Fanny had risen into favour since her engagement; Mr. Marsh, also, had won golden opinions at Lancaster Gate.

"I believe," Fanny replied, speaking for once to the point, "that Frank Jermyn is going to write, himself, to Mr. Pratt, at the first opportunity."

Meanwhile, upstairs in the sitting room, Conny was delivering herself of her opinion that they had all behaved shamefully to Aunt Caroline.

"She had a right to know. And it is very good of her to trouble about such a set of ungrateful girls at all," she cried. "You can't expect everyone besides yourselves to look upon Frank Jermyn as dropped from heaven."

"Aunt Caroline is cumulative – not to be judged at a sitting," pleaded Gertrude.

Very soon Constance herself rose to go.

"I shall not see you again unless you come down to us; which, I suppose, you won't," she said. "We go to Eastbourne on Friday; and afterwards to Homburg. Mama is going to write and invite you in due form."

"It is very kind of Mrs. Devonshire. Lucy and I cannot possibly leave home, but Phyllis would like to go," answered Gertrude; a remark of which Phyllis herself took no notice.

"Well then, goodbye. Lucy, Fred sends his congratulations. Phyllis, my dear, we shall meet ere long. Fanny, I shall look out for your wedding in the paper. Come on, Gerty, and let a fellow out!"

On the other side of the door, her manner changed suddenly.

"Do come home and dine, Gerty."

"I can't, Con, possibly."

"Gerty, of course I can guess about Fred. I knew it was no good, but I can't help being sorry."

"It was out of the question, poor boy."

"Oh, don't pity him too much. He'll get over it soon enough. His is not a complaint that lasts."

There was a significant emphasis on the last words, that did not escape Gertrude.

"You look better, Conny, than when I last saw you."

"Oh, I'm all right. There's nothing the matter with me but too many parties."

"I think dancing has agreed with you."

"I don't know about dancing. I have taken to sitting in conservatories under pink lamps. That is better sport, and far more becoming to the complexion."

"I shouldn't play that game, Conny. It never ends well."

"Indeed, it does. Often in St. George's, Hanover Square. You are shocked, but I do not contemplate matrimony just at present. But I see you agree with *Chastelard* –

> "'I do not like this manner of a dance;
> This game of two and two; it were much better
> To mix between the dances, than to sit,
> Each lady out of earshot with her friend.'"[64]

"Have you been taking to literature?"

"Yes; to the modern poets and the French novelists particularly. When next you hear of me, I shall have taken probably to slumming; shall have found peace in bearing jellies to aged paupers. Then you might write a moral tale about me."

Gertrude sighed, as the door closed on Constance. It was the Devonshires who, throughout their troubles, had shown them the most unwavering kindness; and on the Devonshires, it seemed, they were doomed to bring misfortune.

At the end of August, Fanny was quietly married at Marylebone Church. She would have dearly liked a "white wedding"; and secretly hoped that her sisters would suggest what she dared not – a white satin bride and white muslin bridesmaids. Truth to tell, such an idea never entered the heads of those practical young women; and poor Fanny went soberly to the altar in a dark green travelling dress, which was becoming if not festive.

64. From Swinburne's *Chastelard* (1866).

Aunt Caroline and Uncle Septimus came up from Tunbridge Wells for the wedding, and the Devonshires, who were away, lent their carriage. It was a sober, middle-aged little function enough, and everyone was glad when it was over.

Aunt Caroline said little, but contented herself with sending her hard, keen eyes into every nook and corner, every fold and plait, every dish and bowl; while she mentally appraised the value of the feast.

One result of the encounters with her nieces was this, that she was more outwardly gracious and less inwardly benevolent than before; a change not wholly to be deprecated.

Lucy, with bright eyes, listened, with the air of one who has a right to be interested, to the words of the marriage service, taking afterwards her usual share in practical details. She was upheld, no doubt, by the consciousness of the letter in her pocket; a letter which had come that very morning; was written on thin paper in a bold hand; and in common with others from the same source, was bright and kind; tender and hopeful; and very full of confidential statements as to all that concerned the writer.

Phyllis, pale but beautiful, alternated between languor and a fitful sprightliness; her three weeks at Eastbourne seemed to have done her little good; while Gertrude went through her part mechanically, and remembered remorsefully that she had never been very nice to Fanny.

As for the bride, she was subdued and tearful, as an orthodox bride should be; and invited all her sisters in turn to come and stay with her at Notting Hill directly the honeymoon in Switzerland should be over. Edward Marsh suffered the usual insignificance of bridegrooms; but did all that was demanded of him with exactness.

In the evening, when that blankness which invariably follows a wedding had fallen upon the sisters, Mrs. Maryon came up into the sitting room, and beguiled them with tales of the various brides she had known; who, if they had not married in haste, must certainly, to judge by the sequel, have repented at leisure.

Chapter 17
A Special Edition

We bear to think
You're gone, – to feel you may not come, –
To hear the door-latch stir and clink,
Yet no more you! ....
E. B. BROWNING[65]

It was true enough, no doubt, that Phyllis did not care for Darrell in Lucy's sense of the word; but at the same time, it was sufficiently clear that he had been the means of injecting a subtle poison into her veins.

Since the night of the *conversazione* at the Berkeley Galleries, when he had bidden her farewell, a change, in every respect for the worse, had crept over her.

The buoyancy, which had been one of her chief charms, had deserted her. She was languid, restless, bored, and more utterly idle than ever. The flippancy of her lighter moods shocked even her sisters, who had been accustomed to allow her great license in the matter of jokes; the moodiness of her moments of depression distressed them beyond measure.

65. From Barrett Browning's "Parting Lovers."

At Eastbourne she had amused herself with getting up a tremendous flirtation with Fred, to the Devonshires' annoyance and the satisfaction of the victim himself, whose present mood it suited and who hoped that Lucy would hear of it.

After Phyllis's visit to Eastbourne, which had been closely followed by Fanny's wedding, the household at Upper Baker Street underwent a period of dulness, which was felt all the more keenly from the cheerful fullness of the previous summer. Everyone was out of town. In early September, even the country cousins have departed, and people have not yet begun to return to London, where it is perhaps the most desolate period of the whole year.

Work, of course, was slack, and they had no longer the preparations for Fanny's wedding to fall back upon.

The air was hot, sunless, misty; like a vapour bath, Phyllis said. Even Gertrude, inveterate cockney as she was, began to long for the country. Nothing but a strong sense of loyalty to her sister prevented Lucy from accepting a cordial invitation from the "old folks." Phyllis openly proclaimed that she was only waiting *der erste beste* to make her escape forever from Baker Street.

Phyllis, indeed, was in the worst case of them all; for while Lucy had the precious letters from Africa to console her, Gertrude had again taken up her pen, which seemed to move more freely in her hand than it had ever done before.

So the days went on till it was the middle of September, and life was beginning to quicken in the great city.

One sultry afternoon, the Lorimers were gathered in the sitting room; both windows stood open, admitting the hot, still, autumnal air; every sound in the street could be distinctly heard.

Lucy sat apart, deep in a voluminous letter on foreign paper which had come for her that morning, and which she had been too busy to read before. Phyllis was at the table, yawning over a copy of *The Woodcut,* which was opened at a page of engravings headed: "The War in Africa; from sketches by our special artist." Gertrude sewed by the window, too tired to think or talk. Now and then she glanced across mechanically to the opposite house, whence in these days of dreariness, no picturesque, impetuous young man was wont to issue; from whose upper windows no friendly eyes gazed wistfully across.

The rooms above the auctioneer's had, in fact, a fresh occupant; an ex-Girtonian without a waist, who taught at the High School for girls hard-by.

The Lorimers chose to regard her as a usurper; and with the justice usually attributed to their sex, indulged in much sarcastic comment on her appearance; on her round shoulders and swinging gait; on the green gown with balloon sleeves, and the sulphur-coloured handkerchief which she habitually wore.

Presently Lucy looked up from her letter, folded it, sighed, and smiled.

"What has your special artist to say for himself?" asked Phyllis, pushing away *The Woodcut.*

"He writes in good spirits, but holds out no prospect of the war coming to an end. He was just about to go further into the interior, with General Somerset's division. Mr. Steele of *The Photogravure,* with whom he seems to have chummed, goes too," answered Lucy, putting the letter into her pocket.

"Perhaps his sketches will be a little livelier in consequence. They are very dull this week."

Phyllis rose as she spoke, stretching her arms above her head. "I think I will go and dine with Fan. She is such fun."

Fanny had returned from Switzerland a day or two before, and was now in the full tide of bridal complacency. As mistress of a snug and hideous little house at Notting Hill, and wedded wife of a large and affectionate man, she was beginning to feel that she had a place in the world at last.

"I will come up with you," said Lucy to Phyllis, "and brush your hair before you go."

The two girls went from the room, leaving Gertrude alone. Letting fall her work into her lap, she leaned in dreamy idleness from the window, looking out into the street, where the afternoon was deepening apace into evening. A dun-coloured haze, thin and transparent, hung in the air, softening the long perspective of the street. School hours were over, and the Girtonian, her arm swinging like a bell-rope, could be discerned on her way home, a devoted *cortège* of schoolgirls straggling in her wake. From the corner of the street floated up the cries of the newspaper boys, mingling with the clatter of omnibus wheels.

An empty hansom cab crawled slowly by. Gertrude noticed that it had violet lamps instead of red ones.

A lamplighter was going his rounds, leaving a lengthening line of orange-coloured lights to mark his track. The recollection of summer, the presage of winter, were met in the dusky atmosphere.

"How the place echoes," thought Gertrude. It seemed to her that the boys crying the evening papers were more vociferous than usual; and as the thought passed through her mind, she was aware of a hateful, familiar sound – the hoarse shriek of a man proclaiming a "special edition" up the street.

No amount of familiarity could conquer the instinctive shudder with which she always listened to these birds of ill-omen, these carrion, whose hideous task it is to gloat over human calamity. Now, as the sound grew louder and more distinct, the usual vague and sickening horror crept over her. She put her hands to her ears. "It is some ridiculous race, no doubt."

She let in the sound again.

Her fears were unformulated, but she hoped that Lucy upstairs in the bedroom had not heard.

The cry ceased abruptly; someone was buying a paper; then was taken up again with increased vociferousness. Gertrude strained her ears to listen.

"Terrible slaughter, terrible slaughter of British troops!" floated up in the hideous tones.

She listened, fascinated with a nameless horror.

"A regiment cut to pieces! Death of a general! Special edition!" The fiend stood under the window, vociferating upwards.

In an instant, Gertrude had slipped down the dusky staircase, and was giving the man sixpence for a halfpenny paper. Standing beneath the gas-jet in the passage, she opened the sheet and read; then, still clutching it, sank down white and trembling on the lowest stair.

Noiseless, rapid footfalls came down behind her, someone touched her on the shoulder, and a strange voice said in her ear, "Give it to me."

She started up, putting the hateful thing behind her.

"No, no, no, Lucy! It is not true."

"Yes, yes, yes! Don't be ridiculous, Gerty."

Lucy took the paper in her hands, bore it to the light, and read, Gertrude hiding her face against the wall.

The paper stated, briefly, that news had arrived at headquarters of the almost total destruction of the troops which, under General Somerset, had set out for the interior of Africa some weeks before. A few stragglers, chiefly native allies, had reached the coast in safety, and had reported that the General himself had been among the first to perish.

Messrs. Steele and Jermyn, special artists of *The Photogravure* and *The Woodcut*, respectively, had been among those to join the expedition. No news of their fate had been ascertained, and there was reason to fear that they had shared the doom of the others.

"It is not true." Lucy's voice rang hollow and strange. She stood there, white and rigid, under the gas-jet.

Mrs. Maryon, who had bought a paper on her own account, issued from the shop-parlour in time to see the poor young lady sway forward into her sister's arms.

*****

Those were dark days that followed. At first there had been hope but as time went on, and further details of the catastrophe came to light, there was nothing for the most sanguine to do but to accept the worst.

Gertrude herself felt that the one pale gleam of uncertainty which yet remained was, perhaps, the most cruel feature of the case. If only

Lucy's hollow eyes could drop their natural tears above Frank's grave, she might again find peace.

Frank's grave! Gertrude found herself starting back incredulous at the thought.

Death, as a general statement, is so easy of utterance, of belief; it is only when we come face to face with it that we find the great mystery so cruelly hard to realise; for death, like love, is ever old and ever new.

"People always come back in books," Fanny had said, endeavouring, in all good faith, to administer consolation; and Lucy had actually laughed.

"Your sister ought to be able to do better for herself," Edward Marsh said, later on, to his wife.

But Fanny, who had had a genuine liking for kind Frank, disagreed for once with the marital opinion.

"He was good, and he loved her. She has always that to remember," Gertrude thought, as she watched Lucy going about her business with a calmness that alarmed her more than the most violent expressions of sorrow would have done.

"Dear little Frank! I wonder if he is really dead," Phyllis reflected, staring with wide eyes at the house opposite, rather as if she expected to see a ghost issue from the door.

Fortunately for the Lorimers, they had little time for brooding over their troubles. Their success had proved itself no ephemeral one. As people returned to town, work began to flow in upon them from all sides, and their hands were full. Labour and sorrow, the common human portion, were theirs, and they accepted them with courage, if not, indeed, with resignation. September and October glided by, and now the winter was upon them.

Chapter 18
Phyllis

Die aeltre Tochter gaehnet
"Ich will nicht verhungern bei euch,
Ich gehe morgen zum Grafen,
Und der ist verliebt und reich."
HEINE[66]

"Lucy, dear, you must go."

"But, Gerty, you can never manage to get through the work alone."

"I will make Phyllis help me. It will be the best thing for her, and she works better than any of us when she chooses."

The sisters were standing together in the studio, discussing a letter which Lucy held in her hand – an appeal from the heart-broken "old folks" that she, who was to have been their daughter, should visit them in their sorrow.

66. From "The Homecoming" in Heinrich Heine's (1797–1856) *Buch der Lieder*; Hal Draper's translation reads: "The older daughter says, yawning: / 'I refuse to starve here with you; / I'll go to the Count tomorrow – / He's rich, and in love with me too'"; see *The Complete Poems of Heinrich Heine: A Modern English Version* (Boston: Suhrkamp/Insel, 1982), 88; New, ed., *The Complete Novels*, 543 n. 61.

"It is simply your duty to go," went on Gertrude, who was consumed with anxiety concerning her sister; then added, involuntarily, "if you think you can bear it."

A light came into Lucy's eyes.

"Is there anything that one cannot bear?"

She turned away, and began mechanically fixing a negative into one of the printing frames. She remembered how, on that last day, Frank had planned the visit to Cornwall. Was he not going to show her every nook and corner of the old home, which many a time before he had so minutely described to her? The place had for long been familiar to her imagination, and now she was in fact to make acquaintance with it; that was all. What availed it to dwell on contrasts?

The sisters spoke little of Lucy's approaching journey, which was fixed for some days after the receipt of the letter; and one cold and foggy November afternoon found her helping Mrs. Maryon with her little box down the stairs, while Matilda went for a cab.

At the same moment, Gertrude issued from the studio with her outdoor clothes on.

"No one is likely to come in this Egyptian darkness," she said; "it is four o'clock already, and I am going to take you to Paddington."

"That will be delightful, if you think you may risk it," answered Lucy, who looked very pale in her black clothes.

"I have left a message with Mrs. Maryon to be delivered in the improbable event of 'three customers coming in,' as they did in *John Gilpin*,"[67] said Gertrude, with a feeble attempt at sprightliness.

Matilda appeared at this point to announce that the cab was at the door.

"Where is Phyllis?" cried Lucy. "I have not said goodbye to her."

"She went out two hours ago, miss," put in Mrs. Maryon, in her sad voice.

"No doubt," said Gertrude, "she has gone to Conny's. I think she goes there a great deal in these days."

---

67. Refers to William Cowper's (1731–1800) *The Diverting History of John Gilpin* (1782).

Mrs. Maryon looked up quickly, then set about helping Matilda hoist the box on to the cab.

"How bitterly cold it is," cried Gertrude, with a shudder, as they crossed the threshold.

An orange-coloured fog hung in the air, congealed by the sudden change of temperature into a thick and palpable mass.

"I shouldn't be surprised if we had snow," observed Mrs. Maryon, shaking her head.

"Oh, how could Phyllis be so wicked as to go out?" cried Gertrude, as the cab drove off: "and her cough has been so troublesome lately."

"I think she has been looking more like her old self the last week or two," said Lucy; then added, "Do you know that Mr. Darrell is back? I forgot to tell you that I met him in Regent's Park the other day."

"I hope he will not wish to renew the sittings; but no doubt he has found some fresh whim by this time. I wish he had let Phyllis alone; he did her no good."

"Poor little soul, I am afraid she finds it dismal," said Lucy.

"I mean to plan a little dissipation for us both when you are away – the theatre, probably," said Gertrude, who felt remorsefully that in her anxiety concerning Lucy she had rather neglected Phyllis.

"Yes, do, and take care of yourself, dear old Gerty," said Lucy, as the cab drew up at Paddington station.

The sisters embraced long and silently, and in a few minutes, Lucy was steaming westward in a third-class carriage, and Gertrude was making her way through the fog to Praed Street Station. At Baker Street, she perceived that Mrs. Maryon's prophecy was undergoing fulfilment; the fog had lifted a little, and flakes of snow were falling at slow intervals.

Before the door of Number 20B, a small brougham was standing – a brougham, as she observed by the light of the street lamp, with a coronet emblazoned on the panels.

"Lord Watergate is in the studio, miss," announced Mrs. Maryon, who opened the door; "he only came a minute ago, and preferred to wait. I have lit the lamp." As Gertrude was going towards the studio the woman ran up to her, and put a note in her hand. "I forgot to give you this," she said. "I found it in the letterbox a minute after you left."

Gertrude, glancing hastily at the envelope, recognised, with some surprise, the childish handwriting of her sister Phyllis, and concluded that she had decided to remain overnight at the Devonshires.

"She might have remembered that I was alone," she thought, a little wistfully as she opened the door of the waiting room.

Lord Watergate advanced to meet her, and they shook hands gravely. She had not seen him since the night of the *conversazione* at the Berkeley Galleries. His ample presence seemed to fill the little room.

"It is a shame," he said, "to come down upon you at this time of night."

She laid Phyllis's note on the table, and turned to him with a smile of deprecation.

"Won't you read your letter before we embark on the question of slides?"

"Thank you. I will just open it."

She broke the seal, advanced to the lamp, and cast her eye hastily over the letter. But something in the contents seemed to rivet her attention, to merit more than a casual glance. For some moments, she stood absorbed in the carelessly-written sheet; then, suddenly, an exclamation of sorrow and astonishment burst from her lips.

Lord Watergate advanced towards her.

"Miss Lorimer, you are in some trouble. Can I help you, or shall I go away?"

She looked up, half-bewildered, into the strong and gentle face. Then realising nothing, save that here was a friendly human presence, put the letter into his hand.

This is what he read.

"MY DEAR GERTY, – This is to tell you that I am not coming home tonight – am not coming home again at all, in fact. I am going to marry Mr. Darrell, who will take me to Italy, where the weather is decent, and where I shall get well. For you know, I am horribly seedy, Gerty, and very dull.

"Of course you will be angry with me; you never liked Sidney, and you will think it ungrateful of me, perhaps, to go off like this. But oh, Gerty, it has been so dismal, especially since we heard about poor little Frank. Sidney hates a fuss, and so do I. We both of us prefer to go off on the Q.T., as Fred says. With love from

"PHYLLIS"

As Lord Watergate finished this characteristic epistle, an exclamation more fraught with horror than Gertrude's own burst from his lips. He strode across the room, crushing the paper in his hands.

"Lord Watergate!" Gertrude faced him, pale, questioning: a nameless dread clutched at her.

Something in her face struck him. Stopping short in front of her, in tones half paralysed with horror, he said –

"Don't you know?"

"Do I know?" she echoed his words, bewildered.

"Darrell is married. He does not live with his wife; but it is no secret."

The red tables and chairs, the lamp, Lord Watergate himself, whose voice sounded fierce and angry, were whirling round Gertrude in hopeless confusion; and then suddenly she remembered that this was an old story; that she had known it always, from the first moment when she had looked upon Darrell's face.

Gertrude closed her eyes, but she did not faint. She remained standing, while one hand rested on the table for support. Yes, she had known it; had stood by powerless, paralysed, while this thing approached; had seen it even as Cassandra saw from afar the horror which she had been unable to avert.[68]

Opening her eyes, she met the gaze, grieved, pitiful, indignant, of her companion.

"What is to be done?"

Her lips framed the words with difficulty.

68. Cassandra of Greek mythology.

A pause; then he said –

"I cannot hold out much hope. But will you come with me to – to – his house and make inquiries?"

She bowed her head, and gathering herself together, led the way from the room.

The snow was falling thick and fast as they emerged from the house, and Lord Watergate handed her into his brougham. It had grown very dark, and the wind had risen.

"The Sycamores," said Lord Watergate to his coachman, as he took his seat by Gertrude, and drew the fur about her knees.

Mrs. Maryon, watching from the shop window, shrugged her shoulders.

"Who would have thought it? But you never can tell. And that Phyllis! It's twice I've seen her with the fair-haired gentleman, with his beard cut like a foreigner's. It's what you'd expect from her, poor creature – but Gertrude!"

"They have got the rooms on lease," grumbled Mr. Maryon, from among his pestles and mortars.

Chapter 19

The Sycamores

How the world is made for each of us!
How all we perceive and know in it
Tends to some moment's product thus.
When a soul declares itself – to wit,
By its fruit the thing it does!

ROBERT BROWNING[69]

The carriage rolled on its way through the snow to St. John's Wood, while its two occupants sat side by side in silence. Now that they had set out, each felt the hopelessness of the errand on which they were bound, to which only the first stifling moment of horror, that absolute need of action, had prompted them.

The brougham stopped in the road before the gate of The Sycamores.

"We had better walk up the drive," said Lord Watergate, and opened the carriage door.

By this time, the snow lay deep on the road and the roofs of the houses; the trees looked mere blotches of greyish-white, seen through the rapid whirl of falling flakes, which it made one giddy to contemplate.

69. From Robert Browning's "By the Fire-Side."

"A terrible night for a journey," thought Lord Watergate, as he opened the big gate; but he said nothing, fearing to arouse false hopes in the breast of his companion.

They wound together up the drive, the dark mass of the house partly hidden by the curving, laurel-lined path, and further obscured by the veil of falling snow.

Then, suddenly, something pierced through Gertrude's numbness; she stopped short.

"Look!" she cried, beneath her breath.

They were now in full sight of the house. The upper windows were dark; the huge windows of the studio were shuttered close, but through the chinks were visible lines and points of mellow light.

Lord Watergate laid his hand on her arm. He thought: "That is just like Darrell, to have doubled back. But even then, we may be too late."

He said: "Miss Lorimer, if they are there, what are you going to do?"

"I am going to tell my sister that she has been deceived, and to bring her home with me."

Gertrude spoke very low, but without hesitation. Somewhere, in the background of her being, sorrow, and shame, and anger were lurking; at present she was keenly conscious of nothing but an irresistible impulse to action.

"That she has been deceived!" Lord Watergate turned away his face. Had Phyllis, indeed, been deceived, and was it not a fool's errand on which they were bent?

They mounted the steps, and he rang the bell; then, by the light of the hanging lamp, while the snow swirled round and fell upon them both, he looked into her white, tense face.

"Do not hope for anything. It is most probable that they are not there."

A long, breathless moment, then the door was thrown open, revealing the solemn manservant standing out against the lighted vestibule.

"I wish to see Mr. Darrell," said Lord Watergate, shortly.

"He's not at home, your lordship."

Gertrude pressed her hand to her heart.

"He is at home to me, as you perfectly well know."

"He has gone abroad, your lordship."

Gertrude swayed forward a little, steadying herself against the lintel, where she stood in darkness behind Lord Watergate.

"There are lights in the studio, and you must let me in," said Lord Watergate, sternly.

The man's face betrayed him.

"I shall lose my place, my lord."

"I am sorry for you, Shaw. You had better make off, and leave the responsibility with me."

The man wavered, took the coin from Lord Watergate's hand, then, turning, went slowly back to his own quarters.

Gertrude came forward into the light.

"You must not come in, Lord Watergate."

Her mind worked with curious rapidity; she saw that a meeting between the two men must be avoided.

"I cannot let you go alone. You do not know – "

"I am prepared for anything. Lord Watergate, spare my sister's shame."

She had passed him, with set, tragic face. He saw the slim, rapid figure, in the black, snow-covered dress, make its way down the passage, then disappear behind the curtain which guarded the entrance to the studio.

Gertrude had entered noiselessly, and, pausing on the threshold, hidden in shadow, remained there motionless a moment's space.

Every detail of the great room, seen but once before, smote on her sense with a curious familiarity. It had been wintry daylight on the occasion of her former presence there; now a mellow radiance of shaded, artificial light was diffused throughout the apartment, a radiance concentrated to subdued brilliance in the immediate neighbourhood of the fireplace.

A wood fire, with leaping blue flames, was piled on the hearth, its light flickering fitfully on the surrounding objects; on the tiger-skin rug, the tall, rich screen of faded Spanish leather; on Darrell himself, who lounged on a low couch, his blonde head outlined against the screen, a cloud of cigarette smoke issuing from his lips, as he looked from under his eyelids at the figure before him.

It was Phyllis who stood there by the little table, on which lay some fruit and some coffee, in rose-coloured cups. Phyllis, yet somebody new and strange; not the pretty child that her sisters had loved, but a beautiful wanton in a loose, trailing garment, shimmering, wonderful, white and lustrous as a pearl; Phyllis, with her brown hair turned to gold in the light of the lamp swung above her; Phyllis, with diamonds on the slender fingers, that played with a cluster of bloom-covered grapes.

For a moment, the warmth, the over-powering fragrance of hothouse flowers, most of all, the sight of that figure by the table, had robbed Gertrude of power to move or speak. But in her heart the storm, which had been silently gathering, was growing ready to burst. For the time, the varied emotions which devoured her had concentrated themselves into a white heat of fury, which kindled all her being.

The flames leapt, the logs crackled pleasantly. Darrell blew a whiff of smoke to the ceiling; Phyllis smiled, then suddenly into that bright scene glided a black and rigid figure, with glowing eyes and tragic face; with the snow sprinkled on the old cloak, and clinging in the wisps of wind-blown hair.

"Phyllis," it said in level tones; "come home with me at once. Mr. Darrell cannot marry you; he is married already."

Phyllis shrank back, with a cry.

"Oh, Gerty, how you frightened me! What do you mean by coming down on one like this?"

Her voice shook, through its petulance; she whisked round so suddenly that her long dress caught in the little table, which fell to the ground with a crash.

Darrell had sprung to his feet with an exclamation. "By God, what brings that woman here!"

Gertrude turned and faced him.

His face was livid with passion; his prominent eyes, for once wide open, glared at her in rage and hatred.

Gertrude met his glance with eyes that glowed with a passion yet fiercer than his own.

Elements, long smouldering, had blazed forth at last. Face to face they stood; face to face, while the silent battle raged between them.

Then with a curious elation, a mighty throb of what was almost joy, Gertrude knew that she, not he, the man of whom she had once been afraid, was the stronger of the two. For one brief moment, some fierce instinct in her heart rejoiced.

Phyllis, cowering in the background, Phyllis, pale as her splendid dress, shrank back, mystified, afraid. Her light soul shivered before the blast of passions in which, though she had helped to raise them, she felt herself to have no part nor lot.

Reckoned by time, the encounter of those two hostile spirits was but brief; a moment, and Darrell had dropped his eyes, and was saying in something like his own languid voice –

"To what may I ascribe this – honour?"

Gertrude turned in silence to her sister –

"Take off that – " (she indicated the shimmering garment with a pause), "and come with me."

Darrell sneered from the background; "Your sister has decided on remaining here."

"Phyllis!" said Gertrude, looking at her.

Phyllis began to sob.

"Oh, Gerty, what shall I do? Don't look at me like that. My dress is there behind the screen; and my hat. Oh, Gerty, I shall never get it on; I am so much taller."

With rapid fingers, Gertrude had unfastened her own long, black cloak, and was wrapping it about her sister.

"Great heavens," cried Darrell, coming forward and seizing her hands; "You shall not take her away! You have no earthly right to take her against her will."

With a cold fury of disgust, she shook off his touch.

"Oh, Sidney, I think I'd better go. I oughtn't to have come." Phyllis's voice sounded touchingly childish.

Something in the pleading tones stirred his blood curiously.

"Do you know," he cried, addressing himself to Gertrude, who was deliberately drawing the rings from her sister's passive hands, "Do you know what a night it is? That if you take her away you will kill her? Great God, you paragon of virtue, don't you see how ill she is?"

She swept her glance over him in icy disdain; then going up to the mantelpiece, laid the rings on the shelf.

"I swear to you," he cried, "that I will leave the house this hour, this minute. That I will never return to it; that I will never see her again – Phyllis!"

At the last word, his voice had dropped to a low and passionate key; he stretched out his arms, but Gertrude coming between them put her strong desperate grasp about Phyllis, who swayed forward with closed eyes. Darrell retreated with a muffled exclamation of grief and rage and baffled purpose, and Gertrude half led, half carried her sister from the room, the hateful satin garment trailing noisily behind them from beneath the black cloak.

A tall figure came forward from the doorway; the door was standing open; and the white whirlpool was visible against the darkness outside.

"She has fainted," said Gertrude, in a low voice.

Lord Watergate lifted her gently in his arms. At the same moment, Darrell emerged from the studio, then remained rooted to the spot, dismayed and sullen, at the sight of his friend.

"You are a scoundrel, Darrell," said Lord Watergate, in very clear, deliberate tones; then, his burden in his arms, he stepped out into the darkness, Gertrude closing the door behind them.

Half an hour, later the brougham stopped before the house in Upper Baker Street.

Lord Watergate, when he had carried the fainting girl upstairs, went himself for a doctor.

"I think I have killed her," said Gertrude, before he went, looking up at him from over the prostrate figure of her sister; "and if it were all to be done again – I would do it."

Mrs. Maryon asked no questions; her genuine kindness and helpfulness were called forth by this crisis; and her suspicions of Gertrude had vanished forever.

Chapter 20

In The Sick Room

A riddle that one shrinks
To challenge from the scornful sphinx.

D. G. ROSSETTI[70]

The doctor's verdict was unhesitating enough. Phyllis's doom, as more than one who knew her foresaw, was sealed. The shock and the exposure had only hastened an end which for long had been inevitable. Consumption, complicated with heart disease, both in advanced stages, held her in their grasp; added to these, a severe bronchial attack had set in since the night of the snowstorm, and her life might be said to hang by a thread. It might be a matter of days, said the cautious physician, of weeks, or even months.

"Would a journey to the south, at an earlier stage of her illness, have availed to save her?" Gertrude asked, with white, mechanical lips.

It was possible, was the answer, that it would have prolonged her life. But almost from the first, it seemed, the shadow of the grave must have rested on this beautiful human blossom.

"Death in her face," muttered Mrs. Maryon grimly; "I saw it there, I have always seen it."

---

70. From Rossetti's "Jenny."

Meanwhile, people came and went in Upper Baker Street; sympathetic, inquisitive, bustling.

Fanny, dismayed and tearful, appeared daily at the invalid's bedside, laden with grapes and other delicacies.

"Poor old Fan," said Phyllis; "how shocked she would be if she knew everything. Don't you think it is your duty, Gerty, to Mr. Marsh, to let him know?"

Aunt Caroline drove across from Lancaster Gate, rebuke implied in every fold of her handsome dress.

"I cannot think," she remarked to her friends, "how Gertrude could have reconciled such culpable neglect of that poor child's health to her conscience."

Gertrude avoided her aunt, saying to herself, in the bitterness of her humiliation: "It is the Aunt Carolines of this world who are right. I ought to have listened to her. She understood human nature better than I."

The Devonshires, who had not long returned from Germany, were unremitting in their kindness, the slackened bonds between the two families growing tight once more in this hour of need.

Lord Watergate made regular inquiries in Baker Street. Gertrude found his presence more endurable than that of the people with whom she had to dissemble; he knew her secret; it was safe with him and she was almost glad that he knew it.

Gertrude had written a brief note to Lucy, telling her that Phyllis was very ill, but urging her to remain a week, at least, in Cornwall.

"She will need all the strength she can get up," thought Gertrude. She herself was performing prodigies of work without any conscious effort.

Frozen, tense, silent, she vibrated between the studio and the sickroom, moving as if in obedience to some hidden mechanism, a creature apparently without wants, emotions, or thoughts.

She had gathered from Phyllis's cynically frank remarks, that it was by the merest chance she had not been too late and that Darrell had returned to The Sycamores.

"We were going to cross on our way to Italy that very night," Phyllis said. "We drove to Charing Cross, and then the snow began to fall, and I had such a fit of coughing that Sidney was frightened, and took me home to St. John's Wood."

Gertrude, who had received these confidences in silence, turned her head away with an involuntary, instinctive movement of repugnance at the mention of Darrell's Christian name.

"Gerty," said Phyllis, who lay back among the pillows, a white ghost with two burning red spots on her cheeks, "Gerty, it is only fair that I should tell you: Sidney isn't as bad as you think. He went away in the summer, because he was beginning to care about me too much; he only came back because he simply couldn't help himself. And – and, you will go out of the room and never speak to me again – I knew he had a wife, Gerty; I heard them talking about her at the Oakleys, the very first day I saw him. She was his model; she drinks like a fish, and is ten years older than he is – I put that in the letter about getting married, because I didn't quite know how to say it. I thought that very likely you knew."

Gertrude had walked to the window, and was pulling down the blind with stiff, blundering fingers. It was growing dusk and in less than half an hour Lucy would be home. It was just a week since she had set out for Cornwall.

"Shall you tell Lucy?" came the childish voice from among the pillows.

"I don't know. Lie still, Phyllis, and I will see if Mrs. Maryon has prepared the jelly for you."

"Kind old thing, Mrs. Maryon."

"Yes, indeed. She quite ignores the fact that we have no possible claim on her."

Gertrude met Mrs. Maryon on the dusky stairs, dish in hand.

"Do go and lie down, Miss Lorimer; or we shall have you knocked up too, and where should we be then? You mustn't let Miss Lucy see you like that."

Gertrude obeyed mechanically. Going into the sitting room, she threw herself on the little hard sofa, her face pressed to the pillow.

She must have fallen into a doze, for the next thing of which she was aware was Lucy's voice in her ear, and opening her eyes she saw Lucy bending over her, candle in hand.

"Have you seen her?" she asked, sitting up with a dazed air.

"I am back this very minute. Gertrude, what have you been doing to yourself?"

"Oh, I am all right." She rose with a little smile. "Let me look at you, Lucy. Actually roses on your cheek."

"Gertrude, Gertrude, what has happened to you? Have I come – Oh, Gerty, have I come too late?"

"No," said Gertrude, "but she is very ill."

Lucy put her arms round her sister.

"And I have left you alone through these days. Oh, my poor Gerty."

They went upstairs together, and Lucy passed into the invalid's room, Gertrude remaining in the outer apartment, which was her own.

In about ten minutes Lucy came out sobbing. "Oh, Phyllis, Phyllis," she wept below her breath.

Gertrude, paler than ever, rose without a word, and went into the sick room.

"Poor old Lucy, she looked as if she were going to cry. I asked her if she had any message for Frank," said Phyllis, as her sister sat down beside her, and adjusted the lamp.

"You are over-exciting yourself. Lie still, Phyllis."

"But, Gerty, I feel ever so much better tonight."

Silence. Gertrude sewed, and the invalid lay with closed eyes, but the flutter of the long lashes told that she was not asleep.

"Gerty!" In about half an hour, the grey eyes had unclosed, and were fixed widely on her sister's face.

"What is it?"

"Gerty, am I really going to die?"

"You are very ill," said Gertrude, in a low voice.

"But to die – it seems so impossible, so difficult, somehow. Frank died; that was wonderful enough; but oneself!"

"Oh, my child," broke from Gertrude's lips.

"Don't be sorry. I have never been a nice person, but I don't funk somehow. I ought to, after being such a bad lot, but I don't. Gerty!"

"What is it?"

"Gerty, you have always been good to me; this last week as well. But that is the worst of you good people; you are hard as stones. You bring me jelly; you sit up all night with me – but you have never forgiven me. You know that is the truth."

Gertrude knelt by the bedside, a great compunction in her heart; she put her hand on that of Phyllis, who went on –

"And there is something I should wish to tell you. I am glad you came and fetched me away. The very moment I saw your angry, white face, and your old clothes with the snow on, I was glad. It is funny, if one comes to think of it. I was frightened, but I was glad."

Gertrude's head drooped lower and lower over the coverlet; her heart, which had been frozen within her, melted. In an agony of love, of remorse, she stretched out her arms, while her sobs came thick and fast, and gathered the wasted figure to her breast.

"Oh, Phyllis, oh, my child; who am I to forgive you? Is it a question of forgiveness between us? Oh, Phyllis, my little Phyllis, have you forgotten how I love you?"

Chapter 21
The Last Act

Just as another woman sleeps.
D. G. ROSSETTI[71]

It was not till a week or two later that Gertrude brought herself to tell Lucy what had happened during her absence. It was a bleak afternoon in the beginning of December; in the next room lay Phyllis, cold and stiff and silent forever; and Lucy was drearily searching in a cupboard for certain mourning garments which hung there. But suddenly, from the darkness of the lowest shelf, something shone up at her, a white, shimmering object, lying coiled there like a snake.

It was Phyllis's splendid satin gown, which Gertrude had flung there on the fateful night, and, from sheer repugnance, had never disturbed.

"But you must send it back," Lucy said, when in a few broken words her sister had explained its presence in the cupboard.

Lucy was very pale and very serious. She gathered up the satin gown, which nothing could have induced Gertrude to touch, folded it neatly, and began looking about for brown paper in which to enclose it.

71. From Rossetti's "Jenny" again.

The ghastly humour of the little incident struck Gertrude. "There is some string in the studio," she said, half-ironically, and went back to her post in the chamber of death.

In her long narrow coffin lay Phyllis; beautiful and still, with flowers between her hands. She had drifted out of life quietly enough a few days before; tomorrow she would be lying under the newly-turned cemetery sods.

Gertrude stood a moment, looking down at the exquisite face. On the breast of the dead girl lay a mass of pale violets which Lord Watergate had sent the day before, and as Gertrude looked, there flashed through her mind, what had long since vanished from it, the recollection of Lord Watergate's peculiar interest in Phyllis.

It was explained now, she thought, as the image of another dead face floated before her vision. That also was the face of a woman, beautiful and frail; of a woman who had sinned. She had never seen the resemblance before; it was clear enough now.

Then she took up once again her watcher's seat at the bedside, and strove to banish thought.

To do and do and do; that is all that remains to one in a world where thinking, for all save a few chosen beings, must surely mean madness.

She had fallen into a half stupor, when she was aware of a subtle sense of discomfort creeping over her; of an odour, strong and sweet and indescribably hateful, floating around her like a winged nightmare. Opening her eyes with an effort, she saw Mrs. Maryon standing gravely at the foot of the bed, an enormous wreath of tuberose in her hand.

Gertrude rose from her seat.

"Who sent those flowers?" she said, sternly.

"A servant brought them; he mentioned no name, and there is no card attached."

The woman laid the wreath on the coverlet and discreetly withdrew.

Gertrude stood staring at the flowers, fascinated. In the first moment of the cold yet stifling fury which stole over her, she could have taken them in her hands and torn them petal from petal.

One instant, she had stretched out her hand towards them; the next, she had turned away, sick with the sense of impotence, of loathing, of immeasurable disdain.

What weapons could avail against the impenetrable hide of such a man?

"She never cared for him," a vindictive voice whispered to her from the depths of her heart.

Then she shrank back, afraid before the hatred which held possession of her soul. The passion which had animated her on the fateful evening of Phyllis's flight, the very strength which had caused her to prevail, seemed to her fearful and hideous things. She would fain have put the thought of them away; have banished them and all recollection of Darrell from her mind forever.

It was a bleak December morning, with a touch of east wind in the air, when Phyllis was laid in her last resting place.

To Gertrude all the sickening details of the little pageant were as the shadows of a nightmare. Standing rigid as a statue by the open grave, she was aware of nothing but the sweet, stifling fragrance of tuberose, which seemed to have detached itself from, and prevailed over, the softer scents of rose and violet, and to float up unmixed from the flower-covered coffin.

Lucy stood on one side of her, silent and pale with down-dropped eyes; Fanny sobbed vociferously on the other. Lord Watergate faced them with bent head. The tears rolled down Fred Devonshire's face as the burial service proceeded. Aunt Caroline looked like a vindictive ghost. Uncle Septimus wept silently.

It seemed a hideous act of cruelty to turn away at last and leave the poor child lying there alone, while the sexton shovelled the loose earth on to her coffin; hideous, but inevitable; and at midday Gertrude and Lucy drove back in the dismal coach to Baker Street, where Mr. Maryon had put up alternate shutters in the shop window, and the umbrella-maker had drawn down his blinds.

Gertrude, as she lay awake that night, heard the rain beating against the windowpanes, and shuddered.

Chapter 22
Hope And A Friend

Alas, I have grieved so I am hard to love.
SONNETS FROM THE PORTUGUESE[72]

Gertrude was sitting by the window with Constance Devonshire one bleak January afternoon.

Conny's face wore a softened look. The fierce, rebellious misery of her heart had given place to a gentler grief, the natural human sorrow for the dead.

This was a farewell visit. The next day she and her family were setting out for the South of France.

"I tried to make Fred come with me today," Constance was saying; "but he is dining with some kindred spirits at the Café Royal, and then going on to the Gaiety. He said there would be no time."

Fred had been once to Baker Street since the unfortunate interview with Lucy; had paid a brief visit of condolence, when he had been very much on his dignity and very afraid of meeting Lucy's eye. The re-establishment of the old relations was not more possible than it usually is in such cases.

72. From Barrett Browning's *Sonnets from the Portuguese* (1850).

"How long do you expect to be at Cannes?" Gertrude said, after one of the pauses, which kept on stretching themselves baldly across the conversation.

"Till the end of March, probably. Isn't Lucy coming up to say 'goodbye' to a fellow?"

"She will be up soon. She is much distressed about the overexposure of some plates, and is trying to remedy the misfortune. Do you know, by the by, that we are thinking of taking an apprentice? Mr. Russel has found a girl – a lady – who will pay us a premium, and probably live with us."

"I think that is a good plan," said Conny, staring wistfully out of the window.

How strange it seemed, after all that had happened, to be sitting here quietly, talking about overexposed negatives, premiums, and apprentices.

Looking out into the familiar street, with its teeming memories of a vivid life now quenched forever, she said to herself, as Gertrude had often said: "It is not possible."

One day, surely, the door would open to give egress to the well-known figure; one day they would hear his footstep on the stairs, his voice in the little room. Even as the thought struck her, Constance was aware of a sound as of someone ascending, and started with a sudden beating of the heart.

The next moment, Matilda flung open the door, and Lord Watergate came, unannounced, into the room.

Gertrude rose gravely to meet him.

Since the accident, which had brought him into such intimate connection with the Lorimers' affairs, his kindness had been as unremitting as it had been unobtrusive.

Gertrude had several times reproached herself for taking it as a matter of course; for being roused to no keener fervour of gratitude; yet something in his attitude seemed to preclude all expression of commonplaces.

It was no personal favour that he offered. To stretch out one's hand to a drowning creature is no act of gallantry; it is but recognition of a natural human obligation.

Lord Watergate took a seat between the two girls, and, after a few remarks, Constance declared her intention of seeking Lucy in the studio.

"Tell Lucy to come up when she has soaked her plates to her satisfaction," said Gertrude, a little vexed at this desertion.

To have passed through such experiences together as she and Lord Watergate, makes the casual relations of life more difficult. These two people, to all intents and purposes strangers, had been together in those rare moments of life when the elaborate paraphernalia of everyday intercourse is thrown aside; when soul looks straight to soul through no intervening veil; when human voice answers human voice through no medium of an actor's mask.

We lose with our youth the blushes, the hesitations, the distressing outward marks of embarrassment; but, perhaps, with most of us, the shyness, as it recedes from the surface, only sinks deeper into the soul.

As the door closed on Constance, Lord Watergate turned to Gertrude.

"Miss Lorimer," he said, "I am afraid your powers of endurance have to be further tried."

"What is it?" she said, while a listless incredulity that anything could matter to her now stole over her, dispersing the momentary cloud of self-consciousness.

Lord Watergate leaned forward, regarding her earnestly.

"There has been news," he said, slowly, "of poor young Jermyn."

Gertrude started.

"You mean," she said, "that they have found him – that there is no doubt."

"On the contrary; there is every doubt."

She looked at him bewildered.

"Miss Lorimer, there is, I am afraid, much cruel suspense in store for you, and possibly to no purpose. I came here today to prepare you for what you will hear soon enough. I chanced to learn from official quarters what will be in every paper in England tomorrow. There is a rumour that Jermyn has been seen alive."

"Lord Watergate!" Gertrude sprang to her feet, trembling in every limb.

He rose also, and continued, his eyes resting on her face meanwhile: –

"Native messengers have arrived at head-quarters from the interior, giving an account of two Englishmen, who, they say, are living as prisoners in one of the hostile towns. The descriptions of these prisoners correspond to those of Steele and Jermyn."

"Lucy!" came faintly from Gertrude's lips.

"It is chiefly for your sister's sake that I have come here. The rumour will be all over the town tomorrow. Had you not better prepare her for this, at the same time impressing on her the extreme probability of its baselessness?"

"I wish it could be kept from her altogether."

"Perhaps even that might be managed until further confirmation arrives. I cannot conceal from you that at present I attach little value to it. It was in the nature of things that such a rumour should arise; neither of the poor fellows having actually been seen dead."

"What steps will be taken?" asked Gertrude, after a pause. She had not the slightest belief that Frank would ever be among them again; she and Lucy had gone over forever to the great majority of the unfortunate.

"A rescue party is to be organised at once. The war being practically at an end, it would probably resolve itself into a case of ransom, if there were any truth in the whole thing. I may be in possession of further news a little before the newspapers. Needless to say, that I shall bring it here at once."

He took up his hat and stood a moment looking down at her.

"Lord Watergate, we do not even attempt to thank you for your kindness."

"I have been able, unfortunately, to do so little for you. I wish today that I had come to you as the bringer of good tidings; I am destined, it seems, to be your bird of ill-omen."

He dropped his eyes suddenly, and Gertrude turned away her face. A pause fell between them; then she said –

"Will it be long before news of any reliability can reach us?"

"I cannot tell; it may be a matter of days, of weeks, or even months."

"I fear it will be impossible to keep the rumour from my poor Lucy."

"I am afraid so. I trust to you to save her from false hopes."

"So I am to be Cassandra," thought Gertrude, a little wistfully. She was always having some hideous *rôle* or other thrust upon her.

Lord Watergate moved towards the door.

A sudden revulsion of feeling came over her.

"Perhaps," she said, "it is true."

He caught her mood. "Perhaps it is."

They stood smiling at one another like two children.

Constance Devonshire coming upstairs a few minutes later found Gertrude standing alone in the middle of the room, a vague smile playing about her face. A suspicion that was not new gathered force in Conny's mind. Going up to her friend, she said, with meaning –

"Gerty, what has Lord Watergate been saying to you?"

"Conny, Conny, can you keep a secret?"

And then Gertrude told her of the new hope, vague and sweet and perilous, which Lord Watergate had brought with him.

"But it is true, Gerty; it really is," Conny said, while the tears poured down her cheeks; "I have always known that the other thing was not possible. Oh, Gerty, just to see him, just to know he is alive – will not that be enough to last one all the days of one's life?"

But this mood of impersonal exaltation faded a little when Constance went back to Queen's Gate, where everything was in a state of readiness for the projected flitting. She lay awake, sobbing with mingled feelings half through the night.

"Even Gerty," she thought; "I am going to lose her too." For she remembered the smile in Gertrude's eyes that afternoon when she had found her standing alone after Lord Watergate's visit; a smile to which she chose to attach meanings which concerned the happiness of neither Frank nor Lucy.

Chapter 23
A Dismissal

O thou of little faith, what hast thou done?[73]

Lucy has always since maintained that the days which followed Lord Watergate's communication were the very worst that she ever went through. The fluctuations of hope and fear, the delays, the prolonged strain of uncertainty coming upon her afresh, after all that had already been endured, could be nothing less than torture even to a person of her well-balanced and well-regulated temperament.

"To have to bear it all for the second time," thought poor Gertrude, whose efforts to spare her sister could not, in the nature of things, be very successful.

A terrible fear that Lucy would break down altogether and slip from her grasp haunted her night and day. The world seemed to her peopled with shadows, which she could do nothing more than clutch at as they passed by, she herself the only creature of any permanence of them all. But gradually the tremulous, flickering flame of hope grew brighter and steadier; then changed into a glad certainty. And one wonderful day, towards the end of March, Frank was with them

73. Both New (*The Complete Novels*, 543 n. 68) and Bernstein (*The Romance of a Shop*, 185 n. 1) rightly point to the basis of the quotation, Matthew 14:31, but it is actually from Clough's *Dipsychus* (1850).

once more: Frank, thinner and browner perhaps, but in no respect the worse for his experiences; Frank, as they had always known him – kind and cheery and sympathetic; with the old charming confidence in being cared for.

"And I was not there," he cried, regretful, self-reproachful, when Lucy had told him the details of their sad story.

"I thought always, 'If Frank were here!'"

"I think I should have killed him," said Frank, in all sincerity; and Lucy drew closer to him, grateful for the non-fulfilment of her wish.

They were standing together in the studio. It was the day after Jermyn's return, and Gertrude was sitting listlessly upstairs, her busy hands for once idle in her lap. In a few days April would have come round again for the second time since their father's death.

What a lifetime of experience had been compressed into those two years, she thought, her apathetic eyes mechanically following the green garment of the high school mistress, as she whisked past down the street.

She knew that it is often so in human life – a rapid succession of events; a vivid concentration of every sort of experience in a brief space; then long, grey stretches of eventless calm. She knew also how it is when events, for good or evil, rain down thus on any group of persons. The majority are borne to new spheres, for them the face of things has changed completely. But nearly always there is one, at least, who, after the storm is over, finds himself stranded and desolate, no further advanced on his journey than before.

The lightning has not smitten him, nor the waters drowned him, nor has any stranger vessel borne him to other shores. He is only battered, and shattered, and weary with the struggle; has lost, perhaps, all he cared for, and is permanently disabled for further travelling. Gertrude smiled to herself as she pursued the little metaphor, then, rising, walked across the room to the mirror which hung above the mantelpiece. As her eye fell on her own reflection, she remembered Lucy Snowe's words –

"I saw myself in the glass, in my mourning dress, a faded, hollow-eyed vision. Yet I thought little of the wan spectacle.... I still felt life at life's sources."[74]

That was the worst of it; one was so terribly vital. Inconceivable as it seemed, she knew that one day she would be up again, fighting the old fight, not only for existence, but for happiness itself. She was only twenty-five when all was said; much lay, indeed, behind her, but there was still the greater part of her life to be lived.

She started a little as the handle of the door turned, and Mrs. Maryon announced Lord Watergate. She gave him her hand with a little smile: "Have you been in the studio?" she said, as they both seated themselves.

"Yes; Jermyn opened the door himself, and insisted on my coming in, though, to tell you the truth, I should have hesitated about entering had I had any choice in the matter – which I hadn't."

"Lucy has picked up wonderfully, hasn't she?"

"She looks her old self already. Jermyn tells me they are to be married almost immediately."

"Yes. I suppose they told you also that Lucy is going to carry on the business afterwards."

"In the old place?"

"No. We have got rid of the rest of the lease, and they propose moving into some place where studios for both of them can be arranged."

"And you?"

"It is uncertain. I think Lucy will want me for the photography."

"Miss Lorimer, first of all you must do something to get well. You will break down altogether if you don't."

Something in the tone of the blunt words startled her; she turned away, a nameless terror taking possession of her.

"Oh, I shall be all right after a little holiday."

---

74. From Charlotte Brontë's (1816–1855) *Villette* (1853); see New, ed., *The Complete Novels*, 543 n. 69; Bernstein, ed., *The Romance of a Shop*, 186, n. 1.

"You have been looking after everybody else; doing everybody's work, bearing everybody's troubles." He stopped short suddenly, and added, with less earnestness, "*Quis custodet custodiem*? Do you know any Latin, Miss Lorimer?"

She rose involuntarily; then stood rather helplessly before him. It was ridiculous that these two clever people should be so shy and awkward; those others down below in the studio had never undergone any such uncomfortable experience; but then neither had had to graft the new happiness on an old sorrow; for neither had the shadow of memory darkened hope.

Gertrude went over to the mantelshelf, and began mechanically arranging some flowers in a vase. For once, she found Lord Watergate's presence disturbing and distressing; she was confused, unhappy, distrustful of herself; she wished when she turned her head that she would find him gone. But he was standing near her, a look of perplexity, of trouble, in his face.

"Miss Lorimer," he said, and there was no mistaking the note in his voice, "have I come too soon? Is it too soon for me to speak?"

She was overwhelmed, astonished, infinitely agitated. Her soul shrank back afraid. What had the closer human relations ever brought her but sorrow unutterable, unending? Some blind instinct within her prompted her words, as she said, lifting her head, with the attitude of one who would avert an impending blow –

"Oh, it is too soon, too soon."

He stood a moment looking at her with his deep eyes.

"I shall come back," he said.

"No, oh, no!"

She hid her face in her hands, and bent her head to the marble. What he offered was not for her; for other women, for happier women, for better women, perhaps, but not for her.

When she raised her head, he was gone.

The momentary, unreasonable agitation passed away from her, leaving her cold as a stone, and she knew what she had done. By a lightning flash, her own heart stood revealed to her. How incredible it seemed, but she knew that it was true: all this dreary time, when the personal thought had seemed so far away from her, her greatest personal experience had been silently growing up – no gourd of a night, but a tree to last through the ages. She, who had been so strong for others, had failed miserably for herself.

Love and happiness had come to her open-handed, and she had sent them away. Love and happiness? Oh, those will o' the wisps had danced ere this before her cheated sight. Love and happiness? Say rather, pity and a mild peace. It is not love that lets himself be so easily denied.

Happiness? That was not for such as she; but peace, it would have come in time; now it was possible that it would never come at all.

All the springs of her being had seemed for so long to be frozen at their source; now, in this one brief moment of exaltation, half-rapture, half-despair, the ice melted, and her heart was flooded with the stream.

Covering her face with her hands, she knelt by his empty chair, and a great cry rose up from her soul: – the human cry for happiness – the woman's cry for love.

Chapter 24
At Last

We sat when shadows darken,
And let the shadows be;
Each was a soul to hearken,
Devoid of eyes to see.

You came at dusk to find me;
I knew you well enough....
Oh, Lights that dazzle and blind me –
It is no friend, but Love!

A. MARY F. ROBINSON[75]

Hotel Prince de Galles, Cannes,
April 27th

My dearest Gerty, you shall have a letter today, though it is more than you deserve. Why do you never write to me? Now that you have safely married your young people, you have positively no excuse. By the by, the poor innocent mater read the announcement of the wedding out loud at breakfast today. Fred got crimson and choked in his coffee, and I had a silent fit of laughter. However, he is all right

75. From Agnes Mary Frances Robinson's (1857–1944) poem, "Love Without Wings."

by now, playing tennis with a mature lady with yellow hair, whom he much affects, and whom Papa scornfully denominates a "hotel hack."

All this, let me tell you, is preliminary. I have a piece of news for you, but somehow it won't come out. Not that it is anything to be ashamed of. The fact is, Gerty, I am going the way of all flesh, and am about to be married. Believe me, it is the most sensible course for a woman to take. I hope you will follow my good example.

Do you remember Sapho's words: "J'ai tant aimé; J'ai besoin d'être aimée?"[76] Do not let the quotation shock you; neither take it too seriously. I think Mr. Graham – you know Lawrence Graham? – does care as caring goes and as men go. He came out here, on purpose, a fortnight ago, and yesterday we settled it between us…"

Gertrude read no further; the thin, closely-written sheet fell from her hand; she sat staring vaguely before her.

Conny's letter, with its cheerfulness, partly real, partly affected, hurt her taste, and depressed her rather unreasonably.

This was the hardest feature of her lot: for the people she loved, the people who had looked up to her, she had been able to do nothing at all.

She was sitting alone in the dismantled studio on this last day of April. Tomorrow Lucy and Frank would have returned from Cornwall, and have taken possession of the new home.

Her own plans for the present were vague.

One of her stories, after various journeys to editorial offices, had at last come back to her in the form of proof, supplemented, moreover, by what seemed to her a handsome cheque.

She had arranged, on the strength of this, to visit a friend in Florence, for some months; after that period she would in all probability take part with Lucy in the photography business.

There was no fire lighted, and the sun, which in the earlier part of the day had warmed the room, had set. Most of the furniture and

---

76. According to both Bernstein and New, Levy's source is Daudet's *Sapho* (1884); Bernstein's translation is as follows: "'I have loved so much; I have need to be loved'" (*The Romance of a Shop*, 189 n. 2; New, ed., *The Complete Novels*, 543 n. 72).

properties had already gone to the new studio, but some yet remained, massed and piled in the gloom.

The black signboard, with its gold lettering, stood upright and forlorn in a corner, as though conscious that its day was over forever. Gertrude had been busying herself with turning out a cupboard, but the light had failed, and she had ceased from her work.

A very dark hour came to Gertrude, crouching there in the dusk and cold, amid the dismantled workshop which seemed to symbolize her own life.

She, who held unhappiness ignoble and cynicism a poor thing, had lost for the moment all joy of living and all belief. The little erection of philosophy, of hope, of self-reliance, which she had been at such pains to build, seemed to be crumbling about her ears; all the struggles and sacrifices of life looked vain things. What had life brought her, but disillusion, bitterness, an added sense of weakness?

She rose at last and paced the room.

"This will pass," she said to herself; "I am out of sorts; and it is not to be wondered at."

She sat down in the one empty chair the room contained, and leaning her head on her hand, let her thoughts wander at will.

Her eyes roved about the little dusky room which was so full of memories for her. Shadows peopled it; dream-voices filled it with sound.

Lucy and Phyllis and Frank moved hither and thither with jest and laughter. Fanny was there too, tampering amiably with the apparatus; and Darrell looked at her once with cold eyes, although, indeed, he had been a rare visitor at the studio.

Then all these phantoms faded, and she seemed to see another in their stead; a man, tall and strong, his face full of anger and sorrow – Lord Watergate, as he had been on that never-forgotten night. Then the anger and sorrow faded from his face, and she read there nothing but love – love for herself shining from his eyes.

Then she hid her face, ashamed.

What must he think of her? Perhaps that she scorned his gift, did not understand its value; had therefore withdrawn it in disdain.

Oh, if only she could tell him this: that it was her very sense of the greatness of what he offered that had made her tremble, turn away and reject it. One does not stretch out the hand eagerly for so great a gift.

She had told him not to return and he had taken her at her word. She was paying the penalty, which her sex always pays one way or another, for her struggles for strength and independence. She was denied, she told herself with a touch of rueful humour, the gracious feminine privilege of changing her mind.

Lord Watergate might have loved her more if he had respected her less, or at least allowed for a little feminine waywardness. Like the rest of the world, he had failed to understand her, to see how weak she was, for all her struggles to be strong.

She pushed back the hair from her forehead with the old resolute gesture. Well, she must learn to be strong in earnest now; the thews and sinews of the soul, the moral muscles, grow with practice, no less than those of the body. She must not sit here brooding, but must rise and fight the Fates.

Hitherto, perhaps, life had been nothing but failures, but mistakes. It was quite possible that the future held nothing better in store for her. That was not the question; all that concerned her was to fight the fight.

She lit a solitary candle, and began sorting some papers and prints on the table near.

"If he had cared," her thoughts ran on, "he would have come back in spite of everything."

Doubtless it had been a mere passing impulse of compassion which had prompted his words, and he had caught eagerly at her dismissal of him. Or was it all a delusion on her part? That brief, rapid moment, when he had spoken, had it ever existed save in her own imagination? Worst thought of all, a thought which made her cheek burn scarlet in the solitude, had she misinterpreted some simple expression of kindness, some frank avowal of sympathy; had she indeed refused what had never been offered?

She felt very lonely as she lingered there in the gloom, trying to accustom herself in thought to the long years of solitude, of dreariness, which she saw stretching out before her.

The world, even when represented by her best friends, had labelled her a strong-minded woman. By universal consent she had been cast for the part, and perforce must go through with it.

She heard steps coming up the Virginia cork passage and concluded that Mrs. Maryon was bringing her an expected postcard from Lucy.

"Come in," she said, not raising her head from the table.

The person who had come in was not, however, Mrs. Maryon.

He came up to the table with its solitary candle and faced her.

When she saw who it was her heart stood still; then in one brief moment the face of the universe had changed for her forever.

"Lord Watergate!"

"I said I would come again. I have come in spite of you. You will not tell me that I come too soon, or in vain?"

"You must not think that I did not value what you offered me," she said simply, though her voice shook; "that I did not think myself deeply honoured. But I was afraid – I have suffered very much."

"And I.... Oh, Gertrude, my poor child, and I have left you all this time."

For the light, flickering upwards, had shown him her weary, haggard face; had shown him also the pathetic look of her eyes as they yearned towards him in entreaty, in reliance, – in love.

He had taken her in his arms, without explanation or apology, holding her to his breast as one holds a tired child.

And she, looking up into his face, into the lucid depths of his eyes, felt all that was mean and petty and bitter in life fade away into nothingness; while all that was good and great and beautiful gathered new meaning and became the sole realities.

Epilogue

There is little more to tell of the people who have figured in this story.

Fanny continues to flourish at Notting Hill, the absence of children being the one drop in her cup and that of her husband.

"But, perhaps," as Lucy privately remarks, "it is as well; for I don't think the Marshes would have understood how to bring up a child."

For Lucy, in common with all young matrons of the day, has decided views on matters concerned with the mental, moral, and physical culture of the young. Unlike many thinkers, she does not hesitate to put her theories into practice, and the two small occupants of her nursery bear witness to excellent training.

The photography, however, has not been crowded out by domestic duties; and no infant with pretensions to fashion omits to present itself before Mrs. Jermyn's lens. Lucy has succumbed to the modern practice of specialising, and only the other day carried off a medal for photographs of young children from an industrial exhibition. Her husband is no less successful in his own line. Having permanently abandoned the paintbrush for the needle, he bids fair to take a high place among the black and white artists of the day.

The Watergates have also an addition to their household, in the shape of a stout person with rosy cheeks and stiff white petticoats, who receives a great deal of attention from his parents. Gertrude wonders if he will prove to have inherited his father's scientific tastes, or the literary tendencies of his mother. She devoutly hopes that it is the former.

Conny flourishes as a married woman no less than as a girl. She and the Jermyns dine out now and then at one another's houses; her old affection for Gertrude continues, in spite of the fact that their respective husbands are quite unable (as she says) to hit it off.

Fred has not yet married; but there is no reason to believe him inconsolable. It is rather the embarrassment of choice than any other motive which keeps him single.

Aunt Caroline, having married all her daughters to her satisfaction, continues to reign supreme in certain circles at Lancaster Gate. She speaks with the greatest respect of her niece, Lady Watergate, though she has been heard to comment unfavourably on the shabbiness of the furniture in Sussex Place.

As for Darrell, shortly after Phyllis's death, he went to India at the invitation of the Viceroy and remained there nearly two years.

It was only the other day that the Watergates came face to face with him. It was at a big dinner, where the most distinguished representatives of art and science and literature were met. Gertrude turned pale when she saw him, losing the thread of her discourse, and her appetite, despite her husband's reassuring glances down the table.

But Darrell went on eating his dinner and looking into his neighbour's eyes, in apparent unconsciousness of, or unconcern at, the Watergates' proximity.

The Maryons continue in the old premises, increasing their balance at the banker's and enlarging their experience of life.

The Photographic Studio is let to an enterprising young photographer, who has enlarged and beautified it beyond recognition.

As for the rooms above the umbrella-maker's: the sitting room facing the street; the three-cornered kitchen behind; the three little bedrooms beyond; – when last I passed the house they were to let unfurnished, with great fly-blown bills in the blank casements.

THE END

Reuben Sachs: A Sketch
(1888)

Chapter 1

This is my beloved Son.[1]

Reuben Sachs was the pride of his family.

After a highly successful career at one of the great London day-schools, he had gone up on a scholarship to the University, where, if indeed he had chosen to turn aside from the beaten paths of academic distinction, he had made good use of his time in more ways than one.

The fact that he was a Jew had proved no bar to his popularity; he had gained many desirable friends and had, to some extent, shaken off the provincialism inevitable to one born and bred in the Jewish community.

At the bar, to which in due course he was called, his usual good fortune did not desert him.

Before he was twenty-five, he had begun to be spoken of as "ris ing"; and at twenty-six, by unsuccessfully contesting a hard-fought

1. This quotation from Matthew 3:17/17:5, Mark 9:7, Luke 9:35, 2 Peter 1:17 (see also Mark 1:11, Luke 3:22) is possibly the most significant moment in *Reuben Sachs* in establishing a narrator who, for Cynthia Scheinberg, "seems fully connected to a Christian literary tradition" (see "Canonizing the Jew: Amy Levy's Challenge to Victorian Poetic Identity," *Victorian Studies* 39 (1996): 181). Similarly, for Susan David Bernstein, ed., the quotation "implies that any depiction of Jewish culture and religion is necessarily framed through Christian texts and gentile perspectives" ("Introduction," in *Reuben Sachs,* by Amy

election, had attracted to himself attention of another sort. He had no objection, he said, to the woolsack; but a career of political distinction was growing slowly but surely to be his leading aim in life.

"He will never starve," said his mother, shrugging her shoulders with a comfortable consciousness of safe investments; "and he must marry money. But Reuben can be trusted to do nothing rash." In the midst of so much that was highly promising, his health had broken down suddenly, and he had gone off grumbling to the antipodes.

It was a case of over-work, of over-strain, of nervous breakdown, said the doctors; no doubt a sea voyage would set him right again, but he must be careful of himself in the future.

"More than half my nervous patients are recruited from the ranks of the Jews," said the great physician whom Reuben consulted. "You pay the penalty of too high a civilization."

"On the other hand," Reuben answered, "we never die; so we may be said to have our compensations."

Reuben's father had not borne out his son's theory; he had died many years before my story opens, greatly to his own surprise and that of a family which could boast more than one nonagenarian in a generation.

He had left his wife and children well provided for, and the house in Lancaster Gate was rich in material comfort.

Levy (Peterborough: Broadview Editions, 2006), 34). Moreover, for Linda Hunt Beckman, the novel, "rather than photographing reality, draws on ideas and uses words that inescapably reproduce meanings that result from the way these ideas and words have been used by other users of the language in the past" (*Amy Levy: Her Life and Letters* (Athens: Ohio University Press, 2000), 173). Indeed, Levy clearly hoped that readers would pick up on the fact that the narrator tells the story through the lens of Christian biblical tradition. For other annotated versions of *Reuben Sachs* see Bernstein's comprehensive *Rueben Sachs*, 55–157, and Melvyn New's *The Complete Novels and Selected Writings of Amy Levy 1861–1889* (Gainesville: University Press of Florida, 1993), 197–293.

In the drawing room of this house, Mrs. Sachs and her daughter were sitting on the day of Reuben's return from his six months' absence.

He had arrived early in the day, and was now sleeping off the effects of a night passed in travelling, and of the plentiful supply of fatted calf with which he had been welcomed.

His devoted womankind meanwhile sipped their tea in the fading light of the September afternoon, and talked over the event of the day in the rapid, nervous tones peculiar to them.

Mrs. Sachs was an elderly woman, stout and short, with a wide, sallow, impassive face, lighted up by occasional gleams of shrewdness from a pair of half-shut eyes.

An indescribable air of intense, but subdued vitality characterized her presence; she did not appear in good health, but you saw at a glance that this was an old lady whom it would be difficult to kill.

"He looks better, Addie, he looks very well indeed," she said, the dull red spot of colour on either sallow cheek alone testifying to her excitement.

"I have said all along," answered her daughter, "that if Reuben had been a poor man, the doctors would never have found out that he wanted a sea-voyage at all. Let us only hope that it has done him no harm professionally." She emptied her tea cup as she spoke, and cut herself a fresh slice of the rich cake which she was devouring with nervous voracity.

Adelaide Sachs, or to give her her right title, Mrs. Montague Cohen, was a thin, dark young woman of eight or nine-and-twenty, with a restless, eager, sallow face, and an abrupt manner. She was richly and very fashionably dressed in an unbecoming gown of green shot silk, and wore big diamond solitaires in her ears. She and her mother indeed were never seen without such jewels, which seemed to bear the same relation to their owners as his pigtail does to the Chinaman.

Adelaide was the eldest of the family; she had married young a husband chosen for her, with whom she lived with average contentment.

Reuben was scarcely two years her junior; no one cared to remember the age of Lionel, the youngest of the three, a hopeless ne'er-do-weel, who had with difficulty been relegated to an obscure colony.

"There is always either a ne'er-do-weel or an idiot in every Jewish family!" Esther Kohnthal[2] had remarked in one of her appalling bursts of candour.

The mother and daughter sat there in the growing dusk, amid the plush ottomans, stamped velvet tables, and other Philistine splendours of the large drawing room, till the lamp lighter came down the Bayswater Road and the gilt clock on the mantelpiece struck six.

Almost at the same moment, the door was flung open and a voice cried:

"Why *do* women invariably sit in the dark?"

It was a pleasant voice; to a fine ear, unmistakably the voice of a Jew, though the accents of the speaker were free from the cockney twang which marred the speech of the two women.

"Reuben! I thought you were asleep," cried his mother.

"So I was. Now I have arisen like a giant refreshed."

A man of middle height and slender build had made his way across the room to the window; his face was indistinct in the darkness as he stooped and put his arm caressingly about the broad, fat shoulder of his mother.

"Dressed for dinner already, Reuben?" was all she said, though the hard eye under the cautious old eyelid grew soft as she spoke.

Her love for this son and her pride in him were the passion of her life.

"Dinner? You are never going to kill the fatted calf twice over? But seriously, I must run down to the club for an hour or two. There may be letters."

He hesitated a moment, then added: "I shall look in at the Leunigers on my way back."

"The Leunigers!" cried Adelaide in open disapproval.

"Reuben, there's the old gentlemen. He won't like your going first to your cousins," said his mother.

---

2. On Esther Kohnthal as a reinterpretation of biblical Esther, see Richa Dwor, *Jewish Feeling: Difference and Affect in Nineteenth-Century Jewish Women's Writing* (London: Bloomsbury, 2017), 175–7.

"My grandfather? Oh, but my arrival isn't an official fact till tomorrow. We were sixteen hours before our time, remember. Goodbye, Addie. I suppose you and Monty will be dining in Portland Place tomorrow with the rest of us. What a gathering of the clans! Well, I must be off." And he suited the action to the word.

"Why on earth need he rush off like that to the Leunigers?" said Mrs. Cohen as she drew on her gloves.

Her mother looked across at her through the dusk.

"Reuben will do nothing rash," she said.

Chapter 2

Whatever my mood is, I love Piccadilly.

LONDON LYRICS[3]

Reuben Sachs stepped into the twilit street with a distinct sense of exhilaration.

He was back again; back to the old, full, strenuous life which was so dear to him; to the din and rush and struggle of the London which he loved with a passion that had something of poetry in it.

With the eager curiosity, the vivid interest in life, which underlay his rather impassive bearing, it was impossible that foreign travel should be without charm for him; but he returned with unmixed delight to his own haunts; to the work and the play; the marketplace, and the greetings in the marketplace; to the innumerable pleasantnesses of an existence which owed something of its piquancy to the fact that it was led partly in the democratic atmosphere of modern London, partly in the conservative precincts of the Jewish community.

Now as he lingered a moment on the pavement, looking up and down the road for a hansom, the light from the street lamp fell full upon him, revealing what the darkness of his mother's drawing room had previously hidden from sight.

He was, as I have said, of middle height and slender build. He wore good clothes, but they could not disguise the fact that his

3. From Frederick Locker-Lampson's poem, "Piccadilly," in *London Lyrics* (1857).

figure was bad, and his movements awkward; unmistakably the figure and movements of a Jew.

And his features, without presenting any marked national trait, bespoke no less clearly his Semitic origin.

His complexion was of a dark pallor; the hair, small moustache and eyes, dark, with red lights in them; over these last the lids were drooping, and the whole face wore for the moment a relaxed, dreamy, impassive air, curiously Eastern, and not wholly free from melancholy.

He walked slowly in the direction of an advancing hansom, hailed it quickly and quietly, and had himself driven off to Pall Mall. To every movement of the man clung that indescribable suggestion of an irrepressible vitality which was the leading characteristic of his mother.

There were several letters for him at the club; having discussed them, and been greeted by half a dozen men of his acquaintance, he dined lightly off a chop and a glass of claret, and gave himself up to what was apparently an exceedingly pleasant reverie.

The club where he sat was not, as he himself would have been the first to acknowledge, in the front rank of such institutions; but it was respectable and had its advantages. As for its drawbacks, supported by his sense of better things to come, Reuben Sachs could tolerate them.

It was nearly half past eight when Reuben's cab drew up before the Leunigers' house in Kensington Palace Gardens, where a blaze of light from the lower windows told him that he had come on no vain errand.

Israel Leuniger had begun life as a clerk on the Stock Exchange, where he had been fortunate enough to find employment in the great broking firm of Sachs & Co. There, his undeniable business talents and devotion to his work had met with ample reward. He had advanced from one confidential post to another; after a successful speculation on his own account, had been admitted into partnership, and finally, like the industrious apprentice of the story books, had married his master's daughter.

In these days, the reins of government in Capel Court had fallen almost entirely into his hands. Solomon Sachs, though a wonderful man of his years, was too old for regular attendance in the city, while poor Kohnthal, the other member of the firm, and, like Leuniger, son-in-law to old Solomon, had been shut up in a madhouse for the last ten years and more.

As Reuben advanced into the large, heavily upholstered vestibule, one of the many surrounding doors opened slowly, and a woman emerged with a vague, uncertain movement into the light.

She might have been fifty years of age, perhaps more, perhaps less; her figure was slim as a girl's, but the dark hair, uncovered by a cap, was largely mixed with gray. The long, oval face was of a deep, unwholesome, sallow tinge; and from its haggard gloom looked out two dark, restless, miserable eyes; the eyes of a creature in pain. Her dress was rich but carelessly worn, and about her whole person was an air of neglect.

"Aunt Ada!" cried Reuben, going forward.

She rubbed her lean sallow hands together, saying in low, broken, lifeless tones: "We didn't expect you till tomorrow, Reuben. I hope your health has improved." This was quite a long speech for Mrs. Leuniger, who was of a monosyllabic habit.

Before Reuben could reply, the door opposite the one from which his aunt had emerged was flung open, and two little boys, dressed in sailor-suits, rushed into the hall.

One was dark, with bright black eyes; the other had a shock of flame-coloured hair, and pale, prominent eyes. "Reuben!" they cried in astonishment, and rushed upon their cousin.

"Lionel! Sidney!" protested their mother faintly as the boys proceeded to take all sorts of liberties with the new arrival.

The door by which they had come opened again, and a man's voice cried, half in fun:

"Why on earth are you youngsters making this confounded row? Be off to bed, or you'll be sorry for it!"

Reuben was standing under the light of a lamp, a smile on his face, as he lifted little red-haired Sidney from the ground and held him suspended by his wide sailor-collar.

"It's Reuben, old Reuben come back!" cried the children.

An exclamation followed; the door was flung open wide; Reuben set down the child with a laugh and passed into the lighted room.

Chapter 3

How should Love,
Whom the cross-lightnings of four chance-met eyes
Flash into fiery life from nothing, follow
Such dear familiarities of dawn?
Seldom; but when he does, Master of all.

AYLMER'S FIELD[4]

The Leunigers' drawing room, in which Reuben now found himself, was a spacious apartment, hung with primrose coloured satin, furnished throughout in impeccable Louis XV and lighted with incandescent gas from innumerable chandeliers and sconces. Beyond, divided by a plush-draped alcove, was a room of smaller size, where, at present, could be discerned the intent, Semitic faces of some half-dozen card-players.

In the front room, four or five young people in evening dress were grouped, but at Reuben's entrance they all came forward with various exclamations of greeting.

"Thought you weren't coming back till tomorrow!"

"I shouldn't have known you; you're as brown as a berry!"

"See the conquering hero comes!"

---

4. Alfred, Lord Tennyson's *Aylmer's Field* (1864).

This last from Rose Leuniger, a fat girl of twenty, in a tight-fitting blue silk dress, with the red hair and light eyes *à fleur de tête* of her little brother.

"I am awfully glad to see you looking so well," added Leopold Leuniger, the owner of the voice.

He was a short, slight person of one or two-and-twenty, with a picturesque head of markedly tribal character.

The dark, oval face, bright, melancholy eyes, alternately dreamy and shrewd; the charming, humorous smile, with its flash of white even teeth, might have belonged to some poet or musician, instead of to the son of a successful Jewish stockbroker.

By his side stood a small, dark, gnome-like creature, apparently entirely overpowered by the rich, untidy garments she was wearing. She was a girl, or woman, whose age it would be difficult to determine, with small, glittering eyes that outshone the diamonds in her ears.

Her trailing gown of heavy flowered brocade was made with an attempt at picturesqueness; an intention which was further evidenced by the studied untidiness of the tousled hair, and by the thick strings of amber coiled round the lean brown neck.

This was Esther Kohnthal, the only child of poor Kohnthal; and, according to her own account, the biggest heiress and the ugliest woman in all Bayswater.

Shuffling up awkwardly behind her came Ernest Leuniger, the eldest son of the house, of whom it would be unfair to say that he was an idiot. He was nervous, delicate; had a rooted aversion to society; and was obliged by his state of health to spend the greater part of his time in the country.

Esther used to shrug her shoulders and smile shrewdly and unpleasantly whenever this description of what she chose to consider the family skeleton was given out in her hearing; she told everyone, quite frankly, that her own father was in a madhouse.

Judith Quixano came up a little behind the others, with a hesitation in her manner which was new to her, and of which she herself was unconscious.

She was twenty-two years of age, in the very prime of her youth and beauty; a tall, regal-looking creature, with an exquisite dark head, features like those of a face cut on gem or cameo, and wonderful, lustrous, mournful eyes, entirely out of keeping with the accepted characteristics of their owner.

Her smooth, oval cheek glowed with a rich, yet subdued, hue of perfect health; and her tight-fitting fashionable white evening dress showed to advantage the generous lines of a figure which was distinguished for stateliness rather than grace.

Reuben Sachs had looked straight at this girl on entering the room; but he shook hands with her last of all, clasping her fingers closely and searching her face with his eyes. They were not cousins, her relationship to the Leunigers coming from the father's side; but there had always been between them a fiction of cousinship, which had made possible what is rare all the world over, but rarer than ever in the Jewish community – an intimacy between young people of opposite sexes.

"I thought I had better come while I could. We were before our time," said Reuben as they sat down, the whole party of them grouped close together, with the exception of Ernest, who returned to his solitaire board, a plaything which afforded him perpetual occupation. After several years of practice, he had never arrived at leaving the glass marble in solitary state on the board; but he lived in hopes.

"While you could! Before, in fact, fashion had again claimed Mr. Reuben Sachs for her own," cried Esther.

"I don't know about fashion," answered Reuben with perfect good temper; Esther was Esther, and if you began to mind what she said, you would never know where to stop; "but there are a hundred things to be attended to. I suppose everyone is going to the grandpater's feed tomorrow?"

Everyone was going; then, turning to Leo, Reuben said: "When do you go up?"

"Not till October 14th."

Leopold Leuniger was on the eve of his third year at Cambridge.[5]

"What have you been doing this long?"

"Oh ... staying about."

"Leo has been stopping with Lord Norwood, but we are not allowed to mention it," cried Rose in her loud, penetrating voice, "in case it should seem that we are proud."

Leo, who was passing through a sensitive phase of his growth, winced visibly, and Reuben said in a matter-of-fact way: "Oh, by the by, I came across a cousin of Lord Norwood's abroad – Lee-Harrison;[6] a curious fellow, but a good fellow."

"A howling swell," added Esther, "with a double-barrelled name."

"Exactly. But the point about him is that he has gone over body and soul to the Jewish community."

There was an ironical exclamation all round. The Jews, the most clannish and exclusive of peoples, the most keen to resent outside criticism, can say hard things of one another within the walls of the ghetto.

---

5. See Levy's "Cohen of Trinity" (pp. 832–40).
6. New speculated that in the comical figure of Bertie Lee-Harrison, "Levy is satirizing Eliot" ("Introduction," in *The Complete Novels*, 49 n. 57). However, Hunt Beckman suggests that "Levy may have had in mind Vernon Lee's brother Eugene Lee-Hamilton [1845–1907], whom she disliked, when she named this character" (*Amy Levy*, 310 n. 17). Hunt Beckman's speculation is supported by Levy's correspondence. Indeed, in a letter to her sister, Katie, Levy writes: "Lee-Hamilton has sent me his poems with a well-turned compliment scrawled on the fly-leaf. I called the other day, but thank God, he was out. However I have had a special request to go again. The poems are dreadful, I must look through them, I suppose, before I go" (quoted in Hunt Beckman, *Amy Levy*, 150, 269; see also Christine Pullen, *The Woman Who Dared: A Biography of Amy Levy* (Kingston: Kingston University Press, 2010), 139). Pullen (140) notes that Levy may have been the subject of Lee-Hamilton's romantic interest, pointing to a poem he wrote after her suicide entitled "Fumes of Charcoal": "Then let him ask: 'Oh Amy, in the land / Of the sweet light and of the sweet live air, / Did you ne'er sit beside a friend's wheeled bed, / That you could thus destroy, at Hell's command, / All that he envied you, and choke the fair / Young flame of life, to dwell with the wan dead?'" (quoted in *The Complete Novels*, ed. New, 56; see also Pullen, *The Woman Who Dared*, 140). See Eugene Lee-Hamilton's *Sonnets of the Wingless Hours* (Chicago: Stone & Kimball, 1894), 110–1.

"He says himself," went on Reuben, "that he has a taste for religion. I believe he flirted with the Holy Mother for some years, but didn't get caught. Then he joined a set of mystics, and lived for three months on a mountain, somewhere in Asia Minor. Now he has come round to thinking Judaism the one religion, and has been regularly received into the synagogue."[7]

"And expects, no doubt," said Esther, "to be rejoiced over as the one sinner that repenteth.[8] I hope you didn't shatter his illusions by telling him that he would more likely be considered a fool for his pains?"

Reuben laughed, and with an amused expression on his now animated face went on: "He has a seat in Berkeley Street, and a brand new *talith,* but still he is not happy. He complains that the Jews he meets in society are unsatisfactory; they have no local colour.[9] I said I thought I could promise him a little local colour; I hope to have the pleasure of introducing him to you all."

They all laughed with the exception of Rose, who said, rather offended: "I don't know about local colour. We don't wear turbans."[10]

---

7. Lee-Harrison is presented here "satirically" as a comic figure looking to find a suitable religion (Hunt Beckman, *Amy Levy,* 160). In the next line, Esther is in no doubt that Lee-Harrison will "be considered a fool," much to Reuben's amusement. Later, it is revealed that Lee-Hamilton had been "a High Churchman ..., and hardly knew a Jew from a Mohammedan" (p. 209).
8. From Luke 15:7, 15:10 (Bernstein, ed., *Reuben Sachs,* 64 n. 2). That Levy puts a Gospel reference into Esther's comment is significant in maintaining the notion that in literature "Jewish" characters are constructed according to prevalent "Christian" biblical, literary, and cultural discourses.
9. Levy's point here is that Lee-Harrison is seeking out a popular, mediatised construction of Jews and Judaism and that having a synagogue seat and wearing *talith* still does not match up to the stereotypes and caricatures prevalent in the literature of the period. It is only when Lee-Harrison meets Judith that his expectations are fulfilled. Indeed, according to Reuben, "He [Lee-Harrison] says you exactly fulfil his idea of Queen Esther" (p. 237).
10. Levy here is clearly pointing to an expectation constructed in contemporary literature that "Jews" will be exoticized, "Eastern," "Oriental," etc. (see Nadia Valman, *The Jewess in Nineteenth-Century British Culture* (Cambridge: Cambridge University Press, 2007), 4, 28, 116).

Reuben put back his head, laughing a little and seeking Judith's eyes for the answering smile he knew he should find there.

She had been keeping rather in the background tonight, quietly but intensely happy.

Reuben was back again! How delightfully familiar was every tone, every inflection of his voice! And how well she knew the changes of his face: the heavy dreaminess, the imperturbable air of Eastern gravity; then lo! the lifting of the mask; the flash and play of kindling features; the fire of speaking eyes; the hundred lights and shades of expression that she could so well interpret.

"What do his people say to it all?" asked Leo.

"Lee-Harrison's? Oh, I believe they take it very sensibly. They say it's only Bertie," answered Reuben, rising and holding out his hand to his uncle, who sauntered in from the card room.

He was a short, stout, red-haired man, closely resembling his daughter, and at the present moment, looked annoyed. The play was high and he had been losing heavily.

"Let's have some music, Leo," he said, flinging himself into an armchair at some distance from the young people. Rose, who was a skilled musician, went over to the piano, and Leopold took his violin from its case.

Reuben moved closer to Judith, and, under cover of the violin tuning, they exchanged a few words.

"I can't tell you how glad I am to get back."

"You look all the better for your trip. But you must take care and not overdo it again. It's bad policy."

"It is almost impossible not to."

"But those committees and meetings and things" (she smiled), "surely they might be cut down?"

"They are often very useful, indirectly, to a man in my position," answered Reuben, who had no intention of saying anything cynical.

There was a good deal of genuine benevolence in his nature, and an almost insatiable energy.

He took naturally to the modern forms of philanthropy: the committees, the classes, the concerts, and meetings. He found indeed that they had their uses, both social and political; higher motives for attending them were not wanting; and he liked them for their own sake besides. Outdoor sports he detested; the pleasures of dancing he had exhausted long ago; the practice of philanthropy provided a vent for his many-sided energies.

The tuning had come to an end by now, and the musicians had taken up their position.

Immediately silence fell upon the little audience, broken only by the click of counters, the crackle of a banknote in the room beyond; and the sound of Ernest's solitaire balls as they dropped into their holes.

Mrs. Leuniger, at the first notes of the tuning, had stolen in and taken up a position near the door; Esther had moved to a further corner of the room, where she lay buried in a deep lounge.

Then, all at once, the music broke forth. The great, vulgar, over-decorated room, with its garish lights, its stifling fumes of gas, was filled with the sound of dreams; and over the keen faces stole, like a softening mist, a faraway air of dreamy sensuousness. The long, delicate hands of the violinist, the dusky, sensitive face, as he bent lovingly over the instrument, seemed to vibrate with the strings over which he had such mastery.

The voice of a troubled soul cried out tonight in Leo's music, whose accents even the hard brilliance of his accompanist failed to drown.

As the bow was drawn across the strings for the last time, Ernest's solitaire board fell to the ground with a crash, the little balls of Venetian glass rolling audibly in every direction.

The spell was broken; everyone rose, and the card-players, who by this time were hungry, came strolling in from the other room.

Reuben found himself the centre of much handshaking and congratulation on his improved appearance. He was popular with his relatives, enjoying his popularity and accepting it gracefully.

"No airs, like that stuck up Leo," the aunts and uncles used to say.

"There's a spread in the dining room; won't you stay?" said Rose, as Reuben held out his hand in farewell.

"Not tonight." He turned last of all to Judith, who stood there silent, with smiling eyes.

"Tomorrow in Portland Place," he said, clasping her hand with lingering fingers.

As he walked home in the warm September night, he had for once neither ears nor eyes for the city pageant so dear to him.

He heard and saw nothing but the sound of Leo's violin, and the face of Judith Quixano.

Chapter 4

The full sum of me
Is an untutored girl, unschooled, unpractised.

MERCHANT OF VENICE

Judith Quixano had lived with the Leunigers ever since she was fifteen years old.

Her mother, Israel Leuniger's sister, had been thought to do very well for herself when she married Joshua Quixano, who came of a family of Portuguese merchants, the *vieille noblesse* of the Jewish community.

That was before the days of Leuniger's prosperity; now here, as elsewhere, the prestige of birth had dwindled, that of money had increased. The Quixanos were a large family, and they had grown poorer with the years; very gratefully did they welcome the offer of the rich uncle to adopt their eldest daughter.

So Judith had been borne away from the little crowded house in a dreary region lying somewhere between Westbourne Park and Maida Vale to the splendours of Kensington Palace Gardens.

Here she had shared everything with her cousin, Rose: the French and German governesses, the expensive music lessons, the useless, pretentious "finishing" lessons from innumerable masters.

Later on, the girls, who were about of an age, had gone together into such society as their set afforded; and here, again, no difference had been made between them. The gowns and bonnets of Rose were neither more splendid nor more abundant than those of her poor relation, nor her invitations to parties more numerous.

Rose, it is true, had a fortune of £50,000; but it was a matter of common knowledge that her uncle would settle £5000 on Judith when she married.

The cousins were good friends after a fashion. Rose was a materialist to her fingers' ends; she was lacking in the finer feelings, perhaps even in the finer honesties. But on the other hand, she was easy to live with, good-tempered, good-natured, high-spirited; qualities which cover a multitude of sins.

It will be seen that in their own fashion, and according to their own lights, the Leunigers had been very kind to Judith. She had no ground for complaint; nor indeed was there anything but gratitude in her thoughts of them. If, at times, she was discontented, she was only vaguely aware of her own discontent. To rail at fate, to cry out against the gods, were amusements she left to such people as Esther and Leo, for whom, in her quiet way, she had considerable contempt.

But the life, the position, the atmosphere, though she knew it not, were repressive ones. This woman, with her beauty, her intelligence, her power of feeling, saw herself merely as one of a vast crowd of girls awaiting their promotion by marriage.

She had, it is true, the advantage of good looks; on the other hand she was, comparatively speaking, portionless; and the marriageable Jew, as Esther was fond of saying, is even rarer and shyer than the marriageable Gentile.

To marry a Gentile would have been quite out of the question for her. Mr. Leuniger, thorough-going pagan as he was, would have set his foot mercilessly on such an arrangement; it would not have seemed to him respectable. He was no stickler for forms and ceremonies; though while old Solomon lived a certain amount of observance of them was necessary; you need only marry a Jew and be buried at Willesden or Ball's Pond; the rest would take care of itself.

But, her uncle's views apart, Judith's opportunities for uniting herself to an alien were small.

The Leunigers had of course their Gentile acquaintance, chiefly people of the sham "smart," pseudo-fashionable variety, whose parties at Bayswater or South Kensington they attended. But the business of their lives, its main interests, lay almost entirely within the tribal limits. It was as Hebrews of the Hebrews that Solomon Sachs and his son-in-law took their stand.

In the Community, with its innumerable trivial class differences, its sets within sets, its fine-drawn distinctions of caste, utterly incomprehensible to an outsider, they held a good, though not the best position. They were, as yet, socially on their promotion. The Sachses and the Leunigers, in their elder branches, troubled themselves, as we have seen, little enough about their relations to the outer world; but the younger members of the family, Reuben, Leo, even Adelaide and Esther in their own crude fashion, showed symptoms of a desire to strike out from the tribal duck pond into the wider and deeper waters of society. Such symptoms, their position and training considered, were of course, inevitable; and the elders looked on with pride and approval, not understanding indeed the full meaning of the change.

But as for Judith Quixano, and for many women placed as she, it is difficult to conceive a training, an existence, more curiously limited, more completely provincial than hers. Her outlook on life was of the narrowest; of the world, of London, of society beyond her own set, it may be said that she had seen nothing at first hand; had looked at it all, not with her own eyes, but with the eyes of Reuben Sachs.

She could scarcely remember the time when she and Reuben had not been friends. Ever since she was a little girl in the schoolroom, and he a charming lad in his first terms at the University, he had thought it worthwhile to talk to her, to confide to her his hopes, plans and ambitions; to direct her reading and lend her books.

Books were a luxury in the Leuniger household. We all have our economies, even the richest of us; and the Leunigers, who begrudged no money for food, clothes or furniture, who went constantly into the stalls of the theatre, without considering the expense, regarded every shilling spent on books as pure extravagance.

Reuben indeed was the only person who had any conception of Judith's possibilities, or, of those surrounding her, who even estimated at its full her rich and stately beauty. Their friendship, unusual enough in a society which retains, in relation to women at least, so many traces of orientalism, had sprung up at first unnoticed in the intimacy of family life.

It was not till the last year or two that it had attracted any serious attention. Adelaide Cohen openly did everything in her power to check it; and even Mrs. Sachs, with her rooted belief in her son's discretion, her conviction that he would never fail to act up to his creed of doing the very best for himself, grew anxious at times, and was almost glad of the chance which had sent him off to the antipodes.

Aloud to her daughter, she scouted the notion of any serious cause for alarm.

"It is for the girl's sake I am sorry. That sort of thing does a girl a great deal of harm. It is time she was married."

"She has no money. Very likely she won't marry at all," cried Adelaide, who was dyspeptic and subject to fits of bad temper.

Meanwhile Judith, acquiescent, receptive, appreciative, took the good things this friendship offered her, and shut her eyes to the future. Not, as she believed, that she ever for a moment deceived herself. That would scarcely have been possible in the atmosphere in which she breathed.

She had known from the beginning, how could she fail to know? That Reuben must do great things for himself in every relation of life; must ultimately climb to inaccessible heights where she could not hope to follow.

Her pride and her humility went hand in hand, and she prided herself on her own good sense which made any mistake in the matter impossible. And that he was so sensible, was what she particularly admired in Reuben.

Leo was clever, she knew; and Esther after a fashion; but these two people had an uncomfortable, eccentric, undignified method of setting about things, from the way they did their hair, upwards.

But Reuben had sacrificed none of his dignity as a human being to his cleverness; he was eminently normal, though cleverer than anyone she knew.

For the long-haired type of man, the professional person of genius, this thorough-going Philistine, this conservative ingrain, had no tolerance whatever. She never could understand the mania among some of the girls of her set, Rose Leuniger included, for the second-rate actors, musicians, and professional reciters with whom they came into occasional contact at parties.

She had, it is seen, distinct if unformulated notions as to the sanity of true genius.

And she herself? She was so sensible, oh, she was thoroughly sensible and matter-of-fact!

Esther fell in love half-a-dozen times a season, loudly bewailing herself throughout. Even Rose was not without her *affairs de coeur*; but she, Judith, was utterly free from such sentimental aberrations.

That was why perhaps a man like Reuben, who had not much opinion of women in general, considering them creatures easily snared, should find it possible to make a friend of her.

She understood perfectly Adelaide's snubs, Mrs. Sachs's repressive attitude, Esther's clumsily veiled warnings.

She understood and was indignant. Did they think her such a fool; a person incapable of friendship with a man without misinterpretation of his motives?

But Reuben knew that it was not so; and therein of course lay her strength and her consolation.

It was this openly matter-of-fact attitude of hers which had not only added piquancy to his intercourse with her, but had made Reuben less careful with her than he would otherwise have been.

He had no wish to hurt the girl, either as regarded her feelings or her prospects; nor was the danger, he told himself, a serious one.

She liked him immensely, of course, but she was unsentimental, like most women of her race, and would settle down happily enough when the time came.

He told himself these things with a secret, pleasant consciousness of a subtler element in their relationship; of unsounded depths in the nature of this girl who trusted him so completely, and whom he had so completely in hand. Nor did he hide from himself that she charmed him and pleased his taste as no other woman had ever done.

A man does not so easily deceive himself in these matters, and during the last year or two he had been fully aware of a quickening in his sentiments towards her.

Yes, Reuben knew by now that he was in love with Judith Quixano. The situation was full of delights, of dangers, of pains and pleasantnesses.

A disturbing element in the serene course of his existence, it added a charm to existence of which he was in no haste to be rid.

Chapter 5

Quand il pâlit un soir, et que sa voix tremblante
S'éteignit tout a coup dans un mot commencé;
Quand ses yeux, soulevant leur paupière brûlante,
Me blessèrent d'un mal dont je le crus blessé;
* * * * * * * *
Il n'aimait pas – j'aimais.

M. DESBORDES VALMORE[11]

Old Solomon Sachs awaited his guests in the drawing room of his house in Portland Place.

It was the night after Reuben's arrival, in honour of which the feast was given.

Such feasts were by no means rare events, the old man liking to assemble his family round him in true patriarchal fashion. As for the family, it always grumbled and always went.

He was a short, sturdy-looking man, with a flowing white beard, which added size to a head already out of all proportion to the rest of him. The enormous face was both powerful and shrewd; there was power too in the coarse, square hands, in the square, firmly-planted feet.

11. From Marceline Desbordes-Valmore's (1786–1859) "Souvenir" (1825); see New, ed., *The Complete Novels*, 544 n. 12; Bernstein, ed., *Reuben Sachs*, 72 n. 1.

You saw at a glance that he was blest with that fitness of which survival is the inevitable reward.[12]

He wore a skullcap, and, at the present moment, was pacing the room, performing what seemed to be an incantation in Hebrew below his breath.

As a matter of fact, he was saying his prayers, an occupation which helped him to get rid of a great deal of his time, which hung heavily on his hands, now that age had disabled him from active service on the Stock Exchange.

His daughter, Rebecca, a woman far advanced in middle-life, stitched drearily at some fancywork by the fire. She was unmarried, and hated the position with the frank hatred of the women of her race, for whom it is a peculiarly unenviable one.

Reuben's mother, her daughter and son-in-law, were the first to arrive.

Old Solomon shook hands with them, still continuing his muttered devotions, and they received in silence a greeting to which they were too much accustomed to consider in any way remarkable.

"Grandpapa saying his prayers," was an everyday phenomenon. Perhaps the younger members of the party remembered that it had never been allowed to interfere with the production of cake; the generous slices had not been less welcome from the fact that they must be eaten without acknowledgment.

Montague Cohen, Adelaide Sachs's husband, belonged to that rapidly dwindling section of the Community which attaches importance to the observation of the Mosaic and Rabbinical laws in various minute points.

He would have half-starved himself sooner than eat meat killed according to Gentile fashion, or leavened bread in the Passover week.

Adelaide chafed at the restrictions imposed by this constant making clean of the outside of the cup and platter; but it was a point on which her husband, amenable in everything else, remained firm.

12. Possible reference to Herbert Spencer's (1820–1903) term, "survival of the fittest," which was made popular in the context of social Darwinism (Bernstein, ed., *Reuben Sachs*, 72 n. 2).

He was an anaemic young man, destitute of the more brilliant qualities of his race, with a rooted belief in himself and everything that belonged to him.

He was proud of his house, his wife, and his children. He was proud, Heaven knows why, of his personal appearance, his mental qualities, and his sex; this last to an even greater extent than most men of his race, with whom pride of sex is a characteristic quality.

"Blessed art Thou, O Lord my God, who hast not made me a woman."[13]

No prayer goes up from the synagogue with greater fervour than this.

This fact notwithstanding, it must be acknowledged that, save in the one matter of religious observation, Montague Cohen was led by the nose by his wife, whose intelligence and vitality far exceeded his own. Borne along in her wake, he passed his life in pursuit of a shadow which is called social advancement; going uncomplainingly over quagmires, into stony places, up and down uncomfortable declivities; following patiently and faithfully wherever the restless energetic Adelaide led.

Esther and her mother were the next to arrive. Mrs. Kohnthal was old Solomon's eldest child, a stout, dark, exuberant-looking woman, between whom and her daughter was waged a constant feud.

The whole party of the Leunigers, with the exception of Ernest, who never dined out, was not long in following: Mrs. Leuniger, dejected, monosyllabic, untidy as usual; Mr. Leuniger, cheerful, pompous, important; Rose, loud-voiced, overdressed, good-tempered; Judith, blooming, stately, calm, in her fashionable gown, which assorted oddly, a close observer might have thought, with the exotic nature of her beauty. Leo dragged in mournfully in the rear of his party; he was in one of his worst moods. He hated these family gatherings, and had only been prevailed on with great difficulty to put in an appearance.

"We are all here," cried Adelaide, when greetings had been exchanged, "with the exception of the hero of the feast."

---

13. One of the traditional morning benedictions; see Esther Kohnthals' revision of the benediction on p. 272; see also Bernstein, ed., *Reuben Sachs*, 74 n. 1.

"Who has evidently," added Esther, "a sense of dramatic propriety."

"Reuben is at his club," explained Mrs. Sachs, looking under her eyelids at Judith, who had taken a seat opposite her.

She admired the girl immensely, and at the bottom of her heart was fond of her.

Judith, on her part, would have found it hard to define her feelings towards Mrs. Sachs.

With Reuben she was always calm; in his mother's presence she was conscious of a strange agitation, of the stirrings of an emotion which was neither love, nor hate, nor fear, but which perhaps was compounded of all three.

They had not long to wait before the door was thrown open and the person expected entered.

He came straight across the room to old Solomon, a vivifying presence – Reuben Sachs, with his bad figure, awkward movements, and charming face, which wore tonight its air of greatest alertness.

The old man, who had finished his prayers and taken off his cap, greeted the newcomer with something like emotion. Solomon Sachs, if report be true, had been a hard man in his dealings with the world; never overstepping the line of legal honesty, but taking an advantage wherever he could do so with impunity.

But to his own kindred he had always been generous; the ties of race, of family, were strong with him. His love for his children had been the romance of an eminently unromantic career; and the death of his favourite son, Reuben's father, had been a grief whose marks he would bear to his own dying day.

Something of the love for the father had been transferred to the son, and Reuben stood high in the old man's favour.

The greater subtlety of ambition which had made him while, comparatively speaking, a poor man, prefer the chances of a professional career to the certainties of a good berth in Capel Court, appealed to some kindred feeling, had set vibrating some responsive cord in his grandfather's breast. Such a personality as Reuben's seemed the crowning splendour of that structure of gold which it had been his lifework to build up; a luxury only to be afforded by the rich.

For poor Leo's attainments, his violin-playing, his classical scholarship, he had no respect whatever.

They went down to dinner without ceremony, taking their places, for the most part, as chance directed; Reuben sitting next to old Solomon, on the side of his best ear; Judith at the far end of the table opposite.

Conversation flagged, as it inevitably did at these family gatherings, until after the meal, when crabbed age and youth, separating by mutual consent, would grow loquacious enough in their respective circles.

Reuben, his voice raised, but not raised too much, for his grandfather's benefit, recounted the main incidents of his recent travels, while doing ample justice to the excellent meal set before him.

It might have been thought that he did not show to advantage under the circumstances; that his introduction of "good" names, and of his own familiarity with their bearers was a little too frequent, too obtrusive; that altogether there was an unpleasant flavour of brag about the whole narration.

Esther smiled meaningly and lifted her shoulders. Leo frowned and winced perceptibly, his taste offended to nausea; there were times when the coarser strands woven into the bright woof of his cousin's personality affected him like a harsh sound or evil odour.

But, these two cavillers apart, Reuben understood his audience.

Old Solomon listened attentively, nodding his great head from time to time with satisfaction; Mrs. Sachs, while apparently absorbed in her dinner, never lost a word of the beloved voice; Monty and Adelaide, who, when all is said, were naive creatures, were frankly impressed, and revelled in a sense of reflected glory.

As for Judith, shall it be blamed her if she saw no fault? She sat there silent, now and then lifting her eyes to the far-off corner of the table where Reuben was, divided between admiration and that unacknowledged sense of terror which came over her whenever the fact of Reuben's growing importance was brought home to her. Shall it be blamed her, I say, that she saw no fault, she who, where others were concerned, had sense of humour and critical faculty enough? Shall it be blamed her that she had a kindness for everything he said and everything he did; that he was the king and could do no wrong?

Only once during the meal did their eyes meet, then he smiled quietly, almost imperceptibly – a smile for her alone.

"Mr. Lee-Harrison," said Adelaide, stretching forward her sallow, eager, inquisitive face, on either side of which the diamonds shone like lamps, and plunging her dark, ring-laden fingers into a dish of olives as she spoke; "Mr. Lee-Harrison was staying at our hotel one year at Pontresina. He was a High Churchman in those days, and hardly knew a Jew from a Mohammedan."

"He is a cousin of Lord Norwood's," added Monty, who cultivated the acquaintance of the peerage through the pages of *Truth*.[14] After several years' study of that periodical he was beginning to feel on intimate terms with many of the distinguished people who figure weekly therein.

"A friend of yours, Leo!" cried Adelaide nodding across to her cousin.

She had a great respect for the lad, who affected to despise class distinctions, but succeeded in getting himself invited to such "good" houses.

"I know Lord Norwood," answered Leo with an impassive air, that caused Reuben to smile under his moustache.

"He was at this year's Academy private view, don't you remember, Monty, with that sister of his, Lady Geraldine?" went on Adelaide, undisturbed.

"They are both often to be seen at Sandown," chimed in the faithful Monty, "and at Kempton."

The Montague Cohens, those two indefatigable Peris at the gate,[15] patronized art, and never missed a private view; patronized the turf, and at every race-meeting, with any pretensions to "smartness," were familiar figures.

14. Newspaper.

15. Here, Levy refers to "Peris" in their mythological context, as being denied access to eschatological fulfillment.

There was but a brief separation of the sexes at the end of dinner, the whole party within a short space of time adjourning to the ugly, old-fashioned splendours of the drawing room, where card playing went on as usual.

A game of whist was got up among the elders for the benefit of old Solomon, the others preferring to embark on the excitements of Polish bank with the exception of Leo, who never played cards, and Judith, who was anxious to finish a piece of embroidery she was preparing for her mother's birthday.

Reuben, who had dutifully offered himself as a whist-player and been cut out, lingered a few moments, divided between the expediency of challenging fortune at Polish bank, and the pleasantness of joining the girlish figure at the far end of the room.

Adelaide, shuffling her cards with deft, accustomed fingers, looked up and read something of his indecision in her brother's face.

"There's a place here, Reuben," she called out, drawing her silken skirts from a chair on to which they had overflowed.

She was not a person of tact; her remark, and the tone of it, turned the balance.

"No, thanks," said Reuben, dropping his lids and assuming his most imperturbable air.

It was not his custom to single out Judith for his attentions at these family gatherings, but tonight some irresistible magnetism drew him towards her. It only wanted that little goad from Adelaide to send him deliberately to the ottoman where she sat at work, her beautiful head bent over the many-coloured embroidery.

Leo, lounging discontentedly a few paces off, with something of the air of a petulant child who is ashamed of itself, twisted a bit of silk in his long brown fingers and hummed the air of *Ich grolle nicht*[16] below his breath.

---

16. From Heinrich Heine's *Lyrisches Intermezzo* and put to song in Robert Schumann's (1810–1856) *Dichterliebe.* For the poem, see *The Complete Poems of Heinrich Heine: A Modern English Version*, ed. Hal Draper (Boston: Suhrkamp/Insel, 1982), 57.

"Judith," said Reuben, taking a seat very close beside her and looking straight at her face, "poor Ronaldson, the member for St. Baldwin's, is dangerously ill."

She looked up eagerly.

"Then you will be asked to stand?"

He smiled; partly at her readiness of comprehension, partly at the frank, feminine hard-heartedness which realizes nothing beyond the circle of its own affections.

"You mustn't kill him off in that summary fashion, poor fellow."

"I meant, of course, if he should die."

"Under those circumstances I believe they will ask me to stand. That's the beauty of you, Judith," he added, half-seriously, half jestingly, "one never has to waste one's breath with needless explanation."

She blushed, and smiled naively at the little compliment with its studied uncouthness.

There was something incongruous in the girl's rich and stately beauty, in the deep, serious gaze of the wonderful eyes, the severe, almost tragic lines of the head and face, with her total lack of manner, her little, abrupt, simple air, her apparent utter unconsciousness of her own value and importance as a young and beautiful woman.

"Judith is not a woman of the world, certainly," Reuben had said on one occasion, in reply to a criticism of his sister's; "but neither is she a bad imitation of one." And Adelaide, scenting a brotherly sarcasm, had allowed the subject to drop.

Leo, who had broken his bit of silk and hummed his song to the end, rose at this point, and went from the room without a word.

"Leo is in one of his moods," said Judith looking after him. "I am sure I don't know what is the matter with him."

Reuben, who understood perhaps more of Leopold's state of mind than anyone suspected, of the struggles with himself, the revolt against his surroundings which the lad was undergoing, answered slowly: "He is in a ticklish stage of his growth. Horribly unpleasant, I grant you. But I like the boy, though he regards me at present as an incarnation of the seven deadly sins."

"You know he is very fond of you."

"That may be. All the same, he thinks I keep a golden calf in my bedroom for purposes of devotion."

Judith laughed, and Reuben, his face very close to hers, said: "Can you keep *a* secret?"

"You know best."

"Well, that poor boy is head over heels in love with Lord Norwood's sister."

She looked up with her most matter-of-fact air.

"He will have to get over *that!*"

"Judith!" cried Reuben, piqued, provoked, inflamed by her manner; "I believe there isn't one grain of sentiment in your whole composition. Oh, I know it's a fine thing to be calm and cool and have one's self well in hand, but a woman is not always the worse for such a weakness as possessing a heart."

There was a note in his voice new to her; a look in the brown depths of his eyes as they met hers which she had never seen there before. It seemed to her that voice and eyes entreated her, cried to her for mercy; that a wonderful answering emotion of pity stirred in her own breast.

A moment they sat there looking at one another, then came a rustle of skirts, the sound of a penetrating, familiar voice, and Adelaide was sitting beside them. She had lost her part in the game for the time being, and, full of sisterly solicitude, had borne down on the pair with the object of interrupting that dangerous *tête-à-tête*.

"Reuben," she cried gaily, "I want you to dine with me tomorrow."

"I don't know that I can," he answered ungraciously, the mask of apathy falling over his features which a moment before had been instinct with life.

"Caroline Cardozo is coming. She has £50,000, and will have more when her father dies. You see," turning to Judith, "I am a good sister, and do not forget my duty."

Judith made some commonplace rejoinder, and went on stitching, outwardly calm.

Reuben, bitterly annoyed, tugged at the silks in the basket with those broad, square hands of his, which, in spite of their superior delicacy, were so much like his grandfather's.

"And, by the by," went on Adelaide, nothing daunted, "you must bring Mr. Lee-Harrison to see me, and then I can ask him to dinner."

"I don't know about that," answered Reuben slowly, looking at her from under his eyelids; "he might swallow your Jews; he walks by faith as regards *them* just at present. But as for the rest – a man doesn't care to meet bad imitations of the people of his own set, does he?"

Having planted this poisoned shaft, and feeling rather ashamed of himself, Reuben rose sullenly and went to the card table, where Rose was winning steadily, and Esther, who always sat down reluctantly and ended by giving herself up completely to the excitement of the game, fingered with flushed cheeks her own diminishing hoard.

Adelaide and Judith, each in her way shocked at this outburst of bad temper from the urbane Reuben, plunged into lame and awkward conversation. Only somewhere in the hidden depths of Judith's being a voice was singing of triumph and delight.

Chapter 6

He had a gentle, yet aspiring mind;
Just, innocent, with varied learning fed.

SHELLEY: Prince Athanase[17]

Judith rose early the next morning and put the finishing touches to her embroidery. It was her mother's birthday, and she had planned going to the Walterton Road after breakfast with her gift.

But Rose claimed her for purposes of shopping, and the two girls set out together for the region of Westbourne Grove. It was a delicious autumn morning; Whiteley's was thronged with familiar, sunburnt faces, and greetings were exchanged on all sides.

The Community had come back in a body from country and seaside, in time for the impending religious festivals; the feast of the New Year would be celebrated the next week, and the great fast, or Day of Atonement,[18] some ten days later.

"How glad everyone is to get back," cried Rose. "I know I hate the country; so do most people, only it isn't the fashion to say so."

And she nodded in passing to Adelaide, who, with her gloves off, was intently comparing the respective merits of some dress lengths in brocaded velvet.

---

17. From Percy Bysshe Shelley's poem, "Prince Athanase: A Fragment."
18. Note here that Levy wants to demonstrate the framing of Jewish tradition through a Christian lens; indeed, the term, Yom Kippur, is never used.

Judith smiled rather dreamily, and remarked that they had better go first to the glove department, that for the sale of dress materials, for which they were bound, being so hopelessly overcrowded.

"Very well," cried Rose. Then, in an undertone: "Look the other way; there's Netta Sachs. What a howling cad!" as a bouncing, gaily attired daughter of Shem passed them in the throng.

Rose was in her element; she was an excellent shopping-woman, loving a bargain for its own sake, grudging no time to the matching of colours and such patience-trying operations, going through the business from beginning to end with a whole-hearted enjoyment that was good to see.

Judith, who had all a pretty girl's interest in dress, and was generally willing enough for such expeditions, followed her cousin from counter to counter, with a little amiable air of abstraction.

Was there some magic in the autumn morning, some intoxication in the hazy, gold-coloured air, that she, the practical, sensible Judith, went about like a hashish-eater under the first delightful influence of the dangerous drug?

"What a crowd!" ejaculated Adelaide, coming up to them as she turned from the contemplation of some cheap ribbons in a basket.

She had, to the full, the gregarious instincts of her race, and Whiteley's was her happy hunting-ground. Here, on this neutral territory, where Bayswater nodded to Maida Vale, and South Kensington took Bayswater by the hand, here could her boundless curiosity be gratified, here could her love of gossip have free play.

"We are going to get some lunch," said Rose, moving off; "Judith has to go and see her people."

She, too, loved the social aspects of the place no less than its business ones. Her pale, prominent, sleepy eyes, under their heavy white lids, saw quite as much and as quickly as Adelaide's dancing, glittering, hard little organs of vision.

The girls lunched in the refreshment room, having obtained leave of absence from the family meal, then set out together from the shop.

At the corner of Westbourne Grove they parted, Rose going towards home, Judith committing herself to a large blue omnibus.

The Walterton Road is a dreary thoroughfare, which, in respect of unloveliness, if not of length, leaves Harley Street, condemned of the poet, far behind.

It is lined on either side with little sordid gray houses, characterized by tall flights of steps and bow-windows, these latter having for frequent adornment cards proclaiming the practice of various humble occupations, from the letting of lodgings to the tuning of pianos.

About halfway up the street, Judith stopped the omnibus, and mounted the steps to a house some degrees less dreary-looking than the majority of its neighbours. Fresh white curtains hung in the clean windows, while steps, scraper and doorbell bore witness to the hand of labour.

Mrs. Quixano herself opened the door to her daughter, and drew her by the hand into the sitting room, across the little hall to which still clung the odour of the mid-day mutton.

"Many happy returns of the day, Mamma," said Judith, kissing her and offering her parcel.

"I am sure it is very good of you to remember, my dear," answered her mother, leaning back in her chair and taking in every detail of the girl's appearance; her gown, her bonnet, the tinge of sunburn on her fresh young cheek, a certain indescribable air of softness, of maidenliness which was hers today.

Israel Leuniger's sister was a stout, comely woman of middle-age; red-haired, white-skinned, plump, with a projecting under-lip and comfortable double chin.

She was disappointed with her life, but she made the best of it; loving her husband, though unable to sympathize with him; planning, working unremittingly for her six children; extracting the utmost benefit from the narrowest of means; a capable person who did her duty according to her own lights.

"So Reuben Sachs has come back," she said, after some conversation.

Judith glanced up quickly with a bright, gentle look.

"Yes, and he is ever so much better; quite himself again."

Mrs. Quixano grumbled some inarticulate reply. Personally, she would not have been sorry if he had failed to return from the antipodes.

As may be imagined, she had been one of the first people whom the gossip about Reuben and her daughter had reached.

She had begun to be jealously conscious that there was no one to protect Judith's interests; that, after all, it might have been better for the girl to take her chance in the Walterton Road, than waste her time among a set of people too greedy or too ambitious to marry her.

Twenty-two, and no sign of a husband; only a troublesome flirtation that kept off the rest of the world, and was not in the least likely to end in anything but smoke.

And yet, thought Mrs. Quixano, with a sudden burst of maternal pride and indignation, any man might be proud of such a wife.

With her beauty, her health, and her air of breeding, surely she was good enough, and more than good enough, for such a man as Reuben Sachs, his enormous pretensions, and those of his family on his behalf notwithstanding?

The door opened presently to admit two little dark-eyed, foreign-looking children – children such as Murillo[19] loved to paint – who had just returned from a walk with a very juvenile nursemaid.

They were Judith's youngest brothers, and as she knelt on the floor with her arm round one of them, administering chocolate and burnt almonds, she was conscious of a new tenderness, of a strange yearning affection for them in her heart.

"The girls will be so sorry to miss seeing you," said Mrs. Quixano, taking in the picture before her with her shrewd glance; "they are at the High School, and Jack, of course, is in the City."

Jack Quixano, the eldest of the family, was also its chief hope and pride.

---

19. Spanish painter, Bartolomé Esteban Murillo (1618–1682).

He had taken to finance as a duck to water, and from the humblest of berths at Sachs and Co.'s, had risen in a few years to the proud position of authorized clerk.

It had been evident, almost from the cradle, that he had inherited the true Leuniger ambition and determination to get on in the world, qualities which had shone forth so conspicuously in the case of his uncle Israel, and, unlike the ambition and determination of the Sachs family, were unrelieved by any touch of imagination or self-criticism.

"It is disappointing not to see the girls," answered Judith, who was fond of her sisters, when she remembered them. "But Papa, he is at home? I shall not be disturbing him?"

A moment later, she was standing with her hand on the door of the room at the back of the house, where her father was accustomed to pass his time.

Turning the handle, in obedience to a voice from within, she entered slowly, a suggestion of shyness and reluctance in her manner, and found herself in a tiny apartment, into which the afternoon sun was streaming. It was lined and littered with books, all of them dusty and many dilapidated.

From the midst of this confusion of dust and sunlight rose a tall, lean, shabby figure: a middle-aged man, with stooping shoulders, a very dark skin, dark, straight, lank hair, growing close round the cheekbones, deep-set eyes, and long features.

"Why, Judith, my dear," he said, with his vague, pleasant smile, as she came forward and submitted her fresh cheek to his lips.

"I hope I don't disturb you, Papa. And how is the treatise getting on?"

He shook his head and smiled, and Judith was content with this for an answer. She only asked after the treatise from politeness, not from any interest in the subject.

Long ago in Portugal, there had been Quixanos doctors and scholars of distinction. When Joshua Quixano had been stranded high and dry by the tides of modern commercial competition, he had reverted to the ancestral pursuits, and for many years had devoted himself to collecting the materials for a monograph on the Jews of Spain and Portugal.

Absorbed in close and curious learning, in strange genealogical lore, full of a simple, abstract, unthinking piety, he let the world and life go by unheeded.

Judith remained with her father for some ten minutes. Conversation between them was never an easy matter, yet there was affection on both sides.

Quixano's manners and customs were accepted facts, unalterable as natural laws, over which his children had never puzzled themselves. Some of them indeed had inherited to some extent the paternal temperament, but in most cases, it had been overborne by the greater vitality of the Leunigers. But today the dusty scholar's room, the dusty scholar, struck Judith with a new force. She looked about her wistfully, from the book-laden shelves, the paper-strewn tables, to her father's face and eyes, whence shone forth clear and frank his spirit – one of the pure spirits of this world.

* * * *

When Judith reached home it was already dusk, and afternoon tea was going on in the morning room.

Mrs. Leuniger was absent, and Rose officiated at the tea-table, while Adelaide, her feet on the fender, her gloves off, was preparing for herself an attack of indigestion with unlimited muffins and strong tea.

She had been paying calls in the neighbourhood, clad in the proof-mail of her very best manners, an uncomfortable garment which she had now thrown off, and was reclining, metaphorically speaking, in dressing-gown and slippers.

A burst of laughter from both young women greeted Judith's ears as she entered.

"How late you are," cried Rose. "What filial piety!"

Judith knelt down by the fire smiling, and took her part with spirit in the girlish jokes and gossip.

It was six o'clock before Adelaide rose to go, by which time the attack of indigestion had set in. Her vivacity died out suddenly; her features looked thick, strained, and lifeless; her sallow skin took a positively orange tinge.

"Dear me," she cried ill-temperedly, "I had no idea it was so late. I must fly. I have one or two people dining with me tonight: the Cardozos, the Hanbury-ffrenches – oh, and Reuben finds he can come."

Judith felt suddenly as though a chill wind had struck her; but she called out gaily to Rose, who was escorting Adelaide to the door, that there was time before dinner to practise the new duet.

Chapter 7

On this day shall He make an atonement for you, to purify you; you shall be clean from all your sins.

LEVITICUS xvi. 30.[20]

Herbert, or, as he was generally spoken of, Bertie Lee-Harrison, called at Lancaster Gate on the day of the New Year, to make acquaintance with Reuben's people and offer his best wishes for the year 564–.[21]

He was a small, fair, fluent person, very carefully dressed, assiduously polite, and bearing on his amiable, commonplace, neatly modelled little face no traces of the spiritual conflict which anyone knowing his history might have supposed him to have passed through.

Esther, who happened to be calling on her aunt at the time of Bertie's visit, classified him at once as an intelligent fool; but Adelaide professed herself delighted with the little man, and had had the joy

---

20. Both New (*The Complete Novels*, 544 n. 21) and Bernstein (*Reuben Sachs*, 87 n. 1) highlight that Levy's biblical quotation adds in a "He" that is not present in Torah or the King James Bible. New even suggested that Levy's use of "He" is "deliberate." However, Levy's quotation is actually from the *Forms of Prayer Used in The West London Synagogue of British Jews* and a number of English translations of the traditional liturgy in circulation at the time.

21. According to Bernstein (*Reuben Sachs*, 87, n. 2), it was normal in the period to be unclear about the exact date.

of informing him that she had once met his sister, Lady Kemys, at a garden party.

"Lady Kemys is charming," Reuben said when the matter was being discussed. "Sir Nicholas, too, is a good fellow. They have a place some miles out of St. Baldwin's."

His mind ran a good deal on St. Baldwin's in these days, and on poor Ronaldson, its Conservative member, lying hopelessly ill in Grosvenor Place.

Reuben, it may be added, was true to the traditions of his race, and wore the primrose; while Leo, who knew nothing about politics, gave himself out as a social democrat.

Mr. Lee-Harrison was to break his fast in Portland Place on the evening of the Day of Atonement, when it was old Solomon's custom to assemble his family round him in great numbers.

Adelaide objected to this arrangement.

"It will give him such a bad impression," she said.

"He asked for local colour, and local colour he shall have," answered Reuben, amused.

"It is disloyal to your own people to assume such an attitude regarding them to a stranger. After all, he is not one of us," cried Adelaide, taking a high tone.

"Your accusations are a little vague, Addie; but to tell you the truth I had no choice in the matter. I took him up yesterday to Portland Place, and the old man gave him the invitation. He simply jumped at it."

"Those dreadful Samuel Sachses!" groaned Adelaide.

"Oh, they are a remarkable survival. You should learn to take them in the right spirit," answered her brother.

He was dining that night at the house of an important Conservative M.P., and was disposed to take a cheerful view of things.

* * * *

The Fast Day, or Day of Atonement, is the greatest national occasion of the whole year.

Even those lax Jews who practise their callings on Saturdays and other religious holidays, are withheld by public opinion on either side the tribal barrier from doing so on this day of days.

The synagogues are thronged; and if the number of people who rigidly adhere to total abstinence from food for twenty-four hours is rapidly diminishing, there are still many to be found who continue to do so.

Solomon Sachs, his daughter, Rebecca, and the Montague Cohens worshipped in the Bayswater synagogue; the rest of the family had seats in the Reformed synagogue in Upper Berkeley Street, an arrangement to which the old man was too liberal-minded to take objection.

The Quixano family attended the synagogue of the Spanish and Portuguese Jews in Bryanston Street, with the exception of Judith, who shared with her cousins the simplified service, the beautiful music, and other innovations of Upper Berkeley Street.[22]

The morning of the particular Day of Atonement of which I write dawned bright and clear; and from an early hour, in all quarters of the town, the Chosen People – a breakfastless band – might have been seen making their way to the synagogues.

Many of the women were in white, which is considered appropriate wear for the occasion; and if traces of depression were discernible on many faces, in view of the long day before them, it is scarcely to be wondered at.

It was about ten o'clock when the Leunigers, who had all breakfasted, made their way into the great hall of the synagogue in Upper Berkeley Street, where the people were streaming in, in great numbers. As they paused a moment at the bottom of the staircase leading to the ladies' gallery, for their party to divide according to sex, Reuben came up to them with Bertie Lee-Harrison in his wake.

There was a general hand-shaking, and Reuben, as he pressed her fingers, smiled a half-humorous, half-rueful smile at Judith – a protest against the rigours and *longueurs* of the day which lay before them.

---

22. See the analysis of this chapter on pp. xl–xli.

She managed to say to him over her shoulder:

"How is Mr. Ronaldson?"

"He has taken a turn for the better."

They laughed in one another's faces.

Bertie, struck by the effect of that sudden, rapidly checked wave of mirth passing over the beautiful, serious face, remarked to Reuben as they turned towards the entrance to their part of the building, that the Jewish ladies were certainly very lovely. Reuben said nothing; they were by this time well within the synagogue, but he glanced quickly and coldly under his eyelids at Bertie picking his way jauntily to his seat.

Ernest Leuniger, who was very devout, and who loved the exercise of his religion even more than the game of solitaire, had already enwound himself in his *talith,* exchanged his tall hat for an embroidered cap, and was muttering his prayers in Hebrew below his breath.

Leo, his small, slight, picturesque figure swathed carelessly in the long white garment, with the fringes and the border of blue, his hat tilted over his eyes, leaned against a porphyry column, lost to everything but the glorious music which rolled out from the great organ.

He had come today under protest, to prevent a definite break with his father, who exacted attendance at synagogue on no other day of the year.

The time was yet to come when he should acknowledge to himself the depth of tribal feeling, of love for his race, which lay at the root of his nature. At present, he was aware of nothing but revolt against, almost of hatred of, a people who, as far as he could see, lived without ideals, and was given up body and soul to the pursuit of material advantage.

Behind him, his two little brothers were quarrelling for possession of a prayer-book. Near him stood his father, swaying from side to side, and mumbling his prayers in the corrupt German-Hebrew[23] of

23. Yiddish.

his youth – a jargon not recognized by the modern culture of Upper Berkeley Street.

Reuben and his friend had seats opposite; seats moreover which commanded a good view of the ladies of the Leuniger household in the gallery above: Mrs. Leuniger, in a rich lace shawl, very much crumpled, and a new bonnet hopelessly askew; Rose, in a tight-fitting costume of white, with blue ribbons; Judith, in white also, her dusky hair, the clear, soft oval of her face surmounted by a flippant French bonnet – the very latest fashion.

It was a long day, growing less and less endurable as it went on; the atmosphere getting thicker and hotter and sickly with the smell of stale perfume.

The people, for the most part, stuck to their posts throughout. A few disappeared boldly about lunch time, returning within an hour refreshed and cheerful. Some – these were chiefly men – fidgeted in and out of the building to the disturbance of their neighbours. One or two ladies fainted; one or two others gossiped audibly from morning till evening; but, on the whole, decorum was admirably maintained.

Judith Quixano went through her devotions upheld by that sense of fitness, of obedience to law and order, which characterized her every action.

But it cannot be said that her religion had any strong hold over her; she accepted it unthinkingly.

These prayers, read so diligently, in a language of which her knowledge was exceedingly imperfect, these reiterated praises of an austere tribal deity, these expressions of a hope whose consummation was neither desired nor expected, what connection could they have with the personal needs, the human longings of this touchingly ignorant and limited creature?

Now and then, when she lifted her eyes, she saw the bored, resigned face of Reuben opposite, and the respectful, attentive countenance of Mr. Lee-Harrison, who was going through the day's proceedings with all the zeal of a convert.

Leo had absented himself early in the day, and was wandering about the streets in one of those intolerable fits of restless misery which sometimes laid their hold on him.

Esther was not in synagogue. She had had a sharp wrangle with her mother the night before, which had ended in her staying in bed with *Good-bye, Sweetheart!*[24] for company.

She, poor soul, was of those who deny utterly the existence of the Friend of whom she stood so sorely in need.

24. Rhoda Broughton's (1840–1920) *Good-bye Sweetheart!* (1872).

Chapter 8

My lord, will't please you to fall to?

RICHARD II.[25]

A limp, drab-coloured group was assembled in the drawing room at Portland Place.

It was nearly half-past seven, and it only wanted the arrival of the Samuel Sachses – who came from the St. John's Wood synagogue – for the whole party to descend into the dining room, where the much-needed meal awaited them.

The Leunigers were there, of course, with the exception of Ernest and his mother, who had gone home; the Sachses; the Montague Cohens; Mrs. Kohnthal and Esther, who had left her bed at the eleventh hour prompted by a desire for society; Judith; Mr. and Mrs. Quixano, their son Jack, and two young sisters.

Bertie Lee-Harrison, who had come in with Reuben, pale, exhausted, but prepared to be impressed by everything and everyone he saw, confided to his friend that the twenty-four hours' fast had been the severest ordeal he had as yet undergone in the service of religion – his experiences in Asia Minor not excepted.

Leo, whose mood had changed, overheard this confidence with an irresistible twitching of the lips. He was sitting on the big sofa with his two little brothers, making jokes below his breath to their

25. William Shakespeare's *Richard II.*

immense delight; while Rose, at the other end of the same piece of furniture, was maintaining an animated conversation with her cousin Jack.

Jack Quixano was a spruce, dapper, polite young man of some twenty-four or twenty-five years of age. Perhaps he was a little too spruce, a little too dapper, a little too anxious to put himself *en évidence* by his assiduity in picking up handkerchiefs and opening doors. But few of his family noticed these defects, least of all Rose, on whom he was beginning to cast aspiring eyes, and whom he closely resembled in personal appearance.

The door opened at last, to everyone's relief, to admit the expected guests: a party of six – father, mother, grown-up son and daughter, a little girl and a little boy.

Samuel Sachs was the unsuccessful member of his family.

From the beginning, the atmosphere of the Stock Exchange had proved too strong for his not very strong brains, and his career had been inaugurated by a series of gambling debts.

His father paid his debts and forbade him the office, and he had gone his own way for many years, settling down ultimately in a humble way of business as a lithographer.

He had married a Polish Jewess with some money of her own, and in these latter days, old Solomon made him an allowance, so there was enough and to spare in the home in Maida Vale, where he and his family were established.

They came now into the crowded drawing room with a curious mixture of deference and self-assertion.

To their eminently provincial minds, the Bayswater Sachses, the Leunigers and the Kohnthals were very great people indeed, and they derived no little prestige in Maida Vale from their connection with so distinguished a family.

But as regarded their occasional admittance into the charmed circle, that was a privilege which, though they would on no account have foregone it, was certainly not without its drawbacks.

It was splendid, but it was not comfortable.

Mrs. Sachs was a stout, dark-haired matron, who entirely overshadowed her shambling, neutral-tinted husband. Netta, the eldest daughter, was a black-eyed, richly coloured, bouncing maiden of two or three-and-twenty, wearing a white dress, with elbow sleeves, cut open a little at the neck, and a great deal of silver jewellery.

Alec, her brother, was a short, fair, exuberant-looking youth, with a complexion both glossy and florid, in whom the Sachs's fitness for survival had reasserted itself. He practised painless dentistry with great success in the heart of Maida Vale, and was writing a manual – destined to pass through several editions – on *Diseases of the Teeth and Gums*.

Adèle and Bernard (pronounced Adale and Bernàrd), the two children, strutted in behind the others, in all the glory of white cambric and black velveteen, respectively, much impressed by the situation, but no less on the defensive than the elder members of their family.

There was languid greeting all round; languor, under the circumstances, was excusable; and then the whole party poured down into the dining room, where an abundant meal was set out.

Old Solomon prided himself on his hospitality, and the great table, which shone with snowy linen, gleaming china, and glittering silver, groaned, as the phrase goes, with good things to eat.

There were golden-brown blocks of cold fried fish in heavy silver dishes; rosy piles of smoked salmon; saffron-tinted masses of stewed fish; long twisted loaves covered with seeds; innumerable little plates of olives, pickled herrings, and pickled cucumbers; and the quick eyes of Lionel and Sidney had lighted at once on the many coloured surfaces of the almond puddings, which awaited the second course on the sideboard.

Aunt Rebecca, faint and yellow, behind the silver urns, dispensed tea and coffee with rapid hand; while old Solomon, none the worse for his rigid fast, wielded the fish slice at the other end of the table.

Bertie, respectful, wondering, interested through all his hunger, was seated between Reuben and Mrs. Kohnthal.

Adelaide had chosen her seat as far as possible from the Samuel Sachses, whose presence was an offence to her. They, on their part, regarded her with a mixture of respect and dislike. She never gave them more than two fingers in her grandfather's house, and ignored them altogether when she met them anywhere else. This conduct impressed them by its magnificence, and they followed the ups and downs of her career, as far as they were able, with a passionate interest that had in it something of the pride of possession.

Nor was Adelaide above taking an interest in the affairs of her humbler relatives behind their backs. I cannot help wishing that they had known this; it would have been to them the source of so much innocent gratification.

Reuben, who had his cousin Netta on the other side of him, and whose vanity was a far subtler, more complicated affair than his sister's, was making himself agreeable with his accustomed urbanity, beneath which the delighted maiden was unable to detect a lurking irony.

The humours of the Samuel Sachses, their appearance, gestures, their excruciating method of pronouncing the English language, the hundred and one tribal peculiarities which clung to them, had long served their cousins as a favourite family joke into which it would have been difficult for the most observant of outsiders to enter.[26]

They were indeed, as Reuben had said, a remarkable survival.

Born and bred in the very heart of nineteenth century London, belonging to an age and a city which has seen the throwing down of so many barriers, the levelling of so many distinctions of class, of caste, of race, of opinion, they had managed to retain the tribal characteristics, to live within the tribal pale to an extent which spoke worlds for the national conservatism.

They had been educated at Jewish schools, fed on Jewish food, brought up on Jewish traditions and Jewish prejudice.

Their friends, with few exceptions, were of their own race, the making of acquaintance outside the tribal barrier being sternly

26. See Levy's "Jewish Humour," pp. 921–4 (Bernstein, ed., *Reuben Sachs,* 94 n. 2).

discouraged by the authorities. Mrs. Samuel Sachs indeed had been heard more than once to observe pleasantly that she would sooner see her daughters lying dead before her than married to Christians.

Netta tossed her head defiantly at these remarks, but contented herself with sowing her little crop of wild oats on the staircases of Bayswater and Maida Vale, where she "sat out" by the hour with the very indifferent specimens of Englishmen who frequented the dances in her set.

Generally speaking, the race instincts of Rebecca of York are strong, and she is less apt to give her heart to Ivanhoe, the Saxon knight,[27] than might be imagined.

Bernard Sachs, a very smug-looking little boy, with inordinately thick lips and a disagreeable nasal twang, had been placed between the two young Leunigers, who regarded him with a mixture of disgust and amusement, which they were at small pains to conceal.

"Did you fast all day?" he said, by way of opening the conversation. "I did. I was *bar-mitzvah* last month. Is either of you fellows *bar-mitzvah*?"

"I am thirteen, if that's what you mean," said Lionel, with his most man-of-the-world air. He considered the introduction of the popular tribal phrases very bad form indeed.

"I suppose you were in *shool*[28] all day?" went on Bernard unabashed, and much on his dignity.

"I was only in synagogue in the morning," answered Lionel. Then he kicked Sidney violently under the table, and the two little brothers went off into a series of chuckles; while Bernard, with a vague sense of being insulted, turned his attention to his fried salmon and Dutch herring.

Meanwhile Alec, who had been rather subdued at the beginning of the evening, was regaining his native confidence as the meal proceeded.

---

27. Refers to Walter Scott's (1771–1832) *Ivanhoe: A Romance* (1820).
28. Synagogue (*shul*).

He happened to be sitting opposite Bertie, and having elicited from his neighbour, Mrs. Quixano, the explanation of an alien presence among them on such an occasion, had fixed his attention with great frankness on the stranger.

Very soon he was leaning across the table, and with much use of his fat red hands, and many liftings of his round shoulders, was expatiating to the astonished Bertie on the beauties and advantages of the faith which he had just embraced.

"Mr. Harrison," he cried at last – he preferred to skip the difficulties of the double-barrelled name – "Mr. Harrison, take my word for it, it is the finest religion under the sun. Those who have left it for reasons of their own have always come back in the end. They're bound to, they're bound to!" (He pronounced the word "bound" with an indescribable twang.) "Look at Lord Beaconsfield"[29] – he pointed with his short forefinger – "everyone knows he died with the *shemang*[30] on his lips!"

There was a sudden stifled explosion of laughter from Leo's quarter of the table; and Judith glanced across rather anxiously at Reuben, on whose polite, impassive face she at once detected a look of annoyance.

She was sitting next to her father in the close-fitting white gown which displayed to advantage the charming lines of her arms and shoulders.

Now and then she caught the glance of Mr. Lee-Harrison, who was far too well-bred to obtrude his admiration by staring, fixed momentarily on her face.

The hunger and weariness natural, under the circumstances, to her youth and health had in no way marred the perfect freshness of her appearance; and there was a gentle kindliness in her manner to her father which added a charm, not always present, to her beauty.

29. Benjamin Disraeli (1804–1881), Prime Minster, 1868, 1874–1880; Disraeli was baptised as a child.

30. The Shema.

Perhaps she felt instinctively, what Quixano himself was far too much in the clouds to notice, that no one made much account of him, that it behoved her to take him under her protection. He was one of this world's failures; and the Jewish people, so eager to crown success in any form, so determined in laying claim to the successful among their number, have scant love for those unfortunates who have dropped behind in the race.

The meal came to an end at last, and there was a pushing back of chairs on the part of the men.

Bertie, about to rise, felt himself held down by main force; Reuben was gripping him hard by the wrist with one hand, and with the other was engaged in fishing out his hat from under the table; while Netta, leaning across her cousin, explained with her most fascinating smile that grandpa was going to *bench*.[31]

Bertie, at a sign from Reuben, rose to the situation, and stooping for his own hat with alacrity, drew it from its place of concealment and placed it on his head. By this time all the men had unearthed and assumed their head-gear, with the exception of Samuel Sachs, whose hat by some mischance was not forthcoming; however, to avoid delay, he covered his head in all gravity with his table-napkin.

Bertie glanced round him, from one face to another, puzzled and inquiring.

It seemed to him a solemn moment, this gathering together of kinsfolk after the long day of prayer, of expiation; this offering up of thanksgiving; this performance of the ancient rites in the land of exile.

He could not understand the spirit of indifference, of levity even, which appeared to prevail.

A finer historic sense, other motives apart, should, it seemed, have prevented so obvious a display of the contempt which familiarity had bred.

31. *Bench,* meaning to recite blessings.

Alec had put his hat on rakishly askew, and was winking across to him reassuringly, as though to intimate that the whole thing was not to be taken seriously.

Rose, led on by Jack Quixano, giggled hysterically behind her pocket-handkerchief.

Leo and Esther took on airs of aggressive boredom. Judith, lifting her eyes, met Reuben's in a smile, and even Montague Cohen permitted himself to yawn.

Only old Solomon at the head of the table, mumbling and droning out the long grace in his corrupt Hebrew – his great face impenetrably grave – appeared to take an interest in the proceeding, with perhaps the exception of his son Samuel, who joined in now and then from beneath the drooping shelter of his table-napkin.

Bertie stared and Bertie wondered. Needless to state, he was completely out of touch with these people whose faith his search for the true religion had led him, for the time being, to embrace.

Grace over, the women went upstairs, the men, with the exception of old Solomon, remaining behind to smoke.

Bertie, who was thoroughly tired out, soon rose to go.

"I will make your excuses upstairs," said Reuben.

But the polite little man preferred to go to the drawing room and perform his farewells in person.

"Thanks so much," he said in the hall, where Leo and Reuben were speeding him.

"I hope you have been edified – that's all." Reuben laughed.

"I am deeply interested in the Jewish character," answered Bertie; "the strongly marked contrasts; the underlying resemblances; the elaborate differentiations from a fundamental type – !"

"Ah, yes," broke in Reuben, secretly irritated,[32] his tribal sensitiveness a little hurt, "you will find among us all sorts and conditions of men."

---

32. Hunt Beckman suggests that Reuben's being "secretly irritated" demonstrates Levy's belief that "stereotypical thinking is … foolish" (*Amy Levy*, 173).

"Except perhaps Don Quixote,[33] or even King Cophetua,"[34] added Leo.

"King Cophetua," repeated Reuben in a slow, reflective tone, as the door closed on Mr. Lee-Harrison; "King Cophetua had an assured position. It isn't everyone that can afford to marry beggar-maids."

---

33. Refers to Miguel de Cervantes' (1547–1616) *The Ingenious Gentleman Don Quixote of La Mancha* (1605, 1615).

34. Refers possibly to Edward Burne-Jones' painting, "King Cophetua and the Beggar Maid" (1884), or to Tennyson's poem, "The Beggar Maid," or to Thomas Percy's (1729–1811) ballad, "King Cophetua and the Beggar-Maid"; Levy might also have been referring to the story more generally (see New, ed., *The Complete Novels*, 545 n. 34; Bernstein, ed., *Reuben Sachs*, 98 n. 2).

Chapter 9

Never by passion quite possessed,
And never quite benumbed by the world's sway.

MATTHEW ARNOLD[35]

The party was never prolonged to a late hour on these occasions, and by ten o'clock there was no one left in the drawing room in Portland Place except Mrs. Sachs, Mr. Leuniger, Mrs. Kohnthal and the young people in their respective trains.

The elders had got up a game of whist for the amusement of old Solomon, the termination of which their juniors awaited in conclave at the other end of the room.

Lionel and Sidney meanwhile, sleepy and overfed, quarrelled in a corner over the possession of a bound volume of the *Graphic*.[36]

"Judith," said Reuben, who had taken a seat opposite her, "do you know that you have made a conquest?"

"Is that such an unheard-of occurrence?"

Reuben laughed gently, and Rose cried:

"It is Mr. Lee-Harrison! I know it from the way he looked at supper."

35. Taken from Matthew Arnold's "A Summer Night"; see the discussion of Arnold beginning on p. lxii.

36. Newspaper.

"Yes, it is Bertie." Reuben looked straight in Judith's eyes. "He says you exactly fulfil his idea of Queen Esther."[37]

"Ah," cried Esther Kohnthal, "I have always had a theory about her. When she was kneeling at the feet of that detestable Ahasuerus,[38] she was thinking all the time of some young Jew whom she mashed, and who mashed her, and whom she renounced for the sake of her people!"

A momentary silence fell among them, then Reuben, looking down, said slowly: "Or perhaps she preferred the splendours of the royal position even to the attractions of that youth whom you suppose her to – er – have mashed."

He was not fond of Esther at the best of times; now he glanced at her under his eyelids with an expression of unmistakable dislike.

"I wonder," cried Rose, throwing herself into the breach, "what Mr. Lee-Harrison thought of it all."

"I think," said Leo, "that he was shocked at finding us so little like the people in *Daniel Deronda*."[39]

---

37. The book of Esther states (2:7): "The maiden was shapely and beautiful"; Esther becomes Queen to Ahasuerus, replacing Vashti who has fallen from favour (2:17), but "did not reveal her people or her kindred" based on Mordecai's advice (2:10). When Haman secures Ahasuerus' permission for a decree "to destroy, massacre, and exterminate all the Jews" (3:13), Esther is eventually forced to reveal her Jewish identity (7:3–4). Consequently, Ahasuerus orders that Haman be "impaled … on the stake" (7:9–10) and that although the decree could not be rescinded, Jews could "assemble and fight for their lives" (8:8–11). Thus, "the Jews mustered in their cities to attack those who sought their hurt; and no one could withstand them" (9:2). In sum, with the vanquishing of Haman, "these days were named Purim" (9:26). Levy might also have been drawing on Esther's iconography in contemporary art. In the nineteenth century, Esther was painted by Ernest Normand (1857–1923), Edwin Long (1829–1891), Edward Armitage (1817–1896), Théodore Chassériau (1819–1856), Francesco Caucig (1755–1828), etc. In each of these images the focus is on Esther's beauty and more often than not the imagery is exoticized and sexualised.
38. See above footnote.
39. Levy's point here is that Lee-Harrison's understanding of Anglo-Jewish life is derived from mediatised representations of "Jews"; note Esther and Leo's responses. See also Levy's discussions of George Eliot's *Daniel Deronda* in "The Jew in Fiction" (pp. 918–20) and "Jewish Children" (pp. 929–34).

"Did he expect," cried Esther, "to see our boxes in the hall, ready packed and labelled *Palestine*?"

"I have always been touched," said Leo, "at the immense good faith with which George Eliot carried out that elaborate misconception of hers."

"Now Leo is going to begin," cried Rose; "he never has a good word for his people. He is always running them down."

"Horrid bad form," said Reuben; "besides being altogether a mistake."

"Oh, I have nothing to say against us at all," answered Leo ironically, "except that we are materialists to our fingers' ends. That we have outlived, from the nature of things, such ideals as we ever had."

"Idealists don't grow on every bush," answered Reuben, "and I think we have our fair share of them. This is a materialistic age, a materialistic country."

"And ours the religion of materialism. The corn and the wine and the oil; the multiplication of the seed; the conquest of the hostile tribes – these have always had more attraction for us than the harp and crown of a spiritualized existence."

"It is no good to pretend," answered Reuben in his reasonable, pacific way, "that our religion remains a vital force among the cultivated and thoughtful Jews of today. Of course, it has been modified, as we ourselves have been modified, by the influence of Western thought and Western morality. And belief, among thinking people of all races, has become, as you know perfectly, a matter of personal idiosyncrasy."

"That does not alter my position," said Leo, "as to the character of the national religion and the significance of the fact. Ah, look at us," he cried with sudden passion, "where else do you see such eagerness to take advantage; such sickening, hideous greed; such cruel, remorseless striving for power and importance; such ever-active, ever-hungry vanity, that must be fed at any cost? Steeped to the lips in sordidness, as we have all been from the cradle, how is it possible that anyone among us, by any effort of his own, can wipe off from his soul the hereditary stain?"

"My dear boy," said Reuben, touched by the personal note which sounded at the close of poor Leo's heroics, and speaking with sudden earnestness, "you put things in too lurid a light. We have our faults; you seem to forget what our virtues are. Have you forgotten for how long, and at what a cruel disadvantage, the Jewish people has gone its way, until at last it has shamed the nations into respect? Our self-restraint, our self-respect, our industry, our power of endurance, our love of race, home and kindred, and our regard for their ties – are none of these things to be set down to our account?"[40]

"Oh, our instincts of self-preservation are remarkably strong; I grant you that."

Leo tossed back his head with its longish hair as he spoke, and Reuben went on:

"And where would you find a truer hospitality, a more generous charity than among us?"

"A charity whose right hand is so remarkably well posted up in the doings of its left!"

"Oh, come, that's a libel – and not even true."

"There is one good thing," cried Leo, taking a fresh start, "and that is the inevitability – at least as regards us English Jews – of our disintegration; of our absorption by the people of the country. That is the price we are bound to pay for restored freedom and consideration.[41] The Community will grow more and more to consist of mediocrities, and worse, as the general world claims our choicer specimens for its own. We may continue to exist as a separate clan, reinforced from below by German and Polish Jews for some time to come: but absorption complete, inevitable – that is only a matter of time. You and I sitting here, self-conscious, discussing our own race-attributes, race-position – are we not as sure a token of what is to come as anything well could be?"

---

40. Note the dichotomy Levy sets up here between "'faults'" and "'virtues.'"
41. Levy refers here to the questions posed by the *Haskalah*, political emancipation, and European nationalisms; in these contexts, citizenship brought with it difficult challenges vis-à-vis diversity, assimilation, and secularisation.

"Yours is a sweeping theory," said Reuben; "and at present, I don't feel inclined to go into the rights and wrongs of it; still less to deny its soundness. I can only say that, should I live to see it borne out, I should be very sorry. It may be a weakness on my part, but I am exceedingly fond of my people. If we are to die as a race, we shall die harder than you think. The tide will ebb in the intervals of flowing. That strange, strong instinct which has held us so long together is not a thing easily eradicated. It will come into play when it is least expected. Jew will gravitate to Jew, though each may call himself by another name. If prejudice died, if difference of opinion died, if all the world, metaphorically speaking, thought one thought and spoke one language, there would still remain those unspeakable mysteries, affinity and – love."

Reuben's voice sounded curiously moved, and in his eyes, as he spoke, glowed a dreamy flame, as of some deep and tender emotion.

Judith, leaning forward with parted lips, lifted her shining eyes to his face in a long, unconscious gaze. Reuben with his sword in his hand, fighting the battle for his people, seemed to her a figure noble and heroic beyond speech.

In her own breast was kindled the flame of a great emotion; she felt the love of her race grow stronger at every word.

Reuben, conscious to the fingertips of Judith's presence, of her gaze, which he did not return, was stirred, on his part, with a new enthusiasm.

He praised her in the race, and the race in her; and this was conveyed in some subtle manner to her consciousness.

Thus they acted and reacted on one another, deceiving and deceived, with that strange, unconscious hypocrisy of lovers.

* * * *

The game of whist had come to an end, and everyone rose, preparatory to departure.

"Goodnight, Uncle Solomon," said Reuben's mother. She, too, was a Sachs, who had married her cousin.

"Come along, Mamma," cried Esther yawning, "I am dead beat. The domestic habits of the cobra are not adapted to the human constitution, that is clear."

Reuben was standing in the hall with his mother, as Rose and Judith came downstairs in their outdoor clothes.

"Your carriage is at the door," said Israel Leuniger to Mrs. Sachs as he lit his cigar.

Mrs. Sachs turned to her son:

"Aren't you coming, Reuben?"

"No, but I do not expect to be late." He answered gently and seriously, stooping down and folding a shawl about her shoulders as he spoke.

Mrs. Sachs raised her wide, sallow, wrinkled face to her son's, looked at him a moment, then with a sudden impulse of tenderness, lifted her hand and stroked back the hair from his forehead.

Ah, what had come to Judith, standing in a corner of the hall watching the little scene?

Ah, what did it mean, what was it, this beating and throbbing of all her pulses, this strange, choked feeling in her throat, this mist that swam before her eyesight?

The dining room door, near which she stood, was ajar; moved by the blind impulse of her terror, she pushed it open; and trembling, ashamed, not daring to analyse her own emotions, she sought the shelter of the darkness.

* * * *

While Judith was being driven to Kensington Palace Gardens, lying back pale and tired in a corner of the carriage, Reuben was sauntering towards Piccadilly with a cigar in his mouth.

For the moment, his mind dwelt on the fact that he had not been able to say goodnight to Judith.

"Where did she make off to?" he asked himself persistently.

He was strangely irritated and baffled by the little accident.

As he went slowly down Regent Street, which was full of light and of people returning from the theatres, the thought of Judith took more and more possession of him, till his pulses beat and his senses swam.

Ah, why not, why not?

Children on his hearth with Judith's eyes, and Judith there herself amongst them: Judith, calm, dignified, stately, yet a creature so gentle withal, so sweet, so teachable!

He looked again and again at this picture of his fancy, fascinated, alarmed at his own fascination.

Whatever happened, he would never be a poor man. There was the money which would come to him at his grandfather's death, and at his mother's: no inconsiderable sums. There was his own little income, besides what his practice brought him.

But it was not altogether a question of money. He had no wish to fetter himself at this early stage of his career; his ambition was boundless; and the possibilities of the future looked almost boundless too.

He had an immense idea of his own market value; an instinctive aversion to making a bad bargain.

From his cradle, he had imbibed the creed that it is noble and desirable to have everything better than your neighbour; from the first had been impressed on him the sacred duty of doing the very best for yourself.

Yes, he was in love; cruelly, inconveniently, most unfortunately in love. But ten years hence, when he would still be a young man, the fever would certainly have abated, would be a dream of the past, while his ambition he had no doubt would be as lusty as ever.

Thus, he swayed from side to side, balancing this way and that; pitying himself and Judith as the victims of fate; full of tenderness, of sentiment for his own thwarted desires.

He believed himself to hesitate, to waver; but at the bottom of Reuben's heart there was that which never wavered.

He put the question by at last, wearied with the conflict, and gave himself up to pleasant dreams.

He thought of the look in Judith's eyes, of the vibration in her voice when she spoke to him.

"Ah, she does not know it herself!"

Triumph, joy, compunction, an overwhelming tenderness, set his pulses beating, his whole being aglow.

It was late when, tired and haggard, he reached his home and let himself in with the key.

His mother came out on the landing with a candle.

She did not present a charming spectacle *en déshabille,* her large, partially bald head deprived of the sheltering, softening cap, her withered neck exposed, the lines of her figure revealed by a dingy old dressing-gown.

She gave an exclamation as she saw him; the wide, yellow expanse of her face, with its unwholesome yet undying air, lighted up by the twinkling diamonds on either side of it, looked agitated and alarmed.

"My dear boy, thank God it is you! I have been dreaming about you – a terrible dream."

Chapter 10

Dusty purlieus of the law.

TENNYSON[42]

Leopold Leuniger came slouching down Chancery Lane, his hat at the back of his head, a woebegone air on his expressive face, dejection written in his graceless, characteristic walk, and in the droop of his picturesque head, which was, it must be owned, a little too large for his small, slight figure. He turned up under the archway leading to Lincoln's Inn, and made his way to New Square, where Reuben's chambers were situated.

Reuben, the clerk told him, was in court, but was expected every minute, and Leo passed into the inner room, which was his cousin's private sanctum. It was two or three days after the Day of Atonement, and in less than a week he would be back in Cambridge.

He paced restlessly to and fro in the little dingy room with its professional litter of books and papers, pausing now and then to look out of the window, or to examine the mass of cards, photographs, notes and tickets which adorned the mantelpiece.

Leo was by no means free from the tribal foible of inquisitiveness.

It was not long before the door burst open, and Reuben rushed in, in his wig and gown. The former decoration imparted a curious air of sageness to his keen face, and brought out more strongly its

42. From Tennyson's *In Memoriam* (1850).

peculiarities of colour: the clear, dark pallor of the skin, the red lights in the eyes and moustache.

"Hullo!" said Leo, still standing by the mantelpiece, his hat tilted back at a very acute angle, his restless fingers busy with the cards on the mantelpiece, "a nice gay time you appear to be having, old man: Jewish Board of Guardians, committee meeting; Anglo-Jewish Association, committee meeting; Bell Lane Free Schools, committee meeting – shall I go on?"

Reuben laughed.

"You see, it consolidates one's position both ways to stand well with the Community; and I am a very good Jew at heart, as I have often told you. But if you continue your investigations among my list of engagements you will find a good many meetings of all sorts, which are not communal; not to speak of first nights at the Terpischore and the Thalian."[43]

Leo, abandoning the subject, flung himself into a chair and said: "Ah, by the by, how is Ronaldson?"

"Much the same as ever. It may be a long business. The doctors have left off issuing bulletins."

Reuben took the chair opposite his cousin, then said shortly:

"You have come to tell me something."

"Yes. I have been having it out with my governor."

"Ah?" interrogatively.

"I told him," went on Leo, leaning forward and speaking with some excitement, "that I hadn't the faintest idea of going on the Stock Exchange, or even of reading for the bar; that my plan was this: to work hard for my degree, and then stay on, on chance of a fellowship. Everyone up there seems to think the matter lies virtually in my own hands."

"What did my uncle say to that?"

"Oh, he was furious; wouldn't listen to reason for a moment. I think" – with a boyish, bitter laugh – "that he rather confounds a

43. Possibly theatres or could refer to two of the nine muses in Greek mythology (Bernstein, ed., *Reuben Sachs,* 106 n. 4).

fellow of Trinity with the assistant-master at a Jewish boarding-school. The word 'usher' figured very largely in his arguments."

"I think," said Reuben slowly, "that you are making a mistake."

"Ah," cried Leo, flinging out his hand, "you don't understand. I can't live – I can't breathe in this atmosphere; I should choke. Up there, somehow, it is freer, purer; life is simpler, nobler."

Reuben looked down: "I quite agree with you on that point. All the same, you were never cut out for a University don. Do you want me to tell you that you are a musician?"

Leo blushed like a girl, and his face quivered. He did not altogether approve of Reuben, but Reuben's approval was very precious to him.

Moreover, he greatly respected his cousin's intelligent appreciation of music.

"Do you think so?" he cried. "That's what Norwood says. But there is plenty of opportunity for cultivating music; we have Silver up there, remember. He is immensely kind."

"You might talk it over with Silver. But think it well over and do nothing rash. There is plenty of time between now and taking your degree."

He rose and proceeded to take off his wig and gown.

"I don't know that my advice is worth much," he said, "but I should say a year or two in Germany – Leipzig, Berlin, Vienna – and if by then you feel justified in setting your face against the substantial attractions of Capel Court, no doubt your governor can be brought round."

"You will have to put it to him, Reuben. He believes in no one as he does in you."

"Very handsome of him. But doubtless he will welcome the idea after the usher scheme."

"You will have to paint the splendours of a musical success," cried Leo, his spirits rising, his white teeth flashing as he smiled. "You must employ rather crude colours, and go in for obvious effects – such as the Prince of Wales, the Lord Mayor, and the Archbishop of Canterbury seated in the front row of the stalls at St. James's Hall."

Reuben laughed as he put on his well brushed hat before the glass.

"I will impress upon him how fashionable is the pursuit of the arts in these democratic days." He added slowly, looking furtively at the lad: "And shall I tell him that one of these days you will marry very well indeed?"

Leo rose hastily, jarred, discomposed.

"Aren't you coming to lunch, Reuben?"

"Yes, I am ready." He smiled to himself, and the two young men passed out together into the paved courtyard of the old inn.

They made their way up Chancery Lane into Holborn. Leo hated London almost as vehemently as his cousin loved it. It was the place, he said, which had succeeded better than any other in reducing life to a huge competitive examination. Its busy, characteristic streets, which Reuben regarded with an interest both passionate and affectionate, filled him with a dreary sensation of disgust and depression.

As they sat down to lunch at the First Avenue Hotel, Lord Norwood came into the dining room. He was a tall, fair, aristocratic-looking young man, with a refined and thoughtful face, which, as he advanced towards his friend, broke into a peculiarly charming smile.

Leo exclaimed with impetuosity: "Oh, there's Norwood!" But as the latter approached, he stiffened into self-consciousness; somehow, he did not welcome the juxtaposition of his cousin and his friend. Acting on a sudden impulse, he rose and met the latter half-way, and the two young men stood talking together in the middle of the room.

Reuben, after a moment's hesitation, rose also and joined them. He greeted Lord Norwood, whom he had met once or twice before, with a little emphasis of deference, which was not lost on poor Leo, who hated himself at the same time for noticing it. Lord Norwood returned Reuben's greeting with marked *hauteur*; that cousin of Leuniger's was a snob, was not a person to be encouraged. In the young nobleman's delicate, fastidious, but exceedingly *borné* mind there was no mercy for such as he.

Reuben, though he showed no signs of it, was keenly alive to the fact that he had been snubbed; was alive no less keenly to the many points in favour of the offender.

The Norwoods were people whom it hurt the subtler part of his vanity not to stand well with.

They were not rich, not "smart," not politically important; but in their own fashion they were people of the very best sort, true aristocrats, such as few remain to us in these degenerate days.

For generations they had borne the reputation of high personal character and of scholarly attainment. They were, in the true sense of the word, exclusive; and their pride was of that nature which, as the poet has it, asserts an inward honour by denying outward show.

The friendship existing between Lord Norwood and Leo was founded on mutual admiration.

The Jew's many-sided talent, his brilliant scholarship, his mental quickness, and versatility, above all, his musical genius, had fairly dazzled the scholarly young Englishman, who loved art, but had not a drop of artist's blood in his veins.

Leo, on his part, had fallen down before the other's refinement of mind and soul and body, and before the delicate strength of his character.

It was a strange friendship perhaps, but one which had stood, and was destined long to stand, the test of time.

Meanwhile Reuben, who knew that it is half the battle not to know when you are vanquished, quietly invited Lord Norwood to join them at table.

He pleaded, coldly, an appointment with a friend, and after a few words with Leo, withdrew to a further apartment.

Leo had taken in the slight, brief, yet significant episode in all its bearings, hating himself meanwhile for his own shrewdness, which he considered a mark of latent meanness.

Reuben returned thoughtfully, if quite composedly, to the discussion of his roast pheasant and potato chips.

His method of wiping out a snub was the grandly simple one of making a conquest of the snubber. Persons less completely equipped for the battle of life have been known to prefer certain defeat to the chances of such a victory.

But Reuben was possessed of a bottomless fund of silent energy, of quiet resistance and persistence, which had stood him ere now in good stead under like circumstances.

He appraised Lord Norwood very justly; recognized instinctively the charms of mind and manner which had cast such glamour over him in his cousin's eyes; recognized also his limitations, with an irritated consciousness that he, Reuben, was being judged at a far less open-minded tribunal. In such cases, it is always the more intelligent person who is at a disadvantage – he appreciates, and is not appreciated.

I have no intention of following out Reuben's relations with Lord Norwood, throughout which, it may be added, he had little to gain, even in the matter of social prestige, for he numbered people far more important among his acquaintance. But it was not long before an invitation to Norwood Towers was given and accepted. By one at least of the people concerned, however, the circumstances which had marked the earlier stages of their acquaintance were never forgotten.

* * * * * *

A few days later saw Leo back at Trinity with his lexicon, his violin, and the friend of his heart. Here, he alternately worked furiously and gave himself up to spells of complete idleness; to sauntering, sociable days spent in cheerful, excited discussion of the vexed problems of the universe, or long days of moody solitude. At these latter times, he pondered deeply on the unsatisfactoriness of life in general, and of his life in particular, and underwent a good many uncomfortable sensations which he ascribed to a hopeless passion for his friend's sister.

Lady Geraldine Sydenham was a gentle, kindly, cultivated young woman, who had not the faintest idea of having inspired anyone with hopeless passion, least of all young Leuniger.

She was two or three years older than Leo – a thin, pale person, with faint colouring, a rather receding chin, and slightly prominent teeth.

She dressed dowdily, and even Leo did not credit her with being pretty. Indeed, he took a fanciful pleasure in dwelling on the fact that she was plain, and in quoting to himself the verse from Browning's *Too Late*:

> "… There never was to my mind
> Such a funny mouth, for it would not shut;
> And the dented chin too – what a chin! …
> You were thin, however; like a bird's
> Your hand seemed – some would say the pounce
> Of a scaly-footed hawk – all but!
> The world was right when it called you thin."[44]

Meanwhile in London, Bertie Lee-Harrison was celebrating the Feast of Tabernacles[45] as best he could.

He had given up with considerable reluctance his plan of living in a tent, the resources of his flat in Albert Hall Mansions not being able to meet the scheme.

He consoled himself by visits to the handsome *succouth*[46] which the Montague Cohens had erected in their garden in the Bayswater Road.

44. From Robert Browning's poem, "Too Late."
45. The term, "Feast of Tabernacles," is significant here; Levy clearly wanted to highlight how Sukkot is referred to by a "Christian."
46. Different spelling of Sukkot.

Chapter 11

I do not like this manner of a dance,
This game of two and two; it were much better
To mix between the pauses than to sit
Each lady out of earshot with her friend.

SWINBURNE: Chastelard[47]

The Leunigers were giving a dance at the beginning of November, and the female part of the household was greatly taken up with preparations for the event.

There was much revising of invitation lists, discussion of the social claims of their friends and acquaintance, and the usual anxious beating up of every available dancing-man.

"Addie will bring Mr. Griffiths, and Esther Mr. Peck," said Rose. "They go well, look nice, and one sees them everywhere, although Reuben calls them 'outsiders.'"

Rose loved dances, as well she might, for from the first she had been a success.

Rose, with her fair, plump shoulders and blonde hair, her high spirits and good-nature, her nimble feet and nimble tongue; Rose with her £50,000 and twenty guinea ball-gowns; Rose went down – magic phrase! – as not one girl in ten succeeds in doing.

47. From Swinburne's *Chastelard* (1866).

"I suppose," said Judith, "that the Samuel Sachses will have to be asked?"

She, though of course she had her admirers, was by no means such a success as her cousin.

"Yes, isn't it a nuisance?" cried Rose; "and the Lazarus Harts."

If there is a strong family feeling among the children of Israel, it takes often the form of acute family jealousy.

The Jew who will open his doors in reckless ignorance to every sort and condition of Gentile is morbidly sensitive as regards the social standing of the compatriot whom he admits to his hospitality.

The Leunigers, as we know, were not people of long standing in the Community, and numbered among their acquaintance Jews of every rank and shade; from the Cardozos, who were rich, cultivated, could almost trace their descent from Hillel,[48] the son of David, and had a footing in English society, to such children of nature as the Samuel Sachses.

"We must have Nellie Hepburn and the Strettel girls," went on Rose, consulting her list; "the men all rush at them, though I don't see that they are so pretty myself."

"I suppose they make a change from ourselves," answered Judith smiling, "whose faces are known by heart."

Judith was entering with spirit, with a zeal that was almost feverish, into the preparations for the forthcoming festivity.

She and Reuben had scarcely spoken to one another since the Day of Atonement. They had met once or twice at family gatherings, at which, either by accident, or design on Reuben's part, there had been no opportunity for private conversation.

Perhaps an instinctive feeling that the old relations were imperilled and that no new ones could ever be so satisfactory held them apart.

Meanwhile, Judith unconsciously fixed her mind on the one definite fact that Reuben would be at the Leunigers' dance. It was in the crowded solitude of ballrooms that they had hitherto found their best opportunity.

48. Hillel, foundational rabbi and sage.

The night so much prepared for came round at last, and the house in Kensington Palace Gardens became for the time being the scene of ceaseless activity.

Ernest had gone away into the country with the person who was always talked of as his valet; and Leo, of course, was in Cambridge; but the rest of the family – not excepting Lionel and Sidney, who handed programmes – had mustered in great force to do honour to the event.

From an early hour, poor Mrs. Leuniger had taken up her station in the doorway of the primrose-coloured drawing room, where she stood dejectedly welcoming her guests. She was wearing a quantity of valuable lace, very much crumpled, and had a profusion of diamonds scattered about her person, but had apparently forgotten to do her hair.

Rose, in short, voluminous skirts of pink tulle, and a pale pink satin bodice fitting close about her plump person, defining the lines of her ample hips, was performing introductions with noisy zeal, with the help of Jack Quixano, whom she had constituted her *aide-de-camp*. The Montague Cohens had come early, and Adelaide, in a very grand gown, scrutinized the scene with breathless interest, secretly wondering why more people had not asked her to dance.

Judith was looking very well. Her short, diaphanous white ball-gown, with its low-cut, tight-fitting satin bodice was not exactly a dignified garment, but she managed to maintain, in spite of it, her customary air of stateliness.

Moreover tonight, some indefinable change had come over the character of her beauty, heightening it, intensifying it, giving it new life and colour. The calm, unawakened look which many people had found so baffling, had left her face; the eyes, always curiously mournful, shone out with a new soft fire.

Bertie Lee-Harrison, tripping jauntily into the ballroom, remained transfixed a moment in excited admiration.

What a beautiful woman was this cousin, or pseudo-cousin, of Sachs's! How infinitely better bred she seemed than the people surrounding her!

The Quixanos, as Reuben had told him, were *sephardim*,[49] for whose claim to birth he had the greatest respect. But as for that red-headed young man, her brother – there were no marks of breeding about *him!*

Bertie was puzzled, as the stranger is so often puzzled, by the violent contrasts which exist among Jews, even in the case of members of the same family.[50]

Judith was standing some way off, where Bertie stood observing her, while two or three men wrote their names on her dancing-card.

She was one of the few people of her race who look well in a crowd or at a distance. The charms of person which a Jew or Jewess may possess are not usually such as will bear the test of being regarded as a whole.

Some quite commonplace English girls and men who were here tonight looked positively beautiful as they moved about among the ill-made sons and daughters of Shem, whose interesting faces gain so infinitely on a nearer view, even where it is a case of genuine good-looks.

Bertie waited a minute till the men had moved off, then advanced to Miss Quixano and humbly asked for two dances. Judith gave them to him with a smile. He was a poor creature, certainly, but he was Reuben's friend, and she knew that, in one way at least, Reuben thought well of him: he was one of the few Gentiles of her acquaintance whom he had not stigmatized as an "outsider."

Moreover, Bertie's little air of deference was a pleasant change from the rather patronizing attitude of the young men of her set, whose number was very limited, and who were aggressively conscious of commanding the market.

---

49. The privileging of Sephardic ancestry in *Reuben Sachs* should not be considered unique or innovative. See, for example, Michael Galchinsky on Anglo-Jewish writer, Grace Aguilar (1816–1847), in *The Origin of the Modern Jewish Woman Writer* (Detroit: Wayne State University Press, 1996), and *Grace Aguilar: Selected Writings* (Peterborough: Broadview, 2003). Similarly, see John Efron's *German Jewry and the Allure of the Sephardic* (Princeton: Princeton University Press, 2016).
50. Levy's point here is that Lee-Harrison's understanding of Anglo-Jew life, driven be contemporary media, constructs "Jews" as a homogenous, singular community with little or no diversity. Indeed, Levy highlights here that Lee-Harrison expects a particular "Jewish" *type*.

Bertie, his dances secured, moved off regretfully. He would have liked to sue for further favours, but his sense of decorum restrained him. Had he but known it, he might without exciting notice have claimed a third, at least, of the dances on Judith's card. Hard flirtation was the order of the day, and the chaperons, who were few in number, gossiped comfortably together, while their charges sat out half the night with the same partner.

Rose fell upon Bertie at this point, and fired him off like a gun at one or two partnerless damsels; while Judith, her partner in her wake, moved over to the doorway, where Adelaide was standing with Caroline Cardozo.

It was eleven o'clock and Reuben had not come. Judith had, it must be owned, changed her position with a view to consulting the hall-clock, and perhaps Adelaide had some inkling of this, for she said very loudly to her companion:

"It is a first night at the Thalian; my brother never misses one. I don't expect we shall see him tonight. Young men have so many ways of amusing themselves, I wonder they care about dances at all."

The musicians struck up a fresh waltz, and Bertie came over to claim the first of his dances with Judith.

He danced very nicely, in a straightforward, unambitious way, never reversing his partner round a corner without saying, "I beg your pardon."

Esther, her sharp brown shoulders shuffling restlessly in and out of a gold-coloured gown of *moiré* silk, and with a string of pearls round her neck worth a king's ransom, surveyed the scene with shrewd, miserable eyes, while rattling on aimlessly to her partner and *protégé*, Mr. Peck.

It was indeed a motley throng which was whirling and laughing and shouting across the music, in the bare, bright, flower-scented apartment.

The great majority of the people were Jews – Jews belonging to varying shades of caste and clique in that socially sensitive Community. But besides these, there was a goodly contingent of Gentile dancing men – "outsiders," according to Reuben, everyone – and a smaller band of Gentile ladies who were the fashion of the hour: among the sons of Shem.

("Bad form" was the label affixed by Reuben to these attractive maids and matrons.)

To give distinction to the scene, there were a well-known R.A., who had painted Rose's portrait for last year's Academy; two or three pretty actresses; an ex-Lord Mayor, who had been knighted while in office; and last, though by no means least in the eyes of the clannish children of Israel, Caroline Cardozo and her father.

"'What a pretty girl'? did you say," remarked Esther as the music died away. "Yes, Judith Quixano is very good-looking, but I don't know that she goes down particularly well."

Mr. Peck made some complimentary remark, of a general character, as to the beauty of Jewish ladies.

"Yes, we have some pretty women," Esther answered; "but our men! No, the Jew, unlike the horse, is not a noble animal."

Esther, it will be seen, was of those who walk naked and are not ashamed.[51]

At this point, a fashionably late hour, a new arrival was announced, and in marched Netta and Alec Sachs, their heads very much in the air, the self-assertion of self-distrust written on every line of their ingenuous countenances.

Netta, who had had a new dress from Paris for the occasion, really looked rather well in her own style, which was of the exuberant, black-haired, highly-coloured kind, and was at once greeted by one of the "outsiders" as an old friend.

This was no less a person than Adelaide's particular *protégé*, Mr. Griffiths, who, ignorant of the fine shades of Community class-distinction, engaged Miss Sachs for several dances under the eyes of his mortified patroness. Mr. Griffiths indeed was an impartial person, who, so long as you gave him a good floor, a decent supper, and a partner

51. See Genesis 2:25 (Bernstein, ed., *Reuben Sachs*, 116 n. 1).

who could "go," would lend the light of his presence to any ballroom whatever, whether situated in South Kensington or Maida Vale.

Alec Sachs was less fortunate than his sister. There were plenty of men, and the girls whom he thought worthy of inviting to dance for the most part declared themselves engaged.

This was a new experience to him. His skilful dancing – it was of the acrobatic or gymnastic order – his powers of "chaff" and repartee, above all, his reputation as a *parti,* had secured him a high place among the maidens of Maida Vale.

He stood now, his back to the wall, an air of contempt for the whole proceeding written on his florid face, exclaiming loudly and petulantly to his sister, whenever he had an opportunity: "They don't introduce, they don't introduce!"

Twelve o'clock was striking as Reuben Sachs stepped into the hall, which by this time was filled with couples "sitting out"; a few of them really enjoying themselves, the great majority gay with that rather spurious gaiety, that forcing of the note, which is so marked a characteristic of festivities. Sounds of waltz music were borne from the drawing room, and the draped aperture of the doorway – the door itself had been removed – showed a capering throng of dancers of varying degrees of agility.

Reuben advanced languidly; his face wore the mingled look of exhaustion and nerve-tension which with him denoted great fatigue.

It had been a long day: in and out of court all the morning; two committee meetings, political and philanthropical, respectively, later on; a hurried club dinner; and an interminable first night, with hitches in the scene-shifting, and long waits between the acts.

He had told himself over and over again that he would "cut" the dance at his uncle's, and here he was – alleging to himself as an excuse the impossibility of getting to sleep directly after the theatre.

It was little more than a month that he had been home, and already his old enemy, insomnia, showed signs of being on the track.

Reuben made his way to a position near the foot of the stairs, which afforded a good view of the ballroom.

He could not see Judith, a circumstance which irritated him, as he did not wish to go in search of her.

Beyond, in the crowded refreshment room, he had a glimpse of Rose, who was exceedingly *friande,* giggling behind a large pink ice, while Jack Quixano, a look of conscious waggishness on his face, dropped confidential remarks into her ear. Esther, on the stairs behind him, was delivering herself freely of cheap epigrams to an impecunious partner; and in a rose-lit recess was to be seen Montague Cohen, his pale, pompous, feeble face wreathed in smiles, enjoying himself hugely with a light-hearted matron from the Gentile camp.

The whole scene was familiar enough to Reuben, who from his boyhood upward had taken part in the festivities of his tribe, with their gorgeously gowned and bejewelled women, elaborate floral decorations and costly suppers.

The Jew, it may be remarked in passing, eats and dresses at least two degrees above his Gentile brother in the same rank of life.

The music came to an end, and the dancers streamed out from the ballroom.

Alec Sachs, who had been dancing with his sister, brushed past Reuben in the throng, and the latter was mechanically aware of hearing him say to his partner:

"Mixed, very mixed! A scratch lot of people I call it."

Lionel Leuniger came rushing up to him in all the glory of an Eton suit and a white gardenia.

"So you've come at last, Reuben! You are very late, and all the pretty girls are engaged. Have a programme?"

Reuben did not answer. By this time the ballroom was almost empty, and he could see clearly into the room beyond, where a red cloth recess had been built in from the balcony.

Chapter 12

There are flashes struck from midnights,
there are fire-flames noondays kindle,
Whereby piled-up honours perish,
whereby swollen ambitions dwindle….
* * * * * *
Oh, observe! Of course, next moment, the
world's honours, in derision,
Trampled out the light forever.

BROWNING: Christina[52]

There were two people sitting there, to all appearance completely absorbed in one another. In the distance, Judith's head bending slightly forward, her profile, the curves of her neck and bosom, and the white mass of her gown, were to be seen clearly outlined against the red. And another figure, in close proximity to the first, defined itself against the same background. Reuben started – Judith and Lee-Harrison!

His apathy, his fatigue, his uncertainty as to seeking Judith vanished as by magic. Outwardly he looked impassive as ever as he strolled into the all but deserted ballroom. It would have taken a close observer to perceive the repressed intensity of his every movement.

52. From Browning's "Christina."

There was a draped alcove dividing the front and back drawing rooms where Caroline Cardozo and Adelaide were standing as Reuben sauntered towards them.

"I hardly expected to see you," cried his sister as Reuben stopped and greeted the ladies. Adelaide was not enjoying herself. Her social successes, such as they were, were not usually obtained in the open competition of the ballroom.

"Am I too late for a dance?" asked Reuben, turning with deference to Miss Cardozo.

She handed him her card with a faint smile; there were two or three vacant places on it.

A great fortune (I am quoting Esther), though it always brings proposals of marriage, does not so invariably bring invitations to dance. Caroline Cardozo was a plain, thin, wistful girl, with a shy manner that some people mistook for stand-offishness, who was declared by the men of the Leunigers' set to be without an atom of "go."

Her wealth and importance notwithstanding, she was, as Rose in her capacity of hostess explained, difficult to get rid of.

Reuben, his dance duly registered, stood talking urbanely, while scrutinizing from beneath his lids the pair on the balcony.

A nearer view showed him the unmistakable devotion on Bertie's little fair face, which was lifted close to Judith's; he appeared to be devouring her with his eyes.

And Judith?

It seemed to Reuben that never before had he seen that light in her eyes, never that flush on her soft cheek, never that strange, indescribable, almost passionate air in her pose, in her whole presence.

His own heart was beating with a wild, incredulous anger, an astonished contempt. *He* to be careful of Judith; *he* to beware of engaging her feelings too deeply, *he*, who after all these years had never been able to bring that look into her eyes!

Bertie? It was impossible!

In any case (with sudden vindictiveness), it was unlikely that Bertie himself meant anything; and yet – yet – he was just the sort of man to do an idiotic thing of the kind.

The music struck up, and the dancers drifted back to the ballroom.

Reuben, bowing himself away, turned to see Judith and her escort standing behind him, while the latter, gathering courage, wrote his name again and again on her card.

Reuben remained a moment in doubt, then went straight up to her.

"Good evening, Miss Quixano."

There was a note of irony in his voice, a look of irony on his pale, tense face; the glance that he shot at her from his brilliant eyes was almost cruel.

"Ah, good evening, Reuben."

She gave a little gasp, thrilled, bewildered. Long ago, her searching glance travelling across the two crowded rooms had distinguished the top of Reuben's head in the hall beyond. She knew just the way the hair grew, just the way it was lifted from the forehead in a sidelong crest, just the way it was beginning to get a little thin at the temples.

Bertie moved off in search of his partner, with a bow and a reminder of future engagements.

"May I have the pleasure of a dance?"

Reuben retained his tone of ironical formality, but looking into her uplifted face his jealousy faded and was forgotten.

She held up her card with a smile; it was quite full.

Reuben took it gently from her hand, glanced at it, and tore it into fragments.

Judith said not a word.

To both of them the little act seemed fraught with strange significance, the beginning of a new phase in their mutual relations.

Reuben gave her his arm in silence; she took it, half frightened, and he led her to the furthermost corner of the crimson recess.

The dancers, overflowing from the ballroom beyond, closed about it, and they were screened from sight.

Reuben leaned forward, looking at her with eyes that seemed literally alight with some inward flame. The precautions, the restraints, the reserves which had hitherto fenced in their intercourse, were for the moment overthrown. Each was swept away on a current of feeling which was bearing them who knew whither?

To Judith, Reuben was no longer a commodity of the market with a high price set on him; he was a piteous human creature who entreated her with his eyes, yet held her chained: her suppliant and her master.

A soft wind blew in suddenly through the red curtains and stirred the hair on Judith's forehead.

"Aren't you cold?"

Reuben broke the silence for the first time.

"No, not at all." She smiled, then holding back the red drapery with her hand, looked out into the night.

The November air was damp, warm, and filled full of a yellow haze which any but a Londoner would have called a fog.

Across the yard and a half of garden which divided the house from the street, she could see the long deserted thoroughfare with its double line of lamps, their flames shining dull through the mist.

Reuben watched her. The clear curve of the lifted arm, the beautiful lines of the half-averted face stirred his already excited senses.

"Judith!"

She turned her face, with its almost ecstatic look, towards him, letting fall the curtain.

There were some chrysanthemums like snowflakes in her bodice, scarcely showing against the white, and as she turned, Reuben bent towards her and laid his hand on them.

"I am going to commit a theft," he said, and his low voice shook a little. Judith yielded, passive, rapt, as his fingers fumbled with the gold pin. It was like a dream to her, a wonderful dream, with which the whirling maze of dancers, the heavy scents, the delicious music were inextricably mingled. And mingling with it also was a strange, harsh sound in the street outside, which, faint and muffled at first, was growing every moment louder and more distinct.

Reuben had just succeeded in releasing the flowers from their fastening; but he held them loosely, with doubtful fingers, realizing suddenly what he had done.

Judith shivered, vaguely conscious of a change in the moral atmosphere.

The noise in the street was very loud, and words could be distinguished.

"What is it they are saying?" he cried, dropping the flowers, springing to the aperture, and pulling back the curtain.

Outside the house stood a dark figure, a narrow crackling sheet flung across one shoulder. A voice mounted up, clear in discordance through the mist:

"Death of a Conservative M.P.! Death of the member for St. Baldwin's!"

"Ah, what is it?"

Cold, white, trembling, she too heard the words, and knew that they were her sentence.

He turned towards her; on his face was the look of a man who has escaped a great danger.

"Poor Ronaldson is dead. It has come suddenly at the last. No doubt I shall find a telegram at home."

He spoke in his most everyday tones, but he did not look at her.

She summoned all her strength, all her pride:

"Then I suppose you will be going down there tomorrow?"

Her voice never faltered.

"No; in any case I must wait till after the funeral."

He looked down stiffly. It was she who kept her presence of mind.

"Don't you want to buy a paper and to tell Adelaide?"

"If you will excuse me. Where shall I leave you?"

"Oh, I will stop here. The dance is just over."

He moved off awkwardly; she stood there white and straight, and never moving.

At her feet lay her own chrysanthemums, crushed by Reuben's departing feet.

She picked them up and flung them into the street.

At the same moment, a voice sounded at her elbow:

"I have found you at last."

"Is this our dance, Mr. Lee-Harrison?"

Chapter 13

We did not dream, my heart, and yet
With what a pang we woke at last.

A. MARY F. ROBINSON[53]

Rose, with a candle in her hand, stood at the top of the stairs and yawned.

It was half-past three; the last waltz had been waltzed, the last light extinguished, the last carriage had rolled away.

Bertie, on the road to Albert Hall Mansions, was dreaming dreams; and Reuben, as he tossed on his sleepless bed, pondering plans for the coming contest, was disagreeably haunted by the recollection of some white chrysanthemums which he had let fall – on purpose.

"It has been a great success," said Judith, passing by her cousin and going towards her own room.

Rose followed her, and sitting down on the bed, began drawing out the pins from her elaborately dressed hair.

"Yes, I think it went off all right. Caroline Cardozo stuck now and then, and no one would dance with poor Alec, so I had to take him round myself."

Judith laughed. She had danced straight through the programme, had eaten supper, had talked gaily in the intervals of dancing. Rose got up from the bed and went over to Judith.

53. From Agnes Mary Frances Robinson's "Semitones."

"Please unfasten my bodice. I have sent Marie to bed."

Then, as Judith complied:

"What was Reuben telling Adelaide, and why did he make off so soon?"

"Mr. Ronaldson, the member for St. Baldwin's, is dead. A man came and shouted the news down the street."

Her voice was quite steady.

"What a ghoul Reuben is! He has been waiting to step into that dead man's shoes this last month and more. – 'Reuben Sachs, M.P.' – 'My brother, the member for St. Baldwin's' – 'A man told me in the House last night' – 'My son cannot get away while Parliament is sitting.' – The whole family will be quite unbearable."

Judith bent her head over an obstinate knot in the silk dress-lace. "He is not elected yet," she said.

Rose, her bodice unfastened, sprang round and faced her cousin. "Reuben is as hard as nails!" she cried with apparent inconsequence. "Under all that good nature, he is as hard as nails!"

"Undo my frock, please," said Judith, yawning with assumed sleepiness. "It must be nearly four o'clock."

Rose's capable fingers moved quickly in and out the lace; as she drew the tag from the last hole, she said: "Well, Judith, when are we to congratulate you?"

Judith did not affect to misunderstand the allusion. Bertie's open devotion had acted as a buffer between her and her smarting pride.

"Poor little person!" she said, and smiled.

"You might do worse," said Rose, gathering herself up for departure.

The mask fell off from Judith's face as the door closed on her cousin. She stood there stiff and cold in the middle of the room, her hands hanging loosely at her side.

Rose put her head in at the door –

"Do you know what Jack says?" she began, then stopped suddenly. "Judith, don't look like that, it is no good."

"No," said Judith, lifting her eyes, "it is no good." Then she went over to the door and shut it.

She sat down on the edge of her little white bed, supporting one knee with a smooth, solid arm, while she stared into vacancy.

Nothing had happened – nothing; yet henceforward life would wear a different face for her and she knew it.

It was impossible any longer to deceive herself. Her wide, vacant eyes saw nothing, but her mental vision, grown suddenly acute, was confronted by a thronging array of images.

Yes, she was beginning to see it all now; dimly and slowly indeed at first, but with ever increasing clearness as she gazed; to see how it had all been from the beginning; how slowly and surely this thing had grown about her life; how in the night a silent foe had undermined the citadel.

She had been caught, snared in a fine, strong net of woven hair, this young, strong creature. Her strength mocked her in the clinging, subtle toils.

She got up from the bed slowly, stiffly, and stood again upright in the middle of the room. Forced into a position alien to her whole nature, to the very essence of her decorous, law-abiding soul, it was impossible that she should not seek to strike a blow in her own behalf.

"It is no good," Rose had said, and she had echoed the words.

She did not put her thought into words, but her heart cried out in sudden rebellion, "Why was it no good?"

She went over mentally almost every incident in her intercourse with Reuben; saw how from day to day, from month to month, from year to year they had been drawn closer together in ever strengthening, ever tightening bonds. She remembered his voice, his eyes, his face – his near face – as she had heard and seen them a few short hours ago.

The conventions, the disguises, which she had been taught to regard as the only realities, fell down suddenly before the living reality of this thing which had grown up between her and Reuben. She recognized in it a living creature, wonderful, mysterious, beautiful and strong, with all the rights of its existence. It was impossible that they who had given it breath should do violence to it, should stain their hands with its blood – it was impossible.

She stood there still, her head lifted up, glowing with a strange exultation as her pride reasserted itself.

Opposite was a mirror, a three-sided toilet mirror, hung against the wall, and suddenly Judith caught sight of her own reflected face with its wild eyes and flushed checks; her face which was usually so calm.

Calm? Had she ever been calm, save with the false calmness which narcotic drugs bestow? She was frightened of herself, of her own daring, of the wild, strange thoughts and feelings which struggled for mastery within her. There is nothing more terrible, more tragic than this ignorance of a woman of her own nature, her own possibilities, her own passions.

She covered her face with her hands, and in the darkness the thoughts came crowding (was it thought, or vision, or feeling?).

The inexorable realities of her world, those realities of which she had so rarely allowed herself to lose sight, came pressing back upon her with renewed insistence.

That momentary glow of exultation, of self-vindication faded before the hard daylight which rushed in upon her soul.

She saw not only how it had all been, but how it would all be to the end.

Then once more his low, broken voice was in her ear, his supplicating eyes before her; the music, the breath of dying flowers assailed once more her senses; she lived over again that near, far-off, wonderful moment.

Again, Judith dropped her hands to her side; she clenched them in an intolerable agony; she took a few steps and flung herself face forward on the pillow.

Shame, anger, pride, all were swept away in an overwhelming torrent of emotion; in a sudden flood of passion, of longing, of desolation.

Baffled, vanquished, she lay there, crushing out the sound of unresisted sobs.

From her heart rose only the cry of defeat:

"Reuben, Reuben, have mercy on me!"

Chapter 14

Man's love is of man's life a thing apart;
'Tis woman's whole existence.

BYRON[54]

Judith slept far into the morning the sound, deep sleep of exhaustion; that sleep of the heavy-hearted from which, almost by an effort of will, the dreams are banished.

The first thing of which she was aware was the sound of Rose's voice, and then of Rose herself standing over her with a plate and a cup of coffee in her hand. Judith raised herself on her elbow; a vague sense of calamity clung to her; her eyes were heavy with more than the heaviness of sleep.

"It is ten o'clock," cried Rose. "I have brought you your breakfast. Rather handsome of me, isn't it?"

"Yes, very," said Judith, smiling faintly. "How came I to sleep so late?" It was quite an event in her well-ordered existence; she realized it with a little shock which set her memory in motion.

Judith drank her coffee hastily and sprang out of bed. She went through her toilet with even more care and precision than usual; there is nothing more conducive to self respect than a careful toilet.

Nothing had happened; everything had happened. Judith felt that she had grown older in the night.

54. From Lord (George Gordon) Byron's *Don Juan* (1819–1824).

All day long, people came and went and gossiped; gossiped loudly and ceaselessly of last night's party; more cautiously and at intervals of Mr. Ronaldson's death.

In the evening Adelaide, Esther, and Mrs. Sachs came in, but not Reuben. Not Reuben – she knew her sentence.

That brief moment of clear vision, of courage, had faded, as we know, even as it came. Now she dared not even look back upon it – dared not think at all.

Nothing had happened – nothing.

She fell back upon the unconsciousness, the unsuspiciousness of her neighbours. For them the world was not changed; how was it possible that great things had taken place?

She talked, moved about, and went through all the little offices of her life.

Now and then she repeated to herself the formulae on which she had been brought up, which she had always accepted, as to the unseriousness, the unreality of the romantic, the sentimental in life.

Two or three days went by without any event to mark them. On the fourth, Bertie Lee-Harrison paid a call of interminable length, when Judith, with bright eyes and flushed cheeks, talked to him with unusual animation.

In her heart she was thinking: "Reuben will never come again, and what shall I do?"

But the very next day Reuben came.

It was of course impossible that he should stay away for any length of time.

The Leunigers were at tea in the drawing room after dinner when the door was pushed open, and he entered, as usual, unannounced.

Judith's heart leapt suddenly within her. The misery of the last few days melted like a bad dream. After all, were things any different from what they had always been?

Here was Reuben, here was she, face to face – alive – together.

He came slowly forward, his eyelids drooping, an air of almost wooden immobility on his face. The black frock-coat which he wore, and in which he had that day attended Mr. Ronaldson's funeral, brought out the unusual sallowness of his complexion. There was a withered, yellow look about him tonight which forcibly recalled his mother.

Judith's heart grew very soft as she watched him shaking hands with her aunt and uncle.

"He is not well," she thought; then: "He always comes last to me."

But even as this thought flitted across her mind, Reuben was in front of her, holding out his hand.

For a moment she stared astonished at the stiff, outstretched arm, the downcast, expressionless face, taking in the exaggerated, self-conscious indifference of his whole manner, then, with lightning quickness, put her hand in his.

It was as though he had struck her.

She looked round, half-expecting a general protest against this public insult, saw the quiet, unmoved faces, and understood.

She, too, to outward appearance, was quiet and unmoved enough, as she sat there on a primrose-coloured ottoman, bending over a bit of work. But the blood was beating and surging in her ears, and her stiff, cold fingers blundered impotently with needle and thread.

Reuben finished his greetings, then sat down near his uncle. He had come, he explained, to say "goodbye" before going down to St. Baldwin's, for which, as he had expected, he had been asked to stand.

There was every chance of his being returned, Mr. Leuniger believed?

Well, yes. There was a small Radical party down there, certainly, beginning to feel its way, and they had brought forward a candidate. Otherwise, there would have been no opposition.

Sir Nicholas Kemys, who had a place down there, and who was member for the county of which St. Baldwin's was the chief town, had been very kind about it all. Lady Kemys was Lee-Harrison's sister.

Judith listened, cold as a stone.

How could he bear to sit there, drawling out these facts to Israel Leuniger, which in the natural course of things should have been poured forth for her private benefit in delicious confidence and sympathy?

Esther, who was spending the evening with her cousins, came and sat beside her.

"You are putting green silk instead of blue into those cornflowers," she cried.

Judith lifted her head and met the other's curious, penetrating glance.

"When I was a little girl," cried Esther, still looking at her, "a little girl of eight years old, I wrote in my prayer-book: 'Cursed art Thou, O Lord my God, Who hast had the cruelty to make me a woman.' And I have gone on saying that prayer all my life – the only one."

Judith stared at her as she sat there, self-conscious, melodramatic, anxious for effect.

She never knew if mere whim or a sudden burst of cruelty had prompted her words.

"According to your own account, Esther," she said, "you must always have been a little beast."

Esther chuckled. Judith went on sewing, but changed her silks.

She wondered if the evening would never end, and yet she did not want Reuben to go.

He rose at last and made his farewells.

Judith put out her hand carelessly as he approached her, then, drawn by an irresistible magnetism, lifted her eyes to his.

As she did so, from Reuben's eyes flashed out a long melancholy glance of passion, of entreaty, of renunciation; and once again, even from the depths of her own humiliation, arose that strange, yearning sentiment of pity, with which this man, who was strong, ruthless and successful, had such power of inspiring her.

Only for a moment did their eyes meet, the next she had turned hers away – had in her turn grown cold and unresponsive.

How dared he look at her thus? How dared he profane that holiest of sorrows, the sorrow of those who love and are by fate separated?

Chapter 15

Wer nie sein Brod mit Thraenen ass,
Wer nie die kummervollen Naechte
Auf seinem Bette weinend sass,
Der Kennt euch nicht, ihr himmlische Maechte!

GOETHE[55]

There was a little set of shelves in Judith's bedroom which contained the whole of her modest library, some twenty books in all – *Lorna Doone*;[56] Carlyle's *Sterling*;[57] Macaulay's *Essays*;[58] *Hypatia*;[59] *The Life of Palmerston*;[60] the *Life of Lord Beaconsfield*:[61] these were among her favourites, and they had all been given to her by Reuben Sachs.

Like many wholly unliterary people, she preferred the mildly instructive even in her fiction. It was a matter of surprise to her that clever creatures, like Leo and Esther for instance, should pass whole

55. From Johann Wolfgang von Goethe's (1749–1832) *Wilhelm Meister's Apprenticeship* (1795–1796); see Bernstein, ed., *Reuben Sachs*, 130 n. 1.
56. *Lorna Doone: A Romance of Exmoor* (1869), by Richard Doddridge Blackmore (1825–1900).
57. Thomas Carlyle's (1795–1881) *The Life of John Sterling* (1851).
58. Thomas Babbington Macaulay's (1800–1859) *Critical and Historical Essays* (1843).
59. *Hypatia, or New Foes with an Old Face* (1853), by Charles Kingsley (1819–1875).
60. Henry Lytton Bulwer's (1801–1872) *The Life of Henry John Temple, Viscount Palmerston: With Selections from His Diaries and Correspondence* (1870).
61. *The Earl of Beaconsfield: His Life and Work* (1881), by historian Lewis Apjohn.

days when the fit was on in the perusal of such works as *Cometh Up as a Flower*,[62] and *Molly Bawn*.[63]

But it was not novels, even the less frivolous ones, that Judith cared for.

Rose, whose own literary tastes inclined towards the society papers, varied by an occasional French novel, had said of her with some truth, that the drier a book was, the better she liked it. Reuben had long ago discovered Judith's power of following out a train of thought in her clear, careful way, and had taken pleasure in providing her with historical essays and political lives, and even in leading her through the mazes of modern politics.

Perhaps he did not realize, what it is always hard for the happy, objective male creature to realize, that if he had happened to be a doctor, Judith might have developed scientific tastes, or if a clergyman, have found nothing so interesting as theological discussion and the history of the Church.

Judith stood before her little library in the dark November dawn, with a candle in her hand, scanning the familiar titles with weary eyes. She was so young and strong, that even in her misery she could sleep the greater part of the night; but these last few days she had taken to waking at dawn, to lying for hours wide-eyed in her little white bed, while the slow day grew.

But today it was intolerable, she could bear it no longer, to lie and let the heavy, inarticulate sorrow prey on her.

She would try a book; not a very hopeful remedy in her own opinion, but one which Reuben, Esther, and Leo, who were all troubled by sleeplessness, regarded, she knew, as the best thing under the circumstances.

So, she scanned the familiar bookshelves, then turned away; there was nothing there to meet her case.

62. Broughton's *Cometh Up as a Flower* (1867).

63. Margaret Wolfe Hungerford's (1855–1897) novel, *Molly Bawn* (1878).

She put on her dressing-gown and stole out softly across the passage to Leo's empty room, where she remembered to have seen some books.

Here she set down the candle, and, as she looked round the dim walls, her thoughts went out suddenly to Leo himself, went out to him with a new tenderness, with something that was almost beyond comprehension.

She knew, though she did not use the word to herself, that after some blind, groping fashion of his own, Leo was an idealist – poor Leo!

There were books on a table near, and she took them up one by one: some volumes of Heine, in prose and verse; the operatic score of *Parsifal*;[64] Donaldson on the *Greek Theatre*;[65] and then two books of poetry, each of which, had she but known it, appealed strongly to two strongly marked phases of Leo's mood – *Poems and Ballads*,[66] and a worn green copy of the poems of Clough.[67]

She turned over the leaves carelessly.

Poetry? Yes, she would try a little poetry. She had always enjoyed reading Tennyson and Shakespeare in the schoolroom. So, she put the books under her arm, went back to her room, and crept into her little cold bed.

She took up the volume of Swinburne and began reading it mechanically by the flickering candlelight.

The rolling, copious phrases conveyed little meaning to her, but she liked the music of them. There was something to make a sophisticated onlooker laugh in the sight of this young, pure creature, with her strong, slow-growing passions, her strong, slow-growing intellect, bending over the diffuse, unreserved, unrestrained pages. She came at

---

64. Richard Wagner's (1813–1883) opera, *Parsifal*.
65. John William Donaldson's (1811–1861) *The Theatre of the Greeks* (1836).
66. Swinburne's *Poems and Ballads* (1866).
67. The probable text is *The Poems and Prose Remains of Arthur Hugh Clough: With a Selection from His Letters and Memoirs: Vol. II: Poems* (1869). The volume was edited by his wife, Blanche Smith Clough.

last to one poem, the *Triumph of Time*,[68] which seemed to have more meaning than the others, and which arrested her attention, though even this was only comprehensible at intervals. She read on and on:

> "I have given no man of any fruit to eat;
> I have trod the grapes, I have drunken the wine.
> Had you eaten and drunken and found it sweet,
> This wild new growth of the corn and vine,
> This wine and bread without lees or leaven,
> We had grown as gods, as the gods in heaven,
> Souls fair to look upon, goodly to greet,
> One splendid spirit, your soul and mine.
>
> "In the change of years, in the coil of things,
> In the clamour and rumour of life to be,
> We, drinking love at the furthest springs,
> Covered with love as a covering tree,
> We had grown as gods, as the gods above,
> Filled from the heart to the lips with love,
> Held fast in his arms, clothed warm with his wings,
> O love, my love, had you loved but me!
>
> "We had stood as the sure stars stand, and moved
> As the moon moves, loving the world; and seen
> Grief collapse as a thing disproved,
> Death consume as a thing unclean.
> Twin halves of a perfect heart, made fast
> Soul to soul while the years fell past;
> Had you loved me once, as you have not loved;
> Had the chance been with us that has not been."

The slow tears gathered in her eyes, and forcing themselves forward fell down her cheeks.

Then there was, after all, something to be said for feelings which had not their basis in material relationships. They were not mere

68. Swinburne's "The Triumph of Time," slightly reworded (New, ed., *The Complete Novels*, 547 n. 56); note how Levy has Swinburne guide Judith's crisis.

phantasmagoria conjured up by silly people, by sentimental people, by women. Clever men, men of distinction, recognized them, treated them as of paramount importance.

The practical, if not the theoretical, teaching of her life had been to treat as absurd any close or strong feeling which had not its foundations in material interests. There must be no undue giving away of one's self in friendship, in the pursuit of ideas, in charity, in a public cause. Only gushing fools did that sort of thing, and their folly generally met with its reward.

And this teaching, sensible enough in its way, had been accepted without question by the clannish, exclusive, conservative soul of Judith.

Where your interests lie, there should lie your duties; and where your duties, your feelings. A wholesome doctrine no doubt, if not one that will always meet the far-reaching and complicated needs of a human soul.

And if this doctrine applied to friendship, to philanthropy, to art and politics, in how much greater a degree must it apply to love, to the unspoken, unacknowledged love between a man and woman; a thing in its very essence immaterial, and which, in its nature, can have no rights, no duties attached to it?

It was the very hatred of the position into which she had been forced, the very loathing of what was so alien to her whole way of life and mode of thought that was giving Judith courage; if she could not vindicate herself, she must be simply crushed beneath the load of shame.

On one point, the nature and extent of her feeling for Reuben, there could no longer be illusion or self-deception; she would have walked to the stake for him without a murmur, and she knew it.

She knew, too, that Reuben loved her as far as in him lay; knew, with a bitter humiliation, how far short of hers fell his love.

Yet deep in her heart lay the touching obstinate belief of the woman who loves – that she was necessary to him, that she alone could minister to his needs; that in turning away from her and her large protection, her infinite toleration, he was turning away from the best which life had to offer him.

In the first sharp agony of awakening, Judith, as we know, had recognized that which had grown up between her and Reuben as a reality with rights and claims of its own. And the conviction of this was slowly growing upon her in the intervals of the swinging back of the pendulum, when she judged herself by conventional standards and felt herself withered by her own scorn, the scorn of her world, and the scorn of the man she loved.

A great tear splashing down across the *Triumph of Time* recalled her to herself.

She shut the book and sat up in bed, sweeping back the heavy masses of hair from her forehead.

Often and often, with secret contempt and astonishment, had she seen Esther dissolved in tears over her favourite poets.

Should she grow in time to be like Esther, undignified, unreserved? Would people talk about her, pity her, say that she had had unfortunate love affairs?

Oh, yes, they would talk, that was the way of her world; even Rose who was kind, and her own mother who loved her; no doubt they had begun to talk already.

Then, with a sense of unutterable weariness, she fell back on the pillows and slept.

Chapter 16

.... What help is there?
There is no help, for all these things are so.

A. C. SWINBURNE[69]

"Come over here, Judith, and I will show you something," said Ernest Leuniger as he sat by the fire in the morning room.

It was two days after Reuben's departure for St. Baldwin's, and Ernest had returned from the country that morning.

She went over to him, drawing a chair close to his. Judith was always very kind to him, and he admired her immensely, treating her at intervals with a sort of gallantry.

"Now look at me!" He had the solitaire board on his knee, and a little glass ball, with coloured threads spun into it, between his fingers.

"There, and there, and there!"

Judith bent forward dutifully, watching how he lifted the marbles, one after the other, from their holes.

"Don't you see?"

He looked at her triumphantly, but a little irritated at her obtuseness.

"Oh, yes," said Judith vaguely.

"The figure eight – don't you see?"

He pointed to the balls remaining on the board.

69. From Swinburne's "A Leave-Taking."

"So it is! Where did you learn to do that?" she asked, smiling gently.

"Ah, that's telling, isn't it?" He chuckled slyly, swept the balls together with his hand, and announced his intention of going in search of his man, with a view to a game of billiards.

Judith sank back in her chair as the door closed on him. The firelight played about her face, which, though not less beautiful, had grown to look older. She had been living hard these last few days.

The door opened, and Rose came in with her hat on and a parcel in her hand.

"No tea?" she cried, kneeling down on the hearthrug and holding out her hands to the fire.

"It isn't five o'clock yet."

There was an air of tension, of expectancy almost about Judith which contrasted markedly with her habitual serenity.

Rose turned suddenly. "When, Judith, *when*?" she cried with immense archness.

"I don't know," said Judith quietly.

There had been a dance the night before at the Kohnthals, where Bertie's unconcealed devotion to herself had been one of the events of the hour.

"Judith!" – Rose regarded her with excitement – "do you mean to say he has – spoken? Or are you humbugging in that serious way of yours?"

"Mr. Lee-Harrison has not proposed to me, if that is what you want to know."

Rose unfastened her fur mantle in silence. Something in Judith's manner puzzled her.

"He really is a nice little person," Rose went on after a pause; "such beautiful manners!"

"Oh, he hands plates and opens doors very prettily."

Judith spoke with a certain weary scorn, which Rose accepted as the tone of depreciation natural to a woman who discusses an undeclared admirer.

As a matter of fact, Judith recognized clearly the marks of breeding, the hundred and one fine differences which distinguished Bertie from the people of her set, whose manners were almost invariably tinged with respect of persons – that sure foe to respect of humanity. She recognized them and their value as hallmarks, wondering all the time with a dreary wonder, that anyone should attach importance to such things as these.

For in her heart, she despised the man. His intelligent fluency, his unfailing, monotonous politeness were a weariness to her.

His very readiness to fall down utterly before her, seemed to her – alas, poor Judith! – in itself a brand of inferiority.

"Tea at last," cried Rose, as the door opened. "And Adelaide. What a scent you have for tea, Addie."

Mrs. Montague Cohen swept in past the servant with the tray and took possession of the best chair.

"Mamma is here too," she cried; "she and aunt Ada will be in in a minute."

She drew off her gloves and the two girls rose to greet Mrs. Sachs, who at this point came with Mrs. Leuniger into the room.

Judith gave her hand very quietly to Reuben's mother, then took her seat at some distance from the group round the tea-table, occupying herself with cutting the leaves of a novel that had just arrived from Mudie's.

"Reuben is nominated," cried Adelaide, as she helped herself liberally to tea cake. "We had a telegram this morning."

"He expects to get in *this* time?" said Mrs. Leuniger, her pessimistic mind reverting naturally to her nephew's first unsuccessful attempt at embarking on a political career.

"It won't be for want of interest if he doesn't," said Mrs. Sachs; "Sir Nicholas Kemys and his wife are working day and night for him – day and night."

"And Miss Lee-Harrison, Lady Kemys' sister, *she* seems to be quite specially zealous in the good cause," put in Adelaide with meaning.

Secretly she was mortified at not having been asked down to St. Baldwin's for the campaign, Reuben having met her hints on the subject in a very decided manner. There was some satisfaction in venting her feelings on Judith, for whose benefit her last remark was uttered.

"When is the election?" said Rose, turning to her aunt.

"Not till today week. But I may safely say there is no real cause for anxiety."

"Did you see last night's *Globe*?" cried Adelaide, "and the *St. James's*? They cracked up Reuben no end."

Judith had seen them; she had seen also the *Pall Mall Gazette*, which expressed itself in very different terms.

She had put back *Poems and Ballads* on its shelf, and had taken to reading all the articles respecting the prospects of the St. Baldwin's elections that she could lay hands on.

At least she had a right to be interested in what she had been told so much about, but there were times when she felt, as she read, that her interest was intrusive, a thing to be ashamed of.

"I suppose," said Rose, "that he is too busy to write much."

"We had a letter yesterday – just a line. He seemed in splendid spirits, and has promised to wire from time to time," answered Adelaide.

"A good son," said Mrs. Sachs half tenderly, half jestingly, very proudly, "who never forgets his mother."

So, the talk went on.

Judith sat there listening, cutting open her novel, and throwing in a remark from time to time.

Every word that was uttered seemed a brick in the wall that was building between herself and Reuben.

In this crisis of his career, so long looked forward to, so often discussed, he had no need, no thought of her. Adelaide, Esther, Rose, all had more claim on him than she; she was shut out from his life.

Reuben, disappointed, defeated: in such a one she would always, in spite of himself, have felt her rights. But Reuben, hopeful, successful, surrounded by admiring friends and relatives, fenced in more closely still by his mother's love: from the contemplation of this glittering figure, cruel, triumphant, she turned away in a stony agony of self-contempt.

There was a sound of carriage wheels outside, and Lionel, who had been reconnoitring in the hall, burst in with the announcement, "Grandpapa has come."

Mrs. Leuniger received the news with something like agitation. Old Solomon's visits were few and far between, and now as he came, with pompous uncertainty of step across the room, the whole group by the fireplace rose hastily and went to meet him.

"Reuben is nominated," cried Adelaide, when the old man had been established in a chair.

"Yes, yes," said Solomon Sachs, "so I hear."

He turned to his niece: "He ain't looking well, that boy of yours."

Mrs. Sachs shifted uneasily.

"You saw him just before he went, Uncle Solomon, when he was tired out and not himself. He had been running from pillar to post all the week."

Mrs. Leuniger muttered dejectedly: "He is getting to look like his father."

Old Solomon raised his square hand to his beard, lifting his eyebrows high above the grave, shrewd, melancholy eyes.

Mrs. Sachs started; a sudden look of terror came into her face; the whites of her little hard eyes grew visible.

"Why don't he marry?" said Solomon Sachs after a pause; "why don't he marry that daughter of Cardozo's? She's not much to look at, certainly," he added, and a wave of whimsical amusement broke out suddenly over the large, grave face.

"Yes," put in Mrs. Leuniger, unusually loquacious, "his wife might see that he didn't work himself to death."

"I don't see how he can work less," cried Adelaide; "he has his way to make. And making your way, in these days, means pulling a great many strings."

"Yes," said Mrs. Sachs, relieved by this view of the case, "he must get on."

Judith began to feel that her powers of endurance had their limits. She rose slowly, went over to the fireplace for a moment, threw a casual remark to Rose, and went from the room.

As she made her way upstairs, the postman's knock sounded through the house, and then Lionel came running to her with a letter.

Her correspondence was very small, and she glanced with but faint interest at the little packet in her cousin's hand.

He was carrying it seal upwards, and suddenly her heart beat with a wild, mad beating, and the colour leapt to her pale checks.

She could see that it was sealed with wax. There was only one person that she knew who fastened his letters so. Reuben invariably made use of the signet ring which had belonged to his father, engraved with a crest duly bought and paid for at the Heralds' College.

She took the precious thing in her hand, closing her fingers over it, and smiled radiantly at the little boy.

"Thank you, Lionel."

Her room gained, she locked the door, sat down on the bed, and looked at her letter –

"To Miss Judith Quixano."

The writing was certainly not Reuben's, and he never used the "To."

Then she turned it over and examined the seal, the seal that was totally unfamiliar. She felt a little sick, a little dazed, and leaned her head against the wall.

After a time, she opened the letter and read it.

It was from Bertie Lee-Harrison, who asked her to be his wife.

It was a long letter, and stated, amongst other things, that he had already obtained his uncle's permission to address her.

Old Solomon's words as to his grandson's marriage flashed into her mind. It struck her that these plans for Reuben, for herself, were nothing less than an outrage.

It struck her also that she might marry Bertie.

All her courage had deserted her, all her daring of thought and feeling, in the face of a world where thought and feeling were kept apart from word and deed.

She, too, must fall down and worship at the shrine of the great god Expediency.

For how, otherwise, could she live her life?

Thrust out from Reuben's friendship, from all that made her happiness; shorn of self-respect, of the respect of her world; how could she bear to go on in the old track?

To her blind misery, her ignorance, Bertie was nothing more than a polite little figure holding open for her a door of escape.

Chapter 17

O' Thursday let it be: o' Thursday, tell her,
She shall be married to this noble earl.

ROMEO AND JULIET[70]

The news of Bertie's proposal spread like fire in the family. Rose had a vision of bridesmaids' gowns and of belted earls at the wedding. Lionel and Sidney, who always knew everything without being told, scented wedding-cake from afar, and indulged in a great deal of chaff *sotto voce* at their cousin's expense.

Adelaide was so excited when the news reached her, that she flattened her nose with the handle of her parasol, and exclaimed with her usual directness: "I wonder if the Norwood people will receive her."

Like everyone else, she took for granted that Judith would not be allowed to let slip so brilliant an opportunity.

A little maidenly hesitation, a little genuine reluctance perhaps – for Bertie was not the man to take a girl's fancy – and Judith would give further proof of her good sense; would open her mouth and shut her eyes and swallow what the Fates had sent her.

Poor Mrs. Quixano, greatly agitated, vibrated between the Walterton Road and Kensington Palace Gardens, expending quite a little fortune on blue omnibuses.

70. From Shakespeare's *Romeo and Juliet.*

It took a long time for her brother to convince her that Bertie's spurious Judaism could for a moment be accepted as the real thing.

"He is not a Jew," she reiterated obstinately; "would you let your own daughter marry him?"

Israel Leuniger evaded the question.

"My dear Golda, he is as much a Jew as you or I. Her father is perfectly satisfied, as well he may be – it is a brilliant match."

Mrs. Leuniger realized perfectly the meaning of £5000 a year. Bertie's other advantages, such, for instance, as his connection with the Norwoods, had little weight with her. If he had been one of the Cardozos, or the Silberheims – the great Jewish bankers – she could have understood all this fuss about his family.

"Who are the girls to marry in these days?" Mrs. Sachs said later on, as she, Mrs. Quixano, and Mrs. Leuniger sat in consultation. "If I had unmarried daughters I should tell them they would have to marry Germans."

The extreme nature of this statement did not fail to impress her hearers.

While the matrons sat in conclave in the primrose-coloured drawing room, Judith upstairs in her own little domain was trying to come to a decision on the subject of their discussion.

She had asked for time, for a few days in which to make up her mind, and of these, three had already gone by. But from the first there had always been this thing in her mind, this thing from which she shrank – that she would marry Bertie.

Her loneliness, her utter isolation of spirit in that crowded house where she was for the moment a centre of interest, a mark for observation, are difficult to realize. A severance of home ties had been to a certain extent involved in her change of homes. Her nearest approach to intimate women friends were Rose and Esther. As for the one friend who had wound his way into her reserved, exclusive soul, who had made a path into her enclosed, restricted life, he was her friend no more.

Reuben, oh, humiliation! had shown her plainly that he was afraid of her; afraid of any claims she might choose to base on the friendship which had existed between them. There was always this thought in her mind goading her.

On the faces round her, she read nothing but anxiety that she would make up her mind without delay. She knew what was expected of her.

Sometimes she thought she could have borne it better if someone had said outright:

"We know that you love Reuben; that Reuben loves you after a fashion. But it is no good crying for the moon; take your half loaf and be thankful for it."

It was this absolute, stony ignoring of all that had gone before which seemed to crush the life out of her.

She was growing to feel that in loving Reuben she had committed a crime too shameful for decent people even to speak of.

That Reuben had ever loved her she now doubted. It had all been a chimera of the emotional female brain, of which Reuben, who was subject, as we know, to occasional lapses of taste, had often confided to her his contempt. Yet, even now there were moments when, remembering all that had gone before, it seemed to her impossible that Reuben should do long without her.

If she flew in the face of nature and said "Yes" to Bertie, surely he would come forward and protest against such an outrage.

Every day she devoured the scraps of news which the papers contained respecting the coming election at St. Baldwin's.

Sometimes her mind dwelt on the splendours of the prospect held out before her; splendours which, in her ignorance, she was disposed to exaggerate. Reuben, climbing to those social heights, which for herself she had always deemed inaccessible, Reuben reaching the summit, would find her there before him. That would impress him greatly, she knew.

Let this thought be forgiven her; let it be remembered who was her hero, and how little choice there had been for her in the matter of heroes.

Yet such are the contradictions of our nature, that had the Admirable Crichton[71] stood before her, Don Quixote, or Sir Galahad[72] himself, I cannot answer for Judith that she would not have turned from them to the mixed, imperfect human creature – Reuben Sachs.

So, she sat there swaying this way and that, and then the door opened and her mother came in. Mrs. Quixano, we know, was not pleased at heart, but she had become very anxious for the marriage.

Judith listened passively as the advantages of her future position were laid before her.

Then she made her protest, fully conscious of its weakness.

"I do not like Mr. Lee-Harrison."

"Of course not," said Mrs. Quixano. "I should be sorry to hear that you did. No girl likes her intended – at first."

Judith bowed her head, conscious, ashamed.

Only that afternoon, Rose had said to her: "We all have to marry the men we don't care for. I shall, I know, although I have a lot of money. I am not sure that it is not best in the end."

And she sighed, as a red-headed, cousinly vision rose before her mental sight.

"You are coming home with me," went on Mrs. Quixano, "then we can talk it over comfortably. You mustn't keep the poor man waiting much longer."

Mrs. Leuniger came in as Judith was tying her bonnet strings.

"Judith is coming with me," said her mother.

Aunt Ada drifted slowly across the room to where Judith was standing. She looked at her with her miserable eyes, rubbing her hands together as she said:

"You had better write to Mr. Lee-Harrison before you go. You won't get such an opportunity as this every day."

Judith stared at her aunt in a sort of desperation.

---

71. James Crichton, the "Admirable Crichton" (1560–1582).
72. A knight and member of King Arthur's Round Table.

She, too? Aunt Ada, who all the days of her life had known wealth, splendour, importance, and, as far as could be seen, had never enjoyed an hour's happiness!

She looked at the dejected, untidy figure, with the load of diamonds on the fingers, the rich lace round neck and wrists, the crumpled gown of costly silk.

Aunt Ada still believed in these things then; in diamonds, lace and silk? Did not wring her hands and cry, "all is vanity!"[73]

Hers was truly an astonishing manifestation of faith.

* * * *

Judith sat in her father's study in the Walterton Road.

On the desk before her lay the letter which she had written and sealed to Mr. Lee-Harrison, containing her acceptance of his offer.

A certain relief had come with the deed. She had opened up for herself a new field of action; she would be reinstated in the eyes of her world, in Reuben's eyes, in her own.

She was so strong, so cruelly vital that it never for an instant occurred to her that she might pine and fade under her misery. She would have laughed to scorn such a thought.

Not thus could she hope for escape. A new field of action – there lay her best chance.

Her father came up to her and put his hand on her shoulder. She lifted her mournful glance to his; the kind, vague regard was inexpressibly soothing after the battery of eyes to which she had been recently exposed.

"I hope, my dear," said Joshua Quixano, "that you are quite happy in this engagement?"

"Oh, yes, Papa," answered Judith; but suddenly, as she spoke, the tears welled to her eyes and poured down her face.

73. See Ecclesiastes 1:2. In Tanakh later translations of the line say, "All is futile!"

Such a display of feeling on her part was without precedent. Both father and daughter were exceedingly shy, though in neither case with that shyness which manifests itself in outward physical flutter.

Mr. Quixano, deeply moved, stretched out his arms, and putting them about her, drew her close against him.

"My dear girl, my dear girl, you are not to do this unless you are sure it is for your happiness. Remember, there is always a home for you here. You can always come back to us."

She let her face lie on his breast, while the tears flowed unchecked. His words, the kind, timid, caressing movements with which he accompanied them were sweet to her, though in the depths of her heart she knew that there was no turning back.

Material advantage; things that you could touch and see and talk about; that these were the only things which really mattered, had been the unspoken gospel of her life.

Now and then you allowed yourself the luxury of a fine sentiment in speech, but when it came to the point, to take the best that you could get for yourself was the only course open to a person of sense.

The push, the struggle, the hunger, and greed of her world rose vividly before her. Wealth, power, success – a flaunting success for all men to see; had she not believed in these things as the most desirable on earth? Had she not always wished them to fall to the lot of the person dearest to her?

Did she not believe in them still? Was she not doing her best to secure them for herself?

But she was Joshua Quixano's daughter – was it possible that she cared for none of these things?

Chapter 18

The essence of love is kindness; and indeed it may be best defined as passionate kindness.

R. L. STEVENSON[74]

There is nothing more dear to the Jewish heart than an engagement; and when, four days after the events of the last chapter, that between Judith and Bertie was made public, congratulations flowed in, people called at all hours of the day, and the house in Kensington Palace Gardens presented a scene of cheerful activity and excitement.

The Community, after much discussion, much shaking of heads over the degeneracy of the times, had decided on accepting Bertie's veneer of Judaism as the real thing, and the engagement was treated like any other. If Mr. Lee-Harrison had continued in the faith of his fathers this would not have been the case. Though both engagement and marriage would in a great number of instances have been countenanced, their recognition would have been less formal and public, and of course a fair proportion of Jews would never have recognized them at all.

As it was, the brilliancy of the match was considered a little dimmed by the fact of Bertie's not being of the Semitic race. It showed indifferent sportsmanship, if nothing else, to have failed in bringing down one of the wily sons of Shem.

---

74. From Robert Louis Stevenson's (1850–1894) "On Falling in Love" (1877).

The Samuel Sachses came over at the first opportunity to *wish joy*, as they themselves expressed it, and inspect the new *fiancé*.

It is possible that they were not well received, for Netta gave out subsequently, whenever the Lee-Harrisons were in question: "We don't visit. Mamma doesn't approve of mixed marriages."

The day on which the engagement was announced happened also to be that of the election, and in the course of the afternoon, Adelaide burst in, much excited by the double event.

"An overwhelming majority!" she cried; "Reuben is in by an overwhelming majority."

Then going up to Judith, she gave her a sounding kiss.

"I am so glad, dear," she said gushingly.

Judith submitted to this display of affection with a good grace.

For the last four days she had been living in a dream; a dream peopled by phantoms, who went and came, spoke and smiled, but had about as much reality as the figures of a magic lantern.

As before Bertie's proposal she had been too much preoccupied to be much aware of him, so now she continued to accept his attentions in the same spirit of amiable indifference and unconsciousness. Bertie, as Gwendolen Harleth said of Grandcourt, was not disgusting.[75] He took his love, as he took his religion, very theoretically. There was something not unpleasant in the atmosphere of respectful devotion with which he contrived to surround her.

"Where is your young man?" went on Adelaide, taking a seat close to Judith, and noting with admiration the rich colour in her face, the wonderful brilliance of her eyes.

She felt very friendly towards the girl, who was safely out of her brother's way, and was doing so remarkably well for herself.

Afterwards she observed to her husband: "Judith looked quite good-looking. I always say there is nothing like being engaged for improving a girl's complexion."

"Am I my young man's keeper?" answered Judith lightly. "But I believe he is at Christie's."

75. Characters in *Daniel Deronda*.

"When can you come and dine with us?" went on Adelaide, who had never asked Judith to dinner before. "I will get some pleasant people to meet you. You shall choose your own night. Reuben must come as well – if he is not too jealous."

Adelaide did not mean to be cruel. She honestly believed that before the solid reality of an engagement, such vapour as unspoken, unacknowledged feeling must at once have melted.

And Judith was beyond being hurt by her words.

"I don't know exactly when we can come. Blanche Kemys wants us to go down there for a day or two next week. And we are half promised to Geraldine Sydenham for the week after."

She pronounced these distinguished names thus familiarly with a secret amusement, a sense that there was really a great deal of fun to be got out of Adelaide.

Mrs. Cohen stared open-mouthed, frankly impressed.

She had no idea that Bertie's people would come round without any difficulty in that way, and visions of herself and Monty honoured guests at Norwood Towers began to dance before her mental vision.

Esther, noting the little comedy, smiled to herself. She had perhaps a clearer view of Judith's state of mind than anyone else.

Judith indeed had almost succeeded in banishing thought during the last few days.

The persistent questions: "What will Reuben think?" "When will he know?" were the nearest approach to thought she had allowed herself.

Rose, who was thoroughly enjoying the engagement, and had confided to Judith that, once married, "she would be all right," came in at this point, and in her turn was made acquainted with the results of the election.

"Reuben comes back tonight by the last train, the 12:15," added Mrs. Cohen.

Judith thought: "He knows now."

Lady Kemys would certainly have told him what that morning had been a public fact.

People streamed in and out all the afternoon, greatly disappointed at not finding Bertie.

At six Judith, at the instigation of Rose, went to dress for dinner. Bertie had announced his intention of coming early.

As she shut the drawing room door behind her, the muscles of her face relaxed, she stood a moment at the foot of the stairs like a figure of stone.

Mrs. Sachs, emerging from Mr. Leuniger's private room, where she had been imparting the news of her son's triumph, came upon her thus.

"My dear!" she cried, going up to her.

Judith roused herself at once, and held out her hand with the comedy-smile which she had learned to wear these last few days.

Mrs. Sachs looked up at her, curiously moved. "My dear, I have to congratulate you."

"And I to congratulate you, Mrs. Sachs."

Their eyes met.

Hitherto Judith had been too proud to make the least advance to Reuben's mother, to respond even to any advance the latter might choose to make. But things were changed between them now.

She looked down at the sallow face, the shrewd eyes lifted to hers, almost, it seemed, in deprecation, in sympathy almost.

Her beautiful face quivered; stooping forward, she pressed her lips with sudden passion to the other's wrinkled cheek.

Chapter 19

.... This life's end, and this love-bliss have been lost here.
Doubt you whether
This she felt, as looking at me, mine and her souls rushed together?

BROWNING: Christina[76]

Esther sat a little apart, watching the lovers.

"Does she think he is a cardboard man to play with, or an umbrella to take shelter under?" she reflected. "A lover may be a shadowy creature, but husbands are made of flesh and blood. Doesn't she see already that he is as obstinate as a mule, and as whimsical as a goat?"

And she repeated the phrase to herself well pleased with it.

It was Sunday, the day following that of the election. A great family party had dined in Kensington Palace Gardens, and now were awaiting Reuben in the primrose-coloured drawing room.

Judith, side by side with Bertie, was listening amiably to a fluent account of his adventures in Asia Minor, in which he dwelt a great deal on his state of mind and state of health at the time; while Rose played scraps of music for the benefit of Jack Quixano, who had a taste for comic opera.

Judith was in such a state of tension as scarcely to be conscious of pain. Her duties as *fiancée* were clearly marked out; anything was

76. Again, from Browning's "Christina."

better than those days of chaos, of upheaval, which had preceded her engagement.

Esther's favourite phrase, that marriage was an opiate, had occurred to her more than once during the past week.

"I sat up all night long, and read every word of it. I was determined to make up my mind once for all," Bertie was saying.

Rose, at the piano, put her hand on her hip and hummed a scrap from a music-hall song, while Jack whistled an accompaniment:

> "Stop the cab,
> Stop the cab,
> Woh, woh, woh!"

The hall-door banged to with some violence.

The voices of Lionel and Sidney were heard upraised without:

"Vote for Sachs! Vote for Sachs, the people's friend!"

Then came the sound of another voice –

"My head was like a live coal, and my feet were as cold as stones ..." went on Bertie.

Judith looked sympathetic, and her heart leaped suddenly within her: it had not yet unlearnt the trick of leaping at the sound of Reuben's voice. Lionel flung open the door and capered into the room.

Behind him came Reuben Sachs.

Judith knew nothing more till she and Reuben were standing face to face, holding one another's hands.

Whatever had happened before, whatever happened afterwards, she will remember to the day of her death that in that one moment, at least, they understood one another.

No need for question, for answer, for explanation of motives and feelings.

It was all as clear as daylight, in that strange, brief, interminable moment which to the onlookers showed nothing more than a pale, tired-looking gentleman offering his congratulations on her engagement to a flushed, bright-eyed lady.

Even that sharp battery of eyes could discover nothing more than this.

It was not long before the hall-door closed again upon Reuben.

He flung out into the night.

"Good God, good God!" he said to himself. Not till he had actually seen her had he been able to realize what had happened; to understand what manner of change had come into his life; to see what might have been, and what was.

He had so many things to tell her, which might never now be told. The blind, choking rage of a baffled creature came over him; he sped on, stifled, through the darkness.

Judith, sitting dazed and smiling in the gaslight, said over and over again in her heart:

"Oh my poor Reuben, my poor, poor Reuben!"

At the piano Rose and Jack sang in chorus:

"For he's going to marry, Yum Yum,
    Yum Yum.
Your anger pray bury,
For all will be merry,
I think you had better succumb,
    cumb–cumb!"[77]

* * * *

At the beginning of January there was a wedding at the synagogue in Upper Berkeley Street which excited unusual interest.

The beautiful bride in her white silk dress was greatly admired. She was very pale, certainly, and in her wide-open eyes an acute observer might have read an expression of something like terror; but acute observers, fortunately, are few and far between. The bridegroom, to all appearance, enjoyed himself immensely, going through the whole pageant with great exactness, smashing the

77. From W.S. Gilbert and Arthur Sullivan's *The Mikado* (1885).

wine-glass vigorously with his little foot, and sipping the wine daintily from the silver cup.

Old Solomon Sachs, whose own daughters had been married in the drawing room at Portland Place, but who had no prejudice against the new fashion of weddings in the synagogue, occupied a prominent place near the ark, surrounded by his family.

Reuben Sachs stood close to Leopold Leuniger, a little in the background. His face was absolutely expressionless, unless weariness may be allowed to count as expression. He wanted yet a year or two of thirty, and already he was beginning to lose his look of youth. Leo, it must be owned, paid little attention to the ceremony. His eyes roved constantly to where the bridegroom's family, the Lee-Harrisons and the Norwoods, stood together in a rather chilly group; to where, in particular, Lady Geraldine Sydenham, in her unassertive, unaccentuated costume, leaned lightly against a porphyry column.

Bertie's people had accepted the situation with philosophy, and were really fond of Judith, but they found her family, especially in its collateral branches, uncongenial, if not worse.

On the outskirts of this group hovered Montague Cohen, absolutely rigid with importance. Near him Adelaide tossed her head in its smart new bonnet from side to side, her sallow face and diamond earrings flashing this way and that throughout the ceremony.

She knew that such restlessness was not good manners, but for the life of her she could not resist the temptation of seeing all that was to be seen.

Poor Mrs. Quixano, proud, but vaguely distressed, stood near her husband; while Jack, the picture of nimble smartness, ushered everyone into their places and made himself generally useful.

The wedding was followed by a reception; and afterwards, amid showers of rice from Lionel and Sidney, the newly-married pair set out *en route* for Italy.

Epilogue

It was the beginning of May, a bright, balmy evening, and the London season was in full swing.

The trees in Kensington Gardens wore yet that delicate brilliance of early spring, which, a passing glory all the world over, is in London the glory of an hour.

Under the trees children were playing and calling; out beyond in the road a ceaseless stream of cabs, carriages, carts, and omnibuses rolled by.

The broad back of the Prince Consort, gold beneath his golden canopy, shone forth with unusual splendour; the marble groups beneath stood out clearly against the soft background of pale blue sky.

And in the air – the London air – lingered something of the freshness of evening and of spring, mixed though it was with the odour of dinners in preparation, and with that of the bad tobacco which rose every now and then from the tops of the crowded road-cars rolling by.

The windows of a flat in the Albert Hall Mansions opposite were open, and a lady who was standing by one of them could smell the characteristic London odour, and could hear the sound of the children's voices, the rolling and turning of the wheels, and the shuffle and tramp of footsteps on the pavement below. She stood there a moment, one bare, beautiful hand and arm resting on the back of an adjacent couch, her eyes mechanically fixed on the glistening gilt cross surmounting the Albert Memorial, then she turned away suddenly, the thick, rich folds of her white silk dress trailing heavily behind her. The room across which she moved was small, but bright, and fitted up with the varied and elaborate luxury of a modern fashionable drawing room. Among the articles of *bric à brac*, costly, interesting, or merely bizarre which adorned it, were an antique silver *Hanucah* lamp and a spice box, such as the Jews make use of in certain religious services, of the same metal.[78]

Judith Lee-Harrison, for it was she, went over to the mantelpiece and consulted a little carriage-clock which stood upon it.

It was barely three months since her marriage, though to judge from the great, if undefinable change which had passed over her, it might have been the same number of years.

Her beauty indeed had ripened and deepened, so that it would have been impossible for the least observant person to pass it by, and the little over emphasis of fashion which had hitherto marred the perfect distinction of her appearance, had vanished.

"Mrs. Lee-Harrison would be a beauty if she cared about it," is the verdict of the world to which she had been introduced little more than a month ago.

But it was sufficiently evident that Mrs. Lee-Harrison did not care.

There was something almost austere in the pose of the head and figure, the lines of the mouth, the look in the wonderful eyes.

Those eyes, to a close observer indeed told that Judith had learnt many things, had grown strangely wise these last three months.

Yes, she knew now more clearly what before she had only dimly and instinctively felt: the nature and extent of the wrong which had been perpetrated; which had been dealt her; which she in her turn had dealt herself and another person.

She stood idly by the mantelpiece, staring at the mass of invitation cards stuck into the mirror above it.

One of them told that Lady Kemys would be at home that night in Grosvenor Place at nine o'clock. It was to be a political party, and

78. The wording here makes clear that the narrating voice is *not* Jewish.

like all such gatherings would begin early, for which reason she had dressed before dinner.

She took the card from its place and read it over. Reuben would be there of course.

Well, they would shake hands perhaps; she, for one, would be very amiable; they might even talk about the weather; and would he ask her to have an ice?

She put back the card indifferently; it mattered so little.

She had been home a month from Italy, and, as it happened, she and Reuben had not yet met.

The Lee-Harrisons had dined duly in Kensington Palace Gardens, but Reuben had been unavoidably detained that night at the House.

He had called on her some weeks ago, and she had been out.

But rumours of him had reached her. He had addressed his constituents with great *éclat* in the recess, and was already beginning to attract attention from the leader of his party.

As for more intimate matters, there were reports current connecting his name with Caroline Cardozo, with Miss Lee-Harrison, and with a chorus girl at the Gaiety.

Some people said he was only waiting for old Solomon's death to marry the chorus girl.

The last month, which had been full of new experiences, of social events for Judith, seemed curiously long as she stood there looking back on it.

It came over her that she was in a fair way to drift off completely from her own people; they and she were borne on dividing currents.

A sudden longing for the old faces, the old ties and associations came over her as she stood there; a strange fit of home-sickness, an inrushing sense of exile.

Her people – oh, her people! – to be back once more among them! When all was said, she had been so happy there.

A servant entered with a letter.

Judith, glancing again at the clock, saw that it was nearly eight, and said, as she opened the envelope,

"Has Mr. Lee-Harrison come in?"

He had come in half an hour ago, when she had been dressing, and had gone straight to his room.

The gong sounded for dinner as the man spoke, and a few minutes afterwards Bertie came tripping in, fully equipped for the festivities of the evening.

"Blanche expects us early," said Judith as she swept across to the dining room and took her place at the little round table.

Bertie looked across at her doubtfully, then put his spoon into the excellent white soup before him.

It was the first time for some weeks that they had dined alone together, and conversation did not flow freely.

Bertie looked up again, fixing his eyes, not on her face, but on the row of pearls at her throat.

"My dear, you will be very much shocked."

"Yes?" said Judith interrogatively, eating her soup.

"Reuben Sachs is dead."

"It is not true," said Judith, and then she actually smiled.

* * * *

The room was whirling round and round, a strange, thick mist was over everything, and through it came the muffled sound of Bertie's voice:

"It occurred this afternoon, quite suddenly. I heard it at the club. He had not been well for some time, and had collapsed more or less the last week. But no one had any idea of danger. It seems that his heart was weak; he had been overdoing himself terribly, and cardiac disease was the immediate cause of his death – cardiac disease," repeated Bertie, with mournful enjoyment of the phrase, and pulling a long face as he spoke.

Judith, sitting there like an automaton, eating something that tasted like sawdust, something that was difficult to swallow, was vividly conscious of only this – that Bertie must be silenced at any cost. Anything else could be borne, but not Bertie's fluent regrets.

Another woman would have fainted: there had never been any mercy for her: but at least she would not sit there while Bertie talked of it.

So, she lifted up her face, her stony face, and turned the current of his talk.

* * * *

Dinner came to an end at last and the automatic woman passed across to the sitting room.

Her husband followed her; she stared at him.

"You must take my excuses to Blanche. It is due to my family that I should not appear tonight in public."

"Certainly, certainly; a mark of respect, Blanche will understand. We will neither of us go."

She looked at him in horror, all her force of will gathered to a point: "Go – go! Blanche will expect it. There is no reason for you to stop here."

"My dear girl, do you think I can't stand an evening alone with you? It will be a change, quite a pleasant change."

* * * *

He had gone at last, and she stood there motionless by the mantelpiece, staring at the card for Lady Kemys' "At home."

"Infinite aeons" seemed to divide the present moment from that other moment, half an hour ago, when she had told herself carelessly, indifferently, that she would meet Reuben that night.

It struck her now that all the sorrow of her life, all the suffering she had undergone would be wiped out, would be as nothing, if only she could indeed meet Reuben – could see his face, hear his voice, touch his hand. Everything else looked trivial, imaginary; everything else could have been forgotten, forgiven; only this thing could never be forgiven him, this inconceivable thing – that he was dead.

* * * *

She knew that her agony was not yet upon her, that she was dazed, stunned, without feeling. A dim foreshadowing of what that agony would be was slowly creeping over her.

She moved across to a chair by the open window, and sat down.

The children's voices were silent; the iron gates were shut; the gold cross above the Memorial shone like fire as the rays of the setting sun fell upon it.

And below in the roadway the ceaseless stream of carriages moved east and west. On the pavement the people gathered, thicker and thicker. A pair of lovers moved along slowly, close against the park railings, beneath the shadow of the trees.

The pulses of the great city beat and throbbed; the great tide roared and flowed ever onward.

London, his London, was full of life and sound, a living, solid reality; not – oh, wonder! – a dream city that melted and faded in the sunset.

* * * *

Across the great gulf she could never stretch a hand. Death had thrown down no barriers, had brought them no nearer to one another. Wider and deeper – though before it had been very wide and deep – flowed the stream between them.

* * * *

Nearer and nearer came the sound, nearer and nearer. Where had she heard it before?

There was music in her ears now, the dreamy monotony of a waltz; the scent of dying flowers – tuberose, gardenia – was wafted in from some unseen region. It was a November night, not springtime sunset, and the harsh sound struck upwards through the mist:

"Death of a Conservative M.P.! Death of the member for St. Baldwin's!"

* * * *

Away in Cambridge Leo paced beneath the lime trees, a sick, blank horror at his heart.

Nearer, across that verdant stretch of twilit park, sat a wrinkled image of despair, surely a mark for the mirth of ironical gods.

And here by the open window sat Judith, absolutely motionless – a figure of stone.

Before the great mysteries of life her soul grew frozen and appalled.

It seemed to her, as she sat there in the fading light, that this is the bitter lesson of existence; that the sacred serves only to teach the full meaning of sacrilege; the beautiful of the hideous; modesty of outrage; joy of sorrow; life of death.

* * * *

Is life indeed over for Judith, or at least all that makes life beautiful, worthy – a thing in any way tolerable?

The ways of joy like the ways of sorrow are many; and hidden away in the depths of Judith's life – though as yet she knows it not – is the germ of another life,[79] which shall quicken, grow, and come forth at last. Shall bring with it, no doubt, pain and sorrow, and tears; but shall bring also hope and joy, and that quickening of purpose which is perhaps as much as any of us should expect or demand from Fate.

THE END

79. Judith is pregnant.

Miss Meredith[1]
(1889)

1. *Miss Meredith* was serialised before its publication as a book in *The British Weekly: A Journal of Social and Christian Progress* (April 19-June 28, 1889); see Beth Zion Lask, "Amy Levy," *Transactions of the Jewish Historical Society of England* 11 (1928): 184.

Chapter 1
A Family of Four

It was about a week after Christmas, and we – my mother, my two sisters, and myself – were sitting, as usual, in the parlour of the little house at Islington. Tea was over, and Jenny had possession of the table, where she was engaged in making a watercolour sketch of still life by the light of the lamp, whose rays fell effectively on her bent head with its aureole of Titian-coloured hair – the delight of the Slade school – and on her round, earnest young face as she lifted it from time to time in contemplation of her subject.

My mother had drawn her chair close to the fire, for the night was very cold, and the fitful crimson beams played about her worn, serene, and gentle face, under its widow's cap, as she bent over the sewing in her hands.

A hard fight with fortune had been my mother's from the day when, a girl of eighteen, she had left a comfortable home to marry my father for love. Poverty and sickness – those two redoubtable dragons – had stood ever in the path. Now, even the love which had been by her side for so many years, and helped to comfort them, had vanished into the unknown. But I do not think she was unhappy. The crown of a woman's life was hers; her children rose up and called her blest.

At her feet sat my eldest sister, Rosalind, entirely absorbed in correcting a bundle of proof-sheets which had arrived that morning from *Temple Bar*. Rosalind was the genius of the family, a full-blown London B.A., who occasionally supplemented her earnings as coach and lecturer by writing for the magazines. She had been engaged, moreover, for the last year or two, to a clever young journalist, Hubert Andrews by name, and the lovers were beginning to look forward to a speedy termination to their period of waiting.

I, Elsie Meredith, who was neither literary nor artistic, neither picturesque like Jenny nor clever like Rosalind, whose middle place in the family had always struck me as a fit symbol of my own mediocrity – I, alone of all these busy people, was sitting idle. Lounging in the armchair which faced my mother's, I twisted and retwisted, rolled and unrolled, read and reread a letter which had arrived for me that morning, and whose contents I had been engaged in revolving in my mind throughout the day.

"Well, Elsie," said my mother at last, looking up with a smile from her work, "have you come to any decision, after all this hard thinking?"

"I suppose it will be 'Yes,'" I answered rather dolefully; "Mrs. Grey seems to think it a quite unusual opportunity." And I turned again to the letter, which contained an offer of an engagement for me as governess in the family of the Marchesa Brogi, at Pisa.

"I should certainly say 'Go,'" put in Rosalind, lifting her dark expressive face from her proofs; "if it were not for Hubert, I should almost feel inclined to go myself. You will gain all sorts of experience, receive all sorts of new impressions. You are shockingly ill-paid at Miss Cumberland's, and these people offer a very fair salary. And if you don't like it, it is always open to you to come back."

"We should all miss you very much, Elsie," added my mother; "but if it is for your good, why, there is no more to be said."

"Oh, of course we should miss her horribly," cried Rosalind, in her impetuous fashion, gathering together the scattered proof-sheets as she spoke; "you mustn't think we want to get rid of you." And the little thoughtful pucker between her straight brows disappeared as she laid her hand with a smile on my knee. I pressed the inky, characteristic fingers in my own. I am neither literary nor artistic, as I said before, but I have a little talent for being fond of people.

"I'm sure I don't know what I shall do without you," put in Jenny, in her deliberate, serious way, making round, grey eyes at me across the lamp light. "It isn't that you are such a good critic, Elsie, but you have a sort of feeling for art which helps one more than you have any idea of."

I received very meekly this qualified compliment, without revealing the humiliating fact that my feeling for art had probably less to do with the matter than my sympathy with the artist; then observed, "It seems much waste, for me, of all of us, to be the first to go to Italy."

"I would rather go to Paris," said Jenny, who belonged, at this stage of her career, to a very advanced school of aesthetics, and looked upon Raphael[2] as rather out of date. "If only someone would buy my picture I would have a year at Julian's;[3] it would be the making of me."

"For heaven's sake, Jenny, don't take yourself so seriously," cried Rosalind, rising and laying down her proofs; "one day, perhaps, I shall come across an art-student with a sense of humour – growing side by side with a blue rose. Now, Elsie," she went on, turning to me as Jenny, with a reproachful air of superior virtue, lifted up her paint-brush, and, shutting one eye, returned in silence to her measurements – "now, Elsie, let us have further details of this proposed expedition of yours. How many little Brogi shall you be required to teach?"

"There is only one pupil, and she is eighteen," I answered; "just three years younger than I."

"And you are to instruct her in all the 'ologies?"

Rosalind had taken a chair at the table, and, her head resting on her hand, was interrogating me in her quick, eager, half-ironical fashion.

"No; Mrs. Grey only says English and music. She says, too, that they are one of the principal families of Pisa. And they live in a palace," I added, with a certain satisfaction.

---

2. Renaissance painter, Raphael (1483–1520).
3. An art academy in Paris.

"It sounds quite too delightful and romantic; if it were not for Hubert, as I said before, I should insist on going myself. Pisa, the Leaning Tower, Shelley – a Marchesa in an old, ancestral palace!"[4] And Rosalind's dark eyes shone as she spoke.

"Ruskin says that the Leaning Tower is the only ugly one in Italy,"[5] said Jenny, not moving her eyes from the Japanese pot, cleft orange, and coral necklace which she was painting.

"But the cathedral is one of the most beautiful, and the place is a mine of historical associations," answered Rosalind, her ardour not in the least damped by this piece of information.

As for me, I sat silent between these two enthusiasts with an abashed consciousness of the limitations of my own subjective feminine nature. It was neither the beauties or defects of Pisan architecture which at present occupied my mind, nor even the historical associations of the town. My thoughts dwelt solely, it must be owned, on the probable character of the human beings among whom I was to be thrown. But then it was I who was going to Pisa, and not my sisters.

"Does Mrs. Grey know the Marchesa Brogi personally?" asked my mother, who also was disposed to take the less abstract view of the matter.

"Oh, no, it is all arranged through the friend of a friend."

"I don't like the idea of your going so far, alone among strangers," sighed mother; "but, on the other hand, a change is just what you want."

"What a pity Hubert is not here tonight –that horrid *première* at the Lyceum! We must lay the plan before him tomorrow," struck in Rosalind, who, hopeless blue-stocking as she was, consulted her oracle with all the faith of a woman who barely knows how to spell.

---

4. Percy Bysshe Shelley.
5. Refers to John Ruskin's (1819–1900) comment (107) in *The Seven Lamps of Architecture* (New York: John Wiley, 1849) that "There is but one thoroughly ugly tower in Italy that I know of, and that is so because it is divided into vertical equal parts: the tower of Pisa" (Melvyn New, ed., *The Complete Novels and Selected Writings of Amy Levy 1861–1889* (Gainesville: University Press of Florida, 1993), 548, n. 3).

I went over to my mother and took the stool at her feet, which my sister had just vacated.

"It's going to be 'Yes,' mother; I have felt it all along."

"My dear, I won't be the one to keep you back. But need you make up your mind so soon?"

"Mrs. Grey says that the sooner I can leave the better. They would like me to start in a week or ten days," I answered, suppressing as best I could all signs of the feeling of desolation that came over me at the sound of my own words.

"You will have to get clothes," cried Rosalind; "those little mouse-coloured garments of yours will never do for ancestral palaces."

"Oh, with some new boots and an ulster – I'm afraid I must have an ulster – I shall be quite set up."

"You would pay very well for good dressing," observed Jenny, contemplating me with her air of impartial criticism. "You have a nice figure, and a pretty head, and you know how to walk."

"'Praise from Sir Hubert Stanley,'" replied Rosalind with some irony. "My dear Elsie, I have seen it in your eyes – they are highly respectable eyes, by the bye – I have seen it in your eyes from the first moment the letter came, that you meant to go. It is you quiet women who have all the courage, if you will excuse a truism."

"Well, yes, perhaps I did feel like going from the first."

"And, now that is decided, let me tell you, Elsie, that I perfectly hate the idea of losing you," cried Rosalind with sudden abruptness; then, changing her tone, she went on – "for who knows how or when we shall have you back again? You will descend upon that *palazzo* resplendent in the new boots and the new ulster; the combined radiance of those two adornments will be too much for some Italian Mr. Rochester[6] who, of course, will be lurking about the damask-hung corridors with their painted ceilings. Jane Eyre will be retained as a fixture, and her native land shall know her no more."

---

6. Refers to the character, Edward Fairfax Rochester ("Mr. Rochester"), in Charlotte Brontë's *Jane Eyre* (1847).

"You forget that Jane Eyre would have some voice in the matter. And I have always considered Mr. Rochester the most unpleasant person that ever a woman made herself miserable over," I answered calmly enough, for I was accustomed to these little excursions into the realms of fancy on the part of my sister.

"I think there's a little stone, Elsie, where the heart ought to be," and Rosalind, bending forward, poked her finger, with unscientific vagueness, at the left side of my waist.

"'Men have died and worms have eaten them, but not for love,'"[7] I quoted, while there flashed across my mind a vision of Rosalind sobbing helplessly on the floor a month before Hubert proposed to her.

"*Men*; it doesn't say anything about women," answered Rosalind, thoughtfully flying off, as usual, at a tangent.

"Is it woman's mission to die of a broken heart?" I could not resist saying, for there had been some very confidential passages between us, once upon a time. "The headache is too noble for my sex; you think the heartache would sound pleasanter."

"Elsie talking women's rights!" cried Jenny, looking up astonished from her work.

"Yes; the effects of a daring and adventurous enterprise are beginning to tell upon her in advance."

"We have wandered a long way from Pisa," I said; "but that is the worst of engaged people. Whatever the conversation is, they manage to turn it into sentimental channels."

"I sentimental!" cried Rosalind, opening wide her eyes; "I, who unite in my own person the charms of Cornelia Blimber and Mrs. Jellaby,[8] to be accused of sentiment!"

---

7. From William Shakespeare's *As You Like It* (New, ed., *The Complete Novels*, 548 n. 6).

8. Cornelia Blimber is a character in Charles Dickens' (1812–1870) *Dombey and Son* (1848); Mrs. Jellaby is a character in Dickens' *Bleak House* (1853); see New, ed., *The Complete Novels*, 548 n. 8.

I lay awake that night on my little iron bed long after Rosalind was sleeping the sleep of happy labour. I was a coward at heart, though I had contrived to show a brave front to my little world.

At the thought of that coming plunge into the unknown, my spirit grew frozen within me, and I began to wish that the fateful letter from Mrs. Grey had never been written.

Chapter 2
A Great Event

About ten days after the conversation recorded in the last chapter, I was driving down to Victoria station in a four-wheel cab, wearing the new ulster, the new boots, and holding on my knee a brand-new travelling bag. It was a colourless London morning, neither hot nor cold, but as I looked out with rather dim eyes through the dirty windows, I experienced no pleasure at the thought of exchanging for Italian skies this dear, familiar greyness. At my side sat my mother, silent and pale. Now that we two were alone together – my busy sisters had been at work some hours ago – we had abandoned the rather strained and feverish gaiety which had prevailed that morning at breakfast.

"Now, Elsie, keep warm at night; don't forget to eat plenty of Brand's essence of beef – it's the brown parcel, not the white one – and write directly you arrive."

Between us we had succeeded in taking my ticket and registering the luggage, and now my mother stood at the door of the carriage, exchanging with me those last farewells which always seem so much too long and so much too short.

It must be owned, this journey of mine bore to us both the aspect of a great event. We had always been poor, most of our friends were poor, and we were not familiarized with the easy modern notions of travel, which make nothing of a visit to the North Pole, or a little trip to China by way of Peru. And as the train steamed out at last from the station, my heart sank suddenly within me, and I could scarcely see the black-clothed familiar figure on the platform, for the tears which sprang to my eyes blinded me.

My first new experience was not a pleasant one, and as I lay moaning with sickness in a second-class cabin, I wondered how I or anyone else could ever have complained of anything while we stood on *terra firma.* All past worries and sorrows faded momentarily into nothingness before this present all-engulfing evil. It seemed an age before we reached Calais, where, limp, bewildered, and miserable, I was jostled into a crowded second-class carriage *en route* for Basle. The train jolted and shook, and I grew more and more unhappy, mentally and physically, with every minute. My fellow-passengers, a sorry, battered-looking assortment of women, produced large untempting supplies of food from their travelling bags, and fell to with good appetite. I myself, after some hesitation, sought consolation in the little tin of Brand's essence; after which, squeezed in between the window and a perfectly unclassifiable specimen of Englishwoman, I fell asleep.

When I awoke it was broad daylight, and the train was gliding slowly into the station at Basle.

I was stiff, cramped, and dishevelled, but yesterday's depression had given place to a new, delicious feeling of excitement. The porters hurrying to and fro, and shouting in their guttural Swiss-German, the people standing on the platform, the unfamiliar advertisements and announcements posted and painted about the station, all appeared to me objects of surpassing interest. The glamour of strangeness lay overall. A keen exhilarating morning breeze blew from the mountains, and as I stepped on to the platform it seemed as if I trod on air. With a feeling of adventure, which I firmly believe Columbus himself could never have experienced more keenly, I made my way into the crowded refreshment room and ordered breakfast. I was very hungry and thought that I had never tasted anything better than the coffee and rolls, the shavings of white butter, and the adulterated honey in its little glass pot. As I sat there contentedly, I found it difficult to realize that less than twenty-four hours separated me from the familiar life at Islington. It seemed incredible that so short a space of time had sufficed to launch me on this strange sea of new experiences, into this dream-like, disorganized life, where night was scarcely divided from day, and the common incident of a morning meal could induce, of itself, a dozen new sensations. The rest of that day was unmixed delight. I scarcely moved my eyes from the window as the train sped on through the St. Gothard Pass into Italy. What a wondrous panorama unrolled itself before me!

First, the mysterious, silent world of mountains, all black and white, like a photograph, with here and there the still, green waters of a mighty lake; then gentler scenes – trees, meadows, villages; last of all, the wide, blue waters of the Italian lakes, with their fringe of purple hills, and the little white villas clustered round them, and the red, red sunset reflected on their surfaces.

The train was late, and I missed the express at Genoa, passing several desolate hours in the great deserted station. It was not till eleven o'clock the next morning that a tired, dishevelled, and decidedly dirty young woman found herself standing on the platform at Pisa, her travelling rug trailing ignominiously behind her as she held out her luggage check in dumb entreaty to a succession of unresponsive porters.

The pleasant excitement of yesterday had faded, and I was conscious of being exceedingly tired and rather forlorn. Here was no exhilarating mountain air, but a damp breeze, at once chilly and enervating, made me shiver where I stood.

I succeeded at last, in spite of a complete absence of Italian, in conveying myself and my luggage into a fly, and in directing the driver to the Palazzo Brogi. As we jolted along slowly enough, I looked out, expecting every minute to see the Leaning Tower; but I saw only tall, grey streets, narrow and often without sidewalks, in which a sparse but picturesque population was moving to and fro. But I was roused, tired as I was, to considerable interest as we crossed the bridge, and my eye took in the full sweep of the river, with the noble curve of palaces along its bank, the distant mountains, beautiful in the sunshine, and the clear and delicate light which lay overall.

I had not long, however, to observe these things, for in another minute the drosky had stopped before a great square house in grey stone, with massive iron scrolls guarding the lower windows, and the driver, coming to the door, announced that this was the Palazzo Brogi.

My heart sank as I dismounted, and going up the steps, pulled timidly at the bell. The great door was standing open, and I could see beyond into a gloomy and cavernous vista of corridors.

No one answered the bell, but just as I was about to pull for a second time a gentleman, dressed in a grey morning suit *à l'anglais*, strolled out inquiringly into the passage. He was rather stout, of middle height, with black hair parted in the middle, and a pale, good-looking face. The fact that no one had answered the bell seemed neither to disconcert nor surprise him; he called out a few words in Italian, and, advancing towards me, bowed with charming courtesy.

"You are Miss Meredith," he said, speaking in English, slowly, with difficulty, but in the softest voice in the world; "my mother did not expect you by the early train." Here his English seemed to break down suddenly, and he looked at me a moment with his dark and gentle eyes. There was something reassuring in his serious, simple dignity of manner; I forgot my fears, forgot also the fact that I was as black as a coal, and had lost nearly all my hair-pins, and said, composedly, "I missed the express from Genoa. The train across the St. Gothard was late."

At this point, there emerged from the shadowy region at the back a servant in livery, who very deliberately, and without explanation of his tardiness, proceeded to help the driver in carrying my box into the hall.

The gentleman bowed himself away, and in another moment, I was following the servant up a vast and interminable flight of stone stairs.

The vaulted roof rose high above us, half lost to sight in shadow; everywhere were glimpses of galleries and corridors, and over everything hung that indescribable atmosphere of chill stuffiness which I have since learned to connect with Italian palaces.

Anything less homelike, less suggestive of a place where ordinary human beings carried on the daily, pleasant avocations of life, it would be impossible to conceive. A stifling sensation rose in my throat as we passed through a folding glass-door, across a dim corridor, into a large room, where my guide left me with a remark which of course I did not understand. With a sense of unutterable relief, I perceived the room to be empty, and I sat down on a yellow damask sofa, feeling an ignominious desire to cry. The shutters were closed before the great windows, but through the gloom I could see that the place was furnished very stiffly with yellow damask furniture, while enormous and elaborate chests and writing-tables filled up the corners. A big chandelier shrouded in yellow muslin hung from the ceiling, which rose to a great height, and was painted in fresco. There was no fire, and I looked at the empty gilt stove, which had neither bars nor fire-irons, with a shiver.

It was not long before an inner door was thrown open to admit two ladies, who came towards me with greetings in French. The Marchesa Brogi was a small, vivacious, dried-up woman of middle age, with an evident sense of her own dignity, looking very cold and carrying a little muff in her hands.

She curtseyed slightly as we shook hands, then motioned me to a seat beside her on the sofa. "This is my daughter Bianca," she said, turning to the girl who had followed her into the room.

I looked anxiously at my pupil, whose aspect was not altogether reassuring. She was a tall, pale, high-shouldered young person, elaborately dressed, with a figure so artificially bolstered up that only by a great stretch of imagination could one realize that she was probably built on average anatomical lines. Her hair, dressed on the top of her head and struck through with tortoiseshell combs, produced by its unnatural neatness the same effect of unreality. She was decidedly plain withal, and her manners struck me as being inferior to those of her mother and brother. She took up her seat at some little distance from the sofa, and whenever I glanced in her direction, I saw a pair of sharp eyes fixed on my face, with something of the unsparing criticism of a hostile child in their gaze.

I began to be terribly conscious of my disordered appearance – I am not one of those people who can afford to affect the tempestuous petticoat – and grew more and more bewildered in my efforts to follow the little Marchesa through the mazes of her fluent but curiously accentuated French.

It was with a feeling of relief that I saw one of the inner doors open, and a stout, good-tempered looking lady, in a loose morning jacket, come smiling into the room. She shook hands with me cordially, and taking a chair opposite the sofa, began to nod and smile in the most reassuring fashion. She spoke no English and very little French, but was determined that so slight an obstacle should not stand in the way of expressing her good-will towards me.

I began to like this fat, silly lady, who showed her gums so unbecomingly when she smiled, and to wonder at her position in the household.

The door opened yet again, and in came my first acquaintance, the gentleman in the grey suit.

I was growing more and more confused with each fresh arrival, and dimly wondered how long it would be before I fell off the hard yellow sofa from sheer weariness. The strange faces surged before me, an indistinguishable mass; the strange voices reached me, meaningless and incoherent, through a thick veil.

"She is very tired," someone said in French; and not long after this I was led across half a dozen rooms to a great bedroom, where, without taking in any details of my surroundings, I undressed, went to bed, and fell asleep till the next morning.

Chapter 3
New and Strange Experiences

When I awoke, the sun was streaming in through the chinks of the shutters, and a servant was standing at my bedside with a cup of coffee and some rolls. But I felt no disposition to attack my breakfast, and lay still, with a dreamy sensation as my eyes wandered round the unfamiliar room.

I saw a great, dim chamber, with a painted ceiling rising sky-high above me; plaster walls, coarsely stencilled in arabesques; a red-tiled floor, strewn here and there with squares of carpet; a few old and massive pieces of furniture, and not the vestige of a stove. The bed on which I lay was a vast, four-post structure, mountains high, with a baldaquin in faded crimson damask, and was reflected, rather libellously, in a glass-front of a wardrobe opposite.

"I shall never, never feel that it is a normal, human bedroom," I thought, appalled by the gloomy state of my surroundings. Then I drank my coffee, and, climbing out of bed, went across to the window, and unshuttered it.

An exclamation of pleasure rose to my lips at the sight which greeted me.

Below flowed the full waters of the Arno, spanned by a massive bridge of shining white marble, and reflecting on its waves the bluest of blue heavens. A brilliant and delicate sunshine was shed overall, bringing out the lights and shades, the differences of tint and surface, of the tall old houses on the opposite bank, and falling on the minute spires of a white marble church perched at the very edge of the stream.

The sight of this toy-like structure – surely the smallest and daintiest place of worship in the world – served to deepen the sense of unreality which was hourly gaining hold upon me.

"I wonder where the Leaning Tower is," I thought, as I hastily drew on my stockings, for standing about on the red-tiled floor had made me very cold, in spite of the sunshine flooding in through the windows; "what would they say at home if they heard I had been twenty-four hours in Pisa without so much as seeing it in the distance."

But I did not allow myself to think of home, and devoted my energies to bringing myself up to the high standard of neatness which would certainly be expected of me.

I found the ladies sitting together in a large and cold apartment, which was more homelike than the yellow room of yesterday, inasmuch as its bareness was relieved by a variety of modern ornaments, photograph-frames and other trifles, all as hideous as your latter-day Italian loves to make them. They greeted me with ceremony, making many polite inquiries as to my health and comfort, and invited me to sit down. The room was very cold, in spite of the morning sun, whose light, moreover, was intercepted by Venetian blinds. The chilly little Marchesa had her hands in her muff, while her daughter warmed hers over a *scaldino,* a small earthen pot filled with hot wood ashes, which she held in her lap.

The amiable lady in the dressing-jacket was evidently a more warm-blooded creature, for she stitched on, undaunted by the cold, at a large and elaborate piece of embroidery, taking her part meanwhile in the ceaseless and rapid flow of chatter.

It was rather a shock to me to gather that she was the wife of the charming son of the house; to whom, moreover, a fresh charm was added when it came out that his name was Romeo. I had put her down for a woman of middle age, but I learned subsequently that she was only twenty-eight years old, and had brought her husband a very handsome dowry. The pair were childless after several years of marriage and they lived permanently at the Palazzo Brogi, according to the old patriarchal Italian custom, which, like most old customs, is dying out.

I sat there, stupidly wondering if I should ever be able to understand Italian, replying lamely enough to the remarks in French which were thrown out to me at decent intervals, and encountering every now and then with some alarm the suspicious glances of the Signorina Bianca.

Once the kind Marchesina Annunziata – Romeo's wife – drew my attention with simple pride to a leather chair embroidered with gold, her own handiwork, as I managed to make out.

I smiled and nodded the proper amount of admiration, and wished secretly that my feet were not so cold, for the tiled floor struck chill through the carpet. Bianca offered me a scaldino presently, and the Marchesa explained that she wished the English lessons to begin on the following day. After that I sat there in almost unbroken silence till twelve o'clock, when the casual manservant strolled in and announced that lunch was ready.

The dining room, a large and stony apartment with a vaulted roof, was situated on the ground floor, and here we found the Marchesino Romeo and the old Marchese, to whom I was introduced. The meal was slight but excellently cooked; and the sweet Tuscan wine I found delicious. Romeo, who sat next to me, and attended to my wants with his air of gentle and serious courtesy, addressed a few remarks to me in English and then subsided into a graceful silence, leaving the conversation entirely in the hands of his womenkind.

After lunch, a drive and round of calls was proposed by the ladies, who invited me to join them. The thought of being shut up in a carriage with these three strange women, all speaking their unknown tongue, was too much for me, and gathering courage, the courage of desperation, I announced that unless my services were required I should prefer to go for a walk.

The ladies looked at me, and then at one another, and the good-natured Annunziata burst into a laugh. "It is an English custom," she explained. "You must not go beyond the city walls, Miss Meredith, not even into the Casine; it would not be safe," said the Marchesa; while Bianca looked scrutinizingly at my square, low-heeled shoes which contrasted sharply with her own.

It was with a feeling of relief, some twenty minutes later, that, peeping from the window of my room, I saw them all drive off, elaborately apparelled, in a closed carriage; Romeo, bareheaded, speeding them from the steps.

Then I sat down and wrote off an unnaturally cheerful letter to the people at home, only pausing now and then when the tears rose to my eyes and blurred my sight.

"I hope I haven't overdone it," I thought, as I addressed the envelope and proceeded to dress. "I'm not sure that there isn't a slightly inebriated tone about the whole thing, and mother is so quick at reading between the lines."

I passed across the corridor and down the stair to the first landing, where I lingered a moment. A covered gallery ran along the back of the house, and through the tall and dingy windows I could see a surging, unequal mass of old red roofs.

"How Jenny would love it all," I thought, as I turned away with a sigh.

As I reached the street door, Romeo emerged from that mysterious retreat of his on the ground-floor, where he appeared to pass his time in some solitary pursuit, looked at me, bowed, and withdrew.

"At last!" I cried, inwardly, as I sped down the steps. At last I could breathe again, at last I was out in the sunlight and in the wind, away from the musty chilliness, the lurking shadows of that stifling palace. Oh, the joy of freedom and of solitude! Was it only hours? Surely it must be years that I had been imprisoned behind those thick old walls and iron guarded windows. On, on I went with rapid foot in the teeth of the biting wind and the glare of the scorching sunlight, scarcely noticing my surroundings in the first rapture of recovered freedom. But by degrees the strangeness, the beauty of what I saw, began to assert themselves.

I had turned off from the Lung' Arno, and was threading my way among the old and half-deserted streets which led to the cathedral.

What a dead, world-forgotten place, and yet how beautiful in its desolation! Everywhere were signs of a present poverty, everywhere of a past magnificence.

The men with their sombreros and cloaks worn toga fashion; their handsome, melancholy faces and stately gait; the women bareheaded, graceful, drawing water from the fountain into copper vessels, moved before me like figures from an old-world drama.

Here and there was a little, empty piazza, the tall houses abutting on it at different angles, without sidewalks, the grass growing up between the stones. It seemed only waiting for first gentleman and second gentleman to come forward and carry on their dialogue while the great "set" was being prepared at the back of the stage.

The old walls, roughly patched with modern brick and mortar, had bits of exquisite carving imbedded in them like fossils; and at every street corner the house leek sprang from the interstices of a richly wrought moulding. A great palace, with a wonderful facade, had been turned into a wineshop; and the chestnut-sellers dispensed their wares in little gloomy caverns hollowed out beneath the abodes of princes. Already the nameless charm of Italy was beginning to work on me; that magic spell from which – let us once come under its influence – we can never hope to be released.

A long and straggling street led me at last to the Piazza del Duomo, and here for a moment I paused breathless, regardless of the icy blast which swept across from the sea.

I thought then, and I think still, that nowhere in the world is there anything which, in its own way, can equal the picture that greeted my astonished vision.

The wide and straggling grass-grown piazza, bounded on one side by the city wall, on the other by the low wall of the Campo Santo, with the wind whistling drearily across it, struck me as the very type and symbol of desolation.

At one end rose the Leaning Tower, pallid, melancholy, defying the laws of nature in a disappointingly spiritless fashion. Close against it the magnificent bulk of the cathedral reared itself, a marvel of mellow tints, of splendid outline, and richly modelled surfaces. And, divided from this by a strip of rank grass, up sprang the little quaint baptistery, with its extraordinary air of freshness and of fantastic gaiety, looking as though it had been turned out of a mould the day before yesterday.

Such richness, such forlornness, struck curiously on the sense. It was as though, wandering along some solitary shore, one had found a heaped treasure glittering undisturbed on the open sand.

I strolled for some time spellbound about the cathedral, not caring to multiply impressions by entering, shivering a little in the wind which held a recollection of the sea, and was at the same time cold and feverish. By and by, however, I made my way into the Campo Santo, lingering fascinated in those strange sculptured arcades, with the visions of life and death, of hell and heaven, painted on the walls.

One or two cypresses rose from the little grass-plot in the middle, and in the rank grass the jonquils were already in flower. I plucked a few of these and fastened them in my dress. They had a sweet, peculiar odour, melancholy, enervating.

The bright light was beginning to fail as I sped back hurriedly through the streets.

It was Epiphany, and the children were blowing on long glass trumpets. Every now and then the harsh sound echoed through the stony thoroughfare. It fell upon my overwrought senses like a sound of doom. The flowers in my bodice smelt of death; there was death, I thought, crying out in every old stone of the city.

The palazzo looked almost like home, and I fled up the dim stairs with a greater feeling of relief than that with which an hour or two ago I had hastened down them.

After dinner the Marchesa received her friends in the yellow drawing room.

A wood fire was lighted on the flat, open hearth of the stove, and a side table was spread with a few light refreshments – a bottle of Marsala wine, and a round cake covered with bright green sugar, being the most important items.

About eight o'clock the visitors began to arrive, and in half an hour nine or ten ladies and three or four gentlemen were clustered on the damask sofas, talking at a great rate, and gesticulating in their graceful, eager fashion. Bianca had withdrawn into a corner with a pair of contemporaries, whose long, stiff waists, high-heeled shoes, and elaborately dressed hair, resembled her own. The old Marchese sat apart, silent and contemplative, as was his wont, and Romeo, drawing a chair close to mine, questioned me in his precise, restricted English as to my afternoon walk.

This parliament of gossip, which, as I afterwards discovered, occurred regularly three times a week, was prolonged till midnight, but, kind Annunziata noticing my tired looks, I was able to make my escape by ten o'clock.

As I climbed into my bed, worn out by the crowded experiences of the day, there rose before me suddenly a vision of the parlour at home; of mother sewing by the fireside; of Jenny and Rosalind at work in the lamplight; of Hubert coming in with the evening papers and bits of literary gossip.

"If they could only see me," I thought, "alone in this unnatural place, with no one to be fond of me, with no one even being aware that I have a Christian name."

This last touch struck me as so pathetic that the tears began to pour down my face. But the tall bed, with the faded baldaquin, if oppressive to the imagination, was, it must be confessed, exceedingly comfortable, and it was not long before I forgot my troubles in sleep.

Chapter 4

The New Governess and Her Pupil

The English lesson next morning proved rather an ordeal. It took place in one of the many sitting rooms, a large room with an open hearth, on which, however, no fire was lighted. But with a shawl round my shoulders, and a *cassetta,* or brass box filled with live charcoal, for my feet, I managed to keep moderately warm.

Bianca rather sullenly drew a small collection of reading books, grammars, and exercise-books, all bearing marks of careless usage, from a cabinet, and placed them on the table. Then drawing a chair opposite mine, she fixed her suspicious, curious eyes on me, and said in French –

"Have you any sisters, Miss Meredith?"

"I have two. But we must speak English, Marchesina."

"I always spoke French with Miss Clarke," answered Bianca.

Miss Clarke, as I subsequently gathered, was my predecessor, who had recently left the palazzo after a sojourn of eighteen months, and who, to judge by results, must have performed her duties in a singularly perfunctory fashion.

"Are your sisters married?" Bianca condescended to say in English, looking critically at my grey merino gown, with its banded bodice, and at my hair braided simply round my head.

"No; but one is engaged."

"And have you any brothers?"

"No; not one."

"And I have not one sister, and two brothers, signorina," cried Bianca, apparently much struck by the contrast. "It is my brother Andrea who is so anxious for me to learn and to read books, although I am past eighteen. He writes about it to my father, and my father always does what Andrea tells him."

"Then you must work hard to please your brother," I said, with my most didactic air, examining the well-thumbed English-Italian grammar as I spoke.

"What is the use, when he has been five years in America? Who knows when I may see him? Ah! *molto indipendente* is Andrea – *molto indipendente!*" And Bianca shook her too neat head with a sigh of mingled pride and approbation.

We made a little attack on the grammars and reading books in the course of the morning, but it was uphill work, and I sat down to the piano, feeling thoroughly disheartened.

But the music lesson was a great improvement on the English. Bianca had some taste, and considerable power of execution, and we rose from the piano better friends. A short walk before lunch was prescribed by the Marchesa, and soon I was re-threading the mazes of the Pisa streets, Bianca hobbling slowly and discontentedly at my side on her high heels.

My pupil's one idea with regard to a walk was shops, and now she announced her intention of buying some *torino*, the sweet paste of honey and almonds so dear to Italian palates. As we turned into the narrow street, with its old, old houses and stone arcades, where, such as they are, the principal shops of Pisa are to be found, I could not suppress an exclamation of delight at the sight of so much picturesqueness.

"Ah," said Bianca, not in the least understanding my enthusiasm; "you should see the shops at Turin, and the great squares, and the glass arcades, and the wide streets. I have been there twice. Romeo says it is almost as beautiful as Paris."

The ladies drove out again after lunch in the closed carriage, and again I set out alone to explore the town. This time I penetrated into the interior of the cathedral, spending two happy hours in the dusky richness of the vast building; lost in admiration, now of the soft rich colour of marble and jasper and painted glass; now of the pictures on walls, roof, and altar; now of the grandeur of line, the mysterious effects of light and shadow planned by the cunning brain of a long-departed master.

The weather was much milder than on the previous day, and half a dozen tourists, with red guide-books, were making a round of inspection of the buildings on the piazza.

Two of these I recognized with a thrill to be my own compatriots. They were, to the outward eye, at least, quite uninteresting; a bride and bridegroom, presumably, of the most commonplace type; but I followed them about the cathedral with a lingering, wistful glance which I am sure, had they been conscious of it, would have melted them to pity. Once, as I was standing before Andrea del Sarto's[9] marvellous St. Catherine, the pair came up behind me.

"It's like your sister, Nellie," said the man.

"Nonsense! Nellie isn't half so fat, and she never did her hair like that in her life. Why, you wouldn't know Nellie without her fringe," answered the woman in a superior way as they moved off to the next object of interest mentioned in Baedecker.[10]

They were Philistines, no doubt; but I was in no mood to be critical, and must confess that the sound of their English voices was almost too much for my self-control.

The ladies went out after dinner, and I was left to the pains and pleasures of a solitary evening, an almost unprecedented experience in my career. The next day was Sunday: the family drove to early mass, and an hour or two later I made my way to the English church, the sparseness of whose congregation gave it rather a forlorn aspect.

---

9. Andrea del Sarto (1486–1530), a Florentine Renaissance painter.
10. Probably refers to Karl Baedeker's *Italy: Handbook for Travellers* (1886).

The English colony is small, and consists chiefly of invalids attracted by the mildness of the climate, who at the same time are too poor to seek a more fashionable health resort.

They did not, as may be imagined, present a very cheerful aspect, but the sight of them filled me with a passing envy. Mothers and daughters, sisters, friends; everyone came in groups or pairs, with the exception of myself; I, the most friendless and forlorn of all these exiles.

The chaplain and his wife called on me after I had sent in my name for a sitting, but there was never much intimacy between us.

In the evening of this, my first Sunday away from home, the Marchesa again "received," and once more I sat bewildered amid the flood of unintelligible chatter, or exchanged occasional remarks with Bianca, who appeared to have abandoned her suspicions of me, and had taken up her place at my side.

Chapter 5
Making Friends

I bought a dictionary and a grammar, and worked hard in my moments of leisure. My daily life, moreover, might be described as an almost unbroken Italian lesson, and it was not long before I began to understand what was said around me, and to express myself more or less haltingly in the language of my land of exile. A means of communication being thus opened up between myself and the Marchesina Annunziata, that open-hearted person began to take me into her confidence, and to pour out for my benefit a dozen little facts and circumstances which I might have lived all my life with the voluble, but reserved, Marchesa without ever having learnt.

Of Andrea, the absent son, she spoke often.

"*Molto indipendente!*" she said shaking her head, and using the same expression as her young sister-in-law.

This reprobate, it seemed, flying in the face of family tradition, had announced from the first his intention of earning his own living; had studied hard and with distinction for a civil engineer, and five years ago, refusing all offers of help, had accepted a post in America.

As for Romeo, the elder brother, he also, said his wife, was very clever; had passed his examinations as a barrister. "But, of course," she added, with naive pride, "he would never think of practising."

Romeo, indeed, to do him justice, was troubled by no disturbing spirit of radicalism, and carried on the ancestral pursuit of doing nothing with a grace and a persistence which one could not help but admire.

His mother possessed a fine natural aptitude for the same branch of industry; but the old Marchese, whom, though he spoke but little and was seldom seen, I soon perceived to have a character of his own, passed his days in reading and writing in some obscure retreat on the ground floor.

Bianca, after suspending her judgment for some days, had apparently given a verdict in my favour, for she now followed me about like a dog, a line of conduct which, though flattering, had certainly its drawbacks. The English lessons were always a trial, but they grew better as time went on, and the music lessons were far more satisfactory.

As for me, I began to grow fond of my pupil; she was such a crude, instinctive creature, so curiously undeveloped for her time of life, that one could not but take her under one's wing and forgive her her failings as one forgives a little child.

I had now been a month in Pisa, and the first sense of desolation and strangeness had worn off. There were moments, even now, when the longing for home grew so desperate that I was on the point of rushing off to England by the next train; but I was growing accustomed to my surroundings; the sense of being imprisoned in an enchanted palace had vanished, and had been followed by a more prosaic, but more comfortable, adaptation to environment.

My life moved from day to day in a groove, and I ceased to question the order of things. In the morning were the lessons and the walk with Bianca; the afternoons were looked upon as my own, and these I generally passed in reading, writing letters, and in walking about the city, whose every stone I was getting to know by heart.

Often leaning on the bridge and looking across at the palaces curving along the river, I peopled with a visionary company the lofty rooms beyond the lofty windows.

Here Shelley came with his wife[11] and the Williams',[12] and here it was that they made acquaintance with Emilia Viviani, the heroine of "Epipsychidion."[13] Byron[14] had a palazzo all to himself, whence he rode out with Trelawney, to the delight of the population.

Leigh Hunt[15] lingered here in his many wanderings, and Landor[16] led a hermit life in some hidden corner of the old town.

Claire Clairmont,[17] that unfortunate mortal, who where'er she came brought calamity, vibrated discontentedly between here and Florence, and it seemed that sometimes I saw her, a little, unhappy, self-conscious ghost, looking from the upper windows of Shelley's palace.

And here, too, after the storm and the shipwreck in which their lives' happiness had gone down, came those two forlorn women, Mary Shelley and Jane Williams.[18] Upon the picture of such sorrow I could not trust myself to gaze; only now and then I heard their shadowy weeping in some dim, great chamber of a half-deserted house.

At other times, I returned to my first friend, the great piazza, whose marvels it seemed impossible to exhaust, and for which I grew to entertain a curiously personal affection.

But as the spring came on, and the mild, enervating breezes ousted more and more their colder comrades, I began to long with all my soul and body for the country. The brown hills, so near and yet so far, inspired me with a fervour of longing. I had promised never to go beyond the city walls; even the great park, or Casine, where

---

11. Percy Shelley and Mary Shelley (1797–1851). See New, ed., *The Complete Novels*, on the "Pisan circle" (549 n. 17).
12. Edward Ellerker Williams (1793–1822) and Jane Williams (1798–1894).
13. Teresa ("Emilia") Viviani was the focus of Shelley's *Epipsychidion: Verses Addressed to the Noble and Unfortunate Lady: Emilia V – : Now Imprisoned in the Convent of –* (1821).
14. Lord (George Gordon) Byron; the sentence also refers to Edward Trelawny (1792-1881), another member of the "circle."
15. James Henry Leigh Hunt (1784–1859).
16. Walter Savage Landor (1775–1864).
17. Claire Clairmont (1798–1879).
18. See footnotes 11 and 12 above.

already the trees were bourgeoning, was forbidden ground, though sometimes, indeed, I drove out there with the ladies. The cool and distant peaks of the Apennines drew my heart towards them with an ever-growing magnetism.

The cypresses and ilexes springing up beyond the high white walls of a garden, the scent of spring flowers borne across to me in passing, filled me with a longing and a melancholy which were new to me.

As a matter of fact, the enervating climate, the restricted life and the solitude – for solitude, when all were said, it was – were beginning to tell upon my health. I was not unhappy, but I grew thin and pale, and was developing a hitherto unknown mood of dreamy introspection.

In June, I gathered, the whole Brogi household would adjourn to the family villa near the baths of Lucca. It was taken for granted that I was to accompany them, and, indeed, I had determined on making out my full year, should my services be required for so long.

After that, no doubt, a husband would be found for Bianca, and I could return to England with a clear conscience and quite a nice little amount of savings. Mother should have a deep armchair, and Rosalind a really handsome wedding present; and with my new acquisition of Italian I hoped to be able to command a higher price in the educational market.

The evenings were generally passed in chatter, in which I soon learnt to take my part; and I began to be included in the invitations to the houses of the various ladies who "received," like the Marchesa, on certain evenings of the week.

No subject of gossip was too trivial for discussion; and I could not but admire the way in which the tiniest incident was taken up, turned inside out, battledored this way and that, and finally worn threadbare before it was allowed to drop, by these highly skilled talkers. Talk, indeed, was the business of their lives, the staple fare of existence.

Everyone treated me with perfect courtesy, but also, it must be owned, with perfect coldness.

Bianca, as I said before, developed a sort of fondness for me; and Annunziata included me in her general benevolence – Annunziata, good soul, who was always laughing, when she was not deluged in tears. I fancy the charming Romeo had his drawbacks as a husband.

The Marchesa, with her glib talk, her stately courtesy, was in truth the chilliest and the most reserved of mortals. Of Romeo I saw but little. With the old Marchese, alone, I was conscious of a silent sympathy.

Chapter 6
Costanza Marchetti

One morning after breakfast I found the whole family assembled in the yellow drawing room in a state of unusual excitement. Even the bloodless little Marchesa had a red spot on either shrivelled cheek, and her handsome old husband had thrown off for once his mask of impenetrable and impassive dignity in favour of an air of distinct and lively pleasure.

Bianca was chattering, Romeo was smiling, and Annunziata, of course, was smiling too. Beckoning me confidentially towards her, and showing her gums even more freely than usual, she said: "There is great news. The Marchesino Andrea is coming home. We have had a letter this morning, and we are to expect him within a fortnight."

I received with genuine interest this piece of information. From the first I had decided that the rebel was probably the most interesting member of his family, and had even gone so far as to "derive" him from his father, in accordance with the latter-day scientific fashion which has infected the most unscientific among us.

Bianca was quite unmanageable that morning, and I had finally to abandon all attempts at discipline and let her chat away, in English, to her heart's content.

"I cried all day when Andrea went away," she rattled on; "I was quite a little thing, and I did nothing but cry. Even Mamma cried too. When he was home she was often very, very angry with Andrea. Everyone was always being angry with him," she added presently, "but everyone liked him best. There was often loud talking with Papa and Romeo. I used to peep from the door of my nursery and see Andrea stride past with a white face and a great frown." She knitted her own pale brows together in illustration of her own words, and looked so ridiculous that I could not help laughing.

I judged it best, moreover, to cut short these confidences, and we adjourned, with some reluctance on her part, to the piano.

Lunch was a very cheerful meal that day, and afterwards Bianca thrust her arm in mine and dragged me gaily upstairs to the sitting room.

"Only think," she said, "Mamma is writing to Costanza Marchetti at Florence to ask her to stay with us the week after next."

"Is the signorina a great friend of yours?"

Bianca looked exceedingly sly. "Oh yes, she is a great friend of mine. I stayed with her once at Florence. They have a beautiful, beautiful house on the Lung' Arno, and Costanza has more dresses than she can wear."

She spoke with such an air of naive and important self-consciousness that I could scarcely refrain from smiling.

It was impossible not to see through her meaning. The beloved truant was to be permanently trapped; the trap to be baited with a rich, perhaps a beautiful bride.

The situation was truly interesting; I foresaw the playing out of a little comedy under my very eyes. Life quickened perceptibly in the palazzo after the receipt of the letter from America.

Plans for picnics, balls, and other gaieties were freely discussed. There was a constant dragging about of heavy furniture along the corridors, from which I gathered that rooms were being suitably prepared both for Andrea and his possible bride.

At the gossip parliaments, nothing else was talked of but the coming event; the misdemeanours of servants, the rudeness of tradesmen, and the latest Pisan scandal being relegated for the time being to complete obscurity.

In about ten days, Costanza Marchetti appeared on the scene.

We were sitting in the yellow drawing room after lunch when the carriage drove up, followed by a fly heavily laden with luggage.

Bianca had rushed to the window at the sound of wheels, and had hastily described the cavalcade.

A few minutes later, in came Romeo with a young, or youngish, lady, dressed in the height of fashion, on his arm.

She advanced towards the Marchesa with a sort of sliding curtsy, and shook hands from the elbow in a manner worthy of Bond Street. But the meeting between her and Bianca was even more striking.

Retreating a little, to allow free play for their operations, the young ladies tilted forward on their high heels, precipitating themselves into one another's arms, where they kissed one another violently on either cheek. Retreating again, they returned once more to the charge, and the performance was gone through for a second time.

Then they sat down close together on the sofa, stroking one another's hands.

"Costanza powders so thickly with violet powder, it makes me quite ill," Bianca confided to me later in the day; "and she thinks there is nobody like herself in all the world."

When the Contessima, for that I discovered was her style and title, had detached her fashionable bird-cage veil from the brim of her large hat, I fell to observing her with some curiosity from my modest corner. She was no longer in her first youth – about twenty-eight, I should say – but she was distinctly handsome, in a rather hard-featured fashion.

When she was introduced to me, she bowed very stiffly, and said, "How do you do, Miss?" in the funniest English I had ever heard.

"It is so good of you to come to us," said the Marchesa, with her usual stateliness; "to leave your gay Florence before the end of the Carnival for our quiet Pisa. We cannot promise you many parties and balls, Costanza."

Perhaps Costanza had seen too many balls in her time – had discovered them, perhaps (who knows?), to be merely dust and ashes.

At any rate, she eagerly and gushingly disclaimed her hostess's insinuation, and there was voluble exchange of compliments between the ladies.

"Will you give Bianca a holiday for this week, Miss Meredith?" said the Marchesa, presently.

"Certainly, if you will allow it," I answered, saying what I knew I was intended to say.

Costanza looked across at me coldly, taking in the modest details of my costume.

"And when does the Marchesino arrive?" she asked, turning to his mother.

"Not till late on Thursday night."

Bianca counted upon her fingers.

"Three whole days and a half," she cried.

"On Friday," said the Marchesa, "we have arranged a little dance. It is so near the end of Carnival we could not put it off till long after his arrival."

"Ah, dearest Marchesa," cried Costanza, clasping her hands in a rather mechanical rapture, "it will be too delightful! Do we dance in the ballroom below, or in here?"

"In the ballroom," said the Marchesa, while Annunziata nodded across at me, saying –

"Do you dance, Miss Meredith?"

"Yes; I am very fond of it," I answered, but it must be owned that I looked forward with but scant interest to the festivity. My insular mind was unable to rise to the idea of Italian partners.

Costanza raised her eyeglass, with its long tortoiseshell handle, to her heavy-lidded eyes, and surveyed me scrutinizingly. It had been evident from the first that she had but a poor opinion of me.

"I hope you will join us on Friday, Miss Meredith," said the Marchesa, with much ceremony.

I could not help feeling snubbed. I had taken it for granted that I was to appear; this formal invitation was inexpressibly chilling.

I did not enjoy my holiday of the next few days. I had always been exceedingly grateful for my few hours of daily solitude, and these were mine no more.

The fact that the ladies of the household never seemed to need either solitude or silence had impressed me from the first as a curious phenomenon. Now, for the time being, I was dragged into the current of their lives, and throughout the day was forced to share in the ceaseless chatter, without which, it seemed, a guest could not be entertained, a ball given, or even a son received into the bosom of his family.

Here, there, and everywhere was the unfortunate Miss Meredith – at everybody's beck and call, "upstairs, downstairs, and in my lady's chamber."

"It is fortunate that it is only me," I reflected. "I don't know what Jenny or Rosalind would do. They would just pack up and go." For, at home, the liberty of the individual had always been greatly respected, which was, perhaps, the reason why we managed to live together in such complete harmony.

As for Bianca and her friend, they clattered about all day long together on their high heels, their arms intertwined, exchanging confidences, comparing possessions, and eating *torino* till their teeth ached. In the intervals of this absorption in friendship my pupil would come up to me, throw her arms round me, and pour out a flood of the frankest criticisms on the fair Costanza. To these I refused to listen.

"How can I tell, Bianca, that you do not rush off to the Contessima and complain of me to her?"

"Dearest little signorina, there could be nothing to complain of."

"Of course," I said, "we know that. I am perfect. But, seriously, Bianca, I do not understand this kissing and hugging of a person one moment, and saying evil things of her the next."

Bianca was getting on for nineteen, but it was necessary to treat her like a child. She hung her head, and took the rebuke very meekly.

"But, signorina, say what you will, Costanza does put wadding in her stays because she is so thin, and then pretends to have a fine figure. And she has a bad temper, as everyone knows…"

"Bianca, you are incorrigible!" I put my hand across her mouth, and ran down the corridor to my own room.

Chapter 7

The Home-Coming of the Rebel

The covered gallery which ran along the back of the house was flooded in the afternoon with sunshine. Here, as the day declined, I loved to pace, basking in the warmth and rejoicing in the brightness, for mild and clear as the day might be out of doors, within the thick-walled palace it was always mirk and chill.

The long, high wall of the gallery was covered with pictures – chiefly paintings of dead and gone Brogi – most of them worthless, taken singly; taken collectively, interesting as a study of the varieties of family types.

Here was Bianca, to the life, painted two centuries ago; the old Marchese looked out from a dingy canvas three hundred years old at least, and a curious mixture of Romeo and his sister disported itself in powder amid a florid eighteenth century family group. Conspicuous among so much indifferent workmanship hung a genuine Bronzino[19] of considerable beauty, representing a young man, whose charming aspect was scarcely marred by his stiff and elaborate fifteenth century costume. The dark eyes of this picture had a way of following one

19. Florentine painter, Agnolo Bronzino (1503–1572).

up and down the gallery in a rather disconcerting manner; already I had woven a series of little legends about him, and had decided that he left his frame at night, like the creatures in "Ruddygore,"[20] to roam the house as a ghost where once he had lived as a man.

Opposite the pictures, on which they shed their light, was a row of windows, set close together deep in the thick wall, and rising almost to the ceiling. They were not made to open, but through their numerous and dingy panes I could see across the roofs of the town to the hills, or down below to where a neglected bit of territory, enclosed between high walls, did duty as a garden.

In one corner of this latter stood a great ilex tree, its massive grey trunk old and gnarled, its blue-green foliage casting a wide shadow. Two or three cypresses, with their broom-like stems, sprang from the overgrown turf, which, at this season of the year, was beginning to be yellow with daffodils, and a thick growth of laurel bushes ran along under the walls. An empty marble basin, approached by broken pavement, marked the site of a forgotten fountain, the stone-crop running riot about its borders; the house-leek thrusting itself every now and then through the interstices of shattered stone. Forlorn, uncared for as was this square of ground, it had for me a mysterious attraction; it seemed to me that there clung to it through all change of times and weathers, something of the beauty in desolation which makes the charm of Italy.

It was about four o'clock on Thursday afternoon, and I was wandering up and down the gallery in the sunshine.

I was alone for the first time during the last three days, and was making the best of this brief respite from the gregarious life to which I saw myself doomed for some time to come. The ladies were out driving, paying calls and making a few last purchases for the coming festivities. In the evening Andrea was expected, and an atmosphere of excitement pervaded the whole household.

"They are really fond of him, it seems," I mused; "these people who, as far as I can make out, are so cold."

20. Refers to W.S. Gilbert and Arthur Sullivan's *Ruddigore; or, the Witch's Curse.*

Then I leaned my forehead disconsolately against the window, and had a little burst of sadness all by myself.

The constant strain of the last few days had tired me. I longed intensely for peace, for rest, for affection, for the sweet and simple kindliness of home.

I had even lost my interest in the coming event which seemed to accentuate my forlornness.

What were other people's brothers to me? Let mother or one of the girls come out to me, and I would not be behindhand in rejoicing. "No one wants me, no one cares for me, and I don't care for anyone either," I said to myself gloomily, brushing away a stray tear with the back of my hand. Then I moved from the window and my contemplation of the ilex tree, and began slowly pacing down the gallery, which was getting fuller every minute of the thick golden sunlight.

But suddenly my heart seemed to stop beating, my blood froze, loud pulses fell to throbbing in my ears. I remained rooted to the spot with horror, while my eyes fixed themselves on a figure, which, as yet on the further side of a shaft of moted sunlight, was slowly advancing towards me from the distant end of the gallery.

"Is it the Bronzino come to life?" whispered a voice in the back recess of my consciousness. The next moment I was laughing at my own fears, and was contemplating with interest and astonishment the very flesh-and-blood presentment of a modern gentleman which stood bowing before me.

"I fear I have startled you," said a decidedly human voice, speaking in English, with a peculiar accent, while the speaker looked straight at me with a pair of dark eyes that were certainly like those of the Bronzino.

"Oh, no; it was my own fault for being so stupid," I answered rather breathlessly, shaken out of my self-possession.

"I am Andrea Brogi," he said, with a little bow; "and I believe I have the pleasure of addressing Miss Clarke?"

"I am Miss Meredith, your sister's governess," I answered, feeling perhaps a little hurt that the substitution of one English teacher for another had not been thought a matter of sufficient importance for mention in the frequent letters which the family had been in the habit of sending to America. Andrea, with great simplicity, went on to explain his presence in the gallery.

"I am some hours before my time, you see. I had miscalculated the trains between this and Livorno. Now don't you think this a nice reception, Miss Meredith?" he went on, with a smile and a sudden change of tone.

"No one to meet me at the depot, no one to meet me at home! Father and brother at the club, mother and sister amusing themselves in the town."

His remark scarcely seemed to admit of a reply; it was not my place to assure him of his welcome, and I got out of the situation with a smile.

He looked at me again, this time more attentively. "But I fear you were really frightened just now. You are pale still and trembling. Did you think I was a ghost?"

"I thought – I thought you were the Bronzino come down from its frame," I answered, astonished at my own daring. The complete absence of self-consciousness in my companion, the delight, moreover, of being addressed in fluent English, gave me courage.

As I spoke, I moved over half-unconsciously to the picture in question. Andrea, smiling gently, followed me, and planting himself before the canvas contemplated it with a genuine naive interest that was irresistible.

I stood by, uncertain whether to go or stay, furtively regarding him. "Was there ever such a creature," I thought; "with your handsome serious face, your gentle dignified air for all the world like Romeo's; with your sweet Italian voice and your ridiculous American accent – and the general suggestion about you of an old bottle with new wine poured in – only in this case by no means to the detriment of the bottle?"

At this point the unconscious object of my meditation broke in upon it.

"Why, yes," said Andrea, calmly, "I had never noticed it before, but I really am uncommonly like the fellow."

As he spoke, he fixed his eyes, frank as a child's, upon my face.

As for me, I could not forbear smiling; whereupon Andrea, struck with the humour of the thing, broke into a radiant and responsive smile. I thought I had never seen anyone so funny or so charming.

At this point a bell rang through the house. "That must be my mother," he said, growing suddenly alert. "Miss Meredith, you will excuse me."

I lingered in the gallery after he had left, but my forlorn and pensive mood of ten minutes ago had vanished.

Rather wistfully, but with a certain excitement, I listened to the confused sound of voices which echoed up from below.

Then I heard the whole party pass upstairs behind me, the heels of the ladies clattering in a somewhat frenzied manner on the stones.

Annunziata was laughing and crying, the Marchesa was talking earnestly, the young ladies scattered ejaculations as they went. Every now and then I caught the clear tones of Andrea's voice.

At dinner that night there was high festival. Everyone talked incessantly, even Romeo and his father. We had a turkey stuffed with chestnuts, and the Marchese brought forth his choicest wines. At the beginning of the meal I had been introduced to the new arrival, and, for no earthly reason, neither had made mention of the less formal fashion in which we had become acquainted. Some friends dropped in after dinner, and Andrea was again the hero of the hour – a rather trying position, which he bore with astonishing grace. As for me, I sat sewing in a distant corner of the room, content with my spectator's place, growing more and more interested in the spectacle.

"That Costanza!" I thought, rather crossly, as I observed the handsome Contessima smiling archly at Andrea above her fan. "I wonder how long the little comedy will be a-playing? As for the end, that, I suppose, is a foregone conclusion." Then I bent my head over my crewelwork again. I was beginning to feel annoyed with Andrea for having passed over our first meeting in silence; I was beginning also to wish I had furred slippers like Bianca's, as a protection against the cold floor.

"Miss Meredith," said a voice at my elbow, "you are cold; your teeth will soon begin to chatter in your head."

Then, before I knew what was happening, I was led from my corner, and installed close to the kindling logs. And it was Andrea, the hero of the day, who had done this thing; but had done it so quietly, so much as a matter of course, as scarcely to attract attention, though the Marchesa's eye fell on me coldly as I took up my new position.

"It really does make the place more alive," I reflected, as I laid my head on my pillow that night. "I am quite glad the Marchesino is here. And I wonder what he thinks of Costanza?"

Chapter 8
An Italian Ball

The next day was exquisitely bright and warm – we seemed to have leapt at a bound into the very heart of spring – and when I came out of my room I was greeted with the news that Andrea and the ladies had gone to drive in the Cascine. Annunziata was my informant. She had stayed at home, and, freed from the rigid eye of her mother-in-law, was sitting very much at her ease, ready to gossip with the first comer.

The Marchesina could rise to an occasion as well as anyone else; could, when duty called, confine her stout form in the stiffest of stays, and build up her hair into the neatest of bandolined pyramids. But I think she was never so happy as when, the bow unbent, she could expand into a loose morning-jacket and twist up her hair into a vague, unbecoming knot behind.

"Dear little signorina," she cried, beckoning me to a seat with her embroidery scissors, "have you heard the good news? Andrea returns no more to America."

"He has arranged matters with Costanza pretty quickly," was my reflection; and at the thought of that easy capitulation, he fell distinctly in my esteem.

"He has accepted a post in England," went on Annunziata. "We shall see him every year, if not oftener. Everyone is overjoyed. It is a step in the right direction. Who knows but one day he may settle in Italy?" And she smiled meaningly, nodding her head as she spoke.

The ladies came back at lunch time without their cavalier, who had stayed to *collazione* with some relatives in the town.

The afternoon was spent upstairs talking over the dance which was to take place that evening, discussing every detail of costume and every expected guest. Costanza was as cross as two sticks, and hadn't a good word for anybody. We dined an hour earlier than usual, but none of the gentlemen put in an appearance at the meal. With a sigh of inexpressible relief, I rose from the table, and escaped to the welcome shelter of my room.

"I thought I was glad that Andrea had come," was my reflection; "but today has been worse than any other day."

Then, rather discontentedly, I began the preparations for my toilet.

The little black net dress, with the half-low bodice, the tan gloves, the black satin shoes, were already lying on the bed.

It is all very well to be Cinderella, if you happen to have a fairy-godmother. Without this convenient relative the situation is far less pleasant, and so common as to be not even picturesque. There are lots of Cinderellas who never went to the ball, or, if they did go, were taken no notice of by the prince, and were completely cut out by the proud sisters. Musing thus, with a pessimism which, to do me justice, was new to me, I proceeded to make myself as fine as the circumstances of the case permitted.

"At least my hair is nice," I thought, as I stood before the glass and fastened a knot of daffodils into my bodice; "Jenny always admired it, and the shape of my head as well. I've been pale and ugly, too, for the last few weeks, but my cheeks are red enough tonight. They are only red from crossness, and the same cause has made my eyes so bright, but how is anyone to know that?"

"Why, Elsie Meredith," said a voice suddenly from some inner region of my being, "what on earth is the matter with you? You, who could never be persuaded to take enough interest in your personal appearance! Surely you have caught the infection from that middle-aged Costanza."

With which rather spiteful reflection, I blew out the candles, threw a shawl over my shoulders, and ran downstairs into the ballroom.

I was the first arrival. The room stood empty, and I halted a moment on the threshold, struck by the beauty of the scene.

The walls of the vast chamber were hung from top to bottom with faded tapestry, of good design and soft dim colour. From the painted, vaulted ceiling, which rose to mysterious height, hung a chandelier in antique silver, ablaze with innumerable wax lights. Other lights in silver sconces were placed at intervals along the walls, and narrow sofas in faded gilt and damask bordered the wide space of the floor.

At one end of the room was a musician's gallery, whence sounds of tuning were already to be heard.

Two other rooms led out from the main apartment, both of smaller size, indeed, but large withal, and characterized by the same severe beauty. There was no attempt at decoration, nor was any needed.

Having made a general survey of the premises, I advanced to the middle of the ballroom, and began to feel the floor, across which a faded drugget had been stretched, critically with my foot.

Then I circled round on the tips of my toes under the chandelier, humming the air of "Dream Faces" very softly to myself.

So absorbed was I in this occupation that I did not notice the entrance of another person, till suddenly a voice sounded quite close to my ear, "Well, is it a good floor?"

I stopped, blushing deeply. There before me stood Andrea, looking very nice in his evening clothes.

"Not very good, but quite fair," I answered, recovering my self-possession before his complete coolness.

He smiled quietly.

"I guess you are a person of experience in such matters, Miss Meredith."

"I haven't been to many balls, but we are fond of dancing at home."

"We?" said Andrea, interrogatively.

"My sisters – "

"And brothers?"

"I haven't any brothers."

"And friends?"

"Yes, and friends." I could not help laughing; then thinking that he looked rather offended, I added by way of general conversation –

"How beautiful this room looks. It seems quite desecration to dance in it."

He looked round, and up and down.

"Yes, I suppose it is elegant. I think it very gloomy."

Again, I found myself smiling. There was something so absurd in this mixture of the soft, sweet Italian tones and the very pronounced American accent, not to speak of the occasional flowers of American idiom.

This time, however, Andrea did not appear offended, but smiled back at me most charmingly, then turned to greet his mother, who, the two girls in her wake, came sweeping across the room in violet velvet and diamonds.

"You are down early, Miss Meredith," she said to me without moving a muscle of her face, but making me feel that I had committed a breach of propriety in venturing alone downstairs.

"You look so nice," cried Bianca, who, in blue-striped silk and a high tortoiseshell comb, had made the very worst of herself.

Costanza, shrugging her shoulders, turned and rustled across the room.

I was surprised to see how handsome she looked. With her gown of richest brocade, made with a long train and Elizabethan collar, with the rubies gleaming in her dark hair and in the folds of her bodice, she seemed a figure well in harmony with the stately beauty of her surroundings. As though conscious of her effect, she moved over to the entrance of the inner room, and stood there framed in the arched doorway with its hangings of faded damask. Andrea went at once to her side.

"It's a long time since we have had a dance together, Contessima."

"A long, long time, Marchesino."

Then their voices fell, and there was nothing to be heard but a twittering exchange of whispers.

Bianca put her arm about my waist and whirled me round and round.

"We don't dance the same way," she said, releasing me after a brief but breathless interval.

Annunziata in apple-green brocade and a pearl stomacher was the next arrival, laughing heartily, and flourishing her lace handkerchief as she came. Behind her strolled her husband, handsome, indolent, and grave as a judge. The old Marchese brought up the rear.

The guests began now to arrive; smart, dignified, voluble matrons; smart, expectant girls; slight, serious young civilians, dandling their hats as they came; pretty little officers in uniform, with an air of being very much at home in a ballroom. Romeo brought me a programme, and wrote his name down for the lancers.

Then I stood there rather forlornly while the musicians struck up the first waltz.

At the first notes of the music Andrea left Costanza's side and came towards me.

"He is going to ask me to dance," was my involuntary reflection; "how nice! I am sure he dances well."

"Let me introduce il signor capitano," said Romeo's voice in my ear; and there stood a trim little person in uniform before me, bowing and requesting the honour of the first dance.

"One moment," said Andrea, quietly, as, rather disappointed, I began to move away with my partner; "Miss Meredith, may I see your card?"

I handed him the little bit of gilt pasteboard, virgin, save for his brother's name.

"Will you give me six and ten?"

"Yes."

He returned to Costanza, his partner for the dance, and I and my officer plunged into the throng.

It was not a success. There were no points of agreement in our practice of waltzing, and after a few turns we subsided on to one of the damask sofas, exchanging commonplaces and watching the dancers, whose rapid twists and bounding action filled my heart with despair.

"I shall never be able to dance like that," I reflected. It was by no means an ungraceful performance. They leapt high, it is true, but in no vulgar fashion of mere jumping; rather they rose into the air with something of the ease and elasticity of an india-rubber ball, maintaining throughout an appearance of great seriousness and dignity.

At the end of the dance, my partner bowed himself away, and I withdrew rather forlornly to a corner, hoping to escape unnoticed. Here, however, Romeo again espied me, and led up to me a rather despondent young gentleman – a student at the University of Pisa, I afterwards learned – whom I had observed nursing his tall silk hat in solitude throughout the previous dance.

I explained earnestly that I could not dance Italian fashion; that I preferred, indeed, to be a spectator, and settled down into my corner with some philosophy.

"I dare say Andrea can waltz my way," I thought, looking down at my programme, where the initials A. B. stood out clearly on two of the gilt lines. "It is rather disappointing to have to sit still and look on while other people dance to this delightful music, but it is amusing enough, in its way, and I must keep my eyes open and remember things to tell the girls."

It annoyed me, I confess, a little to meet Costanza's glance of contemptuous pity as she whirled by with a tall officer, and a mean-spirited desire came over me to explain to her that I was sitting out from choice, and not from necessity. The flood of dancers rushed on – those many-coloured ephemera, on which the old, dim walls looked down so gravely – and still I sat there patiently enough, though my eyes were beginning to ache and my brain to whirl.

Annunziata's apple-green skirts, Bianca's blue and white stripes, the Contessima's brocade and rubies, were growing familiar to weariness, so often did they flash before my sight. It was with genuine relief that I welcomed Romeo, who came up to claim the fifth dance, the lancers, for which he had engaged me at the beginning of the evening.

But alas! the word "lancers" printed in French on the programme proved a mere will-o'-the-wisp, and I found myself drawn into the intricacies of a quite unknown and elaborate dance.

Romeo, gravely piloting me through the confusing maze, was all courtesy and patience; but Andrea, who with Costanza was our *vis-à-vis,* seemed entirely absorbed in observing my stupidity.

"And I am really getting through with it very well," was my reflection; "it is all that Costanza who makes him notice the mistakes."

The next dance was Andrea's – a waltz.

"Have you been having a good time, Miss Meredith?" he asked, as we stood awaiting the music. "I lost sight of you till the lancers, just now."

"I have been sitting in a corner, looking on," I answered dismally, but with a smile.

"What!" he drew his brows together.

"It is no one's fault but my own. I can't waltz Italian fashion. Perhaps we had better not attempt it."

For answer, Andrea put his arm scientifically round my waist, piloting me into the middle of the room, where a few couples were already revolving.

"I have yet to find the young lady with whom I could not waltz," he observed, quietly, as we glided smoothly and rapidly across the floor.

Oh, the delights of that waltz! It was one of the intensely good things of life which cannot happen often even in the happiest careers; one of the little bits of perfection which start up now and then to astonish us, plants of such delicate growth that only by an unforeseen succession of accidents are they ever brought to birth. With what ease my partner skimmed about that crowded hall! How skilfully he steered among the bounding complex! Was ever such music heard out of heaven; and was ever such a kind, comfortable, reassuring presence as that of Andrea?

A moment ago, I had been bored, wistful, tired; now I had nothing left to wish for.

"Well," he said, as, the music coming to an end, we paused for the first time; "that was not so bad for an Italian, was it?"

I was so happy that I could only smile, and my partner, apparently not disconcerted by my stupidity, led me into the inner room, installed me in a chair, and seated himself in another opposite.

At the same moment, Romeo came sauntering up to us, throwing a remark in rapid Italian to his brother.

The latter, with a slight frown, rose reluctantly, and the two men went over to the doorway, where they stood talking.

I fell to observing them with considerable interest, these handsome, dark-eyed gentlemen, with their grace and air of breeding, who were at the same time so curiously alike and so curiously different.

In both the same simplicity and ease was felt to cover a certain inscrutability, the frankness a considerable depth of reserve; and in neither was seen a person to be thwarted with impunity. But whereas in Romeo's case the quiet manner was the unmistakable mark of a genuine indolence and indifference, in Andrea's it only served to bring out more clearly the keen vitality, the alertness, the purpose with which his whole personality was instinct.

I had not much time for my observations. In the course of a few minutes, Annunziata rustled smilingly past them, and threw herself and her green skirts into the chair just vacated by her brother-in-law.

The latter shot a quick glance at her, shrugged his shoulders slightly, resumed his conversation with Romeo, and made no attempt to rejoin me.

As for me, my little cup of pleasure was dashed to the ground.

Annunziata, fanning herself and talking volubly, made but a poor substitute for Andrea, and I began to be dimly aware of a certain hostility towards myself in the atmosphere.

The next dance was played, and the next, and still Annunziata sat there smiling. The two gentlemen had long disappeared into the ballroom, and we had the smaller apartment to ourselves.

"I can't stand it any longer," I thought, "even with another waltz with Andrea in prospect." And making an apology to the Marchesina, I stole through a side door upstairs to bed.

Sounds of revelry reached me faint through the thick walls for many succeeding hours; and I lay awake on my great bed till the dawn crept in through the shutters.

"I have been a wallflower," I reflected, "a wallflower, to do me justice, for the first time in my life. And I'm not so sure that, in some respects, it wasn't the nicest dance I ever was at."

Chapter 9

"What Has Happened to Me?"

"Costanza is so cross," said Bianca, drawing me aside, in her childish fashion; "she talks of going back at once to Florence, and I don't know who would be sorry if she did."

"Oh, for shame, Bianca; she is your guest," I said, really shocked.

It was the morning after the ball, and all the ladies were assembled in the sitting room, displaying everyone of them unmistakable signs of what is sometimes called "hot coppers."

I had been greeted coldly on my entrance, a fact which had dashed my own cheerful mood, and had set me seriously considering plans of departure. "If they are going to dislike me, there's an end of the matter," I thought; but I hated the idea of retiring beaten from the field.

I did not succeed in making my escape for a single hour throughout the day. Everyone wanted Miss Meredith's services; now she must hold a skein of wool, now accompany Costanza's song on the piano, now shout her uncertain Italian down the trumpet of a deaf old visitor. I was quite worn out by dinner time; and afterwards the whole party drove off to a reception, leaving me behind.

"Does not the signorina accompany us?" said Andrea to his mother, as they stood awaiting the carriage.

"Miss Meredith is tired and goes to bed," answered the Marchesa in her dry, impenetrable way. I had not been invited, but I made no remark. Andrea opened his eyes wide, and came over deliberately to the sofa where I sat.

There was such a determined look about the lines of his mouth, about his whole presence, that I found myself unconsciously thinking: "You are a very, very obstinate person, Marchesino, and I for one should be sorry to defy you. You looked just like that five years ago, when they were trying to tie you to the ancestral apron-strings, and I don't know that Costanza is to be envied, when all is said."

"Miss Meredith," said his lowered voice in my ear, "this is the first opportunity you have given me today of telling you what I think of your conduct. I do not wonder that you are afraid of me."

"Marchesino!"

"To make engagements and to break them is not thought good behaviour either in Italy or in America. Perhaps in England it is different."

I looked up, and meeting his eyes forgot everything else in the world. Forgot the Marchesa hovering near, only prevented by a certain awe of her son from swooping down on us; forgot Costanza champing the bit, as it were, in the doorway; forgot the cold, unfriendly glances which had made life dark for me throughout the day.

"I had no partner for number ten," went on Andrea, "though a lady had promised to dance it with me. Now what do you think of that lady's behaviour?"

His gravity was too much for my own, and I smiled.

"You suffer from too keen a sense of humour, Miss Meredith," he said, and I scarcely knew whether to take him seriously or not. I only knew that my heart was beating, that my pulses were throbbing as they had never done before.

"The carriage is at the door, Andrea," cried Bianca, bouncing up to us, and looking inquisitive and excited.

He rose at once, holding out his hand.

"Goodnight, Miss Meredith," he said, aloud; "I am sorry that you do not accompany us."

Costanza flounced across the passage noisily; the Marchesa looked me full in the face, then turned away in silence; and even Annunziata was grave. I felt suddenly that I had been brought up before a court of justice, tried, and found guilty of some heinous but unknown offence.

Light still lingered in the gallery, and when the carriage had rolled off, I sought shelter there, pacing to and fro with rapid, unequal tread. What had happened to me? What curious change had wrought itself not only in myself, but in my surroundings, during these last two days? Was it only two days since Andrea had come towards me down this very gallery? Unconsciously the thought shaped itself, and then I grew crimson in the solitude. What had Andrea to do with the altered state of things? How could his home-coming affect the little governess, the humblest member of that stately household?

There in the glow of the fading sunlight hung the Bronzino, its eyes – so like some other eyes – gazing steadily at me from the canvas. "Beautiful eyes," I thought; "honest eyes, good eyes! There was never anything very bad in that person's life. I think he was good and happy, and that everyone was fond of him."

And then again I blushed, and turned away suddenly. To blush at a picture!

Down in the deserted garden the spring was carrying on her work, in her own rapid, noiseless fashion. No doubt it was the spring also that was stirring in my heart; that was causing all sorts of new, unexpected growths of thought and feeling to sprout into sudden life; that was changing the habitual serenity of my mood into something of the fitfulness of an April day.

Alternately happy and miserable, I continued to pace the gallery till the last remnant of sunlight had died away, and the brilliant moonlight came streaming in through the windows.

Then my courage faded all at once. The stony place struck chill, my own footsteps echoed unnaturally loud; the eyes of the Bronzino staring through the silver radiance, filled me with unspeakable terror.

With a beating heart, I gathered up my skirts and fled up the silent stairs, along the corridor, to my room.

Chapter 10
"As Good as Gold"

Leaning out from the window of my room the next morning, I saw Andrea and his father walking slowly along the Lung' Arno in the sunlight.

In the filial relation, Andrea, I had before observed, particularly shone. His charming manner was never so charming as when he was addressing his father; and the presence of his younger son appeared to have a vitalizing, rejuvenating effect on the old Marchese.

And now, as I watched them pacing amicably in the delightful spring morning, the tears rose for a moment to my eyes; I remembered that it was Sunday, that a long way off in unromantic Islington my mother was making ready for the walk to church, while I, an exile, looked from my palace window with nothing better in prospect than a solitary journey to the *Chiesa Inglese*. Annunziata had not gone to mass, and when I came downstairs ready dressed, she explained that she had a headache, and was in need of a little company to cheer her up.

Of course, I could not do less than offer to forego my walk and attendance at church, which I did with a wistful recollection of the beauty and sweetness of the day.

"Have you heard?" she said. "Costanza goes back to Florence tonight. She prefers not to miss the last two days of Carnival, Monday and

Tuesday. So she says," cried the Marchesina, with a frankness that astonished me, even from her; "so she says; but between ourselves, Andrea was very attentive last night to Emilia di Rossa. Costanza ought to understand what he is by now. She has known him all her life; she ought certainly to be aware that his one little weakness – Andrea is as good as gold – is the ladies."

I bent my head low over my work, with an indignant, shame-stricken consciousness that I was blushing. "He is evidently engaged to Costanza," I thought, and I wished the earth would open and swallow me.

"And a young girl, like Emilia," went on Annunziata; "who knows what construction she might put upon his behaviour? It is not that he says so much, but he has a way with him which is open to misinterpretation. Poor little thing, she has no money to speak of, and, even if she had, who are the Di Rossas? Andrea, for all he is so free and easy, is as proud as the devil, and the very last man to make a *mésalliance*. A convent, say I, will be the end of the Di Rossa." And she sighed contentedly.

Was it possible that she was insulting me? Was this a warning, a warning to me, Elsie Meredith? Did she think me an adventuress, setting traps for a rich and noble husband, or merely an eager fool liable to put a misconstruction on the simplest acts of kindliness and courtesy?

My blazing cheeks, no doubt, confirmed whichever suspicion she had been indulging in, but I was determined to show her that I was not afraid. Lifting my face – with its hateful crimson – boldly to hers, I said: "We in England regard marriage and – and love in another way. I know it is not so in Italy; but with us the reason for getting married is that you are fond of someone, and that someone is fond of you. Other sorts of marriages are not thought nice," with which bold and sweeping statement on behalf of my native land, I returned with trembling fingers to my needlework.

To do me justice, I fully believed in my own words. That marriage which had not affection for its basis was shameful had been the simple creed of the little world at home.

"Indeed?" said Annunziata, with genuine interest; "but, as you say, it is not so with us."

My lips twitched in an irresistible smile. Her round eyes met mine so frankly, her round face was so unruffled in its amiability, that I could not but feel I had made a fool of myself. The guileless lady was prattling on, no doubt as usual, as a relief to her own feelings, and not with any underlying intention.

I felt more ashamed than before of my own self-consciousness.

"What is the matter with you, Elsie Meredith?" cried a voice within me. "I think your own mother wouldn't know you; your own sisters would pass you by in the street."

"Andrea ought to know," went on Annunziata, "that such freedom of manners is not permissible in Italy between a young man and young women. He seems to have forgotten this in America, where, I am told, the licence is something shocking."

I wished the good lady would be less confidential – what was all this to me? – and I was almost glad when the ladies came sailing in from mass, all of them evidently in the worst possible tempers.

There was an air of constraint about the whole party at lunch that day. Wedged in between the Marchesa and Romeo, I sat silent and glum, having returned Andrea's cordial bow very coldly across the table. Everyone deplored Costanza's approaching departure, rather mechanically, I thought, and that young lady herself repeatedly expressed her regret at leaving.

"Dear Marchesa," she cried, "I am at my wits' end with disappointment; but my mother's letter this morning admits of but one reply. She says she cannot spare me from the gaieties of the next two days."

"You might come back after Ash Wednesday," said Bianca, who sat with her arm round her friend between the courses, and whose friendship seemed to have been kindled into a blaze by the coming separation.

"Dearest Bianca, if I could only persuade you to return with me!"

"Bianca never makes visits," answered her mother, drily.

"Were you at church this morning, Miss Meredith?" asked the old Marchese, kindly, as the figs and chestnuts were put on the table.

It was the first time that anyone had addressed me directly throughout the meal, and I blushed hotly as I gave my answer.

The departure of Costanza, her boxes and her maid, was of course the great event of the afternoon.

The three gentlemen and Annunziata drove with her to the station, and I was left behind with my pupil and her mother.

A stiff bow from Costanza, a glare through her double eyeglass, and a contemptuous "Goodbye, Miss," in English, had not tended to raise my spirits. To be an object of universal dislike was an experience as new as it was unpleasant, and I was losing confidence in myself with every hour.

Even Bianca had deserted me, and, ensconced close to her mother, shot glances at me of her early curiosity and criticism.

As for the Marchesa, that inscrutable person scarcely stopped talking all the afternoon, rattling on in her dry, colourless way about nothing at all. Speech was to her the shield and buckler which silence is to persons less gifted. Behind her own volubility she could withdraw as behind a bulwark, whence she made observations safe from being herself observed.

I was quite worn out by eight o'clock, when the usual Sunday visitors began to arrive.

With my work in my hand, I sat on the outskirts of the throng, not working indeed, but pondering deeply.

"Miss Meredith, you are very industrious."

There before me stood Andrea, a very obstinate look on his face, unmindful of Annunziata's proximity and Romeo's scowls.

"As it happens, I haven't put in a stitch for the last ten minutes," I answered quietly, though my heart beat.

He drew a chair close to mine.

"You are unfair, Andrea, you are unfair," I thought, "to make things worse for Miss Meredith by singling her out in this way, when you know it makes them all so cross. Things are bad enough for her as it is, and you might forego your little bit of amusement."

I began really to stitch with unnatural industry, bending an unresponsive face over the work in my hand.

"That is very pretty," said Andrea.

"No, no, Marchesino," I thought again, "you are as good as gold, anyone could see that from your eyes; but you have a little weakness, only one – 'the ladies' – and you must not be encouraged."

I turned to Annunziata, who, baffled by the English speech, sat perplexed and helpless.

"Marchesina," I said aloud in Italian, "the Marchesino admires my work."

"I taught her how to do it," cried Annunziata, breaking into a smile. "See, it is not so easy to draw the fine gold thread through the leather, but she is an apt pupil."

"Miss Meredith, I am sorry to see you looking so pale." Andrea dropped his voice very low, adhering obstinately to English and fixing his eyes on mine.

"I haven't been out today."

"What, wasting this glorious weather indoors. Is it possible that you are falling into the worst of our Italian ways?"

"I generally go for a walk."

I rose as I spoke, and turned to the Marchesina. "I am so tired; do you think I may be excused?"

"Certainly, dear child."

Bowing to the assembled company I made my way deliberately to the door. Andrea was there before me, holding it open, a look of unusual sternness on his face.

"Goodnight, Miss Meredith," and then before them all he held out his hand.

Only for a moment did our fingers join in a firm eager clasp, only for a moment did his eyes meet mine in a strange, mysterious glance. Only for a moment, but as I fled softly, rapidly along the corridor I felt that in that one instant of time all my life's meaning had been changed. "As good as gold; as good as gold." These words went round and round in my head as I lay sobbing on the pillow.

Somehow that was the only part of Annunziata's warning which remained with me.

Chapter 11
"Will You Make Me Very Happy?"

I rose early next morning, and without waiting for my breakfast, ran downstairs, made Pasquale, the vague servant, open the door for me, and I escaped into the sunshine.

In the long and troubled night just passed I had come to a resolution – I would go home.

From first to last, I told myself, the experiment had been a failure. From first to last, I had been out of touch with the people with whom I had come to dwell; the almost undisguised hostility of the last few days was merely the culmination of a growing feeling.

In that atmosphere of suspicion, of disapprobation, I could exist no longer. Defeated, indeed, but in no wise disgraced, I would return whence I came. I would tell them everything at home, and they would understand.

That I had committed some mysterious breach of Italian etiquette, outraged some notion of Italian propriety, I could not doubt; but at least I had been guilty of nothing of which, judged by my own standard, I could feel ashamed.

But my heart was very heavy as I sped on through the streets, instinctively making my way to the cathedral.

It was the second week in March, and the spring was full upon us. The grass in the piazza smelt of clover, and here and there on the brown hills was the flush of blossoming peach or the snow of flowering almonds.

In the soft light of the morning, cathedral, tower, and baptistery seemed steeped in a divine calm. Their beauty filled me with a great sadness. They were my friends; I had grown to love them, and now I was leaving them, perhaps forever.

Pacing up and down, and round about, I tried to fix my thoughts on my plans, to consider with calmness my course of action. But this was the upshot of all my endeavours, the one ridiculous irrelevant conclusion at which I could arrive – "He is certainly not engaged to Costanza."

As I came round by the main door of the cathedral for perhaps the twentieth time, I saw Andrea walking across the grass towards me.

A week ago, I had never seen his face; now as I watched him advancing in the sunlight, it seemed that I had known him all my life. Never was figure more familiar, never presence more reassuring, than that of this stranger. The sight of him neither disturbed nor astonished me; now that he was here, his coming seemed inevitable, a part of the natural order of things.

"Ah, I have found you," he said quietly, and we turned together and strolled towards the Campo Santo.

"Do you often come here?" He stopped and looked at me dreamily.

"Often, often. It is all so beautiful and so sad."

"It is very sad."

"Do you not see how very beautiful it is?" I cried, "that there is nothing like it in the whole world? And I am leaving it, and it breaks my heart!"

"You are going away?"

"Yes." I was calm no longer, but strangely agitated. I turned away, and began pacing to and fro.

"Ah! they have not made you happy?" His eyes flashed as he came up to me.

"No," I said, "I am not happy; but it is nobody's fault. They do not like me, and I cannot bear it anymore. It has never happened to me before – no one has thought me very wonderful, very clever, very beautiful, very brilliant; but people have always liked me, and if I am not liked I shall die."

With which foolish outbreak – which astonished no one more than the speaker – I turned away again with streaming eyes.

"Let us come in here," said Andrea, still with that strange calm in voice and manner, and together we passed into the Campo Santo.

A bird was singing somewhere among the cypresses; the daffodils rose golden in the grass; the strip of sky between the cloisters was intensely blue.

"Miss Meredith," said Andrea, taking my hand, "will you make me very happy – will you be my wife?"

We were standing in the grass plot, face to face, and he was very pale.

His words seemed the most natural thing in the world. I ought, perhaps, to have made a protest, to have reminded him of family claims and dues, to have made sure that love, not chivalry, was speaking.

But I only said, "Yes," very low, looking at him as we stood there among the tombs, under the blue heavens.

* * * * * *

"As you came down the gallery, in the sunlight, with the little grey gown, and the frightened look in the modest eyes, I said to myself, 'Here, with the help of God, comes my wife!'"

I do not know how long we had been in the cloisters, pacing slowly, hand in hand, almost in silence. The sun was high in the heavens, and the bird in the cypresses sang no more.

"Do you know," cried Andrea, stopping suddenly, and laughing, "here is a most ridiculous thing! What is your name? For I haven't the ghost of an idea!"

"Elsie." I laughed, too. The joke struck us both as an excellent one.

"Elsie! Ah, the sweet name! Elsie, Elsie! Was ever such a dear little name? What shall we do next, Elsie, my friend?"

"Take me to the mountains!" I cried, suddenly aware that I was tired to exhaustion, that I had had no sleep and no breakfast. "Take me to the mountains; I have longed, longed for them all these days!"

I staggered a little, and closed my eyes.

When I opened them, he was holding me in his arms, looking down anxiously at my face.

"Yes, we will go to the mountains; but first I shall take you home, and give you something to eat and drink, Elsie."

Chapter 12
The Breaking of the Storm

"You are not afraid?" said Andrea, as we turned on to the Lung' Arno and came in sight of the house.

"No," I answered in all good faith, a little resenting the question.

After all, what was there to fear? This was the nineteenth century, when people's marriages were looked upon as their own affairs, and the paternal blessing – since it had ceased to be a *sine quâ non* – was never long withheld.

If Andrea's family were disappointed in his choice, and I supposed that at first such would be the case, it lay with me to turn that disappointment into satisfaction.

I had but a modest opinion of myself, yet I knew that in making me his wife Andrea was doing nothing to disgrace himself; his good taste, perhaps, was at fault, but that was all.

You see, I had been educated in a very primitive and unworldly school of manners, and must ask you to forgive my ignorance.

Yet I confess my heart did beat rather fast as we made our way up the steps into the empty hall, and I wished the next few hours well over.

I reminded myself that I was under Andrea's wing, safe from harm, but looking up at Andrea I was not quite sure of his own unruffled self-possession. A distant hum of voices greeted us as we entered, growing louder with every stair we mounted, and when we reached the landing leading to the gallery, there stood the whole family assembled like the people in a comedy.

To judge from the sounds we heard, they had been engaged in excited discussion, everyone speaking at once, but at our appearance a dead and awful silence fell upon the group.

Slowly we advanced, the mark of every eye, then came to a stop well in front of the group.

It seemed an age, but I believe it was less than a minute, before the Marchesa stepped forward, looking straight at me and away from her son, so as not in the least to include him in her condemnation, and said: "I am truly sorry, Miss Meredith, for I was given to understand that your mother was a very respectable woman."

"Mother!" cried Andrea, with a pale face and flashing eyes; "be careful of your words." Then taking my hand, he turned to the old Marchese, who stood helpless and speechless in the background, and said loudly and deliberately: "This lady has promised to be my wife."

For an instant no one spoke, but there was no mistaking the meaning of their silence; then Romeo called out in a voice of suppressed fury: "It is impossible!"

Andrea, still holding my hand, turned with awful calm upon his brother. Annunziata's ready tears were flowing, and Bianca gazed open-mouthed with horror and excitement upon the scene.

"Romeo," said Andrea, tightening his hold of my fingers, "this is no affair of yours. Once before you tried to interfere in my life; I should have thought the result had been too discouraging for a second attempt."

"It is the affair of all of us when you try to bring disgrace on the family."

"Disgrace! Sir, do you know what word you are using, and in reference to whom?"

"Oh, the signorina, of course, is charming. I have nothing to say against her."

He bowed low, and, as our eyes met, I knew he was my enemy.

"Andrea," said his mother, interposing between her sons, "this is no time and place for discussion. Miss Meredith shall come with me, and you shall endeavour to explain to your father how it is you have insulted him."

"My son," said the Marchese, speaking for the first time, with a certain mournful dignity, "never before has such a thing happened in our family as that a wife should be brought home to it without the head of the house being consulted. What am I to think of this want of confidence, of respect, except that you are ashamed of your choice?"

"Father," answered Andrea, drawing my hand through his arm, "it has throughout been my intention of asking your consent and your blessing. Nor has there been any concealment on my part. From the first I have expressed my admiration of this lady very openly to you all. What is the result? That she is watched, persecuted like a suspected criminal, and finally driven away – she a young girl, a stranger in a foreign land. Can you expect the man who loves her to stand by and see this without letting her know at the first opportunity that there is one on whose protection she can at once and always rely?"

"Andrea," said his mother, "we did but try our best to prevent what we one and all regard as a misfortune. Miss Meredith is no suitable bride for a son of the house of Brogi. Oh" (as he opened his lips as about to protest), "I have nothing to say against her, though indeed you cannot expect me to be lost in admiration of her discretion."

The Marchesa shrugged her shoulders and threw out her hands as she spoke, with an impatience which she rarely displayed.

Andrea answered very quietly: "My mother, this is no time and place for such a discussion. With your permission, I will retire with my father, and Miss Meredith shall withdraw to her own room." He released my hand very gently from his arm, and stood a moment looking down at me.

"You are not afraid, Elsie?" he whispered in English.

"Yes, I am frightened to death!"

"It will be all right very soon."

"Must you leave me, Andrea?"

"Yes, dear, I must."

He went over to his father and gave him his arm. All this time Annunziata was weeping like the walrus in *Alice*,[21] her loud sobs echoing dismally throughout the house.

"Elsie," said Andrea, as he prepared to descend with the Marchese, "go straight to your room."

I turned without a word, and stunned, astonished, unutterably miserable, fled upstairs without a glance at the hostile group on the landing.

Once the door safely shut behind me, my pent-up feelings found vent, and I sobbed hysterically.

Was ever such a morning in a woman's life? And I had had no breakfast.

I was not allowed much time in which to indulge my emotions. Very soon came a knock at the door, and a maid entered with wine, bread, and chestnuts. With the volubility of Italian servants, she pressed me to eat and drink, and when she departed with the empty tray, I felt refreshed and ready to fight my battle to the last. A second knock at the door was not long in following the first, and this time it was the Marchesa who responded to my "Come in."

My heart sank considerably as the stately little lady advanced towards me, and I inwardly reproached Andrea for his desertion.

---

21. Refers to Lewis Carroll's (1832–1898) *Through the Looking Glass* (1872).

Chapter 13
A Skilful Diplomatist

"Miss Meredith," said the Marchesa, taking the chair I mechanically offered her, and waving her hand towards another, "pray be seated."

I obeyed, feeling secretly much in awe of the rigid little figure sitting very upright opposite me.

"What, after all, is the love of a young man but a passing infatuation?"

Thus was the first gun fired into the enemy's camp, but there was no answering volley.

That she spoke in all good faith I fully believe, and I felt how useless would be any discussion between us of the point. I looked down in silence.

"Miss Meredith," went on the dry, fluent tones, which I was beginning to feel were the tones of doom, "I will refrain from blaming you in this unfortunate matter. I will merely state the case as it stands. You come into this family, are well received, kindly treated, and regarded with esteem by us all. In return for this, I am bound to say, you perform your duties and do what is required of you with amiability. So far all is well. But there are traditions, feelings, sacred customs, and emotions belonging to the family where you have been received of which you can have no knowledge. That is not required, nor expected of you. What is expected of you, as of every right-minded person, is that you should at least respect what is of such importance to others. Is this the case? Have you not rather taken delight in outraging our feelings in their most delicate relations; in trampling, in your selfish ignorance, on all that we hold most dear?"

Her words stung me; they were cruel words, but I had sworn inwardly to stand by my guns.

With hands interlocked and drooping head, I sat before her without a word.

"We had looked forward to this home-coming of my son," she went on, branching off into another talk, "as to the beginning of a fresh epoch of our lives, his father and I, we that are no longer young. To him we had looked for the carrying on of our race. From my daughter-in-law we have been obliged to despair of issue. Andrea, suitably married and established in the home of his ancestors, is what we all dreamed one day to see – nor do I even now entirely abandon the hope of seeing it."

With burning cheeks, and an awful sense that a web was being woven about me, I rose stiffly from my seat, and went over to a cabinet where stood my mother's portrait.

I looked a moment at the pictured eyes, as if for guidance, then said in a low voice:

"Marchesa, I have given my word to your son, and only at his bidding can I take it back."

"It does not take much penetration," she replied, "to know that my son is the last person to bid you do anything of the kind. That he is the soul of chivalry, that the very fact of a person being in an unfortunate position would of itself attract his regard, a child might easily discover."

She spoke with such genuine feeling that for a moment my heart went out towards her; for a moment our eyes met, and not unkindly.

"No doubt," she went on, after a pause, and rising from her seat, "no doubt you represented the precautions we thought necessary to adopt, for your own protection as well as my son's, as a form of persecution. If you did not actually represent it to him, I feel sure you gave him to understand that such was the case."

She had hit the mark.

With an agonizing rush of shame, of despair, I remembered my own outbreak on the piazza that morning; how I had confided to Andrea, unasked, my intention of going away, and of the sorrow the prospect gave me.

Had I been mistaken? Had the message of his eyes, his voice, his manner, meant nothing? Had I indeed been unmindful of my woman's modesty? The Marchesa was aware at once of having struck home, and the monotonous tones began again.

"Of course, Miss Meredith, if you choose to take advantage of my son's chivalry, and of his passing fancy – for Andrea is exceedingly susceptible, and, no doubt, believes himself in love with you – if, I say, you choose to do this, there is no more to be said.

"Andrea will never take back his word, on that you may rely. But be sure of this, his life will be spoiled, and he will know it. It is not to be expected that you should realize the meaning of ancestral pride, of family honour. Perhaps you think the sentiments which have taken centuries to grow can wither up in a day before the flame of a foolish fancy?"

She had conquered. Moving over to her I looked straight in her face. My voice rang strange and hollow: "By marrying your son I should bring no disgrace upon him nor his family. But I do not intend to marry him."

She had not anticipated so easy a victory. Her cheek flushed, almost as if with compunction. She held out her hands towards me.

But as for me, I turned away ungraciously, and, going up to the chest, began to lift out my under linen, and to pile it on the bed.

"Marchesa, do not thank me, do not praise me. I do not know if I am doing right or wrong."

"Signorina, you have taken the course of an honourable woman."

I went over to the corner where my box stood, and lifted the lid with trembling hands.

"Marchesa, will your servant find out what hour of the night the train leaves for Genoa? And will he have a drosky ready in time to take me to the station?"

"Miss Meredith, there is no necessity for this haste. You cannot depart like this, and without advising your family."

I laid a dress – the little black dress I had worn at the dance – at the bottom of the box. It ought to have gone at the top, but such details did not occupy me at the moment.

"I trust," I said, "that there may be no difficulties placed in the way of my immediate departure."

She came up to me in some agitation.

"But, signorina!"

"Marchesa," I answered, "you have my promise. Is not that what you wanted?"

I intended a dismissal, I frankly own it, but the Marchesa took my rudeness with such humility that for the moment I felt ashamed of myself.

"You have forced me, Miss Meredith, to speak to you as I have never spoken before to a stranger beneath my roof. To fly in the face of the hospitable traditions of the house – "

There came a knock at the door, and the servant announced that the Marchesino desired to speak with Miss Meredith.

We two women, who both loved Andrea, looked at one another.

"You will have to tell him yourself, signorina; from no one else would my son receive your message." The Marchesa turned away as she spoke.

"I will write to him."

Hastily dismissing the servant with words to the effect that Andrea should be waited on in a few minutes, the Marchesa handed me, in silence, the little paper-case which lay on the table. With uncertain fingers I wrote:

"MARCHESINO, We were both of us hasty and ill-advised this morning. I must thank you for the great honour you have done me, but at the same time I must beg of you to release me from the promise I have made. ELSIE MEREDITH."

I handed the open sheet to the Marchesa, who read it carefully, folded it up, thanked me and went from the room.

Then suddenly the great bed began to waltz, the open box in the corner, the painted ceiling, the chest and cabinet to whirl about in hopeless confusion. I don't know how it came about, but for the first time in my life I fainted.

Chapter 14
Released from Her Vow

It was four o'clock in the afternoon; already the front of the house was in shadow, and the drawing room was cool and dark. Here Andrea and I were standing face to face; both pale, both resolute, while the Marchesa looked from one to the other with anxious eyes.

"You wrote this?" he asked, holding up my unfortunate scrawl.

"Yes, I wrote it."

"And you meant what you wrote?"

"Yes."

He came a little nearer to me, speaking, it seemed, with a certain passionate contempt.

"And you expected me, Elsie, to accept such an answer?"

Before the fire of his glance my eyes fell suddenly. "I have no other answer to give you," I murmured brokenly.

The Marchesa, who had stayed in the room by my own request, glanced questioningly from one to the other, evidently unable to follow the rapid English of the dialogue.

"Is it possible, Elsie, that you have deceived me? That you, who seemed so true, are falser than words can say? Have you forgotten what you said to me, what your eyes said as well as your lips, a few short hours ago?"

"I have not forgotten, but I cannot marry you."

"Then you do not love me, Elsie? You have been amusing yourself."

"If you choose to think so, I cannot help it."

"Elsie, whatever promise you have made to my mother, whatever promise may have been extorted from you, remember that your first promise and your duty were to me."

I shivered from head to foot, while my heart echoed his words. But I had given my word, and I would not go back from it. Never should my mother's daughter thrust herself unwelcomed in any house.

"Have you nothing to say to me, Elsie?"

"Nothing."

"Mother," he cried, turning flashing eyes to the Marchesa, "what have you been saying to her, by what means have you so transformed her, how have you succeeded in wringing from her a most unjust promise?"

"Stay," I interposed, speaking also in Italian, "no promise has been wrung from me, I gave it freely. Marchesino, it seems you cannot believe it, yet it is true that of my own free will I refuse to marry you, that I take back my unconsidered word of this morning. I am no wife for you, and you no husband for me; a few hours of reflection have sufficed very plainly to show me that."

He stood there, paler than ever, looking at me with a piteous air of incredulity. "Elsie, it is not possible – consider, remember – it is not true!"

His voice broke, wavered, and fell; from the passionate entreaty of his eyes I turned my own away.

"It is true, Marchesino, that I will never, never marry you."

Clear, cold, and cruel, though very low, were the tones of my voice; I know not what angel or fiend was giving me strength and utterance; I only know that it was not the normal Elsie who thus spoke and acted.

There was a pause, which seemed to last an age, then once again his voice broke the stillness.

"Since, then, you choose to spoil my life, Elsie, and perhaps (who knows?) your own, there is no more to be said. Far be it from me to extort a woman's consent from her. The only love worth having is that which is given freely, which has courage, which has pride."

Very hard and contemptuous sounded his words. My heart cried out in agony: "Andrea, you are unjust!" but I stood there dumb as a fish, with clasped hands and a drooping head.

"Mother," went on Andrea, "will you kindly summon my father and the others. Miss Meredith, oblige me and stay a few moments; I am sorry to trouble you."

They came in slowly through the open door, the old man, his son and the two younger ladies, anxious, expectant.

Andrea turned towards them.

"My father," he said, "this lady refuses to marry me, and no doubt everybody is content. That she declines to face the hostility, the discourtesy of my family, is not perhaps greatly to be wondered at. It is evident that I am not considered worthy of so great a sacrifice on her part; I do not blame her; rather I blame my own credulity in thinking my love returned. But I wish you all to know," he added, "that I have entirely altered my plans. I shall write off my appointment in England, and shall start tonight for Livorno, on my way to America. My mother, you will kindly send for an *orario* that I may know at what time to order the carriage. Miss Meredith, I bid you goodbye."

He turned round suddenly and faced me, holding out his hand with an air of ceremony.

As for me, I glanced from the dear hand, the dear eyes, to the circle of dismayed faces beyond, then, without a word, I rushed through the open door to my room.

Not daring to allow myself a moment's thought, I fell to immediately packing – fitting in a neat mosaic of stockings and petticoats as though it were the one object of existence.

I do not know if it were minutes or hours before the Marchesa came in, pale and unusually agitated, with no air of enjoying her victory.

"Signorina," she said, "the train for Genoa leaves at 8; I have ordered the carriage for 7:15. You would prefer, perhaps, to dine in your room?"

"I do not wish for dinner, thank you."

"You must allow me to thank you once again, Miss Meredith."

"Do not thank me," I cried, with sudden passion; "I have done nothing to be thanked for."

For, indeed, I was enjoying none of the compensations of martyrdom; for me it was the pang without the palm, as the poet says.[22]

I had fallen in a cause in which I did not believe, had been pressed into a service for which I had no enthusiasm.

"If you will excuse me, Marchesa," I went on, "there are some books of mine in the schoolroom which I must fetch"; and, with a little bow, I swept into the corridor with an air as stately as her own.

Andrea's room was on the same floor as my own, but at the other end of the passage, and I had to pass it on my way to the schoolroom. The door stood wide open, and just outside was a large trunk, which Pasquale, the servant, was engaged in packing, while his master gave directions and handed things from the threshold.

I heard their voices as I came.

"At what time does the train go for Livorno, did you say?"

"At 9, *excellenza*. The carriage will be back in time from the station."

I glided past as rapidly as possible, filled with a certain mournful humour at this spectacle of the gentleman packing his box at one end of the hall, while the lady packed hers at the other.

My room was empty when I regained it, and with a heavy heart I finished my sad task, locking the box, labelling and strapping it.

Then I put on my grey travelling dress, my hat, veil, and gloves, and sat down by the window.

It was only half-past five, and these preparations were a little premature; but this confused, chaotic day seemed beyond the ordinary measurements of time.

---

22. Refers to Elizabeth Barrett Browning's poem, "The Cry of the Children" (New, ed., *The Complete Novels*, 550 n. 24).

A maid-servant, with a dainty little dinner on a tray, was the next arrival on the scene. She set it down on a table near me, but I took no heed. As if I could have swallowed a mouthful!

I was quite calm now, only unutterably mournful. "I have spoilt my life," I thought, as my eyes fixed themselves drearily on the river, the old houses opposite, the marble bridge – once all so strange, now grown so dear; "I have spoilt my life, and for what? Ah, if Mother had only been here to stand by me! But I was alone. What was I to do? Oh, Andrea, do you hate me?"

The tears streamed down my face as I sat. "Oh, my beloved Pisa," I thought again, "how can I bear to leave you!"

Once more came a knock at the door – the little, quick knock of the Marchesa; and as I responded duly, I reflected: "No doubt she comes to insult me with my salary. And the worst of it is, I shall have to take it; for if I don't, how am I to get home?"

She looked very unlike her usual self-possessed self as she came towards me.

"Miss Meredith, my husband wishes to speak to you."

I rose wearily in mechanical obedience, and followed her, silent and dejected, downstairs to the Marchese's room. Here, amid his books and papers, sat the old man, looking the picture of wretchedness.

"Ah, signorina," he said, "what will you think of me, of us all? Of the favour which, very humbly, I have to beg of you? I cannot bear thus to part from my son; he is going far away from me, in anger, for an indefinite time. It is you, and you only, who can persuade him to stop!"

I looked up in sudden astonishment.

"My child, go to him; tell him that he can stay."

"Marchese, I am sorry, but you ask what is impossible."

"I do not wonder," he said, with a most touching yet dignified humility, "I do not wonder at your reply. My wife, it is your part to speak to this lady."

With set lips yet unblanching front, the gallant little Marchesa advanced.

"Miss Meredith, do not in this matter consider yourself bound by any promise you have made to me. I release you from it."

"May not the matter be considered ended?" I cried in very weariness; "that I have come between your son and his family no one regrets more than I. Only let me go away!"

The old man rose slowly, left the room, and went to the foot of the stairs.

"Andrea, Andrea," I heard him call.

"His excellency has not finished packing," answered the voice of Pasquale.

"Andrea, Andrea," cried his father again; then came rapid footsteps, and in a few seconds Andrea stood once more before me.

He turned from one to the other questioningly.

The Marchese took my hand.

"My son," he said, "can you not persuade this lady to remain with us?"

He looked up, my Andrea, and our eyes met; but on neither side was speech or movement.

The old man went on.

"Andrea, it is possible that we did wrong, your mother and I, in attempting to interfere with you in this matter. You must forgive us if we are slow to understand the new spirit of radicalism which, it seems, is the spirit of the times. Once before our wishes clashed; but, my son, I cannot bear to send you away in anger a second time. As for this lady, she knows how deeply we all respect her. Persuade her to forgive us, if indeed you can."

Andrea I saw was deeply moved; he shaded his eyes with his hand, and the tears flowed down my own cheeks unchecked.

"Well, Elsie, it is for you to decide." He spoke at last, coldly, in an off-hand manner.

I was lacking in pride, perhaps in dignity, for though I said nothing, I held out my hand.

"Are you quite sure you love me, Elsie?"

"Quite, quite sure, Andrea."

* * * * * *

"I am so glad," cried Bianca, some ten minutes later, giving me a hug, "I am so glad it is you and not that bad-tempered Costanza."

"We are all glad," said the old Marchese, holding out his hand with a smile, while Romeo and his mother stood bearing their defeat with commendable grace.

* * * * * *

So it came to pass that on the evening of that wonderful day Andrea and I, instead of being borne by express trains to Genoa and Leghorn respectively, were pacing the gallery arm in arm in the sunlight.

We had been engaged in this occupation for about an hour, and now he knew all about my mother and sisters, and the details of the happy life at Islington.

"We will live in England, but every year we will come to Italy," he was saying, as we paused before the Bronzino, which seemed to have taken in the situation.

"I love Italy more than any place in the world," I answered.

A pause.

"We will be married immediately after Easter, Elsie!"

"Andrea, I go home the day after tomorrow."

"And tomorrow," he said, "we will go to the mountains."

THE END

Poetry Collections

Contents

Xantippe and Other Verse
(1881)

Xantippe (A Fragment)[1]

What, have I waked again? I never thought
To see the rosy dawn, or ev'n this grey,
Dull, solemn stillness, ere the dawn has come.
The lamp burns low; low burns the lamp of life:
The still morn stays expectant, and my soul,
All weighted with a passive wonderment,
Waiteth and watcheth, waiteth for the dawn.
Come hither, maids; too soundly have ye slept
That should have watched me; nay, I would not chide –
Oft have I chidden, yet I would not chide
In this last hour; – now all should be at peace.
I have been dreaming in a troubled sleep
Of weary days I thought not to recall;
Of stormy days, whose storms are hushed long since;
Of gladsome days, of sunny days; alas!
In dreaming, all their sunshine seem'd so sad,
As though the current of the dark To-Be
Had flow'd, prophetic, through the happy hours.
And yet, full well, I know it was not thus;
I mind me sweetly of the summer days,
When, leaning from the lattice, I have caught
The fair, far glimpses of a shining sea:

1. "Xantippe: A Fragment" is taken from *The University Magazine* 5, no. 29 (May 1880): 592–7; the poem was also published in *A Minor Poet and Other Verse* (1884; rpt. London: T. Fisher Unwin, 1891), 23–34. See the analysis of "Xantippe" beginning on p. xlv. Xantippe was the wife of the Athenian philosopher, Socrates.

And nearer, of tall ships which thronged the bay,
And stood out blackly from a tender sky
All flecked with sulphur, azure, and bright gold;
And in the still, clear air have heard the hum
Of distant voices; and methinks there rose
No darker fount to mar or stain the joy
Which sprang ecstatic in my maiden breast
Than just those vague desires, those hopes and fears,
Those eager longings, strong, though undefined,
Whose very sadness makes them seem so sweet.
What cared I for the merry mockeries
Of other maidens sitting at the loom?
Or for sharp voices, bidding me return
To maiden labour? Were we not apart,
I and my high thoughts, and my golden dreams,
My soul which yearned for knowledge, for a tongue
That should proclaim the stately mysteries
Of this fair world, and of the holy gods?
Then followed days of sadness, as I grew
To learn my woman-mind had gone astray,
And I was sinning in those very thoughts –
For maidens, mark, such are not woman's thoughts –
(And yet, 'tis strange, the gods who fashion us
Have given us such promptings)....
Fled the years,
Till seventeen had found me tall and strong,
And fairer, runs it, than Athenian maids
Are wont to seem; I had not learnt it well –
My lesson of dumb patience – and I stood
At Life's great threshold with a beating heart,
And soul resolved to conquer and attain....
Once, walking 'thwart the crowded market-place,
With other maidens, bearing in the twigs,

White doves for Aphrodite's[2] sacrifice,
I saw him, all ungainly and uncouth,
Yet many gathered round to hear his words,
Tall youths and stranger-maidens – Sokrates –
I saw his face and marked it, half with awe,
Half with a quick repulsion at the shape....
The richest gem lies hidden furthest down,
And is the dearer for the weary search;
We grasp the shining shells which strew the shore,
Yet swift we fling them from us; but the gem
We keep for aye and cherish. So a soul,
Found after weary searching in the flesh
Which half repelled our senses, is more dear,
For that same seeking, than the sunny mind
Which lavish Nature marks with thousand hints
Upon a brow of beauty. We are prone
To overweigh such subtle hints, then deem,
In after disappointment, we are fooled....
And when, at length, my father told me all,
That I should wed me with great Sokrates,
I, foolish, wept to see at once cast down
The maiden image of a future love,
Where perfect body matched the perfect soul.
But slowly, softly did I cease to weep;
Slowly I 'gan to mark the magic flash
Leap to the eyes, to watch the sudden smile
Break round the mouth, and linger in the eyes;
To listen for the voice's lightest tone –
Great voice, whose cunning modulations seemed
Like to the notes of some sweet instrument.
So did I reach and strain, until at last
I caught the soul athwart the grosser flesh.

2. Greek goddess.

Again of thee, sweet Hope, my spirit dreamed!
I, guided by his wisdom and his love,
Led by his words, and counselled by his care,
Should lift the shrouding veil from things which be,
And at the flowing fountain of his soul
Refresh my thirsting spirit....
                                        And indeed,
In those long days which followed that strange day
When rites and song, and sacrifice and flow'rs,
Proclaimed that we were wedded, did I learn,
In sooth, a-many lessons; bitter ones
Which sorrow taught me, and not love inspired,
Which deeper knowledge of my kind impressed
With dark insistence on reluctant brain; –
But that great wisdom, deeper, which dispels
Narrowed conclusions of a half-grown mind,
And sees athwart the littleness of life
Nature's divineness and her harmony,
Was never poor Xantippe's....
                                        I would pause,
And would recall no more, no more of life,
Than just the incomplete, imperfect dream
Of early summers, with their light and shade,
Their blossom-hopes, whose fruit was never ripe;
But something strong within me, some sad chord
Which loudly echoes to the later life,
Me to unfold the after-misery
Urges, with plaintive wailing in my heart.
Yet, maidens, mark; I would not that ye thought
I blame my lord departed, for he meant
No evil, so I take it, to his wife.
'Twas only that the high philosopher,
Pregnant with noble theories and great thoughts,
Deigned not to stoop to touch so slight a thing

As the fine fabric of a woman's brain –
So subtle as a passionate woman's soul.
I think, if he had stooped a little, and cared,
I might have risen nearer to his height,
And not lain shattered, neither fit for use
As goodly household vessel, nor for that
Far finer thing which I had hoped to be....
Death, holding high his retrospective lamp,
Shows me those first, far years of wedded life,
Ere I had learnt to grasp the barren shape
Of what the Fates had destined for my life.
Then, as all youthful spirits are, was I
Wholly incredulous that Nature meant
So little, who had promised me so much.
At first I fought my fate with gentle words,
With high endeavours after greater things –
Striving to win the soul of Sokrates,
Like some slight bird, who sings her burning love
To human master, till at length she finds
Her tender language wholly misconceived,
And that same hand whose kind caress she sought,
With fingers flippant flings the careless corn....
I do remember how, one summer's eve,
He, seated in an arbour's leafy shade,
Had bade me bring fresh wine-skins....
As I stood
Ling'ring upon the threshold, half concealed
By tender foliage, and my spirit light
With draughts of sunny weather, did I mark
An instant the gay group before mine eyes.
Deepest in shade, and facing where I stood,
Sat Plato,[3] with his calm face and low brows,

---

3. Athenian philosopher tutored by Socrates.

Which met above the narrow Grecian eyes;
The pale, thin lips just parted to the smile,
Which dimpled that smooth olive of his cheek.
His head a little bent, sat Sokrates,
With one swart finger raised admonishing,
And on the air were borne his changing tones.
Low lounging at his feet, one fair arm thrown
Around his knee (the other, high in air
Brandish'd a brazen amphor, which yet rained
Bright drops of ruby on the golden locks
And temples with their fillets of the vine),
Lay Alkibiades[4] the beautiful.
And thus, with solemn tone, spake Sokrates:
"This fair Aspasia,[5] which our Pericles[6]
Hath brought from realms afar, and set on high
In our Athenian city, hath a mind,
I doubt not, of a strength beyond her race;
And makes employ of it, beyond the way
Of women nobly gifted: woman's frail –
Her body rarely stands the test of soul;
She grows intoxicate with knowledge; throws
The laws of custom, order, 'neath her feet,
Feasting at life's great banquet with wide throat."
Then sudden, stepping from my leafy screen,
Holding the swelling wine-skin o'er my head,
With breast that heaved, and eyes and cheeks aflame,
Lit by a fury and a thought, I spake:
"By all great powers around us! Can it be

4. Alcibiades, a politician and general in classical Athens.
5. Ancient Greek figure subject to historiographical debate; Aspasia was the mistress of Pericles and supposedly popular in ancient Greece and active in philosophical circles, but did not hold Athenian citizenship.
6. Pericles: politician, general, and foundational figure of classical Athenian democracy.

That we poor women are empirical?
That gods who fashioned us did strive to make
Beings too fine, too subtly delicate,
With sense that thrilled response to ev'ry touch
Of nature's, and their task is not complete?
That they have sent their half-completed work
To bleed and quiver here upon the earth?
To bleed and quiver, and to weep and weep,
To beat its soul against the marble walls
Of men's cold hearts, and then at last to sin!"
I ceased, the first hot passion stayed and stemmed
And frighted by the silence: I could see,
Framed by the arbour foliage, which the sun
In setting softly gilded with rich gold,
Those upturned faces, and those placid limbs;
Saw Plato's narrow eyes and niggard mouth,
Which half did smile and half did criticise,
One hand held up, the shapely fingers framed
To gesture of entreaty – "Hush, I pray,
Do not disturb her; let us hear the rest –
Follow her mood, for here's another phase
Of your black-browed Xantippe...."
Then I saw
Young Alkibiades, with laughing lips
And half-shut eyes, contemptuous shrugging up
Soft, snowy shoulders, till he brought the gold
Of flowing ringlets round about his breasts.
But Sokrates, all slow and solemnly,
Raised, calm, his face to mine, and sudden spake:
"I thank thee for the wisdom which thy lips
Have thus let fall among us: prythee tell
From what high source, from what philosophies
Didst cull the sapient notion of thy words?"
Then stood I straight and silent for a breath,

Dumb, crushed with all that weight of cold contempt;
But swiftly in my bosom there uprose
A sudden flame, a merciful fury sent
To save me; with both angry hands I flung
The skin upon the marble, where it lay
Spouting red rills and fountains on the white;
Then, all unheeding faces, voices, eyes,
I fled across the threshold, hair unbound –
White garment stained to redness – beating heart
Flooded with all the flowing tide of hopes
Which once had gushed out golden, now sent back
Swift to their sources, never more to rise….
I think I could have borne the weary life,
The narrow life within the narrow walls,
If he had loved me; but he kept his love
For this Athenian city and her sons;
And, haply, for some stranger-woman, bold
With freedom, thought, and glib philosophy….
Ah me! the long, long weeping through the nights,
The weary watching for the pale-eyed dawn
Which only brought fresh grieving: then I grew
Fiercer, and cursed from out my inmost heart
The Fates which marked me an Athenian maid.
Then faded that vain fury; hope died out;
A huge despair was stealing on my soul,
A sort of fierce acceptance of my fate, –
He wished a household vessel – well 'twas good,
For he should have it! He should have no more
The yearning treasure of a woman's love,
But just the baser treasure which he sought.
I called my maidens, ordered out the loom,
And spun unceasing from the morn till eve;
Watching all keenly over warp and woof,
Weighing the white wool with a jealous hand.

I spun until, methinks, I spun away
The soul from out my body, the high thoughts
From out my spirit; till at last I grew
As ye have known me, – eye exact to mark
The texture of the spinning; ear all keen
For aimless talking when the moon is up,
And ye should be a-sleeping; tongue to cut
With quick incision, 'thwart the merry words
Of idle maidens....
                    Only yesterday
My hands did cease from spinning; I have wrought
My dreary duties, patient till the last.
The gods reward me! Nay, I will not tell
The after years of sorrow; wretched strife
With grimmest foes – sad Want and Poverty; –
Nor yet the time of horror, when they bore
My husband from the threshold; nay, not when
The subtle weed had wrought its deadly work.
Alas! alas! I was not there to soothe
The last great moment; never any thought
Of her that loved him – save at least the charge,
All earthly, that her body should not starve....
You weep, you weep; I would not that ye wept;
Such tears are idle; with the young, such grief
Soon grows to gratulation, as, "her love
Was withered by misfortune; mine shall grow
All nurtured by the loving," or, "her life
Was wrecked and shattered – mine shall smoothly sail." ....
Enough, enough. In vain, in vain, in vain!
The gods forgive me! Sorely have I sinned
In all my life. A fairer fate befall
You all that stand there....
                    Ha! the dawn has come;
I see a rosy glimmer – nay! it grows dark;

Why stand ye so in silence? throw it wide,
The casement, quick; why tarry? – give me air –
O fling it wide, I say, and give me light!

A Prayer[7]

Since that I may not have
Love on this side the grave,
Let me imagine Love.
Since not mine is the bliss
Of "claspt hands and lips that kiss,"
Let me in dreams it prove.
What tho' as the years roll
No soul shall melt to my soul,
Let me conceive such thing;
Tho' never shall entwine
Loving arms around mine
Let dreams caresses bring.
To live – it is my doom –
Lonely as in a tomb,
This cross on me was laid;
My God, I know not why;
Here in the dark I lie,
Lonely, yet not afraid.
It has seemed good to Thee
Still to withhold the key
Which opes the way to men;
I am shut in alone,
I make not any moan,
Thy ways are past my ken.
Yet grant me this, to find

---

7. See the analysis of "A Prayer" on pp. lxvi-lxvii.

The sweetness in my mind
Which I must still forego;
Great God which art above,
Grant me to image Love, –
The bliss without the woe.

Ralph to Mary

Love, you have led me to the strand,
Here, where the stilly, sunset sea,
Ever receding silently,
Lays bare a shining stretch of sand;

Which, as we tread, in waving line,
Sinks softly 'neath our moving feet;
And looking down our glances meet,
Two mirrored figures – yours and mine.

Tonight you found me sad, alone,
Amid the noisy, empty books
And drew me forth with those sweet looks,
And gentle ways which are your own.

The glory of the setting sun
Has sway'd and softened all my mood;
This wayward heart you understood,
Dear love, as you have always done.

Have you forgot the poet wild,
Who sang rebellious songs and hurl'd
His fierce anathemas at "the world,"
Which shrugg'd its shoulders, pass'd and smil'd?

Who fled in wrath to distant lands,
And sitting, thron'd upon a steep,

Made music to the mighty deep,
And thought, "Perhaps *it* understands."

Who back return'd, a wanderer drear,
Urged by the spirit's restless pain,
Sang his wild melodies in vain –
Sang them to ears that would not hear....

A weary, lonely thing he flies,
His soul's fire with soul's hunger quell'd,
Till, sudden turning, he beheld
His meaning – mirrored in your eyes!...

Ah, Love, since then have passed away
Long years; some things are chang'd on earth;
Men say that poet had his worth,
And twine for him the tardy bay.

What care I, so that hand in hand,
And heart in heart we pace the shore?
My heart desireth nothing more,
We understand, – we understand.

Felo De Se

With Apologies to Mr. Swinburne[8]

For repose I have sighed and have struggled; have sigh'd and have
struggled in vain;
I am held in the Circle of Being and caught in the Circle of Pain.
I was wan and weary with life; my sick soul yearned for death;
I was weary of women and war and the sea and the wind's wild breath;
I cull'd sweet poppies and crush'd them, the blood ran rich and red: –
And I cast it in crystal chalice and drank of it till I was dead.
And the mould of the man was mute, pulseless in ev'ry part,
The long limbs lay on the sand with an eagle eating the heart.
Repose for the rotting head and peace for the putrid breast,
But for that which is "I" indeed the gods have decreed no rest;
No rest but an endless aching, a sorrow which grows amain: –
I am caught in the Circle of Being and held in the Circle of Pain.
Bitter indeed is Life, and bitter of life the breath,
But give me life and its ways and its men, if this be Death.
Wearied I once of the Sun and the voices which clamour'd around:
Give them me back – in the sightless depths there is neither light
nor sound.
Sick is my soul, and sad and feeble and faint as it felt
When (far, dim day) in the fair flesh-fane of the body it dwelt.
But then I could run to the shore, weeping and weary and weak;
See the waves' blue sheen and feel the breath of the breeze on my
cheek:

---

8. This version is taken from *A London-Plane Tree and Other Verse* (London: T. Fisher Unwin, 1889), 68–70.

Could wail with the wailing wind; strike sharply the hands in despair;
Could shriek with the shrieking blast, grow frenzied and tear the hair;
Could fight fierce fights with the foe or clutch at a human hand;
And weary could lie at length on the soft, sweet, saffron sand....
I have neither a voice nor hands, nor any friend nor a foe;
I am I – just a Pulse of Pain – I am I, that is all I know.
For Life, and the sickness of Life, and Death and desire to die; –
They have passed away like the smoke, here is nothing but Pain and I.

Sonnet[9]

Most wonderful and strange it seems, that I
Who but a little time ago was tost
High on the waves of passion and of pain,
With aching heart and wildly throbbing brain,
Who peered into the darkness, deeming vain
All things there found if but One thing were lost,
Thus calm and still and silent here should lie,
Watching and waiting, – waiting passively.

The dark has faded, and before mine eyes
Have long, grey flats expanded, dim and bare;
And through the changing guises all things wear
Inevitable Law I recognise:
Yet in my heart a hint of feeling lies
Which half a hope and half is a despair.

---

9. Text taken from *A Minor Poet*, 89. "Sonnet" can also be found in Elizabeth Sharp's (1856–1932) *Women's Voices: An Anthology of the Most Characteristic Poems by English, Scotch, and Irish Women* (London: Walter Scott, 1887), 348.

Translated from Geibel[10]

O say, thou wild, thou oft-deceived heart,
What mean these noisy throbbings in my breast?
After thy long, unutterable woe
Wouldst thou not rest?

Fall'n from Life's tree the sweet rose-blossom lies,
And fragrant youth has fled. What made to seem
This earth as fair to thee as Paradise,
Was all a dream.

The blossom fell, the thorn was left to me;
Deep from the wound the blood-drops ever flow,
All that I have are yearnings, wild desires,
And wrath and woe.

They brought me Lethe's water, saying, "Drink!"
"Drink, for the draught is sweet," I heard them say,
"Shalt learn how soft a thing forgetting is."
I answered: "Nay."

What tho' indeed it were an idle cheat,
Nathless to me 'twas very fair and blest:
With every breath I draw I know that love
Reigns in my breast.

10. Title refers to the German poet, Emanuel Geibel (1815–1884). This text is taken from *A Minor Poet*, 90-1.

Let me go forth, – and thou, my heart, bleed on:
A lonely spot I seek by night and day,
That love and sorrow I may there breathe forth
In a last lay.

Run to Death[11]

A True Incident of Pre-Revolutionary French History

Now the lovely autumn morning breathes its freshness in earth's face,
In the crowded castle courtyard the blithe horn proclaims the chase;
And the ladies on the terrace smile adieux with rosy lips
To the huntsmen disappearing down the cedar-shaded groves,
Wafting delicate aromas from their scented finger tips,
And the gallants wave in answer, with their gold-embroidered gloves.
On they rode, past bush and bramble, on they rode, past elm and oak;
And the hounds, with anxious nostril, sniffed the heather-scented air,
Till at last, within his stirrups, up Lord Gaston rose, and spoke –
He, the boldest and the bravest of the wealthy nobles there:
"Friends," quoth he, "the time hangs heavy, for it is not as we thought,
And these woods, tho' fair and shady, will afford, I fear, no sport.
Shall we hence, then, worthy kinsmen, and desert the hunter's track
For the chateau, where the wine cup and the dice cup tempt us back?"
"Ay," the nobles shout in chorus; "Ay," the powder'd lacquey cries;
Then they stop with eager movement, reining in quite suddenly;
Peering down with half contemptuous, half with wonder-opened eyes
At a "something" which is crawling, with slow step, from tree to tree.
Is't some shadow phantom ghastly? No, a woman and a child,
Swarthy woman, with the "gipsy" written clear upon her face;
Gazing round her with her wide eyes dark, and shadow-fringed, and wild,

11. This version was published in 1879; see "Run to Death," *The Victoria Magazine* 33 (May-October 1879): 248–50.

With the cowed suspicious glances of a persecuted race.
Then they all, with unasked question, in each other's faces peer,
For a common thought has struck them, one their lips dare scarcely say.
Till Lord Gaston cries, impatient, "Why regret the stately deer
When such sport as yonder offers? quick! unleash the dogs – away!"
Then they breath'd a shout of cheering, grey-haired man and stripling boy,
And the gipsy, roused to terror, stayed her step, and turned her head –
Saw the faces of those huntsmen, lit with keenest cruel joy –
Sent a cry of grief to Heaven, closer clasped her child, and fled!

* * * * * * * * * * *

O ye nobles of the palace! O ye gallant-hearted lords!
Who would stoop for Leila's kerchief, or for Clementina's gloves,
Who would rise up all indignant, with your shining sheathless swords,
At the breathing of dishonour to your languid lady loves!
O, I tell you, daring nobles, with your beauty-loving stare,
Who ne'er long the coy caresses of the courtly dames withstood,
Tho' a woman be the lowest, and the basest, and least fair,
In your manliness forget not to respect her womanhood,
And thou, gipsy, that hast often the pursuer fled before,
That hast felt ere this the shadow of dark death upon thy brow,
That hast hid among the mountains, that hast roamed the forest o'er,
Bred to hiding, watching, fleeing, may thy speed avail thee now!

* * * * * * * * * * *

Still she flees, and ever fiercer tear the hungry hounds behind,
Still she flees, and ever faster follow there the huntsmen on,
Still she flees, her black hair streaming in a fury to the wind,
Still she flees, tho' all the glimmer of a happy hope is gone.
"Eh? what? baffled by a woman! Ah, *sapristi!* She can run!

Should she 'scape us, it would crown us with dishonour and disgrace;
It is time" (Lord Gaston shouted) "such a paltry chase were done!"
And the fleeter grew her footsteps, so the hotter grew the chase.
Ha! at last! the dogs are on her! will she struggle ere she dies?
See! she holds her child above her, all forgetful of *her* pain,
While a hundred thousand curses shoot out darkly from her eyes,
And a hundred thousand glances of the bitterest disdain.
Ha! the dogs are pressing closer! they have flung her to the ground;
Yet her proud lips never open with the dying sinner's cry –
Till at last, unto the Heavens, just two fearful shrieks resound,
While the soul is all forgotten in the body's agony!
Let them rest there, child and mother, in the shadow of the oak,
On the tender mother-bosom of that earth from which they came.
As they slow rode back those huntsmen neither laughed, nor sang,
nor spoke,
Hap, there lurked unowned within them throbbings of a secret shame.
But before the flow'ry terrace, where the ladies smiling sat,
With their graceful nothings trifling all the weary time away,
Low Lord Gaston bowed, and raising high his richly 'broider'd hat,
"Fairest ladies, give us welcome! 'Twas a famous hunt today."

A Minor Poet and Other Verse (1884)

To a Dead Poet[1]

I knew not if to laugh or weep;
　　They sat and talked of you –
"'Twas here he sat; 'twas this he said!
　　'Twas that he used to do."

"Here is the book wherein he read,
　　The room wherein he dwelt;
And he" (they said) "was such a man,
　　Such things he thought and felt."

I sat and sat, I did not stir;
　　They talked and talked away.
I was as mute as any stone,
　　I had no word to say.

They talked and talked; like to a stone
　　My heart grew in my breast –
I, who had never seen your face,
　　Perhaps I knew you best.

1. According to Melvyn New, the focus of this poem is James Thomson (*The Complete Novels and Selected Writings of Amy Levy 1861–1889* (Gainesville: University Press of Florida), 551 n. 7).

A Minor Poet[2]

"What should such fellows as I do,
Crawling between earth and heaven?"[3]

Here is the phial; here I turn the key
Sharp in the lock. Click! – there's no doubt it turned.
This is the third time; there is luck in threes –
Queen Luck, that rules the world, befriend me now
And freely I'll forgive you many wrongs!
Just as the draught began to work, first time,
Tom Leigh,[4] my friend (as friends go in the world),
Burst in, and drew the phial from my hand,
(Ah, Tom! Ah, Tom! That was a sorry turn!)
And lectured me a lecture, all compact
Of neatest, newest phrases, freshly culled
From works of newest culture: "common good";
"The world's great harmonies"; "must be content
With knowing God works all things for the best,
And Nature never stumbles." Then again,
"The common good," and still, "the common, good";
And what a small thing was our joy or grief
When weigh'd with that of thousands. Gentle Tom,
But you might wag your philosophic tongue
From morn till eve, and still the thing's the same:
I am myself, as each man is himself –

2. See the analysis of this poem beginning on p. lxii.
3. The extract is from William Shakespeare's *Hamlet.*
4. Tom Leigh is also a character in Levy's "In Holiday Humour" (pp. 658–69).

Feels his own pain, joys his own joy, and loves
With his own love, no other's. Friend, the world
Is but one man; one man is but the world.
And I am I, and you are Tom, that bleeds
When needles prick your flesh (mark, yours, not mine).
I must confess it; I can feel the pulse
A-beating at my heart, yet never knew
The throb of cosmic pulses. I lament
The death of youth's ideal in my heart;
And, to be honest, never yet rejoiced
In the world's progress – scarce, indeed, discerned;
(For still it seems that God's a Sisyphus[5]
With the world for stone).
                                        You shake your head. I'm base,
Ignoble? Who is noble – you or I?
I was not once thus? Ah, my friend, we are
As the Fates make us.
                                        This time is the third;
The second time the flask fell from my hand,
Its drowsy juices spilt upon the board;
And there my face fell flat, and all the life
Crept from my limbs, and hand and foot were bound
With mighty chains, subtle, intangible;
While still the mind held to its wonted use,
Or rather grew intense and keen with dread,
An awful dread – I thought I was in Hell.
In Hell, in Hell! Was ever Hell conceived
By mortal brain, by brain Divine devised,
Darker, more fraught with torment, than the world
For such as I? A creature maimed and marr'd
From very birth. A blot, a blur, a note
All out of tune in this world's instrument.

5. Sisyphus, figure of Greek mythology characterized by his futile efforts to roll a boulder up a hill.

A base thing, yet not knowing to fulfil
Base functions. A high thing, yet all unmeet
For work that's high. A dweller on the earth,
Yet not content to dig with other men
Because of certain sudden sights and sounds
(Bars of broken music; furtive, fleeting glimpse
Of angel faces 'thwart the grating seen)
Perceived in Heaven. Yet when I approach
To catch the sound's completeness, to absorb
The faces' full perfection, Heaven's gate,
Which then had stood ajar, sudden falls to,
And I, a-shiver in the dark and cold,
Scarce hear afar the mocking tones of men:
"He would not dig, forsooth; but he must strive
For higher fruits than what our tillage yields;
Behold what comes, my brothers, of vain pride!"
Why play with figures? trifle prettily
With this my grief which very simply 's said,
"There is no place for me in all the world"?
The world's a rock, and I will beat no more
A breast of flesh and blood against a rock....
A stride across the planks for old time's sake.
Ah, bare, small room that I have sorrowed in;
Ay, and on sunny days, haply, rejoiced;
We know some things together, you and I!
Hold there, you ranged row of books! In vain
You beckon from your shelf. You've stood my friends
Where all things else were foes; yet now I'll turn
My back upon you, even as the world
Turns it on me. And yet – farewell, farewell!
You, lofty Shakespeare, with the tattered leaves
And fathomless great heart, your binding's bruised
Yet did I love you less? Goethe, farewell;
Farewell, triumphant smile and tragic eyes,

And pitiless world-wisdom!
For all men
These two. And 'tis farewell with you, my friends,
More dear because more near: Theokritus;[6]
Heine that stings and smiles; Prometheus' bard;[7]
(I've grown too coarse for Shelley latterly:)
And one wild singer of today, whose song
Is all aflame with passionate bard's blood
Lash'd into foam by pain and the world's wrong.
At least, he has a voice to cry his pain;
For him, no silent writhing in the dark,
No muttering of mute lips, no straining out
Of a weak throat a-choke with pent-up sound,
A-throb with pent-up passion....
Ah, my sun!
That's you, then, at the window, looking in
To beam farewell on one who's loved you long
And very truly. Up, you creaking thing,
You squinting, cobwebbed casement!
So, at last,
I can drink in the sunlight. How it falls
Across that endless sea of London roofs,
Weaving such golden wonders on the grey,
That almost for the moment we forget
The world of woe beneath them.
Underneath,
For all the sunset glory, Pain is king.
Yet, the sun's there, and very sweet withal;
And I'll not grumble that it's only sun,
But open wide my lips – thus – drink it in;

6. Ancient Greek poet.

7. Levy is probably referring here to Percy Bysshe Shelley's *Prometheus Unbound* (1820); Johann Wolfgang von Goethe did also publish a poem entitled, "Prometheus." Likewise, Levy was familiar with Aeschylus' *Prometheus Bound*.

Turn up my face to the sweet evening sky
(What royal wealth of scarlet on the blue
So tender-toned, you'd almost think it green)
And stretch my hands out – so – to grasp it tight.
Ha, ha! 'tis sweet awhile to cheat the Fates,
And be as happy as another man.
The sun works in my veins like wine, like wine!
'Tis a fair world: if dark, indeed, with woe,
Yet having hope and hint of such a joy,
That a man, winning, well might turn aside,
Careless of Heaven....
O enough; I turn
From the sun's light, or haply I shall hope.
I have hoped enough; I would not hope again;
'Tis hope that is most cruel.
Tom, my friend,
You very sorry philosophic fool;
'Tis you, I think, that bid me be resign'd,
Trust, and be thankful.
Out on you! Resign'd?
I'm not resign'd, not patient, not school'd in
To take my starveling's portion and pretend
I'm grateful for it. I want all, all, all;
I've appetite for all. I want the best:
Love, beauty, sunlight, nameless joy of life.
There's too much patience in the world, I think.
We have grown base with crooking of the knee.
Mankind – say – God has bidden to a feast;
The board is spread, and groans with cates and drinks;
In troop the guests; each man with appetite
Keen-whetted with expectance.
In they troop,
Struggle for seats, jostle and push and seize.
What's this? what's this? There are not seats for all!

Some men must stand without the gates; and some
Must linger by the table, ill-supplied
With broken meats. One man gets meat for two,
The while another hungers. If I stand
Without the portals, seeing others eat
Where I had thought to satiate the pangs
Of mine own hunger; shall I then come forth
When all is done, and drink my Lord's good health
In my Lord's water? Shall I not rather turn
And curse him, curse him for a niggard host?
O, I have hungered, hungered, through the years,
Till appetite grows craving, then disease;
I am starved, wither'd, shrivelled.
Peace, O peace!
This rage is idle; what avails to curse
The nameless forces, the vast silences
That work in all things.
This time is the third,
I wrought before in heat, stung mad with pain,
Blind, scarcely understanding; now I know
What thing I do.
There was a woman once;
Deep eyes she had, white hands, a subtle smile,
Soft speaking tones: she did not break my heart,
Yet haply had her heart been otherwise
Mine had not now been broken. Yet, who knows?
My life was jarring discord from the first:
Tho' here and there brief hints of melody,
Of melody unutterable, clove the air.
From this bleak world, into the heart of night,
The dim, deep bosom of the universe,
I cast myself. I only crave for rest;
Too heavy is the load. I fling it down.

Epilogue

We knocked and knocked; at last, burst in the door,
And found him as you know – the outstretched arms
Propping the hidden face. The sun had set,
And all the place was dim with lurking shade.
There was no written word to say farewell,
Or make more clear the deed.
                                        I search'd and search'd;
The room held little: just a row of books
Much scrawl'd and noted; sketches on the wall,
Done rough in charcoal; the old instrument
(A violin, no Stradivarius)
He played so ill on; in the table drawer
Large schemes of undone work. Poems half-writ;
Wild drafts of symphonies; big plans of fugues;
Some scraps of writing in a woman's hand:
No more – the scattered pages of a tale,
A sorry tale that no man cared to read.
Alas, my friend, I lov'd him well, tho' he
Held me a cold and stagnant-blooded fool,
Because I am content to watch, and wait
With a calm mind the issue of all things.
Certain it is my blood's no turbid stream;
Yet, for all that, haply I understood
More than he ever deem'd; nor held so light
The poet in him. Nay, I sometimes doubt
If they have not, indeed, the better part –
These poets, who get drunk with sun, and weep
Because the night or a woman's face is fair.
Meantime there is much talk about my friend.
The women say, of course, he died for love;
The men, for lack of gold, or cavilling
Of carping critics. I, Tom Leigh, his friend,

I have no word at all to say of this.
Nay, I had deem'd him more philosopher;
For did he think by this one paltry deed
To cut the knot of circumstance, and snap
The chain which binds all being?

Medea

(A Fragment in drama form, after Euripides)[8]

πάντων δ᾽ ὅς ἔστ᾽ ἔμψυχα καὶ
γνὼμην ἔχὲι γυναῖκές ἐσμεν
ἀθλιώτατον φυτόν[9]

PERSONS
Citizens of Corinth
Medea
Aegeus
Jason
Nikias

First Scene

Scene: *Before* MEDEA's *House.*

(*Enter* MEDEA.)
MEDEA.
Today, today, I know not why it is,

---

8. Refers to Euripides' play, *Medea*; see the analysis of "Medea" beginning on p. xlii. The characters in Levy's "Medea" include, Aegeus, the Athenian King; Kreon, the King of Corinth, and his daughter, Glaukê; Nikias, an Athenian statesperson, and the mythical hero, Jason. See also Marta Villalba-Lázaro's comprehensive analysis of "Medea" in "Radicalizing the Myth: Amy Levy's Medea, the (Un) Assimilated Jewish Victorian Woman," *Women in Judaism: A Multidisciplinary Journal* 15, no. 2 (2018): 1–30.
9. From Euripides' *Medea*. Levy's Greek is very similar to a number of Greek/English translations in circulation in the period. However, Emily McDermott's later reproduction and translation perhaps best characterises Levy's "Medea": "Of all the things alive and that have sense, we women are the most miserable breed" (see *Euripides' Medea: The Incarnation of Disorder* (University Park: Pennsylvania State University Press, 1989), 45–6).

I do bethink me of my Colchian home.
Today, that I am lone and weary and sad,
I fain would call back days of pride and hope;
Of pride in strength, when strength was all unprov'd,
Of hope too high, too sweet, to be confined
In limits of conception.
I am sad.
Here in this gracious city, whose white walls
Gleam snow-like in the sunlight; whose fair shrines
Are filled with wondrous images of gods;
Upon whose harbour's bosom ride tall ships,
Black-masted, fraught with fragrant merchandise;
Whose straight-limbed people, in fair stuffs arrayed,
Do throng from morn till eve the sunny streets.
For what avail fair shrines and images?
What, cunning workmanship and purple robes?
Light of sweet sunlight, play and spray of waves?
When all around the air is charged and chill,
And all the place is drear and dark with hate?
Alas, alas, this people loves me not!
This strong, fair people, marble-cold and smooth
As modelled marble. I, an alien here,
That well can speak the language of their lips,
The language of their souls may never learn.
And in their hands, I, that did know myself
Ere now, a creature in whose veins ran blood
Redder, more rapid, than flows round most hearts,
Do seem a creature reft of life and soul.
If they would only teach the subtle trick
By which their hearts are melted into love,
I'd strive to learn it. I am very meek.
They think me proud, but I am very meek,
Ready to do their bidding. Hear me, friends!
Friends, I am very hungry, give me love!
'Tis all I ask! Is it so hard to give?

You stand and front me with your hostile eyes;
You only give me hatred?
Yet I know
Ye are not all unloving. Oft I see
The men and women walking in the ways,
Hand within hand, and tender-bated breath,
On summer evenings when the sky is fair.
O men and women, are ye then so hard?
Will ye not give a little of your love
To me that am so hungry?

(*Enter* AEGEUS *and* NIKIAS, *on the opposite side.*
MEDEA *steps back on the threshold and pauses.*)

Ha, that word!
'Tis Jason's name they bandy to and fro.
I know not why, whene'er his name is spoke,
Once name of joy and ever name of love,
I wax white and do tremble; sudden seized
With shadowy apprehension. May 't forbode
No evil unto him I hold so dear;
And ever dearer with the waxing years: –
For this indeed is woman's chiefest curse,
That still her constant heart clings to its love
Through all time and all chances; while the man
Is caught with newness; coldly calculates,
And measures pain and pleasure, loss and gain;
And ever grows to look with the world's eye
Upon a woman, tho' his, body and soul.
(*She goes within.*)
(*The two citizens come forward.*)

NIKIAS.
I, in this thing, do hold our Jason wise;
Kreon is mighty; Glaukê very fair.

AEGEUS.
An 'twere for that – the Colchian's fair enough.

NIKIAS.
I like not your swart skins and purple hair;
Your black, fierce eyes where the brows meet across.
By all the gods! when yonder Colchian
Fixes me with her strange and sudden gaze,
Each hair upon my body stands erect!
Zeus,[10] 'tis a very tiger, and as mute!

AEGEUS.
'Tis certain that the woman's something strange.

NIKIAS.
Gods, spare me your strange women, so say I.
Give me gold hair, lithe limbs and gracious smiles,
And spare the strangeness.

AEGEUS.
I do marvel much
How she will bear the tidings.

NIKIAS.
Lo behold!
Here comes our Jason striding 'thwart the streets.
Gods! what a gracious presence!

AEGEUS.
I perceive
The Colchian on the threshold. By her looks,
Our idle talk has reached her listening ears.
(*Enter* JASON. MEDEA *reappears on the threshold.*)

10. Classical Greek deity.

NIKIAS.
Let's draw aside and mark them; lo, they meet.
(*The two citizens withdraw, unperceived, to*
a further corner of the stage.)

MEDEA.
'Tis false, 'tis false. O Jason, they speak false!

JASON.
Your looks are wild, Medea; you bring shame
Upon this house, that stand with hair unbound
Beyond the threshold. Get you in the house.

MEDEA.
But not till you have answered me this thing.

JASON.
What is this thing that you would know of me?

MEDEA.
O I have heard strange rumours – horrible!

JASON.
Oft lies the horror of a tale in the ear
Of him that hears it. What is 't you have heard?

MEDEA.
Almost, for fear, I dare not give it tongue.
But tell me this? Love, you have not forgot
The long years passed in this Corinthian home?
The great love I have borne you through the years?
Nor that far time when, in your mighty craft,
You came, a stranger, to the Colchian shore?
O strong you were; but not of such a strength
To have escaped the doom of horrid death,

Had not I, counting neither loss nor gain,
Shown you the way to triumph and renown.

JASON.
And better had I then, a thousand times,
Have fought with my good sword and fall'n or stood
As the high Fates directed; than been caught
In the close meshes of the magic web
Wrought by your hand, dark-thoughted sorceress.

NIKIAS.
Did you mark that? Jason speaks low and smooth;
Yet there is that within his level tones,
And in the icy drooping of his lids
(More than his words, tho' they are harsh enough),
Tells me he hates her.

AEGEUS.
Hush! Medea speaks.

MEDEA.
O gods, gods; ye have cursed me in this gift!
Is it for this, for this that I have striven?
Have wrestled in the darkness? Wept my tears?
Have fought with sweet desires and hopes and thoughts?
Have watched when men were sleeping? For long days
Have shunned the sunlight and the breaths of Heaven?
Is it for this, for this that I have prayed
Long prayers, poured out with blood and cries and tears?
Lo, I who strove for strength have grown more weak
Than is the weakest. I have poured the sap
Of all my being, my life's very life,
Before a thankless godhead; and am grown
No woman, but a monster. What avail
Charms, spells and potions, all my hard-won arts,

My mystic workings, seeing they cannot win
One little common spark of human love?
O gods, gods, ye have cursed me in this gift!
More should ye have withheld or more have giv'n;
Have fashioned me more weak or else more strong.
Behold me now, your work, a thing of fear –
From natural human fellowship cut off,
And yet a woman – sick and sore with pain;
Hungry for love and music of men's praise,
But walled about as with a mighty wall,
Far from men's reach and sight, alone, alone.

NIKIAS.
Behold her, how she waves about her arms
And casts her eyes to Heaven.

AEGEUS.
Ay, 'tis strange –
Not as our women do, yet scarce unmeet.

NIKIAS.
Unmeet, unmeet? But Jason holds it so!
Mark you his white cheeks and his knitted brows,
What wrath and hate and scorn upon his face!

JASON.
Hear me, Medea, if you still can hear
That seem so strangely lifted from yourself:
But I, that know you long, do know you well,
A thing of moods and passions; so I bear
Once more with your wild words and savage gests,
Ay, and for all your fury speak you fair.
You say you love me. Can I deem it so,
When what does most advantage me and mine
You shrink to hear of? For I make no doubt,

Fleet-footed rumour did anticipate
The tidings I was hastening to bear,
When you, wide-eyed, unveiled, unfilleted,
Rushed out upon me.
Know then this once more:
That I have sworn to take as wedded wife
Glaukê, the daughter of our mighty king,
In this, in nowise hurting you and yours.
For you all fair provision I have made,
So but you get beyond the city walls
Before the night comes on. Our little ones –
They too shall journey with you. I have said.
And had I found you in a mood more mild,
Less swayed by savage passion, I had told
How this thing, which mayhap seems a thing hard,
Is but a blessing, wrapped and cloaked about
In harsh disguisements. For tho' Kreon rule
Today within the city; Kreon dead,
Who else shall rule there saving I alone,
The king's son loved of him and other men?
And in those days Medea's sons and mine
Shall stand at my right hand, grown great in power.
Medea, too, if she do but control
Her fiery spirit, may yet reign a queen
Above this land of Corinth. I have said.

NIKIAS.
Well said.

AEGEUS.
But none the better that 'twas false.

NIKIAS.
I'd sooner speak, for my part, fair than true.

Mark Jason there; how firm his lithe, straight limbs;
How high his gold-curled head, crisped like a girl's.
And yet for all his curled locks and smooth tones
Jason is very strong. I never knew
A man of such a strange and subtle strength.

AEGEUS.
The Colchian speaks no word; and her swart hands,
Which waved, a moment since, and beat the air
In mad entreaty, are together clasped
Before her white robe in an iron clasp.
And her wild eyes, which erst did seek the heav'ns,
And now her lord and now again the earth,
Are set on space and move not. The tall shape
Stands there erect and still. This calm, I think,
Is filled with strangest portent.

NIKIAS.
O ye gods,
She is a pregnant horror as she stands.

AEGEUS.
She speaks; her voice sounds as a sound far off.

MEDEA.
As you have said, O Jason, let it be.
I for my part am nothing loth to break
A compact never in fair justice framed,
Seeing how much one gave and one how much.
For you, you thought: This maid has served me well,
And yet may serve me. When I touch her palm
The blood is set a-tingle in my veins;
For these things I will make her body mine.
And I, I stood before you, clean and straight,

A woman some deemed fair and all deemed wise;
A woman, yet no simple thing nor slight,
By nature fashioned in no niggard mould;
And looked into your eyes with eyes that spake:
Lo, utterly, forever, I am yours.
And since that you, this gift I lavish laid
Low at your feet, have lightly held and spurned –
I in my two arms, thus, shall gather it up
So that your feet may not encounter it
Which is not worthy for your feet to tread!
Yet pause a moment, Jason. Haply now
In some such wise as this your thoughts run on:
I loved this woman for a little space;
Alas, poor soul, she loved me but too well –
It is the way with women! Some, I think,
Did deem her fierce; gods! she was meek enough,
Content with what I gave; when I gave not
Nothing importunate.
Ah, Jason, pause.
You never knew Medea. You forget,
Because so long she bends the knee to you,
She was not born to serfdom.
I have knelt
Too long before you. I have stood too long
Suppliant before this people. You forget
A redder stream flows in my Colchian veins
Than the slow flood which courses round your hearts,
O cold Corinthians, with whom I long have dwelt
And never ere this day have known myself.
Nor have ye known me. Now behold me free,
Ungyved by any chains of this man wrought;
Nothing desiring at your hands nor his.
Free, freer than the air or winged birds;
Strong, stronger than the blast of wintry storms;

And lifted up into an awful realm
Where is nor love, nor pity, nor remorse,
Nor dread, but only purpose.
There shall be
A horror and a horror in this land;
Woe upon woe, red blood and biting flame;
Most horrid death and anguish worse than death;
Deeds that shall make the shores of Hades sound
With murmured terror; with an awful dread
Shall move the generations yet unborn;
A horror and a horror in the land.

JASON.
Shrew, triple-linked with Hell, get you within.
Shame not my house! 'Tis your own harm you work.
(MEDEA *goes within.* JASON *moves off slowly.*
AEGEUS *and* NIKIAS *go off conferring in whispers.*)

Second Scene
Time: After an interval; the evening of the same day.
Scene: A street. A crowd of people running to and fro.

NIKIAS.
O horror, horror, have ye heard the tale?

AEGEUS.
Alas, a bloody rumour reached mine ears
Of awful purport: that the king lies dead –

NIKIAS.
And by his side, his daughter; both caught up
In sudden toils of torment. With his grief
Jason is all distraught; behold her deed,
The swift and subtle tigress!

AEGEUS.
Woe! Alas!
Woe for the state, woe for our Kreon slain,
For hapless Glaukê, for our Jason, woe!
But three times woe for her that did the deed –
Her womanhood sham'd; her children basely wrong'd.

NIKIAS.
Hold back your pity till the tale be told,
For never was there horror like to this.
Ere now in Corinth, haply, you have heard
How she did use for her crime's instruments
The tender boys sprung from great Jason's loins;
Bidding them bear the garments wrought in Hell
As bridal gifts to grace the marriage morn
Of gold-hair'd Glaukê. Serpent! Sorceress!

AEGEUS.
Alas, consider; so the tigress springs
When that her cubs are menaced. 'Twas her love
That wrought the deed – evil, yet wrought for love.

NIKIAS.
Spare me such love. I never yet could deem,
Ev'n ere the horror, that Medea held
The love of human mothers in her breast.
For I have seen her, when her children played
Their innocent, aimless sports about her knees,
Or held her gown across the marketplace,
Move all unheeding with her swart brows knit
And fierce eyes fixed; not, as is mothers' wont,
Eager to note the winning infant ways,
A-strain to catch the babbling treble tones
Of soft lips clamouring for a kiss or smile.

And once I marked her ('twas a summer's morn)
Turn suddenly and, stooping, catch and strain
One tender infant to her breast. She held
Her lips to his and looked into his eyes,
Not gladly, as a mother with her child,
But stirred by some strange passion; then the boy
Cried out with terror, and Medea wept.

AEGEUS.
Your tale is strange.

NIKIAS.
Stranger is yet to come.
How that the Colchian did send forth her sons,
Innocent doers of most deadly deed,
Has reached your knowledge. When the deed was done,
And the dead king lay stretched upon the floor
Clutching his daughter in a last embrace,
Arose great clamour in the palace halls;
Wailing and cries of terror; women's screams;
A rush of flying feet from hall to hall;
The clanging fall of brazen instruments
Upon the marble.
The two tender boys,
Half apprehending what thing had befallen,
Fled forth unmarked, and all affrighted reached
The house of Jason, where Medea stood
Erect upon the threshold. From afar
Sounded and surged the fiercely frighted roar
Of the roused city, and, like waves of the sea,
Grew nearer ev'ry beating of the pulse.
Forth from the inmost chambers fled the slaves,
Made fleet with sudden fear; the little ones
With arms outspread rushed to the Colchian,

And clung about her limbs and caught her robe,
Hiding their faces.
And Medea stood
Calm as a carven image. As the sound
Of wrath and lamentation drew more near,
The pale lips seemed to smile. But when she saw
Her children clinging round her, she stretched forth
One strong, swart hand and put the twain away,
And gathered up the trailing of her robe.
I saw the deed, I, Nikias, with these eyes!
Then spake she (Zeus! Grant that I may not hear
Such tones once more from human lips!). She spake:
"I will not have ye, for I love ye not!"
Then all her face grew alien. Those around
Stood still, not knowing what she planned.
Then she
Forth from her gathered garment swiftly drew
A thing that gleamed and glinted; in the air
She held it poised an instant; then – O gods!
How shall I speak it? – on the marble floor
Was blood that streamed and spurted; blood that flow'd
From two slain, innocent babes!

AEGEUS.
O woful day!

NIKIAS.
Then brake a cry from all about: a wail
Of lamentation. But above the sound
A fierce long shriek, that froze the blood i' the veins,
Rang out and rose, cleaving the topmost cloud.

AEGEUS.
O evil deed! O essence of all evil

Stealing the shape of woman!

NIKIAS.
After that
All is confusion; from all sides surged up
The people, cursing, weeping. 'Thwart the din
Each other moment the strained ear might catch
Medea's name, or Jason's, or the King's;
And women wailed out "Glaukê" through their tears.
Then sudden came a pause; the angry roar
Died down into a murmur; and the throng
Grew still, and rolled aside like a clov'n sea.
And Jason strode between them till he reached
His own home's threshold where the twain lay dead,
Long gazed he on their faces; then he turned
To the hush'd people; turned to them and spake:
(His face was whiter than the dead's, his eyes
Like to a creature's that has looked on Hell)
"Where is the woman?" Lo, and when they sought
Medea, no eye beheld her. And no man
Had looked upon her since that moment's space
When steel had flashed and blood foamed in the air.
Then Jason stood erect and spake again:
"Let no man seek this woman; blood enough
Has stained our city. Let the furies rend
Her guilty soul; nor we pollute our hands
With her accursed body ..."

AEGEUS.
Cease, my friend;
It is enough. You judged this thing aright;
This woman was dark and evil in her soul;
Black to her fiend-heart's root; a festering plague
In our fair city's midst.

NIKIAS.
Spake I not true?

(*Night; outside the city.* MEDEA *leaning against a rock.*)
Here let me rest; beyond men's eyes, beyond
The city's hissing hate. Why am I here?
Why have I fled from death? There's sun on the earth,
And in the shades no sun; – thus much I know;
And sunlight's good.
Wake I, or do I sleep?
I'm weary, weary; once I dream'd a dream
Of one that strove and wept and yearned for love
In a fair city. She was blind indeed.
They say the woman had a fiend at heart,
And afterwards – Hush, hush, I dream'd a dream.
How cold the air blows; how the night grows dark,
Wrapping me round in blackness. Darker too
Grows the deep night within. I cannot see;
I grope with weary hands; my hands are sore
With fruitless striving. I have fought with the Fates
And I am vanquished utterly. The Fates
Yield not to strife; nay, nor to many prayers.
Their ways are dark.
One climbs the tree and grasps
A handful of dead leaves; another walks,
Heedless, beneath the branches, and the fruit
Falls mellow at his feet.
This is the end:
I have dash'd my heart against a rock; the blood
Is drain'd and flows no more; and all my breast
Is emptied of its tears.
Thus go I forth
Into the deep, dense heart of the night – alone.

Sinfonia Eroica[11]

(To Sylvia)

My Love, my Love, it was a day in June,
A mellow, drowsy, golden afternoon;
And all the eager people thronging came
To that great hall, drawn by the magic name
Of one, a high magician, who can raise
The spirits of the past and future days,
And draw the dreams from out the secret breast,
Giving them life and shape.
I, with the rest,
Sat there athirst, atremble for the sound;
And as my aimless glances wandered round,
Far off, across the hush'd, expectant throng,
I saw your face that fac'd mine.
Clear and strong
Rush'd forth the sound, a mighty mountain stream;
Across the clust'ring heads mine eyes did seem
By subtle forces drawn, your eyes to meet.
Then you, the melody, the summer heat,
Mingled in all my blood and made it wine.
Straight I forgot the world's great woe and mine;
My spirit's murky lead grew molten fire;
Despair itself was rapture.
Ever higher,

11. Christine Pullen suggests that this poem and "To Sylvia" below were "inspired" by fellow Cambridge student, Jennie Wetton; see *The Woman Who Dared: A Biography of Amy Levy* (Kingston: Kingston University Press, 2010), 29–30.

Stronger and clearer rose the mighty strain;
Then sudden fell; then all was still again,
And I sank back, quivering as one in pain.
Brief was the pause; then, 'mid a hush profound,
Slow on the waiting air swell'd forth a sound
So wondrous sweet that each man held his breath;
A measur'd, mystic melody of death.
Then back you lean'd your head, and I could note
The upward outline of your perfect throat;
And ever, as the music smote the air,
Mine eyes from far held fast your body fair.
And in that wondrous moment seem'd to fade
My life's great woe, and grow an empty shade
Which had not been, nor was not.
                                        And I knew
Not which was sound, and which, O Love, was you.

To Sylvia[12]

"O love, lean thou thy cheek to mine,
And let the tears together flow" –
Such was the song you sang to me
Once, long ago.

Such was the song you sang; and yet
(O be not wroth!) I scarcely knew
What sounds flow'd forth; I only felt
That you were you.

I scarcely knew your hair was gold,
Nor of the heavens' own blue your eyes.
Sylvia and song, divinely mixt,
Made Paradise.

These things I scarcely knew; today,
When love is lost and hope is fled,
The song you sang so long ago
Rings in my head.

Clear comes each note and true; today,
As in a picture I behold
Your turn'd-up chin, and small, sweet head
Misty with gold.

---

12. See above footnote. "To Sylvia" was originally published in *The Cambridge Review: A Journal of University Life and Thought* 3, no. 65 (March 15, 1882): 289

I see how your dear eyes grew deep,
How your lithe body thrilled and swayed,
And how were whiter than the keys
Your hands that played....

Ah, sweetest! cruel have you been,
And robbed my life of many things.
I will not chide; ere this I knew
That Love had wings.

You've robbed my life of many things –
Of love and hope, of fame and pow'r.
So be it, sweet. You cannot steal
One golden hour.

A Greek Girl

I may not weep, not weep, and he is dead.
A weary, weary weight of tears unshed
Through the long day in my sad heart I bear;
The horrid sun with all unpitying glare
Shines down into the dreary weaving room,
Where clangs the ceaseless clatter of the loom,
And ceaselessly deft maiden-fingers weave
The fine-wrought web; and I from morn till eve
Work with the rest, and when folk speak to me
I smile hard smiles; while still continually
The silly stream of maiden speech flows on: –
And now at length they talk of him that's gone,
Lightly lamenting that he died so soon –
Ah me! ere yet his life's sun stood at noon.
Some praise his eyes, some deem his body fair,
And some mislike the colour of his hair!
Sweet life, sweet shape, sweet eyes, and sweetest hair,
What form, what hue, save Love's own, did ye wear?
I may not weep, not weep, for very shame.
He loved me not. One summer's eve he came
To these our halls, my father's honoured guest,
And seeing me, saw not. If his lips had prest
My lips, but once, in love; his eyes had sent
One love-glance into mine, I had been content,
And deemed it great joy for one little life;
Nor envied other maids the crown of wife:
The long sure years, the merry children-band –

Alas, alas, I never touched his hand!
And now my love is dead that loved not me.

Thrice-blest, thrice-crowned, of gods thrice-loved she – [13]
That other, fairer maid, who tombward brings
Her gold, shorn locks and piled-up offerings
Of fragrant fruits, rich wines, and spices rare,
And cakes with honey sweet, with saffron fair;
And who, unchecked by any thought of shame,
May weep her tears, and call upon his name,
With burning bosom prest to the cold ground,
Knowing, indeed, that all her life is crown'd,
Thrice-crowned, thrice honoured, with that love of his; –
No dearer crown on earth is there, I wis.

While yet the sweet life lived, more light to bear
Was my heart's hunger; when the morn was fair,
And I with other maidens in a line
Passed singing through the city to the shrine,
Oft in the streets or crowded marketplace
I caught swift glimpses of the dear-known face;
Or marked a stalwart shoulder in the throng;
Or heard stray speeches as we passed along,
In tones more dear to me than any song.
These, hoarded up with care, and kept apart,
Did serve as meat and drink my hungry heart.

---

13. This line possibly moves the poem into the context of the Holy Trinity and Christian tradition in order to develop critique; the fact that "gods" is uncapitalised potentially indicates the calling into question of this principal tenet of Christian faith. Thus, the poem can be read in conjunction with "Magdalen" – see below (Luke Devine, *From Anglo-First-Wave towards American Second-Wave Jewish Feminism: Negotiating with Jewish Feminist Theology and its Communities in the Writing of Amy Levy* (Piscataway: Gorgias Press, 2010), 111–2).

And now forever has my sweet love gone;
And weary, empty days I must drag on,
Till all the days of all my life be sped,
By no thought cheered, by no hope comforted.
For if indeed we meet among the shades,
How shall he know me from the other maids? –
Me, that had died to save his body pain!

Alas, alas, such idle thoughts are vain!
O cruel, cruel sunlight, get thee gone!
O dear, dim shades of eve, come swiftly on!
That when quick lips, keen eyes, are closed in sleep,
Through the long night till dawn I then may weep.

Magdalen[14]

All things I can endure, save one.
The bare, blank room where is no sun;
The parcelled hours; the pallet hard;
The dreary faces here within;
The outer women's cold regard;
The Pastor's iterated "sin"; –
These things could I endure, and count
No overstrain'd, unjust amount;
No undue payment for such bliss –
Yea, all things bear, save only this:
That you, who knew what thing would be,
Have wrought this evil unto me.
It is so strange to think on still –
That you, that you should do me ill!
Not as one ignorant or blind,
But seeing clearly in your mind
How this must be which now has been,
Nothing aghast at what was seen.
Now that the tale is told and done,
It is so strange to think upon.

You were so tender with me, too!
One summer's night a cold blast blew,
Closer about my throat you drew
The half-slipt shawl of dusky blue.
And once my hand, on a summer's morn,

14. See the analysis of this poem beginning on p. lxvii.

I stretched to pluck a rose; a thorn
Struck through the flesh and made it bleed
(A little drop of blood indeed!)
Pale grew your cheek; you stoopt and bound
Your handkerchief about the wound;
Your voice came with a broken sound;
With the deep breath your breast was riven;
I wonder, did God laugh in Heaven?

How strange, that *you* should work my woe!
How strange! I wonder, do you know
How gladly, gladly I had died
(And life was very sweet that tide)
To save you from the least, light ill?
How gladly I had borne your pain.
With one great pulse we seem'd to thrill, –
Nay, but we thrill'd with pulses twain.

Even if one had told me this,
"A poison lurks within your kiss,
Gall that shall turn to night his day:"
Thereon I straight had turned away –
Ay, tho' my heart had crack'd with pain –
And never kiss'd your lips again.

At night, or when the daylight nears,
I hear the other women weep;
My own heart's anguish lies too deep
For the soft rain and pain of tears.
I think my heart has turn'd to stone.
A dull, dead weight that hurts my breast;
Here, on my pallet-bed alone,
I keep apart from all the rest.
Wide-eyed I lie upon my bed,

I often cannot sleep all night;
The future and the past are dead,
There is no thought can bring delight.
All night I lie and think and think;
If my heart were not made of stone,
But flesh and blood, it needs must shrink
Before such thoughts. Was ever known
A woman with a heart of stone?

The doctor says that I shall die.
It may be so, yet what care I?
Endless reposing from the strife,
Death do I trust no more than life.
For one thing is like one arrayed,
And there is neither false nor true;
But in a hideous masquerade
All things dance on, the ages through.
And good is evil, evil good;
Nothing is known or understood
Save only Pain. I have no faith
In God or Devil, Life or Death.

The doctor says that I shall die.
You, that I knew in days gone by,
I fain would see your face once more,
Con well its features o'er and o'er;
And touch your hand and feel your kiss,
Look in your eyes and tell you this:
That all is done, that I am free;
That you, through all eternity,
Have neither part nor lot in me.

Christopher Found

1.

At last; so this is you, my dear!
How should I guess to find you here?
So long, so long, I sought in vain
In many cities, many lands,
With straining eyes and groping hands;
The people marvelled at my pain.
They said: “But sure, the woman’s mad;
What ails her, we should like to know,
That she should be so wan and sad,
And silent through the revels go?”
They clacked with such a sorry stir!
Was I to tell? were they to know
That I had lost you, Christopher?
Will you forgive me for one thing?
Whiles, when a stranger came my way,
My heart would beat and I would say:
“Here’s Christopher!” – then lingering
With longer gaze, would turn away
Cold, sick at heart. My dear, I know
You will forgive me for this thing.
It is so very long ago
Since I have seen your face – till now;
Now that I see it – lip and brow,
Eyes, nostril, chin, alive and clear;

Last time was long ago; I know
This thing you will forgive me, dear.

2.

There is no Heaven – this is the best;
O hold me closer to your breast;
Let your face lean upon my face,
That there no longer shall be space
Between our lips, between our eyes.
I feel your bosom's fall and rise.
O hold me near and yet more near;
Ah sweet; I wonder do you know
How lone and cold, how sad and drear,
Was I a little while ago;
Sick of the stress, the strife, the stir;
But I have found you, Christopher.

3.

If only you had come before!
(This is the thing I most deplore)
A seemlier woman you had found,
More calm, by courtesies more bound,
Less quick to greet you, more subdued
Of appetite; of slower mood.
But ah! you come so late, so late!
This time of day I can't pretend
With slight, sweet things to satiate
The hunger-cravings. Nay, my friend,
I cannot blush and turn and tremble,
Wax loth as younger maidens do.
Ah, Christopher, with you, with you,
You would not wish me to dissemble?

4.

So long have all the days been meagre,
With empty platter, empty cup,
No meats nor sweets to do me pleasure,
That if I crave – is it over-eager,
The deepest draught, the fullest measure,
The beaker to the brim poured up?

5.

Shelley, that sprite from the spheres above,
Says, and would make the matter clear,
That love divided is larger love; –
We'll leave those things to the bards, my dear.
For you never wrote a verse, you see;
And I – my verse is not fair nor new.
Till the world be dead, you shall love but me,
Till the stars have ceased, I shall love but you.

Epilogue

Thus ran the words; or rather, thus did run
Their purport. Idly seeking in the chest
(You see it yonder), I had found them there:
Some blotted sheets of paper in a case,
With a woman's name writ on it: "Adelaide."
Twice on the writing there was scored the date
Of ten years back; and where the words had end
Was left a space, a dash, a half-writ word,
As tho' the writer minded, presently
The matter to pursue.
                                        I questioned her,
That worthy, worthy soul, my châtelaine,

Who, nothing loth, made answer.
There had been
Another lodger ere I had the rooms,
Three months gone by – a woman.
"Young, sir? No.
Must have seen forty if she'd seen a day!
A lonesome woman; hadn't many friends;
Wrote books, I think, and things for newspapers.
Short in her temper – eyes would flash and flame
At times, till I was frightened. Paid her rent
Most regular, like a lady.
Ten years back,
They say (at least Ann Brown says), ten years back
The lady had a lover. Even then
She must have been no chicken.
Three months since
She died. Well, well, the Lord is kind and just.
I did my best to tend her, yet indeed
It's bad for trade to have a lodger die.
Her brother came, a week before she died:
Buried her, took her things, threw in the fire
The littered heaps of paper.
Yes, the sheets,
They must have been forgotten in the chest; –
I never knew her name was Adelaide."

A Dirge

"Mein Herz, mein Herz ist traurig
Doch lustig leuchtet der Mai."[15]

There's May amid the meadows,
There's May amid the trees;
Her May-time note the cuckoo
Sends forth upon the breeze.

Above the rippling river
May swallows skim and dart;
November and December
Keep watch within my heart.

The spring breathes in the breezes,
The woods with wood-notes ring,
And all the budding hedgerows
Are fragrant of the spring.

In secret, silent places
The live green things upstart;
Ice-bound, ice-crown'd dwells winter
Forever in my heart.

---

15. The extract is from Heinrich Heine's "The Homecoming"; see *The Complete Poems of Heinrich Heine: A Modern English Version,* ed. and trans. Hal Draper (Boston: Suhrkamp/Insel, 1982), 77. In the Draper edition the quotation reads, "My heart, my heart is heavy, / Though May shines bright on all"; see Levy's translation in "From Heine" pp. 558–9.

Upon the bridge I linger,
Near where the lime-trees grow;
Above, swart birds are circling,
Beneath, the stream runs slow.

A stripling and a maiden
Come wand'ring up the way;
His eyes are glad with springtime,
Her face is fair with May.

Of warmth and sun and sweetness
All nature takes a part;
The ice of all the ages
Weighs down upon my heart.

The Sick Man and the Nightingale[16]

(From Lenau)[17]

So late, and yet a nightingale?
Long since have dropp'd the blossoms pale,
The summer fields are ripening,
And yet a sound of spring?

O tell me, didst thou come to hear,
Sweet Spring, that I should die this year;
And call'st across from the far shore
To me one greeting more?

16. Originally published as "The Sick Man in the Garden," in *The Cambridge Review: A Journal of University Life and Thought* 3, no. 60 (February 8, 1882): 157.

17. Austrian poet, Nikolaus Lenau, a pseudonym of Nikolaus Franz Niembsch (1802–1850); Lenau's poetry is characteristic of *Weltschmerz* (New, ed., *The Complete Novels*, 551 n. 11).

To Death[18]

(From Lenau)

If within my heart there's mould,
If the flame of Poesy
And the flame of Love grow cold,
Slay my body utterly.

Swiftly, pause not nor delay;
Let not my life's field be spread
With the ash of feelings dead,
Let thy singer soar away.

18. "To Death" was originally published in *The Cambridge Review: A Journal of University Life and Thought* 3, no. 60 (February 8, 1882): 157.

A June-Tide Echo

(After a Richter Concert)[19]

In the long, sad time, when the sky was grey,
  And the keen blast blew through the city drear,
When delight had fled from the night and the day,
  My chill heart whispered, "June will be here!

"June with its roses a-sway in the sun,
  Its glory of green on mead and tree."
Lo, now the sweet June-tide is nearly done,
  June-tide, and never a joy for me!

Is it so much of the gods that I pray?
  Sure craved man never so slight a boon!
To be glad and glad in my heart one day –
  One perfect day of the perfect June.

Sweet sounds tonight rose up, wave upon wave;
  Sweet dreams were afloat in the balmy air.
This is the boon of the gods that I crave –
  To be glad, as the music and night were fair.

For once, for one fleeting hour, to hold
  The fair shape the music that rose and fell
Revealed and concealed like a veiling fold;
  To catch for an instant the sweet June spell.

---

19. It is difficult to know which "Richter" Levy is referring to, but it is possibly the conductor, Hans Richter (1843–1916).

For once, for one hour, to catch and keep
    The sweet June secret that mocks my heart;
Now lurking calm, like a thing asleep,
    Now hither and thither with start and dart.

Then the sick, slow grief of the weary years,
    The slow, sick grief and the sudden pain;
The long days of labour, the nights of tears –
    No more these things would I hold in vain.

I would hold my life as a thing of worth;
    Pour praise to the gods for a precious thing.
Lo, June in her fairness is on the earth,
    And never a joy does the niggard bring.

To Lallie[20]

(Outside the British Museum)

Up those Museum steps you came,
And straightway all my blood was flame,
O Lallie, Lallie!

The world (I had been feeling low)
In one short moment's space did grow
A happy valley.

There was a friend, my friend, with you;
A meagre dame, in peacock blue
Apparelled quaintly:

This poet-heart went pit-a-pat;
I bowed and smiled and raised my hat;
You nodded – faintly.

My heart was full as full could be;
You had not got a word for me,
Not one short greeting;

That nonchalant small nod you gave
(The tyrant's motion to the slave)
Sole mark'd our meeting.

---

20. New (*The Complete Novels*, 551 n. 12) speculates that "Lallie" is Violet Paget (pseud. Vernon Lee); alternatively, Pullen argues that "Lallie" is Alice Lloyd, a friend Levy made at Cambridge (*The Woman Who Dared*, 28–9).

Is it so long? Do you forget
That first and last time that we met?
The time was summer;

The trees were green; the sky was blue;
Our host presented me to you –
A tardy comer.

You look'd demure, but when you spoke
You made a little, funny joke,
Yet half pathetic.

Your gown was grey, I recollect,
I think you patronized the sect
They call "aesthetic."

I brought you strawberries and cream,
I plied you long about a stream
With duckweed laden;

We solemnly discussed the – heat.
I found you shy and very sweet,
A rosebud maiden.

Ah me, today! You passed inside
To where the marble gods abide:
Hermes, Apollo,[21]

Sweet Aphrodite, Pan;[22] and where,
For aye reclined, a headless fair
Beats all fairs hollow.

---

21. Classical Greek gods.
22. Greek god.

And I, I went upon my way,
Well – rather sadder, let us say;
The world looked flatter.

I had been sad enough before,
A little less, a little more,
What *does* it matter?

In a Minor Key

(An Echo from a Larger Lyre)

That was love that I had before,
    Years ago, when my heart was young;
Ev'ry smile was a gem you wore,
    Ev'ry word was a sweet song sung.

You came – all my pulses burn'd and beat.
    (O sweet wild throbs of an early day!)
You went – with the last dear sound of your feet
    The light wax'd dim and the place grew grey.

And I us'd to pace with a stealthy tread
    By a certain house which is under a hill;
A cottage stands near, wall'd white, roof'd red –
    Tall trees grow thick – I can see it still!

How I us'd to watch with a hope that was fear
    For the least swift glimpse of your gown's dear fold!
(You wore blue gowns in those days, my dear –
    One light for summer, one dark for cold.)

Tears and verses I shed for you in show'rs;
    I would have staked my soul for a kiss;
Tribute daily I brought you of flow'rs,
    Rose, lily, your favourite eucharis.

There came a day we were doomed to part;

There's a queer, small gate at the foot of a slope:
We parted there – and I thought my heart
Had parted forever from love and hope.

* * * * *

Is it love that I have today?
Love, that bloom'd early, has it bloom'd late
For me, that, clothed in my spirit's grey,
Sit in the stillness and stare at Fate?

Song nor sonnet for you I've penned,
Nor passionate paced by your home's wide wall;
I have brought you never a flow'r, my friend,
Never a tear for your sake let fall.

And yet – and yet – ah, who understands?
We men and women are complex things!
A hundred tunes Fate's inexorable hands
May play on the sensitive soul-strings.

Webs of strange patterns we weave (each owns)
From colour and sound; and like unto these,
Soul has its tones and its semitones,
Mind has its major and minor keys.

Your face (men pass it without a word)
It haunts my dreams like an odd, sweet strain;
When your name is spoken my soul is stirr'd
In its deepest depths with a dull, dim pain.

I paced, in the damp grey mist, last night
In the streets (an hour) to see you pass:
Yet I do not think that I love you – quite;
What's felt so finely 'twere coarse to class.

And yet – and yet – I scarce can tell why
    (As I said, we are riddles and hard to read),
If the world went ill with you, and I
    Could help with a hidden hand your need;

But, ere I could reach you where you lay,
    Must strength and substance and honour spend;
Journey long journeys by night and day –
    Somehow, I think I should come, my friend!

A Farewell

(After Heine)[23]

The sad rain falls from Heaven,
   A sad bird pipes and sings;
I am sitting here at my window
   And watching the spires of "King's."

O fairest of all fair places,
   Sweetest of all sweet towns!
With the birds, and the greyness and greenness,
   And the men in caps and gowns.

All they that dwell within thee,
   To leave are ever loth,
For one man gets friends, and another
   Gets honour, and one gets both.

The sad rain falls from Heaven;
   My heart is great with woe –
I have neither a friend nor honour,
   Yet I am sorry to go.

23. New (*The Complete Novels,* 552 n. 15) suggests that the poem was influenced by Heine's "The Homecoming"; indeed, New's quotation from Draper's translation clearly shows Levy's reliance on Heine for the first verse: "This surely is dreadful weather, / With rain and snow and sleet. / I sit at my window gazing / Out on the darkling street" (see *The Complete Poems,* ed. and trans. Draper, 89).

A Cross-Road Epitaph[24]

"Am Kreuzweg wird begraben
Wer selber brachte sich um."[25]

When first the world grew dark to me
I call'd on God, yet came not he.
Whereon, as wearier wax'd my lot,
On Love I call'd, but Love came not.
When a worse evil did befall,
Death, on thee only did I call.

24. "A Cross Road Epitaph" was originally published in *The Cambridge Review: A Journal of University Life and Thought* 4, no. 96 (May 9, 1883): 353.

25. The extract is from Heine's "Lyrisches Intermezzo"; in *The Complete Poems*, ed. and trans. Draper, 73, the lines read: "He's buried at the crossroad, / He whom his own hand slew." When Dollie Radford's husband, Ernest, translated Heine, Levy immediately requested a copy of the book (Pullen, *The Woman Who Dared*, 51, 53); see Ernest Radford, ed. and trans., *Translations from Heine, and Other Verses* (Oxford: Oxford University Press, 1882). Radford's compilation includes the same translation (7).

Epitaph[26]

(On a Commonplace Person Who Died in Bed)

This is the end of him, here he lies:
The dust in his throat, the worm in his eyes,
The mould in his mouth, the turf on his breast;
This is the end of him, this is best.
He will never lie on his couch awake,
Wide-eyed, tearless, till dim daybreak.
Never again will he smile and smile
When his heart is breaking all the while.
He will never stretch out his hands in vain
Groping and groping – never again.
Never ask for bread, get a stone instead,
Never pretend that the stone is bread.
Never sway and sway 'twixt the false and true,
Weighing and noting the long hours through.
Never ache and ache with the chok'd-up sighs;
This is the end of him, here he lies.

---

26. "Epitaph" was originally published in *The Cambridge Review: A Journal of University Life and Thought* 4, no. 96 (May 9, 1883): 353.

A London Plane-Tree and Other Verse (1889)

To Clementina Black

More blest than was of old Diogenes,[1]
I have not held my lantern up in vain.
Not mine, at least, this evil to complain:
"There is none honest among all of these."

Our hopes go down that sailed before the breeze;
Our creeds upon the rock are rent in twain;
Something it is, if at the last remain
One floating spar cast up by hungry seas.

The secret of our being, who can tell?
To praise the gods and Fate is not my part;
Evil I see, and pain; within my heart
There is no voice that whispers: "All is well."

Yet fair are days in summer; and more fair
The growths of human goodness here and there.

1. The Greek philosopher, Diogenes.

A London Plane-Tree

Green is the plane-tree in the square,
    The other trees are brown;
They droop and pine for country air;
    The plane-tree loves the town.

Here from my garret-pane, I mark
    The plane-tree bud and blow,
Shed her recuperative bark,
    And spread her shade below.

Among her branches, in and out,
    The city breezes play;
The dun fog wraps her round about;
    Above, the smoke curls grey.

Others the country take for choice,
    And hold the town in scorn;
But she has listened to the voice
    On city breezes borne.

London in July[2]

What ails my senses thus to cheat?
What is it ails the place,
That all the people in the street
Should wear one woman's face?

The London trees are dusty-brown
Beneath the summer sky;
My love, she dwells in London town,
Nor leaves it in July.

O various and intricate maze,
Wide waste of square and street;
Where, missing through unnumbered days,
We twain at last may meet!

And who cries out on crowd and mart?
Who prates of stream and sea?
The summer in the city's heart –
That is enough for me.

2. "London in July" was originally published in *The Academy* no. 795 (July 30, 1887): 70.

A March Day in London

The east wind blows in the street today;
The sky is blue, yet the town looks grey.
'Tis the wind of ice, the wind of fire,
Of cold despair and of hot desire,
Which chills the flesh to aches and pains,
And sends a fever through all the veins.

From end to end, with aimless feet,
All day long have I paced the street.
My limbs are weary, but in my breast
Stirs the goad of a mad unrest.
I would give anything to stay
The little wheel that turns in my brain;
The little wheel that turns all day,
That turns all night with might and main.

What is the thing I fear, and why?
Nay, but the world is all awry –
The wind's in the east, the sun's in the sky
The gas-lamps gleam in a golden line;
The ruby lights of the hansoms shine,
Glance, and flicker like fire-flies bright;
The wind has fallen with the night,
And once again the town seems fair
Thwart the mist that hangs i' the air.

And o'er, at last, my spirit steals
A weary peace; peace that conceals

Within its inner depths the grain
Of hopes that yet shall flower again.

Ballade of an Omnibus

To see my love suffices me.
BALLADES IN BLUE CHINA[3]

Some men to carriages aspire;
On some the costly hansoms wait;
Some seek a fly, on job or hire;
Some mount the trotting steed, elate.
I envy not the rich and great,
A wandering minstrel, poor and free,
I am contented with my fate –
An omnibus suffices me.

In winter days of rain and mire
I find within a corner strait;
The 'busmen know me and my lyre
From Brompton to the Bull-and-Gate.
When summer comes, I mount in state
The topmost summit, whence I see
Croesus[4] look up, compassionate –
An omnibus suffices me.

I mark, untroubled by desire,
Lucullus' phaeton and its freight.

3. Andrew Lang's *Ballades in Blue China* (1885).
4. The classical references here and in the next verse are used to indicate horse-drawn carriages.

The scene whereof I cannot tire,
The human tale of love and hate,
The city pageant, early and late
Unfolds itself, rolls by, to be
A pleasure deep and delicate.
An omnibus suffices me.

Princess, your splendour you require,
I, my simplicity; agree
Neither to rate lower nor higher.
An omnibus suffices me.

Ballade of a Special Edition

He comes; I hear him up the street –
    Bird of ill omen, flapping wide
The pinion of a printed sheet,
    His hoarse note scares the eventide.
Of slaughter, theft, and suicide
    He is the herald and the friend;
Now he vociferates with pride –
    A double murder in Mile End!

A hanging to his soul is sweet;
    His gloating fancy's fain to bide
Where human-freighted vessels meet,
    And misdirected trains collide.
With Shocking Accidents supplied,
    He tramps the town from end to end.
How often have we heard it cried –
    A double murder in Mile End.

War loves he; victory or defeat,
    So there be loss on either side.
His tale of horrors incomplete,
    Imagination's aid is tried.
Since no distinguished man has died,
    And since the Fates, relenting, send
No great catastrophe, he's spied
    This double murder in Mile End.

Fiend, get thee gone! no more repeat
 Those sounds which do mine ears offend.
It is apocryphal, you cheat,
 Your double murder in Mile End.

Straw in the Street

Straw in the street where I pass today
Dulls the sound of the wheels and feet.
'Tis for a failing life they lay
Straw in the street.

Here, where the pulses of London beat,
Someone strives with the Presence grey;
Ah, is it victory or defeat?

The hurrying people go their way,
Pause and jostle and pass and greet;
For life, for death, are they treading, say,
Straw in the street?

Between the Showers

Between the showers I went my way,
The glistening street was bright with flowers;
It seemed that March had turned to May
Between the showers.

Above the shining roofs and towers
The blue broke forth athwart the grey;
Birds carolled in their leafless bowers.

Hither and thither, swift and gay,
The people chased the changeful hours;
And you, you passed and smiled that day,
Between the showers.

Out of Town

Out of town the sky was bright and blue,
    Never fog-cloud, lowering, thick, was seen to frown;
Nature dons a garb of gayer hue,
                        Out of town.

Spotless lay the snow on field and down,
    Pure and keen the air above it blew;
All wore peace and beauty for a crown.

London sky, marred by smoke, veiled from view,
    London snow, trodden thin, dingy brown,
Whence that strange unrest at thoughts of you
                        Out of town?

The Piano-Organ

My student-lamp is lighted,
  The books and papers are spread;
A sound comes floating upwards,
  Chasing the thoughts from my head.

I open the garret window,
  Let the music in and the moon;
See the woman grin for coppers,
  While the man grinds out the tune.

Grind me a dirge or a requiem,
  Or a funeral-march sad and slow,
But not, O not, that waltz tune
  I heard so long ago.

I stand upright by the window,
  The moonlight streams in wan: –
O God! with its changeless rise and fall
  The tune twirls on and on.

London Poets
(In Memoriam)

They trod the streets and squares where now I tread,
With weary hearts, a little while ago;
When, thin and grey, the melancholy snow
Clung to the leafless branches overhead;
Or when the smoke-veiled sky grew stormy-red
In autumn; with a re-arisen woe
Wrestled, what time the passionate spring winds blow;
And paced scorched stones in summer: – they are dead.

The sorrow of their souls to them did seem
As real as mine to me, as permanent.
Today, it is the shadow of a dream,
The half-forgotten breath of breezes spent.
So shall another soothe his woe supreme –
"No more he comes, who this way came and went."

The Village Garden[5]

To E.M.S.[6]

Here, where your garden fenced about and still is,
    Here, where the unmoved summer air is sweet
With mixed delight of lavender and lilies,
    Dreaming I linger in the noontide heat.

Of many summers are the trees recorders,
    The turf a carpet many summers wove;
Old-fashioned blossoms cluster in the borders,
    Love-in-a-mist and crimson-hearted clove.

All breathes of peace and sunshine in the present,
    All tells of bygone peace and bygone sun,
Of fruitful years accomplished, budding, crescent
    Of gentle seasons passing one by one.

Fain would I bide, but ever in the distance
    A ceaseless voice is sounding clear and low; –
The city calls me with her old persistence,
    The city calls me – I arise and go.

---

5. Also published in *The Spectator: A Weekly Review of Politics, Literature, Theology, and Art* 62, no. 3163 (February 9, 1889): 199.
6. Refers to Euphemia Malder Stevens, a friend from Levy's time at school in Brighton (Susan David Bernstein, ed., *The Romance of a Shop* (Peterborough: Broadview Editions, 2006), 232 n. 1).

Of gentler souls this fragrant peace is guerdon;
    For me, the roar and hurry of the town,
Wherein more lightly seems to press the burden
    Of individual life that weighs me down.

I leave your garden to the happier comers
    For whom its silent sweets are anodyne.
Shall I return? Who knows, in other summers
    The peace my spirit longs for may be mine?

New Love, New Life[7]

1.

She, who so long has lain
    Stone-stiff with folded wings,
Within my heart again
    The brown bird wakes and sings.

Brown nightingale, whose strain
    Is heard by day, by night,
She sings of joy and pain,
    Of sorrow and delight.

2.

'Tis true, in other days
    Have I unbarred the door;
He knows the walks and ways
    Love has been here before.

Love blest and love accurst
    Was here in days long past;
This time is not the first,
    But this time is the last.

---

7. Originally titled "*Neue Liebe, Neues Leben*" (Linda Hunt Beckman, *Amy Levy: Her Life and Letters* (Athens: Ohio University Press, 2000), 123). The poem is clearly influenced by a verse in Heine's *Buch der Lieder*; indeed, where Heine says, "she sings / Of love and the pain of love," Levy's poem says: "She sings of joy and pain"; see *The Complete Poems of Heinrich Heine: A Modern English Version*, ed. and trans. Hal Draper (Boston: Suhrkamp/Insel, 1982), 7.

Impotens

If I were a woman of old,
What prayers I would pray for you, dear;
My pitiful tribute behold –
Not a prayer, but a tear.

The pitiless order of things,
Whose laws we may change not nor break,
Alone I could face it – it wrings
My heart for your sake.

Youth and Love

What does youth know of love?
    Little enough, I trow!
He plucks the myrtle for his brow,
    For his forehead the rose.
Nay, but of love
    It is not youth who knows.

The Dream[8]

Believe me this was true last night.
Tho' it is false today.
A. M. F. ROBINSON[9]

A fair dream to my chamber flew:
Such a crowd of folk that stirred,
Jested, fluttered; only you,
You alone of all that band,
Calm and silent, spake no word.
Only once you neared my place,
And your hand one moment's space
Sought the fingers of my hand;
Your eyes flashed to mine; I knew
All was well between us two.

* * * * *

On from dream to dream I past,
But the first sweet vision cast
Mystic radiance o'er the last.

* * * * *

8. "The Dream" was originally published in *The Cambridge Review: A Journal of University Life and Thought* 6, no. 130 (October 22, 1884): 29.
9. Refers to Agnes Mary Francis Robinson, a writer Levy became acquainted with through Vernon Lee; see Hunt Beckman, *Amy Levy*, 256–7 n. 3.

When I woke the pale night lay
Still, expectant of the day;
All about the chamber hung
Tender shade of twilight gloom;
The fair dream hovered round me, clung
To my thought like faint perfume: –
Like sweet odours, such as cling
To the void flask, which erst encloses
Attar of rose; or the pale string
Of amber which has lain with roses.

On the Threshold

O God, my dream! I dreamed that you were dead;
Your mother hung above the couch and wept
Whereon you lay all white, and garlanded
With blooms of waxen whiteness. I had crept
Up to your chamber-door, which stood ajar,
And in the doorway watched you from afar,
Nor dared advance to kiss your lips and brow.
I had no part nor lot in you, as now;
Death had not broken between us the old bar;
Nor torn from out my heart the old, cold sense
Of your misprision and my impotence.

The Birch-Tree at Loschwitz[10]

At Loschwitz above the city
    The air is sunny and chill;
The birch-trees and the pine trees
    Grow thick upon the hill.

Lone and tall, with silver stem,
    A birch-tree stands apart;
The passionate wind of spring-time
    Stirs in its leafy heart.

I lean against the birch-tree,
    My arms around it twine;
It pulses, and leaps, and quivers,
    Like a human heart to mine.

One moment I stand, then sudden
    Let loose mine arms that cling:
O God! the lonely hillside,
    The passionate wind of spring!

10. Additionally published in *The Woman's World* 2 (1889): 429. However, note that "Loschwitz" is spelt "Loeschwitz" in *Woman's World*.

In the Night

Cruel? I think there never was a cheating
More cruel, thro' all the weary days than this!
This is no dream, my heart kept on repeating,
But sober certainty of waking bliss.

Dreams? O, I know their faces – goodly seeming,
Vaporous, whirled on many-coloured wings;
I have had dreams before, this is no dreaming,
But daylight gladness that the daylight brings.

What ails my love; what ails her? She is paling;
Faint grows her face, and slowly seems to fade!
I cannot clasp her – stretch out unavailing
My arms across the silence and the shade.

Borderland[11]

Am I waking, am I sleeping?
As the first faint dawn comes creeping
Thro' the pane, I am aware
Of an unseen presence hovering,
Round, above, in the dusky air:
A downy bird, with an odorous wing,
That fans my forehead, and sheds perfume,
As sweet as love, as soft as death,
Drowsy-slow through the summer-gloom.
My heart in some dream-rapture saith,
It is she. Half in a swoon,
I spread my arms in slow delight. –
O prolong, prolong the night,
For the nights are short in June!

11. See the analysis of "Borderland" on pp. lvii–lix.

At Dawn[12]

In the night I dreamed of you;
    All the place was filled
With your presence; in my heart
    The strife was stilled.

All night I have dreamed of you;
    Now the morn is grey. –
How shall I arise and face
    The empty day?

12. Additionally published in *The Woman's World* 3 (1890): 65.

Last Words[13]

Dead! all's done with!
R. BROWNING[14]

These blossoms that I bring,
This song that here I sing,
These tears that now I shed,
I give unto the dead.

There is no more to be done,
Nothing beneath the sun,
All the long ages through,
Nothing – by me for you.

The tale is told to the end;
This, ev'n, I may not know –
If we were friend and friend,
If we were foe and foe.

All's done with utterly,
All's done with. Death to me
Was ever Death indeed;
To me no kindly creed

13. "Last Words" was originally published in *The University Pulpit: Supplement to The Cambridge Review: A Journal of University Life and Thought* 6, no. 141 (February 11, 1885): lxxi.

14. The extract is from Robert Browning's "Too Late."

Consolatory was given.
You were of earth, not Heaven….
This dreary day, things seem
Vain shadows in a dream,

Or some strange, pictured show;
And mine own tears that flow,
My hidden tears that fall,
The vainest of them all.

June

Last June I saw your face three times;
    Three times I touched your hand;
Now, as before, May month is o'er,
    And June is in the land.

O many Junes shall come and go,
    Flow'r-footed o'er the mead;
O many Junes for me, to whom
    Is length of days decreed.

There shall be sunlight, scent of rose,
    Warm mist of summer rain;
Only this change – I shall not look
    Upon your face again.

A Reminiscence

It is so long gone by, and yet
How clearly now I see it all!
The glimmer of your cigarette,
The little chamber, narrow and tall.

Perseus;[15] your picture in its frame;
(How near they seem and yet how far!)
The blaze of kindled logs; the flame
Of tulips in a mighty jar.

Florence and springtime: surely each
Glad things unto the spirit saith.
Why did you lead me in your speech
To these dark mysteries of death?

15. Perseus, hero of Greek mythology.

The Sequel to "A Reminiscence"

Not in the street and not in the square,
    The street and square where you went and came;
With shuttered casement your house stands bare,
    Men hush their voice when they speak your name.

I, too, can play at the vain pretence,
    Can feign you dead; while a voice sounds clear
In the inmost depths of my heart: Go hence,
    Go, find your friend who is far from here.

Not here, but somewhere where I can reach!
    Can a man with motion, hearing and sight,
And a thought that answered my thought and speech,
    Be utterly lost and vanished quite?

Whose hand was warm in my hand last week? ...
    My heart beat fast as I neared the gate –
Was it this I had come to seek,
    "A stone that stared with your name and date;"

A hideous, turfless, fresh-made mound;
    A silence more cold than the wind that blew?
What had I lost, and what had I found?
    My flowers that mocked me fell to the ground –
Then, and then only, my spirit knew.

In the Mile End Road

How like her! But 'tis she herself,
    Comes up the crowded street,
How little did I think, the morn,
    My only love to meet!

Whose else that motion and that mien?
    Whose else that airy tread?
For one strange moment I forgot
    My only love was dead.

Contradictions

Now, even, I cannot think it true,
My friend, that there is no more you.
Almost as soon were no more I,
Which were, of course, absurdity!
Your place is bare, you are not seen,
Your grave, I'm told, is growing green;
And both for you and me, you know,
There's no Above and no Below.[16]
That you are dead must be inferred,
And yet my thought rejects the word.

16. On this line, see Heine's "The Homecoming": "Dead is the good Lord God above us, / And down below the devil's died" (*The Complete Poems*, ed. and trans. Draper, 93).

Twilight

So Mary died last night! Today
    The news has travelled here.
And Robert died at Michaelmas,
    And Walter died last year.

I went at sunset up the lane,
    I lingered by the stile;
I saw the dusky fields that stretched
    Before me many a mile.

I leaned against the stile, and thought
    Of her whose soul had fled.
I knew that years on years must pass
    Or e'er I should be dead.

In September

The sky is silver-grey; the long
    Slow waves caress the shore. –
On such a day as this I have been glad,
    Who shall be glad no more.

The Old House[17]

In through the porch and up the silent stair;
    Little is changed, I know so well the ways; –
Here, the dead came to meet me; it was there
    The dream was dreamed in unforgotten days.

But who is this that hurries on before,
    A flitting shade the brooding shades among? –
She turned, – I saw her face, – O God, it wore
    The face I used to wear when I was young!

I thought my spirit and my heart were tamed
    To deadness; dead the pangs that agonise.
The old grief springs to choke me, – I am shamed
    Before that little ghost with eager eyes.

O turn away, let her not see, not know!
    How should she bear it, how should understand?
O hasten down the stairway, haste and go,
    And leave her dreaming in the silent land.

17. "The Old House" was also published in *The Spectator: A Weekly Review of Politics, Literature, Theology, and Art* 62, no. 3173 (April 20, 1889): 543.

Lohengrin[18]

Back to the mystic shore beyond the main
    The mystic craft has sped, and left no trace.
    Ah, nevermore may she behold his face,
Nor touch his hand, nor hear his voice again!
With hidden front she crouches; all in vain
    The proffered balm. A vessel nears the place;
They bring her young, lost brother; see her strain
    The new-found nursling in a close embrace.

God, we have lost Thee with much questioning.
In vain we seek Thy trace by sea and land,
And in Thine empty fanes where no men sing.
    What shall we do through all the weary days?
    Thus wail we and lament. Our eyes we raise,
And, lo, our Brother with an outstretched hand!

18. "Lohengrin" was first published in *The Academy* no. 724 (March 20, 1886): 201. See the analysis of "Lohengrin" beginning on p. lxv.

Alma Mater[19]

A haunted town thou art to me.[20]
ANDREW LANG

Today in Florence all the air
Is soft with spring, with sunlight fair;
In the tall street gay folks are met;
Duomo and Tower gleam overhead,
Like jewels in the city set,
Fair-hued and many-faceted.
Against the old grey stones are piled
February violets, pale and sweet,
Whose scent of earth in woodland wild
Is wafted up and down the street.
The city's heart is glad; my own
Sits lightly on its bosom's throne.

* * * * * * *

Why is it that I see today,
Imaged as dear as in a dream,
A little city far away,
A churlish sky, a sluggish stream,

19. "Alma Mater" was originally published in *The Cambridge Review: A Journal of University Life and Thought* 9, no. 203 (June 1, 1887): 362.
20. Rewording of Andrew Lang's "Almae Matres"; the original line is "A haunted town it is to me!" (Melvyn New, ed., *The Complete Novels and Selected Writings of Amy Levy 1861–1889* (Gainesville: University Press of Florida, 1993), 553 n. 24).

Tall clust'ring trees and gardens fair,
Dark birds that circle in the air,
Grey towers and fanes; on either hand,
Stretches of wind-swept meadow-land?

* * * * * * *

Oh, who can sound the human breast?
And this strange truth must be confessed;
That city do I love the best
Wherein my heart was heaviest!

In the Black Forest[21]

I lay beneath the pine trees,
And looked aloft, where, through
The dusky, clustered treetops,
Gleamed rent, gay rifts of blue.

I shut my eyes, and a fancy
Fluttered my sense around:
"I lie here dead and buried,
And this is churchyard ground.

"I am at rest forever;
Ended the stress and strife."
Straight I fell to and sorrowed
For the pitiful past life.

Right wronged, and knowledge wasted;
Wise labour spurned for ease;
The sloth and the sin and the failure;
Did I grow sad for these?

They had made me sad so often;
Not now they made me sad;
My heart was full of sorrow
For joy it never had.

---

21. Originally titled "After Heine" and published in *The Cambridge Review: A Journal of University Life and Thought* 6, no. 136 (December 3, 1884): 123–4.

Captivity[22]

The lion remembers the forest,
  The lion in chains;
To the bird that is captive a vision
  Of woodland remains.

One strains with his strength at the fetter,
  In impotent rage;
One flutters in flights of a moment,
  And beats at the cage.

If the lion were loosed from the fetter,
  To wander again;
He would seek the wide silence and shadow
  Of his jungle in vain.

He would rage in his fury, destroying;
  Let him rage, let him roam!
Shall he traverse the pitiless mountain,
  Or swim through the foam?

If they opened the cage and the casement,
  And the bird flew away;
He would come back at evening, heartbroken,
  A captive for aye.

22. See the analysis of "Captivity" beginning on p. lxix. "Captivity" was first published in 1885, see *The Cambridge Review: A Journal of University Life and Thought* 7, no. 163 (December 9, 1885): 142–3.

Would come if his kindred had spared him,
    Free birds from afar –
There was wrought what is stronger than iron
    In fetter and bar.

I cannot remember my country,
    The land whence I came;
Whence they brought me and chained me and made me
    Nor wild thing nor tame.

This only I know of my country,
    This only repeat: –
It was free as the forest, and sweeter
    Than woodland retreat.

When the chain shall at last be broken,
    The window set wide;
And I step in the largeness and freedom
    Of sunlight outside;

Shall I wander in vain for my country?
    Shall I seek and not find?
Shall I cry for the bars that encage me,
    The fetters that bind?

The Two Terrors[23]

Two terrors fright my soul by night and day:
The first is Life, and with her come the years;
A weary, winding train of maidens they,
With forward-fronting eyes, too sad for tears;
Upon whose kindred faces, blank and grey,
The shadow of a kindred woe appears.
Death is the second terror; who shall say
What form beneath the shrouding mantle nears?

Which way she turn, my soul finds no relief,
My smitten soul may not be comforted;
Alternately she swings from grief to grief,
And, poised between them, sways from dread to dread.
For there she dreads because she knows; and here,
Because she knows not, inly faints with fear.

23. "The Two Terrors" was previously published as "Sonnet" in Elizabeth Sharp's *Women's Voices: An Anthology of the Most Characteristic Poems by English, Scotch, and Irish Women* (London: Walter Scott, 1887), 349.

The Promise of Sleep[24]

Put the sweet thoughts from out thy mind,
The dreams from out thy breast;
No joy for thee – but thou shalt find
Thy rest.

All day I could not work for woe,
I could not work nor rest;
The trouble drove me to and fro,
Like a leaf on the storm's breast.

Night came and saw my sorrow cease;
Sleep in the chamber stole;
Peace crept about my limbs, and peace
Fell on my stormy soul.

And now I think of only this, –
How I again may woo
The gentle sleep – who promises
That death is gentle too.

24. Additionally published in *The Woman's World* 3 (1890): 52.

The Last Judgment

With beating heart and lagging feet,
Lord, I approach the Judgment-seat.
All bring hither the fruits of toil,
Measures of wheat and measures of oil;

Gold and jewels and precious wine;
No hands bare like these hands of mine.
The treasure I have nor weighs nor gleams:
Lord, I can bring you only dreams.

In days of spring, when my blood ran high,
I lay in the grass and looked at the sky,
And dreamed that my love lay by my side –
My love was false, and then she died.

All the heat of the summer through,
I dreamed she lived, that her heart was true
Throughout the hours of the day I slept,
But woke in the night, at times, and wept.

The nights and days, they went and came,
I lay in shadow and dreamed of fame;
And heard men passing the lonely place,
Who marked me not and my hidden face.

My strength waxed faint, my hair grew grey;
Nothing but dreams by night and day.

Some men sicken, with wine and food;
I starved on dreams, and found them good.

* * * * * * *

This is the tale I have to tell –
Show the fellow the way to hell.

The Lost Friend

The people take the thing of course,
They marvel not to see
This strange, unnatural divorce
Betwixt delight and me.

I know the face of sorrow, and I know
Her voice with all its varied cadences;
Which way she turns and treads; how at her ease
Thinks fit her dreary largess to bestow.

Where sorrow long abides, some be that grow
To hold her dear, but I am not of these;
Joy is my friend, not sorrow; by strange seas,
In some far land we wandered, long ago.

O faith, long tried, that knows no faltering!
O vanished treasure of her hands and face! –
Beloved – to whose memory I cling,
Unmoved within my heart she holds her place.

And never shall I hail that other "friend,"
Who yet shall dog my footsteps to the end.

Cambridge in the Long

Where drowsy sound of college-chimes
  Across the air is blown,
And drowsy fragrance of the limes,
  I lie and dream alone.

A dazzling radiance reigns o'er all –
  O'er gardens densely green,
O'er old grey bridges and the small,
  Slow flood which slides between.

This is the place; it is not strange,
  But known of old and dear. –
What went I forth to seek? The change
  Is mine; why am I here?

Alas, in vain I turned away,
  I fled the town in vain;
The strenuous life of yesterday
  Calleth me back again.

And was it peace I came to seek?
  Yet here, where memories throng,
Ev'n here, I know the past is weak,
  I know the present strong.

This drowsy fragrance, silent heat,
  Suit not my present mind,

Whose eager thought goes out to meet
    The life it left behind.

Spirit with sky to change; such hope,
    An idle one we know;
Unship the oars, make loose the rope,
    Push off the boat and go....

Ah, would what binds me could have been
    Thus loosened at a touch!
This pain of living is too keen,
    Of loving, is too much.

To Vernon Lee

On Bellosguardo, when the year was young,
We wandered, seeking for the daffodil
And dark anemone, whose purples fill
The peasant's plot, between the corn-shoots sprung.

Over the grey, low wall the olive flung
Her deeper greyness; far off, hill on hill
Sloped to the sky, which, pearly-pale and still,
Above the large and luminous landscape hung.

A snowy blackthorn flowered beyond my reach;
You broke a branch and gave it to me there;
I found for you a scarlet blossom rare.

Thereby ran on of Art and Life our speech;
And of the gifts the gods had given to each –
Hope unto you, and unto me Despair.

The Old Poet

I will be glad because it is the Spring;
 I will forget the winter in my heart –
Dead hopes and withered promise; and will wring
 A little joy from life ere life depart.

For spendthrift youth with passion-blinded eyes,
 Stays not to see how woods and fields are bright;
He hears the phantom voices call, he flies
 Upon the track of some unknown delight.

To him the tender glory of the May,
 White wonder of the blossom, and the clear,
Soft green of leaves that opened yesterday,
 This only say: Forward, my friend, not here!

They breathe no other messages than this,
 They have no other meaning for his heart;
Unto his troubled sense they tell of bliss,
 Which make, themselves, of bliss the better part.

Yea, joy is near him, tho' he does not know;
 Her unregarded shape is at his side,
Her unheard voice is whispering clear and low,
 Whom, resting never, seeks he far and wide.

So once it was with us, my heart! Today
    We will be glad because the leaves are green,
Because the fields are fair and soft with May,
    Nor think on squandered springtimes that have been.

On the Wye in May

Now is the perfect moment of the year.
    Half naked branches, half a mist of green,
Vivid and delicate the slopes appear;
    The cool, soft air is neither fierce nor keen,

And in the temperate sun we feel no fear;
    Of all the hours which shall be and have been,
It is the briefest as it is most dear,
    It is the dearest as the shortest seen.

O it was best, belovèd, at the first. –
    Our hands met gently, and our meeting sight
Was steady; on our senses scare had burst
    The faint, fresh fragrance of the new delight....

I seek that clime, unknown, without a name,
    Where first and best and last shall be the same.

Oh, is it Love?

O is it Love or is it Fame,
  This thing for which I sigh?
Or has it then no earthly name
  For men to call it by?

I know not what can ease my pains,
  Nor what it is I wish;
The passion at my heart-strings strains
  Like a tiger in a leash.

In the Nower[25]

To J. De P.[26]

Deep in the grass outstretched I lie,
    Motionless on the hill;
Above me is a cloudless sky,
    Around me all is still:

There is no breath, no sound, no stir,
    The drowsy peace to break;
I close my tired eyes – it were
    So simple not to wake.

25. Additionally published as "Peace" in *The Woman's World* 3 (1890): 7.
26. Jenny de Pass, a friend of Levy's.

The End of the Day

To B. T.[27]

Dead-tired, dog-tired, as the vivid day
Fails and slackens and fades away. –
The sky that was so blue before
With sudden clouds is shrouded o'er.
Swiftly, stilly the mists uprise,
Till blurred and grey the landscape lies.

* * * * * * *

All day we have plied the oar; all day
Eager and keen have said our say
On life and death, on love and art,
On good or ill at Nature's heart.
Now, grown so tired, we scarce can lift
The lazy oars, but onward drift.
And the silence is only stirred
Here and there by a broken word.

* * * * * * *

O, sweeter far than strain and stress
Is the slow, creeping weariness.
And better far than thought I find
The drowsy blankness of the mind.
More than all joys of soul or sense

27. Bertha Thomas, a friend of Levy's; see Christine Pullen, *The Woman Who Dared: A Biography of Amy Levy* (Kingston: Kingston University Press, 2010), 148, 153.

Is this divine indifference;
Where grief a shadow grows to be,
And peace a possibility.

A Wall Flower[28]

I lounge in the doorway and languish in vain
While Tom, Dick and Harry are dancing with Jane

My spirit rises to the music's beat;
There is a leaden fiend lurks in my feet!
To move unto your motion, Love, were sweet.

Somewhere, I think, some other where, not here,
In other ages, on another sphere,
I danced with you, and you with me, my dear.

In perfect motion did our bodies sway,
To perfect music that was heard alway;
Woe's me, that am so dull of foot today!

To move unto your motion, Love, were sweet;
My spirit rises to the music's beat –
But, ah, the leaden demon in my feet!

---

28. Additionally published in *The Woman's World* 2 (1889): 320. On the content of the poem, see Cheryl Wilson, "Politicizing Dance in Late-Victorian Women's Poetry," *Victorian Poetry* 46, no. 2 (2008): 191–205.

The First Extra

A Waltz Song

O sway, and swing, and sway,
    And swing, and sway, and swing!
Ah me, what bliss like unto this,
    Can days and daylight bring?

A rose beneath your feet
    Has fallen from my head;
Its odour rises sweet,
    All crushed it lies, and dead.

O Love is like a rose,
    Fair-hued, of fragrant breath;
A tender flow'r that lives an hour,
    And is most sweet in death.

O swing, and sway, and swing,
    And rise, and sink, and fall!
There is no bliss like unto this,
    This is the best of all.

At a Dinner Party

With fruit and flowers the board is deckt,
    The wine and laughter flow;
I'll not complain – could one expect
    So dull a world to know?

You look across the fruit and flowers,
    My glance your glances find. –
It is our secret, only ours,
    Since all the world is blind.

Philosophy[29]

Ere all the world had grown so drear,
When I was young and you were here,
'Mid summer roses in summer weather,
What pleasant times we've had together!

We were not Phyllis, simple-sweet,
And Corydon;[30] we did not meet
By brook or meadow, but among
A Philistine and flippant throng

Which much we scorned; (less rigorous
It had no scorn at all for us!)
How many an eve of sweet July,
Heedless of Mrs. Grundy's[31] eye,

We've scaled the stairway's topmost height,
And sat there talking half the night;
And, gazing on the crowd below,
Thanked Fate and Heaven that made us so; –

---

29. Also published as "Philosophy in the Ballroom," in *London Society: An Illustrated Magazine of Light and Amusing Literature for the Hours of Relaxation* 48, no. 284 (August 1885): 175.
30. Refers to Nicholas Breton's (1545-1626) poem, "A Pastoral of Phyllis and Corydon."
31. Probably refers to the character of Mrs. Grundy in Thomas Morton's (1764–1838) play, *Speed the Plough*. In popular usage, "Mrs. Grundy" became a derogatory term.

To hold the pure delights of brain
Above light loves and sweet champagne.
For, you and I, we did eschew
The egoistic "I" and "you;"

And all our observations ran
On Art and Letters, Life and Man.
Proudly we sat, we two, on high,
Throned in our Objectivity;

Scarce friends, not lovers (each avers),
But sexless, safe Philosophers.

* * * * * * *

Dear Friend, you must not deem me light
If, as I lie and muse tonight,
I give a smile and not a sigh
To thoughts of our Philosophy.

A Game of Lawn Tennis[32]

What wonder that I should be dreaming
    Out here in the garden today?
The light through the leaves is streaming, –
    Paulina cries, "Play!"

The birds to each other are calling,
    The freshly-cut grasses smell sweet;
To Teddy's dismay, comes falling
    The ball at my feet.

"Your stroke should be over, not under!"
    "But that's such a difficult way!"
The place is a springtide wonder
    Of lilac and may;

Of lilac, and may, and laburnum,
    Of blossom, – *We're losing the set!*
"Those volleys of Jenny's, – return them;
    "Stand close to the net!"

****

You are so fond of the Maytime,
    My friend, far away;
Small wonder that I should be dreaming
    Of you in the garden today.

32. This poem is also included in *Romance of a Shop*, pp. 87–8.

To E.[33]

The mountains in fantastic lines
Sweep, blue-white, to the sky, which shines
Blue as blue gems; athwart the pines
The lake gleams blue.

We three were here, three years gone by;
Our Poet, with fine-frenzied eye,
You, steeped in learned lore, and I,
A poet too.

Our Poet brought us books and flowers,
He read us *Faust*;[34] he talked for hours
Philosophy (sad Schopenhauer's),
Beneath the trees:

And do you mind that sunny day,
When he, as on the sward he lay,
Told of Lassalle who bore away
The false Louise?

---

33. The dedication is to Levy's friend, Ellen Crofts (Pullen, *The Woman Who Dared*, 57, 60). "To E." was originally published in *London Society: An Illustrated Magazine of Light and Amusing Literature for the Hours of Relaxation* 49, no. 293 (May 1886): 447.

34. Johann Wolfgang von Goethe's play, *Faust*; the line below refers to the German philosopher, Arthur Schopenhauer (1788-1860).

Thrice-favoured bard! to him alone
That green and snug retreat was shown,
Where to the vulgar herd unknown,
Our pens we plied.

(For, in those distant days, it seems,
We cherished sundry idle dreams,
And with our flowing foolscap reams
The Fates defied.)

And after, when the day was gone,
And the hushed, silver night came on,
He showed us where the glow-worm shone; –
We stooped to see.

There, too, by yonder moon we swore
Platonic friendship o'er and o'er;
No folk, we deemed, had been before
So wise and free.

* * * * * * *

And do I sigh or smile today?
Dead love or dead ambition, say,
Which mourn we most? Not much we weigh
Platonic friends.

On you the sun is shining free;
Our Poet sleeps in Italy,
Beneath an alien sod; on me
The cloud descends.

Miscellaneous Poetry

Contents

The Ballad of Ida Grey (1875)

(A Story of Woman's Sacrifice)

Part 1

The nightingale[1] sang tenderly,
    In the gentle evening breeze,
As a knight and maiden saunter'd
    (Arm-in-arm) beneath the trees.
She was clad in samite snowy;
    He, in dazzling armour bright,
And their voices murmur'd softly
    In the shadow of the night.
"Ida Grey" (the man quoth sadly)
    "Thou whose heart is link'd with mine,
"And who lov'st, with such a fondness,
    "This too hasty knight of thine;
"Thy pure soul will shrink in horror,
    "Thy young love will change to hate,
"When thou hearest the dread story,
    "Which I will to thee relate.
"Thou know'st well my kinsman Siegfried,
    "In the glory of youth's prime,
"That tomorrow he will suffer

---

1. The nightingale's song begins both parts of this poem; this might point to Amy Levy's evoking of Heinrich Heine's *Buch der Lieder,* where the nightingale is "ubiquitous" (see David Gallagher, *Metamorphosis: Transformations of the Body and the Influence of Ovid's Metamorphoses on German Literature of the Nineteenth and Twentieth* Centuries (New York: Rodopi, 2009), 222).

"For a foul and bloody crime; –
"That with sounds of shame and horror
"The indignant nations ring; –
"Ida, Ida, he is bloodless,
"*It was I that slew the King!*
"In a moment of mad passion,
"When my brain with wine was hot,
"He had mocked me, and I slew him,
"Aye, I slew him on the spot!
"Then, in guilty, guilty terror,
"From the palace-hall I fled;
"And I left him (noble Siegfried!)
"To support the blame instead.
"Ida Grey! my life's at peril,
"Death may come, – and with death hell!
"And now, ere I fly my country,
"I have come to bid 'farewell.'"
When the knight had finish'd speaking,
There was silence for a space;
Then, retreating further from him,
She look'd up into his face.
Seem'd her voice like rolling thunder,
Burnt her eye with angry flame:
"I renounce thee now forever!
"Go! weak heart, *confess* thy shame."
Heaved her bosom with emotion,
Stood a tear within her eye;
Then, in mournful tones, she added,
"But thou art not fit to die!
"Thou, so wicked and so bloodstain'd;
"Death is only for the good.
"Lo! to shrive thee, will I give thee,
"Knight! mine own chaste maidenhood!"

Part 2[2]

The nightingale sang tenderly,
 In the hollow ev'ning breeze
As a lonely friar saunter'd,
 Sadly, slowly through the trees.
With his shaven head bent earthward,
 Clad in sable gown and stole;
Then in dull and mournful accents,
 Pour'd he forth his bursting soul:
"Curse my selfish weak heart promptings!
 "Curse oh! curse the fatal day,
"When I (craven wretch!) accepted
 "The pure life of Ida Grey.
"Since, the long years, passing slowly,
 "Leave but shadows in their flight;
"While one vision ever hovers
 "Dark around me day and night;
"Still I see the bloody scaffold
 "Rising clear before mine eyes;
"Still I see th' unhallow'd pit-hole,
 "Where the martyr'd maiden lies;
"Still my aching heart re-echoes
 "Tones that for my 'silence' plead
"'Echoes, Headsman, stay thy weapon,
 "'It was I that did the deed!'
"Never stopping, never turning,
 "In her purpose strange and bold;
"Fearlessly she gave her life blood,
 "Like the holy saints of old."
As he spake, burst forth ringing
 From the solemn Cloister bell.

2. Reprinted with permission of The Camellia Collections.

Then he turn'd and murmur'd softly,
"Oh ye glades and trees, farewell!"

* * * * *

And the people, still unconscious
For the noble soul they pray,
And with shudd'ring lips they mention
The pure name of "Ida Grey."
No sweet tears for *her* have glisten'd,
No kind hearts for *her* bewail;
But the little wood-birds listen'd,
It was *they* told me the tale.

Original Definitions: Heroism (1875)

The great *enduring* power, which spurs us on
To meet the hardest suffering and woe
(Entailing sacrifice of all of *Self*)
For conscience', Right's, and God's Almighty sake.

Definitions (1876)

"'Friendship'"

The quiet bond of mutual confidence;
The steady trust, that in the hour of need
Accepts the proffered aid, nor hesitates,
As freely, with its hands and heart to give.

The Shepherd (1880)

(From Goethe)[3]

There was an idle shepherd, fond of sleep,
Who never troubled him about his sheep.
But by a maiden was he captive led
He left the bottle, sleep and hunger fled.

His passion drove him to unrest and flight;
He'd moan and groan and count the stars at night!
But when, at length, the maiden he had ta'en,
Sleep, hunger, thirst—they all came back again.

3. Refers to Johann Wolfgang von Goethe's "The Shepherd's Lament."

From Grillparzer's Sappho (1882)[4]

PHAON.
And who had thought that Hellas' highest maid
On Hellas' lowest youth would deign to glance?

SAPPHO.[5]
Fate and thyself thou wrong'st; forbear to scorn
The golden gifts which gods delight to pour
On cheek and brow, in heart and breast, at birth
Of one by them mark'd out for happiness.
A beauteous body is a beauteous gift,
Ay, and a priceless gem is joy of life:
The daring of bold men, the iron might
Of lords o' the earth, firm will; the strength to bear
'That which the fates have destin'd, fantasy,
(A servant, a chaste handmaid as is meet),
These are the things which deck life's thorny way: –
Life's highest aim is, after all, to live.
Not vainly did the muses choose to bind
The barren laurel-leaf about their brows;
Upon his head, to whom it erst has giv'n
Fair promise of reward of sacrifice,
Cold, without fruit or fragrance, presses it.
Who stands aloft upon the topmost peaks

4. The Austrian playwright, Franz Grillparzer (1791–1872).
5. Sappho, ancient Greek poet subject to neo-classical interest and appropriation in Victorian literature. According to myth, Sappho was supposedly in love with Phaon, leaping into the sea when he rejected her.

In suff'ring stands; poor Art is ever driv'n
To beg of Life's abundance.

ACT 1

SAPPHO.
O Phaon, O Phaon, what did I do to thee?
Peaceful I stood in the fair meads of song,
Alone, and made gold-stringéd melody.
Earth's joy and gladness from on high I saw;
Earth's sorrows could not reach me. And I knew
The flight of Time, the God who never stays,
Not by the hours, but by the spotless blooms
Enwoven in the wreath of Poesy.
Eternal youth was green about my head,
And what I gave to song, song gave to me.
Then comes he, one rough man, and with rude hands
Tears down the golden veil before mine eyes,
Leads me below into the desert waste,
Where is no path nor any print of foot;
And now, the one light shining in the void,
He draws his hand from mine, woe's me! and flees.

ACT 4

From Heine (1882)[6]

My heart, my heart is heavy,
Yet May is bright in the land;
High up on the grey old rampart
'Neath the linden tree I stand.

Below, the moat round the city
Azure-waved, peacefully flows;
A lad in a boat glides onwards,
And fishes and sings as he goes.

Gay-hued, small in the distance,
To right and to left one sees
Houses and gardens and people,
Oxen and meadows and trees.

Women are bleaching linen,
They leap in the grass and bound;
The mill-wheel splashes diamonds,
I hear from afar the sound.

---

6. Taken from Heine's "The Homecoming"; see *The Complete Poems of Heinrich Heine: A Modern English Version*, ed. and trans. Hal Draper (Boston: Suhrkamp/Insel, 1982), 77. The opening two lines, in German, can be found in the quotation that precedes "A Dirge" (pp. 462–3).

There stands by the old grey tower
A sentry box, small and low,
And the sentinel, red-coated,
Is pacing there to and fro.

With his gun he is playing;
It gleams in the sunlight's red;
Now he "presents" it; – now "shoulders" –
I wish he would shoot me dead.

A Ballad of Last Seeing (1883)

It is so very long ago,
    A little thing, I am aware;
I heard the music's ebb and flow,
    I raised my head and saw you there.
Cold was your face, as cold as fair,
    You did not stay to smile or greet;
Sunshine and music filled the air
    The last time that I saw you sweet.

Beneath the arching portico
    Carved round about with carvings rare
You paused a space, then turned to go,
    I watched you down the sculptured stair.
I did not hear the organ's blare
    Sole heard I your departing feet;
I cared so much, you did not care,
    The last time that I saw you, sweet.

ENVOY.

Friend, if indeed it must be so,
    And we no more on earth may meet,
One time was dear to me I know –
    The last time that I saw you, sweet.

In Switzerland (1884)

Above my head the sky is blue
Matching the rippling lake in hue.
All round about the mountains rise,
A green delight to weary eyes.
Here, where the place is warm and fair,
Where soft moss grows, where all the air
Is sweet with pungent scent of pine,
Stretched, prone and passive, I recline.
Around me lies the books and rugs,
The basket, boiler, teapot, mugs,
And all the other things that we
Have carried up for work and tea.
Walled round with tomes of ponderous size,
Her pen the busy Ellen plies.
Kit Marlow[7] is her theme. Enough
I've had of all your dead men's stuff.
Kit Marlow's dead since long ago,
And I'm alive today, I know.
Heigho! I kick my heels i' the sun!
What matter if the work's undone?
Give me warm sweet air, the sound
That Nature whispers soft around,
The lights and shadows in the trees,
And let them write their books that please.

---

7. The playwright, Christopher Marlowe (1564–1593).

Mariana in the Ballroom (1884)

"'He cometh not,' she said."[8]

One o'clock! "Neither hasting nor staying,"
    The dowagers all disappear;
The band the 'third extra' is playing;
    O Frank and you said you'd be here!

There's a sound of champagne-corks a-popping
    Below, like a jovial refrain;
In a corner young Biffins is dropping
    First hints of his feelings to Jane.

And I try to think Freddy beguiling,
    And persuade myself not to look glum;
I am talking and turning and smiling:
    O Frank, and you promised to come!

Yet this evening the ladies are longing
    (I know it) to stand in my shoes;
For the partners *are* pushing and thronging,
    And I've captured young Fred of the Blues.

For Freddy the girls are all dying,
    They jump when he asks them to dance;
And here is he blushing and sighing,
    If I throw him a word or a glance.

---

8. The quotation is taken from Alfred, Lord Tennyson's "Mariana."

He dips and he skips like a swallow;
He has scent on his hands and his hair;
If I danced half the night with Apollo,[9]
Ah me! do you think I should care?

O Frank! yet dear me! for what reason,
I wonder – yes, really I do –
Should a girl who's the belle of the season
Expend so much feeling on you?

For no; you're not handsome precisely,
Although you've such beautiful eyes;
And you quote from the bards very nicely,
But I fancy you're not very wise.

And not my worst foe could assert you
To revel in honours and pelf;
So it seems you have only one virtue
(That's Shakespeare) – that you are yourself!

* * * *

Has the music grown suddenly brighter?
Have they turned on the big chandelier,
That the room's so remarkably lighter?
And I – am I looking severe?

Am I frigid as snowdrifts in Norway?
Am I colder than ice at the Pole?
For Someone stands there in the doorway,
And Someone shall smart in his soul!

---

9. Apollo, classical Greek/Roman god.

I fancied *he* saw too when *I* did
    (This dancing is bad for the nerves;
I'm glad it is done): I've decided
    To treat him the way he deserves.

"Good evening!" I think were you saying
    "Good morning," you phrased it aright;
What tricks with my programme you're playing!
    Pray, sir, do you call it polite?

After Heine (1886)

The stately sentinel cypress
    Stands out against the blue,
The world declares you wronged me,
    And I declared it too.

I've no blame left to utter,
    And no tears left to shed;
The joy, and the shame, and the sorrow,
    They, too, are done with and dead.

So long ago it happened;
    Long since my heart is stone;
And yet beneath the cypress
    I linger here alone.

Your friends forgot; I scatter
    My flow'rs above your grave;
For you to me have given
    That which none other gave.

Translations of Jehudah Halevi (1888)[10]

[1.]
God grant that I may rise again,
Nor perish by Thine anger slain.
This draught that I myself combine,
What is it? Only Thou dost know
If well or ill, if swift or slow,
Its parts shall work upon my pain.
Ay of these things, alone is Thine
The knowledge. All my faith I place,
Not in my craft, but in Thy grace.

[2.]
Lo! My light has pierced to the dark abyss,
I have brought forth gems from the gloomy mine;
Now the fools would see them! I ask you this:
Shall I fling my pearls down before the swine?
From the gathered cloud shall the raindrops flow
To the barren land where no fruit can grow?

[3.]
So we must be divided; sweetest, stay,
Once more, mine eyes would seek thy glance's light.
At night I shall recall thee: Thou, I pray,
Be mindful of the days of our delight.

10. These translations are based on Abraham Geiger's German translations in *Divan des Castiliers Abu'l-Hassan Juda ha-Levi* (Breslau: Kern, 1851); see Linda Hunt Beckman, *Amy Levy: Her Life and Letters* (Athens: Ohio, 2000), 77, 295 n. 6.

Come to me in my dreams, I ask of thee,
And even in my dreams be gentle unto me.

If thou shouldst send me greeting in the grave,
The cold breath of the grave itself were sweet;
Oh, take my life, my life, 'tis all I have,
If it should make thee live, I do entreat.
I think that I shall hear when I am dead,
The rustle of thy gown, thy footsteps overhead.

[4.]
A dove of rarest worth
And sweet exceedingly;
Alas, why does she turn
And fly so far from me?
In my fond heart a tent,
Should aye preparéd be.
My poor heart she has caught
With magic spells and wiles.
I do not sigh for gold,
But for her mouth that smiles;
Her hue it is so bright,
She half makes blind my sight,

* * * *

The day at last is here
Filled full of love's sweet fire;
The twain shall soon be one,
Shall stay their fond desire.
Ah! would my tribe could chance
On such deliverance!

[5.]

Oh! City of the world, most chastely fair;
In the far west, behold I sigh for thee.
And in my yearning love I do bethink me,
Of bygone ages; of thy ruined fane,
Thy vanished splendour of a vanished day.
Oh! Had I eagle's wings I'd fly to thee,
And with my falling tears make moist thine earth.
I long for thee; what though indeed thy kings
Have passed forever; that where once uprose
Sweet balsam-trees the serpent makes his nest.
Oh! That I might embrace thy dust, the sod
Were sweet as honey to my fond desire.

Translation of Heinrich Heine (1888)[11]

They have told thee a-many stories,
  And much complaint have made;
And yet my heart's true anguish
  That never have they said.

They shook their heads protesting,
  They made a great to-do;
They called me a wicked fellow,
  And thou believedst it true.

And yet the worst of all things,
  Of that they were not aware,
The darkest and the saddest
  That in my heart I bear.

11. The translation is taken from Heine's "Lyrisches Intermezzo"; see *The Complete Poems,* ed. and trans. Draper, 59.

Rondel (1888)

(Dedicated to Mrs. Fenwick-Miller)[12]

To change my name was once my heart's desire!
In other days (I own it without shame)
I was a simple maid, who did aspire
To change of name.

My dreams were undisturbed by thoughts of fame;
I was content to listen and admire
While Edwin told me of his hopes and aim.

Of such unworthy weakness now I tire;
I grow to recognize my sex's claim;
Married or single, I do *not* require
To change my name.

12. Feminist journalist and campaigner, Florence Fenwick-Miller; see Hunt Beckman, *Amy Levy*, 137.

A Ballad of Religion and Marriage (1915)[13]

Swept into limbo is the host
Of heavenly angels, row on row;
The Father, Son, and Holy Ghost,
Pale and defeated, rise and go.
The great Jehovah is laid low,
Vanished his burning bush and rod –
Say, are we doomed to deeper woe?
Shall marriage go the way of God?

Monogamous, still at our post,
Reluctantly we undergo
Domestic round of boiled and roast,
Yet deem the whole proceeding slow.
Daily the secret murmurs grow;
We are no more content to plod
Along the beaten paths – and so
Marriage must go the way of God.

Soon, before all men, each shall toast
The seven strings unto his bow,
Like beacon fires along the coast,
The flames of love shall glance and glow.
Nor let nor hindrance man shall know,
From natal bath to funeral sod;

---

13. See the analysis of this poem beginning on p. lxiv. According to Christine Pullen, the poem is Levy's "literary suicide note" (*The Woman Who Dared: A Biography of Amy Levy* (Kingston: Kingston University Press, 2010), 182).

Perennial shall his pleasures flow
When marriage goes the way of God.

Grant, in a million years at most,
Folk shall be neither pairs nor odd –
Alas! we shan't be there to boast
"Marriage has gone the way of God!"

Short Fiction

Contents

Mrs. Pierrepoint: A Sketch in Two Parts (1880)

"Sunt, qui
Crustis et pomis viduas venentur avaras,
Excipiantque senes quos in vivaria mittant."

HORACE, Ep. 1.1[1]

Part 1

Prince's Gate

The funeral was over; the great mourning coaches had deposited their highly respectable burdens at the door of the large house in Prince's Gate, and people, standing in little groups about hall and dining room, were beginning to grow quite conversational, and to forget, in the light from the freshly unshuttered windows, what cause had brought them together.

When a man gets beyond the portion of life allotted to him by public opinion and the Bible, he must not expect to be very deeply mourned when he *does* die; and Mr. Pierrepoint, at whose last rites his friends had just assisted, had outlived by two years those "three score and ten years" of Scripture. Under the circumstances, immoderate grief at his loss was not to be expected; it was reserved for disappointed legatees to mourn, as a waggish cousin, a "briefless barrister," whispered to his neighbour.

1. The Roman poet, Horace; the quotation is from his *Epistles*.

Upstairs the newly-made widow was sitting, with clasped hands and pensive eyes, alone in her dainty boudoir. The sunlight, falling upon her, called up points of gold in the rich brown of her thick, coiled hair, and put to severe test the delicate pureness of her skin. There was a tap at the door, and in answer to her subdued "come in" a tall gentleman entered, whose stout proportions and sleek grey head seemed thoroughly in keeping with his clerical coat and gaiters. Mrs. Pierrepoint rose and stood gravely before him. "Do you want me, uncle?" she said.

"You had better go downstairs, my dear," he answered; "Mr. Wormit is about to read the will."

"Do you think it better that I should be present?"

"Yes, I do," said the Dean, deliberately, "it was your husband's special wish. Now, my dear Minnie, if you are ready, we will go at once;" and, taking her on his arm, he led his niece to the drawing room, where the people, including lawyer Wormit, had assembled. There was a little hush as the widow came into the room; naturally enough she was the subject of no small amount of speculation and curiosity. When a man dies possessed of something like £20,000 a year, his possible inheritors acquire an importance which they have never had before. All eyes turned openly or furtively on to the young figure sitting near the Dean, looking very pale and pathetic in the heavy crape dress.

Then the first tones of the lawyer's voice directed everyone's thoughts to the matter in hand.

It was not a long will; in spite of legal intricacies and repetitions it took hardly ten minutes to read. There were a few legacies to relatives, a few to servants; but the testator had unconditionally bequeathed the bulk of his huge property to his wife – Mrs. Minnie Pierrepoint.

There was a hush, a pause; if the widow had been an object of interest before, she was one of something like awe now; and all eyes were turned upon her. Her face was very pale; her full, red lips pressed tightly together; her bosom rose and fell; for a moment she closed her eyes – that was all. She turned to the Dean and spoke in a low, tremulous voice:

"Please, uncle, would you see to all these people? I have ordered dinner for them at six; I should like to go upstairs."

"Certainly, my dear," said the clergyman, offering her his arm, and looking at her with no little respect – he had had no expectations from the dead man, and consequently could rejoice the more thoroughly in his niece's good fortune. "Certainly. I suppose you will dine in your own room?"

"No, thank you, uncle. Jenkinson will bring me up some tea presently. I am not hungry."

Mrs. Pierrepoint went back into her boudoir, which led into the great empty bedroom. She would stay there alone that evening, and would not dine. Not that, as a rule, she was indifferent to delicate cookery – on the contrary, there was a good deal of the epicure in her nature; it was this very epicureanism which kept her fasting tonight. She had a subtler, more exquisite feast in store for herself; she would not spoil the effect of either banquet by indulging in both at the same time.

There was a soft, golden light in the little room, a soft breath of summer blowing in through the open window; beyond the roofs of the houses she could see the tops of the trees in Kensington Gardens, standing out against a sky bright with all the glory of the declining day. Mrs. Pierrepoint drew a low chair to the open window, and lay back with closed eyes. She could not believe it, could not realise it; that for which she had given up so much was hers at last, her very own, not held at the caprice of a sickly, jealous old man. Only six months, and she was free; long, dreary months of self-repression they had been; but they were over, and her reward was greater than she had ever dared to hope (though, to do her justice, she had never much occupied herself with unworthy speculation). She clasped her hands tightly together, and the fingers of her right hand came in contact with her wedding ring. Poor Mr. Pierrepoint! He must have loved her very much to have made such a will. She really did feel sorry for him, that he had died so suddenly. No one should ever be able to say that she had not respected his memory. She rose and, taking a key from her watchchain, went towards an escritoire standing in a far corner of the room. On the way, she paused before a tall mirror let into the wall, and stood pensively observing her own reflection.

Minnie Pierrepoint was not a tall woman, but the exquisiteness of her proportions made up for any deficiency in height; nor was she very slight for her twenty-two years, indeed, kind friends were fond of prophesying for her an obese middle age, grounding their prophesies on a certain, by no means unbecoming, fullness, and roundness in her form.

She stood for a few minutes, peering gravely into her own large grey eyes, critically observing the curves of her short nose and red lips, which latter, someone had often told her, looked as though "some bee had newly stung them." Perhaps it was this thought which brought the flush to her pale face, and sent her into the corner where stood the escritoire. She sat down on the floor, and unlocking it, pulled out a little drawer whence came a faint scent of rose-leaves, from which she took a packet of letters tied together with a blue riband. She took it out carefully, tenderly, and let it lie on her lap, with her hands lightly crossed above it. Then her thoughts wander far away, beyond the room, beyond Kensington, beyond great, smoky London. She is wandering down a deep Devonshire lane, with its straggling vegetation growing up the sides of its reddish banks. Someone is by her side; and they are laughing and talking softly together. As they emerge from the lane, an ivy-grown church comes in sight. A picturesque old house, built of red sandstone, nestles close by, whence a white-haired clergyman passes out into the churchyard .... Again her thoughts take her back to the deep lane. Once more it is summer, and the same two people are there together, only they are not laughing and talking as before. She is standing still, with downcast face, and her companion, pale and trembling, looks down upon her from his great height ... The train of thought broke off suddenly. Minnie stroked her letters, and pressed them to her lips.

"Poor Frank," she thought, "poor Frank! It was cruel of me to break his heart like that – but I was so young, so easily persuaded; and who can resist the Dean when he becomes argumentative? And Frank – how terrible he looked that day he came home from

Cambridge and heard about it! I don't think I shall ever forget his face in the lane – it makes me shudder to recall it! Will he ever forgive me, I wonder?".... She leaned back against the wall with closed eyes, and a soft smile broke over her face; how inexpressibly sweet it was to be able to let imagination loose and think freely of Frank Quornham, to recall with a less sharp pang of remorse those far-away days before Mr. Pierrepoint had dawned upon her horizon.

Looking back, it seemed to her that she must have been very impulsive, very childish, and very helpless in the hands of the people about her. One's memory is apt to grow rusty with respect to one's old self; we nearly always look upon ourselves as the products of certain causes, setting down anything unsatisfactory to the charge of training and circumstance. "Ah, if my aunt had only whipped me for stealing her horn-book, I should not now be here!" whimpers the wretched criminal on his way to the gallows.

So Minnie forgot the remarkably clear-sighted, intelligent young woman who had given to Mr. Pierrepoint the hand long promised to another; and substituted in her memory a creature of her own imagination – an innocent, unformed thing, much more picturesque, and in every respect more satisfactory.

Long she sat there, deep in such thoughts, with closed eyes and half-smiling lips.

When she awoke from her reverie, the sun had set, and the air was beginning to blow in chilly through the open window. She rose hastily, a little shocked perhaps at her own abstraction; it seemed a sort of disrespect to the old man lying in his newly-made grave, and Minnie, as perhaps you have seen, craved, like most of us, her own respect as well as that of others. If her notions lacked grandeur, if even they may seem to you (oh, high-minded reader!) to have had a tinge of meanness in them, we should set them down to the particular twist which nature and training had given to her mind. She had meant, she told herself, to think over things in a general way that night – her thoughts had insisted on gathering definiteness, and she, half-unconsciously, had given herself up to their delights. There was an irresistible charm in recalling the long past, and in figuring a still happier future. But she checked herself suddenly, and rising, rang the bell for her maid.

"Jenkinson," she said, when the woman appeared, "have any letters come for me?"

"A great number ma'am. I did not like to disturb you."

"Yes, of course. Please bring them up to me now, and light the candles. I shall not want you again tonight." In a few moments she was impatiently turning over a little pile of black-rimmed envelopes, all containing the same stereotyped form of condolence. She opened each one, then shaking her head with a half-disgusted movement, rose, and began pacing the little room with impatient footsteps.

"No sign, no token" (she could not help thinking). "I might have expected it – he is very proud .... I shall have hard work. But one thing I feel, I know – Frank is not a man to love twice; his character was always nobler and stronger than mine; he always seemed so far above me." ... She stopped and buried her face in her hands, while the slow tears trickled through her fingers; then she flung back her head and spoke aloud:

"Only a year – a year – a whole year! Oh, Frank, will you forgive me?" She sank down on her knees, and relieved her excited mind with one of those long fits of sobbing such as only women know.

Part 2

Whitechapel

The way which lies between Prince's Gate and Whitechapel is neither short nor pleasant: there is a whole series of cuts and windings and unexpected turnings to be taken; yet neither locality experiences any serious inconvenience from the comparative inaccessibility of the other.

The glaring July sun beat down upon the pavement, shedding a fierce light on all around; making the staring geraniums in the flower boxes look redder than ever; and bringing out sudden points of brightness in the steel harness and glossy coats of Mrs. Pierrepoint's carriage-horses, which stood impatiently champing before the door of a certain house in Prince's Gate. Jarvis and John, one on the box of the victoria, the other standing on the hot pavement, were by no means in a good temper.

"'Haven't no patience with missus's whims," said the coachman, grumpily; "Whitechapel indeed! And on such a day as this."

"Maybe she's taken to distric' visitin'," suggested John, mildly.

"Not *'er*!" (contemptuously) – "that's not 'er line. Mark my words, she's up to some game or other – " Jarvis never finished that sentence, for at this point the door was flung open, and Mrs. Pierrepoint came forth to the outer air.

"Whitechapel or not Whitechapel" (as Jarvis said) "the missus" had certainly shown no carelessness with respect to toilette that afternoon.

Perhaps some stiff-backed people might have considered her costume hardly suitable to a one-year-old widow; she had cast off the heavy crape dress, bonnet, and mantle, to which she had so rigidly adhered during the first twelve months of her widowhood, and wore some soft transparent web-like material, with a dark lino rippling down it, which lost itself every now and then in the folds. Her hat was soft and feathery, of some graceful, indefinite shape; in the front of her dress were two heavy, half-opened roses of a deep creamy colour.

She stepped into the carriage, and repeated her orders of the morning to the obsequious John, "Number 2, St. Gibb's Buildings, near the Bethnal Green Museum."

An observer more penetrating than the footman might have remarked a rather higher note than usual in the well-trained voice, a brighter sparkle in the eyes, a faint quiver in the full, red lips; but John was thinking about the long, hot journey before him – envying his mistress the lace parasol, which made her look so cool and comfortable.

The carriage rolled from the door; Mrs. Pierrepoint lay back with wide eyes and parted lips, through which came the short, quick breath. She could not think: her head seemed in a confused whirl, half-delicious, half-terrible. Today, today she was to reap the reward of long months of self-denial and self-repression. There would be a struggle – she was prepared for that, for Frank was terribly proud; but of ultimate victory she felt sure. Her whole being seemed in a sweet fever, swayed by a "prodigal inward joy," such as she had not experienced since the old rectory days; a joy enhanced perhaps by its very want of a sure foundation on which to rest.

Absorbed in her own thoughts, it was not till she had been borne far beyond familiar places that she was aware of the change of scene. When she was roused from her reverie by the unaccustomed sights, sounds and smells, she looked around her with a little start of surprise and horror.

Frank a curate in Whitechapel! It seemed impossible. Frank, with his ultra-sensitiveness to external surroundings; his shrinking from anything harsh, or discordant, or unsightly; his keen delight in the soft, the harmonious, the beautiful!

She saw the narrow, crowded streets; the endless rows of houses, from whose every window hard, worn faces of half-starved people were peering; women were leaning far out over the sills, with the disregard of danger characteristic of their class, screaming harshly to over-the-way or street acquaintances. Children swarmed over doorsteps, on the footway, in the roadway, jostling the chaffering crowd round the "costers'" barrows, eliciting oaths from the men, who lounged, smoking and swearing, about the pavement.

Mrs. Pierrepoint shuddered and closed her eyes, and a terrible fear struck her like a chill. What if Frank should be ill, dying? He was always delicate, and the life which he must have been lately leading must have tried him sorely.

What a long way off was her destination! How slowly the carriage was moving! She called to the coachman to drive faster, but he answered that he was going at a greater rate than usual; the neighbourhood was crowded, he dared not increase his pace.

At last they emerged from the more crowded thoroughfares into a closely interlacing network of small streets; to the right, round by the left, to the right again; then the carriage stopped before a dingy block of high, narrow-windowed houses. Mrs. Pierrepoint felt her colour coming and going, and her heart beating faster and faster; she got out and told the man to drive on; then she knocked steadily at a crazy door with a great chalk 2 marked on it. A little pause, which seemed an age, the sound of a scuffle within, followed by the heavy tramp of advancing footsteps, and in another moment Minnie found herself face to face with a worn-out, sullen-looking woman, who stood in silent wonder before her.

"The Rev. Mr. Quornham lives here, I believe?" said Mrs. Pierrepoint in her most conciliatory tones.

The woman's naturally sullen expression gathered definiteness; there were suspicion and hostile questioning in her glance, as she said shortly, "Yes."

"I wish to see him," Minnie went on, with a continued effort at extreme suavity of manner.

The woman put her hands on her hips, and looked uncompromisingly at the dainty figure before her. "Don't know if you can seen 'im, I'm sure, 's gen'ly busy 'bout this time."

"But I wish to see him very particularly – on very urgent business in fact," said Minnie, controlling her irritation, but speaking half a note higher than before.

"'s not had 'is tea yet – 'e never makes much of a dinner, so I give 'im 's tea early." The woman spoke defiantly, yet with a certain undertone of protectiveness and grim tenderness, which the other distinctly felt.

"But will you please tell Mr. Quornham that I am here?" There was a deeper flush on Mrs. Pierrepoint's face, a softer brightness in her eye – everyone it seemed loved Frank, even this hard, worn-out creature.

The woman closed the door; then, without a word, led the way up the dark, narrow stairs, which creaked and shook at every step. On the second storey she stopped before a door and knocked.

No answer, "'e's not in there. I'll tell 'im you've come," panted the sullen janitress, at the same time showing the visitor into the room, and slamming the door upon her.

Minnie was not sorry for the respite; now that the moment had come for which consciously or unconsciously she had shaped the latter part of her life, she felt a vague fear, a terrible anxiety, though deep down in her heart lay the certainty of success, diffusing a strange happiness through all her doubts. She glanced around her with tender scrutiny, and her eyes filled as she noted the pathetic little attempts at refinement amidst the utter poverty of the surroundings. The room was rather large, but miserably fitted and furnished, yet somehow it was stamped with the unmistakeable mark of culture and refinement. The patched window was open, and the scent of mignonette was wafted in from the pots on the sill; two or three fine engravings hung on the wall (one, she remembered with a thrill, she had given him); there was a set of bookshelves with their well-worn books, many of them those little brown-backed, red-leaved volumes, of which she had been rather jealous in the old days; on the table was a blue vase with creamy flowers in it, one of which had fallen on an open volume of "The Earthly Paradise."[2]

Footsteps sounded outside, then the handle of the door turned; her heart beat faster and faster; only by a mighty effort did she raise her eyes to the tall figure advancing towards her.

Some people said, speaking of him not wholly admiringly, that Frank Quornham was like a lily; and the simile was not altogether ill-chosen. Something in the lines of the tall, slight figure, in the curve of the exquisitely graceful neck supporting the fine, fair head with its pale face and long, delicate features, might have suggested the most graceful of all flowers; but there the resemblance ceased; there was no flower-like weakness or mere sweetness in the man's strong, grave face, with its well-controlled lips and deep-set eyes.

He came slowly towards Mrs. Pierrepoint, who rose and stood calm and pale before him. A faint, almost imperceptible flush sprang

---

2. William Morris' poem, *The Earthly Paradise* (1868-1870).

for an instant to his cheek, but slight and fleeting as it was, she saw it, and gave it her own interpretation.

"Mrs. Pierrepoint," he said, bowing gravely, "this is an unexpected pleasure."

Minnie's thought was, "How dreadfully pale and thin he is looking!" Her words were:

"You see it is a case of Mahomet and the mountain. You did not come and see me, so I have come to see you." She spoke lightly and with strict impersonality, carefully steering clear of the familiar "Frank" and the formal "Mr. Quornham."

Frank was puzzled. "Pray sit down," he said, indicating a chair, and speaking with marked formality.

Minnie obeyed, feeling somehow a little chill and frightened; she had told herself over and over again that such would be her reception – her fear had no solid foundation, was only the recurrence of a certain feeling of something like awe which she had always had for Frank, even in the days when she had tyrannised over him.

"I did not know where you lived, till the other day, when the Dean told me," she said; "it must be a great change after Trinity."

"Yes; indeed. College is the little bit of poetry which comes into so many otherwise prosaic lives. It is something to store up in one's memory."

"I can quite think it; one must need a great many pleasant memories in Whitechapel."

"Though even Whitechapel is not without its charms, when one comes to know them."

"I think it would take me a long time to find them out," said Minnie, with a little laugh. She was wondering how she could give the conversation a less impersonal turn, for she felt that very soon the tumultuous inner emotions must burst through the outer crust of composure.

There was a little pause; Mr. Quornham leaned back in his chair, rather wearily; Mrs. Pierrepoint tapped the ground impatiently with her foot. She had meant to be cautious, to lead up to the *dénouement* very slowly and carefully, feeling her ground at every step; but she had miscalculated her own strength – she could bear the silence, the coldness no longer, she must set at rest the wild desires and terrors raging in her bosom. For a moment, she buried her face in her hands, then clasping them tightly together and looking straight at the young man, she spoke in a clear, high voice:

"I daresay you are surprised at seeing me here today, Frank, after all that has happened. If it were to any other than yourself, to anyone less great and noble, I should not have come. I have been very cruel, very wicked – but remember, I was young and inexperienced. Oh, Frank, won't you forgive me? Won't you give me back what you offered me once and I threw away so blindly?... You were willing then to take my worthless self, now I offer you my worthless self and all I have."

Frank Quornham sprang to his feet, the delicate nostrils quivering, the pale cheek glowing for an instant with a pink flush.

Minnie Pierrepoint, too, had risen, and stood exactly facing him; but when she saw that swift action of his she came nearer and looked up into his eyes; a sudden thrill of pain, and dread, and joy passed through her – she spoke quickly, to stay the words on his lips:

"Frank, dear, I can't help being rich!"

She stood with flushed, uplifted face, and extended hands; her breath came and went; there was a half-smile on her parted lips, and a great tear gathered in her eyes, which rolled down her cheek.

Frank Quornham did not hesitate; the flush had faded from his cheek, his whole face was white, even to the lips; but there was no faltering in the low, deliberate voice:

"Mrs. Pierrepoint," he said, "let there be no misunderstanding between us. I hope I should not be guilty of that form of cowardice which sacrifices the happiness of two lives out of fear of the world's judgment. But there is a barrier between us greater than any difference of station could have raised up. Once I trusted you, believed in you, was ready to shape my life for you. By your own act you destroyed that faith; of faith in other things, which you nearly destroyed, I will not speak. I am deeply grieved that this should have happened. I can appreciate the generosity of your offer, but I cannot accept it."

She stood like a statue before him; her hands still extended, her face uplifted towards him; the joyful tear of a moment ago lay on her cheek, the smile was frozen on her lips; but the cheek was ghastly pale, there was no colour in the full lips. She felt as if someone were stabbing her, and her heart-blood was flowing, drop by drop, as she stood.

He had spoken quite gently, quite impersonally; but the scorn, whose expression he had been so careful to repress in voice and words, seemed conveyed to her with all the more force by some subtler means; she felt paralysed by it; suddenly her own acts and motives stood before her in all their miserable smallness, she seemed to feel dimly at something greater and nobler, to see a great gulf stretching between herself and this man, a gulf never to be spanned.

When Frank ceased speaking, there was a pause; he stood with head thrown back, and eyes fixed straight before him; Minnie's arms dropped nervelessly to her side, her head fell on her bosom, she made a few steps to the door; Frank came forward and held it open for her as she passed through; the folds of her dress touched him, and she felt his breath on her forehead in the narrow doorway, but she did not look up …

Back, back through dirty, crowded streets, to stately mansions and pleasant parks.

Forever and forever! She had received her sentence, and there was no reprieve – a relentless though impalpable force held them apart; there was no hope.

On, on; were the hungry women crowding and pushing at the stall, fiercely eager for the cheapest bits of foul meat, more pitiable than this lady leaning back in her luxurious carriage, with the demons of despair and self-contempt gnawing at her heart?

She could see the long years stretching before her, and for the first time she realised what she had forfeited; and her heart sickened as she came within sight of her great house, and thought of the emptiness of all her splendour and her wealth without love.

Euphemia: A Sketch (1880)

"The common burden of humanity, which we have all to bear, falls most heavily on those whose intellectual faculties are developed early."

GOETHE[3]

Prelude

Perhaps it is because my own life has been so uneventful that I have always taken such a keen interest in those of others; have followed out so earnestly the fortunes of men and women with whom I have had personally little connection. Things might have been otherwise, if – but why stir up old memories? Certain it is, that I think no man is to be pitied whose sympathies have been enlarged, even by the cruellest of misfortunes. About sixteen or seventeen years ago, one bleak day in January, it chanced that my nephew Jack and I were walking down a dirty street at the back of one of our large Northern towns, when a block in the narrow way drove us to take refuge in the doorway of one of the tall, dark houses. The little crowd of people,

3. The translation might have been taken from the fifteenth volume of Johann Wolfgang von Goethe's *Dichtung und Wahrheit*; however, the translation is very close to Sarah Austin's own in *Characteristics of Goethe: From the German of Falk, von Müller, &c.*, Volume 1 (Philadelphia: Lea & Blanchard, 1841), 204. Austin (1793–1867) was a translator of German texts.

which had caused the obstruction, was gathered in front of a wall, on which great red and white posters were occasionally to be seen through the moving mass of heads.

Jack suggested that we should investigate the origin of the excitement, and making our way through the little knot of people we found ourselves opposite to the following announcement: –

"Augustus Corbould, Esq. (the celebrated American actor and musician), begs to announce that he has taken the Town Hall, Newchester, for six nights only, and is about to present to the public his renowned entertainment of

Varieties

"In the course of the evening Little Effie Corbould will give her famous recitation of *Lochinvar*,[4] which in the United States and all the capitals of Europe has been pronounced, etc., etc."

"Dear me, dear me," I said, reflectively, as we moved away, "'Gus Corbould turned up again! This is very strange."

"Do you know him, uncle?" asked Jack, a little surprised. "You've never told me about anyone of that name before."

"'Gus Corbould! Dear me, it's very strange," I repeated, musingly.

"No, my boy, perhaps I have never mentioned him to you, but I knew him many years ago, and we had a mutual liking, I think. When I was practising as a doctor in New York City he was my first patient – down with an ugly attack of fever, and thank God, I managed to pull him through."

"Shall you look him up, uncle? Or couldn't we go to the Town Hall tonight, and take a look at Miss Effie, and the other 'Varieties'?" suggested my nephew.

Accordingly, at seven o'clock that evening, we found ourselves installed in the first row of red cushioned seats, waiting for the dingy curtain to rise and reveal the graces of the well-known American

4. Walter Scott's poem, "Lochinvar."

company. *Scrape, scrape,* went a brace of violins in the orchestra, and then the musicians struck up the "Last Rose of Summer."[5] When the curtain rose, displaying "Augustus Corbould, Esq., seated at a piano in readiness for his comic drawing room entertainment," I observed that time and a restless life had begun to mark him pretty severely; this man of three-and-thirty, whom ten years ago I had known as a splendid fellow, looked worn and coarsened; his hair grey, his face unmistakably wrinkled.

When he had left the stage, I fell into a fit of musing oblivious of what was passing before me, till Jack suddenly touched my arm.

"Look there, uncle, there's something magnificent for you."

I glanced up indifferently, and my eye was strangely arrested by what I saw.

A little girl, of about ten years old, was standing alone upon the stage.

In spite of pink ribbons, bright shoes, and sundry other theatrical adornments and graces, the first thing about her which struck me was her very decided plainness. She was rather a tall child of her age (or of what I guessed to be her age), with long, thin, white-clad legs coming from under her short muslin skirts; her long, thin arms were bare, and very brown; very brown too, was the little face, with its great eyes (her one "point"), aquiline nose, and tremulous, quivering mouth. She stood alone, I repeat, her hands clasped in front of her, looking round as if for admiration before beginning her performance. Then came a little round of applause from the audience, which she acknowledged by her heightened colour and sparkling eyes, no less than by a formal curtsey. A pause, then a clear, childish voice gave forth the first lines of *Lochinvar*.

"Poor little monkey," whispered Jack; "I suppose that's Miss Effie. Her father should never allow – "

"I never knew Corbould had a daughter," I interrupted. "He had been married twice when I knew him, but had no children! She can hardly be his daughter."

5. Poem (given music) by Thomas Moore (1779–1852).

"Poor little monkey!" said my nephew again; "she wouldn't recite badly, if it weren't for her airs and graces, – those are really comic."

"Rather pathetic," I answered with a sigh; "the moral health of such a child must be in a terrible condition. Such vanity alone is enough to render diseased the whole nature."

"She seems rather intelligent too, in other respects," said Jack. "Notice the clearness of her enunciation, and her evident appreciation of what's she's saying: though for the matter of that, I daresay every word's been drilled into her."

Miss Effie had now come to the end of the poem, and stood smilingly receiving the plaudits of the spectators, finally disappearing among them, only to return after a few moments and launch forth into "Casibianca."[6] This second performance was less displeasing to me: for a moment she seemed to have forgotten herself, and was actually pathetic, if not eloquent. Before the green curtain had fallen again I had made my way round to the back of the stage, and in a few moments Corbould and I were clasping hands and bursting forth into a flood of reminiscence and enquiry.

"So I see you've married again, Corbould," I said at length, with a glance at Miss Effie, who was chattering excitedly with the "ladies and gentlemen" of the company. He understood my glance.

"Oh, you mean the child?" he answered, indifferently, "But Effie is ten years old, so you see she can be no daughter of mine. Do you remember my brother Dick?"

"Yes, quite well: a fine, eager-looking young fellow."

"Just so; but he did what many a promising young man has done before him – hampered himself by an imprudent marriage; he fell in love with a Jewess in Boston, and married her secretly when he was only nineteen. She was the daughter of a Rabbi, and never brought him a penny. Later on the child was born."

"Then, when last I saw your brother, Miss Effie must have been in existence?"

6. Felicia Hemans' (1793–1835) poem, "Casibianca."

"Just so, only none of us knew anything about it. The pair had fine notions of earning their bread by teaching and lecturing, and keeping little Euphemia, as they called her, away from the stage. Poor things! When cholera broke out in New Orleans, where they'd gone for a few months the summer after the child was born, they were both down with it. Dick sent to me when he was dying, and told me about the marriage, and how he'd meant to tell me as soon as they'd begun to get on a bit in the world. I reckon he'd have had to wait sometime...."

"Then poor little Effie was a dying charge?"

"Just so; and trouble enough she's been to me – a very troublesome child, though astonishingly quick at picking up things, and sharp at seeing through them."

The subject of remark came tripping towards us at this moment. She was evidently accustomed to seeing strangers, and curtseyed to us both with great self-possession.

"Thanks for our treat of tonight," said Jack, speaking and bowing with mock solemnity.

She fixed her eyes keenly on his face, then replied in exactly the same tone:

"And I thank you, also, for honouring us with your presence."

There was a little laugh at this; Corbould looked at us from the corners of his eyes, as much as to say "There's sharpness for you!" and Miss Effie assumed a look of great unconcern.

In the ensuing fortnight (for the *six nights only* had been increased to twelve) I saw a good deal of my old friend Corbould, and a good deal too of his little niece. Perhaps it is because I have so much love for the young things that children are invariably attracted towards me. Strange to say, before I had known her a day, Miss Effie, with all her unchildlike ways and whims, showed very decided proofs of affection for me, and at the end of the fortnight had come to consider my knee specially privileged to bear her little weight. At last, the tents of the travellers were struck, and my two friends went on their march through the great world.

Part 1

Six years had passed away since the "Great American Company" had descended upon us good people of Newchester. I was sitting one morning in my study, when Nephew Jack (now the proud father of two delightful babies) came in to consult me about a certain family in his parish.

We discussed the case at some length: "Thanks very much for your advice," said Jack, preparing to go, "and by the bye, uncle, there's a bit of news that perhaps may interest you – your old friend Corbould has taken the theatre here, for the winter – comes over with a whole company."

"You surprise me," I said, "I will find out when they begin playing, and we'll persuade Mary to leave the babies for a night. I am particularly anxious to go."

* * * * *

About a week after the conversation recorded above, I sat studying the play bill at the Theatre Royal, Newchester; I read it through once, then scanned it carefully again, no use, the name I sought was not there.

"My little friend Effie is not playing tonight, apparently," I said, rather blankly.

"Oh, it's impossible to tell, uncle," replied Jack, indifferently.

"I shouldn't wonder if the Miss Annette Rosabelle who is down for the heroine were no other than an old friend under a new name."

But no – the programme spake truly; the first scene—no Effie. The second scene – Miss Rosabelle, a gorgeous, golden-haired lady, who, making every allowance for lapse of time and stage make up, could not be Euphemia.

At the end of the second act I rose, and made my way round to the back of the theatre. I looked around in vain for a familiar face. Corbould was on the stage, and no "lady" or "gentleman" of the old *Varieties* company was to be seen. As I was moving away, rather sadly, something arrested me. From a dark corner (where were stowed sundry lumber and properties), gleamed a pale woman's face. The face was decidedly a remarkable one – thin and sallow, with fine aquiline features, and great hollow black eyes, which were fixed vacantly on the darkness. Great wisps of black hair fell from under an old hat on to the face and neck; the whole expression was one of dull despair. The owner of the face was a tall young woman, whose raw, undeveloped figure showed to little advantage in the shabby old "ulster" which she wore. She leant against the wall, her hands clasped in front of her, her whole attitude that of a creature who is wearied and hopeless. I gazed at her amazed, saddened, for a moment, hardly knowing if I were committing an absurd mistake in obeying a sudden impulse, and going towards her, with both hands extended:

"Miss Effie," I said, "do you recognise an old friend?"

She started, flushed a little, and looked down questioningly (for I am not by any means a tall man).

"I think I remember your face," she said, slowly, in tones which bore no resemblance to the shrill, childish treble of former years, "but you must forgive me that I do not know your name."

"That is certainly not surprising, since – "

She broke in upon my words.

"I remember you now; you are Dr. H., and you were kind to me six years ago here in Newchester."

"I must congratulate you on a fine memory, Miss Effie."

"Oh, I never forget people" (indifferently.)

"Nor I, and I've often thought of you, my dear, though our acquaintance was so short. Indeed, it was partly the hope of seeing you which brought me here tonight. I see, however, you are not playing."

"One cannot be an infant phenomenon forever," she said, with sudden bitterness, turning her face away a little.

I looked at her keenly for an instant, her tone and manner pained me no less than her appearance. I began to see pretty clearly the state of the case; this poor Euphemia was paying a heavy price for former triumphs.

"My dear," I said at length, "I am sorry to hear you speak like that."

She gave a little shrug.

"What would you have? But I agree with you that it was silly. Now we will go and find my uncle."

But I was not to be put off like that.

"No, no," I said, "we will do nothing of the kind, just at present, I am going to claim the privilege of an old friend. I want to talk to you confidentially, Miss Effie."

"Not that name, call me *Euphemia*," she put in, impatiently.

"Well, then, Euphemia, have you any business here tonight?"

"Oh, no, beyond bringing some things, and I've done that."

"Then if you will allow me, I will walk with you to your lodging, and we can there await your uncle. And on the way, my dear, you shall tell me what you have been doing with yourself these six years."

"There's very little to tell," she said, wearily, as we emerged into the ill-lighted street. "My story is common enough. I went on reciting (poor little ape) for about three years after you saw me, then naturally I outgrew the part of *infant wonder*; I wasn't pretty, and I couldn't dance or sing, so I was just put on the shelf, as it were. It made me very wretched at first; the gradual falling off of the flatteries and applause, and petting, but I have got over it long ago. I am only worn out and very tired."

She spoke quite simply, though with a ring of unconscious pathos in her voice.

"Worn out!" I said, straining at a cheerfulness which I did not feel, "You talk like a very young person, Euphemia. You are sixteen and here am I nearly sixty, expecting, should God spare me, to get still much profit and pleasure from my life."

"You forget," she said, "what my life has been; that I was pulled open by impatient hands, that would not wait for me to develop."

She possessed a certain refinement of speech and accent, which I could not help observing, even while deeply interested in what she was saying.

Affecting not to grasp her meaning, I merely said, "but you have not accounted for the last three years at all satisfactorily."

"Oh! Their story is blank enough. Always moving from place to place; seeing daily new people, and knowing none. My uncle found it convenient for him that I should be 'domestic:' – well, you're a man, and perhaps do not realise what that means. I had begun life (like most other people) with great hopes, great beliefs, great aims.

Why talk of such things? you know what they come to in the end; how, after a certain point, one's experience is a whole series of findings out, – as though we took a child to the back of the pantomimic scenes, and showed him the paste board and tinsel, and human fairies. But I weary you."

"My dear, my dear," I said mournfully, "you only see the surface...." Then I stopped short. How could I preach of general principles of goodness and beneficence to this creature, crushed so utterly under her own particular sorrows? She went on with her story; "After two years – so dark that I cannot bear to think of them, I fell ill of low fever in Manford. I heard people say that I was going to die, but I knew I should live.... I longed for death, but I knew that it was far off.... Then we left Manford and came here. That's all I can tell you."

By this time we had reached the door of Corbould's lodgings, and my companion led me through a dark passage, into a little room, where the dim lamplight revealed a table spread for supper.

Carelessly laying aside hat and "ulster" Euphemia stooped down to turn up the lamp. I watched her keenly by the uncertain light. Divested as she was of the uncompromising outer garments, I was surprised to observe crude hints of beauty in the lines of the figure, and the poise of the really fine head on the shapely neck; though, I will frankly say, that by reason of her worn and neglected appearance she produced none of those pleasant impressions which young ladies of her age are apt to do.

She bade me be seated, and went about sundry domestic offices in a dull, spiritless manner; then her uncle came in, and I had no further opportunity of private conversation with her that night, only as we parted, I said, detaining her hand for a moment: "I may come and see you tomorrow, my dear?"

"If you care to come," was the weary answer, "it's very good of you to ask. Perhaps the best time is the morning; when everyone is at rehearsal. Good night."

I found my young friend the next morning seated among sundry ragged books and blotted papers, which however seemed but little to interest her, for her pen lay idle in her hands, and her eyes were fixed dreamily before her. She started and blushed when she saw me, and brought forward a chair with a little stir of cordiality, I did not waste time beating about the bush – I went straight to the subject which had brought me there. "Euphemia," I said, "I have been thinking over what you were telling me last night, you don't know how shocked and grieved I was, at hearing a young thing like you talk in that tone. Don't resent it as an impertinence if I scold you severely."

"O, not at all, Dr. H." (with a hopeless little smile.)

"My dear," I went on, "do you know what conclusion I came to? That you think the world a dark place, because you no longer enjoy the excessive praise and applause which you formerly did." I spoke as sternly as I could, keenly watching her face meanwhile.

She coloured a little and said "I think you are wrong, Dr. H., those sort of things don't colour one's views of life, generally; though they may sink into and help to spoil the shape, particularly, that is all."

"Then, my dear, am I to think that your unhappiness arises from a misconception? From a want of that understanding which comes to most of us sooner or later (thank God!) of the principles of beneficence, of harmony, of justice, underlying all things?"

She threw back her head with scornful impatience: "Beneficence, harmony, justice; can we people who live in the world ever say those words out of a sermon or an epigram?

"Beneficence? When more than the half of mankind groans and suffers under the weight of burdens too hard to bear:

"Harmony? When everything is discordant and incomplete. Don't we all come into the world with fine healthy appetites for happiness, and aren't we nearly all sent out of it unsatisfied, like hungry children going supperless to bed?

"Justice! Look round you and talk of justice; aren't all our instincts cruel and unjust? Don't we shrink from the finest soul shut up in an unpleasant body? – "

"My dear, my dear," I interposed, "you are carried away by your own words."

She resumed more calmly:

"I daresay you are thinking of a God who shall make all things complete hereafter. Shall I tell you frankly that I see no reason for such belief? If the world be under guidance, should we rather not judge it to be under the guidance of evil beings? I read a poem once called *Caliban upon Setebos*,*[7] which expresses my meaning more clearly. The ancients had a greater understanding of the principles which govern life, when they made their Zeus a profligate, and their Here[8] a shrew."

This little outburst of schoolgirl knowledge startled me, and drew my attention from metaphysics to metaphysician.

"You have been reading?" I asked rather bluntly.

She coloured, proudly I thought;

"I have always read in a general sort of way – any books I could get hold of. Lately, I have tried to study more systematically for the furtherance of – of certain plans of mine."

I took up several of the books lying on the table: a German dictionary and a copy of *Goetz von Berlichingen* (the latter much annotated in lead pencil);[9] an early edition of Robert Browning's poems, and a tattered copy of the *Eton Latin Grammar*, with "F. Thorpleigh" scrawled on the flyleaf.

"Rather a queer mixture," she said, in answer to my puzzled glance, "but you see I have to take whatever comes in my way. An old musician

---

7. Levy's "*" indicates that Robert Browning is the author of the poem. "Caliban upon Setebos" is also used in "Out of the World" (pp. 703–8) and "Cohen of Trinity" (pp. 832–40).
8. Refers to the classical Greek goddess, Hera.
9. *Goetz von Berlichingen* – Goethe's play.

who went about with us for some years, taught me a little German, and I sometimes try to keep it up. Dr. Thorpleigh, who attended me while I was ill in Manford, gave me the other two. He found out that I was interested in other things than cooking and mending, or even reciting, and helped me a little with my studies."

"That was very good of him; but unfortunately one can't go on being ill and having doctors forever."

This was quite a random shot – nothing more than one of those attempts at facetiousness which belong to my age; but, once uttered, I would have given anything to have recalled it. Not that Euphemia blushed, or smiled, or looked self-conscious. It was only that a livid pallor, in which the blood forsook lip and cheek, passed over her face, and for a moment, she leaned her hand, as if for support, against a chair. In the course of our conversation, she had risen, and taken up her position before the fire.

"Here is a discovery," I thought. "Ah, Miss Effie, you will learn one day that people whose blood is so ready to ebb and flow at a word, are by no means 'worn out.'" I merely said: "But you have not given up trying to study?"

"Sometimes I make attempts in that direction," she replied, in a quick, low voice; "but there's a sort of little imp who always springs up between me and my work, and asks, *What for*?"

Ah! Once I had known that little imp too well, I had used to call him *Cui bono*?

"Don't listen to him," I said, vigorously, "take no notice of him and he will soon cease to trouble you. Work for work's sake – " At that moment, Corbould's entrance put an end to my impromptu sermon.

It was some days before I again found time to call on Euphemia. She was alone in a little closet at the back of the dining room, kneeling before an open trunk, while books and clothes were piled carelessly about the floor. She rose hastily as I entered, and before we had shaken hands, I observed that a slight, at first indescribable change had come over her. On closer examination, I saw that her hair had been brushed and tied back, and that she had put on a linen collar. She blushed a little at my scrutiny, and begged that I would excuse the room and its disorder – she was making preparations for a speedy departure.

"What, going, my dear?" I said, rather surprised, "I thought your uncle had decided to stay here all the winter."

"Yes; he intends doing so," was the reply, "but I – I have altered my plans; I am going back to Manford, to an old cousin of mine who was good to me when I was ill: she is ill now herself, and wants someone to look after her." She lifted a great pile of books as she spoke, and went on rather quickly: "I have been thinking about what you and – someone else, said about *working for work's sake*. I suppose that's the only course open to one.... looked at from outside, there can be no object desirable enough to rouse one to labour. I'm just going to try to fill up my fifty or sixty years of life with work."

"You are doing wisely," I said. "By and bye you will come to love the work for its own sake. I see," I added, cheerfully, "that you are taking a great many books with you: you have endless resources in such companions."

"Yes," she said, in a dull voice, still standing upright before me with the pile of books in her hands.

"And you will come one day to be very grateful for those fifty or sixty years of life, which (in all probability) are before you."

"Yes," she said again, in exactly the same tone as before: then a deep flush passed over her face – her burden fell with a crash to the floor.... "What are they? Wise, *dead* books:" she cried; "I want to *live*:" She sank shuddering on to a trunk, which lay near, and covered her face with her hands.

What could I do for this untaught, egotistical creature? How answer her wild, personal cry of sorrow, by telling her of the broad human sympathies of the glorious inner life, which alone can make the world tolerable to most of us.

As I left her that day, she held out both hands, and bent her face towards mine: "Thank you always, good kind friend," she said.

Part 2

"Nec fera tempestas toto tamen horret in anno;
Et tibi, crede mihi, tempora veris erunt."
OVID[10]

In the course of the next two or three years I did not see Euphemia, though occasional letters (which grew rarer and rarer with the lapse of time) came to me from great, smoky Manford. The first of these were actually little less gloomy than the writer's conversation, though far less openly morbid, and were even relieved by sudden touches of humour.

"I suppose my life is no worse than that of a great many," she wrote once, in answer to a question of mine; "I am sixteen, and without hope, that is all."

Later on, the letters seemed cheerfuller in tone:

"I am working hard," she told me, "at domestic as well as merely personal work. Work is the only thing to minister to a mind diseased, I suppose."

At the end of about two years the letters ceased, as most letters do cease, where the writers have no opportunity of seeing one another.

But I was destined to see Euphemia again. About a year after our correspondence had ceased, I was summoned by urgent business to Manford, and determined to also avail myself of the opportunity of visiting my friend, and fixed upon a certain afternoon to pay the proposed visit.

But on the day in question, I found I had miscalculated the time which my business would take me, and only succeeded in getting free in time for dinner. "Never mind," I thought, "I will go by a later train tomorrow. Tonight I will try and amuse myself as best I can." I consulted the waiter about the latter, and finally followed his advice of dropping in at the theatre.

10. The Roman poet, Ovid. On the potential influence of Ovid's *Metamorphoses* on Heinrich Heine, see David Gallagher, *Metamorphosis: Transformations of the Body and the Influence of Ovid's Metamorphoses on German Literature of the Nineteenth and Twentieth* Centuries (New York: Rodopi, 2009).

The house, I noticed, was remarkably full, and I had had some difficulty in securing my stall, which (by chance) was in the front row. I was tired and lay back, with closed eyes, not even troubling to glance at the playbill in my hands, after I had seen that the piece about to be performed was somewhat ambitiously styled, "Inspired."

I was woke from a half doze by the rather too vigorous sounds of the orchestra, and in a few moments the curtain, rising, revealed the stage fitted up as an artist's studio. A young man, in velvet jacket, and longish hair, moves about among the canvases and easels: at length he throws himself into a chair, and falls into a stage-reverie on his hopes, his aims, his inspirations. The door opens slowly, and a tall young woman enters: she is simply dressed in dark, trailing garments, with a soft line of white at wrist and throat; the thick, dark hair is coiled high on the shapely head, exposing wonderfully graceful curves of neck. She speaks, and her voice is soft and rich, with a subtle underthrill of pathos; she tells of *her* hopes, *her* aims, *her* inspirations – of the wrongs of her sex, which she shall set right, of the disjointed times, which she shall make whole.

I cannot give any exact account of the play which was played that night. Suffice, that it was the story of a man and woman's suffering – of noble young souls gone astray, of ambitious young hearts buying a bitter experience.

I had only eyes for that woman's graceful figure, only ears for that woman's rich voice, only admiration for that woman's power and self-possession amidst the tumult of applauding voices. As the curtain fell for the last time, there rose a great cry of *author*! And when I glanced up, I saw Euphemia, standing calm, pale, and dignified, before the shouting people.

I had had no difficulty in approaching vain little Miss Effie, of the Newchester Town Hall – nor the melancholy figure at the back of the Newchester Theatre; but it was some time ere I could gain access to Euphemia, successful author and actress, surrounded as she was by a congratulatory little group of admirers. I was shown into her private room, and waited somewhat impatiently for her arrival. She came at last. As she pressed my hand, and looked into my face with a cordiality which had something of tenderness in it, I could observe (what I had not seen before), certain lines and marks about her face, which one does not often see in the face of a girl who is not yet twenty.

In a few moments we were deep in conversation. Of herself she spoke little; only from a few stray words, and from the tell-tale face before me, did I gather that Euphemia had fought a hard battle – and had won it. Presently she broke in rather abruptly, rather inconsequently, I thought:

"Do you remember a conversation we had one day in Newchester – the part about the books, I mean?"

"Yes, my dear, very well."

"And about an old Latin grammar, with a name scrawled in it?"

"Yes, my dear. What then?"

"Only, only that I am going to marry Frank Thorpleigh."

"My dear! This is news, indeed."

She rose from her seat, and turning a little away from me, spoke in a low voice.

"It was very strange, very wonderful. Do you remember how miserable and how wicked I was on that morning? I thought my misery was the ruins of an old life. I think now it was the beginning of the new life springing up in me. I did not know what I wanted, did not understand...."

A pause – then she went on: –

"You advised me well. Work was the best thing for me. With work I might have got the lesser happiness, with which, alas! so many have to be content.

> "For many a man, on earth desireth sore
> To have some mate upon the toilsome road,
> Some sharer of his still increasing load;
> And yet, for all his longing and his pain
> His troubled heart must seek for love in vain,
> And till he dies, still must he be alone." – *The Earthly Paradise.*[11]

11. A poem by William Morris.

Her voice had sunk very low; she seemed to have forgotten my presence; then she went on again:

"It was most strange – most wonderful. He had sought me (even the wretched creature that I then was) in vain, till six months ago. Then only did we meet again.... In three weeks (when my engagement with Mr. Smith will be over) we shall be married. The next week we sail for my country, the country of my parents."

"For America?"

"Yes, for Iowa. There is a young, wild colony out there, sadly in need of a doctor."

"It will be rough work."

"We know it; few would undertake it – but of course Frank would go where he could do most good."

"And you, Euphemia," I said, doubtfully; "do you mean to say that you are about to retire permanently at the outset of such a brilliant career?"

She laughed quite merrily, and there came into her eyes a look which one does not often see, with man or woman.

"Oh, Dr. H., with all your wisdom I see you don't understand us women. What is fame to us? Does it satisfy the hunger at our hearts for love, the wild craving in our souls for protection and guidance, for something in our turn to protect and guide? Fame and a brilliant career don't fill up our lives – we want something else; though as regards myself, I don't believe I should ever have got them. I wasn't acting, I did that part well because it was myself – that is all."

The door opened, and Frank Thorpleigh came into the room. Tall, fair, slight, with a wonderfully refined, though rather pathetically thin face, he made a striking contrast to the dark-haired woman at his side.

So I leave my heroine and her hero, standing hand in hand on the threshold of a new life.

Between Two Stools (1883)

From Miss Nora Wycherley, *Pembridge Square, W.*,
to Miss Agnes Crewe, *Newnham College, Cambridge.*

June 4th.

My dear Agnes,

What a relief, to be quiet and alone in one's room; to lock the door; to take up one's pen and have a little peaceful talk with one's best friend!

Since we parted at the station (is it really only two days ago?), life has been all hurry and bustle; all dressmakers, bootmakers, and milliners; and perhaps, under the circumstances, that is the best state of affairs possible. Like the young ladies in the novels, one can pretend to "forget." Forget! Agnes, I believe the Fates have cursed me with the boon – terrible in any case, twice terrible in the case of a woman – the boon of constancy!

Mamma was very shocked at my dress when I got home, and insisted on my going off to the dressmaker's directly after lunch. I was wearing, as you know, the beautiful sage-green which our Hall so admires. The absence of stays and crinolette almost wrung tears from the various members of my family. If it had been worthwhile, I should have protested; but is anything worthwhile? So I allowed myself to be borne off to Madame Stéphanie's like a lamb to the sacrifice. What does it matter? With the new dress, I suppose I put on the new life, unwholesome, artificial, violating all laws of beauty; the sordid London streets, the sordid London faces, these I shall have to endure all my life long. And it is only a few days ago since we walked down the lime-avenue together, and watched the sun set behind the elm-trees in the "*Backs*"; since we puzzled over Plato on the lawn, and read Swinburne on the roof in the evenings. Only a few days! Is it not rather a hundred years?

Agnes, I have never had any concealments from you, and I know you to be fully aware even of what I have not told you in so many words. With regard to a certain person, you will tell me – will you not? – all you see and hear of him. Remember, it is all I shall have in the way of pleasure till I die; the few scraps you can collect for me, the few scraps I have myself collected for memory to hug.

Tonight I went to a big dance in Westbourne Terrace. I did not wish to go, reflecting that skeletons are apt to be out of place at feasts, but I yielded finally to Mamma's request, and submitted to the ordeal. As I was standing at the window after dinner, before going up to dress, somebody passed in a hansom. At first I did not recognise him, and stared vaguely, till he bowed, and then – oh, Agnes! – I saw it was Mr. Talbot! I think it was the sight of him made me so desperate afterwards. The music, the lights, the crowd, and that terrible pain at my heart, all these combined to make me a little mad. I am not quite sure what I said and did; I believe it was nothing to offend Philistine sensibilities, but personally I feel rather debased and degraded. I know my sister "rallied" me – as our dear Sir Charles Grandison[12] hath it; "chaffed" *she* calls it – all the way home. Now I come to think of it, I *did* dance a great many times with some impossible man – his name I believe was Mr. Broke – who assumed rather the manners of a grand Turk,[13] and paid me some quite coarse compliments.

Oh, what a relief to get back to solitude, even when solitude means the old terrible pain, the old awful longing! Yet is it not something to have "known the best and loved it?" – to have seen what is noblest, highest, and purest in the world, and to have felt it to the depth of one's being?

---

12. See Samuel Richardson's (1689–1761) *The History of Charles Grandison* (1753).
13. Offensive term associated with orientalist discourses.

[*Here follow several pages which, for the reader's sake, we have thought best to omit.*]

I am glad to say we leave London for Switzerland next week. Please excuse these outpourings of

Your very sorrowful
NORA.

Pembridge Square, October 16th.

Dear Agnes,

Is it possible that four months have elapsed since I wrote to you? And if I remember rightly, my last letter was neither very sane nor very dignified. I must confess that Switzerland is a disappointment; it is all so obvious; one has seen the whole thing so often on workboxes, in albums, and at the theatre. The scenery wants restraint, reserve; the green trees, the conical mountains, the blue-green lakes; they are crude, glaring, wanting in subtlety. Give me Thames in October, or Cam in May, and I will not ask you for the Alps. But this is by the way. After thoroughly "doing" Switzerland in true barbarian, British-tourist fashion, we went to Brighton, and now at last behold us under our own roof-tree.

Yes, my dear Agnes, I have perforce permanently taken up my abode among the Philistines! I do not pretend to like it; but perhaps, like most other things, it has its consolations. Do you not admire the philosophic, not to say chastened, attitude of your friend? I say, perhaps it has its consolations, but I have not yet discovered them.

I have gathered together my Lares and Penates[14] in a little room at the top of the house, where I mean to work every day. It is nothing like the dear old den at Cambridge, but I have hung up your "Melencolia"[15] and the Burne-Jones head;[16] have ranged my

14. Refers to household Roman deities, probably figurines.
15. An engraving by Albrecht Dürer.
16. Refers to Edward Burne-Jones.

Greek books and poets – my sister nearly fainted when she saw some of them – along the shelves; and have no doubt that in time I shall grow very fond of it. Yes, a refuge, a place to be alone in, is most of all what I need. I am in the very heart and centre of Philistia – I make no pretence of concealment about it. Everybody is quite respectable, rather dull, and just a little vulgar. We do not go in for noble ideals and high notions; but on the other hand, we eschew large vices, leaving *them* for our better-born townsfolk on the other side of the Park. No, we are not wicked; we are only on a rather low level of moral and intellectual culture, and present, perhaps, to the thoughtful observer a more depressing spectacle than a den of thieves. Observe the fine satire of the "we"; I am, as you see, developing a pretty turn for cynicism. Who would not under the circumstances?

Personally I find myself rather desolate. I am willing enough to smoke the pipe of peace with the Philistines, but the Philistines will have none of me. They distrust me: the girls think I want to "come it over" them; and the young men are continually on the look-out for covert snubbing. One is afraid to call a thing by its right name for fear of being thought pedantic; it is not young-ladylike to have one's facts right or one's sentences logical. A pretty haziness, a charming inconsequence – these are the qualities the Philistine male would fain see in his womankind.

I went last night to a dinner party in Cleveland Square, where I was subjected to a quite unreserved cross-examination on the subject of myself, my plans, Newnham, etc. One cannot accuse these people of a shrinking delicacy; if they want to know anything, why, they ask it! There is a beautiful frankness in the way they make known their likes and dislikes, their wants and objections. A ballroom is like a battle field, where it is *vae victis*! Indeed; no quarter is given, and the weakest goes, very literally, to the wall. I find myself getting quite interested in the struggle sometimes.

There is nothing to be done I suppose, but "to put one's soul in a place out of sight," and go on one's way to the end. Perhaps I shall get educated up to the whole concern, one day. Meanwhile, I have given up one hope, that I shall ever *forget*. The gods – it was a cruel whim – have given me a constant heart. The thought of a certain person is with me night and day – a strong undercurrent flowing perpetually in the depths of my being. It is something, in this sordid world, to have such a pure and noble image enshrined in one's heart, even if it be only a source of pain.

How I envy you up there! Cambridge looks her best, I think, in October when the leaves are red. Pray write soon and tell me all the news.

Yours affectionately,
NORA.

That Mr. Broke I told you about, (and who took me in to dinner yesterday), has just sent me a great bouquet of hot-house flowers.

Pembridge Square, November 12th.

My dear Agnes,

I cannot tell you how I rejoiced to receive your letter, redolent as it was of the most beautiful place in the world! Let me congratulate you, dear, on your brilliant suggestion for a new reading of that terrible passage in the "Agamemnon."[17] No wonder Mr. Dalrymple is proud of his pupil!

I am sorry, how sorry you can perhaps faintly conceive, to hear of the continued ill-health of Mr. Talbot. Can nothing be done? Can I do nothing? Oh, it is crudest of all to sit here quietly and feel that I may not even stretch out a hand to help him. Euripides was right when he made Medea say that we women are the most wretched of living things.

Your expressions of pity and sympathy for and with myself are very soothing, though they make me feel that perhaps I have a little

17. Greek tragedy by Aeschylus.

overstated my case. The people about me, generally speaking, are dull and in a certain sense vulgar, but of course there are exceptions. Some of them are clever and amusing. That Mr. Broke, for instance, he is very clever – in his own way quite remarkably clever. And his society is agreeable – sympathetic even, to a certain extent. Of course, I do not mean to say that his soul possesses the delicate bloom, his mind the subtle perceptiveness, his feelings the wonderful fineness of another person we know of. The nature of Stephen Broke is not, indeed, to be compared to that of Reginald Talbot; and I do not fancy the atmosphere of professional and commercial London to be exactly conducive to the preservation of psychic bloom. There is a push, a coarseness, a hurry and bustle in this land of Philistia that necessarily knock off the finer edges of character. But why am I running on like this about souls and feelings, and instituting impossible comparisons? Mr. Broke is a very pleasant person to pass an hour or two with; that is all that concerns me; all that can henceforward concern me about any man alive – except one. And he is nice-looking; yes, I think so, though he does not at all come up to one's idea of a "young god." But in a general, rough sort of man's way, his appearance is distinctly pleasing: I mean, he is big and straight, has a pleasant, intelligent face, with good eyes, and wears his clothes the right way – and they are the right sort of clothes. Perhaps you would think him coarse. He certainly marks his preferences very broadly, and has a tendency to give a personal turn to the conversation. I wish, too, there were not quite so much of the Turk in his attitude towards our sex, both individually and collectively; but I know the highest form of chivalry is only possible to the highest nature; and besides, one must allow for a man's associations. Chivalry, indeed, is very little understood in my part of the world. A woman is held to have no absolute value; it is relative, and depends on the extent of the demand for her among members of the other sex. The way the women themselves acquiesce in this view is quite horrible. I need not say that, personally, I am in very little request; that I am caviare to the general is perhaps the most delicate way of stating it. I am neither a beauty, an heiress, nor a crack dancer, nor do I possess the peculiar mixture of skill and daring which go towards making a successful flirt. Nobody wants a girl for her soul and a rather fine critical perception.

Mr. Broke and I talk to one another a good deal, and dance together sometimes, though he says his dancing days are coming to an end next year, when he will be thirty-five. Have you ever tried sitting on the stairs? We never used to sit on the stairs at perpendiculars. It is something of an experience, a new phase, almost, of existence. There is a great clatter and pushing and moving all about; everybody is in gala dress and gala spirits; the air is alive with music, heavy with the scent of flowers, bright with the light of many candles. You are alone in a crowd – you, and another person. You go and sit down in a little corner among pink lights and ferns, or on some dim-lit landing, and talk about everything under the sun – the weather, the last engagement, your soul if you like – all the time conscious that it is not quite real, that either may go off at a tangent should the conversation grow too serious. It is really a very interesting experience, even for those who, like myself, regard life solely from the spectator's point of view.

I am afraid you must think me sadly degenerate; but it is no good to sit in a corner all day and weep for what one has not got. Perhaps, Agnes, you think I am beginning to forget. But no; on second thoughts, I believe you to know me too well. Only write me better news of a certain person, and I shall be happy – comparatively.

Yours affectionately,
NORA.

Pembridge Square, January 20th.

Dear Agnes,

I was very disappointed at not seeing you this vacation. I had hoped to be able to ask you to stay with me, but my sister's friend,

Sybil Juniper, occupied the spare room through the whole five weeks. Sybil is a most exasperating little person, very pretty in a heterodox manner, with fluffy fair hair, pink-and-white skin, and quite abnormally small waist and feet, at which last-mentioned members my whole family is pleased to sit adoringly. I cannot join in the general worship, and am in consequence considered sinister and a little spiteful. But what rational person could bring themselves to accept this charming, empty-headed, rattling creature as "legal tender for a human being" – to quote George Eliot?[18]

I may indeed be wrong in my judgment of her, for one often strikes suddenly upon a human soul after groping hopelessly about in the deposit of worthless stuff which time and the world have contrived to keep above and around it. Such a soul, for instance, I have found in Stephen Broke. Under the crust of worldliness, under all the little coarsenesses and cynicisms, there beats a very human heart with blood of the right degree of redness. I do not mean that he is great and noble, I mean that he is more than a painted image, ingeniously constructed as to brain, with a spring which only the touch of self-interest can move. I mean that he is a real human being, more or less faulty certainly, but good in the main; and the discovery gives me a more than mere aesthetic pleasure. I am beginning to regain something of my lost faith in the great mass of humanity; perhaps I was a little hasty in my first judgments; perhaps there are various ways of excellence, or perhaps it is I myself who am grown coarser and less sensitive to fine moral differences.

But is it not possible that what seems like change and infidelity to old ideals, is development and increased width? Because we perceive the beauties of the valley, have we of necessity less admiration for the snow-capped mountain? But why do I run off into such nonsense? When a lady plunges into metaphor, there is no knowing what may happen to her and her coherency. Here is my maid come to tell me to dress for the dance tonight, so goodbye for the present....

---

18. The quotation is from George Eliot's *Daniel Deronda*.

Two A.M. – I have just come back from the dance, and though it is very late, I find it quite impossible to make up my mind to go to bed. I have been very much disturbed, very much shocked, altogether more moved than I thought was possible under any circumstances save one. When I got into the room tonight, almost the first person I saw was Mr. Broke. I was glad to see him, and glad when he asked me to dance, because he is bright and genial and interesting. He knows so much, has seen so much, is so exceedingly vital and "all round," that one can excuse a great many things for the sake of the pleasantness of his society. But tonight he did not seem at all inclined to be amusing. He was quite serious, rather surly in fact, and led me off to the conservatory in a sort of right-is-might fashion that was almost brutal. I began to feel frightened, strangely moved and agitated. In the conservatory a very wonderful thing happened. Agnes, in justice to him I cannot tell you what he said to me, indeed I have a very confused remembrance of the whole affair; I only know this, that he asked me to be his wife! Oh, but it was terrible – I could never have imagined beforehand how terrible! I was suddenly conscious of being acted upon, conscious that here was a force to which, if I were not careful, I should yield myself. I told him that what he asked was impossible. At first he simply did not believe me; then he grew very white, and his eyes – they are such beautiful eyes! – fastened on my face with a searching gaze that filled me with a strange emotion: terror, but not wholly terror, whose very vagueness made it no less powerful. "Will you reconsider," he said at length, "and give me your answer another time?"

And then I told him that I was very sorry if I had made a mistake; that I had grown to regard myself as a mere looker-on at life; that my own personal history was long ago at an end. He laughed a little at this. "Let me take you to the dancing room," he said; and when we reached it he made me a deep bow, with the remark: "I have laboured under a misconception. I beg your pardon," and disappeared among the crowd of dancers.

Oh, I was so miserable, I could have cried there and then, but there was nothing for me to do but to go on dancing till the carriage came.

Mr. Broke stayed for about half an hour; once my partner and I knocked up against him in a doorway, when he bowed very deeply and apologised for being in the way.

Am I not pursued by a cruel Fate? If it had not been for a previous occurrence, I believe I could have liked this person. It is a terrible thing to deliberately turn away from love – from the love of a good man; and Stephen Broke is good and clever and handsome, and I have unwittingly done him a wrong – possibly earned his contempt in the bargain. Oh, Agnes, my heart aches as I thought it could never ache again. All this is, of course, strictly confidential. I suppose it would be more discreet to lock it up in one's own breast, but I should die if I could not tell someone.

Your sad and affectionate
NORA.

Pembridge Square, January 30th.

My dear Agnes,

This letter reaches you from a very sad and unhappy person, from a person who would hesitate before she swore that square was not round, and that black was not white. Thank you for your reply to my letter, and for the information respecting Mr. Talbot. My sorrow for the distressing incident I confided to you seems to strike you as excessive. The fact is, even you, dear Agnes, do not understand – not, however, through any want of perception on your part – it is I who have never done justice to Mr. Broke in my letters to you.

And now prepare yourself for a shock. Prepare to be surprised, disgusted, disappointed. Perhaps after the confession I am about to make I shall forever have lost my place in your esteem; nevertheless, I am irresistibly compelled to make it. Last night I went to dinner at the Cunliffes' in Cavendish Square. The Cunliffes are not quite in our own set, being, to tell the truth, in a rather better one, but we occasionally dance and dine at one another's houses on the strength of an old friendship between Mamma and Mrs. Cunliffe.

I was very glad to go out. I had been miserable, so strangely miserable all the week, not even daring to confide my woes to those about me; Mamma and my sister would have been very shocked to hear of the "good chance" I had thrown away.

To return to the events of last night, for that it was an eventful evening I think you will own.

"You are late, dear," said Mrs. Cunliffe, rustling forward as I came in in my willow-green dinner-dress, which I know goes well with my hair and complexion, although my people *do* think it hideous. I was beginning some explanation about Mamma and the carriage when suddenly I felt my face flush violently, and my words began to tumble over one another's heels. Fortunately for me, Sybil Juniper came in at the moment, and my hostess went on to her, without, I think, noticing my confusion. Do you know what I saw?

I saw two men talking together by the mantelpiece, of whom one was Stephen Broke, and the other Reginald Talbot!

For the next few minutes life was a dream. In a dream I shook hands with Mr. Talbot and returned Mr. Broke's icy bow. (What right—what right has he to be so cruel, so intolerant, so unjust?) I found myself contemplating the two sharply contrasted figures as though they had been those of a picture or a drama. (Let me say, in justice to my own breeding, that I had taken a chair at a respectful distance from the mantelpiece, and was exchanging dream-syllables with Sybil Juniper.)

Reginald Talbot – tall, graceful, unutterably refined, with that half-dreamy, half-critical air which you know so well – confronted me as an image from my past, nay, from the depths of my own being. He was so familiar and yet so strange. Stephen Broke, with his air of *bien-être,* his wide-awake face (a little pale and stern tonight), his whole presence breathing as unmistakably of London and a full, active life, as did the other's of academic cloisters and refined seclusion – Stephen Broke, I suppose, cut a very sorry figure! Oh, Agnes, Agnes, how shall I tell you? Very soon the shape of the dream shifted a little, and I found myself walking in to dinner on Mr. Talbot's arm, mechanically exchanging polite commonplaces with him. We took our seats at the long, flower-covered table opposite Sybil and Mr. Broke, who were almost invisible behind the leaves of a great green plant. I tried to wake up from the dream. I told myself that this was the moment for which I had been longing with all my being; that here beside me was the man whose image had never left my heart through many weary months of absence; on whose lightest word, on whose smile or frown, my whole existence hung; for whose sake I had thrust away something unutterably great and precious! Oh, Agnes, how can I go on?

I listened to his words, and found them courteous and intelligent; I looked at his face, and saw that it was refined and handsome; but the spell was broken, he was no longer a *presence*, but a *person*. I can tell you exactly the shape of his head, the colour of his eyes, and I may remark that his nose is not so good as I had believed. I was sitting next to Reginald Talbot, talking to him with the greatest ease in the world, meeting his frank glances with glances no less frank, and all the time I was hardly conscious of it! Was vividly conscious, indeed, of nothing save the presence of Stephen Broke on the other side of the table; of the words that he was saying, of the rapid glances that he shot at me from time to time through the big plant.

An awful sense of humiliation, of terror, rushed across me. What had I done? And then it flashed through my mind that here again was the old, old story of substance and shadow!...

I wonder how I got through that dinner – I really do. I know I became suddenly very animated, and quite surprisingly brilliant – a sort of amateur Sydney Smith or Theodore Hook,[19] or any of those people whose friends collect their "table-talk" into big books. Mr. Talbot seemed quite pleasantly surprised; indeed it is rather my impression that I made passionate love to Mr. Talbot!

---

19. Authors Sydney Smith (1771–1845) and Theodore Edward Hook (1788–1841); see Melvyn New, ed., *The Complete Novels and Selected Writings of Amy Levy 1861–1889* (Gainesville: University Press of Florida, 199), 556 n. 11.

He told me what I already knew, that he had given up Cambridge for a term or two on account of his health. We talked of you, and you will be glad to hear that Mr. Dalrymple confided to him that you were the only woman he had ever come across who understood the meaning of fine scholarship. (Don't blush and push up your spectacles in that delighted way, my dear!)

Oh, I wish I cared about fine scholarship! But I don't; I can't; it's no use to pretend I do; and what is worse, I do not think I ever did. Is not this the saddest thing of all? To wake up and find oneself a sham?

Agnes, whatever may be your scorn for me, it cannot exceed my own.

All through that wretched evening the miserable farce went on. Mr. Broke devoted himself to Sybil Juniper (what can such a man find to say to such a girl, I wonder?), and Mr. Talbot establishing himself at my side, displayed an appreciation of my society that would have driven me mad with delight only a few short months ago. But what is Mr. Talbot to me? Nothing – absolutely nothing; a polite nonentity, having no connection with the shadowy creation of my own brain before which I was once pleased to fall down and worship. I have no doubt that he is admirable, all, more than we used to think him; but he is nothing to me. Perhaps I have grown coarser, have fallen away from my own ideals; perhaps I never *was* so superfine as I once believed. "Coarse," "brutal," are not those the words I have frequently thought fit to make use of with regard to a certain person?

I ought to be whipped for a miserable prig; but indeed my punishment is a harder one than whipping

Oh, Agnes, why did I not see it before? Why did you not see it? You must have understood! But it is too late, too late; I have thrown away the most precious treasure a woman can have, and there is no getting it back. If only he would have a little pity on me, only shake hands and be friends! I held out my hand in the hall tonight on my way to the door, but he would not see it, and gave me a deep bow, with his eyes very wide open.

Do you remember poor Guinevere's words? –

> "That passionless perfection, my good lord!
> I wanted life and colour, which I found
> In Lancelot . . ."[20]

Oh, Lancelot, Lancelot,[21] you are very cruel! Excuse these egotistic outpourings. My heart is very full.

Your miserable and ashamed
NORA.

Pembridge Square, April 6th.

My dear Agnes,

Accept my very warmest congratulations on your engagement to Mr. Dalrymple, and my best wishes for that joint edition of Plato, which I fully expect will set the whole world of learning on fire. You cannot, dear, imagine how refreshing it is to hear of happy people; to reflect that after all there is sometimes such a thing as happiness in the world. I have not written before because I have not had the heart; I have been very miserable. After that unhappy evening at the Cunliffes', things got worse and worse. I was continually meeting Mr. Broke, and each time we met only served to confirm to me the discovery I had made too late. There may be better men (personally I don't think there are), but Stephen Broke is the one man in the world for me. Is love blindness or increased vision, I wonder?

As for Mr. Broke, I think he has altogether ceased to regret the answer I gave him that night in the conservatory. I cannot help believing that he was sorry – yes, really sorry – at first, and that his very pronounced delight in the society of Sybil Juniper was not quite genuine. It is genuine enough now. He is always with her, is always to be found where she goes.

20. A misquote of Alfred, Lord Tennyson's poem, "Lancelot and Elaine" (New, ed., *The Complete Novels*, 556 n. 12).

21. Refers to Lancelot, a knight of King Arthur's Round Table.

Is constancy confined to the dull people, to the Dobbins of this great Vanity Fair,[22] I wonder? But who am I to talk of constancy?

As chance would have it, I saw a great deal of Reginald Talbot during his stay in London. The Fates, who are vulgar enough to enjoy a practical joke, decreed that I, of whose presence he had formerly seemed supremely unconscious, should suddenly become to him an object of some interest.

He is not in our set, but I saw him continually in Cavendish Square (Mrs. Cunliffe suddenly acquired a sort of *grande passion* for me!), and when the Cunliffes went to Torquay last month they invited me to accompany them. Reginald Talbot, who is some connection and a great favourite, was also one of the party.

Oh, Agnes, we have often and often talked about the irony of Fate, but never before had I realised it to its full extent. Here was I walking with, talking with, passing my whole days in the society of a person, to catch a glimpse of whose unresponsive face I would once have walked from China to Peru. And now that he was here, continually beside me – now that his face was by no means unresponsive – I could have seen him depart forever without a pang; nay, I could have hailed his departure with delight, if it had been followed by the arrival of another person, on whom, at one time, I was wont, forsooth, to look down; whom I was fond of reproaching with a want of superfineness. And yet, even viewed dispassionately, Mr. Talbot is undoubtedly a pleasant and worthy person. He is cultivated, generous, kindly, intelligent; nevertheless, I was always conscious of a certain want in him.

Perhaps it is that his atmosphere is too rarefied for me, but do you know that he struck me at times as crude, colourless, a little cramped and academic? He is altogether too much in one's own notation, as you would phrase it. A woman likes to be deferred to, to have her ideas treated respectfully; but on the other hand, she likes to be taken possession of, regulated, magnificently and tenderly scorned, even, at times. We have been slaves so long that we rather

22. Captain William Dobbin, a character in William Makepeace Thackeray's *Vanity Fair* (1847–1848); see New, ed., *The Complete Novels*, 556 n. 13.

enjoy, metaphorically speaking, the application of a little brute force on the part of our lords and masters.

Don't faint, Agnes! and pray have a little mercy on Mr. Dalrymple. When there is a dispute about the Plato commentaries, whose version will be adopted? Do you not perceive that I am growing very sportive – quite "gamesome," as Orlando puts it? –

> "But if I laugh at any mortal thing,
> 'Tis that I may not weep …."[23]

Ha, ha! I wax Byronic! Take my merriment for what it is worth, and let me proceed.

In spite, then, of the kindness of the Cunliffes and the very real pleasure I had in the society of Mr. Talbot, I was very miserable down at Torquay. I used to read "Felise"[24] almost every night, and cry over it about as often, especially over one verse:

> "Let this be said between us here:
> One love grows green when one turns grey;
> This year knows nothing of last year;
> Tomorrow has no more to say
> To yesterday."

Is it not a terrible poem? and yet I think it is the story of many women's lives.

The day after I got home, a sad and surprising event happened. I received a letter from Mr. Talbot asking me to be his wife. I cannot tell you how it distressed and disturbed me. Perhaps my first feeling was one of profound irritation at the sorry trick the Fates had been playing me. Last year, if it were only last year! I thought and re-read the letter, which was indeed a model of fine feeling and delicate taste.

---

23. Taken from Lord (George Gordon) Byron's *Don Juan*; see New, ed., *The Complete Novels*, 556 n. 14.
24. Algernon Charles Swinburne's poem, "Félise" (see New, ed., *The Complete Novels*, 556 n. 15).

Was I to send away love for the second time? – The love of a good and upright man? Who knows how one's feelings may change?

Women generally *do* get to love their husbands more or less after a time, provided only the absence of certain positive evil qualities. This, as you know, is a doctrine I have always hated as unworthy of people with minds and souls, but now I found myself seriously considering it.

I had lost all faith in myself, my feelings, and even my "soul." Mr. Talbot will never know the narrow escape he had of being accepted. Finally I put the letter in my pocket and deferred answering it. I was going to a musical party that evening and would give myself time to consider it. The musical party decided me.

Stephen Broke was there, and, for the first time since *that night,* he came up and shook hands with me. I saw at a glance that Richard was himself again;[25] he was politely cordial, though if anything a shade quieter than usual, but perhaps that was from an instinctive impulse not to indecently flaunt his newly-found freedom in my face. And it is only two months ago since – But we move very rapidly in London.

But however that may be, I knew from the moment I touched his hand and looked into his face, that Reginald Talbot's fate was decided. If, after what has happened, I did not shrink from making any positive assertion about myself, I should say that Stephen Broke is not only the one man that I *can,* but also the one man that I have ever loved. One cannot love a shadow, you must acknowledge. I did not speak to Mr. Broke again that night – he was on the stairs with Sybil Juniper the whole time – but when I reached home I sat down and wrote off my letter unhesitatingly. I am sorry if I have given pain to anyone so good and noble as Mr. Talbot; but the pain cannot, I think, be of long duration. He will see that he has made a mistake, that I was never worthy of him.

---

25. According to New (*The Complete Novels,* 556, n. 16) this line is either in reference to William Shakespeare's *Richard III,* Andrew Lang's "A New Shakespeare," or Colley Cibber's (1671–1757) 1699 version of *Richard III* (the latter probably inspiring Lang).

Oh, Agnes, do you smile at my pitiable plight? I confess myself that I cannot help smiling a little sometimes, though the situation is tragic enough.

In plain English, I have played the fool, and I am suffering for it. Between my two stools I have fallen most woefully to the ground. I dare say I shall get up again one day, and that even all trace of the bruises will have vanished, but that sort of reflection does not console one very much at the time.

Meanwhile I am left stranded. Everyone is talking of the approaching engagement of Mr. Broke to Sybil Juniper; and Mr. Talbot has started for Rome.

You have had my full and free confession, and doubtless hold your own opinions, have come to your own conclusions on the subject. But I should not like you to think that I am broken-hearted; by no means; I am only disgusted, sorry, and just a little sick of everything.

My best regards and best wishes to Mr. Dalrymple.

Your humbled and saddened
NORA.

P.S. – Oh, how my heart *does* ache in spite of the philosophic views! Heartache is worse than toothache even, and you know what Shakespeare says about that. – N. W.[26]

---

26. The reference is to Shakespeare's *Much Ado About Nothing*: "'there was never yet a philosopher / That could endure the toothache patiently'" (quoted in New, ed., *The Complete Novels*, 557 n. 17).

The Diary of a Plain Girl (1883)

May 20th. – It's a shame and a shame! I can't feel like the girls in books, and it's no use trying! You know what the plain girls in books do. Why, they are just resigned and cheerful, and think that nothing matters about themselves. "I'm only Jane or Susan or Martha," they say (they have always got that sort of name), "and all that I care for in the world is my beautiful darling, my sweet sister Rosamund!" Now I don't feel a bit like that about Dahlia. I don't think it fair that because her hair's yellow and mine is no colour in particular, and because her face is pink and white and mine isn't; in short, because she is the best-looking girl in town, and I am about the plainest, I don't think it fair, I say, that she should always have the best of everything. I want things as much as Dahlia. Why can't people's wants be proportioned to their power of getting what they want, I wonder? Mamma and Dahlia and everybody seem to think that *mine* are, or at least ought to be. Dahlia always says to me after parties, "Was it not quite too delightful?" To which I generally reply, "No, it was horrid!" And everyone thinks me cross.

Mamma and Aunt Alicia are continually advising me to read and improve my mind. Nobody advises Dahlia to improve *her* mind. O dear, what a horrid girl I am! I ought to be cheerful and content, and pleased with other people's good fortune, I suppose. But I am not resigned, not the least bit in the world. O, I wish I were not so wicked! Tonight I think I hated Dahlia. It was only for a moment;

but I hated her. She came in, half an hour ago, in her dressing gown, and wanted to "talk it over." I was sitting by the fire, with my dress on, just as I had flung myself down when we first came home, and I wasn't feeling lively. Dahlia looked so beautiful in her clinging pink gown, with all her hair falling about her face like a golden mist, that I could have cried. And her face was so soft and pink and smiling, and her eyes so bright, that I could have fallen on her neck and kissed her. But I hated her all the time. She came up to me and knelt by the fire, and began to laugh softly to herself, as she often does when she's pleased.

"O Milly, Milly, wasn't it a nice party?" she said.

I looked down at her, and moved my chair back an inch or two.

"It was a *beast* of a party!" I called out.

Dahlia was extremely shocked. I knew she would be, and that is why I said it. She got up at once, and sailed out of the room, looking severely good and proper. Dahlia always manages to be in the right. I had the worst of it again, as usual. I began to hate myself worse than I had been hating Dahlia. But really it was very hard for me tonight at Lady Chigwell's. Everyone said it was going to be *the* dance of the season, and that a very great personage was to be present. Dahlia was mad about going, and about her new dress from White's. I had not a new dress, and I thought I did not want to go; but when it came to the last I found that I did. I could not help feeling pleased and excited, though I knew it was of no use. Ralston Owens sent us both flowers. They came just when we were dressed. Dahlia laughed to herself, and said she wondered if candles didn't feel a little sorry sometimes for the poor burnt moths. How dare she talk like that? Mr. Owens is worth ten of her other lords-in-waiting.

Mamma and Aunt Alicia were ready dressed in the hall when we came down. They made Dahlia turn round and round to show her dress. It was a white one, soft, with lots of lace and real roses. Mamma and Auntie nodded at one another approvingly, whispering and smiling; and Dahlia said,

"Nobody has noticed my bouquet. Mr. Owens sent it."

"One of the Clanmore Owens?" asked Aunt Alicia, looking like a wise old owl, inappropriately clad in green satin and diamonds.

"No, dear, one of the Yorkshire Owens of Ralston Towers, you know. His father is Sir Henry Owens. *She* was one of the Beauchamp Ralstons, you remember."

"Yes, yes, to be sure," said Aunt Alicia, nodding again. Then she suddenly chose to become aware of me for the first time. "What, you too, Milly? Did Mr. Owens send you a bouquet too?"

"Yes, wasn't it kind of him?" said Dahlia, bending her triumphant golden head over the flowers in her hand. Mamma and Auntie began a sort of duet with alternating lines, like people in an opera.

"How exceedingly kind of him!"

"You must remember to thank him, Milly."

"So nice and thoughtful."

"Mr. Owens never forgets anyone."

I didn't say anything, but I could have thrown the bouquet at their heads and knocked the feathers off. It was as much as I could do to get quietly into the carriage. Why couldn't they mind their own business? Crowds of people were already there when we got to Lady Chigwell's. The place was full of light and jewels and bright colours, of sweet cool scents and gay sounds. It took us nearly five minutes to get upstairs; there was such a crush, and people kept on stopping us to get a chance for Dahlia's programme. The band was playing "Dolores" when we reached the drawing room, and everyone looked so happy and nice. I began to feel perfectly wild. I tried to keep myself under, as it were, but it was no good. There was a mirror just facing us as we went up to say "How do you do?" to Lady Chigwell, and I saw two figures reflected in it for a moment – a tall Dahlia in white, and a short Milly in blue; but I turned away my head. I wasn't going to look when I felt so rampant. Of course Dahlia was absorbed in an instant. I caught a glimpse of golden hair and white lace, apparently the centre of a crowd of black-coated figures, each of whom appeared to be making violent efforts to get hold of a little white-and-gold book, which was circulating among them.

I had just such another white-and-gold book in my hand, but nobody seemed particularly anxious to secure it. Jack Dale and Charley Coates, and one or two others, sauntered up and put down their names for waltzes. My spirits sank rapidly enough. Things were going as they usually did with me, as I knew they would. I tried to dance with those dull awkward boys, who kept treading on my toes or tearing my dress; and every now and then I found myself sitting by Mamma and Aunt Alicia. I don't think the saddest music ever composed can be half so sad as waltz music when you're not waltzing, only looking on at other people. It beats all the funeral marches and dirges and requiems in the world. It is torture music, and the happy people dancing round are torturers, exquisitely cruel torturers. Once, when I hadn't a partner, Alfred Chigwell brought up a sort of boy and introduced him. He was very plain and quite stupid, but he seemed to think it a great hardship for him and a great honour for me. I heard him telling another man afterwards "that Alfred had been trotting out the 'wallflowers' for his benefit all the blessed night, and that he couldn't stand much more of this sort of thing." Ugly fool! Who wanted him?

It got worse as the evening wore on. Mamma and Aunt Alicia went down to supper. Mamma made me come with her and Uncle William: as if I could have eaten anything! When we came up again in about half an hour we found Aunt Alicia already at her post. She had her eyeglass up, and her green feathers were nodding.

"Who's that young man with Dahlia?" she said; "they seem to be always dancing together."

"O, that's Lord Linfield!" answered Mamma, trying not to appear pleased.

"And the one who is speaking to her now? He only came in a moment ago. The pale young man, with a moustache?"

I turned my head in Dahlia's direction. I didn't wait to hear Mamma's well-known formula – "That's Ralston Owens – Sir Henry Owens of the Towers, you know. *She* is one of the Beauchamp Ralstons." Aunt Alicia's description – not very graphic, perhaps – was enough. Yes, there he was, standing by the doorway with Dahlia and Lord Linfield. I wonder why he came so late? I had thought he could not be coming at all. Of course he went straight up to Dahlia. I saw her hold up her programme and shake her head. She thinks herself very fine, refusing to dance with him, I daresay. He looked ever so much nicer than Lord Linfield. Lord Linfield is called Adonis in his regiment, I believe; he's six foot high, with pink cheeks and a straight nose, lots of moustache, and no forehead. I like a sensible manly face, with a head that looks as though it had brains inside; and I don't care for your very tall men. I hoped Ralston would not see me; I tried to get behind Aunt Alicia's green satin, but it was not any good; he came up to us at once – I knew he would. There's a proverb about a rose and some clay,[27] which I couldn't help thinking of.

"Will you give me the next dance, Miss Milly?" said Mr. Owens, when he had shaken hands all round.

I was tired – O, how tired! – of that rout-seat. But I wasn't going to be taken pity on by Ralston Owens. "No, thank you; I am not dancing," I said, and turned away my face. O, I am ashamed to write it down. All my face had grown red – red as fire – and I felt a sort of lump in my throat. O, if he saw! He sat down next to me. I thought he looked a little pale and sad; his face is always grave. How *dare* Dahlia not dance with him?

"Have you thanked Mr. Owens for your flowers?" said Aunt Alicia.

"Thank you for the flowers," I said very crossly, because I was nearly crying.

He smiled.

"You'd better come down and have some supper," he returned, by way of answer.

"I've been down."

27. The "proverb" that Levy is probably referring to goes as follows: "O beautiful royal Rose, / O Rose so fair and sweet! / Queen of the garden art thou, / And I – the Clay at thy feet!"; this short poem was written by Julia Dorr (1825–1913); see J.K. Hoyt and Anna Ward, *The Cyclopaedia of Practical Quotations* (New York: I.K. Funk and Co. Publishers, 1882), 152.

I was getting ruder and ruder. What right had he, or anyone else, to patronise me? He didn't speak for a long time after that, and at last he got up and went away.

Mamma was getting cross and sleepy. She and Aunt Alicia yawned and yawned, like the traditional chasm. They both began to scold me. "Hadn't I even manners?" cried Mamma.

"And Mr. Owens, who had been so kind about the flowers!" snapped Auntie.

All this time the hideous gay music went on uninterruptedly. We stayed late, as we always do. Once, when Mamma rose to go, Dahlia came up and said,

"O Milly! let's beg for one more waltz. I could go on all night! Couldn't you?"

I didn't say anything at all, and Aunt Alicia scolded me again.

Well, I'm home at last, and thank goodness, I'm beginning to get sleepy over this old scribbling. When I'm asleep I shall be just as well off as Dahlia or anyone. I wish I could go to sleep and never wake. Why, it's quite light! How cold my feet are!

May 21st. – I felt ashamed of myself somehow when I woke this morning. I carried Dahlia's breakfast into her room, and tried not to think about anything. Mamma called me downstairs, and lectured me after breakfast. She said I was a disgrace to the family and her training. That I had no more breeding than a housemaid. That a woman who is not beautiful has her own career to make. That a well-bred and charming woman can always hold her own in society, whatever be her physical disadvantages. O, it's all very well to talk! Ought one to go on smiling and smiling at grumpy people, and talking and talking to people who are giving you one-tenth of their attention, and striving and striving to be noticed, when no one is in the least conscious of your presence! O, I wish it were last year, and I were seventeen again! Perhaps when I am twenty-five I shall be resigned and chastened, and shall not want things any more. But I don't want to be twenty-five.

The weather was glorious today. I cried and cried after Mamma's lecture; then I opened the window and looked out. The air was soft and sweet; the sky was all blue and silver; the Park opposite so brilliantly, yet so delicately green; there were some birds singing, and some people passing on horseback. I began to long and long worse than ever. I think I always want things most in the spring, when the weather is fine. Presently Dahlia came in in her riding-habit. She wore a bunch of violets, and was very fresh and smiling. I thought she looked like a vision of spring, standing with the light from the window full on her face, wrapped round in sunbeams and an odour of violets.

"I'm going to ride, Milly," she said. "I suppose you will be in the Row with Mamma?"

"You know I hate the Row," I said. I did not mean to be cross, but somehow I could not help it.

When Dahlia had gone I shut the window and pulled down the blind. I wanted to forget that there was anything beautiful, anything worth having in the world. The Row indeed! With the beautiful contented people walking about and making one *ache* with admiration and loneliness! I thought I would try to improve my mind. Ugly girls generally go a great deal to church, or pass examinations, or visit poor people. I hate churches and clergymen, I shouldn't know what to say to a poor person when I had got to his house, and I am not even a clever girl. I made a plunge at Mill's *Political Economy,* but the Wages Fund got mixed up with the Row, and I could not take in the advantages of Division of Labour[28] for wondering who Dahlia was riding with. I went down to the library for a more interesting book; I met Ralston Owens in the hall. He had ridden over with a message from his mother, asking us to join their picnic tomorrow. He's always coming here for something or other.

I felt ashamed to see him after last night. I hoped he had forgotten my crossness; people do not generally remember anything about me, excepting that I am Dahlia's sister.

---

28. The philosopher and politician, John Stuart Mill (1806–1873); the "Division of Labour" and "Wage Fund" are discussed in his *Principles of Political Economy* (1848).

"Dahlia's gone to the Row," I said, when we had shaken hands. "And you?"

"I am going into the library to choose an improving book."

He laughed; his eyes have the most beautiful expression when he laughs. It really is very strange when one comes to think of it; taken feature by feature, and limb by limb, Mr. Owens isn't at all handsome, but he has the trick of seeming better-looking *as a whole* than anyone else. I wonder how he manages it?

"Miss Milly," he said, "am I a Philistine if I suggest that a day like this is more improving than all the books that were ever written?"

"I hate fine weather, Mr. Owens."

"I don't believe you, Miss Milly."

He followed me into the library, and said "Might he help me choose a book?" I thought again about the rose and the clay. I never yet knew a young man who wasn't glad of a chance of hanging about the house. We had a long talk. He said there was only one set of hopeless people in the world – the people who were satisfied with themselves. He said that bad people who tried to be good often turned out the best of all. But I don't think by badness he meant envy and crossness and hatred. I don't believe he quite knows what meanness is. I began to forget all about Dahlia, till she came in, and then I wished I was dead. Mamma came in too, and asked Ralston to lunch. I hoped he would not stay, but he said "Yes," at once. I kept on wishing I was dead all lunchtime. He and Dahlia talked and talked. Dahlia chose to be very gracious; she had heard about the picnic from Lord Linfield this morning. "How delightful! How kind of Lady Owens!" she said.

When Mr. Owens had gone Dahlia began to walk about the room, smiling to herself. "He waited all the morning, Milly?" she said once. "Poor, poor Ralston!" How *dare* she? Can't even Dahlia see what he is?

May 22nd. – If there's a thing I hate, it's a picnic. Now, at dances and "at homes," if nobody wants you, there you are—you know what to expect all the evening. It isn't pleasant – it's hateful, but not the most hateful thing of all. At a picnic you must always be doing something; there is no sitting still and making up one's mind to the worst.

I wonder if anywhere there can be a worse torture than tramping along with a grumpy person who has got fastened on to you somehow, and is wild with crossness at the event; or with a polite person bored to death and vexed, but trying hard to conceal his feelings, while you see his eyes roving round in search for means of escape, or dwelling longingly on somebody else's bonnet in front?

It is bad enough, too, though not so bad as the other thing, to trudge along a little way behind with two people who have forgotten all about you, or wish you were somewhere else.

The best hope that a picnic holds out to people like me is to get mixed up with the chaperones, and even they would rather be without one. When I was dressed this morning for the Owens' picnic I made up my mind to face the worst, and take a long look in the glass. (I never look in the glass, on principle, before going out – it's too depressing.) At first it wasn't so bad as I expected. I saw an ordinary little girl enough in a plain hat and frock; nothing to excite notice one way or the other. And then Dahlia came in behind and put her head over my shoulder, and my face looked gray – positively gray – like a mouse, and I seemed to shrivel up into a sort of dwarf. Dahlia had on a big hat with real roses under the brim, and a pink cambric gown, all lace and embroidery and bunches of ribbon. "Is it fair? Is it fair?" I thought, and turned away from the glass.

We got to Waterloo Station at about ten. Everyone was waiting on the platform. Lord Linfield was there, and he made for our party at once, and so did Ralston Owens. Mrs. Morton, the new beauty, was present, and she and Dahlia rushed, figuratively, into each other's arms, utterly ignoring the eager little throng of men who hovered about them.

We got out at Leatherhead Station. Carriages had been ordered to meet us, but there were not enough for us all, so the younger members of the party had to walk on to Box Hill. First, we paired off for the walk. Lord Linfield made a rush at Dahlia at once; but when she saw him coming, she turned to Ralston, who was standing near me, and proposed that he and she should lead the way. Of course, Ralston was off like a shot. Everybody else went off in twos, until there was no one left but Lord Linfield and me. We looked at one another blankly for a minute, then I walked a step or two forward; he slouched up to my side; and finally, we found ourselves walking drearily along, making (O satire!) to the outside eye another link in the chain of amorous "Pärchen." It *was* a little comic, I can't help owning.

It was very, very hot, and the way was hilly. We trudged along doggedly and almost in silence. Once Lord Linfield said, "It's a very fine day;" and I answered, "Yes; so fortunate!" – which, I think, was about the sum of our conversation. How we hated one another! His lordship's pink and white face looked absolutely black; and I don't think he ever once moved his eyes from Dahlia's hat-brim at the head of the little procession. It was some consolation to me to reflect that I was hating *him* quite as much as he did *me*, and I couldn't help despising him a little bit at the same time. Why couldn't he go the other side of Dahlia instead of sulking with people who didn't want him?

After lunch we all got up for a walk. Dahlia and Mrs. Morton became at once the centres of two little groups of would-be escorts. I was standing a step or two off with Ada Coates.

"Mr. Owens," called out Dahlia's clear voice, "you promised to show me that view you were telling me about."

Ralston, who was talking to Mamma, sprang up and went over to Dahlia. They went down the hill, together with Alfred Chigwell and Mrs. Morton and a few others, Lord Linfield following slowly behind – sullen and offended, but still following. I continued to stand by the tree. Ella Chigwell and Ada Coates were conferring in whispers on the other side.

"She's playing a dangerous game," said Ada.

"What game?" asked Ella, who is rather stupid.

"Don't you see? She's dying to hook Lord Linfield, and she's playing off Ralston Owens against him."

I moved away; I was feeling sick at heart.

I got mixed up in a party with Ella Chigwell and the Dale boys. We roved about aimlessly enough. I kept a little behind, while Ella chattered away to Jack and Tom; I suppose they were enjoying themselves, but it sounded very stupid. I fell behind altogether at last, and sat down under a tree; I knew I shouldn't be missed. I sat there, and thought and thought. I wondered if Ada Coates's spiteful remark about Dahlia could be true. And then I fell to wondering about things in general – about justice and injustice, goodness and badness, happiness and unhappiness. I think I got quite a philosopher under that tree. "Nothing matters," I said at last aloud; then I threw myself on the grass and sobbed. I knew it *did* matter, awfully; I knew I cared about things with all my heart and soul. When at last I got up I saw that all the sky had grown gray, and a dull wind came whistling through the trees. I plodded back to the trysting-place, cold and weary. When I got there, it was deserted! Even the chaperones and lunch-baskets had vanished. I looked at my watch, and saw that it was a quarter past the time appointed for the general meeting. A feeling of fear, wretchedness, and indignation passed over me. I had been forgotten! Looking up, I perceived a scattered band of people disappearing down the hill. It was my own fault about being left behind, perhaps; but I felt very injured.

"O, why can't I stay here and die, like the Children in the Wood?"[29] I thought. "Why must I always go where I am not wanted?"

It began to rain – a chill sharp rain that slapped one's face spitefully. I set off down the hill. I was nearly crying with weariness and an awful sense of loneliness. I seemed to see the world and all the people and all the planets on one side, and myself on the other, fighting with them, struggling for my wretched little existence.

Someone came running very quickly up the hill – a man, with a cloak on his arm. It was Ralston Owens, and he came up to me and caught my hand.

---

29. See "Babes in the Wood; Or, The Norfolk Tragedy," in Thomas Ingoldsby, *The Ingoldsby Legends or Myths and Marvels* (London: Richard Bentley & Son, 1879), 350–6.

"Miss Milly, do you know what a fright you have given us? I understood you had gone on in front with the Dales, until I saw Jack just now."

He looked so noble and kind and gentle as he stood there; I felt he was like an angel from heaven who had come down to save me. I could not trust myself to speak; my lips were quivering; there was a lump in my throat.

He wrapped the cloak around me, and fastened it with his dear clever fingers. I was trembling all over, and then a terrible thing happened – I couldn't really help it – a big tear rolled over my eyelid, and fell on to his hand. O, I hope – I hope he thought it was the rain! He didn't seem to notice it.

We walked slowly down the hill. He made me take his arm. I felt wonderfully warm and safe and protected. I don't think if a dragon with flaming jaws had rushed out on us, I should have been frightened.

"Mr. Owens," I ventured to say at last, "it's cold and raining, and you haven't an overcoat." I know how easily he takes cold, poor darling!

"One could hardly calculate on such weather, even in an English May," he answered lightly.

"Mr. Owens," I said rather breathlessly, and growing very red, "I wish you would put on my silk handkerchief; I'm quite, quite warm in the cloak – really." I had a white silk handkerchief knotted loosely round my throat, which I pulled off with the disengaged hand and held out to him.

He took it quite gravely, thanked me, and tied it round his throat.

We went on rather silently. I wished the walk would never end. I had forgotten all about Dahlia.

"Miss Milly," he said at last, with a sudden earnestness in voice and manner, "I want to ask you a very special question. I've been wanting to ask it you all day."

My heart stood still; my short-lived joy died out. I knew what was coming – it had come so often before: Could I – did I know anything of the state of my sister's feelings? Would I exert all my influence in the suppliant's behalf? Would I keep him informed on certain matters from time to time, etc.? I had borne up patiently enough under this vicarious love-making; but today I felt I could not, would not, bear it. I would keep this one walk at least unspoiled in my memory; it might be the only good thing I should have in my life, but I was determined to have it.

"Mr. Owens," I cried foolishly, "it is so wet, we had better get on."

"I want you to answer my question, Miss Milly."

"O Mr. Owens," I said desperately, "don't – don't ask me any questions now. I will answer anything you like tomorrow, only not now."

I suppose something in my voice told him how terribly in earnest I was. I daresay he thought me mad, but he did not say anything about the question again.

So I have taken one beautiful thing into my life, a precious treasure for evermore. I shall always be a lonely woman, I suppose; but I have walked over the Downs for more than an hour alone with Ralston Owens. I have had something worth living for. Mr. Owens forgot to give me back the handkerchief. I wish I had it. I hope he will not send it to be washed.

Dahlia knocked at the door an hour ago, and I pretended to be asleep. I *could* not see her tonight.

O, if only – if only –

May 23rd. – Something very wonderful has happened today; so wonderful that I cannot believe that this is the same world and the same room and the same girl as yesterday. (The grammar of that sentence is a little strange, I know; but I'm too happy to mind about grammar.) How can I write it down – this wonderful thing which is singing and singing in my heart, but which I have not the courage to put into words?

Ralston Owens likes me best – better than Dahlia – than anyone in the world, he says. It is very strange. I cannot understand it at all; but I am so happy that I do not know what to do.

I was very miserable when I got up this morning. I felt flat and gray after yesterday's sad little bit of happiness. Dahlia was cross and tired, and Mamma scolded me for "hiding myself away" at the picnic, and giving Mr. Owens the trouble of fetching me. We were a wretched breakfast party.

After breakfast I went to my room and tried to read. I don't think I understood a word, though I followed the printed lines and turned over the pages. I could think of nothing but that walk over the Downs.

"O, it isn't fair – it can't be fair!" I cried out at last, shutting up the book and rising from my chair. "Starved bodies die and are at peace; but a starved soul will go on living and living, getting hungrier and hungrier as the years go by. How often have I seen such a soul peering out of a pair of unlovely eyes in a woman's plain and withered face! I shall grow to look like those gray, sad women one sees everywhere about, I suppose – unnoticed sort of creatures, sitting wearily in the world's corners. Sometimes they are cross and sour, and sometimes resigned and patient. I *won't* be patient. I won't acquiesce in my fate. I've as much right to be happy as Dahlia or anyone else."

Someone knocked suddenly at the door, and Mamma came in, looking very solemn and important.

"Milly," she said, "brush your hair and make yourself tidy; someone wishes to speak to you in the library."

Then she went away without a word.

I lingered some moments outside the library door, with my hand on the handle. I felt a vague sort of terror; Mamma had been so mysterious and oracular.

When, at last, I summoned courage to open the door and walk into the room, I saw someone standing by the window with his back towards me. It was Ralston Owens, and my heart began to beat very fast. He came forward at once, and took my hand, smiling, but not speaking.

My heart was beating faster and faster.

"How do you do, Mr. Owens?" I said.

He took both my hands into his, but he did not smile this time.

"Milly, I have come to ask you that question you would not listen to yesterday."

I looked up at him, and our eyes met. A wonderful revelation flashed over me. I understood it all in a moment.

What followed I cannot write. One cannot write such things even in one's diary.

I am no longer curious as to how people feel in heaven. I know now.

We had to go to Aunt Alicia's dance tonight, and when Ralston and I were waiting for Mamma and Dahlia before starting, I could not help asking him if he minded my being plain. He took my hand, and led me up to the glass. I was surprised at the face which greeted me; my cheeks were rosy, my eyes were bright, I was *almost* nice looking. Was Ralston a magician? I thought; and then I remembered that Dahlia was not there.

"Ralston, are you sure you do not mind?"

"I'm bearing up under the affliction, Milly."

"And you won't be sorry when people compare me with Dahlia?"

"I shall be very proud of my beautiful sister, but I shall love my wife too much to know that she is anything but herself."

"Ralston, really, really, I can't believe it!"

But, strange to say, in a few short hours I have grown to believe it; it seems the most natural thing in the world, as though we had belonged to one another from the beginning of all time. I would not change with Dahlia or anyone. I am glad I am not beautiful, excepting for Ralston's sake, and he says he doesn't mind.

O, I hope, I hope I shall be a good wife to him. I think that being good will be the easiest thing in the world now. I feel so safe and sure and strong. Dahlia may sneer at a girl who is so happy over her one lover; but how can I mind about anything now, seeing that I possess the best, the most precious, and, alas, the rarest thing in the world?

Sokratics in the Strand (1884)

τί δῆτ᾽ ἐμοὶ ζῆν κέρδος; … …
… … κρείσσον γὰρ εἰσάπαξ θανεῖν,
ἢ τὰς ἁπάσας ἡμέρας πάσχειν κακῶς.[30]
Prom. Vinct. 1. 747.

"I do assure you, Whipple, if I knew a safe and perfectly painless way of popping out of this world into some comfortable quarters in the next, I'd do it."

TOM COBB[31]

It was half-past nine when Vincent, emerging from the gate of the Temple, proceeded to thread his eager way through the crowded mazes of the Strand.

Yellow-haired, shrill-voiced women were jostling one another along the pavement; young men of the type known as "masher" hung about the bar-room and theatre entrances; and the newsboys were

30. The quotation is from Aeschylus' *Prometheus Bound*; New, using the Loeb Classical Library version, translated the quotation as follows: "What gain have I than in life … Better it were to die once and for all than linger out all my days in misery" (quoted in *The Complete Novels*, 557 n. 18). Levy's source is most probably R. H. Mather's *The Prometheus Bound of Aeschylus* (Boston: John Allyn, 1883), 42; this source has informed the text.

31. W.S. Gilbert's play, *Tom Cobb or, Fortune's Toy*, which opened in 1875; *Tom Cobb* is also referred to in "Cohen of Trinity" (pp. 832–40).

calling out the latest news with a grim emulation of horrors: "Terrible Railway Accident," bawled *Globe*; "Double Murder in Mile End," yelled *Echo*; "Loss of 2,000 Lives," shrieked *Evening Standard*, vague but triumphant.

Vincent, moving in the eager, persistent fashion peculiar to him, deftly worked his way through these flowers of fashion and waifs of doom, till he reached the opening of a small passage not far from Charing Cross Station. The passage was dark and narrow, but Vincent dived into its depths with a certain air of usage, nor did he pause till he found himself before a gloomy contracted house at the further end. The house was in darkness, save where a light burned from one of the lower windows and another glimmered faintly from an attic above. Mounting one little flight of steps, Vincent knocked vigorously though not clamorously at the door.

The light from the solitary streetlamp opposite fell on him as he stood there in his evening dress, light overcoat and lustreless black hat; a tall spare frame, not robust nor largely moulded, but sinewy, and suggestive of immense reserves of strength; shoulders that stooped a little; the face, of a healthy pallor, clean-shaven, save for the neat and sparse "legal" whisker; the features well-cut and large; the mouth flexible and eminently forensic; the eyes shrewd and strong, also forensic. He looked, indeed, what he was, – an active and successful young barrister.

Scarcely had the echo of his knock died away in the little passage, when the door was flung open and a figure appeared in the gloomy entry. "Hullo, Vincent?" questioned a man's voice; the tones were despondent, but curiously shrill.

"Yes, 'tis I. I thought I'd look you up as I happened to be passing." Vincent's distinct clear-cut accents sounded with contrasting cheerfulness. Making their way through the narrow hall, the two men turned into a small, low room where a lamp was burning on a table by the window. Vincent took possession of a chair by the table; there were books on it, besides the lamp, and pens and paper and a half-filled jar of birdseye. "Well my Cicero,"[32] said the owner of the room, moving about rather restlessly, "and how wags the world with you? Do we see our way to the woolsack as clearly as ever?"

Vincent laughed, removed his hat, and passed his fine flexible hand across his eyes: "My dear Horace, I'm almost fagged out! What with being in Court all day and finding something that must be done when he gets back to Chambers, a barrister's life is not a happy one. I only found time to get something to eat – a chop at the 'Rainbow' an hour ago, and I expect to be at it again when I get home tonight."

"Poor fellow!" said Horace, with mock compassion, "and what necessitates this enduing of war paint?" He indicated Vincent's costume with a wave of his hand, and taking up the hat from the table, became completely absorbed in opening and shutting it.

"O, I'm going to dance with the Philistines at Kensington. It brushes the cobwebs away, and is good for one's work. My dear fellow, you don't look up to the mark." Vincent leaned back as he spoke, then suddenly stretched forward and put out his hand: "Horace, let me know the worst at once; – *what*, precisely, are your designs on my hat?"

The person addressed stopped in the midst of his aimless wanderings, laid down the unfortunate gibus with a laugh, and leaning up against the chimney piece, proceeded to relight his pipe. He was an undersized, slightly-built man of from five to seven-and-twenty. His head, rather large for the frame supporting it, was well-set and of singularly beautiful shape, as were also the thin, nervous hands; his longish hair was cut and combed with an evident eye to effect, and the fine throat had a trick of lifting itself as though for the benefit of an imaginary spectator. There were marks of ill-health in the unnatural brightness of his eyes and the pallor of his face, and suggestions of poverty both in the bare, small room and its furniture, and the faded fantastic dressing-gown which served him for costume. "Not up to

32. The Roman senator and philosopher, Cicero.

the mark?" he said, in reply to Vincent's exclamation; "about up to my usual mark, I should say."

"Well, and what's the news?" Vincent affected to ignore the last observation.

"They've returned me my comedy for the 'Bijou,'[33] and Biggs of the *Luminary* says he's had enough of the 'Social Sketches.'"

Vincent tapped the table softly with his trim fingernails; then, "Shall I be honest with you?" he said. "I think if you worked more, and more steadily, that these sort of things wouldn't happen."

"My dear fellow, it's all very well for a nicely-constructed bit of mechanism like yourself to talk," answered Horace, with a short laugh; "the truth is, you successful experiments of creation don't understand the difficulties of us failures. 'Steady work!' What wouldn't we give to be able to work steadily, we unfortunate victims of the 'poetic temperament' without the poetry? We 'martyrs by the pang without the palm,' and all that?"[34]

"This is pure nonsense, Horace, and you know it is. You are wasting your life and your health, not to speak of your money. Make an effort before it is too late."

"It was too late from the beginning, old man."

"Don't be a fool. I don't think I ever knew anyone with fairer chances at starting. You know what we all thought of you at Cambridge."

"Oh, I'm quite aware that appearances are against me. I'm a striking instance of the Irony of Fate, of the little rift within the lute, the little speck in garnered fruit, etc.,"[35] and Horace laughed rather bitterly as he spoke. "Yes, I know," he went on more gravely, "that if the scale had dipped ever so little to the other side all would have been very different. The grapes of Tantalus[36] are the only fruit the gods have given me.

33. Theatre.

34. The quotation is taken from Elizabeth Barrett Browning's "The Cry of the Children."

35. The line is from Tennyson's "Merlin and Vivien" in *Idylls of the King* (New, ed., *The Complete Novels*, 557 n. 23).

36. Figure of ancient Greek mythology.

I can smell them, and see them, but I shall never reach them. There is no life for me, I have had enough of life." His voice rose hoarse and shrill; he flung himself into a chair by the table and stared gloomily in front of him. "Byron and Shelley and Keats;[37] it was granted to them all to die young!" murmured poor Horace, whose poems were unanimously rejected by the editors.

Vincent suppressed a desire to smile. It was part of the pathos of Horace that he always made you want to laugh when he was most miserable, and now the sight of the despairing little figure swirling about in the fantastic dressing-gown, talking of Shelley and Keats in brotherly fashion, proved almost too much for his friend's gravity.

"Yes," went on Horace, taking up his restless walk, "There is no doubt about it. I have had enough of life. Honestly, I don't see my way either to use or happiness in the world. There's something wrong with the machine – a flaw somewhere – it won't work. I'm going to try melting it down into the general crucible. There is some good material, and with fresh combination who knows what masterpiece might come to light?"

"Oh, so it's Waterloo Bridge is it? There's a want of originality about the scheme which I should not have expected of you."

"I'm not a witness, Vincent, to be slain by the shafts of the forensic wit. I fancy I'm in earnest, somehow. Seriously, everything considered, it seems the best course open to me."

"I think I should reconsider the matter, Horace. We can't always fly in the face of nature with impunity."

"Are you preaching hell-fire, old man?"

"Something not unlike it. Nature outraged has a little way of avenging herself."

"Oh, I've thought of that too. Had my fit of being frightened at the modern bogeys, disembodied spirits, thwarted development, etc. Have considered the pleasant possibility that

37. John Keats (1795–1821).

> 'This anguish fleeting hence
> Unmanacled by chains of sense'

may be

> 'Fixed and frozen to permanence.'[38]

But don't we presume a little? Is it so easy to outrage nature in our own persons after all? And aren't we altogether too fond of meddling with her workings in the case of other people; for instance, when we control the natural healthy impulse of insane persons to destroy themselves." Vincent laughed aloud, and Horace, who had half intended a sally, joined in the merriment. "And it seems to me likewise," he went on, growing suddenly grave, "that the suicidal impulse of miserable people is by no means to be deplored or regarded as a monstrosity. Here am I, one little link in the great chain, and, somehow or other, an undue share of the common anguish has accumulated in me. It is fit and natural that I should collapse, subside, what you will."

"But you don't collapse – that's the point. A boiler bursts when it's too full of steam. An unhappy man goes on living."

"Perhaps it has never occurred to you, Vincent, that a man is a more complex product than a boiler. Reason and what we call 'choice' are his unfortunate lot."

"Exactly. Yet reason how he will, of one thing I am convinced, that the instinct against suicide, stronger than any mere logical conclusion, will always lie at the root of his nature. Of course a man takes his chance in these matters. Personally, I should not care to fly in the face of such an instinct."

"Vincent, do you remember the high diving-stage at Cambridge? When I stood up there all the body of me used to cry out against that final plunge. Yet I knew it was very unlikely to hurt me, and the doctors assured me that diving was good for my health. Don't you see,

38. New (*The Complete Novels*, 557 n. 24) notes that this is a misquotation of Tennyson's "Two Voices."

it's only the same thing over again? Perhaps the instinctive parts of me shrink from the big plunge into the dark river; but, on the other hand, much thought and bitter experience have taught me my unfitness for life. Yes, a haunting sense of unfitness – that's the phrase I've been wanting all along."

Horace leant up against the mantelpiece as he spoke; his eyes stared with vague brilliance in front of him; the words flowed from him shrill but deliberate.

"Am I to set aside all that my judgment tells me for the sake of a blind instinct, which after all is a purely local and temporal one? I take no joy in life, Vincent; on the contrary, it is an unutterable burden; and now that my mother is dead there is no human being to whom my existence affords a shadow of enjoyment. And I know my own nature too well by now to think that time is likely to bring amelioration of my lot. Quite the contrary. Certainly, my circumstances are not particularly good at present, but the radical evil lies in myself, in my own nature. Body and soul, there is a flaw in the machine which prevents successful normal action."

Vincent laughed a little: "Don't talk as if you were a steam engine. I'll tell you what it is, old man; you're morbid and out of health."

"Exactly; you restate the case. I'm morbid and out of health." Horace drew a chair to the table and pushed the birdseye and a churchwarden towards his friend. "Let's talk of something else, old man," he said, with a laugh, "and refresh ourselves with a cup that not only cheers but at times also inebriates."

"Thanks, no, I don't think I will," answered Vincent, who was engaged in setting fire to a big Havana, "I must be off soon. Try one of these cigars. I tell you what it is, Horace," he went on, "you've a delicate constitution, body and soul, and it takes you a long time to get over your youthful ailments. Believe me, what you are suffering from, I think I can guess at it, more or less, is merely the disease of youth. I've been through it all myself" (he puffed with some complacence at the big cigar), "but I happen to have a good digestion and to be morally something of a pachyderm, so I've got over it without being much the worse. Unfitness for life! You are so awfully greedy, you poets, you expect too much from life, and when you don't get it think all the world has gone wrong. Of course life is a disillusion, a disappointment for most of us. The only way is to treat it as a game which it is just worthwhile to play as long as one doesn't cheat. I'm playing the game of barristering, of success in life, at present, and trying to think I care immensely about the result. And now," he added, drawing out his watch, "it is eleven o'clock and I must be off to take my turn at that pretty little pastime called Flirtation."

Horace's eyes rested wistfully on the healthy and vivacious countenance of his friend, and a rather grim smile played about his lips as the happy Vincent rose and laid one shapely hand on his shoulder; "I shall be in next week, old man, to see what we can do in the matter of work. There's a sub-editorship Watson was telling me about – but never mind tonight. Meantime keep up your pecker and remember that Hamlet was a wise man after all. Don't be nervous, I'm not going to quote 'To be or not to be.'"[39]

"Then you advise the abandonment of the short-cut-to-the-Shades idea?"

"Distinctly, you might come out at a blind alley, if not worse."

"At any rate, there would be decent company. Chatterton and Cleopatra,[40] not to speak of a whole horde of heathen Chinese."

Vincent laughed and waved his hand in reply as he made his way into the dark street. Horace watched the vital well-knit figure out of sight, then turned with a sigh into the gloomy house. Fragments of sound floated up now and then from the great human sea a few yards off; here and there a light flashed and glimmered in the distance. For a moment, a mighty anguish, an unutterable yearning for the life which was so near and yet so far, rose up within him and almost overpowered him. He flung himself down by the table and taking up a volume

39. From Shakespeare's *Hamlet*.

40. Both Cleopatra and the poet, Thomas Chatterton (1752–1770), committed suicide (New, ed., *The Complete Novels*, 557 n. 27).

of *Die Welt als Wille und Vorstellung*[41] which lay near, hurled it across the room. There were times when he liked to nurse and dandle his sorrow; to feed it with philosophy; to mature it with metaphysics; but tonight his own despair made him afraid.

* * *

The circumstances of poor Horace's death are, by now, too well-known to need recital. Opinions differed, as we know, on the subject, but my own belief is, that however much his mode of life may have tended to hasten it, he did nothing by any individual act to bring about the final catastrophe. Poets, and those afflicted with the so called "poetic temperament," although constantly contemplating it, rarely commit suicide; they have too much imagination. The click of the self-slaughterer's pistol (I speak with due allowance for metaphor) is oftener to be heard in Mincing Lane and Capel Court than in the regions of Grub Street and Parnassus Hill.

Vincent continues to flourish. It is whispered in legal circles that the next silk-gown – but I must not reveal professional secrets.

41. Arthur Schopenhauer's seminal text.

Olga's Valentine (1884)

1.

"Good morrow to thee, Valentine!" cries Maud, nodding her yellow head at me as I take my seat at the family breakfast table.

"Is it really the 14th?" I say indifferently, drawing the toast rack towards me with a languid hand.

"O Olga, this looks like old age indeed!" protests Maud, who is not twenty-eight, but eighteen; who has a pink-and-white skin, and sweet laughing eyes; who still sips her sparkling wine of life in happy ignorance of the *vanitas vanitatum*[42] at the bottom of the pot.

"Valentines are only for children and servants," I say sternly, while my father grumbles from behind his *Morning Post*. "Nine o'clock, and the postman not come! Valentines, indeed! The whole nonsensical business ought to be put a stop to by law."

"How do things come from Paris?" inquires my brother, in that mystic financial jargon which is so baffling to the outsider.

"Flat!" says my father, with a groan, and subsides behind the newspaper again.

A gloomy silence falls upon the assembled company at this announcement, broken only by the subdued capering of Freddy, who is anxiously awaiting the postman's arrival. Freddy is our youngest born – an unnecessary unconnected person – nineteen

42. Latin for "vanity of vanities" (Ecclesiastes 1:2).

years younger than I, and nine years younger than Maud. Truth to tell, we as a family are not very fond of him; indeed, I think it would be difficult for anyone, without the tender maternal bias, to be fond of Freddy. He is a pale-faced precocious child, with an interest more keen than kindly in the affairs of his neighbours, and decided if unformulated views on the survival of the fittest theory, and the inevitable juxtaposition of walls and weakness. At this present moment he is engaged in simulating a series of "postman's knocks" with his knuckles on the table, observing meanwhile, with calm enjoyment, the various degrees of annoyance produced on us all by the performance – a performance which only ceases when a genuine rat-tat sends the performer flying breathless from the apartment. He re-enters in another moment, his holland blouse freighted with a miscellaneous assortment of packages, which he proceeds to slowly distribute.

"Here's a blue letter for you, Pa, and a newspaper for Jack," he says importantly, fumbling among his treasures; "and two boxes for Maud, a long one and a short one. No, Olga, there's nothing for you; old maids don't have valentines. Here's a letter for you, Ma; and all the rest are for Master Freddy Carpenter;" with which last announcement he buries his big head in the pile of fancy envelopes, on each of which – ah, the pathos of it! – I recognise a more or less skilful disguise of the maternal handwriting.

"Well, Maudie," I say, repressing the least little elderly pang, and smiling across at my sister, "and what form does their devotion take this time? Is it caramels or chocolate, or only loves and doves from De la Rue?"

Maud looks up breathless from her treasures.

"O Olga, such perfect gloves – three pairs of them, and ten buttons each! I wonder who can have sent them! And here's a box of Parma violets from Frank at Nice, poor boy!" and the pretty face grows thoughtful as she speaks. For only last year Frank could waltz and sing glees, and look tenderly into bright eyes, with the best of them; and now he is sighing out his life by that "tideless, dolorous, midland sea,"[43] which has murmured the death-lullaby of so many human beings.

"They will do nicely for the Chalmers' tonight," I say cheerfully; "a touch of pale colour is just the thing for that white frock of yours."

"A bunch on the left shoulder," begins Maud impressively, "a knot on the fan, and another on the sash – "

Here she is interrupted by a series of impish chuckles from Freddy, whose mirth, owing to a temporary absence of front teeth, is even more unpicturesque than usual.

"O my!" cries the charming child, "here's a valentine for Olga, after all; it got mixed up with mine. It doesn't look much of a one, though, after all."

"Will you please to give me my letter, and *not* to meddle with other people's correspondence?" I say, flushing a little with anger, and holding out my hand for the thick square envelope which the sportive Freddy waves backward and forward before me.

"Give Olga her letter, there's a dear boy," interposes my mother, touching the cream jug suggestively.

In another moment the family gnome, as Jack tenderly designates his younger brother, is being luxuriously plied with spoonfuls of cream, and I am rapidly perusing the contents of my envelope. These I transcribe for the benefit of the reader.

"Charing Cross Hotel, Feb. 13.

"Dear Miss Carpenter, – I have now been in London a week, and am venturing to recall myself to those friends who are kind enough to welcome such an absentee. I hear from my friend Mrs. Chalmers that you and your family continue to reside in St. John's Wood Road. May I do myself the pleasure of calling on you tomorrow evening after dinner? My engagements will not admit of morning calls. With kind regards to your family, – Yours sincerely, JAMES DIXON."

---

43. A line from Swinburne's poem, "The Triumph of Time."

When I have read it, I hand the letter, which is written in a strong square hand, in silence to my mother. She wrinkles her brows a little as she reads it.

"James Dixon?" she says rather puzzled; "is that the Mr. Dixon who used to come here so often six or seven years ago? He went away very suddenly, if I remember. It would have been more usual to have written to me," adds my mother, who has a sort of timid respect for Mrs. Grundy.[44]

"You can't see him tonight, at any rate," cries Maud, who is reading the little note in her turn; "the Chalmers' dance is a Cinderella, and I'm not going to be late."

"Old Dixon coming back?" says my brother, looking up from his stirred eggs. "He went off travelling in the East or something, didn't he? That was seven years ago; he must be getting on."

"I remember him when I was ever so little, and he was quite a fogey then," observes Maud, with the calm contempt of her eighteen years.

"Will you give me the note, please?" I say quietly. (Does anyone see that my hand is shaking?) "Don't be anxious, Maudie; I'm not going to fail you. I will write to Mr. Dixon at once." And I rise from the table, letter and all, with perhaps a touch of added colour on either cheek. As I go out, Freddy's murmured comment falls upon my ear:

"I knew it couldn't be a valentine, after all."

2.

It is half-past eight by the dining room clock. My father is snoring in his fireside armchair, Freddy has gone to bed, and I am drawing on my sober Swedish gloves, and wondering when my sister means to put in an appearance.

"Olga, my dear," says my mother, surveying me rather anxiously, "haven't you anything lighter or brighter – say a white dress like Maud's,

44. Character in Thomas Morton's *Speed the Plough*, which premiered in 1798.

for instance? I don't like to see young people in dingy colours, whatever the fashion may be."

I look down at my discreet fawn-coloured nun's cloth, and smile rather sadly.

"But, mother dear, I don't think anyone else would call me a 'young person,' unless I were seeking a housemaid's situation," I add feebly.

My mother looks distressed; but at this point the door is flung open, and attention is diverted from my staid and respectable garments; for Maud is standing before us, a dazzling vision of youth and joy and beauty, all pink cheeks and golden hair and white fluffy drapery.

"Do I look respectable?" she asks rather breathlessly, fastening her last glove-button, and giving a little pat to the knot of poor Frank's violets on her shoulder. "You know it is such a shockingly unearthly hour for a dance, they can't expect one to have time to dress like a Christian."

"O, I think you'll do. She's just passable, isn't she, mother?" I say critically; whereupon silly Maud grows very red, and drags me off to the hall, where Susan is waiting with the shawls.

"O Olga, isn't it fun?" she says, carefully arranging the fluffy skirts as the carriage rolls away from the door. "I never *can* quite realise, do you know, that I'm grown up and going to a party on my own legitimate hook, as Jack says. It seems only yesterday that I was a little girl in bed, and you used to come to my room with a candle and show yourself before you went to parties. I wonder, did you ever like it as much as I do?"

"I daresay I did, Maudie."

"I wonder, shall I ever grow *not* to like it very much, Olga?"

"It is possible, Maudie."

"But you don't dislike it, do you? And you won't mind if I stay till the end tonight, will you?"

"Just as you like, my dear. I always think what Shylock[45] says about Jews applies equally to old maids: 'Sufferance is the badge of all our

---

45. See the discussion on p. lv.

tribe.' Don't look distressed, Maudie; you know I'm only in fun;" and I lay a remorseful *gant de Suède* on my sister's delicate white glove.

But in another five minutes she has forgotten all about Shylock and old maids, about Jews and Gentiles, except indeed the particular little throng of black-coated Christians who are carrying on fierce, if bloodless, warfare for the possession of her programme. My programme is also filling, slowly perhaps, but very surely. I have never known the delights of being wallflower, though, no doubt, they are yet in store for me. Once, I think, I enjoyed a certain amount of social success; now my success, such as it is, can only be called a *succès d'estime*. Old friends rushing by on their way to the new faces pause to ask for a dance from the elderly young lady who once – would you believe it! – was quite a pretty girl. (O cruel injustice of Fate, which decrees so short a term of youth to womanhood!) Little boys, whose early youth one has comforted with bullseyes and toffee, come gallantly forward as partners for the gay dance; and, lastly, the hundred and one victims of Maud's bright eyes are fain to console themselves, in the absence of the divinity, with the reflected glory of the divinity's sister.

"O, if I were only a chaperone – at least it would be more dignified," I think wearily, as I meekly accept an ice from the hands of a little youth in a big collar. I recollect him in drab knickerbockers and plaid stockings! "*They* are allowed to sit down and go to sleep; *they* have not to pretend they are enjoying themselves. Or a man – O, if I were only a man, the veriest fogey in the doorway, it would be better than this. O my dear girls," I add mentally, as I hand the empty plate to my escort, "you are having a good time now, but take warning. Marry, die, go to Girton – anything; only, whatever you do, don't grow into elderly young ladies."

My reverie is broken off at this point by the approach of my sister, who leads a dapper young man in her wake. He is small and fair, with a tall collar and tiny boots – a very perfect specimen of the ballroom "masher."

"Olga," cries kind little Maud, "I want to introduce Mr. Dude-Snooks. I hope you've a dance left on your card. He dances like an angel" (in breathless *sotto voce*). "Yes, I think it's our dance, Mr. Collett;" and off goes Maud to the strains of Waldteufel's[46] last.

Meanwhile Mr. Dude-Snooks and I are left facing one another rather hopelessly.

"Ah, may I have the pleasure?" begins the hapless youth, fumbling with his programme, and looking as though he wanted to flee.

"I have No. 17," I reply, in all humility; but at this point I forget all about Mr. Dude-Snooks and No. 17; I forget that this is Mrs. Chalmers' "Valentine Cinderella," and that I am Maud's chaperone. For aught I know, it might be Olga Carpenter, aged twenty-one, who holds out her hand in greeting to the tall stalwart man who has just made his way to her from his hostess's side.

"Miss Carpenter!"

"Mr. Dixon!"

"You got my note?"

"And you got mine?"

"And this is my answer to it." He smiles down at me, the old smile. No doubt, as Maud says, he is a fogey, but he has a pleasing smile nevertheless.

"I – I am very glad to welcome you back," I say demurely, repressing with an iron hand all signs of that strange inward agitation which was natural enough in the Olga of seven years ago, but is quite out of place in that respectable chaperone Miss Carpenter.

"Won't you come and sit in the conservatory? I remember you used to be fond of conservatories;" and James Dixon comes closer with extended arm, to the great relief of Mr. Dude-Snooks, who hastens to seek a more congenial partner. "It will be so nice to talk about old times," I say primly, as we ensconce ourselves among the ferns and lanterns.

"Will it?" His eyes rest a moment on mine. Yes, he is growing old; even by the dim rose-light I can see the marks on his face, the silver lines in his drooping moustache.

---

46. French composer, Charles Émile Waldteufel (1837–1915).

I look down at my fan, and pause a minute before I say, "Yes, I think so. They were pleasant times, were they not?"

He does not answer, but looks straight at me, saying, "Miss Carpenter, do you know what I expected when I came home? I expected to find you married!"

I wince a little. Surely *he* is not going to start a subject so threadbare and unprofitable!

"Indeed!" I say coldly, and not lifting my eyes.

James Dixon leans forward: "Olga, forgive me. He was always a shifty thoughtless fellow. I never thought him bad enough for *that*."

"Of whom are you speaking?"

"Of Humphrey Clay, whom you had promised to marry when I left England."

"I do not understand you. Three times I told Humphrey Clay that I could never be his wife."

"Olga, Olga, think what you are saying. He came to me one night seven years ago. He told me he loved you, that you returned his love. I was not young, I was not rich. What chance did I ever have against such a rival? The next week I sailed for the East."

"And you never came and said goodbye – not even that. O, you were not just to me, not just to me!"

James Dixon rises to his feet, a low groan escapes him.

"Olga, Olga, it is not true – "

I have also risen, pale but quiet; he has seized both my hands in his, and holds them in a strong grasp.

"James, it is all over, it is too late!"

"Olga, it shall not be too late."

"Ah, but it is! I'm not the same woman you knew and loved. James, I've grown sad and bitter, old and disappointed. The years have not been kind to me."

"Olga, my dear, I love you – I have always loved you – "

I cannot write any more.

"Olga," cries Maud, as the carriage rolls homeward, "I've had the most delightful time in the world! Tom Vandeleur sent the gloves; I was determined to find out, and I did! And, O, I was so sorry for you, poor dear, being carried off by that old man – after I'd introduced Mr. Dude-Snooks, too!"

"Mr. Dude-Snooks was glad enough of the escape," I say dreamily.

"I remember Mr. Dixon quite well," goes on Maud; "he used to give me sweets when I was little. He was quite old even then."

"Was he?"

"Yes, a perfect fogey, wasn't he?"

"Perhaps; I don't know. How was I to tell? O Maud, I'm a fogey too, and it's natural one should consort with one's kind, isn't it?"

Then I break down and tell her all. No doubt it is very prosaic, very middle-aged, very uninteresting. Maud tries hard to be sympathetic, but I am quite aware of that secret feeling in her heart which is more like compassion than sympathy. And when James comes next day, and everything is explained and settled, I note, with some amusement, the subdued and doubtful manner with which my family supports the news.

As for me, why, I can afford to laugh, can I not? I even think I kiss Freddy in the hall as he asks, with simulated naïveness, if "that is the old man I am going to marry?"

Yes, Freddy, I can forgive that, and much besides; for was it not from your infant hands that I received my precious "valentine"?

In Holiday Humour (1884)

"Come, woo me, woo me; for I am in holiday humour, and like enough to consent."

AS YOU LIKE IT[47]

"Is my hat straight, Marian?"

"I should tilt it rather more forward if I were you. That hat's a little too strong-minded for my taste, Olivia."

"And the bow of my sash, is that straight too?"

"You have grown very particular all of a sudden;" and Marian, pausing in the midst of her own toilette, fastened a direct, rather meaning gaze on her sister's face. Olivia's gray eyes encountered the gaze steadily, almost defiantly, but a faint blush sprang to her pale cheek.

"I don't know what you mean, Marian," she said.

"O, I wasn't meaning anything at all! But you look very nice this morning, Livy. I wonder if Mr. Sydney Tresidder likes cream-coloured gowns and terracotta Liberty sashes?"

Olivia laughed in spite of herself, bending a rather flushed face over her many-buttoned glove. "Marian," she said, "you will never be ready at this rate. The steamer is almost due, and – "

"And a certain young man in tweed knickerbockers and a straw hat has been walking up and down the Pension garden for the last

47. Shakespeare's *As You Like It.*

half-hour. Say I not sooth?" cried Marian, deliberately adjusting each chestnut curl on her white forehead.

"You are very silly," said Olivia, but again she blushed and smiled as she spoke.

"Mr. Sydney Tresidder would be a trifle flattered if he knew what roses the mere mention of his name could call into bloom," answered Marian, still intent on the curls. "Frailty, thy name is Livy![48] 'But three months dead!' Olivia, how about the industrious young man in Paper Buildings who cannot afford to take holidays in Switzerland?"

For a moment there was silence. Olivia walked across the sunny little room and stood by the open window. "The – the person in Paper Buildings has given up caring – if he ever cared," she said, and there was an odd sound in her voice, "and so have I." She leaned on the window-ledge when she had spoken, growing very intent on the prospect outside. And, indeed, it was fair enough. Before her lay the lake, that fairest Lake of the Four Cantons, wide, blue, sparkling in the morning sunlight; the wooded slopes and snow-crowned peaks rose on all sides; directly opposite, Pilatus reared his hoary head; and beyond, in the dim distance, towered the Jungfrau from among a virgin company of sister peaks.

"It's going to be awfully hot," said Marian very volubly, as she tied on her hat. "I wish we'd gone somewhere up the mountains like sensible people. No persons in their senses would think of establishing themselves on the shore of the lake in such weather. And an expedition into Lucerne! The hottest place in the world except this."

"How many of us are going?" asked Olivia, turning round again, and showing a rather grave face.

"O, there will be the Tresidders, of course – Nelly and Fanny and your Mr. Sydney," Marian answered – "and Mr. Collett (that makes four), and Tom Leigh and Miss Meldrum. She is the chaperon, Mamma says, but we are not to let her know it."

"Poor Miss Meldrum!" said Olivia softly.

---

48. A play on Shakespeare's *Hamlet*: "Frailty, thy name is woman!"

The Pension Sonnenthal was assembled in a body on the shore of the lake as the two girls came down the wooden steps: Olivia tall and grave in her cool dress, with the sash from Messrs. Liberty's and the hat that was "a little strong-minded;" Marian, bright-eyed, light-footed, faultlessly got up as was her wont.

"We thought you were never coming, Miss Longcroft," cried a blue-eyed young man in flannels, stepping out from the little group of people towards which the girls were making their way. And then followed much handshaking and laughter, and congratulatory remarks on the weather. Tom Leigh of the blue eyes and flannels flitted about among the ladies with knots of Alpenveilchen and Alpenrosen. Miss Meldrum, in a highly starched gown and shady hat, smiled upon the little company, to which, all unwitting, she was to play propriety. Miss Meldrum's smiles were by no means perennial; sometimes, indeed, she was a little moody, a little sour perhaps, as virginity at forty is apt, alas! to be: but today she smiled. A tall young man, brown eyed, brown skinned, wearing tweed knickerbockers and a straw hat, stood by Olivia Longcroft's side with an air of supreme contentment on his good-looking face. And I may here take occasion to remark, that not only on the lawn of the Pension Sonnenthal, but on the steamer, when they had taken their places later on, the brown tweed suit and straw hat contrived somehow or other to maintain a close proximity to the cream-coloured gown and terracotta sash.

"Here we go!" cried Tom Leigh, as the steamer made off from the landing place.

The young people were in high spirits; they scampered from one end of the boat to the other; they bought fruit of the dull-eyed peasants; they made a great many jokes about nothing at all. Caroline Meldrum, establishing herself as though by instinct in one of the corner seats (poor Caroline, whose life was all corners and third places!), looked on rather glumly at the antics of her companions. The sun danced and sparkled on the water; the mountains stood out very white and green against the bright blue sky; a couple of Italians were playing violins, trilling out pretty shapeless songs in their bird-like voices as they played. Olivia Longcroft lay back in the chair which Sydney Tresidder had brought her, and smiled up at him with a face from which all traces of its early gravity had completely vanished.

"Isn't it lovely!" she said.

"Yes, I think so; perhaps it's all rather too much like a lithograph, but I'm not very critical today, somehow;" and the brown tweed suit slowly stretched itself alongside the canvas chair, so that the straw hat was about on a level with the knee of the cream-coloured gown.

"It spoils everything to criticise it, I think," said Olivia, looking down at the brown eyes lifted towards her.

"This from a modern young lady who has been to Girton! The Millennium approaches! Miss Longcroft, we will not criticise. We will forget for today that we are the pampered children of an effete civilisation. We will play that Mr. Ruskin is a myth and Mr. Pater a nightmare."[49]

"And we will admire everything, even to that good lady's apparel," answered Olivia, glancing from the brown eyes to a sturdy peasant-woman hard by, and thence to the eyes again.

Tresidder looked across at the woman and laughed aloud. She wore a short wide skirt of excruciating plaid, and a velvet bodice adorned with coloured beads; a huge umbrella and flapping hat with rose-coloured streamers completed this tasteful costume.

The boat puffed and paddled its way along the windings of the lake, till by and by the houses of Lucerne – Lucerne the city of the lamps, Lucerne the home of perpetual holiday – could be discerned gleaming white against the pineclad hills. And very soon our merry band of pleasure-seekers had exchanged the sunny deck of the steamer for the no less sunny streets of the festive little town. They wandered up and down the parade; they stood to watch the people arriving at the Schweizerhof; they lingered on the old bridges and inspected the gay little shops. Tresidder (whose unobtrusive maintenance of a desired

49. Scholar, author, and critic, Walter Pater (1839–1894).

proximity was a marvel of skill) expended a small fortune on the purchase of wooden bears and Thorwaldsen lions. The young man was in the wildest spirits; his sisters regarded him with some alarm and protested against his extravagance. Miss Meldrum's smiles had subsided by now; she was hot, cross, and tired, and wanted her luncheon. She wondered what was the fun of it all that the young people should be so mightily pleased. It seemed dull and stupid enough.

They lunched in a shady garden affording a distant glimpse of the lake; there were coffee and omelettes, honey and ices, and great piles of scarlet mountain strawberries. Tresidder sat opposite Olivia, smiling aimlessly throughout the meal. I am aware that in books, when two young people are interested in one another, they are given to exchange glances long and intense, or swift and fraught with tragic meaning. A more commonplace experience has taught me that a recurrent and meaningless smile, far off indeed from the immortal smile of Tito and Romola,[50] is, under the circumstances, a far more frequent phenomenon. It is a sad thing to have to record of one's hero, but I must confess that Sydney Tresidder persistently grinned from beginning to end of that luncheon. He grinned vaguely when he handed Miss Longcroft her portion of omelette; he smiled fatuously when he asked her for the salt. Over Olivia's face, too, the ripples and sparkles played ceaselessly. For these silly smiles are so remarkably catching, even when you are twenty-two and have been to Girton.

"Is there some joke between you two?" cried Miss Meldrum sharply.

(Poor Caroline, into the muddy depths of whose small eyes nobody had ever cared to gaze!) The two young people were covered hopelessly with confusion.

Tresidder rose with scarlet face, and pushed back his chair. "Has everybody finished luncheon?" he said, taking out his watch; "because it's time we set off to do the lions."

"The Lion, I suppose you mean," cried Leigh, also rising; "and there's the cathedral, and a garden which has some mysterious connection

50. Refers to George Eliot's *Romola* (1862–1863).

with the glacial period." Miss Meldrum excused herself rather stiffly, on the plea of fatigue. She would go and sit under the trees on the parade, and they would meet her at the landing stage at five o'clock.

Tresidder and Olivia made no excuse, but they drifted away from the sightseers, somehow or other, and found themselves strolling together down the shady parade.

"Thorwaldsen and the glacial period, Miss Longcroft! 'Dost thou like the picture?' I mean, do they not sound as music in your ears?" There was a half-satirical tone in Tresidder's voice as he spoke.

"They – they are very interesting." Olivia wondered why her voice faltered as she brought out the stupid little sentence.

"I repeat, Thorwaldsen and the glacial period. And I am going to cut you off from them, Miss Longcroft, to hold you back from them for today, perhaps for all the ages; for who knows when you may revisit Lucerne? We agreed not to be critical, did we not? I want you to enjoy the sunshine with me, and think about nothing at all. You are like Cassius,[51] I believe – you think too much."

They had made their way down to the low wide wall of gray stone which skirts the parade, and stood a moment gazing down into the lucid depths below.

Miss Meldrum, from her bench under the trees, watched them with a sort of dull vexation as they leisurely took their seats on the wall, Olivia propping herself luxuriously against a square post; Tresidder taking up his position opposite, and leaning forward as though to catch every word or smile she might be pleased to let fall. Caroline, urged perhaps by a desperate instinct to snatch at something which was pleasure, had provided herself with a basket of apricots, and was eating away with a sort of fierce steadiness. The little barefooted children hung round with envious and admiring eyes. Fortunate lady, who could afford a whole basket of fruit for her own consumption! A warm white glow, which lent a peculiar air of unreality to the scene,

---

51. Allusion to Shakespeare's *The Tragedy of Julius Caesar*, referring to Gaius Cassius Longinus, one of the lead conspirators responsible for the assassination of the play's namesake.

had succeeded to the garish sunlight of the morning. The lake lay strangely colourless and still below. Above, there was not a scrap of blue to be seen in the sky. All around a profound silence was reigning. And there was silence also between the two young people lounging contentedly on the wall. Olivia leant back and sighed with a dreamy enjoyment; she felt strangely happy, strangely at peace with herself and all the world. And Olivia had lived long enough in the world to appreciate the bits of happiness as they came to her. Her life had not been a tragic one, but it had had its complications. Perhaps she was not habitually a very cheerful person; rather given to take life too seriously, both as regarded its pains and its pleasures. And though she did not realise it at the moment, there was the charm of contrast and comparison to add keenness to her present enjoyment.

Meanwhile Tresidder was fumbling lazily in his half-dozen pockets. "I want to show you a letter I had this morning," he said at length, with rather uneasy carelessness; "I thought I had it with me. I want your advice about answering it." Olivia looked at him questioningly, then suddenly lowered her eyes. "It was from some fellows at St. Moritz," the young man went on, in the same tone; "they want me to join them there, and go for a week's walking in the Bernese Oberland."

"Shall you go?" No sooner had she spoken them than Olivia wished the words recalled.

"That depends entirely on you." There was no mistaking the tone this time. The smiles had ceased to play about his face; the brown eyes looked up at her in all seriousness as he leaned forward, taking both her hands in his strong grasp. For a moment there was silence. Olivia turned away her head, and looked across the wide smooth lake to the pineclad hills and snow-crowned peaks bathed in the still, warm whiteness of the mystic afternoon. Her face was flushed, her eyes were bright, her heart was beating with unusual rapidity; she did not draw away her hands. How beautiful it all was! she thought: she had had misgivings at times, but there was no doubt about it; it was a fair and well-ordered world after all! How happy she had been today, yesterday, the last three weeks! And this kind, handsome, high-spirited young man at her side – who looked at her so lovingly with his beautiful eyes; who listened so attentively to every word that she spoke; who was so thoughtful in a hundred ways – how far was he responsible for this new calm happiness? Would not life, passed with such a companion, be sweet indeed? How beautiful the mountains were, and the lake! How kind, how gentle, how clever he was!

And so it came to pass that Olivia Longcroft and Sydney Tresidder between them decided that the latter should *not* make that journey to St. Moritz, should entirely abandon the notion of that walking tour in the Bernese Oberland.

I shrink from conjecturing how long those two young people might have lingered together on the wall, if Miss Meldrum (who, happily, had slumbered through a certain interesting crisis) had not woke with a start to find the afternoon considerably advanced, the sky like lead, and the atmosphere suggestive of nothing so much as a vapour-bath. She came rapidly across the parade, shading her eyes from the glare, and holding out her watch towards them: "Miss Longcroft, Mr. Tresidder! It is half-past five; half an hour later than we appointed to meet the others at the landing place. I have been wondering when you would feel inclined to make a move."

They rose up like people in a dream, obediently following in Miss Meldrum's wake along the parade. But lo and behold! When they reached the landing stage, there was not a trace of the rest of their party to be seen. "I have no doubt," said Tresidder, "that they have gone by the five-o'clock steamer, and left us to our fate. I'm not sure that we don't deserve it, are you, Miss Meldrum?" Caroline tossed her head; she was beginning to suspect that that afternoon's siesta of hers had not passed unnoticed; but indeed her suspicions were groundless. A dark-eyed young man, in picturesque boatman's costume, came up to Tresidder, pouring out a torrent of hideous Swiss-German *patois*, rather to the Englishman's bewilderment. Sydney turned away half-laughing, and addressed himself to Caroline; indeed, there was something quite like rudeness in the way in which he completely ignored Miss Longcroft's presence, throwing her never so much as a word or a glance. "The fellow wants us to go back in that absurd cockleshell of his," he said, "one of those ridiculous sham gondolas with two gondoliers. What do you think of it, Miss Meldrum?"

Caroline hesitated and objected: it would take a long time; they would be late for *table d'hôte*.

"The lake is as smooth as glass. We shan't be more than three-quarters of an hour at the utmost, the fellow says." Tresidder distinctly inclined towards the boat. Nobody had consulted Olivia, perhaps because she was keeping in the background, dreamy-eyed and silent; but she did not seem to notice the omission. Well, the end of it was that they yielded to the boatman's wiles, and were soon well out in the middle of the lake, the light flat boat moving rapidly across the still surface of leaden-hued water. The two boatmen stood up strong and sturdy, skilfully wielding the long poles; Tresidder sat opposite the ladies, talking vigorously to Miss Meldrum, while he inwardly recalled the smile in Olivia's eyes, the touch of her fingers when he had handed her into the boat a few minutes before. Suddenly Caroline paused in the midst of a sentence.

"I am sure I felt a drop of rain."

"By Jove! So do I now." Tresidder looked up at the sky as he spoke.

"And I," said Olivia, speaking for the first time.

"We all felt a drop of rain, like Goldsmith's dinner party, who 'all kept a corner.'"[52] Sydney spoke lightly, but his face had grown grave.

It was the work of a moment; a transformation-scene – a deed of magic. The sky had grown purple, and seemed as though it would descend and close round them. The gray still water was turbid and black, save where an ominous white line could be descried making its way in the direction of the boat. The fair lake was horrible, monstrous, swollen out of all proportion; the very mountains were thin, shadowy, insignificant; the lake, the sky had swallowed up the landscape.

And now the rain and hail came pouring down – a hard stinging sheet; the lightning flashed, the thunder rolled and crashed

52. Refers to Oliver Goldsmith's (1728–1774) poem, "The Haunch of Venison."

among the hills; a stiff breeze sprang up, lashing the water into formidable waves. The little craft – flat-bottomed, ill-trimmed, light as a shell – rocked and plunged, leaped and swirled. The boatmen, with faces set in a grim smile, pulled at the oars like a pair of furies. Miss Meldrum began to grow hysterical, and attempted making jokes. Tresidder, leaning all his weight on his own side of the boat, held it down by main force with both his hands. Only once he stretched out a hand and touched Olivia's; but it lay stiff, cold, unresponsive in her lap. She was sitting bolt upright, motionless, with pale face and dilated eyes, the very embodiment of cold and silent horror. Once Sydney managed to whisper, "Whatever happens, we are together;" but the words were either lost in the rush and roar of wind and water, or they fell on indifferent ears, for Olivia made no sign. The men pulled and strained at the oars, striking out for the nearest point at which to land; but the boat was making no perceptible way. What tragic ending was destined for the day so joyously begun?

To make a long story short, and put an end to the reader's suspense, I will say at once that our travellers were not drowned; only drenched to the skin, and at least an hour late for that *table d'hôte* which, for Miss Meldrum at least, constituted so important an item in the day's work.

"Did you know," said Tresidder, as he lifted Olivia, wet and trembling, from the boat – "did you know that there was great danger?"

"Yes, I knew," she said, in a low voice; then they plodded in silence along the wet shore till the Pension Sonnenthal was reached.

Later that night, when they had changed their clothes, dined, described their adventures, and been duly lionised by the Pension – later on, Olivia and Sydney stole out together on to the veranda which overlooks the lake. The storm had passed, and a flood of silver moonlight lay on the peaceful scene. Now and then a distant report, followed by a rather feeble shower of sparks, told of fireworks at the big Pension up the mountain opposite. They stood in silence a moment; then Olivia spoke.

"Mr. Tresidder, I want to tell you something."

"Miss Olivia Longcroft, I am at your service."

"Do you remember the wall at Lucerne this afternoon, and what we said there?"

"O, I have forgotten it completely! My dearest Olivia, is anything the matter?" He took both her hands, and drew her towards him, smiling down at the earnest face uplifted to his.

"O Mr. Tresidder, forgive me! I have been rash, foolish. I have made a promise it is impossible for me to keep. I cannot marry you."

He let fall her hands, and put his own on her shoulders.

"Do you think you have brought me out here to listen to such things?" He spoke lightly, but there was an odd sound in his voice.

She moved a step or two away from him.

"Mr. Tresidder, don't think too badly of me. How shall I tell you? Out there at Lucerne this afternoon life was so different; it looked all holiday, all sunshine; and I – I was so happy!"

He came nearer to her, and would have taken her hand, but she drew it away.

"But afterwards, in the boat, when I thought I should be drowned, it was different. Things grew awfully real again. I felt then that it was all a mistake about you and me. I did not think about you; I was frightened – I did not want to die. It made no difference that you were with me."

Her voice died away, but she stood looking up at him steadily with glowing gray eyes.

For answer, he stooped and took her in his arms.

"My darling, do you think you are going to get rid of me as easily as all this? You don't know yet with whom you have to deal." Then, changing his tone – "Olivia, go to bed at once, this instant; go to bed, and sleep away those silly fancies. My dear" (his voice changed again), "you are tired, upset, overwrought. Tomorrow morning I will speak with you about this, but not tonight."

She freed herself from his embrace.

"But it is tonight that I must speak. Mr. Tresidder, you make it very hard for me. I must tell you all, it seems. In the boat – in the boat, I – I thought of someone else!"

There was a pause; the moon went suddenly behind a cloud, and the place grew dark. She could see the outline of his tall figure as he stood motionless, with bent head, before her.

"Mr. Tresidder, will you forgive me?"

No answer.

"Mr. Tresidder, do you think me very bad – very base?"

"I think that you have made me very unhappy, Miss Longcroft."

They stood there a moment in silence; then he shrugged his shoulders, threw up his head, and came towards her with outstretched hand.

"Miss Longcroft, I must say goodbye" (a listener would hardly have thought it was the same voice which had pleaded so tenderly a few moments before). "I must be up early tomorrow morning to catch the first steamer. I wonder if I can send a telegram to St. Moritz tonight? You will make my adieus for me to your people, in case I do not see them?"

"Goodbye, Mr. Tresidder."

He held her hand a moment in his, then slowly made his way through the open window into the deserted *salle-à-manger*. On the threshold he paused.

"Thank you for a pleasant holiday, Miss Longcroft."

"And thank *you* very much, Mr. Tresidder."

In Retreat (1884)

A Long Vacation Experience

Convent of St. Odile,
Odilienberg, Vosges,
July

My dear Blanche,[53]

Your letter, with its reproaches, was forwarded me here from home. Poor thing! I pity you. Even Camford and our dear Princess Ida's university[54] cannot compensate for mountain sunlight and the shadow of pine forests. And I was never fond of Long Vacation term. And now I suppose you want to know about our reading-party of two, which excited so much scorn on your part when you heard of it.

53. Christine Pullen suggests that the author of the letter, "Melissa," is Levy, while "Psyche" is her friend, Blanche Smith; see *The Woman Who Dared: A Biography of Amy Levy* (Kingston: Kingston University Press, 2010), 80. Lady Blanche and Lady Psyche are characters in Tennyson's *The Princess* (1847) and in the consequent W. S. Gilbert and Arthur Sullivan opera, *Princess Ida; or, Castle Adamant,* which premiered in 1884 (Susan David Bernstein, ed. *The Romance of a Shop*, by Amy Levy (Peterborough: Broadview Editions, 2006), 216 n. 2). For Linda Hunt Beckman's analysis of "Levy/Melissa" see pp. 122-4 of *Amy Levy: Her Life and Letters* (Athens: Ohio University Press, 2000).

54. See above footnote. "Camford" and "Princess Ida's university" are possible allusions to Newnham College. The term, "Camford," refers to Oxford and Cambridge and comes from Thackeray's *The History of Pendennis* (1848-1850).

When we got as far as Strasburg, Psyche declared that she believed you were right after all, and that Odilienberg was a mythical place. I told her to gather her rosebuds;[55] we were to pass the night at Strasburg, and need take no thought for the morrow and St. Odile.

O, Strasburg is the most delightful place in the world! One seems to have stepped into a picture by Dürer[56] or Holbein.[57] I half expected to see an antic Death come hop-hopping down the narrow street, with the quaint old houses and carved chimneys, where the storks stand, looking as if they were carved themselves.

Psyche made some delightful verses about it, which she is going to send to the *Camford Review*.

Early next morning we took the train to Barr, a little picturesque Alsatian town. From Barr we hired a remarkable "one-hoss shay," which bore us and our luggage, by a long winding route, to our destination. Psyche got quite excited at finding herself in the "Blue Alsatian mountains," hummed that everlasting tune from beginning to end,[58] and made sentimental allusions to "that lovely waltz with Frank!"

In revenge I quoted Browning:

"When you've passed the cornfield country,
Where vineyards leave off, flocks are packed,
And sheep-range leads to the very base
O' the mountain, where, at a funeral pace,
Round about, solemn and slow,
One by one, row after row,
Up and up, the pine-trees grow;
So, like black priests up, and so
Down the other side again."[59]

55. Allusion to Robert Herrick's (1591–1674) "To the Virgins, to Make Much of Time"; in the poem, the line reads: "Gather ye rose-buds ..."
56. Albrecht Dürer.
57. Hans Holbein the Younger (1497–1543), Renaissance artist and printer.
58. "The Blue Alsatian Mountains" is a song by composer, Michael Maybrick (1841–1913), popularly known by his pseudonym, Stephen Adams.
59. Robert Browning's "The Flight of the Duchess."

That is a very good description of the scenery we passed through. I do so love pine trees, especially when, as here, they grow on a red soil, amid red rocks. Red sandstone of a peculiar soft shade is very abundant in the Vosges; Strasburg Cathedral is built of it, and many other buildings of less importance.

After about three hours' drive, our carriage drove through a small archway, and stopped before an unpromising gray wall, with a little door in it. There was no bell. No one came out to meet us; various stray persons of very *bourgeois* aspect hung about to watch us dismount. We felt lost and bewildered. At this point an American lady, who had come up for the day, "guessed" we had better go in search of the Mother, but observed that she thought there was no room for us in the convent. Dismayed, we passed through the little door, and found ourselves in a small quadrangle, of which three sides were formed by a low gray building, the fourth by a small chapel of the same melancholy gray. In one corner a door stood open, through which we passed, and found ourselves in a vaulted stone passage, whitewashed, and fraught with strange odours. A red-cheeked nun, in the black cape, gray dress, and blue apron of the order, told us, in horrible *patois,* to seek the Mother in the garden. There, indeed, we found her – a wicked-looking old woman, with a malevolent eye, which no amount of *Aves* and *Paternosters* has taught to look in any other direction than that of the main chance.

She showed us our rooms herself; they are large and airy, and command a view of a pineclad hill on the right, and a great plain like a map below, which stretches as far as the Black Forest mountains. We live *en pension,* and pay six marks a day, which is dear for this part of the world.

Apparently, the use of the bath is unknown among the sisters of the Order of St. Odile. Psyche's travelling "tub" was regarded with amazement, and the Mother assured us that it would be impossible to let us have water for it. We remarked that this was a point on which we must insist.

"*Dann gehen Sie in den Hohwald,*" said the Mother, with a wicked chuckle.

Hohwald is a sophisticated little place some miles off, where the discontented visitor to Odilienberg is verbally relegated by the

Mother. However, we did not go to Hohwald, and we did get our bath-water.

We had arrived in the afternoon, and were very hungry by seven o'clock, when the supper or *Abendessen* is served.

Feeding, like all the other arrangements, is a very promiscuous affair at the convent. Rough plenty, a greater abundance of meat than of knives, of bread than of platters, is the order of the day. It is served in a refectory, with a vaulted stone roof like the corridor, and fragrant with the same curious odours. Our fellow-guests, some twenty in number, are chiefly Alsatians, of the small *bourgeoisie,* I should say. The nuns wait at table in a kindly, fussy, unsystematic fashion eminently characteristic of them. These poor souls can no more understand division of labour than they can give you a direct answer. There is generally a concentration of food at one end of the table, and absolute famine at the other. Psyche says it is the want of masculine influence which is to blame; but Psyche was always a traitor to the cause.

The food itself is extremely mysterious; "curious meat," as Mr. Swinburne's Clerk says in *The Leper,*[60] would best describe it. Curious meat, and still more curious sauces; salads most curious of all. An uncanny flavour pervades everything, from the nondescript soup to the fossil fantastic cakes – heart-shaped, cross-shaped, bird-shaped – which, together with cheese, constitute dessert.

Psyche came into my room at seven o'clock the next morning with a woeful expression on her face. The night had been passed in vain and ceaseless warfare with animals such as Mr. Keating shows us so nicely magnified in the advertisement of his invaluable powder. I owned to a like experience, and we went gloomily enough down the red-sandstone stairs. If the supper arrangements be "promiscuous," what is one to say of the breakfast?

There is no cloth on the table beyond its normal oilskin cover; but it is covered with long loaves of bread, guiltless of butter, or even plates! If you want to eat, you snatch at a loaf, hew off a slice of the

60. Swinburne's poem, "The Leper."

consistency of wood, betake yourself to your large white bowl and soupspoon, and wait till your coffee is brought you.

After our first breakfast we fetched our books, and established ourselves in the garden, resolutely bent on work. Psyche made elaborate arrangements with cushions on the ivy-grown gray wall, and I fortified myself with a rampart of lexicons. The garden is planted with little squares of cabbages and suchlike unpoetic growths. Presently a nun came out, and began pulling up roots, with the disregard of time which is everywhere observable. She was old and pale, but had a nice cheerful face. There is a small supplementary chapel in the garden, and soon a funny little man dressed as a monk emerged from it, with a crowd of peasant "pilgrims" at his heels. I looked at the procession, then at Psyche: her eyes were straying from Quain's *Anatomy*;[61] but she cast them down hastily when I turned my head.

The convent-door opened, and another nun came into the garden. She had a fat red face, on which rested a lurking simper; there was a great loaf under one arm, a wine bottle under the other. As she passed the brother, she cast him an ineffable glance from under her demure eyelids. Psyche shut up her book with a bang.

"Throw *Anatomy* to the dogs; I'll none of it!" she cried desperately.

I cast down my lexicon.

"Who cares for ancient Greece? We are in the Middle Ages!" I said, springing to my feet. After that we gave ourselves up to the spirit of the hour, and thoroughly explored the convent. There is a great kitchen, presided over by a tall Sister, a wilderness of provisions and pots and pans; but much of the food-preparation is carried on at deal tables in the corridor, where the pounding of roots, scraping of herbs, and washing of plates seems never to cease. There is an infinity of cooks spoiling any quantity of broth. A door at the end of the corridor leads into a little dim stone passage looking down on a small inner chapel, and containing a ghastly effigy of St. Odile enclosed in a glass sarcophagus.

Beyond this is the library, a picturesque stone-vaulted room, with stained-glass windows and a quantity of books. Some of these are

61. Jones Quain's *Elements of Anatomy* (1828).

old and valuable. A vellum-bound Livy[62] looked rather tempting, and I was surprised to find a *Théâtre de Voltaire*[63] hobnobbing with the holy fathers.

There are all sorts of unexplored passages, where clothes are hung to dry, linen is stored, etc., and whence rats occasionally emerge at night. Dinner, which is barbarously served at 12.30, was a more abundant edition of last night's supper.

The old Mother hovered about us during the meal, poking her witch's face into that of some unfortunate guest. Fortunately for us, she has a decided preference for the men, who do not seem grateful for her attentions. Psyche says she is a great flirt; but I should be sorry to endorse such an opinion.

She is a very well-known character in the neighbourhood, but hardly a popular one. The people say she is unkind to the poor, and tyrannical with the nuns, and she has a great reputation for "canniness." To do her justice, she is wonderfully keen and active for her age; but she is an undoubted despot, with all the faults of her qualities.

Psyche was anxious to account for the presence of the little monk in the garden, which she considers highly improper. It seems that there is a small band of brothers living in the convent, who perform the service in the chapel and help in the garden. They are bound by no vows, are merely ordinary peasants "in retreat." In the morning they wear blouses for their work; later in the day they appear as full-blown monks. Did you ever hear of such laxity in a convent? I believe St. Odile is regarded with great disfavour by the bishop, who naturally enough objects to the mixture of soul-saving and hotel-keeping, an arrangement which has gone on for the last thirty years. There are rumours that the place is to pass into the hands of an hotel proprietor; so I suppose the days of this most unique establishment are numbered. I am glad to have seen it and to have lived here; it is an interesting experience, and in many ways a pleasant one. The air is very good.

---

62. The Roman historian, Titus Livy; the text would be his *History of Rome*.
63. The plays of the Enlightenment philosopher, Voltaire (1694–1778).

There are some beautiful walks in the neighbourhood – old ruins to dream in, old towns to explore, endless pine forests to wander in. Psyche and I feel quite set up by our fortnight's stay. And though the prices seem rather high at starting, we have decided that the place is cheap. If not generous, the old Mother is just, and our bills are quite clear from the usual list of "extras." Tomorrow we start for the Black Forest. Cyril and Florian[64] are to meet us at Freyburg, which will be delightful; Cyril is Psyche's brother, as you know. Psyche sends her love, and so does your idle

MELISSA.

P.S. If you want to know more about St. Odile, read Katherine Lee's book, *In the Alsatian Mountains.*[65]

---

64. Characters in Tennyson's *The Princess* and Gilbert and Sullivan's *Princess Ida.*
65. Katherine Lee's *In the Alsatian Mountains: A Narrative of a Tour in the Vosges* (1883).

In the Black Forest (1884)

Gasthaus zum Titisee
Altenweg, Baden,
August

My dear Blanche,

We were very glad to get away from the nuns and from that mongrel Alsace, with its mixture of race, language, and coinage.

Cyril and Florian, looking horribly German in their students' caps, met us at the Freyburg Bahnhof, and insisted on driving us all over the town, in spite of the excessive heat. I quite fell in love with Freyburg – a bright sunny little place, with gardens and villas, and wide rambling streets. Psyche considers my admiration for it the mark of a frivolous taste, and clings to her preference for grim old Strasburg.

At five o'clock the next morning we set out for Titisee on the top of a tall diligence, driven by a light-hearted coachman in the wonderful shiny hat that the German post official is doomed to wear in the service of his Kaiser.[66] Cyril and Florian were there to see us off – a great piece of devotion when one reflects on the early hour and their slothful habits.

66. Kaiser Wilhelm I (1797–1888).

We had a wonderful six hours' drive, begun in a mysterious morning world of mist and silence, ending in the full blaze of an August noontide. The post-road winds slowly upwards among pine-clad hills, sunny meadows, and tall gray cliffs. The most beautiful part is through a pass called the Hoellenthal, where one is completely shut in by the frowning gray rocks.

Alas! All good things must pass. The Goths and Visigoths[67] are actually at work on a railway which will not spare the Hoellenthal itself. In another year or two the yellow coaches will be seen no more on the road to Titisee; light-hearted coachmen with shiny hats will have completely vanished; there will be nothing but smoke and steam, and the grimy faces of the engine-drivers. I begin to sympathise with Grandpapa's laments over the good old coaching days.

There were only two other passengers besides ourselves outside the diligence – a married couple, not long past the honeymoon stage, I should say; the woman shrill, sharp-featured, with light hair and eyelashes, very voracious over the ham sandwiches and hard-boiled eggs with which her husband plied her; very vigilant over the husband, a meek and cheerful little person, evidently much in awe of his wife. I was determined to talk to the man, in spite of the she-dragon, and assailed him with questions in my fluent German – Psyche says it was a positive case of assault.

The woman expressed much shrill surprise at the fact of our travelling alone.

"And you always go *ganz allein*? Without a gentleman?" And she clutched at her miserable specimen of manhood with complacent triumph.

You can imagine our scorn. I wonder when the German Hausfrau will consider the question of casting off the yoke!

It was nearly eleven when the coach set us down at the door of our destination, a picturesque pinewood hotel on the borders

67. Migratory Germanic peoples arising during the Roman Empire.

of a beautiful lake set amid the hills. No sooner had we collected our belongings round us than the polite host appeared, and informed us, in unexceptionable English, that the hotel was full. Psyche sat down on the boxes in despair. I suggested immediate return to Freyburg. Finally a compromise was effected; we were to leave our luggage at Titisee, and pass the night at the Black Bear, an extremely primitive posting-inn, half a mile away. Soon we espied the familiar form of Gama,[68] in all the glory of a Camford boating-suit, who administered consolation in the form of a row on the lake, and escorted us later on to the Bear. We slept in a wonderful room, smelling of cows and pine wood, and furnished with no fewer than four beds. Psyche says she was kept awake all night by the sighing of the cows, who were only divided from us by a thin partition. But everything was clean in its way, and the cooking was really excellent.

We are now thoroughly established at Titisee, and have come to the conclusion that we like it. Would you like to know what we are doing with ourselves?

After an early simple breakfast we generally go for a row on the lake in one of the unwieldy tubs, which are the only available craft. Then we read till one o'clock, the hour for dinner – the usual midday "stodge" so dear to the heart of the Teuton. The meal, I may remark, is invariably well cooked and badly served. After dinner we lounge, walk, and bathe till supper time, and there is usually no very large gap between supper and bed.

Don't we sound healthy, wealthy, and wise? No tea, no cram, no midnight oil. I hope everybody at Princess Ida's University will profit by our example.

The people here are mostly Germans, and we are too busy and too ignorant to explore them. Of course there is the usual English family – father, mother, daughter, and grown-up sons, who sit at a

68. Character in Tennyson's *The Princess* and Gilbert and Sullivan's *Princess Ida.*

separate table, play tennis, and apparently try hard to delude themselves into thinking they are in their native land.

Hilarion[69] is living at a village on the top of the hill, a mile or two off. He fetched us for coffee at his inn the other day; it was such a beautiful walk through shady pine woods, and such a sweet little straggling village, lying amid the hills. These Black Forest folk are charming, very frank and homely, and quite ignoring differences of rank. Indeed, some of the old peasant families are very proud in their way, and not at all disposed to bow down before the stranger on these hills which they have guarded for so many generations.

One day we made an excursion to Lenzkirch, a so called town some miles off, where clock-making and straw-plaiting are carried on. We were refused admittance to the factories, so had to content ourselves with exploring the sunny straggling little place, lying asleep in the noontide heat. Intrepid Psyche asked permission to go over the village school, and we were graciously led into the classrooms where the lessons were going on. In one of them a stern young schoolmaster, with a clever, sad face, was teaching arithmetic to a class of very small boys. O, what dull little brains under the round flaxen skulls! What insuperable difficulties presented by the problem of taking two from five! No wonder the poor young schoolmaster gnashed his teeth and rolled his eye with rage. We talked to him after the lesson, and found him intelligent, but gloomy. Psyche has all sorts of romantic theories about him. Afterwards we saw him drilling the boys outside the schoolhouse, administering cuffs with a practised skill that would have killed the germs of romance in any heart but Psyche's. But she made off at once for the village shop, bought a cartload of nasty sweets, and asked her pedagogue for permission to distribute them among his flock. It was not till she had employed her extremest arts of persuasion that the stern young disciplinarian would give his consent. You may imagine the delight of the youngsters. No doubt they thought the English ladies

69. Character in Gilbert and Sullivan's *Princess Ida*.

in the thick boots and Liberty handkerchiefs were escaped lunatics or munificent fairies.

Girls and boys learn together in the school, but only the latter are taught drilling, which is a great pity: don't you think so?

When we went away Psyche presented her schoolmaster with a rose, which he sniffed with ostentatious gratitude till we were out of sight.

I quoted "Maud Müller"[70] as we went back:

> "Of all sad words of mouth or pen,
> The saddest are these – it might have been."

Psyche was cross, and said I spoiled everything by self-consciousness!

Last night we had a concert, when our English-speaking host – who, pardon me, is a host in himself – charmed us all by his performance on the violin. I think, if I could play like that, I should not want to keep an hotel. Of course some of the ladies sang – songs about spring, and roses, and nightingales (who ever knew a German song that had not a nightingale in it?), and there was a mild performance on the piano.

Do you feel inclined to leave Camford and join us here for a week or two? I am sure it would suit you. It is such a fair, smiling, home-like country, with its fragrant woods and meadows, its quiet villages nestling among the hills; its babbling streams and running brooks – such a contrast to that grim Vosges country, with its solitary ruins and endless forests, and where there was always a skull carved at the base of the wayside crosses. We have planned an expedition to the Feldberg, the highest mountain in the Black Forest. We shall probably take our bags and stay overnight, and attempt to see the sunrise, as one does on the Rigi. I only hope we shall be more successful than one usually is on the Rigi.

70. A poem by John Greenleaf Whittier (1807–1892).

This letter is running to inordinate length, and it is nearly post-time. Psyche joins with me in love to you and all at Princess Ida's. She hopes I have not been libelling her. – Yours ever,

MELISSA.

Revenge (1885)

Chapter 1

Charlotte Cuts Bread And Butter[71]

"Cherry, my dear, it is half-past eight," said the rector, as he came into the parlour, watch in hand.

"I'm quite ready, Papa; it's only just time, and Miss Theodora is never punctual."

Cherry was standing in the middle of the room, while the other children, Maggie and Patrick and little Hal, revolved slowly round her.

"Miss Hawkins has made your gown splendidly!" said fifteen year-old Maggie, adjusting for the hundredth time her sister's fresh, white flounces.

"Hurray! Isn't she a swell!" cried Patrick, standing before her with wide-spread knickerbockered legs.

"Hurray, hurray!" echoed little Hal, dancing about vaguely in his short petticoats.

The rector patted his daughter's cheek, sighed and smiled; "Well, Cherry, I suppose you are to be grown up after tonight," he said; "a woman of the world who has been to balls."

71. From Thackeray's poem, "Sorrows of Werther," a satire of Goethe's *The Sorrows of Young Werther* (1774).

Cherry lifted her radiant face to his, and put her hand into her father's. It said a great deal for her youthful prettiness that it had emerged so triumphantly from Miss Hawkin's handiwork. Fortunately, it is not till after seventeen that most of us begin to be dependent on our dressmakers.

"I suppose Miss Theodora will wear her pearls. I wonder what dress she will put on?" mused Maggie.

"Miss Theodora will look lovely whatever she wears!" cried Cherry. "Now, Patrick, promise me not to tease Hal; and you must let Maggie put you to bed directly I've gone. Maggie will give you your suppers at once."

"Miss Lascelles is late," said the rector, taking out his watch again.

Maggie, with a matronly air, had neared the sideboard and begun operations on the home-baked loaf. Hal watched her with big eyes, then began to whimper as the approaching separation from Cherry was brought home to him by this unwonted proceeding.

"What's the matter, my darling?" cried Cherry, as, overcome with the sudden sense of desolation, Hal buried his head with a rush and a roar, in his sister's trim flounces.

"I don't want Maggie's bread and butter – it's nasty!" said naughty Hal between his sobs.

"Oh Hal, that isn't good. It's very kind of Maggie to give you your supper. See, how could I cut it with my gloves on?"

"I think he'd better go to bed without any supper at all," said Maggie offended, handing a great slice to the less sensitive Patrick.

Cherry, oblivious of the new frock, and in defiance of all educational codes, had taken Hal into her arms and was administering alternate kisses and moral remarks. "He is going to be a good boy," she announced at last, setting down the little tousled bundle which looked rather ashamed of itself; "he's going to bed like a lamb, and won't wake up till the morning." She moved to the sideboard as she spoke and took up the bread knife.

"You'll spoil your gloves and it's more than he deserves," said the sterner Maggie.

Cherry took off her gloves and set to work on the loaf.

"The carriage has come I heard wheels and now they have stopped," cried Maggie.

"Give me some, too," said Patrick, who had finished his first slice.

"My dear, Jane has gone to the door," protested the rector.

"In a minute, Papa," said Cherry, still intent on her loaf. Then she lifted her eyes, and as she did so, a deep flush sprang to her cheek. Someone was standing in the doorway, uncertain apparently, whether to enter; a stranger, a formidable presence, in a dress-coat, with a brown beard, with glittering eyeglasses that did not altogether hide the amused smile in the eyes behind them. A dragon with flaming tail could scarcely have been a more startling apparition on the familiar threshold! Cherry's knife paused midway; the expectant Patrick forgot his hunger in astonishment.

The stranger came forward with a little bow. "I must ask pardon for intrusion. I am Miss Lascelles's envoy; I believe I am speaking to Miss Dangerfield?"

"I must apologise for my servant's stupidity," said the short-sighted rector coming across the room, and sparing poor Cherry from answering this overwhelming personage; "my daughter will not keep you a moment. Pray be seated."

"I am ready now," said Cherry, drawing on her gloves.

"Don't eat too much supper!" cried Patrick, with his mouth full.

"Come home in the morning!" said Hal, dancing round with a renewed sense of the festivity of the occasion.

*****

"I can't see you, but I'm sure you look charming," said a sweet, languid voice from the depths of the great, gloomy carriage, as the stranger handed in little Miss Dangerfield and established himself opposite the ladies.

"Miss Theodora, it's so kind of you to take me. Papa thinks so too," cried Cherry, with a little flutter.

"It's so nice to have you with me," said the voice, and a slender-gloved hand caressed Cherry's sturdy arm.

"Are we going to the *Stag* or the *Crown*?" asked the stranger, whose eyeglass was glittering in the gloom just opposite Cherry, in a way that rather alarmed her.

"To the *Stag*, we have given up having balls at the *Crown*."

"Ah, it's a long journey to the *Stag*."

"Not more than two miles, Ferdinand."

"Then it used to be longer ten years ago, Theodora! I drove there, if you remember, on the box of this very carriage, on just such a clear November night as this. It was the longest drive I ever had in my life."

A sigh, the flutter of a perfumed fan in the depths of the carriage.

Miss Lascelles leaned forward, and the lamplight fell on her clear-cut face, on the pearls in her ears, on the shimmering plush of her cloak.

"I'm afraid you must have forgotten to wrap the fur round your knees," she said, with a certain solicitude, as of retrospective regret.

"It is possible, Theodora. Ah, well, I have had many strange journeys since then."

"Mr. Clarke is a great traveller," said Miss Lascelles, turning graciously to Cherry, whom perhaps she had not thought worthy of a formal introduction.

"He has not rested the sole of his foot for ten years," said a voice from the direction of the eyeglass.

"That is a long time," ventured timid Cherry.

"Mr. Clarke has been to all sorts of out-of-the-way places," went on Miss Lascelles; "to Persia and Arabia and Syria. We are all hoping that he has brought home some sketches."

"I sketched a good deal from memory the first year or two, but there was a sameness in the subject," said Ferdinand Clarke, drily, "but I have a whole portfolio of drawings from the East, if anyone wants to see them. I didn't know you cared for such things, Theodora."

"I always liked your sketches. It used to make me quite unhappy that they were so much better than mine, when we went out painting together."

"What ages ago that seems! Well, I've brought enough Sheikhs and Shahs and sandy deserts to last you a lifetime."

"Have you brought them with you, Ferdinand? That is delightful. Perhaps you will show them to me – and Miss Dangerfield? – I am sure you would wish to see them, wouldn't you, Cherry?"

"Oh, very much indeed," said blushing Cherry.

"You must come to lunch tomorrow," went on Miss Lascelles, no doubt between us we can persuade Mr. Clarke to unpack his portfolio."

"I'm afraid I can't come, Miss Theodora. It doesn't do for me to be away at dinner-time!"

"Then come in later, and have some tea;" Miss Lascelles patted her friend's hand as she spoke and looked across at Ferdinand Clarke with eyes that seemed to say: "Is she not a dear, simple creature: But you mustn't laugh!"

When they got to the *Stag*, Cherry's colour came and went with a strange, new excitement as she followed Miss Lascelles upstairs to the dressing room. Her own little cloak was unfastened in a moment, and she was not anxious about the state of her hair and complexion. She wondered how Theodora could be so patient as she slowly divested herself of her rich mantle, and lingered before the mirror, adjusting her pale, fluffy hair, and the laces on her bodice. Ferdinand Clarke was waiting for them outside as the two women emerged for the dressing room. Cherry, round-eyed, rosy, very fresh and sweet in the ill-made white frock; Theodora, tall, slender, distinguished, splendid with pearl-grey satin and glittering pearls – a pretty, faded, discontented-looking woman, whose graceful head was always a little on one side; whose languid voice held always a note of gentle complaint. Ten years ago Theodora Lascelles had been held one of the most charming women in the county; not beautiful, not clever exactly, but fascinating in a sweet, feminine way, with little sprightlinesses that passed for brilliance. But she had passed the fatal boundary line which divides the twenties from the thirties without fulfilling any of the matrimonial expectations entertained of her, and many people hinted freely at a romance; at the tale of a woman who had loved not wisely, but too well; of a lover who had loved and ridden away.

The dancers were resting between the dances as the Manor House party made its way up the ballroom to where the more distinguished section of the company was assembled. Miss Lascelles was surrounded at once; Ferdinand Clarke watched her closely as she went through the various greetings, with her little, languid manner, so thoroughly well-bred in spite of a certain flimsiness. Theodora was still popular it seemed. People were still anxious to shake hands with her, to talk to her, to ask her to dance. And how young she was in spite of the haggard lines on her face; and yet it was not the old Theodora. Perhaps he was too loyal to acknowledge to himself that a gracious maturity might with advantage have replaced a certain stale juvenility which clung to her.

He had loved her all his life; was he to put her under a microscope and label her as a stunted growth?

Cherry had got over her fears, which indeed, had never prevailed to any extent. Kind Cherry had always found the world remarkably kind. Now her brown eyes danced with innocent satisfaction as the young men crowded about her, filling up her card with their names.

"Theodora," said Ferdinand Clarke, "will you keep the fifteenth dance for me."

"I have given it away already. But you can have the fifth or sixth."

"No, it's the fifteenth I want and mean to have. It's a longstanding debt."

"But I have promised it to Colonel Ralph."

"You were not always so conscientious in these matters, Theodora."

"But you were always a very obstinate person, Ferdinand!"

He laughed: "Perhaps if you told the Colonel that that dance was promised ten years ago – "

"Ferdinand, you are unkind!"

She turned away with a little flush; Clarke knew that he had won. Then he made his way to where Cherry stood amid her crowd of youngsters. "Can you spare a dance to an antediluvian person, who doesn't know a waltz from the Highland fling?" he said.

She turned a blushing, questioning face towards him. He seemed a very formidable person beside the eager young men.

"Haven't you one left for me, Miss Dangerfield?"

"There is one," said Cherry; "the fifteenth."

"And that happens to be the single dance for which I am engaged."

"Perhaps you will have the sixth extra?" timidly.

"Ah, that delusive 'sixth extra!' No, no, Miss Dangerfield. Old birds are not to be caught with chaff. Ah – well." He bowed and walked off with a vague sense of disappointment.

The evening wore on. Cherry was dancing every dance; Miss Lascelles danced a little and strolled about a great deal; Ferdinand Clarke did not dance at all; he leaned in the doorway surveying the scene with unseeing eyes, while his thoughts wandered back to just such another festivity in which he had shared.

Ten years ago! It was the same room, in many instances the same people; – there was Theodora, here was he, Ferdinand, lounging about the doorway just as he had done before.

Ten years ago! Then, he had been wild with passion and pain, mad with unutterable longing, cruelly, fiercely jealous. Now, he could look across calmly enough at Theodora opposite, trifling with her fan and talking languidly to Colonel Ralph. And yet, for the ten years in which he had been a wanderer on the face of the earth, the thought of her had never been long away from him. For him she had always been the one woman in the world. When his long wanderings had ended a few months ago, his first thought had been of Theodora; his first impulse, when he heard she was still unmarried, to seek her. Could it be that this gift, for which he had so long thirsted, was to be his at last? "Poor soul, she has suffered," he thought, looking at the worn face and recalling its former careless vivacity; "poor soul, – if one could make her happier."

On her part, Theodora had gone back to that other ball of ten years back. Ah, how happy she had been! True, she had paid for that happiness with all the peace and content of her life, but it had been worthwhile. At least she had thought so once. Latterly she had begun to doubt. She looked across at Ferdinand. Why had he come? What a loyal and kindly soul was his! He, at least, was always the same, whatever other people might be. Was he the same indeed? Was he not a hundred times stronger, surer, better-looking? Did her heart cry out to her the bitter woman's cry, "he has grown and I have dwindled!" as she sat there thinking of long ago; of the lover who had spoilt her life; of the lover whose life she had done so much to spoil?

"This is our dance," said Ferdinand, coming across to her.

"You see, I do pay my debts sometimes," she said, as they strolled into the rose-lit anteroom.

"There are some debts that one can't always pay. Ah, Theodora, no doubt it seemed a small thing, but you were very cruel."

"It is you who are cruel now, Ferdinand."

"Perhaps I mean to be. Do you know what that dance meant to me? It was the only one you would give me – a miserable quadrille, low down on your card – but you promised it three days before, with one of your sweetest smiles. I lay awake hugging the thought of it, I dreamed of it for three nights. All through that evening at the ball I stood alone, watching you and counting the moments. When the time for our dance came round you told me I had made a mistake! I laughed in your face at that."

The laces on her bodice fluttered; her lips and nostrils quivered. "I only danced with one person that night," she said in a low voice.

Ferdinand was silenced; she had made him feel a brute by this unexpected admission. He knew no details, but he could guess roughly at the outlines of her story. It was a terrible misfortune to be born a woman, he thought. A most unloverlike attitude of mind had he but known it.

Cherry came into the room with her attendant cavalier. Theodora rose from her seat. "Are we disturbing you?" cried Cherry, preparing to beat a retreat.

"No," she said, with a thin smile; "we old fogies were taking refuge from the dancing. But it is over now," and she swept from the room, Clarke following thoughtfully in her train.

*****

"Goodnight, Miss Charlotte," said Ferdinand, as he bade farewell to Cherry, in the hall at the Rectory that night. "Tomorrow come Katzenjammer and Arab sketches."

Cherry was puzzled. "He forgot my name," she thought, rather humiliated, as she went upstairs to bed.

At the Manor House, Miss Lascelles sat down before the mirror. "Does he see the wrinkles as plainly as I do?" she cried, peering at herself. "Does he know how few people have loved me? How weary I am of this life? Is it possible that he has not changed?"

In the room next to her Ferdinand Clarke was saying to himself, with a sigh: "Poor Theodora, poor soul!"

It is significant when a man applies such an epithet to the woman he has loved.

Chapter 2

Othello And Desdemona[72]

At half-past three the next day, Cherry came tripping into the big drawing room at the Manor House. Theodora, languid and graceful, lay back in an armchair by the great fireplace, interposing a light screen between her face and the blaze. Ferdinand, in a velvet coat, stood near her on the rug. They were not talking as Cherry came in rosy and fresh from her walk, with a pleased, shy look in her eyes. Miss Lascelles suffered herself to be kissed and even deigned to offer a caress.

At the Manor House, little Miss Dangerfield was a privileged person; perhaps it was that she brought incense to that tawdry, tinsel shrine, where so few came now to worship. Ferdinand Clarke wheeled a low chair for Cherry to the little table where lay his portfolio, and brought a stool for her feet.

72. Characters in Shakespeare's *Othello*.

"Oh, thank you," said Cherry overwhelmed.

"We are going to take advantage of the light and look at the sketches before tea," said Theodora, drawing her chair nearer to the table; "now, Ferdinand, we are all attention."

Clarke knelt down on the rug beside her and opened the portfolio.

"Charming, charming! How you have improved!" cried Theodora, turning over the sketches.

Cherry said nothing. She was all eyes and ears as Clarke held up the sketches one by one, and proceeded with his exposition. Perhaps he was carried away by his subject; perhaps by the eager intentness of one of his listeners; it is certain that he grew remarkably eloquent, it may even be a little garrulous, as he told the story of his ten years' adventure.

Theodora put up her screen to hide a yawn; she was unutterably bored.

"Is she pretending?" she thought, looking sharply at Cherry. She was not accustomed that people, least of all Ferdinand Clarke, should display so much interest in dull impersonalities in her presence. She began to feel it as a slight. Not the most poignant reproaches, the most remorseless probing of old wounds would have hurt her as this absorption in Sheikhs and Shahs. "Did men ever care. Could he have cared, when he was so busy painting his little pictures, keeping account of his adventures?" She fell back at last on watching his face, and dwelling on the memories which it recalled. Ten years ago she might have feigned an interest in sandy deserts and murderous Arabs, but ten years ago people never talked to her about such things. The fading light put an end at last to the discourse.

"It has been delightful," said Theodora, with a ghost of one of the old smiles. "Please Ferdinand, ring the bell. I am sure you must want some tea after your exertions."

"I'm afraid I have been unconscionably tedious," he answered; "I had almost got back to the East again."

"It is as well that it was 'almost.' What would the lion-hunting London ladies have done, if they had lost their distinguished traveller?"

"I am quite indifferent as to what ladies in London may think or do," said Ferdinand, shortly, and Theodora was mollified.

Clarke walked back with Cherry in the dusk to the Rectory, and, at her timid invitation followed her into the lamp-lit parlour where the children were waiting tea for their sister.

"Oh Papa," she said, "I wish you had been there. Mr. Clarke has been telling us about Syria, and Arabia, and Persia."

Before he left, it was arranged that Ferdinand should bring over his sketches to the Rectory on the afternoon of the following day.

As they undressed that night, the rector's little daughters discussed the events of the day.

"I don't like your Mr. Clarke," said critical Maggie, "he is always laughing at one behind those horrid eyeglasses."

"I think he is very nice," answered Cherry, demurely; "I was terribly afraid of him at first, but he is so kind, one can't be afraid for long."

"Mrs. Duncan says he is going to marry Miss Theodora," went on Maggie.

Cherry blew out the candle and got into bed without so much as a "goodnight."

Chapter 3

Cherry Decides

Ferdinand Clarke sauntered about the Manor House garden, his hands in his pockets, his pipe in his mouth. He was thinking of Theodora; of Theodora past, of Theodora present, of Theodora as she might be in the future. It was no new occupation; she had been the subject of his thoughts pretty constantly for the greater part of his life. She had played fast and loose with him, had done much to spoil the best years of existence for him, but there was nothing but pity and tenderness in his thoughts of her. There was no doubt, poor woman, that she had altered considerably; that her temper was uncertain, that she took no interest in anything beyond the merest personalities. "The scoundrel!" said Clarke to himself; "the scoundrel, I always read his soul in his good-looking face."

He found himself wishing most heartily that things had gone well with Theodora; that he had come back to find her prosperous, blooming, married. As it was, could much happiness accrue if they agreed to join together their spoiled lives? Well, such chance of happiness as lay there should be hers. Clarke was a modest man, but he did not think this time to plead in vain with Theodora.

Upstairs, Miss Lascelles paced her room, strangely agitated. "Has he come to rescue me? Am I beyond rescue," was the half-formed thought in her brain. The love which had spoilt her life was dead, long, long ago. Only an unutterable weariness and emptiness remained.

* * * * *

Ferdinand Clarke came out from the Rectory that afternoon with a look of deep thought on his face. Something in Cherry's eyes had moved him strangely. "Does she know how much they say, those brown eyes of hers? Child, is it the truth they speak? Is it possible, or am I a vain old fool?"

Could it be that life yet held in store for him more than broken ends, old cast clouts of happiness? Pshaw! The whole thing was absurd. But he would go to town the next day, and, for the present at least, he would not speak to Theodora.

* * * * *

Two days after Ferdinand Clarke's departure, Cherry came to see Miss Lascelles. She came by appointment; it was the day on which Theodora usually attempted to impart to her little friend something of her own dabbling knowledge of water-colour painting.

"Oh, I can't give you your lesson today, child," the elder woman cried; "I have a headache – a shocking headache!"

"Oh, I am so sorry!" cried Cherry, kissing the slender hand.

"Oh, don't worry me. I hate so much pretence! The world is all pretence!"

Cherry was much distressed. Theodora drew her towards her with some remorse. "You look pale yourself, child. There are great circles under your eyes. Take care of your complexion. It is the best gift God gives a woman. Heaven pity her when she has outlived it!"

Cherry was greatly shocked; the idol was descending from the pedestal. Theodora's quick vanity saw something of her thought; she took the girl in her arms and kissed her.

"Ah, forgive me, I am a cross old woman. Little Cherry, you mustn't leave off loving me."

Then followed much tenderness between the two women.

"I have a message for you," said Theodora presently; "Mr. Clarke bade me make his farewells to you."

"Mr. Clarke has gone?"

"He went the day before yesterday," answered Theodora, intent on her own thoughts.

"He gave me two of his most beautiful sketches," said Cherry, turning away her face, which was no longer pale.

"How kind," said Theodora indifferently. Cherry's incense, the flattery of her innocent worship, were all very well; Cherry's little personal affairs were another matter. Sometimes, indeed, Miss Lascelles affected a gracious and exaggerated interest in them; but she had not sufficient energy today. She was thinking of Ferdinand. Would he fulfil his half-promise of returning the next week?

It is easy enough to be constant in a desert; in London it is another affair.

*****

Cherry stood disconsolately in the wintry garden holding little Hal by the hand. Her face was pale still; the circles were deeper than ever under her eyes. This last week had made her sadly wise. For seven nights she had sobbed herself to sleep; already she began to foresee a time when there would be no more tears; only a dull, empty aching through the long days.

"Won't it be summer soon?" asked Hal, depressed by the pervasive November dreariness.

"Not for a long, long time, my darling," said Cherry, kissing him. "Ah, your face is as cold as ice! Run, Hal, run and get warm."

"You can't catch me," said Hal, in a challenging tone, setting off down the path.

Cherry, with her heavy heart, went dutifully in pursuit, round the garden, round again; then, at the garden gate, Hal was overtaken and captured.

Just at that moment someone was standing, with his hand on the latch, about to enter; a respectable Philistine, in a tall hat, with a double-eyeglass, with a short brown beard.

"Mr. Clarke!" said Cherry, with a swift, glad smile, holding out her little cold hand.

I think she would have been shocked had she known how much her eyes told him. But Ferdinand Clarke was not shocked at all; he knew that in that moment Cherry had decided her own fate and his.

*****

It was settled that very day. I will not speak of the Rector's surprise, of Cherry's great gladness, of Ferdinand's deep content. After tea the two happy people strolled up and down the dusky road outside the house. Once or twice Ferdinand glanced across at the lights of the Manor House glimmering in the distance. He wished that letter to Theodora were written. She would never know that he had been on his way to her that afternoon; that it was almost by chance he had stopped at the Rectory. Suddenly he drew up his head and recited slowly:

> "Werther had a love for Charlotte
> Such as words could never utter;
> Would you know how first he met her!
> She was cutting bread and butter."[73]

"Charlotte!" said Cherry, "you are so fond of that name. You said 'Goodnight Miss Charlotte' after the ball."

He told her the story over which so many of us have laughed and cried.

"Only," he said in conclusion, "in this case there is no Albert, at least, I think not?"[74] He smiled down at her half-questioningly.

"No, there is no Albert," said Cherry decidedly; "but you – Mr. Clarke, Ferdinand – did you ever – ? but of course you did!" cried world-wise Cherry.

"Yes, of course I did," he answered, and, stooping, kissed her forehead.

73. From Thackeray's poem, "Sorrows of Werther."
74. "Albert" isn't mentioned in Thackeray's poem but is Charlotte's partner in Goethe's novel.

Easter-Tide in Tunbridge Wells (1885)

Mount Edgcumbe, Tunbridge Wells,
April

Dear Psyche,

Please cancel your order at the stationer's for foreign note-paper, and do not trouble to lay in a supply of 2½d stamps. It is not going to be Rome, it is not going to be the Riviera; Ortrud[75] and I have given up our more ambitious plans, and have settled down quietly in the homely Kentish country for our Easter holiday. And what, I hear you ask, are your reasons for this meek and uninteresting proceeding? Lack of funds, lack of time, and a most plentiful lack of energy. Moreover, I by no means share your truly insular conviction that "abroad" (vague and vast region!) is the only place to go to in search of enjoyment. I have every intention of "putting in a good time" without crossing the Channel for it, or even the river Tweed.

The place is new to Ortrud, but I was here last year with Adeline[76] (who has gone the way of all flesh and got married), and we have been fortunate enough to secure the old lodgings. Fortunate, I say. Picture it, you cockney! – a white, irregular wooden house, all windows and corners, standing alone on a high shoulder of gorse-covered down. All around stretches the wide, green country, rising, falling – woodland and meadow and waste. There are wonderful lights and shadows, mists,

75. Levy possibly uses the name, Ortrud, in reference to Richard Wagner's *Lohengrin*.
76. Levy possibly uses the name, Adeline, in reference to Byron's poem, *Don Juan*.

hazes, splashes of colour, such as I verily believe one sees nowhere out of old England. Here and there a house gleams white through the trees, or a straggling scarlet line marks where a village nestles against the hill-side. Fresh breezes – capricious, uncertain, full of the vague fragrance of early spring – come blowing across to us; above, the birds chirp and flutter cheerfully; below, the roofs of the old town gleam like gold in the sunlight. Tunbridge Wells! What a charming, old-world sound it has! How fraught with suggestions of

> "The tea-cup times of hood and hoop,
> And when the patch was worn!"[77]

And it looks even better than it sounds; a queer, little casual, place, all ups and downs and unexpected turnings, with delightful old-fashioned houses starting up in the most unlikely regions.

Then, of course, there is the Pantiles, that odd little parade, with its shops, its colonnade, its bulging house-fronts, and the chalybeate spring at one end, where you can drink water out of a glass for a penny if you are genteel, or out of a tin mug for nothing if you are vulgar.

A few stray spinsters, a few nursemaids, an occasional "old buck" – who clings, no doubt, to the belief that "the Wells" are the height of fashion – were sunning themselves here this morning, marching up and down in time to an emphatic brass band.

I sat down on a seedy wooden bench and tried to picture the gay folk who once thronged the old pavement, flirting, fluttering, drinking the waters; curtseying, bowing, rustling their silks and clinking their swords; talking their smart eighteenth-century talk, and paying their prodigious eighteenth-century compliments; being bored, and sick and sorry very often, I make no doubt.

Fanny Burney[78] was here – don't you remember? – with Mrs. Thrale,[79] who bought an inkstand at a "toyshop" for the wonderful little girl who came to breakfast with them. I think the lively and observant

77. The extract is from Tennyson's poem, "The Talking Oak."
78. Prolific author, Frances Burney (1752–1840).
79. Hester Thrale, author (c. 1740–1821).

Burney (I never *can* bring myself to like her) must have been in her element in such a centre of gossip and scandal as "the Wells" were in those days. Only think of it! – all fashionable society concentrated in one or two small towns, Tunbridge, Bath, Cheltenham! What a paradise for the paragraph-mongers, who in these degenerate days must survey mankind from China to Peru when the holiday season sets in, if they mean to furnish the usual fare of spicy personalities.

I expect the glimpse of Bath life one gets in "The Rivals"[80] gives us some notion of existence at the other fashionable watering places of the day. Other times, other manners! I for one cannot help thinking that there is a great deal to be said for our own nineteenth century, in spite of the picturesque rivalry of good old times.

But I am prosing on dreadfully, vainly trying to express what Thackeray has said so charmingly in his little Roundabout Paper, "Tunbridge Toys."[81] Do read it at once if you do not know it. And talking of Thackeray reminds me that the people in "The Virginians," the Warringtons, and Hetty and her sister,[82] must be reckoned among the distinguished visitors to Tunbridge Wells. They seem quite as real, to me at least, as Johnson[83] and Burke[84] and Goldsmith,[85] as all the fine and clever people who dwell, no less than they, in the land of shadows. Poor Hetty! I think her little, silent, undramatic story, without beginning or middle or end to speak of, contains a higher tragedy, touches more deeply the roots of human pathos, than a hundred tales of weeping heroines, betrayed by their lovers or tortured by the pangs of an overwrought self-consciousness.

I seem to see your face, dear Psyche, as you read. I see its growing weariness, scorn, disgust. You ask for the bread of news, and I give you the stone of maundering reflections! I plead guilty, but I put in

80. Richard Brinsley Sheridan's (1751–1816) play which premiered in London in 1775.
81. See Thackeray's *Roundabout Papers* (1864).
82. Refers to Thackeray's *The Virginians: A Tale of the Last Century* (1857–1859).
83. Samuel Johnson (1709–1784), or "Dr. Johnson": prolific writer, poet, philosopher, and author of *A Dictionary of the English Language* (1755).
84. Edmund Burke (1729–1797), architect of classical conservatism.
85. Oliver Goldsmith.

a plea for extenuating circumstances. What incidents, not of a startling nature, but worthy of the barest record, are likely to befall two sober British spinsters of sedentary habits and respectable character. With us – this confession is terrible but true –the absorbing question is that of our bodies, what we shall eat and drink! You don't know how tiresome it is catering for two people who are at the same time frugal and hungry. We both of us can remember irregular verbs in at least four languages, and Ortrud has whole scenes from Wagner's operas by heart, but somehow we always forget that potatoes are the accepted adjunct for meat, and that, although man does not live by bread alone, it is as well to order some from the baker. As for the beef and mutton question it is too terrible, too complicated, too hopeless! We seemed at first to see a vision of perpetual chops looming before us. Then Ortrud plucked up heart, and taking matters in her own hands, ordered a sturdy round of beef, whose presence, although it gives splendour to our board, is beginning to grow monotonous.

> "And still their house affairs would draw them thence!"

Poor Desdemonas, there is not the least vestige of an Othello in this spinster-ridden place.[86]

By-the-by, I think Othello would feel a little bored if he found himself here; it is the place for churches, for bath chairs, for photographs of the Royal family; but it is not by any means the place for moving accidents by flood and field.

But such as it is, it does very well for us. We take long walks in the beautiful, spring country; we potter about among the provision shops, we sun ourselves on the Pantiles when the band is playing; we have even (tell it not in Gath nor in Camford!) borrowed a novel of Miss Broughton's[87] from the circulating library, which Ortrud is eagerly devouring, and out of which she regales me with choice extracts, as

86. The quotation and the characters are from Shakespeare's *Othello*.

87. Novelist Rhoda Broughton.

I studiously pore over Goethe's "Wahrheit und Dichtung"[88] or the leading article of the *Pall Mall Gazette!* Our sitting room has two windows, two easy chairs, and a sofa. Everything is clean and pleasant, not at all suggestive of the normal British "lodgings."

We pay two guineas a week, which seems very dear, does it not, after those wonderfully cheap hotels in the Vosges and the Black Forest; but cheap and nasty always go together in this expensive country of ours. I must leave off and write to Adeline, who, no doubt, is anxious for news of her old haunt. She is in Japan now, which seems a long way to go, even for a husband.

Ortrud joins with me in love, and hopes that you and Blanche are having a pleasant "vac."

Yours,
MELISSA

88. "Truth and Poetry": Goethe's autobiography, *Aus Meinem Leben: Dichtung und Wahrheit* (1811).

Out of the World (1886)

The Falcon Inn,
St. Mawgan-in-Pydar,
Vale of Lanherne, Cornwall.
October

Dearest Psyche,

Your most meagre little note, announcing your arrival in town, was forwarded to me here. Alas, my friend! We seem fated never to meet, like the pathetic little man and woman in the weather-prophet toy of one's youth; I used to feel so sorry for the poor woman as she emerged from her gay house, prophesying sunshine, only to find that her mate, in obedience to some cruel and inscrutable law of his being, had withdrawn at her approach! Shall I read you a sermon on that toy? It would not be difficult, but you shall be spared for this once.

To speak quite plainly, while you were disporting yourself in the country, I was languishing in town, and now the situation is reversed. Yes, I have lost every claim to consideration as a person of fashion, and must confess to having stayed in London all through August and September. I will not trouble you with any account of the various complications which led to my abandonment of the usual "flitting"; suffice, that they arose in about an equal degree from "the eternal lack of pence," and the engagement and marriage of my sister Josephine. I had determined to follow the example of several millions of my fellow-townsfolk, and do without a holiday altogether; but when the excitement of wedding preparations was over, and the culminating catastrophe of wedding functions had "supervened;" when the boys had gone back to school, and a company of sparrows discussing the rice on the pavement outside was the only reminder of what had occurred, a great blankness fell upon my soul.

I found that, like Lady Clara Vere de Vere, I was sickening of a vague disease, but, not being possessed of "boundless wealth," my case was even more pitiable than that of the sweet-eyed enchantress.[89]

Genuine Cockney as I am, I began to

> "Loathe the squares and streets
> And the faces that one meets"[90]

with an unutterable loathing. "Anywhere, anywhere out of the world,"[91] I cried; and then it was that someone suggested this place as likely to meet the wants of a seedy and penurious spinster desirous of rest and change. So, one day, now about two weeks ago, I found myself speeding westward across the October country, and on the afternoon of the morrow (for I had passed the night with kind friends at Plymouth) I alighted at a little wayside station, where a waggonette from the Falcon Inn awaited me. A long drive across a beautiful autumnal country, a cautious descent into a green and placid valley, and the carriage drew up before a little oblong stone house, with an unobtrusive sign board above the door. A kind hostess came out to meet me and led me into a charming room, with books, and flowers, and pictures, and a log fire blazing merrily in the grate. Presently, a dimpled maid appeared bearing on her tray a dainty meal wherein homemade bread and clotted cream figured largely, and where a fragrant teapot crowned the whole. I began to feel that my rash and sudden flight from town was

89. The sentence refers to Tennyson's poem, "Lady Clara Vere de Vere."
90. From Tennyson's poem, "Maud."
91. Closing line of French poet, Charles Baudelaire's (1821–1867) "Anywhere Out of the World."

turning out more satisfactorily than many a planned and premeditated holiday. The two weeks that I have been here have only served to confirm and deepen the first pleasant impression; but the happiest holiday, like the happiest nation, is apt to have no history, and I am taking mine ease at mine inn at the expense of my correspondents!

You are one of the rare people who like "descriptions," which makes the lack of adventure less of a stumbling-block in writing to you, although, on the other hand, I was never a good hand at describing. Well, dear, as to the landscape, it is very big, and very green, and very uninhabited-looking. Down in my valley, my Vale of Lanherne (a nice romantic name, is it not? Sounds as though there ought to be a maid of Lanherne!) there are elm-trees, and little rushing brooks with moss-grown, fern-tufted banks and bridges; but beyond there is nothing but wave upon wave of downs, intersected by deep lanes, and terminating in one direction in tall slatey cliffs overhanging the Atlantic Ocean. As for the cottages, they are few and far between, and quite uninteresting – small, square blocks of stone and cement, slate-roofed, drab-tinted. Their distinguishing feature is that you never find two on the same level; each little house is stuck about at random on a little shelf of its own. The people are pleasant and good-looking, especially the men and the children; if our friend Gambogia were here, she would have half the village "sitting" to her in no time. I think I see you smile ironically as you read. "And this Cockney is deceiving herself, and thinks to deceive me" you are saying; "this person, who has a confessed preference for chimney-tops to tree-tops, is pretending to enjoy herself in a rustic solitude in the heart of October." No, dear, frankly, I am *not* playing at Wordsworth,[92] not trying to "get at one with nature," as one used to in the old days, before one had come to recognize one's limits; and I *do* enjoy my diurnal *Pall Mall*, and am not in the least indifferent to my weekly *Academy*. But I am genuinely interested in the hitherto unknown aspect of life which a village community such as ours presents.

92. The poet, William Wordsworth (1770–1850).

I have given up all attempts at work, though I occasionally *improve my French!* Do you remember our paper-backed library in the Black Forest last year? My kind hostess has instructed me in bread-making and cream-scalding, and is quite capable of giving instructions in a great many other things. We mix Matthew Arnold with our pastry, and wage war on questions of "the infinite" as we chop meat for pies; all this morning we were up to the eyes in argument, and up to the elbows in flour! It is quite refreshing to find people honestly interested in thinking out things for themselves, after the *tout-est-dit* attitude of the intellectual Londoner. It recalls the dear old days at Princess Ida's. Ah! Those fierce old fights round the fire! ... Malthusia has five children now, and never talks political economy; Agnostica has gone over to Rome; Democratica has married a capitalist and cuts all her old friends... "But, tush! I am puling," as Mr. Rutland Barrington says in the "Sorcerer."[93]

This afternoon I went up to the convent of Lanherne, which, screened by many trees, directly faces the "Falcon." In this fine old building, with its delicate stonework, delicately tinted by the hand of Time, are immured twenty ladies, nuns of the Carmelite order. The woman who showed me the chapel and burial ground (I was not allowed to penetrate into the building itself) spoke with enthusiasm of convent existence. It was a beautiful life, she said – for those who had the vocation! Did she propose taking the veil?

Alas! She had not the "vocation"!

Near the convent, and originally belonging to it, is the beautiful church with its tower of mellow stone and its grass-grown graveyard. Our idiot boy (of course we have an idiot boy, though his name is not "Foy")[94] was craning his long thin neck over the churchyard wall as I came through the lych-gate, an hour ago; the sun was setting behind the tall elms; the children were playing by the gold-tinted brook; a company of geese was promenading the road, engaged in animated

93. Rutland Barrington was an actor in Gilbert and Sullivan's *The Sorcerer*.

94. Refers to Wordsworth's poem, "The Idiot Boy."

conversation; a little farther on I could see that anomalous being, the village policeman (he is a most spurious-looking object), wisely passive as usual, and the rector's wife was speeding up the hill with a basket on her arm: nothing could have been more peaceful or rustic, but do you know what happened to me? I thought I heard a distant newsboy calling out Special Editions and terrible catastrophes! My case strikes me as more pathetic than that of poor Susan who imagined a river flowing through Cheapside![95]

I have had one really important experience – I have seen the Sea. Oh yes, I know that one used to go annually to the "seaside" in one's youth and ply one's wooden spade near the bathing machines; that one has fretted and strutted on a good many "Esplanades," and lain prostrate in many a "Ladies' Cabin," in later years; but that was quite another thing. Two miles' walk over the downs brought me to a long sandy tract, interspersed with brackish pools and rank grass. Over the sand I sped, in the face of a great sou'-wester, breathless, eager, towards the long creamy breakers.

A great solitary sea was churning and booming away at the base of the dark cliffs; nothing but sky, and ocean, but cliff and crag to be seen. No pier, no breakwater, no houses, save a lonely coast-guard's hut in the distance. The sight took away one's breath more effectually than the sou'-wester itself. I understood, for the first time, what poets mean when they write about the sea. This was no bathing pond for Cockneys, but the "great sweet mother, mother and lover of men, the sea," whose "sweet hard kisses are strong like wine," whose "large embraces are keen like pain."[96] I had quite a little rapture, all by myself, for which, alas! I paid with a bad headache next day.

"Is this the mighty ocean – is this all?" I wonder if Landor[97] knew the north-west coast of Cornwall?

---

95. Refers to Wordsworth's poem, "The Reverie of Poor Susan."
96. From Swinburne's "The Triumph of Time"; Levy uses the same poem in "Olga's Valentine" (pp. 650–1) and in *Reuben Sachs* (p. 276).
97. Refers to Walter Savage Landor's "Gebir."

Excuse these musings of a solitary, and write soon; or you might pay me a visit. You could ride and drive to your heart's content. Personally, I am satisfied to jog about the lanes in a disreputable-looking donkey-cart. The donkey is sturdy if obstinate, and can be brisk on occasion; and the hedgerows, crowning the deep lanes, are in all their autumn glory of russet leaves, red berries, gleaming blackberries, and purple sloes. In the midst of this October wealth it is strange to see such survivals of summer as flowering honey-suckle; and the cottage gardens are aglow with fuchsias and hydrangeas.

In any case I shall see you soon. Much as I admire the superior peace, simplicity, and beauty of a country life, I know that my own place is among the struggling crowd of dwellers in cities. I am like Browning's "icy fish" in "Caliban" – do you remember? – who

> "Longed to 'scape the rock stream where she lived
> And thaw herself within the lukewarm brine....
> Only she ever sickened, found repulse
> At the other kind of water...."[98]

With which effusion I conclude.

Write! I have a morbid craving for the postman. He only comes once a day!

Yours ever,
MELISSA.

98. From Robert Browning's poem, "Caliban upon Setebos."

Another Morning in Florence (1886)[99]

(Dedicated to Mr. Ruskin)

A dull grey morning. Melissa, looking out from the tall old house opposite the Pitti Palace, sees damp pavements, damp roofs, and a forest of damp green umbrellas rising up from the cabs on the cab-stand opposite. "It is positively too dark for Santa Croce. Ruskin says we must have sunlight," cries Melissa, in her most pessimistic tones.

Hannamoria, the scribe and optimist, comes to the rescue. "Santa Croce won't run away; meanwhile, let us go to Santa Maria Novella, and look at Giotto's[100] St. Anna."

"Very well. Let us start at once."

"I confess I tremble," says Hannamoria, who loves her jest. "What is it your Ruskin says of the St. Anna? 'If you can be pleased with this, you can see Florence; but if not, you can never see it.' Are you prepared to go home if you don't like it?"

"You may laugh at Ruskin," answers Melissa, as she puts on her hat and tucks the precious volume under her arm; "you may laugh at Giotto, if you like. There is nothing to prevent you from laughing at Raphael. I wonder that you don't."

---

99. See the discussion on p. lxxvi.

100. The painter, Giotto (1267–1337).

"Your knowledge of the relation of cause and effect seems imperfect," is the Sphinx-like reply, as they go down the stone stairs into the street.

The rain has ceased, and the clouds are lifting, but the Arno flows dull and turgid as they cross the bridge to the Via Tornbuoni – that terribly sophisticated thoroughfare, with its cosmopolitan shops and polyglot shopmen. Melissa forgets her artistic enthusiasm, and lingers at every step; now at a jeweller's, now at a photographer's, now at a tempting old book-stall. A splendid officer goes by, his soft blue cloak falling in statuesque folds about him. "Only an Italian can wear a cloak. What a beautiful people it is," she cries.

From the street corner comes a whiff of violets. Flowers lie exposed for sale on the ledge of a tall grey building – anemones, violets, scarlet Florentine lilies – a mass of delicate colour against the gloom. Melissa stops to buy, and is thoroughly cheated by the dark-eyed graceful salesman, who looks as if he had stepped out of a picture at the Uffizi[101] or Pitti.[102]

Santa Maria Novella is reached at last. They pause a moment to examine the façade, then make their way into the great old building. Melissa immediately opens her copy of "Mornings in Florence."[103]

"We are to 'walk straight up the church,'" she announces in a loud whisper, "'and go in behind the great marble altar.'"[104]

It is dark behind the altar, and Hannamoria, who is myopic, complains that she cannot see the frescoes, Ghirlandagio's[105] "farrago of Tweedledum and Tweedledee."[106]

101. Museum and art gallery.
102. A palace in Florence.
103. See John Ruskin's *Mornings in Florence: Being Simple Studies of Christian Art, for English Travellers*, 6 Vols (Orpington: Grant Allen, 1875–1877).
104. The quotations are from Ruskin's *Mornings in Florence: Being Simple Studies of Christian Art, for English Travellers: II. The Golden Gate* (Orpington: Grant Allen, 1875), 3.
105. Florentine Renaissance artist, Domenico Ghirlandaio (1448–1494).
106. Ruskin, *Mornings in Florence*, 30.

"It doesn't matter much," says Melissa Consolatrix; "we are only to look at them because they are rather vulgar and make a good contrast to the Giottos. Now we must ask the sacristan to take us into the Green Cloisters; at least *you* must, for my knowledge of the *lingua Toscana* will not carry me so far."

There is no sacristan visible; but Melissa descries a man engaged with a broom, whom Hannamoria and the polyglot addresses in very choice Italian, to quote her own words and Hamlet's.[107]

Chiostro verde? Yes, he has the key. Will the ladies step through this doorway? He will send the *custode* to them at once.

The great door shuts behind them with a sound that calls forth a perfect orchestra of echoes. The rain has begun to fall, and pours steadily on to the grass-plat, with its central solitary tomb of grey marble; the arching cloisters look dreary enough, with their mouldering frescoes and pavement of tombstones. There is an arched aperture in the wall, big and dark, through which the vaults below can be dimly discerned. "I don't like this place," says Melissa in a low voice, and creeps under the ample wing of her friend.

"We must turn off into this little passage on the right," Hannamoria observes, in her most matter-of-fact tones, "and 'ask for the tomb of the Marchesa Stiozzi Ridolfi.'"[108]

"There is no one to ask," comes the faint response. "I wonder why the *custode* has not come."

"It is much more pleasant without him," Hannamoria answers, as they turn into the gloomy little arcade which branches off from the main cloister; "the frescoes are behind the tomb, in the recess, Ruskin says."[109]

"Look!" cries Melissa, stopping suddenly, and turning pale.

At the furthest end of the passage looms a tall figure, draped, and gleaming very white in the darkness. Motionless it stands, one arm uplifted to the vaulted roof above.

---

107. Refers to Shakespeare's *Hamlet*.
108. Ruskin, *Mornings in Florence*, 28.
109. Ruskin, *Mornings in Florence*, 28.

Hannamoria peering through her eyeglass grows a shade less courageous than before.

"It is one of those white monks one sees at funerals," Melissa says as they advance a step or two. "No; it is only a statue, but it is sufficiently ghastly."

"It *is* ghastly," confesses her companion.

A door opens suddenly in an unexpected place; a veritable monk passes across the cloister and disappears behind another door, equally unexpected; he waves the ladies aside and says something unintelligible as he goes. The mysterious black and white presence seems to belong as little to the world outside as the sculptured effigies on the marble tombs.

The Ridolfi tomb is discovered at last, and behind it, sure enough, are the famous Giottos – St. Anne in her brown and white bed, St. Joachim at the Golden Gate. Melissa whips out Ruskin again, and vibrates between page and picture as she looks at Giotto alternately with her own eyes and her author's.

Presently, up comes a huge black cat and begins to mew piteously.

"Horrid thing!" cries Melissa with a shudder. The faithful Hannamoria chases it with her umbrella, and it flies to a little desolate patch of grass and shrubs opposite, into which the rain is pouring steadily.

"I wish the *custode* would come," repeats Melissa uneasily. "This is such a horrid place one can't really enjoy the pictures."

"And the light is so bad," laments the myopic one, "it is no good trying to see them properly."

"I think I understand a little what Ruskin means about Giotto, though, don't you?"

"Yes, a little. I think we have seen all we want to."

"Yes; we can always come again."

They emerge into the main square of the cloisters. The rain is falling in torrents on to the grass-plat; every now and then comes an echoing splash as a water-pipe sends an unusually big torrent into the court.

Melissa runs up the steps to the door and fumbles with the latch.

"It is locked!" she says, and turns a little pale.

"Of course it is," Hannamoria answers stoutly; "if we knock the man will come and let us out." She applies her knuckles to the panel, but there is no response.

"Louder, louder," urges Melissa; "they will never hear us through this noisy rain."

Five minutes of fruitless knocking: the great oaken door never so much as shakes.

"Oh!" cries Melissa tremulous, "what shall we do?"

"Do?" says her friend, "why, try the door that the monk came through, of course."

A return to the little cloister of the tombs. More knocking at an unimpressionable door; the door opposite is also tried and found locked. Melissa's terrors are growing every minute. At last, she sinks down in despair on a flight of steps and buries her face in her handkerchief.

"We shall never get out of this place, Hannamoria, never!"

"What nonsense."

"That man locked us in for the purpose. I see it now."

"Absurd. What motive could he possibly have had?"

"I can't pretend to your charming simplicity. You know what Italians are."

Drip, drip, plash, plash, goes the rain. Miaw, miaw, the great black cat has come near again and lingers about them. He has brought a comrade, a white cat, as swollen and bloated as himself, who peers up at our prisoners with inquisitive countenance. All the doors have been tried and found wanting; that is to say, all are hopelessly shut fast.

Melissa has left off lamenting and sits in stony despair near the main door, which she has ceased to belabour with her umbrella. Hannamoria maintains an iron front, but she does not enjoy the situation. A distant clock strikes two.

"We have been here just two hours," says Melissa in a low voice.

Opposite, above the arcade of the cloister, rise irregular red roofs, and a white plaster wall set with little windows. There is a hopelessly empty and deserted look about it all, but the sight of it causes Melissa's spirits to rise.

"Hannamoria," she says, "I have an idea. We might climb those water-pipes to the roofs and then signal for help outside."

Her friend answers not; why shall she dash this last hope to the ground? She knows that they both shrink at stiles and are hopelessly "stumped" by a five-barred gate, but why mention it?

"Yes," she answers vaguely. "I suppose it is the street outside, I hear sounds of various kinds. If only that door there leading to it were open."

"Hannamoria!"

"Yes."

"That door that you were speaking about – see."

"Well?"

"It has a fan-light – and the fan-light is broken."

"Yes, but it is hopelessly out of reach, and the hope is small."

"There are some chairs in the cloister; you shall stand on one and hold me up, and I will put my head through the fan-light and scream."

"We can *try*, certainly."

But alas, Hannamoria can no more stand on a rickety chair and hold up her friend than she can fly.

"Oh!" cried Melissa, wringing her hands and pacing up and down, "what shall we do? What shall we do? Think of it—in a few hours it will begin to get dark, here in this place, among these tombs, and they are modern tombs!"

"I don't see that that makes it any worse," says poor Hannamoria, at her wits' end.

"Indeed it does," Melissa cries, argumentative in the midst of her woe and panic; "a modern tomb is an infinitely ghastlier object than an ancient one. And those cats! And that figure!"

Meantime an idea seems to have struck Hannamoria. She has drawn out her handkerchief, and is engaged in tying it on to the handle of her umbrella. In another moment she has remounted the chair and the handkerchief is waving feebly from the fanlight.

"Scream!" urges Melissa. "Yell at the top of your voice."

Hannamoria lifts up her voice, not very heartily, then suddenly is silent.

"The handkerchief has dropped off!"

"Nevermind," cries Melissa, seizing the umbrella and tying on her own handkerchief, "let me come." She leaps to the chair, which rocks wildly, pokes the umbrella through the aperture, and gives vent to a prolonged and polyglot wail of anguish: "Help! Aux secours! Inglese!"

For some time, her efforts are vain, then a sound of a voice speaking an unintelligible tongue is heard on the other side of the door.

"Inglese, Inglese" shrieks Melissa, waving more zealously than ever.

Then the voice dies away. Melissa dismounts broken-hearted.

"Someone has come and gone away again."

"Perhaps they will come back with a key."

"No," says poor Melissa, "we are locked in here on purpose. Oh! Hannamoria, can't you understand?"

She strides off along the cloister, leaving her friend by the empty chair. "There is nothing," she thinks, "with which one could kill oneself if the worst came to the worst."

"Melissa!" It is Hannamoria's voice that floats across to her. And what is that that she sees! Is it possible? The great door is bursting asunder, the fissure widens, and outside in broad daylight stands their faithless friend of the broom, grinning all over his handsome face.

But where, he asks, is the *custode*? He had sent him to the ladies immediately. The base man had failed to go.

Well, it did not matter now who had played them false, sacristan or janitor. They fee him joyfully, regardless of deserts, and walk across the piazza with a sense of freedom known only to those who have not always been free.

"Oh! Those tombs, I shall never forget them," Melissa says.

"I am very hungry," Hannamoria answers calmly. "I wonder what the *trattoria* man has brought us for dinner."

"It was all Ruskin's fault," Melissa observes irrelevantly.

Lost and Won (1886)[110]

The annual lawn-tennis "tournament" is the great social event of West Keltshire. It is more exclusive than the cricket match and possesses the advantage over that function of a feminine interest. It takes place, moreover, on the lawn of the Abbey itself, and not only the natives, but a great many people from London are wont to assist at it, both as combatants and spectators. Every West Keltshire man will understand the allusion to "the" Abbey. For the benefit of the uninitiated, I must explain that I refer to Watergate Abbey, once the seat of the Earls of Watergate, at present the property of Sir Benjamin Coriander, a name familiar to every denizen of Mincing-lane, and of the region, scorned of novelists and writers for the society papers, known as Tyburnia.

The August afternoon sunlight begins to grow mellow; the cloudless blue sky takes a softer tone; a balmy freshness makes itself felt in the air. The people gathered round the lawn, with its well-marked courts and taut net, shift and rustle and murmur a little with an added sense of comfort. An air of pleasant expectation pervades the whole assembly. All faces are turned towards the big tent at one end of the lawn, where a crowd of young people, in Lawn-tennis costume, clusters beneath the striped canvas. The favourite event of the favourite function is about to come off, – the contest for the gold racket brooch, whose possession marks the winning of the Ladies' Championship.

110. Reprinted with permission of The Camellia Collections.

The two candidates, whose prominent position is the result of much hard labour, are standing side by side in the tent, and present a striking contrast. Vi Venables is a Londoner, a Kensingtonian, in fact, bred and born. She is rather short, largely built, and stands firm on a pair of solid feet. Her face, shaded by a tousled, flaxen fringe, is wide, red, and what the French would call *couperosé*. She has a high voice, and an air of great self-possession, and receives much attention from a pair of men in flannels at her side. One of these is fair and colourless, with prominent teeth. He is Percy (*alias* Poppy) Flinders, and Miss Venables talks of him quite simply as "her mash." The other man is short and stout, sleek, dark, middle-aged, with a prominent eye and a suggestive manner. His name is Arthur, or rather Tarts, Dalkeith; and he also is enrolled among the followers of the fair Violet. Elinor German, the second competitor, is a West Keltshire girl, the daughter of a neighbouring vicar. She is tall and slim; a novelist would describe her as *svelte*, with hair like spun gold and a colourless complexion. Her fringed lids have a way of drooping, and, when she looks up, there is always something unexpected and astonishing in the sight of the big, grey eyes, as with the black eyes of Mdlle. Pierrot, in *Le Petit Chose*.[111] At present, an air of suppressed excitement, of extreme tension, pervades her whole person, as she stands nervously fingering her racket, and responding rather disjointedly to the remarks of a tall, fair, young man at her side. Her opponent, on the other hand, is, to quote her own phrase, as cool as a cucumber, and has her two admirers well in hand. The lack of outward attractions notwithstanding, Vi Venables is a person of considerable social value. She can play Lawn-tennis and billiards; can dance, skate, row, stage-manage an amateur company, and play a waltz or an accompaniment, better than any girl of her set. When it is added that these various accomplishments are always at the service of her friends, it will be seen that Miss Venables works sufficiently hard for her living. She has, moreover, a complete set of affairs of the heart always on hand. A bedroom confidence to a bosom friend, for the time being, has summed up her present position in

111. Alphonse Daudet's *Le Petit Chose* (1868).

this respect: "Poppy Flinders and Tarts Dalkeith are mashed on me, and I am mashed on Eustace Williams!" Eustace Williams is the tall young man with the delicate, fastidious face, and dreamy yet critical blue eyes, that we saw a moment ago in conversation with Elinor German. He is a college don, the son of a local squire, and is but rarely seen in West Keltshire. Vi Venables makes open love to him, after the manner of her kind; but he has never been heard to express himself on the subject of that enterprising young woman. A bell rings; there is a rustle among the audience, a stir in the tent.

"Is it ten buttons or six?" demands Mr. Flinders of the departing Vi.

"Ten, of course."

"I believe you're funking," says the dark-eyed Tarts with a sleek chuckle.

"I'm always such a timid fawn, am I not?" she responds, over her shoulder. "Ta-ta, ta-ta! Mr. Williams, you've never wished me luck!" Elinor raises her eyes, an instant, to the young don's face; then the two girls walk across to the courts, each in her cream-white flannel gown and gold-coloured cap and girdle. The Lawn-tennis players in the tent subside on the ground, with the exception of Eustace Williams, who leans against a striped tent-pole, completely unconscious of his own share in the game.

> We women are too apt to look to one;
> We strain our natures at doing something great,
> Far less because it's something great to do
> Than haply that we so commend ourselves
> To some one friend.[112]

How is the vainest of men, who has anything like his fair share of healthy masculine objectivity, to realise the complete, the unanswerable, the most humiliating truth of this sentiment, itself the frank and melancholy utterance of a woman?

---

112. From Barrett Browning's *Aurora Leigh* (1857).

An unusual interest attaches to the contest, each opponent representing in her own person one of the two distinctly marked sections of the audience. Sir Benjamin Coriander has made himself a position in the county with his money, energy, and unquestionable good-will.

The county, being very much of a beggar, has had to renounce the luxury of choice. It swallows Sir Benjamin and his friends, but it makes a wry face over them in private.

Miss Venables opens fire with a clean, swift, low service, which is duly returned, and then the fray begins in earnest. The method of warfare of the two combatants is characteristic.

Vi Venables, planted firm on her wide, india-rubber-soled feet, hardly troubles herself to move. She seems to have some magnetic attraction for the ball rather than to make any conscious effort to reach it. Cool, keen and wary, she is always in the right place, though, if by chance a ball is hopelessly out of reach, she lets it go, without any vain expenditure of force in its pursuit.

Elinor German, on the other hand, plays like a genius, – perhaps, I should say, like a Kelt. She is all over the court, skimming and darting like some graceful bird, trying at everything, performing miracles of good play and miracles of bad.

Set No. 1 is closely contested. The play is pretty equal at first; then Elinor fails suddenly, misses everything, and serves five times running into the net. When everything looks at an end for her, she rallies with equal suddenness, and comes in victor with a brilliant fire of volleys. Vi Venables wins the next set, after a hard fight; and now the third decisive set only remains to be played. By this time people are thoroughly excited, and all eyes are fixed with breathless interest on the two well-matched combatants on the lawn. They are standing in the middle of the court, exchanging a few brief words across the net, before the umpire summons them to the fray. Even Miss Venables displays some marks of agitation. There is a deeper flush on her wide, red cheeks, and her keen eyes are unusually bright. Elinor, on the contrary, is very pale, with great circling eyes, their black pupils dilated. The umpire calls "play!" The exchange of courts is again effected, the fire of balls renewed.

"Five games all, deuce!" cries the umpire. Everyone strains forward; not a stroke is lost on that eager assembly. It is Elinor's service, and she stands at the outer corner of the court, very white and tense, serving the ball from her swiftly in a diagonal line towards her opponent. It goes straight into the net; so does the next ball, and the next. In this manner the game is finished, and Miss Venables' "advantage-game" is proclaimed.

The next game opens with a low, swift service, followed by a long rest, which Elinor terminates to her own advantage with a small miracle in the way of back-handers. She misses the next ball, a comparatively easy one, and returns the third with such vigour that it flies beyond the limits of the court. Then follows a series of hard-fought rests, in which Vi's nerve and coolness are finally triumphant; and the contest ends, amid prolonged cheering and a general stampede on to the lawn. Miss Venables, flushed and voluble, is led off to the tent by a train of admirers, and is soon to be seen with a bumper of claret-cup in one hand and in the other a handkerchief, with which she is mopping her brow.

"Well played, by Jove!" cries Poppy Flinders.

"It was neck and neck," remarks Dalkeith; "Nelly German knows how to get over the rough ground, but she wants staying power."

"Neat little filly, Miss German," adds Mr. Flinders.

Vi Venables looks round with a scrutinising eye, while duly attending to these remarks. Then she tucks her handkerchief in her belt, hands the empty glass to Poppy, and steps forward with prompt decision.

"Mr. Williams!"

The young man turns and regards her questioningly. Unabashed, she holds out her hand, looks straight in his eyes, and says –

"Mr. Williams, you are the only person who has not shaken hands with me."

"Oh," answers Eustace, coolly, "I am quite willing to supply the omission, if you wish it." He extends a long, white hand, with a little air of astonishment; then goes out of the tent.

Where does he go? In pursuit of that slender, drooping, hurrying figure which disappears among the labyrinthine paths of the shrubbery.

"Nelly!" he calls, as he overtakes her; and, when she looks up, trying to smile, he sees that her eyes are full of tears.

"Nelly, you silly child!" he cries, with shocking familiarity. It is long since he has used the old name, and her pale cheek flushes a little at the sound.

"Not quite so silly, nor so ungenerous, as I seem," she answers, with sweet impulsiveness; "but I am very tired and sorry, – it is no good to pretend that I am not sorry."

She breaks off suddenly, and sways towards him. He is just able to catch the fainting girl in his arms.

* * * * *

There is a dance that night at the Abbey. Vi Venables, in a shining cuirass of black satin, and short, voluminous skirts of black net, is, to use her own expression, in great form. A big gardenia, the gift of Mr. Flinders, is fastened in the front of her extremely *decolleté* bodice, where the golden racket gleams conspicuously among a host of narrow brooches and jewelled safety pins. She makes a great deal of noise with Poppy Flinders, and "sits out," innumerable dances with the dark and dangerous Tarts. Nor does she fail to offer her congratulations to Eustace Williams and Elinor German, whose newly-announced engagement is the event of the evening.

The sympathy of every right-minded person goes, of course, with the modest girl who lost her game and won her lover. This is just as it should be, and just what I intended. But, perhaps, the thoughtful reader will agree with me in perceiving a touch of pathos, nay, of tragedy, in the less pleasing picture of Vi Venables. As she lays her hard cheek on the pillow tonight, she recalls the faces of Eustace and Elinor, when they came back from the shrubbery that afternoon. She remembers that she is twenty-nine next birthday; and she wonders why none of the numerous people who have "mashed" her have ever gone the length of a proposal. She reflects that they are dreadfully poor, she and her mother, in the little house in that part of Brompton, which calls itself Kensington. And then, in the midst of these cogitations, she falls off to sleep. Sleep long and soundly, poor battered Violet, luckless holder of the golden racket, and champion Lawn-tennis player of the ladies of West Keltshire.

A Meadowshire Romance (1886)[113]

Chapter 1

There is no one so beautiful as Kitty, no one in the whole world. She might be a queen, I think, with that grave, yet simple, dignity of manner; that straightforward kindliness, which is apt to have a touch of graciousness in it; that absolute, yet unconscious, air of liberty and independence.

At twenty-five she is more beautiful than at eighteen, with a serene and mellow loveliness to which only a small proportion of the vast horde of "pretty girls" can ever hope to attain.

Kitty is an heiress, her father, Colonel Pembroke, being one of the richest men in the whole countryside, and she his only daughter. She is, as I have said, extremely beautiful. Yet the fact remains that Kitty is twenty-five and unmarried.

"You have refused half the county," I say, "and given the other half to understand that you will none of it. Do you mean to braid St. Catherine's hair,[114] Miss Pembroke, or are you waiting for the fairy prince to come galloping up the Manor House drive in quest of you?"

"I don't know," says Kitty, fixing her sweet, calm eyes, with the delicious gleam of humour in them, on my face, "I have always meant

113. Reprinted with permission of The Camellia Collections.
114. Refers to Catherine of Siena (1347-1380), who cut her own hair in protest against her parents' wish that she should be married.

to be married; I think it is best. But St. Catherine seems to be our patron saint, – yours and mine, Agnes, – after all."

We are on the lawn in front of the Manor House, enjoying the delicious mellowness of the August afternoon; the well-seasoned red-brick of the old walls making a becoming background for Kitty, as she lounges gracefully in her gold-coloured draperies, with the knot of dark-red carnations at her throat. The small, regal head, with its nut-brown hair, the delicate, oval face and long throat, the serene grace of the whole figure, make up a picturesque whole, as irresistible to me as it is familiar. Our cane garden chairs are set on the margin of the lawn itself, where a Lawn-tennis net hangs slack between the posts, and innumerable balls lie scattered about the old, velvety turf. Our rackets, moreover, rest on our knees, but there has been no attempt at a game, for which I, for one, am profoundly thankful. To have points given you and then to lose every set, is a sport which must soon pall on the most humble-minded of mortals. And I, Agnes Pembroke, am humble-minded enough, heaven knows. Ever since I can remember, I have had one thought, one interest in life, – my beautiful cousin. To wait on her, hand and foot, to worship her; to pray for her; to bask in the light of her kindly, humorous smiles; these things have made up the sum of my happiness. Some masculine satirists notwithstanding, a lovely and attractive woman is apt to receive much homage from her own sex, – homage which, from the nature of the case, is altogether of a more delicate quality than that which the other sex thinks fit to bestow upon them.

"With their usual sense of justice," says Thackeray, "ladies argue that, because a woman is handsome, therefore she is a fool."[115] Such an argument has never been mine. On the contrary, I have observed a tendency on the part of Fortune to heap up her favours on a single individual. The good-looking people are apt to be also the most intelligent; and not infrequently they are the rich ones as well. Perhaps, my theory of life, which differs, I think, from the accepted one, is drawn too directly from my own experience to be of much universal value. For not only is Kitty beautiful, while I am distinctly plain; not

115. The quotation is from Thackeray's *Vanity Fair*.

only is she her father's heiress, while I am dependent on his bounty; but there is no single thing which she does not do a hundred times better than I can. In Lawn-tennis, photography, and tricycling (three chief interests in Meadowshire), down to making a pudding or darning a stocking, she is immeasurably and incontestably my superior. It is true that my cousin lacks a certain mediocre skill in piano-playing, but then she has never chosen to practise, having, as she says, neither ear nor patience for music.

To return to the sunny lawn of the Manor House, where I left us sitting, before I began to moralise.

"Kitty," I say, as a sudden thought strikes me, "is it not strange that the Verrekers haven't returned our call?"

"They left a whole bundle of cards yesterday, when we were out," she answers; "big, broad ones with 'Lady Verreker,' and little narrow ones with 'Sir Claude Verreker,' nicely printed on them. Are you satisfied?"

She looks straight in my face as she speaks, and I reply, with some resentment, "I believe you are the only girl in the county who would have forgotten to mention such a fact." Kitty laughs her sweet, half-ironical laugh, and looks into my eyes with her most provoking expression: "Bold thing! I believe you have every intention of setting your cap at this young and wealthy Sir Claude."

"O, Kitty, how can you talk like that? It is quite coarse," I cry, blushing scarlet. But I know that Kitty has a different accusation against me in her heart, and that, as the children say, she "knows that I know." "O, Kitty! However, I cannot pretend to your sublime indifference on the subject of the only thing like an event which we have had in Meadowshire for the last ten years."

"But you know how it is, Agnes," says Kitty. Even if one gets up a little excitement about new neighbours, they always turn out as dull as everyone else in the end. It is all very well for a simple young thing like you, but I have had too many disillusions in such matters to be able to produce even a semblance of enthusiasm."

I twist my racket about in my hand a little crossly. My tyrant is in one of her most provoking moods.

"We all know you are very old, and very *blasée*," I say, with a fine attempt at satire. Kitty laughs lazily; I rack my brains for a retort. We are on the verge of a mild, one-sided quarrel, when the appearance of a third person on the scene creates a diversion, and indefinitely postpones the catastrophe. The newcomer is Nancy Field, the rector's daughter, a pert, bucolic miss, whose soul has never soared higher than Lawn-tennis and Sunday school, and who has only the vaguest notions of existence outside Meadowshire. I am not at all fond of Nancy, and Kitty's smiling toleration of her is for me one of the minor troubles of life. Reader, I may as well make the confession at once, – perhaps, you have already discovered it, – I am not even an amiable person. Miss Field comes tripping towards us, wearing a jaunty gown of striped flannel, a sailor-hat perched above her round, rosy face, and a business-like apron with deep pockets. Her racket and rubber shoes are lashed knowingly together, and a most irritating air of bustling complacency pervades her whole person.

"Good afternoon, Kitty. How-do, Aggie?" (with a nod). "Never mind about getting out of those delicious chairs," cries Nancy, taking possession of a third, and nestling comfortably in its cushioned depths.

"O! Kitty, have you forgotten about our practice? You are never going to play in that gown?"

"Let us think about playing after tea. Meanwhile, please tell me some news."

"Oh! I don't know about news," answers Miss Field; "but isn't it delightful about the Verrekers?"

"Delightful?"

"Yes, that they of all people should have taken the Grange. Mamma has been always so afraid that it would get into the hands of some *parvenu*; she says that nearly always happens in these days. Isn't it shocking? And generally with the biggest places in the country. But the Verrekers are everything that they should be. Immensely rich, thorough-going Tories; such a good old family. They belonged originally to Meadowshire; lived here in the reign of Queen Elizabeth,

Papa says, and now they have come back to their old county. I think that is so nice."

The voluble Nancy pauses, with an air of great satisfaction, and I say slowly: – "And there will be actually a new young man on the scene. A highly desirable young man."

"Have you called, Kitty?" asks Miss Field, ignoring my remark.

"Yes, but they were out."

"We were more fortunate. They were at home; at least, Lady Verreker and her niece were. We were charmed."

"I did not know there was a niece," Kitty says, with some show of interest.

"Indeed there is; a Miss Mabel Twyne, a most formidable person. Only fancy, she is champion of the Valeshire Ladies, and owns no less than six prize rackets. She means to play for Meadowshire next month. What do you think of that?"

"That is really news," says Kitty, sitting upright in her chair. "Have you seen her play?"

"No; but I am convinced that she is a great swell. Kitty, we *mustn't* let her beat us; it would be a disgrace to the county."

"We will practice morning, noon, and night," says my cousin slowly, with that air of subdued eagerness which is her nearest approach to enthusiasm. "Here is Grampus with the tea; after we have drunk it, we will begin at once." The old butler sets down the tray on a light garden table in front of me, and Colonel Pembroke comes through the open window in search of his afternoon cup. In his middle-aged, masculine way my uncle is every inch as good looking as his daughter; tall, slight, soldierly, with straight features and a well-poised head; the *beau idéal* of a handsome English gentleman.

Nancy greets him with effusion; his daughter beams upon him; I hand him his tea in the big breakfast cup which towers above all the others in the tray. Kitty tells him of Miss Mabel Twyne and her vaunted prowess in the lawn-tennis-court, a piece of news which he supports with great equanimity.

"That is a matter which concerns you ladies," he says. "I want to know about Sir Claude Verreker; his lawn-tennis, his hunting, his skill with the tricycle. Am I, are all of us Meadowshire gentlemen destined to be beaten on our own ground?"

"I am not at all sure that you are not," cries Miss Field. "I hear on all sides that he is a perfect marvel; that he used to be called Crichton-Verreker[116] at Cambridge, because he did everything better than everyone else!"

"Terrible person!" observes Kitty while the Colonel, stroking his moustache and smiling, begs for more information concerning the paragon.

"O! He has every virtue under the sun!" goes on Nancy, delighted to have such an attentive audience; "I think they called him Sir Galahad sometimes, as well as Crichton."

Kitty and her father burst out laughing.

"O! Pray go on," says the latter, amused.

"You know he is very, very rich," proceeds Nancy, not at all disconcerted, "and immensely philanthropic. Papa has been talking to him already about the parish and is quite touched by the noble and generous view he takes of things. He is very clever as well and plays the piano like an angel; there's something for you, Agnes!"

"Where did you glean all this information?" I say, looking down into my teacup.

"Partly from Tom Daly, who was at the University with him; partly from Lady Yorrick, who knows them in London. Everything one hears adds confirmation to it."

"Does anyone say if he is good looking?" I ask, with studied carelessness, helping myself to a slice of cake as I speak.

"No, I haven't heard. I suppose he is."

Nancy is really distressed at her ignorance on this important point.

"And is he engaged to his cousin, Miss Twyne?"

116. Refers to James Crichton, the "Admirable Crichton," a youthful genius who was murdered in 1582 at the age of twenty-one.

I become absorbed in the discussion of my piece of cake, displaying quite a greedy interest in the matter of currants. Nancy looks really shocked at this suggestion, which evidently strikes her for the first time.

"O! No; I have never heard so. There is no reason to suppose such a thing," she says, disconcerted for once in her life.

Kitty gets up suddenly from her chair. "Agnes, are you under the impression that Nancy is in the witness-box, and that you are an eminent Q.C.?" she asks, with fine scorn. "O! What a set of gossips we are. Nancy, I am ready when you are." She sweeps across the lawn in her trailing, clinging draperies, and proceeds to wind up the net.

"You're never going to play in that gown, Kitty?"

"O! Yes I am." She draws the long, gold-coloured train through her belt, and takes up her position at a corner of the court.

I lean back in my chair, dreamily, and watch the two figures on either side of the net, as they advance, retreat, and double in pursuit of the ball. But my thoughts are very far from the game, with its recurring complications of "fault" and "let," of "line-ball" and "out of court." Nancy has a silly and exaggerated way of putting things, I know; is not, in the least, a trustworthy person where her neighbours' affairs are concerned; but surely even she cannot speak entirely without foundation. A fairy prince; I have always been convinced that Kitty would be content with nothing less. Is it possible that Fate, with unusual benevolence, has wafted him to our very doors? My imagination is apt to run away with me, especially where my cousin is concerned; and long before the game is over I have suppressed every sign of my own desolation and jealousy, have renounced all claims to Kitty and installed her as mistress of the Grange, with an embodiment of all perfections for her husband.

"Kitty," says the Colonel at dinner, that night, "by the bye, oughtn't we to – er – be a little neighbourly to those new people at the Grange? What do you think, my dear?"

"O! Certainly," answers Kitty, very calmly; "we might ask them to dinner next week. Whom shall we have to meet them?" And a matter-of-fact discussion ensues between father and daughter. Later in the evening, as I sit playing in the dusk, Kitty comes and sits beside me, and lays her dear head on my shoulder.

"Play that sad thing of Chopin's;[117] you know the one I mean, Aggie."

"What such a cheerful person wants with music like that, I don't pretend to know," I remark, when I have brought the little piece to a close. "Life can't be sad for you, Kitty."

"O no, not sad; very pleasant, but a little unsatisfactory."

Grampus comes in with the lamp, followed by the footman, with candles.

"Now you can write your note to the Verrekers," I say, shutting up the piano.

Kitty laughs, "Oh you transparent person!"

"When you look at me like that, Kitty, I don't know if you are the simplest person in the world, or quite the most cunning!"

"I have no such doubt respecting you, Agnes!"

I throw my arms about her and kiss her sweet face. "Kitty, Kitty; you are terrible sometimes! Do you remember Matthew Arnold's 'Urania'?

> She smiles and smiles, and will not sigh,
> While we for hopeless passion die;
> Yet she could love, those eyes declare,
> Were men but nobler than they are?"[118]

"Air! What a horrid rhyme, Agnes, and what a horrid person you are always trying to make me out!"

Chapter 2

The coachman is despatched next morning with a bundle of notes, containing invitations to dinner to our various neighbours, including the interesting strangers at the Grange.

---

117. Composer, Frédéric Chopin (1810–1849).
118. Matthew Arnold's poem, "Urania."

"And now," says Kitty, shutting up her writing-case, and turning round on her chair, "now that I have done my duty, what have you to propose in the way of pleasure? What are your plans for this morning, Agnes?"

"We might go for a walk through the wood, and across the meadows towards Haycroft."

"Yes, so we might: and it would be a good opportunity for taking the jelly to old Mrs. Binfield."

"O, very well," I say, not with the best grace in the world. Kitty's *protégés* are the bane of my life. There is no getting her an hour to oneself for them. "O, very well. Mrs. Binfield is an old hypocrite, and as prosperous as you are; but we'll take her the jelly, if you like."

Kitty laughs, amused, and I say, rather crossly, "I don't know why it is, but you are always most amiable to the very nastiest people."

"Perhaps," says Kitty, gravely, "it is because they are most in need of amiability. But don't let us waste this beautiful weather. Be off, Aggie, and put on your things."

A few minutes later, we are walking briskly up the hill together in the direction of Haycroft Wood, my cousin with a basket on her arm, which she steadily refuses to entrust to my care. Kitty wears a blue cambric gown this morning, and a large hat covered with the same material; a knot of her favourite clove carnations is at her belt, their dark red colour harmonising admirably with the soft tones of the dress, and with the yellowish tints of her long tan gloves.

It is a glorious day. Even my own rather gloomy spirits rise as we step along the fragrant autumnal paths; the thick vegetation glistens with dew, and already, alas! shows signs of increased richness and variety of tint. Here and there a comfortable red cottage rises square between the trees. Thatched roofs, leaded panes, tumbledown architecture, – such picturesque abominations are unknown at Haycroft, where aesthetics have long ago succumbed to sanitary science.

"It is a pity," I say, "that Sir Claude Verreker should have stumbled on a place which will afford so little scope for his philanthropy."

"Oh, I daresay there is room for improvement," answers Kitty, carelessly enough; "I don't think we are perfect, even in Haycroft." She stops short, as she speaks, before the gate of a well-kept cottage-garden, lifts the latch and walks down the trim path to the snug little crimson dwelling. I prefer to remain outside in the lane, enjoying the delicious freshness, the mellowing haze, the nameless charm of the autumn morning. Kitty emerges in about a quarter of an hour with a benevolent face and an empty basket.

"Well, and did Mrs. Binfield appreciate your little attention?" I ask, as we proceed on our way to Haycroft Wood.

"I decline to discuss Mrs. Binfield with you," says Kitty, severely; "you are as bad as the rest of the world, Aggie; fond of giving a dog a bad name and hanging him."

"When everybody is agreed that so-and-so is a thoroughgoing scamp, the chances are not exactly in favour of his being the most delightful person in the world, Kitty."

"I think it is one's duty to judge of people for oneself," says my cousin. Indeed, if this proud young person has a fault, it is her obstinate disregard of the world's opinion in such matters; her refusal to accept popular favourites on trust. Add to this her own extreme fastidiousness, and it will be seen that the circle of Kitty's intimate friends cannot be a wide one. Halfway through the wood we meet Nancy Field, who dances up to us with radiant face and an air of extreme importance.

"How do you do? Lovely morning! Shall I meet you at the Grange this afternoon?" she cries, in a breath.

"No," says Kitty gravely. She is a punctilious young person at heart, and such an informality as an invitation from the Verrekers would by no means have found favour in her eyes.

"Of course, I'm only going in a quiet, friendly way," says Nancy, guessing the other's thought, "to practice Lawn-tennis with Miss Twyne. I thought, perhaps – "

"I don't know Miss Twyne." Kitty looks bored; this persistent cropping up of the new neighbours is becoming rather a nuisance. "Goodbye, Nancy, and don't forget your practice with insignificant me tomorrow morning."

"O, Kitty! – " Miss Field is, in all simplicity, actually beginning an apology, which our rapid forward march succeeds in averting.

"How can you endure that girl?" I cry, when we are out of hearing.

"'Juxtaposition is great,'"[119] quotes Kitty; "there, Agnes, I've quoted your favourite poet for you; don't you think you might get up a little more amiability on the strength of it?"

We have emerged from the wood by this time, and are striking across the meadows to the main road. The fine morning tempts us to a walk of unusual length, and very soon we have passed beyond Haycroft village, and are walking along the wide country road, with its border of low green banks and tangled hedges. In the distance rise the red and grey chimneys of the Grange, its vast bulk almost hidden by trees, save for the occasional gleam of a mullioned window and the glimpse, here and there, of mellow brickwork. On one side of the building its high red wall skirts the road, breaking up the line of banks and hedges; but the entrance gates are on the other side, at some distance from the house.

We have soon reached the Grange; then have left it far behind us. Now all signs of human habitation have disappeared, and we have the scene to ourselves. Presently a solitary figure is espied making its way towards us, – a slouching man's figure, swinging a heavy-looking wallet in one hand. He walks along the road slowly enough, with a jaded, sulky step, unaware of our presence, although we are painfully alive to the fact of his approach.

"Kitty," I say, in a low voice; "A tramp!"

---

119. Kitty's quotation is from Arthur Hugh Clough's poem, "Amours de Voyage."

We have no snakes in Meadowshire; infuriated bulls are never found straying about our public highways; I have never heard of a mad dog; with all the more intensity, therefore, do the local fears concentrate themselves on our one object of terror, the tramp.

"Let us go on a little, and then, if you like, turn back, without looking flurried," answers Kitty, with her usual unruffled air. This is a great concession on her part, and I am considerably relieved.

Suddenly, the man, hearing perhaps the distant sound of our voices, looks up and sees us. He hastens his pace unmistakeably at the sight, and in a few moments we are presented with a distinct view of his person. He is a shaggy, ill-conditioned looking creature, of the usual Bill Sykes type,[120] with a massive, underhanging jaw, and unutterably wicked little eyes, which, as he approaches, are fixed full on my beautiful cousin.

"Let us turn now," says Kitty, below her breath. We do so in silence, and walk on rather breathlessly, the sound of the tramp's advancing footsteps growing every moment more distinct.

Not a soul to be seen down that long, solitary road! Suddenly the sound of the footsteps ceases, and, urged by an irresistible impulse, I look over my shoulder.

"O Kitty, he is putting stones in his wallet!"

"How could you be so silly as to look round? No doubt he is amusing himself with our terrors," says Kitty, *sotto voce*; but she is getting over the ground at a good pace. Thank Heaven, here comes a man on a tricycle! A brief respite, I think, from our fate.

"Shall we call to him?" I venture to suggest.

"Of course not; there is no reason; and now we have time to reach a more populous part of the road."

The tricycle spins out of sight. Nearer and nearer come those terrible footsteps; so near that we dare not remark on them to each other. Another respite; a dogcart, driven by a farmer, goes rapidly by. Oh, why did we not signal to him?

It is like a nightmare, I think, our breathless, silent scamper down the interminable road, with those footsteps ever in pursuit.

120. Character in Charles Dickens' *Oliver Twist* (1838).

In pursuit? They have come up to us by now, and a harsh, low voice is sounding in Kitty's ear. I look up at her; she is pale, and, though outwardly calm, I know, from the expression of her face, that she is very, very angry.

By this time we have reached the high red wall of the Grange, and a faint hope of rescue from the distant house flashes across my mind.

Suddenly Kitty stops short, and faces her pursuer.

"I cannot hear what you are saying," she says; "what is it that you want?"

The man shoots a menacing glance at her from his small, evil eyes, and swings his wallet suggestively, his hissing flood of talk for the moment arrested.

Faint and sick with terror, I clutch at Kitty's hand.

"Come away, come away, my darling!" She puts her arm round me and draws me to her; the man glares at her like a wild beast.

"We have no money with us," says Kitty, simply. The man retreats a step or two, then stands as if in act to spring.

There is no mistaking the expression of the cruel face, the attitude of the figure threatening, with the wallet-arm slightly swung back. With a cry of rage and terror I fling myself in front of Kitty, holding back her hands with mine.

"You shall not touch her! You shall not dare to touch her!"

An inarticulate torrent of hoarse speech flows from the man's lips. He raises on high the heavy wallet; in another moment it would have gone ill with one or both of us; but at this point, as if conjured up by magic, a figure appears on the top of the wall, drops neatly down between us and our assailant, and says, in a clear, determined voice, "Be off at once, you coward!" Rather to my surprise, Bill Sykes turns immediately on his heel, making off at an astonishingly good pace, and our rescuer, raising his straw hat, comes forward with the coolest, most imperturbable air in the world. "I am so sorry that you should have been annoyed," he says, addressing himself, of course, to Kitty. "Fortunately, these gentlemen are as brave as they are amiable, and I don't think he will trouble you again."

"We both of us thank you very much," answers Kitty, rather faintly; she is leaning against the wall, pale with half-shut eyes; "but how – ?"

"Where in the world did I spring from?" he says, helping her out with her faltering question. "By the merest luck I happened to be looking for Lawn-tennis balls among the bushes under the wall, and heard what was going on on the other side. Fortunately, I managed to swing myself up by a plum tree just in time, though it was a close shave I can tell you!"

As he speaks, he looks straight at Kitty through his double eyeglass with a pair of singularly bright and expressive eyes. Kitty gives him one of her frank, grave glances, and makes a feeble attempt at a reply.

He interrupts her for the second time: "Now, please, don't trouble to say anything, most particularly 'Thank you.' But I can see you have both had a horrid fright, and no wonder. You must allow me to take you back to the Grange, and see that you are driven home."

While Kitty is faintly protesting against this plan, and assuring him of our perfect ability to return on foot to the Manor House, I am taking stock, with all my eyes, of the stranger.

He is a small man, jaunty, self-satisfied, with an unmistakable air of London about his whole person. He has a keen, ugly, mobile face, redeemed only by the eyes; and even they are partly hidden by the *pince-nez*, with its black cord. His small, neat figure suggests activity and nimbleness rather than strength, and at present is clothed in a white flannel suit and black and white striped *blazer*: a Trinity Hall *blazer*, as I afterwards learn. As I look at him a chill thought strikes me. He is Sir Claude Verreker! Alas for my baseless visions, my airy hopes! Alas for my dreams of Sir Galahad and the Fairy Prince![121] I watch the little person before me, his wiry shape, his eager face, and sparkling eyes. I listen to his confident, cheerful tones, not wholly free from suggestions of London; I watch and listen with a sort of fascination of hatred. It is very ungrateful of me, in the circumstances, is it

121. Levy might here be referring to Thomas Arne's (1710–1778) *The Fairy Prince* (1771), or possibly an earlier version by Benjamin Johnson (1572–1637), *Oberon: The Faery Prince* (1611).

not? But I am so bitterly disappointed! Yes, in the strength of my disappointment, I have entirely got over my fright, and am impatiently wondering why poor, pale Kitty does not cut short the man's arguments by setting off at once for home.

A compromise is at length effected. Our deliverer is allowed to escort us back as far as Haycroft, not a step further, the rest of the journey being off the high road and out of the beat of tramps. He leaves us reluctantly enough at the further end of the village, and we go on our way as before.

"How stupid of me," says Kitty, whose colour has returned, and who has quite recovered her self-possession; "I ought to have asked him to call, so that Papa might thank him."

"There won't be much difficulty in repairing the omission. I suppose he is Sir Claude Verreker?"

"I suppose so."

"O Kitty, what a dreadful little person!"

"Agnes, I will not listen to such base ingratitude." She smiles down at me with inscrutable eyes.

"And quite vulgar, quite Londoney! O Kitty, the Verrekers are people of family!"

"Who have been repairing their broken fortunes at a London banking-house for the last hundred years or so."

"And so short!"

"Does it takes six feet to make a hero?"

"O, of course, you are never like other people! Never disappointed, never – "

"Was it I that built such hopes on the fancied paragon? But I think we are talking a great deal of nonsense. Let us be thankful for our escape, and grateful to that kind, small person, whoever he may be, who rescued us so opportunely."

She laughs her merry, humorous laugh, and opens the gate of the Manor House grounds.

Colonel Pembroke is shocked and frightened when he hears our story, and threatens to put a veto on all unchaperoned expeditions;

but to this his daughter objects so very firmly that he is obliged to yield to her arguments.

As I am sitting in the garden, after lunch, Kitty comes through the drawing room window, waving a long, thick envelope in her hand.

"Guess what I have here, Agnes."

"A proposal of marriage from Sir Claude Verreker?"

"Agnes, your jokes (it was meant for a joke?) tend to breadth. I don't think I shall let you see this."

"Just as you like."

She takes up her position on the grass at my feet, and holds up the envelope for my closer inspection.

It has the Verreker arms on it; but truth to tell, my interest in our neighbours has waned considerably since this morning's encounter.

"Do you say they can come, or can't?"

"Can, of course," I reply.

She breaks the seal daintily.

"My poor Agnes, here is a blow for you. They are going up to town for that day and the next. And you were so anxious for them to come."

"Kitty, you are possessed. That tramp has gone to your head. You are on the verge of a brain-fever."

Kitty blushes a little.

"Agnes, you are the most amusing person in the world."

She looks up at me with her sweet eyes, and smiles. I stoop down and kiss her. What else is to be done in the circumstances?

"Don't try to look like the Sphinx,[122] Kitty; it doesn't suit your style of beauty."

---

122. Levy could here be pointing to neoclassical uses of the sphinx in art and literature; in the late-Victorian period the sphinx symbolised female sexuality, eroticism, animalism, and even the "*femme fatale*" (Norbert Lennartz, "Oscar Wilde's 'The Sphinx'–A Dramatic Monologue of the Dandy as a Young Man?" *Philological Quarterly* 83, no. 4 (Fall 2004): 417). Heine deployed the "Sphinx" in his preface to the *Buch der Lieder* to symbolise "A lovely woman. Her white eyes / Spoke of desire grown wild; / Her lips gave silent promises / Her mute lips arched and smiled"; however, danger is ever present in that the "Sphinx" is "Terror and lust cross bred! / In body and claws a lion's form, / A woman

Chapter 3

"Kitty, – Kitty! are you ready?"

"My dear, the carriage has been waiting for ten minutes!"

My uncle and I are standing at the foot of the stairs, ready-dressed and impatient. It is a week since the events of the last chapter, and we are all bound for a Lawn-tennis party at the Grange. It is not often that my cousin lingers over her toilette, for, like most beautiful people, she is singularly free from vanity; but this afternoon she is keeping us waiting.

"At last!"

The Colonel, who has a truly military respect for punctuality, does his best to look severe as his daughter comes serenely downstairs. Kitty wears a white serge gown and a sailor hat with white ribbons; her only ornament, a long, blue brooch of Roman mosaic, fastening the lace at her throat. I like her best in the trailing, richly-tinted gowns which she usually affects, and which are much better suited to her than the jauntily simple costume, which fashion and convenience, for once joining hands, have decreed as "the only wear" for Lawn-tennis.

"Never mind," is my mental comment, as I take my seat opposite her in the big barouche. "If *that person* was Sir Claude, what does it matter if my darling is not looking quite so well as usual."

"Papa," says Kitty, as we bowl along between the hedgerows, "what is the meaning of this? No flannels, no racket, no shoes!"

"My dear," says the Colonel, drily, "my Lawn-tennis days are over. It was a fine game ten years ago; but you young folks have grown too clever by half, and, except for a quiet knock-up with a crony now and then, I have decided to renounce the racket."

"My dear Colonel, what rubbish!"

---

in breast and head" (*The Complete Poems of Heinrich Heine: A Modern English Version*, ed. Hal Draper (Boston: Suhrkamp/Insel, 1982), 7). For Paul Peters, Heine's "Sphinx" is "the ultimate revelation of the feminine" and something "to which he is constantly and irresistibly drawn" (see "A Walk on the Wild Side: Heine's Eroticism," in *A Companion to the Works of Heinrich Heine*, ed. Roger Cook (Woodbridge: Camden House, 2002), 68–9). Levy uses "the Sphinx" image to similarly point to Kitty's irresistible nature.

"It is exceedingly respectful, the younger generation, is it not?" answers my uncle, appealing to me; "but we don't like swift services and Renshaw smashes, do we, Agnes? We prefer a nice slow ball, tossed sky-high, with perhaps a very deliberate and transparent 'twist' thrown in, by way of flavour!"

"I wish I could get off playing!" I say, a little ruefully; while Kitty observes, severely – "That is quite absurd of Papa, when he knows he plays better than all of us, when he chooses."

In a few minutes we are at the Grange; in a few more are standing in a long, low room, among a crowd of chattering tea-drinking people, for the most part young and attired in Lawn-tennis costumes. Lady Verreker, a tall and stately personage, receives us with due courtesy, and a young girl, in blue and white flannel, comes over from the further end of the room at our entrance, and is introduced to us as "My niece, Miss Twyne."

"Mabel," says Lady Verreker, when the little ceremony is accomplished, "where is Claude?"

"He and Mr. Pole are winding up the nets and getting out the balls."

Lady Verreker looks vexed, then turns to speak to the Colonel, while Mabel, proceeding to discharge the duties of hospitality towards Kitty and me, leads us to the more crowded part of the room, where we find ourselves in a vicious circle of handshaking.

I manage to subside at last into my usual corner, a coign of 'vantage whence I can carry on my observations of men and things. That is our revenge, that of people who are shy and unpopular – to observe; he were a churl, indeed, that grudged it us.

There is Nancy Field, in her parti-coloured flannels, noisy and ineffectual as ever; she has secured that idiot, Tom Daly, and is giggling contentedly with him by the window. To do her justice, she is guilty of no undue fastidiousness, is not in the least inclined to quarrel with her social bread and butter. Quantity, not quality, is her aim. "A man's a man for a' that, and a' that,"[123] in Miss Nancy's eyes. My

123. Refers to the poem, "A Man's a Man for a' That," by Robert Burns (1759–1796).

sweet Kitty is standing opposite me, and is trying to maintain conversation with Mabel Twyne; no easy task, I should say, with such a monosyllabic young person.

Miss Twyne is a tall, well-made girl of nineteen, with an air of perfect health and perfect strength about her such as one rarely sees in nineteenth century damsels. She reminds me of those statues of youthful Greek athletes that have come down to us, – mere splendid animals, magnificent boys, with an almost sulky look of scarcely expressed contempt for weaker mortals on their handsome, impassive faces.

* * * * * * * * *

In the midst of my reflections the door opens, and two men come, one by one, into the room. First, a small, eager person, with a sparkling eye (ah! I knew too well he would come); then a tall, slender young man, whose brown head overtops that of everyone else in the room by several inches.

In a minute, the newcomers have made their way to our part of the room, and Miss Twyne is presenting them in due form.

"Sir Claude Verreker, – Mr. Pole."

Kitty's eyes have met the bright eyes behind the *pince-nez*; then both young people break into an irresistible laugh.

As for me, I have begun to breathe freely again, and already my busy imagination is at work.

The hero of last week's adventure is – Mr. Pole. As for the real Sir Claude, in respect of his outer man, at least, he more than comes up to my expectations.

Men are ugly creatures, take them all in all, even Englishmen, who pride themselves on being a tolerably good-looking race. But Sir Claude Verreker, unlike most of his sex, is really deserving of the epithet, beautiful. Graceful, exquisitely proportioned, unmistakably thoroughbred; with his well-cut, expressive face, his charming smile, and perfect voice, he seems cut out for a hero of romance, and fitted to realise the daydreams of the most exacting of women.

Meanwhile, amid considerable merriment, Mr. Gilbert Pole is fighting his battles o'er again, for the benefit of his two listeners, Kitty and Sir Claude.

– "I hadn't the remotest idea of what was actually going on, on the other side," he is saying, "but thought I'd take a look. I swung up by the plum-tree like a cat (pity we've lost our prehensile faculty!), took a flying leap from the very top of the wall, and landed – "

"Where you always do; on your feet!" says Sir Claude.

"No, at Miss Pembroke's!"

"The Fates were always fond of you, Gillie!"

"It was not the Fates who sent me after those balls, if you recollect!"

Led by Miss Twyne, people are now beginning to stream out through the windows on to the lawn, and I am borne, like the rest, on the tide.

Two well-defined courts, placed at convenient distances from each other, are marked out on the old, elastic turf; the nets stretched high and taut across them respectively. We are more than eight players, and there is some delay in making up the sets.

"Please leave me out; I prefer to look on!" cries Nancy Field, in noisy self-denial. Miss Twyne measures her with her calm, cold eye; and, for once in her life, Nancy blushes.

Thank goodness, I am not let in for playing, Kitty and I, between us, having managed to convince the others of the genuineness of my refusal; and presently I find myself comfortably ensconced in a deep low chair, with Sir Claude Verreker stretched on the grass at my feet. The situation is, for me, an unusual one; and, did I not feel so overwhelmed, I think I should enjoy it. In the court facing us, Kitty and Tom Daly are carrying on vigorous warfare with Mabel Twyne and Gillie Pole (everyone calls him Gillie); and a battle no less fierce rages on the other side of the lawn.

"Don't you ever play?" asks Sir Claude, lifting his eyes to mine, –

> Those eyes of deep, soft, lucent hue.
> Eyes too expressive to be blue,
> Too lovely to be grey.[124]

"Only when a fourth is wanted; generally as a handicap."

He laughs. "But your cousin, she plays a capital game, I see." He is following her with his eyes as he speaks.

"Oh, Kitty is an enthusiast."

"Which side are you prepared to support, Miss Pembroke?"

"Take my advice, and lay long odds on us," calls out Mr. Pole, whose quick ears have caught the question.

Sir Claude laughs. Why do they all laugh at the sallies of this dreadful little person, instead of being disgusted?

"I don't know," I answer, deliberately ignoring the proffered tip; "Kitty and Mr. Daly play a respectable all-round game; Miss Twyne plays better than either, but then" (lowering my voice) "her partner is not to be depended on."

"Oh, Gillie is neat enough at the net, though I agree with you that his back-court game is weak, and he has that fatal tendency to over-volleying."

"Take care what you are saying!" cries the voice that is never silent for long. "Well played, Miss Pembroke!"

Mr. Pole is, so to speak, in full force; performing marvels of agility at the net, flashing light remarks across the court, and keeping both ladies constantly supplied with balls, with the gallantry common to small men. He has discarded the modest black and white college *blazer* in which we first beheld him, and wears a striking coat of many colours, the colours of the Middle Temple Lawn-Tennis Club, as I afterwards learn, for Gillie, as might be guessed, is at the bar, where, according to Sir Claude, he is beginning to make his mark.

The game goes on with unabated vigour, but presently I find myself forgetting all about it; forgetting everything under the sun, in fact, save a pair of blue-grey eyes uplifted to mine, a thrilling voice sounding in

124. Taken from Arnold's poem, "On the Rhine."

my ear, a smile, more charming than ever before lighted up human face, flashing from time to time across my dazzled consciousness.

> What matter if I go mad?
> I shall have had my day.[125]

Some people's days are only hours; what then?

The game is over at last, and Miss Twyne and her partner are demanding our congratulations.

"I gave you the straight tip, didn't I, Miss Agnes?" cries Gillie, delighted with his success.

"Miss Agnes," indeed! I affect not to hear the remark. The contest in the other court is over too, and the players, joined by stragglers from various parts of the garden, come trooping across in our direction. With one accord the men swarm round Mabel Twyne. Whatever other qualities this young woman may possess, that of attractiveness to the opposite sex is certainly hers. I have long ago given up trying to fathom the mysterious laws of sexual attraction, otherwise this fact might cause me astonishment; but I cannot help feeling some pangs of vicarious jealousy of Mabel's fresh young beauty, of her calm consciousness of strength; above all, of her nineteen years. In such cases, be sure, a woman's thoughts fly straight to age.

My Kitty looks a little pale and tired, I think, as she comes up to me with a smile on her face, her great eyes shining with unusual brilliancy. Sir Claude springs to his feet and offers her a chair; there is an unmistakable look of admiration in his eyes. Meanwhile Miss Twyne, Gillie Pole, and one or two other admirers, are strolling towards the terrace, where the elders are seated, and where a pair of footmen are laying out a table with an assortment of "cups."

"You must be thirsty," says Sir Claude to Kitty; "may I get you something to drink, or shall we go over there?"

Kitty rises, by way of answer; and, when I have declined to join them, the two handsome people walk slowly across the turf together.

---

125. Taken from Tennyson's poem, "Maud."

"What a lovely pair they make!" says a well-known voice in my ear. Nancy Field has not succeeded in securing an escort to the terrace, and is taking refuge in my society.

"Why, even their back-views are beautiful, Agnes!"

"Yes," I say, dreamily. I am beginning to account satisfactorily to myself for the defection of the men to Miss Twyne. Considering that Kitty has refused them nearly all, some in so many words, some by implication, it is scarcely to be wondered at! is my reflection; and Sir Claude, – ah, Sir Claude! – it is evident that he admires her! They say (that is, again, the male satirists), that, when a woman is well and kindly disposed towards a man, she is anxious to cut him off from attractive people of her own sex; to interpose her own personality, however lacking in charm, between him and the rest of womankind.

I have made no secret of the extreme kindliness with which Sir Claude inspires me; and one result of this is that I wish him the best thing that I know. Kitty is the best thing that I know in the world: so I wish him Kitty.

When thirsty people have taken their fill of shandygaff, "cup," or light wine, there is a general return to the courts, and two new sets are formed. This time Miss Twyne sits out, and her cousin plays, – from my own point of view, a change for the worse. There is no ignoring Mabel's presence, comparatively silent as she is. Hers is a personality that makes itself felt; I am oppressed, almost crushed, by it. Downright, unimaginative, conscious of a thoroughly successful career, she radiates, almost unconsciously, a scorn for people less well-provided by Nature with weapons for the universal struggle. Where your thorough-going, healthy Philistine puts you to such disadvantage is that, while you are capable of appreciating his good points, he is utterly unable even to perceive your own.

"How well your cousin plays!" she says, after one of the big gaps in our conversation.

"Yes, and your cousin, too," I respond.

"O, Claude! Of course."

Another pause, during which I watch Sir Claude's swift, clean strokes, and the admirable restraint with which he regulates his course of action. He is Kitty's partner, Nancy Field and Gillie Pole playing opposite to them, – a sufficiently unequal contest.

It occurs to me that Nancy and the vivacious Gillie would be an excellent pair; I store up the suggestion for Kitty.

The winning of the game was a foregone conclusion, and everyone looks glad when it is over; then we stroll towards the house *en masse*. There is a cold dinner at eight, served in the beautiful, cedar-panelled dining room, with its great marble fireplaces of the time of Charles II. Claude takes in Kitty; I am assigned to Gillie Pole. He makes the best of a bad job, as no doubt he considers it, and rattles on cheerfully enough, with occasional lapses of silence, during which he stares down the table at Kitty in a manner which would be exceedingly impertinent, if she were not so far off. We go home soon after dinner. It is arranged that the whole party is to play Lawn-tennis at the Manor House on the following Saturday. I follow Kitty to her room, but she is pale and tired, and disinclined to talk. So I leave her, after a long goodnight embrace, and betake myself to my own little chamber.

But the dawn creeps up the sky before I am able to close my eyes in sleep.

Chapter 4

"It looks very much like rain, very much indeed!" says Nancy Field, shaking her weatherwise head, and looking up at the grey sky. Saturday afternoon has come round, and Nancy is our first guest, considering herself sufficiently intimate at the Manor House to put in an appearance at a provokingly early hour.

"I hope it won't rain," answers Kitty, who is looking her very best this afternoon, in spite of her lawn-tennis costume. "We have asked them to stop and dine, and if we are to have them on our hands all that time!" –

"Besides," says Nancy, "I am dying for a game. I want to beat Miss Twyne. Is it not fortunate, Kitty, that she can't play for Meadowshire this year?"

"What a cowardly sentiment! But why can't she play?"

"Don't you know?" Nancy's sense of importance swells visibly, like the old woman in "Pickwick."[126] "Don't you know that they are all going to Scotland at the end of the month?"

"No," says Kitty.

Is it my imagination, or do her eyes droop a little, and does the faintest flush rise to her cheek as she speaks?

Since the Lawn-tennis party at the Grange, three days ago, we have seen something of our new neighbours. Lady Verreker came over the next morning to inspect the Colonel's orchids, and Sir Claude accompanied her. Yesterday afternoon we met the whole party on the lawn at the Rectory, in obedience to a summons from Nancy, archly indited on diminutive notepaper, with a teapot, two rackets crossed, and *Come early* printed at the top.

The arrival of the Dalys puts an end to further private conversation, and a scratch game is immediately organized, Nancy and Tom *versus* Jane Daly and the Colonel, Kitty and I taking our places as spectators on the margin of the lawn.

My cousin looks at the players, and I look at her, scrutinising her from top to toe.

"Kitty, take off that stiff, sailor-hat?"

"Do you want me to have sunstroke?"

"There isn't a vestige of sun, unfortunately."

"My nice little Lawn-tennis hat! Why are you so spiteful about it?"

"It makes a horrid hard line across your face. At your time of life, Miss Pembroke, people must study appearances."

"Yes" says Kitty, quite sadly; "that is true." And she removes the offending headgear as she speaks. I open my eyes with astonishment; the tone, the action, are so unlike my Kitty.

126. Refers to Dickens' *The Pickwick Papers* (1837).

"Kitty!" She grows aware of my scrutiny, aware of my perception of something unusual in her own manner, and laughs rather nervously.

"Well, Agnes, are you satisfied?" Then suddenly a crimson flush spreads over her face from brow to chin. I turn away my head, and grow absorbed in the construction of my racket. What is the meaning of this strange pang at my heart?

******

The Verrekers have come; Kitty and the Colonel have gone in to receive them, and I am left to entertain the other guests to the best of my powers. For once in my life I am thankful for the presence of Nancy Field, whose incessant chatter renders unnecessary any attempts at conversation on my part.

"We ought all to be ashamed of ourselves!" she is saying. "Such shocking defeats as we have been suffering! Did your single with Sir Claude come off, Mr. Daly?"

"Don't ask me about it, Miss Nancy," answers the young man, colouring slightly and turning away from the speaker.

"O! But it was just as bad with me and Mabel!" Nancy is fond of rushing into sudden, one-sided intimacies. "Just as bad. Papa looked on and was quite shocked."

They are coming; he is coming! O! Nancy, my dear, talk on as much as ever you like.

Their voices are distinctly audible; so is the rustle of a woman's gown.

"Yes, I think Kitty means to play for the county, Mr. Daly."

They are stepping through the open window on to the lawn. First comes the colonel, with Lady Verreker, in grey; then Miss Twyne, in mauve, with Gillie Pole at her heels; lastly, Sir Claude and Kitty, both of them very grave and formal.

There is a general handshaking, and a Cassandra chorus arises on the subject of the weather.

"It will rain, to a dead certainty!" cries Gillie Pole, casting up his queer little twinkling face to the sky. "Miss Pembroke, we deserve better treatment at your hands."

"I am very sorry, Mr. Pole."

"Let us invoke Jupiter Pluvius,"[127] says Tom Daly, who has enjoyed a classical education. No one laughs but Nancy, who comes to the rescue with a giggle, hereby saving the unfortunate youth from realising to the full the flatness of his little joke. We have only one court at the Manor House, and it is some time before a set is formed. At last, after much discussion, Nancy and Sir Claude are pitted against Tom Daly and Miss Twyne, leaving Jane Daly and Mr. Pole on our hands.

The Colonel has retired to the conservatory with Lady Verreker, where, no doubt, they are indulging their common passion for orchids. Jane is pouring a long story about her choir-practice into my unwilling ears, and Grampus is setting out the table with tea and what a writer in the *Daily Telegraph* would call other "potables."

"Please take me round the garden, Miss Pembroke," says the unabashed Gillie, looking straight at Kitty in the uncompromising fashion he affects. Kitty rises smiling, but, if I am not mistaken, a little reluctantly, and the ill-matched pair stroll off together down the path, and are soon lost to sight.

Meanwhile, the pale grey of the sky is deepening to a distinct ink colour, and a wet little breeze comes blowing across the lawn. Then an undecided sort of drizzle sets in, which drives Miss Daly, with me in her wake, into the drawing room, whence we can watch the enthusiastic players, bent on finishing their game. I am bored, rather cold, and generally miserable; and I wish that Kitty would come in, especially as she has no hat on. At last, a smart shower of raindrops quells even the ardour of the four players on the lawn, and a general run is made for the house, to the accompaniment of a series of high-pitched giggles from the breathless Nancy.

127. Mythological Roman deity, Jupiter.

"I wonder what Kitty is doing!" I exclaim, involuntarily, addressing no one in particular. Sir Claude turns round very sharply.

"Your cousin – ?"

"She is in the garden with Mr. Pole, and there is no place where they could possibly take shelter."

"Perhaps they are standing under a tree."

"And she has no hat on!" I answer, irrelevantly.

Sir Claude looks unmistakeably concerned.

"Let me go out with an umbrella. And Gillie, too! He is not strong; he will get wet."

He speaks with that tone of indescribable affection which he always employs with regard to his friend; and I feel vaguely irritated.

"There they are!" It is Nancy who speaks, and Sir Claude is arrested on his way to the door.

Kitty and her escort are to be seen coming across the lawn, with a calmness of gait which is rather astonishing, considering the state of the weather.

"Have you actually left off playing for a drop of rain like this?" cries Mr. Pole, with affected surprise, as they enter the drawing room; Kitty with the raindrops glistening in her hair, and a look of polite boredom, I rather fancy, on her face.

"Gillie, you are wet through." Sir Claude speaks in an undertone, but the words reach my ear. He has taken his friend aside, and is feeling the chest and shoulders of that precious person with some apparent anxiety. Why on earth do they all make such a fuss about him?

"On the contrary, my dear fellow, I am as dry as a bone. This coat is extremely thick."

Gillie supports his friend's marks of attention with equanimity, almost with condescension, and in a few moments is engaged in handing round tea with his usual air of briskness and *bonhomie*. Half an hour, an hour goes by, and the rain shows no sign of abating. A wistful group, rackets in hand, is gathered at the window, looking out on the spongy lawn and iron-grey heavens. A few people have given up the vigil, and are to be seen scattered about the big oak-panelled drawing room.

Mabel Twyne and Gillie Pole have been absorbed in one another on a distant ottoman for the last half-hour; Lady Verreker is giving me her opinions on Meadowshire tradesmen; while Kitty and Sir Claude are maintaining what looks like a sufficiently earnest conversation by the mantelpiece. Kitty laughs, and talks frankly enough with Mr. Pole; but in her manner with Sir Claude there is an indescribable touch of reserve, almost of coldness, enough to drive away a more commonplace man, or one bent on mere amusement, and the gratification of his own vanity.

Ah! I know her so well, my stately Kitty; kind, amiable, playful even, up to a certain point; but, beyond that point, – as hard as adamant.

I either hate or love you so,
I can't be merely civil.[128]

Kitty may deceive other people, may deceive even Sir Claude, with that calm and haughty air of hers; but she cannot deceive me. I, who have watched her so closely, so constantly, – I, at least, can understand. There is a look in her eyes, a thrill in her voice, that I have never seen, never heard, before today. Gazing on her transfigured face, I realise for the first time that hitherto there has been something lacking to her beauty; that delicate, crowning touch which makes perfection. And Sir Claude? There is no mistaking the look in his eyes, the air of breathless attention with which he receives her every word, the vibration in his tones as he answers her.

Looking up at them from the depths of my own little grey life, through the mists of my own sorrow, I note, almost with a shock, the unconscious grace, the unconscious pathos, with which their dawning love invests them.

* * * * * *

An adjournment to the billiard room, proposed by the Colonel, and seconded by Gillie, puts an end to the hopeless watch by the window;

128. From Barrett Browning's poem, "Amy's Cruelty."

and very soon we have plunged into the intricacies of a game of pool. There is a great deal of noise from Nancy, and various jokes about "losing lives," on the part of Mr. Pole; and someone succeeds in cutting the cloth. I am heartily glad when the whole thing is over, and we are able to dispose ourselves about the room as we like. Some of the party form themselves into a group at a writing table near the window, where they become absorbed in a low-toned, ceaseless conversation. Sir Claude and I find ourselves side by side on one of the high leather divans, a situation which rather takes away my breath.

"How beautiful your cousin is!" The remark escapes my companion's lips almost involuntarily. He glances across at Kitty, who is explaining the mysteries of the new billiard-marker to the open-mouthed Nancy.

"She is very much admired."

"She is the most beautiful woman I have ever seen." Sir Claude speaks with low-toned earnestness, as though to rebuke me for the tameness of my acquiescence. Great heavens, does he think I am jealous of Kitty?

"Don't you like billiards any better than Lawn-tennis?" he says, at length, after a gloomy little pause.

"O, I hate games."

"What a sweeping assertion!" (I wish he would not smile into my eyes). "May I ask why?"

"I invariably lose at them. Perhaps, that has something to do with it."

He laughs, but his low, musical laugh is drowned in a peal of noisy merriment from the group at the other end of the room.

"What *are* you people about?" asks Kitty, gaily, going over to them as she speaks.

"A plot, a plot!" cries Nancy.

"Quite right, Miss Field!" answers Gillie, from the table.

Please to remember
The Fifth of November, –[129]

129. Rhyme recalling Guy Fawkes' treason.

"We've heard that before," exclaims Sir Claude, rising, and strolling across the room; "you are not original, Gilbert Pole."

Everyone has gathered round the table, and uninitiated outsiders are assailing the conspirators with questions.

"Silence in court!" cries out Gillie, rapping the table with a paper knife, and rising to his feet.

"No 'shop,' my dear fellow," from Sir Claude.

"I think you had better tell them, Miss Twyne," says Gillie, with an injured air.

Mabel shakes her head, in laughing refusal; and, after further persuasion, Mr. Pole unfolds his scheme. This is nothing less than the organization of a Lawn-Tennis Meeting, to take place a week from today.

"You see," adds Gillie, "we are all horribly sold that we can't be here for the county meeting. Some of us have designs on Northern partridges, and some of us '(ruefully)' must seek, perforce, the dusty purlieus of the court of law. Gentlemen, I appeal to you – "

"Not a bit of good, Gillie; we have hearts of flint."

"And no lachrymal glands to speak of," concludes Gillie, quite undisturbed by the cutting short of his eloquence. Both Sir Claude and Kitty enter heartily into the scheme, the former even offering the lawn of the Grange for the scene of action, provided his mother has no objection. A strictly professional conversation prevails, and I have to listen, with the best grace I can summon, to endless talk of "Ladies' Singles," "Gentlemen's Doubles," and "Ladies' and Gentlemen's Handicaps."

When we separate to get ready for dinner, things are no better in the bedrooms. I try to get a few words with Kitty, but she retires, as it were, behind a battery of Lawn-tennis jargon, and I go down to dinner in a thoroughly bad temper. It is worse than ever at dinner, where the elders are drawn into the scheme, which meets, strange to say, with their unqualified approval. Perhaps, it has occurred both to Lady Verreker and the Colonel that a union between their two families would not be inappropriate. My dear uncle is no matchmaker.

People with daughters like Kitty never are; but he has an old-fashioned belief in a happy marriage as the crowning joy of existence. As for me, whom the dearth of men has allowed to go in, in peace and solitude, I am desirous enough, heaven knows, of seeing a satisfactory end to the romance just begun. But is all this hideous fuss necessary for bringing, as the phrase goes, my hero and heroine together? Are the presence of Nancy, of the Dalys, above all, of Gillie Pole, absolutely indispensable? Should not true lovers be drawn, each by the other, as the magnet draws the needle, without, forsooth, the intervention of "Tournaments" and such unromantic paraphernalia?

Someone (Nancy, I think), suggests "a little music," after dinner; whereupon Gillie Pole, who is certainly good-natured and appears to love his kind, seeks me out in my corner and urges me to play. "Now, please do, Miss Agnes! All Meadowshire has told me about you, and I am dying to hear you."

"You will, won't you, Agnes?" asks Kitty, looking down at me half questioningly.

"Kitty, I can't; I simply can't!"

"I am horribly disappointed," says Gillie.

"If someone will play first, – I am tired." I hate making a fuss, emphasising my insignificance, as it were, in any way whatever; but the prospect of sitting down to the piano is, at this moment, too terrible for words. Kitty understands, and Mr. Pole is sufficiently quick-witted not to press the matter. He turns off the subject, kindly enough, and calls upon Sir Claude for a performance. And then, for five minutes, I am in heaven. Five minutes! A lifetime, an eternity! Such moments are not to measured....

"Thanks, most awfully, Verreker," says Gillie, in quite a serious tone, when the last notes have died away. I look at Kitty; she sits opposite me, motionless, with eyes glowing in the gathering dusk. The candles at the piano make the only points of light in the long, twilit room, where shadowy forms are distinguishable in various attitudes of repose. A few are gathered round the piano, showering various complimentary remarks on Sir Claude. The latter gets up after a few minutes, looking a little bored.

"Now, Gillie!"

It appears that Mr. Pole, in addition to his other accomplishments, possesses in perfection the art of whistling. "I hear he whistles chords," whispers awe-struck Nancy.

"His vocal organs must be constructed on a unique principle," I rejoin; "but is it possible that he is going to whistle *now*, after that other music?"

It is quite possible, it seems; and soon Mr. Pole, the centre of an admiring audience, is launching forth on the airs of "Trial by Jury."[130] This done, he gives us "The Sorcerer,"[131] and winds up with selections from "Lohengrin,"[132] "Rip Van Winkle,"[133] and "The Messiah."[134] It must be acknowledged that the performance is excellent of its kind, and, in other circumstances, I might have laughed with the rest at the delight and success with which the performer went through it, looking for all the world like some small, bright-eyed bird. But after Chopin, and Schumann,[135] and Sir Claude!

"Now, Miss Agnes, after my good example – "

"Oh, I will play, if you like, Mr. Pole."

Some instinct, some irresistible desire to give vent to the conflicting emotions which have beset me throughout the day, guides my steps to the piano.

I do not know how long I play. Perhaps it is hours; perhaps only minutes. Never before have I made such music; and, when I cease, there is profound silence in the room.

130. Gilbert and Sullivan's *Trial by Jury*.
131. Gilbert and Sullivan's *The Sorcerer*.
132. Richard Wagner's *Lohengrin*.
133. Dion Boucicault's reworking of Joseph Jefferson's adaption of Washington Irving's *Rip Van Winkle*.
134. George Frideric Handel's *Messiah*.
135. Robert Schumann.

Chapter 5

"Shall I order you a tub, Diogenes?[136] I am writing to the Army and Navy Stores."

It is Kitty who speaks; Kitty, in her blue morning-gown, seated before the dainty, inlaid writing-table which adorns her boudoir.

"There is the water-butt at hand, if you want to get rid of me," I respond, with a dismal attempt at facetiousness, and looking out drearily on to the lawn, where net, balls, and rackets bear witness to our morning's occupation. The people from the Grange have been over for a "practice," and have only just left, and for the last two hours I have been delighting my eyes with the spectacle of Mr. Pole jumping backward and forward over the net in the intervals of playing. Sufferance is the badge of all our tribe (the tribe of old maids, I mean); but there are limits even to my powers of endurance, and the last week has strained them to their utmost limits. "If the present state of things were to continue much longer, I should grow hysterical, or commit suicide, or mysteriously disappear," is my reflection, as Kitty calmly goes on writing her orders for a perfect arsenal of Lawn-tennis balls. As may be guessed, for the last six days, nothing has been spoken of or thought of but the coming "tournament," nothing done without reference to that all-important event. "Practice" at the Grange, at the Manor House, at the Rectory, morning, noon, and night; measuring of courts, weighing of rackets, drawing up of programmes. Even the elders have been drawn into it, and are displaying a zeal beyond their years. Colonel Pembroke is to be referee and head man generally; Lady Verreker has organised a small dance, and invited a huge house-party to do honour to the occasion. As for me, I have been, perforce, in the thick of it, and am even to display my talent for missing balls in a "Ladies' Handicap Double," whatever that may be.

O, how I hate it all! What a nightmare it has grown! Claude's uniform courtesy, and the light in his eyes when he looks at Kitty;

136. Refers to the philosopher, Diogenes, who took to living in a tub.

Mabel Twyne's cold patronage; Gillie Pole's exuberant good nature; these are the elements which have gone to make up my waking dream. Hitherto, when I have been unhappy, when that dreadfully thin skin of mine has been galled by a careless world, I have had one resource, one place to go for comfort and consolation; Kitty, Kitty, whose very presence has always been as healing balm to my wounds. But now, it is Kitty herself, who makes the crown of all my woes; who is, as it were, the last traditionary straw which breaks the camel's back. The last few days have wrought a complete transformation in my cousin. The old sweet serenity, the old clear-eyed calm, which made her such a stronghold for weaker mortals, seem to have deserted her. Kitty is pale, with strange, bright eyes and dark rims under them. She starts at unexpected sounds, blushes, grows pale to the lips on the most trifling pretexts; has little fits of high spirits and long ones of depression; is nervous and anxious about her appearance; in short, if the records of novelists are to be believed, shows every symptom of being attacked by a complaint no less common than it is interesting. "Why is she so anxious, so doubtful?" I think, perhaps a little bitterly. "To anyone not afflicted with her peculiar sort of blindness, it is plain enough that she has no reason to despair. Ah! yet, – why does he linger? Does he also doubt?" And it is hard, hard; none the less so that it is the fulfilment of my own dearest wish that is making my heart to ache so cruelly.

> Habes totâ quod mente petisti,
> Infelis![137]

To lose them both, both!

* * * * * *

The weather is all that can be desired. Perhaps, Tom Daly has been invoking his favourite deity; perhaps, it is merely in the natural course

137. Taken from the *Aeneid* by the Roman poet, Virgil; the quotation also precedes a poem by Edith Nesbit (1858–1924), "The Depths of the Sea."

of things; but certainly, as Gillie Pole says, if we had written a prescription for our day, and ordered it to be made up by the Higher Powers, we could not have been more thoroughly suited in this respect.

Our quiet Meadowshire lanes present a scene of unwonted festivity all the county having consented to put on its best attire, and declare a holiday in honour of the Tournament. The garden and terrace at the Grange are thronged with gaily-dressed people, among whom the destined performers are to be distinguished by the band of blue ribbon which adorns the arm of each, men and women alike.

"Now let me find you a good seat in the tent, Miss Agnes, before it begins; you don't come on till the last, and you mustn't tire yourself," says Gillie Pole, who looks very spruce and cheerful; his eyeglasses glittering in the sun; his little striped cap jauntily set on his head. To give a certain person his due, Gillie is kind, unaffectedly kind. Old people, shy people, very young people; he has a good word and a smile for them all, and is prepared to be genuinely interested in their affairs.

"I am glad to hear you giving such sensible advice to my imprudent cousin," says Kitty, strolling up to us and smiling. She is looking very beautiful this afternoon and very self-possessed. I think few people would suspect the unnatural excitement, the extreme tension underlying her calm, dignified, rather abstracted manner.

"Perhaps, Miss Pembroke herself would deign to accept advice of a kindred nature from a humble friend?" says Gillie, staring at her, the ill-bred creature, with undisguised satisfaction.

Sir Claude is standing a few paces from our group, but makes no attempt to join it. Beyond a formal shake of the hands, he has taken no notice of Kitty this afternoon, but has divided his time between his duties as host and a long colloquy with Mabel Twyne. His beautiful face is singularly cold and impassive, and it appears to me that his glance, too, instead of seeking her, as usual, rather aims at avoiding my cousin. I am a tiro in such matters, but are these the signs of extreme emotion, or of – something less desirable? A thought too terrible for words flashes across my brain. Are Kitty's one hundred and one lovers to be avenged at last? Is she destined to come to a sad end, like the fastidious "Lady of the Lea" in the song, who, as everyone knows,

> Broken-hearted, drooped and died,[138]

for the sake of one man who would none of her? My heart almost ceases to beat, a mist swims before my eyes at the bare notion.

Sir Claude, my saint, my hero, Sir Claude, – that commonplace sinner, that insidious social pest, – a serious flirt! Perish the thought! But, O! How I wish that everything were over, and my Kitty's happiness assured? After all, now that there is some question of taking sides in the matter, I realised that the old love in my heart is infinitely stronger than the new.

Presently Nancy Field comes bustling over to us, thoroughly impressed with the importance of her own position as sharer in today's festivities.

"I'm in shocking form," she announces. "Papa and I had a knock-up in the garden this morning, and I was absolutely nowhere. What a lot of people! I declare I feel quite frightened. Don't you, Miss Twyne?" (The "Mabel" is reserved for the owner's absence).

"No, I don't think so," answers Miss Twyne, with a little stolid, superior smile. She has only just joined our group, and I have not yet done admiring her thoroughly well-groomed appearance. Today, for the first time, I am struck by the resemblance between her and her cousin; and, why I don't quite know, the impression produced by it is, to me, extremely painful.

"The invincible Miss Twyne has no cause for fear," cries Gillie; "but my own heart confesses to undue palpitation at prospect of these jousts."

"If one could only be anonymous and invisible, like the Black Knight in 'Ivanhoe,'"[139] giggles Nancy, with elaborate coyness.

---

138. From W. H. Bellamy's "The Lady of the Lea."

139. Refers to Scott's *Ivanhoe: A Romance.*

"Not even a vizor to hide one's blushes, in this harsh nineteenth century," says Gillie, drily; "nor a helmet," looking with sudden intentness at Kitty, and lowering his voice, "on which to fasten one's lady's sleeve."

Kitty drops her eyelids, and an irritated desire to box the ears of this presuming person takes complete possession of me. Meanwhile Sir Claude has crossed over to the terrace, and is apparently making himself highly agreeable to a pair of young ladies in rose-coloured *crêpe*.

It is possible, of course, that, like Tennyson's heroine,[140] he is proud only because he is kind; but I must confess that this "new departure" (as the journalists say) on the part of our host fills me with indescribable anxiety. Colonel Pembroke, notebook in hand, joins us at this stage of affairs. "Everything is ready, I think," he says, taking out his watch; "I may let them ring the bell in five minutes."

"I believe everything is in perfect order, Colonel," answers Gillie. "I have just been talking very seriously to the ball-boys, who are always dangerous on these occasions. I made them shake in their little shoes, and I think there is now nothing to fear in that quarter."

"Gillie!" Sir Claude has come up behind and has laid his hand on his friend's shoulder. "Hadn't we better begin?" There is a general move to the tent on the part of the players, Gillie leading the way with Mabel Twyne, and Sir Claude coming up with Nancy. This promises to be a most unsatisfactory afternoon, in spite of the weather.

An expectant silence, an anticipatory rustle, is observable on the part of the audience; Gillie is seen to bestow a last admonition to the ball-boys, who grin at him with unfeigned delight and without manifesting the least mark of alarm. Colonel Pembroke strides across to the umpire's post; a bell rings; the four chosen players leave the tent, and the first event of the afternoon is soon in full swing.

For a full, true and particular account of the Lawn-tennis "Tournament," I must refer my readers to the pages of the *South Meadowshire*

140. Probably refers to Princess Ida in Tennyson's *The Princess.*

Argus and Haycroft Gazette. There, at their leisure, they can digest the three-and-a-half closely-printed columns, which tell, with considerable technical glibness, how the games were lost and won;—how Sir Claude Verreker's uncertain play created profound surprise and disappointment among the audience; how Miss Mabel Twyne covered herself and Valeshire with glory; how Mr. Gilbert Pole came to grief in the singles, but did good service in the doubles; above all, how Miss Katherine Pembroke surpassed herself throughout the afternoon, vindicating the honour of her county against the formidable newcomers. There were no professional reporters on the ground, and the authorship of the article must remain a mystery. However, as Tom Daly has taken to assuming the forbidding airs of a Sir Philip Francis, whenever it is mentioned, we are not without a clue to the identity of our local Junius.[141]

It is dusk before the last round of the last event comes to a close, and we have to hurry back to the Manor House at once, for dinner and dressing; Lady Verreker's dance being fixed for an early hour. But when, in obedience to a previous arrangement, I hasten down the drive to the carriage, I find no one but the Colonel.

"How tiresome of Kitty! Where can she have got to?"

"She will be here in a moment, no doubt," says my uncle, even as he speaks Kitty's tall figure comes slowly down between the laurels towards us.

"Papa, Agnes, will you drive on? I am going to walk, – it is only a little way."

There is a strange catch in her voice, a note almost of entreaty in her tones; her upturned face is pale in the twilight.

"My dear, you will be so tired!" The poor Colonel speaks a little ruefully. She takes a hand of each of us; – "Papa, Agnes, you must forgive me for leaving you. I – I have promised to walk!" The Colonel trusts his daughter implicitly. He accepts his fate in silence, and in another minute my uncle and I are bowling along the dusky road in solitary

141. Refers to Philip Francis (1740–1818), possibly behind the pseudonym, "Junius."

splendour. Scarcely a word is exchanged between us during the drive; but I think our thoughts are touching one another pretty closely.

> Once I thought she was proud,
> Only because she was kind.

These lines persist in buzzing in my head over and over again. Ah! Kitty, ah! Claude, how goes it with you both along the twilight paths, between the dusky hedgerows?

My heart stops beating. I clench my hands at the thought, then turn away, ashamed, from even a visionary contemplation of the unknown paradise.

"Agnes, Agnes, open the door, dear."

"In a minute, Kitty."

I get up from the chair by the open window, where I seated myself mechanically when I came in half an hour ago, and, going over to the door, admit my cousin in silence.

"In the dark, Aggie! And still in your flannel gown!"

"Never mind about that, Kitty. Wait a moment; I want to look at you."

I light a candle, and hold it up to my cousin's face, who blinks her bright eyes in sweet protest.

"You look like Moses, Kitty, when he came down from the Mount."

Kitty laughs softly.

"I didn't know you were present on that occasion, Agnes."

I have set down the candle, and my cousin, coming up to me, puts both hands on my shoulders, and looks straight into my eyes.

"Can you guess, Aggie?"

"I think I can."

"Well?"

"O Kitty, dearest, I am so glad!"

"Now, that's delightful! I was sometimes afraid that you wouldn't be altogether pleased!"

"O Kitty!" She puts her arms round me, and draws me to her.

"Agnes, I can't believe it, it seems too wonderful. You know (you have all my secrets!) that there never was anyone else. I began to be afraid that I was a woman without a heart! And then, all of a sudden, this wonderful thing happens!" She pauses a moment, then resumes; – "I have been a great nuisance to you, this last week, haven't I, Aggie? Dear, you don't know what it is, – I hope you will some day, – it makes one so afraid! I had never really believed it till today. I thought, perhaps, Miss Twyne – !"

"What nonsense, Kitty! A timid person would have known better!"

She goes on dreamily: – "It was the same from the first; from the very moment, I do think, when he appeared, like Jack in the box, on the top of that wall!"

"Kitty!"

"What is the matter, Agnes?"

"Nothing, nothing!" I disengage myself from her arms rather breathlessly, and move back a few paces.

"Agnes, dear child, what is it?"

I burst out laughing. It occurs to me that I have been wasting a good deal of sentiment in a general way, as Mr. Pole would express it.

"O, Agnes!" Kitty recoils, hurt.

"Never mind, Kitty, I thought it was Sir Claude, that's all."

"O, poor Sir Claude!" The confession slips involuntarily from her lips.

"Go away, go away, Kitty, and let me make myself smart for tonight. And I have already decided on my wedding present, an *édition de luxe* of the "Midsummer Night's Dream!"[142]

* * * * * * *

Mr. and Mrs. Gilbert Pole are, to all appearances, extremely happy. They have a delightful house on Campden Hill, and every morning

142. Shakespeare's *A Midsummer Night's Dream.*

the cheerful Gillie is to be seen careering down to chambers on the top of a green omnibus.

Sir Claude did not go to Scotland, but set off on a tour round the world. The Grange is shut up once more, Lady Verreker and her niece being at present in Florence, where they have been joined by Sir Claude. A marriage between the two cousins was announced as "arranged" in last Wednesday's *Morning Post*. As for me, I go on very much in the old way; save that there is no Kitty, no Lawn-tennis, and, as far as I am concerned, no more romances in Meadowshire.

THE END

At Prato (1888)

The radiant March daylight had begun to fail, and a luminous twilight was stealing over Prato.

Ivan Callander put up his camera and box of slides, and bore them into his hotel, leaving the strolling player and his wife, to whom he had unconsciously presented a formidable rivalry, in undisputed possession of the Piazza. Presently Ivan reappeared, strolling across to the cathedral, his hands in the pockets of his light shooting clothes, his hat pushed over his fair, sunburnt face. The people were beginning to swarm, Italian fashion, into the great straggling square, and to gather in the doorways of the little old houses; and this time Ivan's tall, unmistakably English figure passed unnoticed in the throng.

He lingered a moment, to survey the scene on the steps of the cathedral, and was about to enter the building, when he was arrested by the sight of a figure strangely at variance with its surroundings advancing in his direction. A woman, tall, slight, presumably young, beautifully dressed in the English fashion, and alone.

Assured that she was making her way towards himself, Ivan advanced a step or two and raised his hat. She bowed slightly, then addressed him in the unmistakable tones of an English gentlewoman. "Pray pardon my troubling you. Would you kindly tell me if there be a hotel where I could wait for the next train to Florence? I have lost my party and the train, and I cannot speak Italian."

A delicate bloom of reserve and timidity overlay the trained self-possession of her manner. Her face was hidden by a veil, but an unspeakable fragrance of grace and beauty exhaled from her whole person. Callander hastened to declare himself at her service, and in a few minutes had led her up the innumerable dusky stairways of the hotel into a big, musty sitting room. She sat down by one of the several tables, elaborately set out for potential dinner-guests, and leaned her little head on her hand.

"Thank you so much," she said. "Oh, that is six o'clock striking! There is no train, I think, till eight?"

"I am afraid not," he answered. "Of course you could take the tram; but there would be no gain in speed, and great loss in comfort."

"I will wait for the train." She drew off the glove from her right hand, and a diamond that glittered on her delicate forefinger shot its light into the gloom. Ivan found himself conjecturing as to the nature of the rings on the gloved left hand.

"You will want something to eat," he said; and at her request ordered bread and coffee of the solitary waiter.

Then, "Please open the window," she said, with her charming, great-lady air of conferring a favour by a command. When he had done so she walked across to it, and leaned out with inimitable grace of pose.

He hesitated a moment, then followed her.

"May I stay here?"

"Please do. I am afraid it is I who am disturbing the peace of your dining room."

"Oh, we are very primitive in Prato; I dined at noon. But, if you will allow me, I will drink my coffee here."

The window overlooked the piazza, and immediately beneath it the strolling players were performing to a large and vociferous audience.

It was dusk, and lights were beginning to appear in the houses and round the great marble fountain in the centre. A torch gleamed on a hawker's barrow, lighting up his wares, – yellow beans in a green basin, pale melon-pips, eggs, and a dark mass of dried prunes. A seller of chestnut cake, his tin tray slanted under his arm, was driving a roaring trade. Life in Prato was at its busiest.

"What a strange little faraway place it is!" mused Ivan, leaning out of the opposite corner of the window. "To think that it was once the rival of Florence!"

She ignored the historical allusion.

"Little? I found it terribly big, – those tall grey streets, so old and so endless! We were wandering about all the afternoon."

She shuddered.

Ivan felt a growing curiosity as to the component parts of the first-person plural. He merely said: "It is an admirable place for taking photographs, and not too hackneyed."

"We came to see the cathedral and Donatello's[143] open-air pulpit. Have you photographed them? It must be charming to make photographs."

She turned her face towards him, affording him a tantalising view of a white, cleft chin, and a veiled symmetrical outline of face. A burst of applause mounted up from the crowd below, drowning their voices.

"What a little it takes," said Ivan, when the tumult had subsided, "to amuse these people. This clown has been here, with short intervals, since midday."

"I have been watching him," she answered, "and wondering what it is that he does."

"Absolutely nothing. He never comes to a climax. He can't do the simplest tricks of his trade."

"Perhaps he is clever and amusing. I wish I could understand Italian."

Ivan permitted himself some assumption of masculine superiority.

"There are cases," he said, "where ignorance is bliss."

Her eyes, through her veil, rested a moment intently on his face, then resumed their contemplation of the players below.

"There is that nameless charm about the fellow," Ivan went on, "that goes further than wit or skill – the best gift the gods can give us."

"Ah! you think so?"

143. Donatello (1386–1466), Florentine Renaissance sculptor.

"See how prettily he puts his hand on his wife's shoulder – poor jaded, faded creature – and petitions in her name for subscriptions."

"No doubt he is cruel to her when they are alone."

"They say these Italians are good to their women."

For a moment there was silence; then, suddenly turning to him, with a charming air of gaiety, she said, "He is Pascarèl; I am certain of it! Do you know Pascarèl?"[144]

The change of tone, her almost childish pleasure at the supposed discovery, the swift, graceful movement of her head and neck, bewildered the young man and dazzled him. He answered, looking at her with his honest grey eyes, "Yes, it's a capital book of its kind. One ought to read it in Florence; that and 'Romola.'"[145]

"I never could read 'Romola.' It's too much like an Italian *chiesa*, half museum, half church."

The waiter came into the room bearing coffee and a lighted candle. They sat down at a great round table.

Ivan watched her furtively. Her movements, the little daintinesses of her toilet, were a constant surprise to him. She put up her arm, displaying more fully the lines of her supple figure in its well-cut tailor-made gown, and drew out the pearl pin which fastened her veil.

By the solitary candle Ivan saw a pale, perfect face, shaded by soft dark hair, lighted by dark, inscrutable eyes. The unusual yet regular face belied the conventionality of her dress and manner.

Across the young man's excited consciousness flashed these words of Bacon's: "There is no excellent beauty that hath not some strangeness in the proportion."[146]

"I am afraid," was all he said, "that they have given us horribly bad coffee."

"It is very – unusual." She looked up at him, and smiled for the first time. He felt himself grow pale.

144. *Pascarèl: Only a Story* (1873), by Ouida (Maria Louise Ramé, 1839–1908).

145. Eliot's *Romola.*

146. From Francis Bacon's (1561–1626) "Of Beauty"; see his *Essays.*

"And the bread is bad, too!" he said.

"The famous bread of Prato, that Baedeker[147] recommends. I have lost another illusion."

The buzzing of the crowd below sounded through the open window; the cathedral bell began to toll.

"There is going to be a funeral. There always is a funeral in Italy," said Ivan.

Her beautiful, strange eyes widened wistfully.

"Imagine," she said, "to have lived and died in Prato!"

The waiter came with the bill, and she handed her little purse to Ivan. His fingers thrilled as he touched it.

She, on her part, resumed her place by the window.

"See, it is already night," she said, when he joined her. "What a dear little curve of a moon, and more stars than I can count! And always Pascarèl."

"It is dark over yonder at Fra Lippo's,"[148] he answered. "Is he looking out of window, I wonder? or perhaps he is supping with Donatello?"

She turned to him, mystified: "Have you been long in Prato?"

"Since yesterday. Tonight I take the up-train to Milan on my way home."

A pause. Then, "You are, perhaps, an artist?" she said.

"No, only a professor."

She looked at him with an air of serious scrutiny. "You are not like the other professors I have seen!"

His cheek flushed, his pulse beat high, he laughed a little. "My laurels are recent. I am yade professor at Cambridge. My name is Ivan Callander."

"My name is – Elinor."

He answered quite simply, "It is a beautiful name, I hope you don't allow it to be spoilt by abbreviation."

---

147. Probably refers to Karl Baedeker's *Italy: Handbook for Travellers* (1886).

148. Refers to the painter, Filippo Lippi (c. 1406–1469), the subject of Robert Browning's poem, "Fra Lippo Lippi."

She turned her face away with some haughtiness; it looked paler than ever in the moonlight. "I have not considered the question," she said.

The funeral procession was coming across the piazza: a red flare of tapers; the pale gleam of the priests' robes; the dark mass of the black brothers bearing the coffin. A sound of chanting was borne to them across the laughter of the crowd, as the player went on, unmoved, with his performance. Some of the people drifted away to this counter-attraction, and followed it into the cathedral.

Two black brothers, masked and hooded, stood sentinel on the steps, lifting up and down their tall tapers.

Ivan was strangely moved. Some influence or combination of influences was at work within him, setting his faculties in motion, straining his perceptions to their utmost keenness.

The scene, with its weird contrasts, imprinted itself forever on his brain, – the wide crowded piazza, livid with torchlight, pale with moonlight; on one hand, a masque of life, on the other, a masque of death, passing each other by without concern or recognition; the glimpse of curving hills beyond the city street; and over all the solemn loveliness of an Italian night.

For some moments, there was silence between the two people at the window; for Ivan, at least, a living, throbbing silence, more full than speech. Then she whose name was Elinor, sighing deeply, said with a strange quiver in her sweet tones, "Do you think he is at rest, that dead person?"

"I think so," he said.

Their faces, that fronted one another, were very close together as they leaned forward in the moonlight. Ivan's glance met the mystic, shining eyes of his companion in a long gaze.

The clock struck half-past seven.

"Madam," said Ivan, in a low, vibrating voice, "it is exactly an hour and a half that I have known you. In half an hour we part. But first I must tell you this: I love you. Need we part forever? I have not much to offer. Such as it is, my whole life is yours – for you to take or refuse."

His voice died away. She leaned forward, motionless, speechless, with intense eyes shining from a white face. He resumed:

"You think me, no doubt, presumptuous, a madman, to say this to you here, in this place, under these circumstances. My love must be its own justification. I cannot make fine speeches to you. If you will not take my love take my service; that, too, is yours, forever. Elinor, forgive me for saying this. I have read in your sweet eyes that you are not happy. Let that also be my justification."

Again silence. Then, very slowly, she said:

"I will tell you something. I am not a good woman."

The chanting of the priests came through the open doorway of the cathedral, and mingled with a clink of falling coins – the clown's poor harvest.

"You do not know what you are saying," said Ivan hoarsely. It seemed that his heart had ceased to beat.

"My friend," she laid her fingers on his ice-cold hand, "I am beyond the reach of all love and all service. Shall I tell you? I was married to a hard man of twice my own age. He gave me a great name; it is mine still. That is his revenge; he will not take away his name. There was someone else. I had known him always – he was young, and poor, and very charming. He was not good, – I have never known a good man except you, – and he tempted me, and I – "

"And you," burst forth Ivan, scarcely knowing what he said, "you are with him, and can never be his wife?"

"Not with him" – she looked into his eyes – "with someone else."

"My God!" Ivan drew himself up from his stooping posture and strode into the room.

The candle flickered and went out.

In a moment he was again at her side. She had not moved.

"Elinor, will you let me help you? I have a sister, a good woman; let me take you to her."

"I must tell you all, it seems," she said a little wearily. "We came here today on one of our aimless excursions, and I told myself that it should be the last. We passed you at noon in the square. You looked strong and kind, and I thought – "

"By Heaven!" he cried, "you shall not tell me this!"

Someone in the crowd laughed out shrilly.

"I must go, Mr. – Callander. I shall miss the train."

She turned from the window, seeking a response, but Ivan had flung himself down by the table, with arms drawn forward and head prone.

"Goodbye." She laid her hand lightly on his shoulder, and perceived that his whole great frame was shaken by mighty sobs.

At her touch he started to his feet, the moonlight showing his haggard face. Then, catching her hands in his, he pleaded with all his man's strength, his man's passion, for the right to save her.

She stood with her back to the window, upright and rigid, her face in darkness. Once or twice she seemed to tremble.

At last, "I will do what you wish," she whispered.

She was to journey with him at once to Milan, where his sister awaited him. The train was due in twenty minutes. They went in silence down the stairs, across the piazza towards the station.

At the cathedral steps she paused.

"A moment," she said, and went into the building where the funeral service was drawing to a close.

Kneeling down near the doorway, she covered her face with her hands. Ivan knelt by her side with closed eyes, and prayed as he had forgotten how to pray.

The tramp of feet close to his ear roused him. The people were passing through the door in the wake of the funeral.

"Come," he said.

She did not answer.

He rose to his feet, and turned to raise her.

She had disappeared.

All through that night Ivan sought her in vain. From that day to this he has never seen her face. She had vanished, as a dream vanishes, leaving no trace behind.

Sometimes he wonders if it were indeed a living woman, or a beautiful, sad vision, that talked with him that night in Prato.

Meanwhile, Ivan Callander's friends shake their heads over the change in him; unaccountable, indescribable, yet in some painful and subtle manner, a change affecting his whole personality.

The Recent Telepathic Occurrence at the British Museum (1888)

1.

She lay dying; soon she would be dead, and her secret would have died with her.

All about her, her friends were weeping, or standing with pale faces from which they strove to keep back the tears. For each she had a look, a word, a pressure of the hand. For the absent there were little gifts and messages of farewell; it seemed that none were forgotten.

Yet, for him whom first and most she remembered, there was no token of remembrance. It is often so with women.

Through long and weary days had she kept her own counsel; now, at the last, there should be no betrayal of her womanhood. The secret which lay hidden in her heart was a hard and cruel one, crushing with its weight the tender breast, sapping the young life at the very spring. Nevertheless, the fact that *it* too must die with the rest of her was what made the thought of death a bitter one.

By-and-by, when they had left her, all save one silent watcher, when she herself had grown too weak for speech, she heard the passionate voice of her secret crying out to her in the stillness.

"Oh, my love, my love," it said, "and must it be so? That all hope and chance depart this hour for evermore? That the mighty force in my breast shall be as it had never been?

"Almost it seems that in dying I play a traitor's part! That there must have been virtue in the love with which I encompassed you; you, that knew or heeded it not. Now that great love shall hover no more about you, poor human creature, knowing not your own forlornness.

"And what was the cloud that came between us?

"Cruel, oh, you were cruel! But you were mine, and I was yours, though the truth of this knowledge may never dawn in your heart. Oh, love, there is so much that I would have done for you...."

The daylight was growing dim, and came in grudgingly through the pane; in her seat the silent watcher stirred wearily; and the body of the dying woman shook and quivered with a mighty yearning.

2.

The Professor was young (as Professors go), but already he was growing bald at the temples; and much poring over manuscripts had made eyeglasses a necessity for eyes that once had been keen as a hawk's.

And this afternoon his back ached with stooping, his head throbbed, he was conscious of unusual weariness.

Leaning back in his chair, he let the pen fall from his hand, while his glance wandered round the vast reading room, with the domed roof and book-lined walls, the concentric circles of catalogue cases and radiating lines of the reading-desks.

How familiar it all was to him! The thick atmosphere, the smell of leather, the dusty people who bustled and dawdled, whispered and flirted, and whose faces he knew by heart.

A more miscellaneous throng, perhaps, that of these seekers of literary honey, than you anywhere else find pursuing its avocations under one roof.

"How dark it is!" grumbled the Professor. "Why do they always wait to the last moment before lighting up? And what a tramping and a whispering on all sides! It's the women – they've no business to have women here at all," he added, as a clergyman and a law-student passed by in loud consultation.

That woman there, for instance, standing near him at the outer circle of the catalogue desks; what did she mean by staring at him in that unearthly fashion?

She here! She, of all people; here, of all places in the world!

What had brought her? What cursed feminine impulse had prompted her to disturb him, to come between him and his work? – His work, which was all he lived for now.

Pshaw! She wanted, no doubt, the answer to an acrostic, the pattern of some bygone fashion for a ball.

And did she expect him to fly to her side with offers of help, that she fastened on him that lingering, wistful glance of appeal?

"Get thee behind me, Satan,"[149] said the Professor to himself, and turned to the books of which he was so weary.

At the same moment the great dim globes suspended from the roof grew white, and their radiance was spread throughout the hall.

The Professor raised his head, and involuntarily his eyes sought the woman with the wistful face.

She was not there.

Strange! His seat was the last of the row towards the centre of the room; she had been, therefore, quite near him, and he had heard no sound – no oft-vituperated rustle of feminine skirts.

The Professor sprang to his feet, and snapped his eyeglass on the bridge of his nose.

She should not escape him thus; for once, from his own lips, she should hear what he thought of her – with her own lips should make what reply she could.

There was something of exaggeration in his rage. His lips twitched a little, as he made his way to the centre of the room, a good point of observation.

149. This term is also used by Levy in *The Romance of a Shop* (p. 89).

The Professor came back to his seat with a curious look on his face; mechanically he restored the books at the desk, received the tickets, put on his hat, and made his way from the Museum.

A few hours later someone stopped him in the street and told him that she was dead.

The streetlamps, the shop lamps, the red flashing lights of the cabs swam and reeled before his eyes in chaotic brightness, and then, somehow, he was stumbling up the dark staircase of his lodging to his room.

Oh, the wasted days, the wasted loves, the wonderful wasted chances!

Crouched there by the table, his head bowed over the papers and manuscripts, he saw it all as by a flash – saw it, and understood.

She had thought that it would die with her, the poor secret, so jealously guarded. Love stronger than death,[150] and for once more merciful, had betrayed her.

For two people knew it now – her secret, which was also his.

150. See Song of Songs 8:6.

Griselda (1888)[151]

Chapter 1

"The shadow of a monarch's crown is softened in her hair."[152]

"What is the good of a birthday without presents?" I ask disconsolately, leaning a pair of shabby elbows on the shabby tablecloth.

"I never could see any good in birthdays myself," answers my brother, the Hon. Patrick MacRonan, setting light to a very indifferent cigarette, and looking at me compassionately with his dark blue eyes. "They must be especially unpleasant to a girl, I should say. Poor old Grizel, she's getting on in life, and nothing to show for it!"

"I used to think twenty such a terrible age when I was seventeen," I say, casting myself back in our one armchair, a precarious structure of stained deal and horsehair. "Oh, Pat, Pat, my dear old Pat, why weren't we born common folk who might have kept a shop, or stood on our heads, without exasperating the names of a lot of old ancestors?"

"Hark to the daughter of a hundred Irish kings; to the Hon. Griselda MacRonan, sister to the most noble Viscount Goll, and

151. This version is taken from *Temple Bar: A London Magazine for Town and Country Readers* 84, no. 334 (September 1888): 65–96; "Griselda" was also published in *The Living Age* 64, no. 2312 (October 20, 1888): 143–59, and serialised in *The Evening Star* from October 27 to 17 November 1888.

152. From Barrett Browning's "Lady Geraldine's Courtship" (New, ed., *The Complete Novels*, 558 n. 30).

niece to half the peerage of the Emerald Isle!" cries Patrick, puffing hard at his strong-smelling cigarette.

"A great deal of good it does one!" I cry, looking round at the dreary little lodging-house parlour. "It was bad enough when we had to let Ronantown because of those poor creatures of tenants and their rents; but when it comes to hiding away like this, and to dear old Goll's hanging about the Chancery Court all day for what he may never get—why, then I declare I sometimes wish we had been born grocers!"

"You might at least confine your wish to yourself. *I* never wish I had been born a grocer!" says a clear proud voice from the other end of the room, as my sister Katherine sends a scornful glance from her beautiful eyes at the reclining figure in the "easy"-chair. "And, Griselda," she goes on, raising her handsome head from her sewing, "you have no right to talk in that way about Goll. He is doing his best for us all. The money is ours, and must fall to us if there is any justice in the land."

"In the meantime," says Patrick, "I can't say I find Welby a particularly pleasant land of exile, especially since you and Goll are so determined we shall not soil that ancient purple of ours by contact with other people's brand-new satins."

"You know as well as I do," answers Katherine, "that the people in Welby are not of our own sort. We have no right to begin acquaintances which it would be impossible for us even to acknowledge afterwards. There can be nothing in common between us and the townspeople."

"I don't expect they would be grateful for any little attentions we might show them," I cry. "You forget, Katie, that to them we are only the MacRonans, obscure Irish strangers, in poor lodgings."

"My dears, haven't we had enough of this discussion," says my mother, who is darning stockings at the table. As she speaks, her gentle face flushes, and I feel guilty.

Of all the many shifts, contrivances and humiliations of our poverty, this is the one that has entered like iron into my mother's proud soul – that it has been deemed expedient to drop our lawful style and title, and present ourselves to the Welby world as Mrs., Mr., and the Misses MacRonan.

"It is a miserable business," Goll had said on the morning of his departure for London; "but it would never do in a place like this to let the people know who we are. Afterwards, when you come to take your right place in the world, it might be unpleasant in many ways." And mother submits, as we all have submitted, to this handsome, tyrannical brother of ours, ever since I can remember.

"I have some news! Would anyone like to hear it," I ask, breaking in on the uncomfortable pause which has followed my mother's remark. "A most important, exciting, unique piece of news."

"Aw, really!" drawls Patrick, assuming his most man-of-the-world air. "Aw, of course we shall be most happy to hear anything Miss MacRonan may have to tell us."

"Now, don't be silly, Pat. When I got to the Watsons' this morning, I found everybody up in arms; servants running to and fro, and Margaret Watson careering up and down stairs in that fussy way of hers. The pervading excitement had penetrated even to the schoolroom, where the table was covered with all sorts of glass pots like fish-bowls. The children were more troublesome than usual over their lessons, and at last little Jo, unable to contain himself any longer, informed me that 'Mamma had a party tomorrow night.' I reproved him severely and made him go on with his dates."

"Oh! a fine school-marm you must be, Miss Grizel! Now I come to think of it, you are the very image of Miss O'Brien. Don't you remember poor old O'Brien and the schoolroom at Ronantown?"

"Don't interrupt, Pat. I went down before lunch to give Margaret Watson her singing, and in the middle of the lesson Mrs. Watson came in, with her most gracious smile on, and said — what do you think she said?"

"I am on the rack to know."

"Well, she said, 'Miss MacRonan, I am giving a little party tomorrow night in honour of the New Year. I should be so pleased if you would join us!'"

I pause and look round at my audience. Katherine's head is bent over her sewing; my mother is threading a needle with great deliberation; Pat gives a prolonged whistle.

"And what did you say?" he asks after a pause.

"Oh, I thanked her, and – told her my arrangements did not depend on myself," I answer rather hurriedly, "and that I would write this afternoon."

Pat whistles again; my mother and sister proceed with their work in silence.

"Is it possible," says Katherine at last, raising her proud head and looking at me; "is it possible, Griselda, that you wish to go to – this party?"

"Mrs. Watson meant to be kind; it would have been ungracious to refuse straight away," I answer evasively; "and besides—oh, Katie, I *do* feel a little dull sometimes!"

"My dear," says my mother, "of course it is out of the question that you should go. Think how shocked your brother would be. He would be vexed enough if he knew that you had persuaded me to allow you to teach these Watsons – very good people, no doubt, but not of our world. Come, Griselda, write a gracious little note at once, and say that you do not go out. And word it carefully; I should not wish you to hurt anyone's feelings."

"'Hurt anyone's feelings'! Oh, you dear, proud mother! Don't you see that Mrs. Watson's point of view cannot be the same as ours? She will think I have no gown, if she thinks at all," I cry ruefully.

"She will be quite correct on that point," says Katherine.

"But I have a gown," I protest. "The white tarlatan did very well for Ronantown; surely it would be good enough for Welby."

"It's a very pretty gown, and shure it is," cries Patrick, launching into his favourite brogue. "Och, do ye remember the dancing at Ronantown, and Teddy MacMorna – the rogue!"

"Oh, don't talk of it, Pat," I cry, "my feet begin to dance at the very name of Teddy MacMorna," and I give a sigh to the memory of that fascinating but impecunious youth, as I take up a pen and slowly inscribe date and address on a sheet of paper.

"Dear Mrs. Watson, – " Then I look round at my family. They have made me desperate and left me but one course open.

"Mother," I cry, laying down my pen; "you will be shocked, I know, but I want to go to this party. I want to go dreadfully!"

"My dear," says my mother, distressed, "I confess you surprise me. I do not think you would enjoy yourself among those people. And it would not be just to them."

"But, Mother, it is not a little matter, so unimportant one way or the other. It is such a long time since I have danced, I think I have forgotten how to dance."

"If you will only have a little patience, Griselda, you will have as much dancing as even you can desire."

"I cannot imagine, Griselda," says my sister, "how you can for a moment wish to go."

"I confess," I answer, "that I am a little surprised at my own depravity. But, Katie, think of waltzing, of waltzing to real music, on a real floor."

"With a partner who will shovel you out your money at the Bank the next morning, or bring you a mustard poultice when you have a cold. I cannot say that the notion dazzles me."

"It is not much money they will shovel out to me! And you know I never catch cold, Katie."

During this discussion Patrick has remained silent, but he comes suddenly forward and flings himself into the breach.

"Let her go, mother," he says. "By the time we are in London she may be forty and have the gout. No one can dance with the gout." Whether it is Patrick's advocacy or my mother's tender-heartedness that pleads for me, I know not. I only know that in a few minutes more she has yielded, and I have gained my point. "Patrick," I say, the note of acceptance being written, "let us go out and post it, before tea."

Pat gives a yawn and nods an affirmative to my invitation, and in a few minutes he and I are speeding through the damp, dismal streets of the dismal little town. We go up the high street to the post office, past Boulter's Bank with the lighted plate-glass windows, and pause at the grocer's to buy a pot of jam, which I manage to conceal under my cloak.

"Patrick," I say, "I wish Mamma and Katie would take another view of my teaching the Watson family. And I wish it were possible to tell Goll. I hate secrets, especially from him."

"He is a good fellow," answers Pat, "with not an atom of the elder brother about him. He never wants anything for himself, and of course he expects us to respect his prejudices."

We walk on a little in silence; then he bursts out again with some impatience:

"It's a shame you should have all the work, Grizel, it is indeed! You know, when I saw there was no immediate prospect of Sandhurst, I wanted to try emigration, the Backwoods, or the Gold Fields, or something of the sort. But Goll said, 'Wait,' and he pointed out that mother and you girls could not be left alone. I will wait another six months, Grizel, and if nothing is settled, I shall get Uncle Fitz to pay my passage to America."

"You might get work at home, Pat."

"It would be more difficult. I'm not much of a hand at anything but riding and shooting and dancing—at using my legs and arms, in short, and not my brains. My sort of talents pay better abroad than at home, I believe. It's *you* have all the cleverness, Grizel."

"Oh, Pat," I say, "I am not clever at all. How can I help knowing French when I have had Antoinette to dress me all my life? And is it any credit to a MacRonan if he or she knows more about music than most people? I think we are all born *singing*! And music and French are my only accomplishments."

"Yes, you do know how to sing," says Pat with condescension; "and I suppose tomorrow night you will be expected to sing for your supper like the young man in the nursery rhyme, whose enforced celibacy has so often moved me to tears:

> "'Little Tommy Tucker sings for his supper; …
> How shall he cut it without e'er a knife?
> How shall he marry without e'er a wife.'"

"'How shall she marry without e'er a husband,' ought to be the modern version, in these days of surplus female population," I say feelingly; "but, Pat, do you think the Watsons will expect me to sing tomorrow!"

"Haven't a doubt! I say, Grizel, you ought to be grateful to me. I almost wish I were going myself; though, to be sure, there's not a pretty girl in Welby, excepting Katherine and – well, perhaps Katherine's sister."

"Do you really think me pretty, Pat?" I say anxiously, for this has always been a doubtful point in our family.

"You're not like Katherine, certainly," Pat answers judicially.

"No one would think of wanting to model your head as that English Lord did Katie's at Dublin. But there's something rather pleasing about you on the whole. I like the way your dimples dance about, and your hair curls round your forehead, and your eyes shine; – I think I may say without flattery, my dear Grizel, that your eyes are the crown and glory of the MacRonan family."

"Oh, Pat!" I cry, overwhelmed, and nearly dropping my jam-pot. "It is such a long time since anyone has said anything nice to me! If I were not afraid of attracting undue attention, I should give you a kiss this very moment!"

Chapter 2

A Welby Festival

It is New Year's eve; a clear, cold night. The Honourable Griselda MacRonan is engaged in adorning her youthful person with such garments of festival as her scanty resources afford. Her fingers are rather stiff, for there is no fire in the small grate; moreover the cracked looking-glass on the wall is both so minute and so misleading as to be a hindrance rather than a help to successful hair-dressing; add to these discomforts the absence of a maid, and insufficient light, and no wonder the business of the toilet proceeds neither quickly nor satisfactorily.

"I am coming, Pat; don't be impatient, there's a dear boy," I cry, wrestling with that rebellious, dusky, Irish hair of mine with both hands, and squinting to obtain a view of myself in the mirror, which presents me with a pleasing image of a young woman with lopsided cheeks, and a twisted mouth. "I am sorry to keep you waiting."

The door opens, and Katherine comes in.

"Why didn't you ask me to help you, you silly child?" she says rather sadly. "I did not even know you had gone up to dress."

"I did not think you would wish to come, Katie."

"I think you are unwise to go; but I would sooner you did not look a little fright, as you are going," she answers, while her clever fingers twist up the abundant hair, and adjust the white tarlatan gown, which is more crumpled than I had realised.

I give Katherine a kiss of silent gratitude and put my arm round her waist as we go down the little staircase together.

"She thought to break the Welby hearts
For pastime e'er she went to town!"[153]

cries Pat as we enter the sitting room.

"Don't be silly, Pat. Seriously, do I look a fright?"

"The gown isn't much, to be sure," answers Pat candidly; "but you don't look half bad, and your eyes are shining like – like the fifth of November."[154]

"Goodnight, mother," I cry, kissing her; "don't look distressed, please don't, or I shall feel remorseful. I shall be like Jane Eyre,[155] you know – without Rochester."

"I should hope so!" says my mother with a shudder. "Oh, my dear, I hope I am not doing wrong in letting you go."

******

153. Rewording of Tennyson's poem, "Lady Clara Vere de Vere."
154. Guy Fawkes Night.
155. Refers to Charlotte Brontë's *Jane Eyre*.

The Watsons' big white villa is a blaze of light as our fly makes its slow way up the carriage drive. The French windows of the drawing room are shut fast, but a confused sound of music and merriment has struggled out into the chilly garden, where a little crowd of shabby people stands gazing intently at the unshuttered windows.

The Watsons are important people in Welby, for, together with their cousin, Mr. Fairfax, they represent the "Co." of Boulter's Bank in the High Street, and from time immemorial "Boulter's," I hear, has taken the lead of Welby society.

"Don't be late, Pat," I say with some trepidation as the plate-glass panelled door is flung open. "I promise not to keep you waiting a moment."

Pat gives my hand a sympathetic squeeze, and I step into the gaily-paved, gas-lit hall. Little Charlotte, my pupil, comes running in while I am removing my cloak in the schoolroom – converted for the evening into a dressing room. She wears an aggressively stiff, white frock, with pink ribbons, and pink ribbons adorn her elaborately crimped hair; she brings in with her an overpowering odour of Patchouli scent, and carries a smart fan in her little gloved hand.

"Oh, Miss MacRonan," she cries, dancing about on the toes of her bronze boots, "it's such a grand party – fifty ladies and gentlemen; I heard Mamma telling Cousin Jack."

She skips across the room, then comes back to the toilet-table, where I am smoothing out the crumpled folds of my gown before the mirror.

"You have a white frock too, Miss MacRonan. Don't you wish you had some pink ribbons?"

"I wish you wouldn't make the candles flicker so," I say, regarding the poor tarlatan with some dismay.

"*I* think you're pretty, Miss MacRonan," announces my pupil with magnificence. "Margaret doesn't, nor Mamma, but I do."

I begin to laugh, and forget all about my gown in a sudden sense of the ludicrousness of the situation.

The door is pushed open, and Jo, my other pupil, rushes in, in all the glory of a black velveteen suit and white kid gloves.

"Come along, Miss MacRonan," he cries, seizing my hand in its long Swedish glove. "Aren't you glad you've come to our party?"

Charlotte takes possession of my other hand, and thus unannounced, between the two children I am led to the scene of action.

Miss Watson comes across the room on her high heels as I enter, and greets me with infinite condescension. Her short, wide skirts of pale silk, her bright velvet bodice, are redolent of that same sickly perfume with which her younger sister has made fragrant her small person. A knot of wired roses and maidenhair fern is fastened under her ear; she carries a huge black fan in her mittened hand.

"We are going to dance," she says; "everyone has paired off. I will introduce some gentlemen later on. Lottie, find Miss MacRonan a seat."

With a sinking heart I survey the scene before me. Gas, gas: that is my first impression—any amount of gas flaring hard, in the big central chandelier, in the gilt branches that project on all sides from the walls; filling the room with a horrible, stifling heat, casting unnatural radiance on the grass-green carpet, guiltless of drugget, on which the dancers are disporting themselves. In one corner of the room stands a rosewood piano, on which Mrs. Watson is performing a remarkably deliberate polka, beating time with her great, smart head, and lifting her jewelled fingers very high in the air. Various groups of middle-aged people adorn the walls, and with few exceptions they also are smilingly beating time to the inspiring strains. But it is on the dancers that my attention is chiefly concentrated. Two dozen short-skirted, perfumed young women, a dozen warm young men in ill-made dress-coats, are gravely careering up and down the green carpet, endeavouring to keep time to the timeless music. In consequence of the overwhelming female majority, many of the young ladies are dancing with one another, making valiant efforts to look as if they enjoyed it.

With a sudden rush of memory, that brings the tears to my eyes, I am back in the old hall at Ronantown. I see the great shadowy room, with the oak-panelled walls, the well-worn oaken floor, the dim light shed by the sparse candles in their big silver sconces. I see Katherine and the MacMorna girls in their simple, shabby, graceful gowns; I see Patrick and Teddy MacMorna light-footed, light-hearted, slim and cool; I see Goll, his handsome face aglow, as his white hands fly over the keyboard, and the bitter-sweet waltz music rolls forth to lose itself in the echoes of the high roof.

"They were right," I think with a great sigh; "I ought not to have come."

The linked sweetness of Mrs. Watson's polka has at length drawn itself out. The good-natured musician has risen and made her way to the middle of the room. "Ladies and gentlemen," she announces in her loud voice, "if you will be so good as to step into the next room you will find some refreshment waiting for you. Margaret, lead the way."

"Pink ices," cries Jo very audibly, addressing himself to Charlotte, but making this announcement for the general benefit; "and wafers, and punch!"

There is a movement towards the door. From my corner I watch the couples streaming out in the direction of the promised land; I recognise the two Miss Boulters, the acknowledged queens of Welby society, each of whom has managed to secure a cavalier for escort; Margaret Watson flounces by with young Boulter, a stout, florid youth with an insinuating eye; Jo and Charlotte strut out together arm in arm with a funny imitation of their elders. And little Jane Eyre sits unnoticed in her corner, with – shall it be owned? – a certain sense of mortification and indignation in her breast.

"You will be a little humbler after this, Griselda MacRonan," I say to myself; "you will begin to recognise that there is considerable difference between Lord Goll's sister and a shabby little governess in an old gown.... Pshaw! I shall be growing cynical next, and I have always hated cynics."

"Miss MacRonan," says a kind voice, "won't you come into the next room and have some refreshment?"

A pair of gentle brown eyes are looking down at me from a gentle brown-bearded face; an attractive face, though it is neither very young nor very handsome. Its owner is Mr. Fairfax, of the Bank, the children's Cousin Jack. We have never been introduced to one another, but I have seen him several times at the villa, where he is a great favourite with my small pupils.

"Yes, please," I say, in answer to his little question, and feeling quite grateful as I take the arm he rather awkwardly offers. It would be impossible to resent the small infringement of etiquette on the part of this respectful and fatherly person; is he not Mr. Fairfax, of the Bank, and I his cousin's unknown Irish governess?

"What can I get you?" asks Mr. Fairfax gravely, when he has carefully piloted me to a seat in the next room. I have already found out that he is a man of action rather than of words, but there is something soothing in his silent services.

"I will have an ice, please," I say. "I have a faint hope that it will make me a little cooler; only a very faint one."

He smiles, amused, as though I had said something witty, and goes off to do my bidding.

"You have not been long in Welby, I think?" he says, as I eat my ice with a despairing sense of growing hotter every moment. It is about the first independent remark he has offered for the last five minutes.

"Six months. I am beginning to get tired of Welby; six months is such a long time."

"Oh, a very long time! Miss MacRonan, I often see you pass my window in the morning."

"I am very punctual, am I not?" I say. "Punctuality is the one virtue on which I pride myself. Ask Jo and Charlotte."

"Who's talking about me?" breaks in a shrill, excited voice. "I say, Miss MacRonan, don't go telling tales! Cousin Jack, would you like to be a fool? Here's a jolly fool's-cap for you!" A small velveteen form has mounted the chair near which Mr. Fairfax is standing, and in another instant two dirty little gloved hands have placed a disreputable tissue adornment on the respectable brown head of my escort.

Cousin Jack absolutely blushes, and glances at me with a look of entreaty, as he removes the undignified headgear, and administers a mild rebuke to the offender.

Miss Watson comes up to me as I re-enter the drawing room, and asks me to sing. I remember Pat's warning, and my heart sinks. Sing! Before these people, in this glaring room, at that jingling piano! It is evident, however, that a refusal is not expected of me; and accepting the situation with my usual philosophy, I draw off my gloves, and sit down to the instrument.

"I will give them something they can understand," I say to myself, and launch into "The Last Rose of Summer."[156] The dear old song! It has carried me away from the vulgar villa, from Welby. I am back at Ronantown. Goll is playing the accompaniment, and Teddy MacMorna is turning over the leaves. The candles flicker in their silver sockets; the firelight dances on the dim old walls....

"Bravo! bravo! encore!" My song has come to an end, and with it my reverie. A dozen voices are clamouring praise, a dozen people crowding round me. I look up, and my glance meets two kind, brown eyes.

"Thank you," says Cousin Jack very simply. I have no reason now to complain of being overlooked, and with the usual feminine "contrariness," begin to sigh for my former obscurity. I do not like these familiar, eager people, who are demanding introductions, or dispensing altogether with such an insignificant formality. I do not like their jokes, their criticisms, worst of all their flattery. I wish that nice, awkward Mr. Fairfax would come to my rescue, but he only stands on the outskirts of my little circle, looking very grave, and never exerting himself to offer a remark.

"Now I call your singing A 1," says young Boulter, looking at me from the corners of his eyes; "quite another matter, between you and me, to our friend Miss Margaret's."

Is it possible, or does there lurk in his eye what only requires a little encouragement to develop into a wink? It is needless to add that this encouragement is not forthcoming.

"I do a little in the singing line myself," he continues unabashed, "and I do assure you I haven't half your nerve. I always say there's

156. Thomas Moore's poem and song.

only two occasions when a man feels funky; that's one. Do you know when the other is?"

"It would be interesting to learn," I say, looking my companion straight in the face.

"When a gentleman pops the question to a lady – eh?"

A little pause; Mr. Boulter is vaguely aware that his sally is not a success, and I am secretly conscious of victory. But I am not elated. Looking round, I perceive that the other people have dropped off, and that Mr. Boulter and I are standing together by the piano. A sense of shame rushes over me, and it is with genuine delight that I observe Cousin Jack making his way towards me with an elderly lady on his arm.

"My sister wants very much to know you," he says abruptly.

Miss Fairfax is a squarely built woman of middle age, with a kind, homely face, and a quiet manner. She is simply but richly dressed in a black silk gown, with a gold chain round her neck, and a big brooch fastening her lace collar. She holds out her hand and smiles at me with her brown eyes, which are like her brother's.

"My dear, you have given us such a great treat," she says.

"I am so glad you liked the song, Miss Fairfax."

"You sing beautifully, Miss MacRonan, and you are not ashamed to sing in your own language. We ignorant people who do not understand Italian are grateful to you for that."

"Ashamed of the dear Irish song! That would be impossible for an Irishwoman," I say, laughing.

"I wonder if you would think it worth your while to come and see a lonely old woman, Miss MacRonan?"

I think of Goll, of Katherine. Surely even they could have no objection to my responding to the kindness of this gentle old lady. "I should be very pleased to come," I say promptly, "and to sing to you if you would care to hear me."

"Will you drink tea with me tomorrow, Miss MacRonan, at five o'clock? I live at number fourteen in the High Street, next door to the Bank."

Scarcely have I accepted this invitation, when Margaret Watson comes up and says, not very amiably, "Can you play dance music, Miss MacRonan?"

"Yes, I can," I answer with alacrity, for the prospect of dancing with Mr. Boulter and his friends is not an inviting one, and in a few minutes more Jane Eyre is at the piano, obediently dashing her way through the "Starlight" waltzes, the "Bric à Brac" polka, and the "Patience" quadrilles; resisting all entreaties on the part of the men to join in the dancing.

"Supper, supper!" announces Mrs. Watson as the "grand chain" is brought to a close. "Gentlemen, choose your partners for supper. It is quite ready."

To my horror and surprise, the thick-skinned Boulter makes his way in my direction.

Fortunately, however, Mrs. Watson arrests him ere he reaches the piano.

"I haven't forgotten you, Mr. Boulter," she says confidentially. "Lobster salad – such a beautiful lobster salad!"

He touches his forehead jocosely with his forefinger. "Thank you, marm! I'm off to find a fair lady to eat it with."

But he is too late, and only escapes from his hostess's clutches to see his victim disappear into the dining room on the arm of Mr. Fairfax.

Supper is a saturnalia of which I only carry away the vaguest recollection. Mrs. Watson sits at the head of the great table struggling with a turkey, while her lord and master dispenses lobster salad from opposite. There is a great deal of gas, a great deal of laughter, and a great deal of champagne with the label of the Welby grocer on the bottles. My escort is silent but active, and supplies not only myself, but half-a-dozen cavalierless young women, with good things. Somebody makes a speech about the new year, and somebody else responds. There is a general assumption of paper caps from the costume crackers, and healths are drunk freely in the doubtful champagne.

The maid-servant's confidential announcement that there is a young gentleman waiting for me in the hall falls upon my ear as the gladdest of glad tidings, and I make my escape while the others are in the full tide of feasting.

"Well?" says Pat, drawing up the window of the fly, as we go down the drive.

"Pat, they were quite right – I ought not to have gone. It was horrid!"

"And who was the fellow who brought you across the hall?"

"Mr. Fairfax, at the Bank. He was very kind."

"Oh, I remember him now," says Patrick; "I saw him there when I went to draw the quarterly instalment of our princely income."

Chapter 3

Number Fourteen, High Street

I enliven the family breakfast-table next morning with a vivid account of last night's festivity. In consideration of my mother's feelings I omit the incident of Mr. Boulter; but I carefully describe the costumes and customs of the company, and rehearse Mrs. Watson's polka on the table-cloth till even Katherine cannot refrain from smiling. Only my mother looks grave and troubled. "My dear," she says at last in her gentle voice, "is it kind, is it dignified, to make fun of these poor people, who, after all, offered you the best they had?"

"Mother," I cry, blushing scarlet, "you are quite right. I ought to be ashamed of myself; I *am* ashamed of myself! Pat, leave off laughing; don't you see how unutterably mean it is to make a joke of these people's hospitality?"

My mother looks very grave when I tell her of Miss Fairfax's invitation and my own acceptance of it. "It would have been impossible to refuse without being ungracious," I protest; "and I am not sure that I wished to refuse."

"By your own showing, Griselda, these people are not fit associates for you."

"The Fairfaxes are different, Mother. They are not bad imitations of smart folk, like the rest. They are just simple and natural."

"It is a great responsibility for me, Griselda."

"Dear Mother," I cry with some remorse, "am I such a rebel, such a dangerous character? I think I am as proud as any of you, if not quite as fastidious; can you not trust me? Only do not ask me to hurt the feelings of a gentle old lady who has shown me kindness."

And my mother's objections are silenced.

At five o'clock in the afternoon of the same day, Patrick walks with me up the High Street and leaves me at the door of number fourteen, which stands directly on the left of Boulter's Bank.

It is a square, sober, Georgian house, with a square brown door, raised from the street by a single shallow step. A neat maid admits me into the cosy, lamp-lit hall, and leads me across it to the sitting room.

Miss Fairfax rises as I enter, and gives me cordial welcome. "It is very kind of a young thing like you to take pity on an old woman," she says. I cannot but admire the kindly tact which is so anxious to make the little governess ignore all difference between herself and the prosperous banker's sister.

The room, like the rest of the house, presents an air of solid, unobtrusive comfort which is wholly strange to me. It is an example, I suppose, of that English middle-class prosperity of which I have heard so much and seen nothing at all. The great mahogany sideboards are polished like mirrors; the steel fender and fire-irons shine as bright as silver; a big clock ticks on the mantelshelf, and above it hangs an oil-painting of a brown-eyed old woman in a Quaker cap.

"That is a portrait of my mother," says Miss Fairfax. "She belonged to the Society of Friends, but my brother and I were brought up as Congregationalists."

I am not much the wiser for this explanation, but I receive it respectfully. Talk flows on gently after this. Miss Fairfax is not a brilliant or fluent talker – she retails no spicy gossip, she asks no questions; but she says nothing but what is kindly; there is something inexpressibly soothing in her whole attitude. At my own suggestion,

I go over to the little piano and sing three or four songs, the Irish, Scotch, and English ballads for which she has expressed a preference.

Cousin Jack comes in while I am singing and stations himself by the piano. His everyday coat suits him far better than the country made dress-clothes of the previous night. He looks almost good-looking as, the music having ceased, he sits by the fireside, and the ruddy light plays over his brown beard and blunt, straight features.

Tea is a solemn, solid performance, quite different from the trifling informal affair with which one usually connects five o'clock. A white cloth is spread on the mahogany table; the neat maid adorns it further with plates of cake and bread and butter; with glass jars of preserve; with an old-fashioned tea-service and an impressive silver teapot. We all take our seats at the abundant board, and the feast is treated with the observance due to a "square meal."

Mr. Fairfax is rather silent, but is kind enough to greet with a smile the mildest and most trivial attempts at sprightliness on my part. Miss Fairfax beams on us from behind her teapot.

After tea Cousin Jack leads me round the room, displaying his little treasure of china, and the few pictures which adorn the wall.

"Oh, how delightful!" I cry, stopping short before a big wire-covered bookcase standing in a deep recess. "Mr. Fairfax, it is so long since I have seen any books, excepting Blair's 'Grave' and the 'Course of Time';[157] may I look through these?"

Cousin Jack, with his slow smile, unlocks the bookcase, and says: "Perhaps you would care to borrow some of them. I should be very pleased if you would. I don't know if there is anything there likely to interest you."

They are nice, old-fashioned books, well bound and carefully kept. I pick out a tall, grey copy of Lamb's essays,[158] and an early edition of Miss Burney's *Evelina*.[159] "Will you lend me these?" I say.

157. Refers to Robert Blair's (1699–1746) poem, *The Grave*, and Robert Pollok's *The Course of Time* (New, ed., *The Complete Novels*, 558 n. 34).

158. Charles Lamb's (1775–1834) *Essays of Elia* (1823).

159. Burney's *Evelina, or the History of a Young Lady's Entrance into the World* (1778).

"With pleasure. I see you have chosen 'Elia.' It is a great favourite of mine."

"Charles Lamb is an old dear!"

"I quite agree with you. Sometimes when I come in here tired out from business, I find nothing rests me so much as a little chat with my old friend in the bookcase."

"We are not a very reading family," I say; "at least, I am fond of books, and so is G – , my eldest brother." I grow red and confused at thought of the incautious remark which I have nearly let slip. A sudden look of grave and puzzled questioning comes into the brown eyes at sight of my scarlet cheeks and lifted eyebrows.

"No, we don't care for books as a family," I go on recklessly; "we are musical or nothing. And we can all dance. Perhaps you don't consider that a very valuable accomplishment?"

"I know very little about dancing, Miss MacRonan."

At this point the clock on the mantelpiece gives seven distinct strokes, and I start in some dismay at the sound.

"Oh, it is seven o'clock, Miss Fairfax," I cry, going over to my hostess; "they will be expecting me at home. I half expected my brother to call for me, but I think he cannot be coming."

"I wish you could have stayed later," says Miss Fairfax, rising, and helping me on with my hat and cloak, which I have previously removed; "but I suppose we must not detain you. I hope you will come very soon and very often."

"May I? It has been delightful!" I say, stooping to receive the little abrupt kiss she half-shyly bestows on me.

Cousin Jack follows me into the passage, takes his hat, opens the door, and steps with me into the street.

"Mr. Fairfax," I protest, "please don't trouble to come with me. It is quite a little way." (Why, oh why, has Patrick omitted to fetch me?)

"It is dark," he answers quietly, and possessing himself of the books in my hand. "It isn't fit for you to walk up the High Street alone."

We walk along almost in silence. I feel a little offended and a little frightened. There is something rather interesting in the situation. Cousin

Jack gives me one of his slow smiles, and hands me back the books as we part at the door of my lodgings. I do not "ask him in," nor does he seem to expect it; no doubt he is aware that the run of Eden Street apartments are not suitable for the reception of visitors of his importance.

I meet Patrick on the stairs, evidently in a tremendous hurry.

"It's never you, Grizel, come home by yourself at this time of night!" he exclaims, peering at me in the paraffin-laden gloom.

"Mr. Fairfax brought me home."

Pat whistles. "Why on earth couldn't you wait for me, Griselda?"

"Why on earth couldn't you come in decent time?" I retort; "I had been there long enough for a first visit. I didn't know when you might take it into your head to put in an appearance."

Chapter 4

A Telegram

The weary winter days go on; there is only a week of February left.

Goll's letters are short, uncertain, vague, indefinably anxious and reserved. That a decision of some sort must shortly be arrived at, he does not seem to doubt; it is only that he has ceased to express himself with the old confidence as to the probable nature of that decision.

"Griselda," says Katherine one afternoon as I am drawing on my gloves in our joint bedroom, "how can you be so cheerful? I sometimes think you ought not to be so cheerful."

"Oh, Katherine," I cry remorsefully, "do you think I am not sorry for you all?"

"It is your own affair as much as ours, poor little Grizel."

"Ah, but I have my work. You can have no idea what a consolation it is! I am afraid it makes me appear unfeeling."

"This dreadful suspense!" says poor Katherine, pacing the squalid room.

"Griselda, how can you bear it?"

"I put it out of my head, Katherine."

"You put it out of your head?" cries my sister; "you are a wonderful philosopher for your time of life!"

"Katie," I say impetuously, "I hate to think of it. I never think of it when I can help. It hurts my pride to feel that everything depends on a mere turning up of the cards. We can do something ourselves with our own lives."

Katherine looks at me with her sad, beautiful eyes. "Grizel," she says, "I believe you are a good girl – I am sure you are a brave one. But you are very young. I am not old myself, you will say; but I know that fighting with Fate, as you would put it, is a hard battle; that the victory is very uncertain."

"Is any fight worth fighting which is not hard, or where victory is certain, Katherine?"

"Oh, Grizel, you are a child! You cannot understand," cries my sister, resuming her march up and down the room: a tall, slender figure, which even the shabby gown and sordid surroundings cannot deprive of its queenly grace.

I go downstairs very sorrowfully, and make my way into the street with a guilty sense of pleasant expectation which it is impossible entirely to repress. Why will one part of my heart persist in feeling happy while the other is aching for my people with all its might? Goll may lose his suit, we may all be reduced to beggary, but the sun will shine as brightly as ever, the first pulses of spring will not cease to beat in one's blood; kind voices will cheer us with friendly words, kind eyes will continue to smile upon us; there will be many things worth living for left in the world. Tonight I am going to tea with the Fairfaxes. It is tacitly understood among us that I shall accept Miss Fairfax's invitations without scruple. I have passed many happy, peaceful hours in the cosy, firelit parlour in the High Street, and have grown to regard the brother and sister in the light of friends. On their part they are perfectly kind and natural, and accept without comment the strict reserve which, alas! I am obliged to maintain with regard to my circumstances and family. I pass a delightful evening with my friends, and at nine o'clock Cousin Jack walks home with me as usual.

"If I believed in presentiments," I observe, as we go up the street, "I should say something was about to happen."

"But don't believe in them," he answers; "things are very well as they are. 'No news is good news,' is it not?"

"I am a Kelt, Mr. Fairfax, and even in the nineteenth century we Kelts cling to our superstitions."

"Have you seen a – a Banshee, Miss MacRonan? That's good Irish, isn't it?"

I laugh with open scorn. "One doesn't *see* Banshees, Mr. Fairfax; one hears them! They come wailing – wailing over marsh and moor on dark nights. Oh, it's enough to make your blood run cold! There's one at Ronantown, and sometimes – " I stop short and become violently interested in the red-glass lamp of the Welby doctor's surgery.

"Goodnight," says my escort presently, taking my hand and looking down at me with those kindly, half-humorous eyes of his; "and please don't have any more presentiments."

We are standing on the doorstep of my dwelling, and Cousin Jack begins to struggle with the ineffectual bell as he ceases speaking.

Mrs. Price greets me with some excitement as I enter the gloomy little hall.

"It came this very minute, miss," she says; "I was just about to take it up to your Mamma."

"What is it, Mrs. Price?"

She lays her hand solemnly on my arm, leads me to the solitary paraffin lamp, and thrusts something thin and soft into my fingers.

A bit of yellow paper, a little envelope, a telegram addressed to "Mrs. MacRonan." In these days of frequent telegraphing that is not enough to fill any sensible mortal with alarm. Perhaps not; only something tells me that I hold our fate folded up in this harmless-looking missive. With a careless word to Mrs. Price I go slowly upstairs; my heart beats with strange rapidity, my head is in a whirl; the dreary little group round the sitting room fire exclaims with one voice on my entrance:

"My dear Griselda, has anything happened?"

"Griselda, are you ill?"

"Have you seen a ghost, Grizel?"

"This will never do," I think, and answer with as much indifference as I am able: "I came upstairs rather quickly. I am a little out of breath, that is all. By-the-by, Mother, this has just come for you."

My mother's face grows white to the lips; her hand trembles as she takes the telegram from mine and lays it down in silence on the table.

"I think it would be as well to open the telegram," cries Pat, with a fine assumption of masculine common-sense, and laying his hand on Katherine's shoulder, who sits, white and motionless, bringing her needle repeatedly through the same point in her work.

"You had better open it, Patrick," says my mother, shading her eyes with her hand.

He breaks it open deliberately, extracts the scrap of pink, scrawled paper and proceeds to read aloud the message:

"'From Gerald MacRonan to Mrs. MacRonan, Eden Street, Welby.

"'The verdict has just been given in our favour. Thank God, all is over. I shall be with you tomorrow at twelve o'clock.'"

Dead silence for a minute; the next, my mother is sobbing in Katherine's arms.

* * * * * *

"I like old Goll's caution," cries Patrick, who is pacing the room with a radiant face and shining eyes. "It's a case of the ruling passion strong in death: 'Gerald MacRonan to Mrs. MacRonan!'"

"My dear boy," says my mother anxiously, "pray do not relax our caution. We shall only be here a few days longer, I suppose; there is no need to let anyone into our secrets."

It is twelve o'clock, and though we usually go to our rooms as the clock strikes ten, tonight not one of us seems to have the remotest recollection of bed.

"Oh, mother," says Katherine, "I may say it now, may I not? I have hated it all so dreadfully."

"I will confess," answers my mother, with unusual emphasis, "that these last months have been to me a time of terrible unhappiness."

"Horrid little place!" cries Katherine, who looks ten times handsomer than she did this morning; "horrid street, horrid room, horrid magenta cloth and horsehair chairs!"

"This outburst is very unusual in a person of your staidness," remarks Patrick; and I feel bound to protest: "Poor little fright of a Welby! It's unkind to abuse it for what it can't help. I dare say it has its good points, if one only knew!"

"I believe Grizel has rather enjoyed herself!" says Pat; "she always was fond of adventures."

"I hope you girls will be presented at an early Drawing Room," says my mother; "I was eighteen when I was introduced."

"And we are quite *passées*, are we not, Katie? You are actually twenty-two and I am twenty," I answer flippantly.

"Girls are allowed to be older in these days," announces Pat; "Goll said so himself the last time he was here."

"I wonder where we shall live," says Katie, and my mother answers: "It is many years since I was in London; but Grosvenor Square always seemed to me the most charming place to live in."

"Of course we shall go to Ronantown for the hunting?" says Pat; "at least, when that wretch of a tenant has had his three years."

"Oh, for a 'real good' gallop," I remark sleepily, stretching my arms and giving a great yawn. "Goodnight, Mother; I hope this is not all a dream, but I feel by no means sure."

"Bird of ill-omen, cease thy croaking," cries Pat in his most wide-awake tones as I go from the room, candle in hand. But, in spite of that yawn, I am unable to sleep when I get to bed.

Is it that visions of the brilliant future are dancing before my dazzled imagination? Am I dreaming waking dreams of pearls and presentation gowns; of Grosvenor Square and Buckingham Palace; of dances in great houses with handsome, light-heeled partners?

Strange to say, I am thinking of none of these things. To say that I am thinking at all would be to give too definite a name to the vague mixture of regret and surprise which fills my breast: regret, for the life of labour and struggle, which already seems to lie far behind me; surprise, at my own sensations, at the recollection of the false ring in my own gaiety which has jarred upon me all the evening, though my family have seemed quite unaware of it.

The door opens and Katherine's entry puts an end to my reverie. Her face is flushed, her eyes are shining like sapphires; she steps with light, elastic tread, very different from the weary, lagging pace she has fallen into during these latter months.

She falls on her knees by the bedside, and bends her beautiful glad face towards me.

"Grizel," she cries, "you have been braver than I. I have been a coward! I am ashamed of myself."

"It wasn't courage on my part, Kitty. It was simply that I never hated it as you did."

"Oh yes, I have hated it! It has hurt me and humbled me; sometimes I have wished to die."

"Poor Kitty! and now everything is turning out well like events in a novel."

"Ah, but those events with which novelists chiefly occupy themselves are yet to come!"

This is very flippant indeed for Katherine, and I stare at her in astonishment before I turn round and go to sleep.

Chapter 5

Cousin Jack

We are all restored to our sober senses the next morning, and take our seats at the breakfast table with a subdued radiance, very different from the light-headed rapture of the previous evening.

"I am going to my work as usual," I announce, as I make my entrance on the cheerful scene; "I want to say goodbye to Jo and Charlotte. They are not very nice children, but I have a sort of liking for them."

"Goll will be here before you have returned," objects Katherine.

"I don't mean to hide anything from Goll. And it is more polite to explain to Mrs. Watson in person the reason of my abrupt departure."

"What are you going to tell her, Grizel?"

"I shall tell her that we are obliged to suddenly leave Welby."

"She will probably question you, after the manner of her kind."

"Oh, I will be very cautious, Katie; and then no more caution for the rest of one's life!"

I go down Eden Street; up the High Street; past Boulter's Bank, where young Boulter throws me a nod, half-sulky, half-impertinent, from the doorstep; past number fourteen; and onwards to the villa.

Mrs. Watson is surprised and annoyed at my news; she considers she had a right to expect longer "notice." Am I aware that, in the eye of the law, I am not entitled to the fraction of my salary due to me? Do I know that it is only because of her clemency that I am destined to receive it? Can I not possibly manage to give Margaret Watson her singing lesson this afternoon?

I submit to these remarks with a meekness eminently becoming in a young governess, and promise to return at four o'clock for a final lesson with Miss Watson.

Patrick opens the door to me when I get home, and putting his arm round my waist, compels me to join him in a waltz across the impossible little passage.

"Pat," I cry breathlessly, "is he here?"

"He is," answers my brother, drawing me to a seat beside him on the bottom stair. "And I say, Grizel, he knows everything about you."

"I am so glad! And how did he take it?"

"For a moment his cheek blanched; his lip quivered. All the blood of all the MacRonans began to boil audibly in his veins. But fortunately the general good humour has influenced even *his* frigid breast. I believe, my dear, you are to be forgiven."

We scamper upstairs together and enter the sitting room. I precipitate myself into the arms of a tall person, who steps forward to meet me.

"My dear, darling Goll!"

"Little rebel," he says, kissing me several times; then holding me from him and looking down at my face: "Strong-minded young woman, what have you to say for yourself? Well, you haven't spoiled your complexion, at any rate, which makes it comparatively easy to forgive you. Why, Grizel, you are prettier than ever!"

"And you – you are beautiful, Goll!"

"The MacRonan mutual admiration society. Am I eligible as a member?" enquires Patrick with scorn.

"*I* shall certainly black-ball you," I cry, nodding at him from the shelter of Goll's strong arms.

Gerald MacRonan, Viscount Goll, is, I firmly believe, the most beautiful person in the United Kingdom. As he stands there, tall and strong, in the little room, his incongruity with his surroundings comes out to a startling degree.

We all take our seats at the table. The extreme resources of Welby have been taxed to produce a luncheon worthy of our guest. There are roast chicken and early peas, a Périgord pie from the grocer's, and two bottles of champagne – not from the grocer's.

"Well, mother, what do you say to leaving this charming spot on Monday, the day after tomorrow?" asks Goll, who sits at the head of the table and carves with great splendour.

She turns her proud, glad eyes to his face. "Just as you like, my dear boy. The question is, where are we to go?"

"We had better go straight to London. There is a furnished house to be had in Clarges Street, which might do for the present. Lady Shannon told me of it. She kindly gave me permission to telegraph to her in the event of your consenting to take it. She will secure it and have it made ready."

"How exceedingly kind of Lady Shannon."

"Everyone has been remarkably kind," answers Goll, who has a fine unconsciousness of his own charms. "People from whom one had no right to expect it have shown us the greatest consideration. Then I may telegraph?"

"Certainly, my dear boy. The girls and I had better get everything in London."

"I shall at once seek the embrace of Mr. Smallpage," announces Pat; "I shall go straight from the station to his Temple of the Graces."

"Goll," I say, "are we very rich?"

He considers a moment. "In these days of Sir Georgius Midases[160] I don't think we are what is called 'very rich.' We have the means, and more than the means, of living according to our position. Have you grown mercenary, Grizel?"

"Grizel is a Socialist," cries Pat; "she would like to distribute the family funds among the deserving poor. She is a person of views."

Goll laughs. "Ah, London is the place for views. You will have plenty of opportunity for airing your theories, Grizel."

"And if one hasn't any theories to air? Katherine, just take away Pat's glass. The champagne is having a bad effect on his over-excited brain."

A chorus of protest greets me when I announce my intention of going to the Watsons' in the afternoon. "I feel that Mrs. Watson has been badly used," I say in explanation. "Clearly, I ought to have told her, when she engaged me, that my sudden departure was probable."

---

160. Refers to George du Maurier's (1834–1896) satirical cartoon character, Sir Gorgius (sometimes spelt differently) Midas; the character, or caricature, "a Jewish *nouveau riche* vulgarian," appeared in du Maurier's *Punch* cartoons (Donald Read, *The Age of Urban Democracy: England 1868–1914* (Abingdon: Routledge, 1994), 29–30). On du Maurier's fixation with "Jews and Jewishness within the framework of Englishness and artistry," and his exploitation of antisemitic imagery to "critique English society," see Sarah Gracombe, "Converting Trilby: Du Maurier on Englishness, Jewishness and Culture," *Nineteenth-Century Literature* 58, no. 1 (June 2003): 90–1 and *passim*; see also Daniel Pick's *Svengali's Web: The Alien Enchanter in Modern Culture* (New Haven: Yale University Press, 2000).

To my surprise, Goll is inclined to take my part. "There is something in what you say, Grizel. *Noblesse oblige.*"

Miss Watson goes through her lesson rather sulkily, asks me a few pointed questions on the subject of my departure from Welby, and informs me that her "Mamma" will see me in the morning room. As I make my way across the hall a confused noise of merriment reaches me, from the direction of the schoolroom. The unmistakable shrill tones of Jo and Charlotte fall upon my ear, mingled with a fuller, deeper sound – the sound of a man's voice, of a voice that I know.

"Cousin Jack, Cousin Jack," is borne across to me, "swing me; it's my turn now, not Lottie's."

I turn the handle of the morning room door and find myself in the presence of Mrs. Watson. When she has written me out my meagre little cheque (of which, by-the-by, I feel remarkably proud) she takes both my hands in hers, draws me towards her, and imprints a sounding kiss on my forehead. "Goodbye, my dear, and good-luck go with you. We're all sorry to lose you; and I was a little short this morning, but naturally I was vexed at being left in the lurch as it were. However, I'm not saying it's your own fault, Miss MacRonan."

"Goodbye, Mrs. Watson. I shall often think of you all, and of Welby."

She goes with me into the hall, whither the children and Cousin Jack have migrated. Mr. Fairfax comes across and shakes hands with me, and the children fling themselves on me with expressions of farewell.

"Joey, open the door for your governess," says his mother. The child sets to struggling with the door-fastening.

"Never mind, Jo, I can do it myself," I say, in a voice full of suppressed indignation; there is a choking sensation in my throat, my eyes smart, my hands tremble. "To stand there like that, and never a word of farewell! Cousin Jack, are you no better than the rest of the world? You lazy, strong man, to let me struggle with this big, heavy door! Oh, I hope you are feeling ashamed!"

From the open door of the morning room behind comes the very audible sound of Mrs. Watson's voice: "Ah, poor thing, it's a difficulty of some sort or other, I'll be bound. Jack, you mark my words, there is something fishy in that direction."

I shut the door and dash down the tall white steps into the dusky garden. Two great tears have forced themselves into my eyes, and are stealing slowly down my cheeks.

Down between the laurels I go, with a tread to which anger lends its buoyancy; my head held very high, my eyes very wide open. The big iron gates of the garden are closed. I stand fumbling vaguely with the heavy latch. Footsteps are coming down the gravel behind me – quick, firm footsteps; in another moment a voice is in my ear: "Miss MacRonan, allow me to help you."

We pass out together, in silence, on to the twilit road.

"Miss MacRonan, what is this I hear about you?"

"Ah, and what have you been hearing, Mr. Fairfax?"

"That you are going away!"

"It is certainly true. Will your sister be at home tomorrow afternoon?"

He does not answer. He stops short in the road and seizes both my hands in his. "Griselda, will you stop here with me?"

The blood rushes to my head; there is a loud singing in my ears, a mist before my eyes; my only answer is a little gasping sob.

"It isn't much I have to offer you, my dear. I am older than you, I am a dull fellow; but I will make you happy, I will make you happy, Griselda!"

He draws me towards him, closer, closer; the brown eyes look down into mine: "I will take such care of you, my darling; my brave, little girl..."

Hitherto I have remained as one spellbound; at these words a little, sharp cry breaks from my lips. I struggle to free my hands from his. "Mr. Fairfax, pray, pray, do not!" The tears are streaming down my face; my hands tremble and flutter in his grasp.

"Griselda, I can't let you go!"

"Oh, it is impossible! You are asking what is impossible!"

"Griselda, I can't go away from you with that answer. Perhaps you don't love me well enough – I don't expect that. But you shall love me one day; you shall, indeed!"

"Mr. Fairfax, you don't understand. It is not a – personal matter with me!"

"Not a personal matter, Griselda?"

"There is a – family complication!"

To my great surprise he greets this solemn announcement with a short laugh. He lets go of my hands, lays his own on my shoulders, and looks down at me with shining eyes.

"What has that to do with you and me, Griselda? We are not a family complication, you and I. I want you, Griselda, you, yourself. I shall always hold it the greatest honour, as well as the greatest happiness of my life, if you will come to me."

His hands drop to his side; his voice, which has vibrated as with a very passion of tenderness, dies away; we stand facing one another in silence. What can I say? What is there for me to say? This generous heart is offering everything – home, shelter, a boundless treasure of love – to the little waif, the little lonely Irish girl; and she, forsooth, turns away in denial from the goodly gift!

A sudden pathetic, humorous sense of the ludicrousness of the situation comes over me; I begin to laugh hysterically.

"Griselda!" he cries, hurt, shocked, "is that all you have to say to me?"

In an instant I am sober again. "Mr. Fairfax, how can I ever thank you for your noble kindness, for your generosity? But I must not, I have no right to take what you offer. It would be wrong, wicked!"

A vision of Goll's angry, haughty face rises before me; another vision of those joyful faces round the fire in Eden Street. Is it for me to mar their long-deferred happiness?

"Griselda," cries Cousin Jack rather hoarsely, "can you expect me to accept such an answer? Say: 'Jack, I do not love you; I never can love you as long as I live; I do not want your love.'"

My heart beats wildly. Oh, what is this strange, keen joy stealing in upon the misery, the anguish, which fills my heart? "Mr. Fairfax," I say, trying to control my unsteady voice, "why do you want me to say things which would be cruel and – untrue? I love you, I shall always love you, as the kindest, truest friend a woman has ever had. And what you have said to me makes me very proud as well as very sorry." My voice dies away; I turn abruptly and set off walking down the lonely road. In an instant he is at my side.

"Griselda," he says in an altered voice, "am I too late? Is there someone who has already won this great happiness? Ah, I might have guessed!"

"Oh no, no! there is no one, no one at all!"

A longing to tell him everything, to repay his generosity with the honesty which at least is its due, comes over me. But the thought of Goll, of his injunctions, of his labour in our behalf, restrains me. I am torn in two.

"Mr. Fairfax," I cry, "be merciful! Don't ask me again. It is more than I can bear!"

"Can you give me no better answer, Griselda?"

"No, no. Oh, I know I must appear foolish, thoughtless. I know some explanation is due to you, but I can give you no explanation."

"Then I have asked for too much, Griselda. You will not trust me with your happiness?"

"I cannot."

We walk on in silence. I cannot see the kind, sad face in the gloom; but I know – ah, how well! – how it looks.

"Is this to be the last time!" he says as we stand together before the door of the house in Eden Street. By the light of the street lamp I can see his pale face as it bends over me; the hurt look in the beautiful eyes stabs my heart like a knife.

"May I come and see your sister tomorrow afternoon?"

"Come. I will leave you in peace, only let me say this: if, at any time, there is anything I can do to serve you, it will be my greatest happiness to do it. If you are in trouble, if you need help, there is always one person to whom you can apply. Griselda, there will be nothing too hard for me to do for you. Will you promise to ask me for help? Will you promise, Griselda?"

"I promise."

Without another word, we part. Like a person in a dream, I make my way upstairs to the landing, where Goll confronts me, pale and stern, outside the sitting room door.

"Griselda," he says, "with whom were you talking outside the street door?"

"With Mr. Fairfax" (dreamily).

"And pray who may 'Mr. Fairfax' be?" (with cold contempt).

"He is a friend of mine."

"Then I presume he is a friend of your family?"

"He is my friend alone."

"You can have no friends who are not also those of your family."

I open the sitting room door and walk in. Goll follows me, his eyes blazing with anger.

"You have no right to walk about the public streets with a man who can be nothing more than a casual acquaintance, and your own inferior," he says stormily.

"My inferior!" I laugh a little. "Goll, I decline to argue this matter with you; you think perhaps you know a great deal about life, about the world; I say, you know nothing at all about human beings. And you to laugh at these provincials – Oh, Goll, that is almost amusing!"

"Griselda," cries my poor mother, "surely you are forgetting yourself. Your brother has given you no cause to speak so to him."

"Mother," I answer, turning towards her, "why don't you speak; why don't you tell Goll the truth? Mr. Fairfax is my friend. Oh, I am proud of my friend! He has helped me through these dark days with his kindness; it has been no secret, Mother. Before we knew what was to happen, when things were beginning to look desperate, you were glad enough, all of you, yes, *glad*, that I had found these kind people – "

"Griselda!" cries my brother, stepping forward and laying his strong hand across my wrists, "do you know what you are saying? Do you know what insults you are offering your mother?"

Our angry eyes flash to one another's.

"Goll," I cry, "it is your fault, yours. Let me go, let me go! You are hard, ungrateful! – and I had made this sacrifice for you – "

I do not know what I am saying; wresting my hands from his grasp, I fly from the room, up the stairs, to the shelter of my little bare garret.

"Oh, Goll," I sob, as I lie face downwards on the bed; "after what I have done for you, after what I have given up for your sake! Oh, Jack, my kind, noble, generous friend, I have hurt you, I have done you wrong. But you are not the only person who is hurt, who is wronged! Jack, my darling, I love you! I love you! I love you!"

Chapter 6

"Very rich he is in virtues, very noble – noble certes,
And I shall not blush in knowing that men call him lowly born."

E. B. BROWNING[161]

It is all over the place. How the secret has oozed out, nobody knows; whether through our own imprudence, or our landlady's eavesdropping propensities, is uncertain. The pork-butcher next door touches his hat to Patrick and calls him "My Lord," to his immense delight; whenever one of us appears at the window, the little dressmaker opposite rushes to her wire-blind and stares over it at the illustrious apparition. (Fortunately it is Sunday, and it is to be hoped that this "hindering of needle and thread" will not have any very serious consequences.) Mrs. Price curtseys deeply whenever she meets us on the stairs; Jane, the maid-of-all-work, eyes us open-mouthed, as

161. Taken from Barrett Browning's "Lady Geraldine's Courtship" (New, ed., *The Complete Novels*, 558 n. 36).

she brings in the matutinal bacon. Pat, returning from an early stroll, reports the unmistakable signs of interest which have everywhere followed his usually obscure progress; he had never believed himself to be one of the people destined to wake up and find themselves famous; henceforward he will put faith in Beaconsfield[162] and the "unexpected."

"It really is no joking matter," frowns Goll, who is deeply vexed. "This staying in Welby has been an unfortunate business from beginning to end. But I did not see, at the time, what other arrangement to make. All our choice lay in a choice of evils."

As for me, I say nothing at all – I am in disgrace, and sit at Goll's elbow with my eyes on my plate. Breakfast passes off rather gloomily. Reaction has set in after our previous course of high spirits, and we are beginning to realise that even £30,000 a year has its troubles. After breakfast I am taken solemnly aside and forgiven. I apologise to my mother, and Goll kisses me on my forehead, in a baptismal sort of way. Katherine and my mother decline to face the curious gaze of the Welby public, and Patrick announces his intention of taking what he calls a Sabbath holiday. So Goll and I set off together for church; I, trotting along meekly enough at his side, with a lurking, ludicrous feminine sense that all the wrong has not lain in one direction in spite of that magnificent "forgiveness."

All eyes are directed towards us, not only on our entrance, but also (alas for Welby piety!) throughout the service. Even my own insignificance fails to pass unnoticed, and Goll creates a positive furore among the feminine part of the congregation. I cannot help observing these things, for while my brother goes through the business of devotion with the solemnity and thoroughness which characterise his every action, I find it impossible to concentrate my attention on my Prayer-Book, and my heavy eyes stray aimlessly about the church from beginning to end of the service.

162. Benjamin Disraeli.

There is the usual smart, perfumed crowd at the door as we make our way from the church. I follow meekly in Goll's stately footsteps, rather abashed by the extremely frank and unreserved staring to which we are subjected, and which my brother treats with the genuine indifference of ignorance. Margaret Watson gives me a nod, half-resentful, half-admiring; young Boulter, who is with her, grows red to the eyes, and raises his hat in a sheepish, grudging fashion, very different from his normal jauntiness.

Jo and Charlotte are to be heard from afar, loudly discussing what seems to be the all-important topic in Welby, though their small persons are not visible in the throng.

"Her brother's a duke, and her mother's a duchess!" proclaims Lottie.

"And she's a princess!" cries Jo.

"What nonsense! She's only a countess."

"She's a very grand person anyhow. Almost as grand as the Queen."

I pass on beyond the sound of their voices. I do not even smile. I have no smiles left today, not even in the midst of so much which is absurd.

There is one thought buzzing in my brain, a little thought, but it leaves no room for any other; it has buzzed, buzzed all the morning "like brain-flies" – it never ceases for a moment.

"Does he know? What will he think?"

We are passing the Congregational Chapel, which stands at the top of the High Street, and the people are streaming out through the narrow entrance.

I can see Miss Fairfax's ugly bonnet and respectable black silk as they make their way through the crowd, and behind them comes a tall person in a tall hat – Cousin Jack, in all the ill-cut glory of his Sunday clothes.

Does he know? Something in the pale face tells me – Yes.

What does he think? Ah, if I only knew!

"Hadn't we better cross the road to make room for these good chapel-going folk," says unconscious Goll with condescension.

"Oh, never mind," I answer hurriedly; too nervous to know what I am saying. Miss Fairfax has been detained on the doorstep by a friend; the two old ladies stand chatting amicably in the sunshine; Jack waits patiently by her side, looking in front of him gloomily enough. Across the heads of the little crowd our eyes have to meet. Only for an instant; the next I have turned away my face and am hurrying on with my brother.

I have cut Mr. Fairfax dead.

"Goll, Goll," I cry; "do you know what I have done?"

"What on earth is the matter with you, Griselda? Are you going into hysterics?"

"Goll – you saw that tall man, with the beard, and – the eyes!"

"He stared at us with more than the usual impudence – if that is the fellow you mean."

"It was Mr. Fairfax!"

"Indeed, Griselda."

"And – and I cut him dead!"

Goll gives vent to a few feeble generalities on the subject of my sex. "You may not be aware," he says with irony, "that, to a lady, there are medium courses open between cutting a man dead and walking about the streets with him at night."

"Goll, it was all your fault!"

"Are you crying in the streets? Griselda," he goes on, suddenly changing his tone, "do you know what inference, what shocking inference, it is almost impossible not to draw from your conduct of today and of last night?"

"I don't know! I don't care! Let me go, Goll; don't hold my arm like that! What! You won't let me go?"

"I certainly should be sorry to detain you by force," he says, dropping my arm coldly. "Griselda, I am deeply shocked!"

But I do not heed him; I scarcely hear his voice; I am conscious of nothing but a pale face, and questioning brown eyes, an avenging phantom floating before my tear-dimmed vision.

Without a word I turn from my brother, and strike off in an opposite direction. He follows me, white and angry.

"Where are you going, Griselda?"

"Let me go, Goll; I am only going across the meadows. Let me be alone a little or I shall say things I shall be sorry for. I will be back by two o'clock."

Slowly, reluctantly, he turns away. I tear down the little narrow street with aimless haste, the little street which leads to the flat fields and dull-hued hedgerows which surround the town.

I sit down on a solitary stile, heedless of the cold wind, which blows my hair about and makes my nose red. The sense of discomfort consoles me; I feel it is no more than I deserve. Footsteps come up the path behind me – slow, sauntering footsteps; a few paces from the stile they come to a sudden stop.

I turn my head, and see – Mr. Fairfax. He is standing quite still. Our eyes, which are about on a level, meet in a long look.

"Mr. Fairfax," I say, impotently.

He raises his hat and smiles faintly.

"Do you want to pass?" I say, with my head still turned towards him over my shoulder.

He swings himself over the stile, disregarding the aid of the step, and stands facing me.

"Miss MacRonan, I believe I have to congratulate you!"

"It would be more appropriate for you to box my ears!" I think; but I say: "What do you think of me, Mr. Fairfax? Do you know I cut you in the street just now?"

"Oh!" he says, with a little smile, "did you?"

I feel horribly, cruelly, and, I may add, deservedly snubbed; the blood rushes to my face.

"I didn't think very badly of you, Griselda. I – I understood that you might feel – afraid of me after what I said to you yesterday."

"We are like people talking in a different language," I think; "how could he ever understand my mean and base jargon!" A rush of love and yearning and regret comes over me. "Cousin Jack," I say (the sweet, childish name coming unbidden to my lips) – "Cousin Jack, will you marry me?"

He comes nearer and looks into my face. A strange mixture of wistful tenderness and humour lies in his eyes. "Oh no, Griselda," he says, and shakes his head, and smiles a little.

I get down from my stile and turn away from him.

"You – you are very cruel to me," I say in a choked voice; "do you like to make me ashamed? I know – I know that I am not worthy, that I never shall be; but yesterday – "

He takes my hands in his and makes me turn towards him; his eyes glow with a strange, wonderful light; his low voice vibrates with some deep and strange emotion.

"Griselda," he says, "my dear little girl, be reasonable. Yesterday and today are different, you know very well. What I offered you, I offered, God knows, with a whole heart. But I did not know – what I know now. My dearest, there lies a happy, beautiful life before you; I am glad that it should be so. And it has made me happier to have known you; you must look back without any sorrow or remorse on a friend who has loved you very dearly, and who does not want to be remembered in connection with unpleasant things."

"Mr. Fairfax, as you say, yesterday and today are different. Before you spoke to me I hardly knew what was in my heart; and when you spoke I was frightened and glad all at once. And then I thought of Goll, of my brother, of what he would say; for I love him very much, and he means to do the best for us all."

My voice breaks down; Jack's deep tones come across my quavering treble: "And you were right; you have duties, ties to think of."

"Mr. Fairfax, I have thought and thought since then. I have grown very wise since last night."

"Griselda!"

"Mr. Fairfax, are you sure that you meant what you said yesterday?"

"Oh, hush, Griselda!"

I go nearer to him and look up in his face.

"There is only one thing clear," I say; "this can have nothing to do with Goll. Cousin Jack, I love you."

The brown eyes meet mine; oh, who shall tell what unspeakable things are spoken in that long gaze?

"No," he says at length, very slowly, "it has nothing to do with Goll." Then he takes me in his arms, and holds me close against his breast.

Postscript

It was a long time before poor Goll could reconcile himself to what had happened. Those were sad days enough – the days before my marriage. I think my mother ceased to regret my choice as she grew to know my dear Jack, but Katherine never got over the shock of (oh, irony!) my *mésalliance*.

After the first six months we left Welby for the sweet home in Berkshire, where we have since lived. Miss Fairfax lived with us till her death last autumn. Margaret Watson married young Boulter, and they have gone to live in the old house in the High Street, much I believe to the former's disgust.

Katherine is a great lady now, and we pay one another short, uncomfortable duty visits at stated intervals. Pat runs down often to Berkshire and entertains us with accounts of his social triumphs and varied experiences. He is very fond of his small nephew, a young person who promises to be the image of his Uncle Goll, save for his great brown eyes. Uncle Goll himself pays us occasional visits. He leads an active political life, and his wife is the cleverest and most beautiful woman in London. He and Jack are quite fond of one another.

As for me, I wonder if a happier woman ever lived. I often marvel at the injustice of Fate which has favoured me so unduly.

It is Jack's birthday today; he is forty years old, and there are several grey hairs in his beard. I was twenty-five last winter. We are quite a middle-aged couple.

Addenbrooke (1889)

I'll never do you wrong for your own sake.

ALL'S WELL THAT ENDS WELL.[163]

1.

Lydia could not help wondering why on earth Addenbrooke should be so anxious to marry her.

She was standing at the window, her eyes mechanically following the familiar, insignificant figure of the Professor, as he plodded down the gravel walk to the gate; and when he had passed from view she sat down in the nearest chair and continued her reflections. It was very strange. She had no love to give him, and had told him so, quite frankly; he must know, as everyone knew, of that miserable affair with Lawrence Fleming; was he not Fleming's intimate friend, the last person who had seen him before he went to Africa?

Moreover, her glass had taken to reflecting a woman who was sad and pale and old before her time; surely not the woman with whom a man would be expected to wish to begin his life.

When we have become to ourselves a daily burden, it is so hard to realise that our presence can be desired of others.

And yet she had been aware of Addenbrooke's devotion from the days of the good, but obstinate little boy with a taste for chemical

163. From Shakespeare's *All's Well that Ends Well.*

experiments, to those of the modest young man, who lurked unobtrusively in doorways for the purpose of saying goodnight to her, and was always at hand to fill up vacancies. She had been aware of it, but had given it little heed; now, in her loneliness, her sorrow, the thought of that devotion moved her strangely.

She had seen herself drifting on to middle age, haggard, loveless, unloved; that sorriest of spectacles, the emotional woman whose emotions have wrecked her. Addenbrooke and Addenbrooke's love interposed themselves like a shield between her and her fate.

She had given him no answer, but she knew by now what her answer would be.

The door opened, and Mrs. Grey, her mother, came into the room.

She sat down in silence – a chill, comfortless presence – and regarded her daughter from the distance.

These two women lived together without profit or pleasure to either. Mrs. Grey was capable of making sacrifices, but she lacked the priceless gift of homemaking; while Lydia, on her part, chafed beneath the restrictions of a relationship in which neither affinity nor affection bore a part.

"So it was to be Johnny Addenbrooke after all," reflected Mrs. Grey; "a Gower Street professor of no particular distinction." Well, Lydia was getting on: and if a girl means to marry, she had better manage to do so before she is five-and-twenty. And there had been nothing, it seemed, in that affair with young Fleming. Mrs. Grey was disappointed. It is true that Fleming's father kept a glove-shop in Regent Street, whereas the Addenbrookes had been gentlefolks for generations; but nobody minded that sort of thing in these days. Lawrence Fleming went everywhere, did everything; his new book from Africa had made him more of a lion than ever; hence he was more to be desired as a husband than poor Johnny, who went nowhere to speak of, and did nothing but his work.

Lydia rose slowly and went over to the writing table.

As she took up her pen, the whimsical thought struck her that, when the other children had carried their pence to the sweet-shop,

Johnny had always preferred to invest his capital in mysterious compounds at the chemist's. A faint smile hovered about her lips as she wrote. When the letter was finished she laid her head a moment on the desk and shut her eyes. The old dream, from which she was turning forever, had rushed with cruel vividness into her consciousness:

> Behüt dich Gott, es wär zu schön gewesen;
> Behüt dich Gott, es hat nicht sollen sein.[164]

She rose, stiff and cold, and went over to her mother.

Lydia was a graceful creature, tall, slight, faintly coloured; some people thought her beautiful, others could see no beauty in her whatever.

"Mamma," she said, in her strange, pathetic voice; "Professor Addenbrooke has asked me to marry him, and I have written to say 'yes.'"

2.

Addenbrooke was spending the evening as usual with Lydia at St. John's Wood. They were alone together, Mrs. Grey having discreetly retired to her room, and the talk between them flowed with the ease of intimacy and affection.

It was now three weeks since their engagement, and already something of Addenbrooke's calm happiness was beginning to be reflected in Lydia's face. She appreciated, what only women can appreciate, the consciousness of making another's happiness by the mere fact of her presence. That is, I think, a pleasure too subtle for the masculine palate. Now, as she laid her hand lightly on his, she enjoyed, as it were, a reflection of the delight which she knew herself to be conferring by the act.

164. Taken from Joseph Victor von Scheffel's (1826–1886) *Der Trompeter von Säckingen* (1853).

"Johnny," she said, "will you let me tell you tonight what I have always meant to tell you? About myself and – that other person." She finished her phrase thus vaguely, not doubting but that Addenbrooke had mentally rounded it off with greater accuracy; somehow, her lips refused to utter the name of Lawrence Fleming.

"My dear," he answered gently, "tell me nothing which distresses you. I don't want to know. I know you have been very unhappy; but one day, I assure you, you are going to be happier than ever."

She smiled half sadly. "Johnny, let me tell you. I think I ought. Perhaps, when you have heard, you will want to go away from me – from a woman who has been so cruelly humiliated."

He laughed, drawing closer to her in the firelight.

"Since that's it, Lydia, perhaps you'd better tell me!"

He saw that she would never rest till she had disburdened her mind of the old, unhappy things, about which personally he had small desire to learn.

They were so infinitely touching, these poor women and their love stories; their anxious interpretation of looks and words and smiles; their pathetic, careful gathering-up of crumbs so carelessly scattered.

So Lydia, with half-averted face, began her story in the strange uncertain voice which, from his boyhood upwards, had had power to thrill John Addenbrooke to the inmost depths of his being.

"It is nearly a year ago," she began, "at the Meades' place in Warwickshire. I arrived on March the 28th, and stayed a week. It began from the beginning. When I walked into the drawing room, where he was standing by the tea table, it seemed that I had walked into a new and strange and wonderful world. I lived in that world for a week, and it was like a lifetime. Looking back, it astonishes me how everyone else at once accepted the situation. Then, I no more questioned it than I questioned the rising of the sun. The day came when I was to go, and he had said nothing definite to me. I, living in my Fool's Paradise, was neither surprised nor afraid. At last, an hour before I left, he took me in his arms, yes, Johnny, yes – he took me in his arms and kissed my lips, and told me that he would follow me the next day."

"That's enough," said Addenbrooke, in a low voice; "he was a brute. Let us hear no more about him."

"There is nothing more to hear," she answered with bitterness, "that is the end of my story. A week later I heard he had gone abroad."

Addenbrooke put his arm about Lydia, and drawing her head to his shoulder stroked her hair backward and forward with his kind hand.

Her recital had pained him. He knew the perfidy of his sex, but this particular offender had gone beyond all recognised limits; limits which, in his own person, Johnny had always refused to recognise. The thought of the misery inflicted on his proud, sensitive, passionate Lydia made him sick with anger and speechless with sympathy. He rose at last, and, buttoning up his coat, tried to speak in tones of reassuring cheerfulness.

"By the by, Lydia, Fleming has come back. You remember Lawrence Fleming? They are making quite a lion of him on account of his new book. He's just the sort of man to enjoy being lionised."

Lydia looked at him, speechless, and he went on:

"I expect he will be turning up at my rooms in the course of a day or two. He left a portmanteau with my landlady before he sailed. Good-night, my own dear girl." And he held out both his hands.

Lydia looked at him sharply and with rising vexation.

She had found out long ago that subtle hints were quite thrown away upon Johnny; but surely, surely he must know the truth.

Either he was the most consummate actor or the densest person living.

It was impossible to entertain seriously the idea of Addenbrooke as a consummate actor.

3.

Addenbrooke had rooms in Gower Street; a sitting room and a bedroom, divided by folding doors. The whole apartment had begun life as what house-agents call a spacious double drawing room, and bore yet the marks of its former state of existence.

The mantelpiece, which now supported a host of bottles, variously shaped and filled, was of white marble, heavily carved – summoning up to the imaginative mind visions of gilt clocks and candlesticks under glass shades.

The walls, hung with white watered paper, were divided into panels by strips of gold beading; and from the ceiling a shrouded chandelier depended from a twelfth-cake-like decoration in white-and-gold plaster.

Addenbrooke had drawn his writing table, with the lamp on it, close to the fire, and had settled down to a long night's work. It was the evening following Lydia's confession, and he was too busy to get up to St. John's Wood. He sighed at the thought of this, then plunged into the pile of papers, which not only covered the table, but overflowed into several neighbouring chairs.

He had not been long at work when the door was flung open, and a man entered the room.

"Still in these gilded halls, Johnny!" said a voice, which was not quite so drawling nor so full of quiet humour as the speaker seemed to intend.

"Fleming, by all that's wonderful!" cried Addenbrooke, rising with extended hand.

The newcomer was a large, heavily built young man, with dark hair, and a complexion, originally florid, burnt crimson by the African sun.

He was distinctly handsome, though the lower part of the face was a trifle heavy, and there was a lack of finish about the ears and nostrils.

"Sit down," said Addenbrooke, clearing a chair, and resuming his own seat.

"Examinations, ugh!" Fleming flicked with his large finger at the papers on the desk. "If it's not your own exams, it's other people's, poor old Johnny!"

Fleming had the greatest contempt for examinations, in which, indeed, he had always conspicuously failed to distinguish himself; the less brilliant Addenbrooke having a commonplace knack of getting into the first class, which is often the way with your dull, plodding fellows.

These two men had been friends, after a fashion, since their first term at the university. In those days Fleming had been a raw, unhappy, self-conscious young man, subject to miserable, hideous fits of shyness, and secretly ashamed of the paternal glove shop.

Now, perhaps, he was too fond of talking about the glove shop; of drawing jocose comparisons between himself and a well-known glover's son[165] of Stratford-on-Avon; and the only remaining mark of his shyness was a certain emphasis of self-confidence. Addenbrooke's affection for him was rather a survival from earlier days than anything else; though Johnny, it must be owned, was uncritical, and, unlike many persons, imposed a far less severe standard of conduct on his friends than on himself.

"Where do you hang out?" asked Addenbrooke, gathering together the despised examination papers.

"I have been down at Twickenham with my people. Can't stand much of that, you know. I am looking out for chambers somewhere Bond Street way; and Mrs. Baxter is going to put me up here for a night or two."

"Oh, good. You know Mrs. Baxter has that portmanteau of yours?"

"Yes; she's fetching it now, I believe, from the lumber room. There are some papers in it I want to look at tonight."

Fleming leaned back in his chair, his eyelids drooping moodily, as they had a trick of doing; then he said discontentedly:

"Haven't you got anything to tell a fellow? You London people are all the same. One goes away and lives what seems a lifetime – it's so cram-full of experience – and when one gets back, not a soul remembers if it was last week or last year they met you at the Jenkinsons' dinner party."

"From what I hear, you've no cause to complain, Fleming."

165. Shakespeare.

"Oh, of course, one's pestered with invitations from a lot of silly women one never heard of!" grumbled the new lion; "but isn't there anything in the shape of news?"

"Well," said Addenbrooke, slowly; "there is one piece of news, but I don't know that it's interesting. I am thinking of getting married."

Addenbrooke had never been a shy man; he was only very modest, and he had not accustomed his friends to take an interest in his affairs.

Fleming opened his eyes full and stared his friend in the face.

There was always something startling in his appearance under these circumstances; perhaps because his eyes were so rarely shown – perhaps because of some quality in the eyes themselves. They were curiously bright and very brown – not a black *manqué*, but a beautiful, unusual brown.

Looking at them, it was easier to realise the power, such as it was, which Lawrence Fleming possessed over his fellow creatures.

"Addenbrooke," he said, leaning forward, and speaking with sudden intensity, "as you value your peace of mind, have nothing to do with women!"

He flung himself back, laughing a little, and letting fall his eyelids. In a few minutes he burst into a fierce tirade against the whole female sex, taking Addenbrooke's announcement merely as a text.

Even Johnny was disappointed at this lack of interest on the part of his friend; but remembered having heard that Lawrence had been hard hit before he went to Africa – that nothing less, indeed, than a broken heart had sent him forth to those distant shores.

Then, before Addenbrooke knew what was happening, Fleming had plunged into the very heart of his own particular grievance.

"It was last year," he said, "at a country house. It began from the moment she came into the room. I don't pretend that she was the first; but it was different, somehow. I am not even sure that she was good-looking; but there was something about her – if you cared at all – well, you cared! She stayed a week, and at the end of the time I told her, more or less directly, that I loved her. I was to see her the next day in London. The next day, as it happened, I was prevented by my mother's serious illness. I wrote and told her this, begging her to fix a day for my visit. She made no reply; and four days later I called at the house, to be told she was out of town. The next day I accepted the offer of the *Waterloo Place Gazette*, and went out to Africa. I'm sure I don't know why I cared. She wasn't worth it; she had given me every encouragement – had even allowed me to kiss her. I suppose there was a richer fellow on hand, or one whose father didn't happen to keep a shop!"

Fleming rose, shrugging his shoulders. Addenbrooke remained silent. The voice of Mrs. Baxter, announcing that the portmanteau was in Lawrence's room, came as a relief to both.

"By the by," said Johnny, in a low voice, as the other felt for his keys; "all this took place at the Meades' in Warwickshire, from March the 28th onwards?"

"Oh," answered Lawrence, with some vexation, pausing on his way to the door; "I suppose you know all about it like the rest of the world!" And he went from the room.

4.

Addenbrooke remained behind, pacing the ridiculous, incongruous apartment, while an unwonted storm of emotion raged within him.

The parts of the puzzle lay, fitted together, in his hand; it only remained for him to step forward and proclaim the solution of a most commonplace enigma. An inefficient postman, a careless housemaid – on some such undignified trifle had the whole complication hung, like many another complication before it.

No doubt, sooner or later, the missing clue would come to light, when he himself had made its discovery of no importance whatever.

Had he been of a melodramatic turn of mind, Addenbrooke might have laughed aloud at the irony of the situation.

His own dream was shattered forever; but of that, for the moment, he scarcely thought.

What he saw most clearly was this: that, by his own act, he must make Lydia over into the hands of a man unworthy of her – unlikely to make her happy; to think of whom in connection with her seemed contamination.

But the man whom Lydia loved withal!

There was the sting, the shock, that for the moment took away his breath, and made him pause, pale, motionless, in his walk.

Then suddenly, before the modest and uncritical mind of Addenbrooke flashed in vivid colours the image of two men – of himself and his friend.

He saw Lawrence Fleming, with his showy, unreliable cleverness, his moral coarseness; the man stood before him revealed in all his second-rateness.

And he saw himself, John Addenbrooke, as he had always been, in the dignity of his irreproachable life – of his honest, patient labour.

He looked on this picture and on that, and knew each for what it was worth.

Then ensued in the peaceful breast of Addenbrooke a terrible war of thoughts and emotions.

Life, which had hitherto been a simple matter enough, a mere case of doing your duty and minding your own business, had assumed a complexion of cruel difficulty.

And yet he knew that the more obvious aspect of the matter was not a complicated one.

Lydia no more belonged to him than a dog who had followed him home and had been claimed by its master.

He was bound, in common honour, to reveal the facts of which he had accidentally become possessed.

Should he go to Lydia and say, "This man, whom you prefer so infinitely to myself, is far less worthy of you than I. He has not led a bad life, as men go, but he has not led a good one …."? Men of the world do not do such things, but then Addenbrooke was not a man of the world.

And if he had no other right over Lydia, had he not that of his own lifelong love and of her three weeks' tolerance of it?

The door opened to admit Lawrence Fleming. He had changed his coat, and bore a bundle of papers and a pipe in his hand.

"Any tobacco?" he said, taking the empty seat at the writing-table.

Addenbrooke nodded towards a jar on the mantelpiece, continuing his troubled promenade across the room.

It was dawning, painfully, but surely, on his mind that his hands were indeed tied; that it only remained for Lydia to choose between them.

"But it is I who would have made her happy!" thought poor, obstinate Johnny.

"Any matches?" said Fleming, with his fingers in the tobacco jar.

Johnny made no answer, and the other fumbled in the pocket of his coat.

"By God!"

This time Addenbrooke was roused, and came over to the table. "What's up?" he said.

Fleming pointed in silence to a stamped and addressed envelope lying at his feet.

Johnny picked it up, with a dull sense of relief that matters had been more or less taken out of his hands. He knew, before he looked at it, that it was addressed to Miss Grey, and that it was Fleming's customary carelessness in the matter of posting his letters which had wrought the mischief.

Lawrence was much excited. "It had slipped behind the lining of the pocket! I have just taken the coat from my portmanteau. O that poor girl, that poor girl! What must she have thought of me all this time?"

Addenbrooke faced him suddenly. "Do you intend," he said, in a low voice, "endeavouring to repair the mischief?"

It is possible that he had a low opinion of Fleming's constancy.

"I will go to her tomorrow!" cried Lawrence.

A sudden pang of personal anguish, an intolerable sense of bereavement, shot through Addenbrooke.

He thought: "After all, perhaps, I am nothing but a jealous-devil who begrudges my girl her happiness!"

Aloud he said: "There may be difficulties at first. In fact, Miss Grey is engaged to be married."

Fleming rose, with an exclamation.

The two men stood facing one another: Lawrence, flushed, excited; Johnny, pale, with tense eyes and nostrils.

"Lydia engaged! Lydia! The women are all alike. Could she have no patience, no trust, but she must needs throw herself away in a fit of *pique* on some fellow who is not worthy of her!"

"She is engaged to me!" cried Addenbrooke, with sudden passion. "And, by Heaven, I think it is I who am too good for her!"

The passion of such men as Addenbrooke is a terrible thing.

Fleming quailed before it. He gathered up his papers in silence and went from the room.

5.

Mrs. Grey swept up to Addenbrooke as he stood with his hand on the knob of the drawing room door.

"Oh, Professor Addenbrooke, I am so sorry!" she cried.

"So am I," he answered curtly.

It was two days after the events of the last chapter. Lydia had made her choice, and now, at her own request, was to take farewell of Addenbrooke.

As she came forward, with flushed cheeks and shining eyes, to meet him, it struck him that she resembled the picture of a Bacchante[166] he had seen somewhere. A Bacchante in a tailor-made gown, with the neatest of cuffs and collars – poor Johnny!

"I wished," she said, when their greeting was over, "to thank you with all my heart."

"And I," he said, "wish to tell you this. Do not think that I merely took advantage of you. I believed that I could make you happy – I believe it still."

166. Ecstatic followers of the Dionysus cult.

She smiled sadly, and Addenbrooke broke into a sort of laugh.

"O Johnny, Johnny!" she cried.

He had no intention of being pitied, even by Lydia.

"Don't distress yourself about me, Lydia," he said; "I have had my chance. Perhaps I ought to tell you that I do not think you have chosen the better man."

They talked a little, aimlessly; then Addenbrooke held out both his hands in farewell. It was Lydia who, drawing him towards her, kissed his face for the last time.

She knew, as he stood there facing her, that he was passing out of her life forever. For the moment he seemed transfigured, no longer insignificant; a tender but inscrutable presence – pitying, ironical. Some inarticulate voice in her heart cried out to him not to leave her; unconsciously she put out her hand, and then he was gone.

Not long after Fleming was with her.

He had his arm about her waist and was kissing her lips as Addenbrooke had never kissed them.

Cohen of Trinity (1889)[167]

The news of poor Cohen's death came to me both as a shock and a surprise.

It is true that, in his melodramatic, self-conscious fashion, he had often declared a taste for suicide to be among the characteristics of his versatile race. And indeed in the Cambridge days, or in that obscure interval which elapsed between the termination of his unfortunate University career and the publication of *Gubernator*, there would have been nothing astonishing in such an act on his part. But now, when his book was in everyone's hands, his name on everyone's lips; when that recognition for which he had longed was so completely his; that success for which he had thirsted was poured out for him in so generous a draught – to turn away, to vanish without a word of explanation (he was so fond of explaining himself) is the very last thing one would have expected of him.

1.

He came across the meadows towards the sunset, his upturned face pushed forward catching the light, and glowing also with another radiance than the rich, reflected glory of the heavens.

A curious figure: slight, ungainly; shoulders in the ears; an awkward, rapid gait, half slouch, half hobble. One arm with its coarse

167. See the analysis of this short story beginning on p. xxxi.

hand swung like a bell-rope as he went; the other pressed a book close against his side, while the hand belonging to it held a few bulrushes and marsh marigolds.

Behind him streamed his shabby gown – it was a glorious afternoon of May – and his dusty trencher-cap pushed to the back of his head revealed clearly the oval contour of the face, the full, prominent lips, full, prominent eyes, and the curved beak of the nose with its restless nostrils.

"Who is he?" I asked my companion, one of the younger dons.

"Cohen of Trinity."

He shook his head. The man had come up on a scholarship, but had entirely failed to follow up this preliminary distinction. He was no good, no good at all. He was idle, he was incompetent, he led a bad life in a bad set.

We passed on to other subjects, and out of sight passed the uncouth figure with the glowing face, the evil reputation, and that strange suggestion of latent force which clung to him.

The next time I saw Cohen was a few days later in Trinity quad. There were three or four men with him – little Cleaver of Sidney, and others of the same pattern. He was yelling and shrieking with laughter – at some joke of his own, apparently – and his companions were joining in the merriment.

Something in his attitude suggested that he was the ruling spirit of the group, that he was indeed enjoying the delights of addressing an audience, and appreciated to the full the advantages of the situation.

I came across him next morning, hanging moodily over King's Bridge, a striking contrast to the exuberant figure of yesterday.

He looked yellow and flaccid as a sucked lemon, and eyed the water flowing between the bridges with a suicidal air that its notorious shallowness made ridiculous.

Little Cleaver came up to him and threw out a suggestion of lecture.

Cohen turned round with a self-conscious, sham-tragedy air, gave a great guffaw, and roared out by way of answer the quotation from *Tom Cobb*:

"The world's a beast, and I hate it!"[168]

2.

By degrees I scraped acquaintance with Cohen, who had interested me from the first.

I cannot quite explain my interest on so slight a knowledge; his manners were a distressing mixture of the *bourgeois* and the *canaille*, and a most unattractive lack of simplicity marked his whole personality. There never indeed existed between us anything that could bear the name of friendship. Our relations are easily stated: he liked to talk about himself, and I liked to listen.

I have sometimes reproached myself that I never grew fond of him; but a little reciprocity is necessary in these matters, and poor Cohen had not the art of being fond of people.

I soon discovered that he was desperately lonely and desperately unapproachable.

Once he quoted to me, with reference to himself, the lines from Browning:

> … hath spied an icy fish
> That longed to 'scape the rock-stream where she lived,
> And thaw herself within the lukewarm waves,
> O' the lazy sea….
> Only she ever sickened, found repulse
> At the other kind of water not her life,
> Flounced back from bliss she was not born to breathe,
> And in her old bonds buried her despair,
> Hating and loving warmth alike.[169]

168. From Gilbert's *Tom Cobb or, Fortune's Toy*.

169. From Browning's poem, "Caliban upon Setebos."

Of the men with whom I occasionally saw him – men who would have been willing enough to be his friends – he spoke with an open contempt that did him little credit, considering how unscrupulously he made use of them when his loneliness grew intolerable. There were others, too, besides Cleaver and his set, men of a coarser stamp – boon companions, as the storybooks say – with whom, when the fit was on, he consented to herd.

But as friends, as permanent companions even, he rejected them, one and all, with a magnificence, an arrogant and bitter scorn that had in it a distinctly comic element.

I saw him once, to my astonishment, with Norwood, and it came out that he had the greatest admiration for Norwood and his set.

What connection there could be between those young puritans, aristocrats and scholars, the flower of the University – if prigs, a little, and *bornés* – and a man of Cohen's way of life, it would be hard to say.

In aspiring to their acquaintance one scarcely knew if to accuse the man of an insane vanity or a pathetic hankering after better things.

Little Leuniger,[170] who played the fiddle, a Jew, was the fashion at that time among them; but he resolutely turned the cold shoulder to poor Cohen, who, I believe, deeply resented this in his heart, and never lost an opportunity of hurling a bitterness at his compatriot.

A desire to stand well in one another's eyes, to make a brave show before one another, is, I have observed, a marked characteristic of the Jewish people.

As for little Leuniger, he went his way, and contented himself with saying that Cohen's family were not people that one "knew."

On the subject of his family, Cohen himself, at times savagely reserved, at others appallingly frank, volunteered little information, though on one occasion he had touched in with a few vivid strokes the background of his life.

I seemed to see it all before me: the little new house in Maida Vale; a crowd of children, clamorous, unkempt; a sallow shrew in a

170. Leopold Leuniger is also a character in *Reuben Sachs* and the unpublished, "Leopold Leuniger: A Study"; see the discussion beginning on p. xxxi.

torn dressing-gown, who alternately scolded, bewailed herself, and sank into moody silence; a fitful paternal figure coming and going, depressed, exhilarated according to the fluctuations of his mysterious financial affairs; and over everything the fumes of smoke, the glare of gas, the smell of food in preparation.

But, naturally enough, it was as an individual, not as the member of a family, that Cohen cared to discuss himself.

There was, indeed, a force, an exuberance, a robustness about his individuality that atoned – to the curious observer at least – for the presence of certain of the elements which helped to compose it. His unbounded arrogance, his enormous pretensions, alternating with and tempered by a bitter self-depreciation, overflowing at times into self-reviling, impressed me, even while amusing and disgusting me.

It seemed that a frustrated sense of power, a disturbing consciousness of some blind force which sought an outlet, lurked within him and allowed him no rest.

Of his failure at his work he spoke often enough, scoffing at academic standards, yet writhing at his own inability to come up to them.

"On my honour," he said to me once, "I can't do better, and that's the truth. Of course you don't believe it; no one believes it. It's all a talk of wasted opportunities, squandered talents – but, before God, that part of my brain which won the scholarship has clean gone."

I pointed out to him that his way of life was not exactly calculated to encourage the working mood.

"Mood!" he shouted with a loud, exasperated laugh. "Mood! I tell you there's a devil in my brain and in my blood, and Heaven knows where it is leading me."

It led him this way and that at all hours of the day and night.

The end of the matter was not difficult to foresee, and I told him so plainly.

This sobered him a little, and he was quiet for three days, lying out on the grass with a lexicon and a pile of Oxford classics.

On the fourth the old mood was upon him and he rushed about like a hunted thing from dawn to sunset winding up with an entertainment which threatened his position as a member of the University.

He got off this time, however, but I shall never forget his face the next morning as he blustered loudly past Norwood and Blount in Trinity Street.

If he neglected his own work, he did, as far as could be seen, no other, unless fits of voracious and promiscuous reading may be allowed to count as such. I suspected him of writing verses, but on this matter of writing he always maintained, curiously enough, a profound reserve.

What I had for some time foreseen as inevitable at length came to pass. Cohen disappeared at a short notice from the University, no choice being given him in the matter.

I went off to his lodgings directly the news of his sentence reached me, but the bird had already flown, leaving no trace behind of its whereabouts.

As I stood in the dismantled little room, always untidy, but now littered from end to end with torn and dusty papers, there rose before my mind the vision of Cohen as I had first seen him in the meadows, with the bulrushes in his hand, the book beneath his arm, and on his face, which reflected the sunset, the radiance of a secret joy.

3.

I did not see *Gubernator* till it was in its fourth edition, some three months after its publication and five years after the expulsion of Cohen from Trinity.

The name, Alfred Lazarus Cohen, printed in full on the title page, revealed what had never before occurred to me, the identity of the author of that much-talked-of book with my unfortunate college acquaintance. I turned over the leaves with a new curiosity, and, it must be added, a new distrust. By-and-bye I ceased from this cursory, tentative inspection, I began at the beginning and finished the book at a sitting.

Everyone knows *Gubernator* by now, and I have no intention of describing it. Half poem, half essay, wholly unclassifiable, with a force, a fire, a vision, a vigour and felicity of phrase that carried you through its most glaring inequalities, its most appalling lapses of taste, the book fairly took the reader by storm.

Here was a clear case of figs from thistles.[171]

I grew anxious to know how Cohen was bearing himself under his success, which must surely have satisfied, for the time being at least, even his enormous claims.

Was that ludicrous, pathetic gap between his dues and his pretensions at last bridged over?

I asked myself this and many more questions, but a natural hesitation to hunt up the successful man where the obscure one had entirely escaped my memory prevented me from taking any steps to the renewal of our acquaintance.

But Cohen, as may be supposed, was beginning to be talked about, heard of and occasionally met, and I had no doubt that chance would soon give me the opportunity I did not feel justified in seeking.

There was growing up, naturally enough, among some of us Cambridge men a sense that Cohen had been hardly used, that (I do not think this was the case) he had been unjustly treated at the University. Lord Norwood, whom I came across one day at the club, remarked that no doubt his widespread popularity would more than atone to Cohen for the flouting he had met with at the hands of Alma Mater. He had read *Gubernator*; it was clever, but the book repelled him, just as the man, poor fellow, had always repelled him. The subject did not seem to interest him, and he went off shortly afterwards with Blount and Leuniger.

A week later I met Cohen at a club dinner, given by a distinguished man of letters. There were present notabilities of every sort – literary, dramatic, artistic – but the author of *Gubernator* was the lion of the

171. From Matthew 7:16: "Do men gather grapes of thorns, or figs of thistles?" See Susan David Bernstein, ed., *Reuben Sachs,* by Amy Levy (Peterborough: Broadview Editions, 2006), 186 n. 1; "Cohen of Trinity" is reprinted, with commentary, in Bernstein's appendices, 181–9.

evening. He rose undeniably to the situation, and roared as much as was demanded of him. His shrill, uncertain voice, pitched in a loud excited key, shot this way and that across the table. His strange, flexible face, with the full, prominent lips, glowed and quivered with animation. Surely this was his hour of triumph.

He had recognised me at once, and after dinner came round to me, his shoulders in his ears as usual, holding out his hand with a beaming smile. He talked of Cambridge, of one or two mutual acquaintances, without embarrassment. He could not have been less abashed if he had wound up his career at the University amid the cheers of an enthusiastic Senate House.

When the party broke up he came over to me again and suggested that I should go back with him to his rooms. He had never had much opinion of me, as he had been at no pains to conceal, and I concluded that he was in a mood for unbosoming himself. But it seemed that I was wrong, and we walked back to Great Russell Street, where he had two large, untidy rooms, almost in silence. He told me that he was living away from his family, an unexpected legacy from an uncle having given him independence.

"So the Fates aren't doing it by halves?" I remarked, in answer to this communication.

"Oh, no," he replied, with a certain moody irony, staring hard at me over his cigar.

"Do you know what success means?" he asked suddenly, and in the question I seemed to hear Cohen the *poseur*, always at the elbow of, and not always to be distinguished from, Cohen stark-nakedly revealed.

"Ah, no, indeed."

"It means – inundation by the second-rate."

"What does the fellow want?" I cried, uncertain as to the extent of his seriousness.

"I never," he said, "was a believer in the half-loaf theory."

"It strikes me, Cohen, that your loaf looks uncommonly like a whole one, as loaves go on this unsatisfactory planet."

He burst into a laugh.

"Nothing," he said presently, "can alter the relations of things – their permanent, essential relations .... 'They *shall* know, they *shall* understand, they *shall* feel what I am.' That is what I used to say to myself in the old days. I suppose, now, 'they' do know, more or less, and what of that?"

"I should say the difference from your point of view was a very great one. But you always chose to cry for the moon."

"Well," he said, quietly looking up, "it's the only thing worth having."

I was struck afresh by the man's insatiable demands, which looked at times like a passionate striving after perfection, yet went side by side with the crudest vanity, the most vulgar desire for recognition.

I rose soon after his last remark, which was delivered with a simplicity and an air of conviction which made one cease to suspect the mountebank; we shook hands and bade one another goodnight.

*****

I never saw Cohen again.

Ten days after our renewal of acquaintance he sent a bullet through his brain, which, it was believed, must have caused instantaneous death. That small section of the public which interests itself in books discussed the matter for three days, and the jury returned the usual verdict. I have confessed that I was astonished, that I was wholly unprepared by my knowledge of Cohen for the catastrophe. Yet now and then an inkling of his motive, a dim, fleeting sense of what may have prompted him to the deed, has stolen in upon me.

In his hour of victory the sense of defeat had been strongest. Is it, then, possible that, amid the warring elements of that discordant nature, the battling forces of that ill-starred, ill-compounded entity, there lurked, clear-eyed and ever-watchful, a baffled idealist?

A Slip of the Pen (1889)

1.

It was all Dicky Carshalton's fault.

In many respects an amiable youth, he cannot be said to be possessed of the finer feelings, and perhaps is not aware of the extent of the discomfort he produces in more sensitive people. A frequenter of parties of every description, he is fond of varying the monotony of the social routine by various little practices. Of these, his favourite, not, alas! peculiar to himself, is commonly known as spoiling sport. Whenever Dicky sees a pair of people who appear to take particular delight in one another's society, showing a tendency to seek unto themselves retreats, he is never satisfied until, by some bold stroke or cunning stratagem, he has succeeded in separating them; or, at least, in destroying their enjoyment for the rest of one evening.

The happy possessor of an exhaustless supply of self-confidence and the most brazen impudence – the objects of his attack, moreover, being, from the nature of their position, comparatively defenceless – it is needless to add that, though Dicky has his failures on record, they are greatly outstripped in numbers by his successes. So there is nothing wonderful in the fact that Dicky was at the bottom of that unfortunate affair with Jack and Ethel.

Matters had long been in a delicate and critical state between those young people. Jack had told himself over and over again that Ethel was a flirt, and that he, for one, had no intention of adding himself to the list of her victims; while Ethel had relieved her feelings by repeatedly assuring herself that Jack was a cross fellow who cared for nothing but his books, and was quite impervious to the charms of womanhood.

But that night at the Warringtons' things really did seem to be taking a turn for the better. Ethel had boldly turned her back on half-a-dozen other admirers, and Jack, looking down into her honest eyes, was rapidly forgetting the doubts and fears which had tormented him during the past months.

There is no knowing what might not have happened, had it not been for Dicky, who came up to them at this hopeful stage of affairs, his shoulders in his ears, his hair brushed to a nicety, and with the most unmistakable look of mischief in his prominent eyes.

"Good evening, Miss Mariner," he said, taking Ethel's hand in his and squeezing it with *empressement*; and then the two poor things, suddenly awakened from their dream, stood there chill and helpless while Dicky fired off his accustomed volley of chaff, and Ethel, with feminine presence of mind, ventured on one or two little pop-guns on her own account.

"Miss Mariner," he said at last, with a satisfied glance at Jack's sullen face, "have you been into the conservatory? They've put a lot of pink lamps, and there's the most scrumptious *tête-à-tête* chair you can imagine."

Poor Ethel looked up at Jack, who stood by, furious and sulky.

"He is only too glad to get rid of me. He hasn't the ordinary kindness to rescue me from this bore. And I have been so horribly amiable to him," she thought in despair.

"If she likes that popinjay, let her go with him! I'm sorry for her taste, that's all," reflected Jack, and in another minute Ethel found herself actually seated in the *tête-à-tête* chair with Dicky, whose large eyes were rolling triumphantly in the light of the rose-coloured lamps.

She did not succeed in making her escape till it was time to go home. Jack was nowhere to be seen, and she drove back in the chill grey morning with the heaviest heart she had known for many days.

2.

"Ethel," said her mother at breakfast the next morning, "did you have a pleasant time at the Warringtons'?"

"Oh, yes, Mamma," said Ethel drearily. She was pale and heavy-eyed; I think she had not slept all night.

"And who were there?" went on Mrs. Mariner, helping herself to buttered eggs with cheery briskness.

Ethel enumerated various people. "And Dicky Carshalton," she concluded, "and Jack Davenant."

The last name slipped out with exaggerated carelessness; and yet it was whirring about in the poor girl's head, and had been doing so for the last five or six hours, like an imprisoned blue-bottle in a glass. "Jack – Jack – Jack Davenant." Was she never to have another definite thought again?

"By-the-by," said Mrs. Mariner, as she rose from table, "will you send a note to Florence Byrne? I want her to lunch here tomorrow at half-past one – the Singletons are coming."

Ethel moved to the writing-table, blushing faintly. She remembered that Mrs. Byrne was Jack Davenant's cousin.

"Half-past one, recollect," cried her mother, as she rushed from the room.

Ethel listlessly took up her pen, and pulled a sheet of paper towards her. It was not stamped with the address, but she failed to notice this, and began at once –

"My dear Mrs. Byrne."

Then she stopped short, and the buzzing in her brain went on worse than ever.

The note got written at last, all but the signature, and then she began to wonder dreamily if she should sign herself "Yours very sincerely," or "Yours affectionately."

"Ethel, Ethel!" cried her mother, putting her head in at the door, "I am going out. Give me the note for Florence; I can take it to the post."

Guilty and ashamed, Ethel seized her pen and wrote hastily, but in a bold hand –

"Yours very sincerely,
"JACK DAVENANT."

3.

Mrs. Byrne neither came to lunch, nor answered the Mariners' invitation. Mrs. Mariner expressed surprise at this want of courtesy, and apologised to the Singletons for having no one to meet them.

"Are you sure, Ethel, you told her the right day? Florence is in town, I know, and it is so unlike her to be rude."

"I think it was all right, Mamma," Ethel replied vaguely, and never gave another thought to the matter.

But on the morning of the next day, as she was practising her singing in the great holland-shrouded drawing room, the door was flung open to admit a benign and comely lady, who advanced smiling towards her.

"Mrs. Byrne!" cried Ethel in some surprise, getting off the music-stool.

Mrs. Byrne established herself comfortably in a deep armchair, then beckoned the young girl mysteriously with a well-gloved finger: "Come over here, Ethel."

Ethel drew a low stool to the other's side, and sat down, smiling but mystified.

Mrs. Byrne played a little with the clasp of the silver-mounted handbag which she carried, from which, having at last succeeded in opening it, she produced a stamped envelope addressed to herself.

"Do you know that handwriting?" she said, flourishing it before Ethel's astonished eyes.

"It is my own; I wrote to ask you to lunch," poor Ethel answered simply; while the thought flashed across her mind that Mrs. Byrne had probably gone mad.

"Read it, then," cried that lady, with an air of suppressed amusement which lent colour to the notion.

Ethel unfolded it quickly, then sat transfixed like one who receives a sudden and fatal injury. For before her horror-stricken eyes glared these words, in her own handwriting: "Yours very sincerely, JACK DAVENANT."

"What does it mean?" she cried at last in a hoarse voice, for it seemed that some fiendish magic had been at work.

"That's what I want to know," Mrs. Byrne answered more, gently. "I received this note the day before yesterday. There was no address, and the handwriting was certainly not Jack's. Nor is my cousin in the least likely to invite me to lunch at his chambers. So I wrote off to him at once, and told him to drop in to dinner if he had anything to say to me."

Ethel had risen to her feet, and was standing with a little frozen smile on her face; but at this point she broke in hurriedly –

"Did you show him – Mr. Davenant, the letter?"

Mrs. Byrne nodded. She was not a person of delicate perceptions, and had come here bent on a little harmless amusement; but somehow the amusement was not forthcoming.

Ethel clasped her cold hands together in a frenzy of despair. She knew that Jack was familiar with her handwriting; had he not made little criticisms, severe and tender, on the occasional notes of invitation which she had addressed to him?

"Jack said he knew nothing about the note, and hadn't the ghost of an idea what it meant."

"Oh, Jack, Jack," cried Ethel's heart in parenthesis, "what must you think of me?"

Mrs. Byrne went on: "Grace Allison came in later, and the mystery was cleared up. She swore to your handwriting, and we concluded you had done it in a fit of absence of mind. Poor old Jack, how she did chaff him!"

Ethel was trying to recover her presence of mind.

"How could I have made such a stupid mistake?" she said, with a short laugh. "I suppose I was pursuing some train of thought. I had met your cousin at a party the night before – you know how it is."

Mrs. Byrne was sorry for the girl's distress.

"It's a mistake anyone might have made, though you must own it was rather funny. However, I can assure you this – it won't get any further. Jack is scarcely likely to tell, and Grace has sworn on her honour."

Ethel laughed again, meaninglessly. As far as she was concerned, the whole world was welcome to know it now. No deeper disgrace could befall her. "I wonder if he is shrieking with laughter, or merely sick with disgust," the poor girl thought, when her obtuse and amiable visitor had at last departed, "Oh, how I hate him, how I hate him!" which was hard on Jack, considering that his own conduct in the matter had been irreproachable. But Ethel was in no mood for justice. It seemed to her that she had utterly betrayed and disgraced herself; that never again could she venture to show herself in a world where Florence Byrne, Grace Allison, and, above all, Jack Davenant lived, moved, and had their being.

Sick with shame, hot and cold with anguish, poor Ethel sat cowering in the great drawing room like a guilty thing.

4.

Ethel astonished her family at dinner that evening by enquiries as to the state of the female labour-market in New Zealand.

Uncle Joe, a philanthropic parson, who happened to be of the party, delighted to find his pretty niece taking an interest in a subject so little frivolous, delivered himself of a short lecture on the subject.

Ethel sighed at hearing that there was so little demand for the work of educated women (save the mark!) in that distant colony, and began to turn her thoughts towards Waterloo Bridge.

"Ethel funks on being an old maid. She knows that positively *any* girl can lasso a husband in New Zealand," her brother Bob remarked in a challenging tone.

But Ethel bore it with uninteresting meekness; perhaps, she told herself, she *was* a husband-hunter after all!

After dinner, she put on her hat and stole out into the street. She had been indoors all day, and could bear it no longer. The June evening was still as light as day, and simple-minded couples were loitering with frank affection in Regent's Park. She had not gone far before she saw a large familiar figure bearing down in her direction.

"Oh, how I hate him – I hate him!" she thought again, while her heart beat with maddening rapidity. "If he has a spark of kindness in him, he will pretend not to see me."

But Jack, for it was he, made no such pretence. On the contrary, he not only raised his hat, but came up to her with outstretched hand. She put her cold fingers mechanically into his, and scanned his face; there was neither mirth nor disgust in it, and the thought flashed across her, chilling, while it relieved her, that he probably attached little importance to an incident to which she, knowing her own secret, had deemed but one interpretation possible. And then, before she knew what had happened, Jack was walking along by her side, pouring out a torrent of indignant reproaches as to her desertion of him in favour of Dicky Carshalton at the Warringtons' party.

"It is you," cried Ethel with spirit, for the unexpected turn of affairs restored her courage, "it is you, Mr. Davenant, who were unkind, to stand by and let old friends be victimised, without striking a blow in their behalf! Pray what did you expect me to do? Was I to have said, 'No, thank you, Mr. Carshalton, I prefer to stay here with Mr. Davenant?'"

"And, if you had said it, would it have been true?"

She changed her tone suddenly.

"Dicky is *such* a bore! I think I prefer anyone's society to his."

He stopped short in the path, seizing both her hands, and looking down at her with stern and passionate eyes.

A close-linked couple strolling by remarked to one another that there had been a row, then refreshed themselves with half-a-dozen kisses.

"Ethel," said Jack, in an odd voice, "it's no use pretending. You *do* think of me sometimes; I happen to know it."

She was looking up at him; but at this allusion the sweet face flushed and drooped suddenly.

"Ethel," – Jack's voice sounded stranger and stranger; was he going to laugh or cry? And why on earth did he speak so low – "Ethel, do you know what signature I should like to see to your letters?"

This was too much.

"No, I don't!" – she lifted her flushed face; the cruel tears shone and smarted in her eyes.

"Can't you guess?"

"No."

The momentary defiance had died; a very meek whisper came from the pale lips.

"Can't you guess? Then shall I tell you, Ethel? 'Ethel Davenant' – that's what I should like to see at the bottom of all your letters. Shall I ever see it?"

"Jack!"

Further explanation is needless. When next they met Mr. Carshalton, both Jack and Ethel were beyond the reach of his manoeuvres.

Eldorado at Islington (1889)[172]

1.

The houses in the terrace were of grey stucco, with bow-windows and flights of steps out of all proportion to their size.

The main road ran along the bottom, and the remaining two sides were bounded by stretches of blank wall, above which a few sickly plane trees were fluttering their leaves in the August air.

Eleanor Lloyd, from her window in the roof, could see not only the wall and the plane trees, but, by dint of craning her neck, the High Street itself, with its ceaseless stream of trams and omnibuses. There was a public house at the corner, and, as the door swung backward and forward, Eleanor caught glimpses of the lively barmaid behind her tall white tap handles. A group of flower girls, with uncurled feathers and straight fringes, stood outside on the pavement, jesting with the 'busmen and passers by. Eleanor, who was a "lady," (Heaven help her) used sometimes to envy the barmaid and the flower girls their social opportunity.

This evening, over everything, over the sordid street, the dusty trees, the clustering roofs – over the girl at the window with her pale face, strong young shoulders, and shabby gown – brooded the spirit of the tired summer.

172. Possible reference to Edgar Allan Poe's (1809–1849) poem, "Eldorado."

The summer, which, by stream and sea, is lusty from June to September, drags on weary and dispirited through its later weeks in the city.

The hot, gusty, grit-laden air blew from the east; it moved querulously among the plane trees, and lifted at intervals the hair on Eleanor's forehead.

She had been sitting there all the afternoon, and now the sun was setting. There was nothing for her to do. Her little pupils in the neighbouring square had gone to the sea; her brothers and sisters played noisily in the basement parlour; even poor Eddy had fallen asleep on the sofa, with the crutch, that was of so little use to him, at his side.

And now, as a great red flame lit up the west, there came over Eleanor one of those half-rapturous fits of longing, those fierce yearnings for happiness, which most of us know in youth; which are not noble, not beautiful, perhaps; certainly in no way to be encouraged; which are only infinitely cruel and infinitely sad.

So the cry went up from her, the human, passionate cry from this helpless, fluttering creature caught – oh, the irony of it! – in a pitiless network of suburban streets.

A man with bent, shabby shoulders and lagging gait, turned up the terrace from the High Street.

At the parlour window of the Lloyds' house a worn out looking woman, with a patient face, watched him and sighed.

In their youth, no doubt, the husband and wife had dreamed of other things than those long years of ceaseless labour with their scant reward.

Hard-working, unassuming, delicately just, he was not, perhaps, of the stuff of which rich men are made.

The children clamoured up into the parlour to greet their father. Eddy held out a little thin hand from the sofa; Eleanor, with the dreams still in her dazzled eyes, slid into the darkened room – darkened on behalf of carpet and curtains – and took her place at the tea table.

"Did you see your letter, father?" said the wife, as she lifted the teapot of Britannia metal.

Mr. Lloyd, who had taken the long blue envelope from the mantelpiece, laid it unopened beside his plate.

The room was very hot, and the blind flapped drearily in the wind. There was a household loaf on the table, some thick, thin-spread bread-and-butter, and a dish of watercress – a tough and sinewy August growth.

Even the children tackled the meal languidly, and after a few minutes their father set down his cup, took up his letter, and broke the seal.

A long, closely-written sheet of paper unrolled itself beneath his hand. He straightened the glasses on his tired eyes and began to read. He read it once, he read it twice, then lifting a perplexed face, said faintly –

"Mother, what does this mean?"

She was at his side, leaning over him, in a moment. She, too, read the letter, then stood strangely silent.

"Children," said their father, "a wonderful thing has happened. It seems that I am a rich man. My brother, from whom I parted in anger many years ago, is dead. He died as he had lived – alone; but at the last remembered me and forgave me...."

His voice died away; and the wife, looking from her children's faces, on which a radiant comprehension was slowly dawning, to her husband's prematurely grizzled head, burst suddenly into weeping.

"My wife," he said – taking her into his arms – "there is no more cause to weep."

2.

Mrs. Lloyd brushed her husband's coat and hat the next morning even more carefully than usual, with a view to his visit to the lawyer.

"If it had come sooner!" she thought, as she watched the bent, beloved figure down the street.

Then she went back to her household duties.

The burden of those long years was not to be shaken off in an hour. She had stiffened, perhaps, into a habit of sorrow and of poverty; it is certain that she laboured faithfully throughout the day at her sordid cares – scarcely able to realise the strange fortune which had befallen them.

But not so the children. For them the good news was a reality. They drew together, building their castles in the air, which, unlike such erections generally, had foundations of solid gold, and even in their unsubstantial upper storeys were fitted up with a sagacity characteristic of the early-wise children of the poor.

Eddy, from his sofa, spoke wistfully of marvellous cures, of health-giving breezes, of great doctors whose services he could now command. Eleanor moved about the house with new life, speaking little, but dreaming, dreaming, dreaming through the summer hours.

The wonderful day sped to its close. Once more the family gathered round the tea table, the tired father taking his seat at the head.

"Did you go to that lawyer, father? A nice fellow he must be, I should say!" cried Eddy, who was a privileged person.

"And, father, did you tell them at the office that you are not going there anymore?" added Eleanor, with a new gladness in her voice, a new light in her eyes, which today, at least, were the eyes of a pretty girl.

"Your father is tired," said the mother, seeing that her husband neither moved nor spoke, but sat with his elbow on the table, shading his face with his hand.

"No, no," he said quickly, "I am not tired...."

Then, lifting his head suddenly, he spoke out with curious harshness –

"Wife, children, you must put today and yesterday out of your heads. It has all been a mistake."

Half-imploring, half-defiant, he swept the dismayed circle of faces with his glance; then, dropping his eyes, went on –

"The money was never ours, never could be ours. It was the fruit of cruelty and extortion; it was wrung from the starving poor. It is money that no honest man can touch."

He covered his face with his hand, and there was silence in the room.

Then, all at once, the youngest of the children broke into loud crying, and Eleanor, with flaming cheeks and blazing eyes, sprang to her feet.

"I knew it!" she cried, and the anger and sorrow of her voice were sad to hear. "I knew it could not be true that we were going to be happy. It is a shame, a shame, but I knew it!" And she went from the room.

Her father followed her into the narrow passage, shutting the door behind them.

She stood silent, motionless, with her forehead pressed to the wall.

He stretched out a tired, trembling hand and laid it on her shoulder.

"My dear" – the harsh note of pain had faded from his voice; it was only very wistful and weary – "My dear, I am very sorry. But you would not wish it otherwise, I know."

He was a man of few words – simple, timid, little given to demonstrations of affection.

"You do not wish it otherwise?" he said again.

No answer; but he felt the shoulder shaking with sobs beneath his touch.

In the poor girl's simple heart she held her father's decision as absolutely without alternative, as he had done himself. Her anger was impersonal, directed against Fate, and at the pathetic sound of her father's voice she had melted into tears.

Meantime, in the parlour, the mother comforted her children. It was Eleanor who had believed in Eldorado, and yet who had cried, "I knew it!" The mother, whose heart had throughout refused to accept the glad tidings, made no such proclamation. She quieted the crying child, handed Eddy his tea, and taking up the loaf, began to cut it.

This evening the sun had been allowed to stream in through the window, regardless of the poor carpet and curtains. Perceiving this, Mrs. Lloyd laid down her knife and, stirred by the familiar thrifty instinct, walked firmly across the room and quietly drew down the blind.

Wise in Her Generation (1890)

1.

It was a charming party at Mrs. Westerleigh's; a good floor, a good band, and a respectable set of people. I wore my new gown from Russell and Allen's – no *débutante* foam of tulle or net, but a really handsome confection in white corded silk, the sort of thing which exactly suits my style, Nature never having cut me out for the part of *jeune fille*. We arrived a little late, but a great many people seemed to have room for my name on their programmes; indeed, throughout the evening I enjoyed the rather novel sensation of a ballroom success. Not that I set much value on such a bit of social gilt-gingerbread. All very well for boys and girls in their first season, but by no means fitted to satisfy the appetite of persons arriving at years of discretion.

The dancing had stopped when we got into the room, and I stood for a few moments in the doorway making up my book for the events of the night. Regy Walker was negotiating with me for the supper dances, when the Shands were announced. I looked up, without moving a hair, and saw them within a yard of me – Philip and Philip's wife.

The latter I observed to be slight and pale; not ugly, of course, for in these days even heiresses cannot afford to be ugly, but generally insignificant. But her maid, her tailor, and her corset-maker are evidently the best of their kind.

I don't know how long Regy Walker and I stood there adjusting our ball cards; perhaps a minute, perhaps a hundred years. Then the room went round suddenly, and I found myself shaking hands with Philip.

Our eyes met; he smiled his wonderful smile. It might almost have been last year. But it can never be last year again.

Last year, Philip, you were a hard-working, ambitious young man of whom great things were already prophesied at the Bar; this year you are a person of importance – your fortune made, your position assured. Last year I was a one-idea'd young person in a white frock, who blushed and smiled with undisguised delight when her friend approached her; who had smiles and blushes for no one else; whose days were full of vague, delicious happiness; whose wakeful nights were sweeter than nights of dreams. This year I am a woman who knows her weakness, knows also her strength, and has had her experience.

It is the third day, and I have risen again.[173]

Without knowledge of life there can be no true enjoyment of life. Life, I maintain, in the face of the sentimentalists, to be an acquired taste. For the educated palate there are all sorts of gustatory surprises – olives, caviar, a host of sauces – far more delicious than, if not quite so wholesome as, the roast meat and boiled pudding of domesticity. You were right, Philip; and I, who once believed myself your victim, crushed beneath the Juggernaut-car of your ambition – I was wrong.

Meanwhile, I have left us – Philip Shand and Virginia Warwick – shaking hands with one another, and smiling into one another's faces, with almost exaggerated amiability.

"Am I too late for a waltz?"

"There is only number eleven left."

"A quadrille! I ask for bread, and you give me a stone."[174]

I wrote down his initials on my card, and he made off, smiling brilliantly.

---

173. Biblical allusion to the resurrection of Jesus.

174. The symbology here is probably in reference to Matthew 7:9.

I stood looking after him with a curious sense of unreality, divided between a desire to laugh aloud, and another – to go from the room, from the house, to some vague, impossible region of darkness and silence and solitude. At the same moment, I grew aware of a pair of wide-open grey eyes, fixed upon myself with unconventional intentness, from the distance. Their owner was a tall, fair, weedy young man, whose whole appearance was indefinably different from that of the surrounding people. It was not long before Mrs. Westerleigh swept up to me with this unknown young man in her wake.

"Sir Guy Ormond – Miss Warwick."

We both bowed, and he asked me for a dance, with a fervour quite disproportionate to the request.

"Some poor little waif of a swell!" was my reflection, as he wrote his name against the twelfth waltz – the only unclaimed dance on my card.

For it must be owned that we were that night a distinctly middle-class gathering, a great mixed mob of Londoners; no mere Belgravian birds of passage, but people whose interests and avocations lay well within the Great City.

"May I take you in to supper later on?" said Sir Guy earnestly.

"Yes, please," I answered, giving him a glance almost as serious as his own. Certainly, there is no game so amusing as that which Philip taught me to play last year. At the opening of the eleventh dance Philip came up to me.

"You don't want to dance this thing?"

He lowered his voice to the old confidential pitch; but his manner was a shade less confident than of old. After all, why not? I hate quadrilles, and I like to talk with Philip.

"If you will allow me," he said, as we strolled off to the conservatory, "I will introduce you to my wife."

And then I found myself bowing and smiling to a colourless person, who bowed and smiled in her turn, and announced her intention of calling on me at an early date.

A few minutes later I was in the conservatory, lounging in a delicious chair; a becoming pink lantern swung above my head. Opposite me, his chair drawn close to mine, sat a well-groomed gentleman in evening dress, with expressive eyes and a vivacious, intelligent face. A charming picture of manners, is it not?

Little by little I gave myself up to the pleasure of the moment, which, when all is said, was considerable.

He is not the Philip of last year, but he has the same eyes and the same voice. The Philip of last year never, indeed, existed, save in my imagination; but I have caught the trick of *bien-étre* in the society of this person who looks like him; of basking in the glow of that radiant vitality, the warmth of that magnetic presence.

"May I take you in to supper?" said Philip presently.

"I have arranged to go in with Sir Guy Ormond."

He looked at me curiously.

"The bloated aristocrat! But perhaps he is a friend of yours?"

"I was introduced to him tonight."

"He's a good fellow; a little sentimental and dilettante, but you can afford to be sentimental on thirty thousand a year."

Thirty thousand a year! Sir Guy was a person of more importance than I had imagined. I dropped my eyes to my fan, and Philip went on in his familiar, mocking fashion: –

"Do you love blue books? Are you devoted to poor law reports? What is your opinion of Toynbee Hall?[175] And when, Miss Virginia Warwick, were you last at the People's Palace?[176] By such paths lies the way to the royal favour."

I looked up and met the glance, mocking and serious and curiously intent, of his brilliant eyes. At the same moment, someone brushed through the ferns and lounges to where we sat, and announced himself as my partner for the next waltz.

It was Sir Guy Ormond.

---

175. Philanthropic institution in Spitalfields, London.
176. Theatre in Mile End, London.

Philip rose at once, with an air of ostentatious magnanimity, a flourish of *fair play* in every line of him. The look in his eyes stung me. Was he insulting me, this polite person, bowing himself gracefully away? But after all, is there any deeper wrong, any crueller insult left for him to offer?

Let me write it down, once for all, that we must remain forever unspoken, unexpressed.

If a man stabs you, or robs you, or injures your fair fame, do you take these things at his hands in silence? Even if he escape the world's punishment, do you smile upon him in the face of the world?

Idle questions, no doubt!

And I – I shall go on smiling at Philip to the end of the chapter!

2.

I wonder, sometimes, that we do not go oftener to the bad, we girls of the well-to-do classes.

If you come to think of it, it is a curious ordeal we pass through at the very outset of our career. Take a girl in the schoolroom and see what her life is.

A dingy room, dowdy dresses, bread and butter, and governesses! In all the household there is, perhaps, no person of less importance than she. Then, one day, this creature, knowing nothing of the world, and less, if possible, of herself, is launched on the stream of fashionable or pseudo-fashionable life. At what has been hitherto her bedtime, she is arrayed gorgeously, whirled through a gas-lit city, and finally let loose in a crowded ballroom, there to sink or swim. There are lights, jewels, heavy scents, and dreamy, delicious music; it is all a whirl, a clatter, a profusion. And there are a great many people, gay, good-looking, well dressed. One person comes to her again and again. He is a great deal older than she, with all the assurance of strength and experience. Deferential and tyrannical, he entreats and commands at one and the same time. And he has a strange power of sympathy, a wonderful insight into her innocence; knows her better than herself, it seems, this charming, clever person. Everywhere he follows her about; with every look, with every tone, he says: "*I love you.*"

She does not know why she is so happy. All day long she dreams, dreams, or gossips of the night to come. If she thinks at all about it, she thinks prim thoughts such as have been instilled into her, and which have nothing to do with what she feels. The natural promptings of her modesty she mistakes for resistance to this unknown force, which is drawing her to itself as inevitably as the magnet draws the needle. With her little prudish defences, she believes herself equipped for any fray; she feels so strong, and, O God, she is so weak! One day a bolt falls from the clear sky; he is going to be married to a woman of fortune, of good connections; he is away in the country wooing his rich bride.... Pshaw, what a rhodomontade!...[177]

All the girls, nearly, have gone through it; everyone knows how Carrie lost her looks after she came home from Cowes, and how Blanche fell off to a skeleton the year Fred Birch was married. Carrie looked blooming enough in the park the other day in her new carriage; and Blanche is fatter than her husband, which is saying a great deal. Not go to the bad? But perhaps a good many of us *do* go after all, though the badness is not of a sort which demands the attention of philanthropists, such, for instance, as Sir Guy Ormond.

Sir Guy Ormond is very strong on all social questions. He is also an Agnostic, and a Socialist of an advanced type. He regards the baronetcy conferred on his father, a benevolent mill-owner at Darlington, in the light of a burden and an indignity.

How do I come by my facts? I gleaned them from no less a person than Sir Guy himself, in the course of two dances and a hasty supper.

The limpid fluency of that young man's discourse is something astonishing. However, he is quite intelligent, in a stupid way, and quite good. Not an atom of vice in his composition, I should say, and not an atom of humour.

---

177. Levy's use of this derogatory term probably comes from Henry Fielding's (1707–1754) *The History of Tom Jones, a Foundling* (1749).

Mrs. Philip Shand called on me some days after the Westerleighs' party. She has that air of petulance, of protest, that I have often noticed in very rich people. They have got into the way of expecting too much.

> "You set a golden cage for happiness,
> And, lo, the uncertain creature flutters by
> To settle on your neighbour's hand, who has,
> Perhaps, no cage at all."

So much for the vanity of riches.

Mrs. Philip was polite enough in her vague, dumb way, and hoped we should meet that night at the Roehamptons' dinner party. We did meet, and Philip was told off to take me in. I accepted the fact coolly enough, and he bore himself towards me with an air of ostentatious restraint; but finding it not so effective as he had, perhaps, supposed, he dropped into one of his moralising moods, which, to do him justice, are rare.

Philip has his faults, but he is not a bore; yet, like most of his sex, he is not without possibilities in that direction. "In a civilisation like ours," went on Philip, between his mouthfuls of *quenelle*, "there can be no middle course. You must go with the tide or drift into some stagnant backwater and rot. It's the old story of survival of the fittest."

"Survival of the toughest," I interposed flippantly; but he continued: "If you want anything worth having, you must make for it and fight for it. If you don't get it for yourself, no one else will. Not that it is an unkind world. Quite the contrary. There is a great deal of kindness going about one way and another."

"Exactly," I answered; "but the best of us can only be benevolent by fits and starts; our own pains and pleasures, like the poor, are always with us. Under the influence of a whim or a passion, people will do a great deal for one another. But for thoroughgoing, untiring support of one's own interest, there is, after all, no one like oneself."

He looked at me, with an air of shocked and affectionate concern. "Don't," he said; "don't! It doesn't do for a woman to talk like that!"

After dinner, Mrs. Philip, evidently a dutiful wife, asked me to go with them next day to a private view at the Institute. I said yes without hesitation; and at the end of the evening Philip reminded me of the engagement. He had risen to say good night to me, and stood holding my hand, with no undue pressure, certainly, but not without a gentle reluctance to let it go.

I told you once, Philip, that I loved you, did I not? Not in words, it is true, but with perfect frankness, nevertheless. Perhaps, to put it very plainly, you think that I love you still.

But, indeed, you would be wrong.

Only, this thing I know: that life can hold no such moment in store for me as those bygone moments when my hand thrilled to yours; when our eyes flashed and lingered in mysterious meeting; when the air about us was tense with the unspoken and the unrevealed.

3.

The Shands called for me at the appointed time, and I drove with them to the Institute, where the usual private-view crowd was assembled.

As we were going in, I was attracted by the sight of two people on a bench overlooking the staircase.

The long head, and straight, tow-coloured hair; the pale face, equine profile, and earnest manner were unmistakable; it did not take me half a second to recognise Sir Guy Ormond. I recognised his companion also; a discontented-looking woman, eccentrically dressed. It was Medora Grey, the poetess.

Poor, poor Medora! Having enacted for a great many years, and entirely without success, the part of *jeune fille*, she has lately adopted that of *esprit fort*, and no doubt Sir Guy (simple soul!) affords her ready appreciation.

Heaven save me from the laurels of third-rate female celebrity! Unless she happens to be Patti or Lady Burdett-Coutts,[178] or Queen

178. The opera singer, Adelina Patti (1843–1919); Angela Georgina Burdett-Coutts (1814–1906) was a wealthy philanthropist (New, ed., *The Complete Novels*, 559 n. 47).

Elizabeth, there is only one way of success open to a woman: the way of marriage.

Sir Guy, unless my vanity be mistaken, looked as if he would very much like to join our party, but Medora had no intention of releasing him. No doubt she had schemes of bearing him back to Bedford Park, there to discuss bad cigarettes and questionable philanthropy in the shaded light of an aesthetic "den."

He *did* escape, however, a little later on, and joined us in the big room, when I soon found that he had quite as much to say about art as about philanthropy.

Philip's face began to display unmistakable signs of boredom and irritation, but, as for me, I listened and looked, put intelligent questions, and made brief but pertinent answers, which seemed to annoy Philip even more than the aesthetic discourse.

What, indeed, had become of Philip's magnanimity?

He fidgeted about me, changing from side to side, trying to attract my attention by various devices.

Presently Sir Guy and I strolled outside together, and stood leaning on the balustrade watching the people swarm up and down the great staircase.

Philip was soon at my elbow, wanting to know if I had had enough of it, in tones that admitted of but one reply. "I am quite ready to go," I said, and looked him full in the face with a sudden thrill of triumph and resolve.

Am I to witness yet further developments of that highly organised product, Mr. Shand?

Having introduced me to my first experience, is he about to initiate me into further knowledge of life and character, as seen under conditions of highly artificial civilisation?

Highly artificial? The Dog and the Manger[179] is an old-world story, adapted to quite a simple state of society – but I do myself too much honour!

179. Fable with ancient origins telling of a dog who refuses to allow other animals access to a manger to eat the hay, even though the dog has no plans to eat it (see New, ed., *The Complete Novels*, 559 n. 48).

Meanwhile, Sir Guy stood there pressing an invitation on the whole party of us for an At Home at Toynbee Hall.[180] Men of his type and Philip's are like oil and vinegar; the invitation, and the acceptance with which, after some demur, it was met, are, I think, significant.

"That prig!" said Philip in the carriage, later on.

"Poor Sir Guy!" I laughed lightly. I was in good spirits. It was no polite fiction when I told my hostess that I had thoroughly enjoyed myself.

4.

Sir Guy Ormond evidently admires me – so much so that a less experienced person might be inclined to jump at conclusions on the subject. But I know very well that a man does not go about the world with thirty thousand a year and a baronetcy without having some idea of his own value; and with all his high-flown theories, the son of the Darlington mill-owner has his share of shrewdness and caution. He is whimsical, too, and obstinate, like all men of his stamp; and having, moreover, such a passion for female society generally, must often, in all innocence, have roused unfounded hopes in the female breast particularly. Not that, accidental advantages apart, he is the sort of man that women naturally take to. Perhaps it is that he assumes towards them an attitude so few are capable of appreciating; he respects them.

As for me, I like him genuinely; he is such a good fellow; I wish sometimes that he were rather less so.

My room is full of blue books, pamphlets, and philosophical treatises. "Sesame and Lilies"[181] and Clifford's "Essays"[182] are hobnobbing on the table; the "Bitter Cry of Outcast London"[183] and a report

180. Set up by Henrietta Barnett (1851–1936) and Samuel Barnett (1844–1913) in 1884 in the East End of London to tackle endemic poverty.

181. Ruskin's *Sesame and Lilies* (1865).

182. William Kingdon Clifford's (1845–1879) *Lectures and Essays* (1879).

183. Andrew Mearns' anonymous pamphlet on poverty in London, published in 1883 (New, ed., *The Complete Novels*, 559 n. 50).

of the Democratic Federation[184] stand together on the shelf. This is an age of independence and side-saddles; but how often is woman doomed to ride pillion on a man's hobby-horse!

Philip stands by and notices everything with his quick eyes. And I – is it at the cost of dignity that I permit myself so much intimacy with Philip?

But Philip amuses me more than anyone I know; and I suppose that I amuse Philip – am sure of it, in fact – or he would have turned his back on me ages ago. But while I think of it, is it possible that in her mild, inarticulate fashion, Mrs. Philip is beginning to hate me? This must be seen to at once. I have no intention of playing a losing game a second time with Philip. Indeed, I am acquiring such skill with games generally that Philip begins to respect me as he never respected me before. Sometimes I think he is a little afraid of me, and goes so far as to doubt if he has done the best for himself after all.

We should have been a well-matched pair; between us we might have moved the world!

5.

In a world of surprises, there is perhaps nothing which astonishes us so much as our own feelings.

I have begun with a sententiousness worthy of Sir Guy himself, but my pinions refuse to sustain me at so giddy a height.

Let me, then, come down to facts.

The letter came on the 18th of June, by the first post. It is as well to be exact. I recognised the handwriting, and put it in my pocket unopened. When, in the privacy of my own room, I broke the seal, I found what I had half expected.

In eight closely written pages Sir Guy Ormond made me a formal offer of marriage.

184. Social Democratic Federation (SDF), founded in 1881 by the antisemitic Henry Mayers Hyndman (1842–1921); see Satnam Virdee, "Socialist Antisemitism and its Discontents in England, 1884–98," *Patterns of Prejudice* 51, no. 3–4 (2017): 356–73.

Wordy, egotistical, pompous, it was, in the main, an honest and a generous letter.

I read it once, twice, then sat staring mechanically at myself in the glass opposite.

It was the moment of my triumph; I had won my game; it only remained for me to stretch out my hand and claim the stakes.

The reflection of my face caught my vision; its expression was scarcely one of triumph. And surely there must be some mistake in the calendar, some trick in the sand and quicksilver; I was not twenty, with smooth cheeks – I was a hundred years old, and wrinkled!

Still I sat there staring, a dull dismay, a stony incredulity taking possession of me.

For gradually it was brought home to me that by no possibility could I accept Sir Guy's offer.

I will take no undue credit to myself; I had no choice in the matter; I simply could not do it!

6.

"Have you posted my letter, Célestine?"

"Yes, Mademoiselle; shall I put out your gown?"

"I am not going out tonight, after all."

Not to face Philip! Philip – this is the hardest part of all – who will think I have played my game and lost; who will undergo a mixed moment of disappointment and gratified pique as the state of the case dawns on him, then turn away with a shrug from a commonplace and uninteresting failure. These are mean thoughts! But have I ever pretended to magnanimity?

I am sorry for what I have just done – I shall be sorry for it all the days of my life!

A year hence, no doubt, I shall be capable not only of stalking, but also of killing my game; then, in all probability, there will be no game to kill.

I gave myself every chance; I waited a week; something stronger than myself withheld me from giving the answer I wished to give. I am defeated, a traitor to my own cause, having brought nothing but dishonour from the fray.

*****

Let me open the window, and lean out to the stars.

Stars, you have often seen me weep, but tonight I have no tears to shed.

Something falls to the ground with a crash.

Only some books of Sir Guy's – the poor books he is so fond of, and writes his name in with a flourish.

(I am not sure that there are not some tears left, after all! Yet, can there be much pathos over a person with thirty thousand a year?)

Let me lean my forehead against the cool window ledge, and hide my face from the stars.

Have I, too, been cruel? Have I also been the means of showing another human being the darker possibilities of his own soul?

Would it have been better, after all, to complete the wrong I had begun?

If I had loved you – but ah! My poor Sir Guy, that could never be, could never have been.

Here, with closed eyes and hidden face, and head bared to the night breeze, let me shut out thought.

The wind is soft and very sweet; there is no sound save the distant murmur of the Great City.

Black, black in its heart is the City; the blackness of man's heart is revealed in its huge, hideous struggle for existence.

Better be unfit and perish, than survive at such a cost.

*****

"No, thank you, Célestine. I will shut the window; and I shall not want you again tonight."

Essays

Contents

Junior Prize Review (1875)[1]

Aurora Leigh

A Poem In Blank Verse By Mrs. Browning

As a poet we see Woman in her most favourable light; her mind is better constituted for that refinement, that delicacy of touch which is so essential to poetry: and though she may lack the grandeur and the strength which characterize bards of the other sex, yet in her own peculiar genius she stands unrivalled. Elizabeth Barrett Browning comes foremost in the rank of women poets, not only in her own country but in all the world. Steadily advancing in her career she finally crowned her other efforts with the wonderful work which has contributed so largely to her fame – "Aurora Leigh," her masterpiece, and the subject of this paper. Its characterizing feature is boldness of opinion, and originality of thought and style (which however sometimes descend to affectation and mannerism). Mrs. Browning maintains that it is the duty of poets to "represent their age, not Charlemagne's;[2] this live, throbbing age," for, she continues, "King Arthur's self was commonplace to Lady Guinevere, and Lancelot[3] to

1. See Elizabeth Barrett Browning's *Aurora Leigh* (1857).
2. Charles the Great (747-814), Holy Roman Emperor.
3. The legend of King Arthur, his wife, Guinevere, and knight of the Round Table, Lancelot. The quotation is from *Aurora Leigh*.

minstrels seemed as flat as Fleet Street to our poets." The characters of this *novel in verse* are all distinctly drawn, finely coloured, and carefully worked out; in "Aurora" we have a proud, struggling, impulsive woman, caring for only two things, her art (she is a poet) and her love, which *pride* prevents her from acknowledging, even to herself, until after many years of trouble have elapsed. "Romney" is a fine portrait of a rigid and egotistical philanthropist; scorning everything beyond the path of duty he has marked out for himself, he labours under some delusive idea, which causes him to make a vain effort to unite the social classes in the persons of himself and "Marian Erle," who is intended as a representative of the lower (as Lord Howe and Lady Waldemar are of the higher) grades of life. There is a vein of shrewd satirical humour running through it, relieving the sombre character of the story. It is a task of no little difficulty to justly review such a work; to eulogise it (when its fame is so established) would be out of place; and to analyse it thoroughly requires much deep thought, for the woman of genius evidently intended her writings for him who takes the trouble to understand them, for which trouble he is amply rewarded.

Some of the Italian scenes are exquisitely, though simply, described; she possesses the rare power of bringing scenes and persons before the imagination with an expression, a line! Of one fault we must accuse the authoress – a very common one at the present time – that of introducing too many learned allusions, etc.; it is perhaps more excusable in a *woman* than in a *man*; for it is only natural she should wish to display what public opinion denies her sex – a classical education. Our short space forbids any further comment; but we must conclude by recommending "Aurora Leigh" to all who have not read it, as an interesting, improving, and graphic work of genius.

Junior Prize Essay (1876)

Essays On The Character Of David

Junior Prize Essay

Perhaps the essential element of David's character is its strong human interest, for, whilst we unquestioningly reverence Abraham and Moses, it is with David alone that we sympathise.[4] The whole tenor of his somewhat romantic life[5] is of itself calculated to awaken our interest: and we must also recognise the fact that, though one of the noblest of men, he was by no means faultless – vainglory, thoughtless cruelty,[6] and even disobedience to the God who had

4. The opening sentence hints that even at a young age, Levy had been imbued with the foundational ideals of German Reform Judaism, biblical criticism, and the historical-critical approach of the *Wissenschaft des Judentums* movement; note the distinction between "human interest" and unquestioning "reverence."
5. One of King Saul's courtiers describes David as (1 Samuel 16:18) "skilled in music; … a stalwart fellow and a warrior, sensible in speech, and handsome in appearance, and the LORD is with him."
6. In commanding Saul's army, David is so popular that "The women sang as they danced, and they chanted: Saul has slain his thousands; / David his tens of thousands!" (1 Samuel 18:7). As King, David defeats the Jebusites and in capturing Jerusalem orders: "'Those who attack the Jebusites shall … [strike down] the lame and the blind, who are hateful to David'" (2 Samuel 5:6–8); consequently, David defeats the Philistines, the Moabites, King Hadadezer of Zobah, the Edomites, Ammonites, and Amalekites (8:1–14).

done so much for him,[7] are among his most striking sins,[8] but these he atoned for, and repented with such a noble acknowledgment of wrong[9] that, like the dark shadows of a beautiful picture, they only seem to show up the whole. In every phase of David's career we note some new trait of his character which circumstance has called forth: the boy who one day risks his life for his flock,[10] and the next for his people,[11] with equal valour, less commands our esteem than the man forgiving the enemy who so deeply wronged him.[12] His friendship for Jonathan, too, shows the strong human affection of which he was capable.[13] In the Psalms, with their poetic piety and wonderful

---

7. In 1 Chronicles 21:1–2, "Satan arose against Israel and incited David to number Israel"; in response to David's calling for a census, God is "displeased about this matter and He struck Israel" (21:7).
8. With Bathsheba pregnant and David's hope that her husband, Uriah, would assume the child was his dashed, David arranged for him to be killed in battle, ensuring their consequent marriage (2 Samuel 11:4–27).
9. In facing God's wrath over the census, the punishment of "pestilence," and the prospect that Jerusalem might be destroyed, David issues a plea: "'Was it not I alone who ordered the numbering of the people? I alone am guilty, and have caused severe harm; but these sheep, what have they done? O LORD my God, let Your hand fall upon me and my father's house, and let not Your people be plagued!'" (1 Chronicles 21:14–17). David then goes on to establish "an altar to the Lord," invoking divine clemency (21:26–27).
10. In responding to Saul's doubts, David avows "Your servant has been tending his father's sheep, and if a lion or a bear came and carried off an animal from the flock, I would go after it and fight it and rescue it from its mouth." David then goes on to apply the same logic, invoking God's protection, to the "Philistine," Goliath (1 Samuel 17:33–37).
11. David, against all odds, defeats Goliath, "champion of the Philistine forces," by invoking God and utilising "sling and stone"; when Goliath is "dispatched," the Philistine army hastily retreats (1 Samuel 17:4, 46–51).
12. Most notably, having cornered Saul in a cave, David opts to "cut off the corner of Saul's cloak" and against the wishes of his soldiers refuses to harm "'the LORD's anointed'"; David then uses the piece of cloak to show Saul that he never intended to kill him, leading to reconciliation (1 Samuel 24:1–23).
13. 1 Samuel 18:1–5 states that "Jonathan's soul became bound up with the soul of David; Jonathan loved David as himself"; accordingly, Jonathan and David form

imagery, we are grieved to perceive a revengeful spirit, which would scarcely have been anticipated from the David of earlier years.[14]

His pathetic, child-like faith is decidedly the brightest spot in his character – to the darker ones have we already alluded, and in conclusion can only add that, faulty as he was, in the life of David we have one of the grandest moral lessons of Scripture.

---

a close "pact," with the former even donating his "cloak and tunic," "sword, bow, and belt" to David, consequently leading to a string of unparalleled military successes.

14. See, for example, Psalm 55, in which David begs: "Let Him incite death against them; / may they go down alive into Sheol!" (55:16); similarly, see Psalm 109 for David's plea: "May his days be few; / ... May his children be orphans, / his wife a widow. / May his children wander from their hovels, begging in search of [bread]" (109:8–10, *passim*).

Jewish Women and Women's Rights (1879)

1.

To The Editor Of The "Jewish Chronicle"

Sir, – Will you allow me to make a few remarks in your columns on a letter which appeared last week in the *Jewish Chronicle*, bearing on the subject of "Women's Rights"? Your correspondent (while owning himself ignorant of the full meaning of the term) starts with a deprecation, and, at the same time, desires a definition of it. His impression that, "what is claimed" is "perfect equality… with Man," is to a great extent a correct one: but, beyond this, he appears to have misconstrued the question.

Thus, he is mistaken in thinking that "coercion into marriage" (as he expresses it) is the great ground of complaint among women; it is rather the obstacles which are placed to hinder "from attaining higher culture," and "sharing in the sterner struggles of life," those women, who, from circumstance or temperament, do not marry. "Marriage," writes your correspondent, "has been defined in Parliament as the principal means of livelihood at present open to women"; some people might be inclined to regard this as a melancholy statement, with the hard fact of – I should not like to say how many – millions of surplus women (in the British Isles alone) staring us in the face. What is to become of this surplus? With regard to working-women, "ש" suggests, for "the higher classes" the "imparting of education" (in plain words, "governessing," a notoriously ill-paid drudgery, for which only peculiar minds are really fitted), and, "to a certain extent," the medical profession; which latter is barred and blocked to the sex (in this country) by about every means which the ingenuity of man could devise. Would it be "inconsistent with the reserve that the social experience of generations imagines," if the broad field of free competition were opened to both sexes? If woman be, indeed, "the weaker," she will not fail to "go to the wall." Without daring to make any positive assertion about such an unsettled question as the relative mental and physical powers of the Man and Woman, we can say that in those few cases where women have had equal chances of developing, the men have not always "beaten them in a canter." Caroline Herschell[15] and Jeanne Pascal[16] shared in the highest of their brother's calculations; Mrs. Somerville[17] (a self-taught genius, by the way) was ahead of many of the scientists of her day; since the London University Classes for Jurisprudence and Political Economy have been opened to both sexes, the traditionally weaker one has, in several instances, carried off the prizes; the first year that women had access to the Royal Academy School of Art, Miss Osborn[18] won the gold medal; of the eleven girls who went up for this year's London Matriculation, ten passed, and about half the boys failed; and we have, besides, to consider the great disadvantages under which most women labour, and the comparative smallness of the number of those who have, as yet, tried to cast off the yoke remaining from ages when physical power was almost always in the ascendant.

---

15. The German astronomer, Caroline Herschell (1750–1848).
16. According to Susan David Bernstein, Levy possibly refers here to a relation of the French mathematician, Blaise Pascal (1623–1662), though it is difficult to be sure (Bernstein, ed., *Reuben Sachs*, by Amy Levy (Peterborough: Broadview Editions, 2006), 172 n. 2). "Jewish Women and 'Women's Rights'" (both letters) are included in Bernstein's appendices, 171–5.
17. Scientist and polymath, Mary Fairfax Somerville (1780–1872); see Bernstein, ed., *Reuben Sachs*, 172 n. 3.
18. The artist, Emily Mary Osborn (1828–1925).

I would now touch upon another point of your correspondent's argument; following out his idea that "women have their sphere," he would condemn all those to whom "work is not a pecuniary necessity," to the cares of domestic life and the performance of works of charity. But I doubt if even the great thought of becoming in time a favourable specimen of the genus "maiden-aunt" would be sufficient to console many a restless, ambitions woman for the dreary performance of work for which she is quite unsuited, for the quenching of personal hopes for the development of her own intellect. To those who urge that she may find ample vent for herself in her own immediate circle, and with no definite aim in view, we point out the melancholy crowd of *femmes incomprises,* so characteristic of the age.

Of the third question on which "ש" touches, I have little to say, not having sufficiently considered it; but it might appear just, to some minds, that those who have to pay taxes should also have some voice in deciding by whom those taxes should be imposed. – Yours obediently,

Brighton
AMY LEVY

2.

To The Editor Of The "Jewish Chronicle"

Sir, – In your correspondent "ש's" letter of this week he has again, unfortunately, shown a misconception of the question at issue. I did not in a former communication, nor do I at present, assert the equality of the male and female intellect; it is so evidently a question which has yet to be proved, that it would be idle to discuss it, such discussion could be only theoretical. The three instances of great women which I quoted (from a host of others) were merely to show the development of which the female mind is actually capable: such cases are, naturally, exceptional (genius, unhappily, is not the rule), but they might be thought to add to the daily increasing mass of evidence that, with higher training than she has hitherto enjoyed, woman may reach the same intellectual standard as man. Nor do I see that by citing the cases of Jael,[19] Joan of Arc[20] and the Maid of Saragossa,[21] it has been proved that she has hitherto *not* been shut out from such training by the ascendance of physical power. The first instance is that of the murderess of a sleeping man; the second, that of a half-mad visionary transformed by the superstition of her age into an inspired being, is altogether exceptional – far more exceptional, indeed, than cases of women of literary or scientific genius; the third is too comparatively modern to affect the question at all.

Had it not been for your correspondent's remarks on the subject, I should hardly have touched on this part of the argument; it appears to me to have little to do with the practical part of the question, which is merely one of justice.

Following out his somewhat crude notions respecting the "sphere" and "mission" of women, "ש" hints at an ideal state of society, where man and woman have each their clearly defined functions, and are, in their mutual relations, like "perfect music unto noble words." Unfortunately, we do not live in Utopia; we have to deal with facts, not theories, and it is a great fact that there has sprung up a large class of intelligent, capable women who are willing and able to perform work from which they find themselves shut out by the tradition of ages – women, who are destitute of their "natural protectors," or whose aims lie outside the circle which convention has marked out for them. The growth of such a class seems to point to the higher development of woman, to the fact that she is beginning to wake up to the sense of her own responsibility as a human being. All that she claims is freedom of competition; and I was not aware that she had, as yet, had a chance of "proving her incapacity for entering upon

19. Biblical Jael who presents the dead Canaanite general, Sisera, to Barak, having driven a tent peg into his head (see Judges 4:17–22).
20. Heroine of the Hundred Years' War and national symbol of France, Joan of Arc (1412–1431).
21. Agustina Raimunda Maria Saragossa Domènech (1786–1857): Spanish national heroine during the Peninsula War.

a competitive struggle with man." That society is beginning to acknowledge the justice of her claims, the rapidly increasing innovations in her favour testify: witness the opening of degrees to women at the London University, the establishment of Newnham Hall and Girton College, etc. I do not deny that your correspondent's ideal of woman is a noble one, nor that "there are thousands of women contented with their lot"; but we must not allow ourselves to be carried away by the beauty of the ideal from the claims of the actual. Because it is a grand and beautiful thing that woman should spend her life in self-sacrifice, we have no right to compel all women to do so, to regard as social outcasts those members of the sex who do not work in the old grooves. Your correspondent himself owns that we never hear of *un homme incompris*. This acknowledgment strengthens my argument; it is, I believe, the sense of cramped and restrained energies (energies which may lie in other directions than the domestic) which has given rise to the large class of *femmes incomprises*. I repeat the term – for me it has no unpleasant associations.

I fear that "ש" has fallen into the female error (as he considers it) of "letting out the gist of his letter" at its conclusion. When he alludes to women who are "delightful companions to men, and charming members of society, by reason of culture and intelligence," he appears to think that such have reached the whole aim and end of female education; he, like many others, has

> "Misconceived the question like a man
> Who sees a woman as the complement
> Of his sex, merely 'He' forgets too much.
> That every creature, female as the male,
> Stands single in responsible act and thought
> As also in birth and death."[22]

Yours obediently,
AMY LEVY
Brighton.

22. From Barrett Browning's *Aurora Leigh*.

Newnham College (1881)[23]

1.

The Daily Life

The Cantab revisiting his university will be surprised to see on what a few years ago was a lonely country road, turning off somewhere near the back of King's College, two imposing red-brick buildings, which stand exactly facing one another in all the ascetic glory of "Queen Anne" architecture. These buildings are the North and South Halls, and together make up Newnham College, the unromantic realisation of the Ladies' College, which Tennyson first shadowed forth in his "Princess."[24] Their history can be given in a few words, which we quote from the "Newnham College Calendar," for 1880: – "The North and South Halls are built at Newnham on sites of two acres and a half and two acres respectively. Together they give accommodation for the principal and vice-principal, resident lecturers, and about seventy students. Each student has one room, which serves both as a bedroom and study, and in each house there are a library, a dining hall, and other common rooms. The buildings of the North Hall include lecture rooms. The laboratory and gymnasium of the South Hall are open to all students of the college. Newnham Hall, now called the South Hall of Newnham College, was opened under

---

23. Reprinted with permission of The Camellia Collections.
24. Alfred, Lord Tennyson's poem, *The Princess* (1847).

the care of Miss Clough[25] in 1875. In 1879 it was resolved to build a second house, which was opened in October 1880. Mrs. Henry Sidgwick[26] has undertaken the care of the North Hall, with the office of vice-principal of Newnham College."

Here, then, in these two buildings, one tall and smoke-darkened, the other two-storied, and looking as though it had just emerged from a box of Nuremberg toys, the woman undergraduate (as she loves to call herself, though she has no legal university standing) works and plays, hopes and despairs, through the few years of her studentship.

Perhaps we shall convey the best idea of the life of a Newnham student by closely following her through a day's work.

For all but the abnormally industrious, the day begins with breakfast, which is at eight o'clock. Woe betide the sleepy student who comes down late; she may consider herself lucky if she secures enough bread and coffee to satisfy her; such things as marmalade, bacon and toast will have been seized by the early risers, for these fair girl (under) graduates are a predatory horde, and believe in the principle of "first come first served." After breakfast people generally lounge, play tennis (each hall has a large court), or read the papers till nine. Lecture and "reading" go on till luncheon, an informal meal, the time of which changes according to that of the lectures.

After luncheon is the time for general idleness; tennis, shopping, and lounging are favoured even by the most industrious students. At three o'clock the gong sounds for tea, but the students often prefer to drink it in one another's rooms. After tea those who have not lecture "read" till dinner, excepting a few, who, being musical, sentimental, or merely indolent, stroll down to King's Chapel to hear the beautiful evening service in the grand old building.

Dinner is at 6:30, when everybody is supposed to be present. The interval between dinner and evening tea is a time specially marked out for recreation. Sometimes the five little dining tables are pushed

---

25. Anne Clough (1820–1892), first Principal of Newnham College, 1871–1892.

26. Eleanor Mildred Sidgwick (1845–1936), second Principal of Newnham College, 1892–1910.

against the wall, and everyone dances to the sound of the piano specially stationed in the corner of the dining hall. "Rather a slow affair – girls dancing among themselves!" we imagine some scarce-fledged cavalier saying, who declares in the same breath that the life is worried out of him with invitations to "hops." But, dear sir, let us assure you, in spite of the absence of you and your confrères, the "girls" manage to enjoy themselves very much.

Waltzing is, perhaps, not so much practiced as the more barbaric dances, such as "mazourkas," "schottisches," and even "reels." A few dance really well, but all are zealous; and spectacled learning – throwing aside her pen – "pirouettes" and "chassées" with all her heart.

"Reading" is resumed from eight till ten. From ten till eleven is the social hour, when "cocoa-parties," Shakspere[27] readings, etc., are the order of the day, and the students grow sentimental, speculative, or just sleepy, over one another's fires.

So much for six days of the week; Sunday has a distinct character of its own.

Each "woman" wakes with a dim sense of "something going to happen," till a certain sudden aroma wafted in through the ventilator above the door dispels the pleasant "dimness," and reminds her that it is Sunday, and that there are sausages for breakfast. The morning is taken up with church and chapel; each student is expected to have a regular place of worship and to inform the principal of her hall respecting it. At two o'clock comes dinner – rather an infliction, for civilized people always find it a little hard to sit down to hot mutton and hot tart in broad daylight. Sunday afternoon is generally taken up with walking, tea parties, visits, etc. Most people go again to church in the evening, and a cold supper is served at eight. So ends a very pleasant day.

Of course this sketch of Newnham life is very rough and general. Each student or set of students has her or its separate work, pleasures, etc., and each member of the college probably leaves it with a different impression. Nor have we here space to more than allude to the many

27. William Shakespeare; Levy's spelling was vogue for the period and considered more genuine on the basis of historical documents.

"societies" which exist in both halls, and which are such a marked feature of college life. The most important of these is the United Debate Club, composed of all the students of the college, which meets twice a term (in the North and South Halls alternately) to discuss questions of social and political interest. In another article we hope to give a sketch of the Newnham student, and an account of her work.

2.

The Students

I am aware that there exists no little curiosity concerning the woman undergraduate, and that all sorts of strange theories are afloat about her, from that of the lady who wished that Newnham students "didn't smoke and drink so much *in the morning(!)*" downwards. She has been pictured alternately as red-nosed, blue-spectacled, and aggressive, as golden-haired, smiling, and fond of flirtation; as a sort of "overground" incapable,[28] as a female Admirable Crichton;[29] but I have observed all these counterfeit presentments of her to have one common attribute – that of vast learning from Mr. du Maurier's charming Girtonians deciphering their Greek valentine[30] to Mortimer Collins's "Chloe," who pathetically asks permission to study the theory of tides in the evening if she condescends to play croquet with the more frivolous members of her sex in the daytime:

> ".... at night 'tis no great boon;
> Let me study how the moon
> Sways the surf!"[31]

---

28. Probably refers to Edward Bulwer-Lytton's (1803–1873) *The Coming Race* (1871).
29. James Crichton.
30. Refers to a *Punch* cartoon by George du Maurier entitled: "St. Valentine's Day at Girton."
31. From Edward James Mortimer Collins' (1827–1876) poem, "Chloe M.A.," in *The Inn of Strange Meetings* (1876).

At the risk of disappointing my readers, I must say that I have never observed anything very abnormal about the Newnham student; she is perhaps, on the whole, a little better read, a little more capable of grasping the problems of life than young ladies whose minds are wholly taken up with the last ball and the newest fashion; but I have never heard her "humming binomial theorem," nor seen her drinking anything stronger than tea at college parties.

But as generalities are mostly idle, and always unsatisfactory, I will now proceed to roughly classify some of the "undergraduates" as far as in me lies.

Of course there is a large element of downright, business-like people, who come up with their eyes fixed on one goal – a good certificate – and when they have attained it they go their way rejoicing, as they would have done if their place of study had been Bradford or Leeds, instead of this rich, beautiful Cambridge, with its stately grandeur, its glorious memories, and its ever-flowing stream of fresh young life.

Then there is the dilettante student, who chiefly spends her time in decorating her room and devising picturesque costumes. She generally patronises lectures on art and moral science, and goes about imbibing (as she fondly believes) "general culture" by some easy and subtle process. She is rather a rare specimen, but by no means an unpleasant one, as she generally has the most comfortable room, the choicest books, and is always ready to converse with and console poor "over-ground" mortals.[32]

A great number of the students are girls who have come up straight from school, eager for work and play – energetic alike in lecture room, tennis court, and gymnasium – they may be compared to average male undergraduates. These are only a few types of students; it is impossible to enumerate the various elements which go to make up the mass of Newnham collegians. All students are alike zealous in the decoration of their rooms, and it is rather interesting to notice how these rooms get

32. See above, footnote 28.

to partake of the nature of their owners. It is not difficult, for instance, to roughly determine the state of mind of a "woman" who adorns her chairs with Berlin-wool antimacassars, or her walls with coloured prints from the *Graphic*, nor of her whose boots and towels, papers and provisions are strewn about in sublime confusion. On the whole, however, the rooms are fairly neat and pretty, and though a casual observer might be chiefly struck by their strong family resemblance, the deeper critic will delight to mark the signs of individuality among them, to cull the unlikeness from the likeness. There is a general leaning towards Japanese wares of all sorts, particularly fans, trays, and blue pots, which are cheap, and impart an "aesthetic" air. One or two of Mr. Burne-Jones's[33] pictures, too, seem to be great favourites, for one meets them on a good many walls. As for books, the Brownings[34] appear on more than one set of shelves, and so does Heine's "Buch der Lieder,"[35] while "C.S.C.'s" imitable "Fly Leaves"[36] are held in great honour. Peacock's feathers abound, and so do portraits of Irving,[37] Ellen Terry[38] and Shelley.[39] In the North Hall the as yet unparalleled walls afford great scope to people with a turn for mural decoration, and throughout the college ingenuity is taxed to its utmost to supress all signs of the fact that the pleasant sitting rooms perform a double function, and are mere prosaic bedrooms at night. The North Hall students are more fortunate [than their] neighbours over the way, for their furniture has been chosen with a careful eye; chintz covers turn the low, wooden beds into sofas in the daytime, while jug and basin lurk coyly in a dainty little cabinet which no one would suspect of being a subtle combination of wash-handstand and toilet table; delightful old brass-handled bureaux serve the threefold

33. Edward Burne-Jones.
34. Robert Browning and Elizabeth Barrett Browning.
35. Heinrich Heine's *Buch der Lieder*.
36. Charles Stuart Calverley's (1831–1884) *Fly Leaves* (1872).
37. Actor, Henry Irving.
38. Actress, Alice Ellen Terry (1847–1928). Terry was painted by, among others, George Frederic Watts, who she was briefly married to; see, for example, "Choosing," "Ophelia," etc.
39. Percy Bysshe Shelley.

purpose of wardrobe, desk and writing table. But the South Hall was furnished with less regard for the artistic tendencies of the "cultured" Newnhamite, and many an aesthetic soul has been wrung to its core by the discovery of a full-grown chest of drawers (white handles, light-painted wood and all!) in its room.

It (the chest, not the soul), may be covered with chintz; it may be concealed with screens, but its possessor will always have an uneasy consciousness of its presence.

Another point on which the Newnhamite prides herself is her "parties," and these are of various kinds. There is the formal afternoon tea, when strangers are bidden within the sacred precincts of the college; there is the evening revel, when kindred spirits gather round the cocoa-pot and talk about their work and "their souls;" there is the orange party, which would have terribly shocked the good ladies of Cranford;[40] and lastly the delicious jam party, where learned fair ones grow merry over alarming quantities of jam and biscuits.

Just now, a spirit of revelry pervades the college, for only last Thursday did we hear the good news that the Senate had decided (by an immense majority) to grant women the right of being examined by the University and of having their names published in the class lists. There had been some fear among us before the voting, for it had been rumoured that the strength of the opposition was very great, and when the good news came we were wild with excitement. Both halls were illuminated at night, and the college danced all the evening at the North Hall. Next week I hope to give some account of the work of the students.

40. Refers to Elizabeth Gaskell's (1810–1865) novel, *Cranford* (1853).

3.

"Lecture"

Since last week a great change has come over the spirit of the Newnham student's dream. Hitherto there has been no fixed course of study, and people have worked at their pet subjects unhaunted by "Paley,"[41] "Extras," and the other torments of a Cambridge undergraduate's life. But it was decreed in the Senate House on that glorious Thursday, of which everyone has heard by now, that no woman should be examined in the Tripos papers who had not previously passed the "Little Go," or obtained an honour certificate in the Cambridge Higher Local Examinations, passing in Groups C and B (mathematics and languages). So this term mathematical classes have been organised for unhappy people whose souls are yearning for Plato or Mill;[42] and classical classes for those devoted to "the hard-grained Muses of the cube and square." Everything seems upside-down; embryo wranglers go about feverishly murmuring, "ὁ, ἡ, Τὸ," and youthful Porsons[43] are trying to realise that the angles at one base of an isosceles triangle are equal, as are also the angles at the other sides of the base if "those sides" be "produced!" Lectures are, generally speaking, delivered in the three spacious lecture rooms on the right wing of the North Hall; some college lectures have been lately thrown open to ladies, who, however, may not attend them unchaperoned.

At the University lectures the audience is principally made up of members of the fair sex – both "town and gown" – who by tacit arrangement do not sit in the same part of the room as the men.

The Newnham College lecturers are chiefly those fellows of colleges – some of them men of mark in the world of learning – who take an interest in the cause of the higher education of women, though during the last few years lecturers have arisen from among the women themselves. Miss Scott,[44] of Girton, teaches mathematics, and there

41. Philosopher, William Paley (1743–1805).
42. John Stuart Mill.
43. Refers to classical scholar, Richard Porson (1759–1808).
44. Mathematician, Charlotte Scott (1858–1931).

are resident lady-'ecturers on classics, history, and moral science, and two ladies to give assistance in natural science.

To give an idea of how the work of teaching is carried on, I will briefly describe a lecture on some of the principal subjects, beginning with classics. It is a Greek class, and about fifteen or sixteen young women have assembled to hear a lecture on the "Antigone."[45] The lecturer, after giving back corrected "prose" papers to their respective writers, calls upon the members of the class in turn to construe, say, ten or twelve lines apiece of the play.

Questions are put, and notes given on parsing, syntax, corrupt passages, etc., and every line is carefully gone over by the lecturer himself. The characteristic of Cambridge scholarship is "accuracy" (as that of Oxford scholarship is "elegance"), and no eccentricity or complicatedness in a turn of phrase, however minute, is allowed to pass unnoticed. Sometimes one is irresistibly reminded of Mr. Browning's grammarian, who

> "Properly based *o u n*, and
> Gave us the doctrine of the enclitic *De*;"[46]

Or of the old scholar who on his deathbed regretted that he had not devoted himself to the dative case!

In many of the lectures, however, there is a happy mingling of the "soul" and "body" of the subject.

Mathematical lecturers demonstrate on the blackboard to their pupils, discuss papers, and set problems to be solved in class, as indeed is the custom of mathematical lecturers all the world over. In such subjects as history and the various branches of moral science connected discourses are delivered, and examination and essay papers are set.

Natural science people spend a great deal of their time in practical work at the college and Cavendish laboratories, and the Woodwardian Museum. Lectures rarely exceed an hour in length, though students often work for many hours together at the laboratory.

45. Antigone, daughter of Oedipus in Greek mythology.

46. From Robert Browning's poem, "A Grammarian's Funeral" (albeit misquoted).

Besides lectures, a good deal of private coaching goes on for the more advanced students, especially for those whose triposes are approaching; two or three people often sharing a "coach" between them.

The number of hours in the day given up to working varies according to the health, inclination and powers of the students. Six hours' hard work is reckoned a very fair average, though some people get through a great deal in four, and others, again, sit at their books for eight or nine hours a day. There was once an unhappy student who worked for two years at the rate of ten hours per diem, and twice failed to pass group A of the Higher Local Examination – and no wonder! "Fresh women" have rather a tendency to work late at night, but they soon find out the mistake of the plan, and, speaking generally, I may say that work does not go on after ten o'clock p.m., or begin later than nine a.m.

Students, as a rule, find it both more pleasant and more advantageous to work in twos and threes, and it is wonderful what mirth can be got out of the driest subjects when this is done; I actually saw two people sitting convulsed over Caesar's "De Bello Gallico"[47] the other day, which, I confess, surprised me a little, as I had never before learnt to look at the bald Roman in the light of a humourist.

There are several college societies of an "improving" nature which fulfil their functions by no means despicably, such as German clubs, "Shakespere[48] readings," etc., and with their mention I must bring to an end these brief and desultory remarks on a subject worthier of a more skilful pen than mine.

All I have attempted to do is to point out the general aspect of things as they are at Newnham College. To have any adequate idea of the influences, the advantages, the delights of the place, one must be a student, and a student of at least a year's standing; to fully appreciate them one must know them for many years.

(– *x.*)

---

47. Julius Caesar's commentary on the Gallic Wars.

48. See above footnote 27; Levy's spelling changes here from the earlier "Shakspere" to "Shakespere."

James Thomson: A Minor Poet (1883)

1.

A few months ago there died very miserably in London a poet called James Thomson. He was neither the idol of a literary clique nor the darling of society's drawing rooms; he was only a poet of wonderful originality and power, and his death created but little stir.

There is nothing very remarkable in this; Homer,[49] we know, had to beg his bread; contemporary cavaliers held Milton[50] not too highly; and I cannot claim for James Thomson the genius of a Homer or a Milton. He is distinctly what in our loose phraseology we call a minor poet; no prophet, standing above and outside things, to whom all sides of a truth (more or less foreshortened, certainly) are visible; but a passionately subjective being, with intense eyes fixed on one side of the solid polygon of truth, and realising that one side with a fervour and intensity to which the philosopher with his birdseye view rarely attains.

Had circumstances been otherwise, I cannot say what might have been the development of a nature so large and strong; with due allowance of sunshine, who knows what fruit might have ripened on a soil so rich and deep? But James Thomson was a poor Scotchman, of humble origin, of straightened means, with every social disadvantage. From first to last, his life was a bitter and sordid struggle; the Fates

49. Homer, ancient Greek poet.
50. John Milton (1608–1674), poet renowned for *Paradise Lost* (1667).

had given him to fight one of the dreariest, weariest fights in which man has ever drawn sword. The Fates were cruel; but the result of their cruelty is a product so moving, so wonderful, so unique, that we do not cry out against them; rather are we dumb before the horrible complexity of their workings.

James Thomson is essentially the poet of mood; he has symbolised, as no poet has done before him, a certain phase of modern feeling, I was going to say of modern pessimism, but the word scarcely covers the sense.

"The City of Dreadful Night,"[51] his masterpiece, as it is a poem quite unique in our literature, stands forth as the very sign and symbol of that attitude of mind which we call Weltschmerz, Pessimism, what you will; *i.e.*, the almost perfect expression of a form of mental suffering which I can convey by no other means than by the use of a very awkward figure – by calling it "grey pain," "the insufferable inane" which makes a man long for the "positive pain." Most of us at some time or other of our lives have wandered in the City of Dreadful Night; the shadowy forms, the dim streets, the monotonous tones are familiar to us; but to those who have never trod its streets, the poet's words can be little else than "a tale of little meaning tho' the words are strong."

> "If any cares for the weak words here written,
> It must be someone desolate, fate-smitten.....
> Yes, here and there some weary wanderer
> In that same city of tremendous night,
> Will understand the speech, and feel a stir
> Of fellowship in all disastrous flight."

The poet recognises his own limits. These limits, it may be objected, are very narrow. He dwells on a view of things which is morbid, nay false, which does not exist for the perfectly healthy human being.

51. For the full version see Thomson's *The City of Dreadful Night and Other Poems* (London: Reeves and Turner, 1880), 1–55.

But philosophy teaches us that all things are as real as one another, and as unreal.

> *"ὁρῶ γὰρ ἡμᾶς οὐδὲν ὄντας ἄλλο πλὴν*
> *εἴδωλ' ὅσοιπερ ζῶμεν ἢ κούφην σκιάν."*[52]

The fact that such a state of mind exists is enough; it is one of the phenomena of our world, as true, as false, as worthy, as unworthy of consideration as any other:

> "For life is but a dream, whose shapes return,
> Some frequently, some seldom, some by night,
> Some by day, some night and day; we learn,
> While all things change and many vanish quite,
> In their recurrence with recurrent changes
> A certain seeming order; where this ranges
> We count things real." – *City of Dreadful Night*

The city, with its dark lagoon, its waste of glistening marshes, its boundary where "rolls the shipless sea's unrest," its vast unruined streets where the lamps always burn tho' there is no light in the houses, rises before us, a picture distinct, real in itself, real in the force of its symbolic meaning. The wanderer goes down into the city; all is dim and shadowy; the dismal inhabitants, whose faces are "like to tragic masks of stone," are few and far between, holding little intercourse with one another, communing each man with himself, "for their woe broods maddening inwardly and scorns to wreak itself abroad." The wanderer follows in the footsteps of one sad being who appears to be walking with some intent, and presently stands successively before the spots where Faith and Hope and Love have died. Then the perplexed

52. From Sophocles' *Ajax*; Melvyn New, using the Loeb Classical Library's version, translated the passage as follows: "'Alas! We are living mortals, what are we / But phantoms all or unsubstantial shades'" (see *The Complete Novels and Selected Writings of Amy Levy 1861–1889* (Gainesville: University Press of Florida, 1993), 560 n. 2). Levy's original source was probably R. C. Jebb's *Sophocles: The Ajax* (London: Rivingtons, c. 1880), 23; this item has been used to inform the text.

question escapes him: "When Faith and Love and Hope are dead indeed, can life still live?"

The answer is a striking example of the wonderful blending of sound and meaning, of outward and inward sense, which marks the poem.

> "As one whom his intense thought overpowers,
> He answered coldly; 'Take a watch, erase
> The signs and figures of the circling hours:
> Detach the hands, remove the dial face;
> The works proceed until run down: altho'
> Bereft of purpose, void of use, still go.'"

The wanderer passes on, leaving his guide pursuing the self-same dismal round, and makes his way to a spacious square (the insistence on the great size of the city is noteworthy) where a man is standing alone and declaiming aloud with mighty gestures.

"No hope can have no fear" is the text of the speech; the lonely soul can go on its way indifferent, hardened, through the glooms and terrors of this world; it is only when love comes that death and the fear of death can move and sway us. I quote one of the earlier verses of this tragic recital:

> "As I came through the desert thus it was:
> As I came through the desert, eyes of fire
> Glared at me, throbbing with a starved desire;
> The hoarse, and heavy, and carnivorous breath
> Was hot upon me from deep jaws of death;
> Sharp claws, swift talons, fleshless fingers cold
> Plucked at me from the bushes, tried to hold:
> But I strode on austere,
> No hope could have no fear."

The wanderer goes on his way finding everywhere the same brooding shadow of nameless horror. Hell itself is eagerly sought, a much-desired goal, as a refuge from the void agony of the city. He makes his way into a vast cathedral, where a preacher is addressing the shadowy multitude with words of good cheer. Yes, here in the City of Dreadful Night these are good tidings that he brings: there is no God; no "fiend with names Divine" made and tortured us; "we bow down to the universal laws"; there is no life beyond the grave, and each man is free to end his life at will.

Silence follows the speaker's words; then suddenly breaks forth a shrill and terrible cry:

> "In all eternity I had one chance,
> One few years' term of gracious human life,
> The splendour of the intellect's advance,
> The sweetness of the home with babes and wife.
>
> The social pleasures with their genial wit,
> The fascination of the worlds of art,
> The glories of the worlds of nature lit
> By large imagination's glowing heart....
>
> All the sublime prerogatives of man....
>
> This chance was never offered me before,
> For me the infinite Past is blank and dumb,
> This chance recurrent never, never more,
> Blank, blank for me, the infinite to-come;
> And this sole chance was frustrate from my birth,
> A mockery, a delusion."

There is no mistaking such writing as this; it goes to the very heart of things; it is for all time and all humanity.

I will not attempt to follow further the course of the poem. The passage which closes it on Dürer's "Melancolia"[53] is worthy of its text; I can say no more.

The value of the poem does not lie in isolated passages, in pregnant lines which catch the ear and eye and linger in the memory; it is as a complete conception, as a marvellously truthful expression of what

53. Albrecht Dürer's engraving, the figure of which is symbolic of "Melancolia."

it is almost impossible to express at all, that we must value it. And the truthfulness is none the less that it has been expressed to a great extent by means of symbols; the nature of the subject is such that it is only by resorting to such means that it can be adequately represented. Mood, seen through the medium of such draughtsmanship and painter's skill, is no longer a dream, a shadow which the sunbeams shall disperse, but one side of a truth.

The City of Dreadful Night is always standing; ceaselessly one or other human soul visits and revisits the graves of Faith and Hope and Love; ceaselessly in the vast cathedral does the preacher give forth his good tidings to that shadowy congregation, and ever and anon rises up the shrill sound of agonised protest from their midst.

From the aesthetic point of view this poem is the consummation of James Thomson's art; but there is much work of his full of infinite possibilities and half-frustrated fulfilment to which the student of human nature will turn with ever greater interest. For the nature of James Thomson was so wide and rich, his intellect so quick and far reaching, and there is, moreover, such great chastity of thought, such large nobleness about the man. Here is no mere poetic weakling kicking against the pricks, but a great human soul, horribly vital and sensitive in all its parts, struggling with a great agony.

2.

From Homer downwards poets have received but sorry treatment at the hands of the Fates, and James Thomson's life was a terribly hard one even for a poet. Here was a man of great powers, of great passions, hemmed in and thwarted on every side by circumstances petty in themselves, but, like Mercutio's wound,[54] "enough." It was many years before he could publish the volume containing the City of Dreadful Night, for the prosaic reason of want of money. His considerable

54. Character in Shakespeare's *Romeo and Juliet.*

knowledge of Italian, German, and Spanish were acquired painfully and in after life, and yet he has caught the spirit of his spiritual kinsmen Heine and of Leopardi,[55] as no other poet has succeeded in doing.

"Only once," says one of his friends, "did I see Thomson smile with purely personal pleasure. It was when he received a letter beginning 'dear fellow-poet,' and signed 'George Eliot.' I never thought there was a spark of vanity in him till then."

"The talent," says Emerson, "sucks the substance."[56] Such a talent as that of James Thomson must have been a heavy burden for any but the strongest to bear under the most favourable circumstances; and when we consider the dark and narrow circumstances of his lonely life we can only stand aghast. For, if one comes to think of it, it is appalling what infinite and exquisite anguish can be suffered by a single human being who is perhaps sitting quietly in his chair before us, or crosses our path in the sunny street and fields. The human organism is so complex; there are so many strings to vibrate to the touch of pain; the body and soul of man are such perfect pain-conductors. And all through the work of James Thomson we hear one note, one cry, muffled sometimes, but always there; a passionate, hungry cry for life, for the things of this human, flesh and blood life; for love and praise, for mere sunlight and sun's warmth.

> "Sweet is to sing, but believe me this,
> Lips only sing when they cannot kiss."[57]

No, this is not the highest utterance, the word of the great artist struggling towards completion; rather is it the under, coarser cry of the imperfect human being, crushed beneath a load which he is not formed to bear.

---

55. Giacomo Leopardi (1798–1837), Italian philosopher and poet.
56. The quotation is from Ralph Waldo Emerson's (1803–1882) "The Superlative," in volume ten, *Lectures and Biographical Sketches*, in *The Works of Ralph Waldo Emerson* (1883).
57. From Thomson's "Art"; see *The City of Dreadful Night*, 131–3.

> "Statues and pictures and art may be grand,
> But they are not the life for which they stand,"[58]

he sings; and Grillparzer, saddest of poets, whose substance the talent sucked like a very vampire, strikes the same note when he makes his Sappho say: "*Und Leben ist ja noch des Lebens höchstes Ziel.*"[59]

In the two groups of lyrics, "Sunday at Hampstead" and "Sunday up the River,"[60] this intensely human side of the poet comes out in a marked degree; the verses, which show distinctly his kinship with Heine, are so full of sunshine and beauty and a most exquisite love. And here I would remark that as regards love James Thomson desired only the best. In youth he loved a woman. She died early, and he loved her memory till the end of his own life. There is a little poem called "Mater Tenebrarum,"[61] not very remarkable for artistic beauty, in which the poet lies sleepless on his bed at night "famished with an uttermost famine for love," which is startling with excess of truth, absolutely rough with pain; we seem to see the blood and sweat on the page as we read.

In the poem called "Our Ladies of Death," the poet stands aloof from the strife; the weary nerves and muscles are for a while relaxed; he looks around with the wide, sad gaze of deeper knowledge, and asks for nothing save perfect, dreamless rest. It is no longer the passionate rebel against fate, stung to agony by the thousand petty shafts of circumstance, who is speaking; for a moment a voice stronger and fuller issues from the weary lips. Only a few months ago the group gathered round James Thomson's grave and heard these words, the utterance of him they mourned, read out in the dreary graveyard.

---

58. From "Art."
59. From Franz Grillparzer's *Sappho* (1818); see Levy's "From Grillparzer's Sappho" (pp. 556–7).
60. For the poems, "Sunday at Hampstead" and "Sunday up the River," see *The City of Dreadful Night*, 78–94, 95–116.
61. For "Mater Tenebrarum" see Bertram Dobell, ed., *The Poetical Works of James Thomson: The City of Dreadful Night*, Volume II, by James Thomson (London: Reeves and Turner, 1895), 388–90.

> "Weary of erring in this desert life,
> Weary of hoping hopes forever vain,
> Weary of struggling in all-sterile strife,
> Weary of thought which maketh nothing plain,
> I close my eyes and calm my panting breath,
> And pray to thee, O ever-quiet Death,
> To come and soothe away my bitter pain."[62]

The rest, so long sought, so long desired, had come at last.

And for us, what is there for us to do now that the great agony is over? We read the books of the dead man, close them, and turn away. They are books over which one wrings the hands in despair. There is so much and yet so little. As we read them, the old question, the old plaint rises to our lips:

> "Who shall change with tears and thanksgivings
> The mystery of the cruelty of things?"[63]

But there is another question, less vast and vague, though perhaps not much easier to answer, which must occur to us at the same time. How comes it that in a day like our own, when the shrill, small voices of a legion of bepraised versifiers are heard all around – how comes it that this man of such large powers, such truth, such force of passion and intellect, such originality, should have been entirely overlooked for the greater part of his life, and even at its close so scantily recognised? Certainly he lacked one graceful finish of our latter-day bards; the pretty modern-classical trick, the prettier trick of old-French forms were unknown to him. We know that the mingled odours of livery-stables and surgery, said to linger about Keats,[64] have stunk in

62. From Thomson's "To Our Ladies of Death"; see *The City of Dreadful Night,* 56–66.

63. New speculated that this quotation was taken from a "Greek tragedy" (*The Complete Novels,* 560 n. 11), but it looks to be a misquotation of Algernon Charles Swinburne's poem, "Anactoria," a woman actually mentioned in Sappho's Fragment 16; see also Swinburne's "Sapphics."

64. John Keats.

the nostrils of one fastidious critic. James Thomson, says report, did not speak the Queen's English with the precision that one would desire; it is certain that he began life as an army schoolmaster, and never rose to be anything higher than a commis-voyageur. And it is certain also that here and there in his verse (and very often in his prose) he breaks out into absolute vulgarity – into a nudity of expression which he has neither the wit nor the taste to drape in the garb of ancient Greece or mediaeval France.

Rough and unequal he certainly is, but that he understood the meaning of perfect work he has shown us in the few gem-like translations from Heine,[65] and in some of his own lyrics, written in Heine's vein. And the weird, powerful poem, "In the Room,"[66] is almost perfect as it stands.

But even his warmest admirers cannot claim for James Thomson a light touch, a fine taste, a delicate wit. "When he laughs," says one critic, "it is a guffaw." To tell the truth, he is always terribly in earnest. The hot-house emotions of "culture" are entirely unknown to him, and I cannot help thinking that it is because of this very earnestness, this absolute truthfulness of feeling and expression, that James Thomson will take a recognised place among our poets, when the mass of our minor bards shall have been consigned by a ruthless posterity to oblivion.

James Thomson, as we know, died miserably. Respectable people shook their heads over him in death, as they had done in life. It was not to be expected that they could feel much sorrow for a man who, it was averred, had drunk himself to death.

But his few friends speak of the genial and loving spirit; the wit, the chastity, the modesty and tenderness of the dead man. To us,

---

65. For the translations of Heine, see "Attempts at Translation from Heine," in *The City of Dreadful Night*, 163–84, and "Translations from Heine" in John Robertson, ed., *Poems, Essays, and Fragments*, by James Thomson (London: A. & H. Bradlaugh Bonner, 1892), 55–71; see also in the same volume, "How Heine Forewarned France," 196–201.

66. For "In the Room," see *The City of Dreadful Night*, 67–77.

who never saw his face nor touched his living hand, his image stands out large and clear, unutterably tragic: the image of a great mind and a great soul thwarted in their development by circumstance; of a nature struggling with itself and Fate; of an existence doomed to bear a twofold burden.

Paul Heyse (1883)

To The Editor Of The "Jewish Chronicle"

Sir, – It may interest your readers to know that the greatest literary light of modern Germany – Paul Heyse – is the offspring of a mixed marriage.[67] His father was an eminent philologist, his mother a Jewess. The Jewish nature, with its strange pride and strange humility; its surprising toughnesses and no less surprising sensibilities; its curious mixture of mart and temple; its quaint juxtaposition of the sublime and the ridiculous; the Jewish nature in full has not descended to Heyse, but his Jewish blood has perceptibly leavened his whole individuality.

Readers of Heyse's philosophical novel "Kinder der Welt,"[68] will remember the marriage of its hero Edwin with Zillah, the refined and sensitive Jewess; and it is interesting to know that in this union Heyse has attempted to depict that of his own father and mother.

Yours obediently,
KERAN NUMI.[69]

---

67. Prolific German author, Paul Johann Ludwig von Heyse (1830–1914).
68. Heyse's *Children of the World* (1882).
69. A pen name used by Levy (Linda Hunt Beckman, *Amy Levy: Her Life and Letters* (Athens: Ohio University Press, 2000), 166).

The New School of American Fiction (1884)

There has lately sprung up on the other side of the Atlantic a remarkable growth of novel-literature; intensely modern, intensely self-conscious, but full of cleverness withal, and quite unique in flavour. It has many admirers, many imitators, and its prophets and elders assure us, that not only is it the fiction of the future, but the only fiction, indeed, which can be *warranted genuine.*

> "The art of fiction," says Mr. Howells,[70] in his startling little article on Mr. Henry James,[71] "has in fact become a finer art in our day than it was with Dickens and Thackeray, and we could not now suffer the confidential attitude of the latter, nor the mannerism of the former, any more than we could endure the prolixity of Richardson, or the coarseness of Fielding.[72] These great men are of the past, they and their methods and interests. The new school derives from Hawthorne[73] and George Eliot rather than from any other, but it studies human nature much more in its wonted aspects, and finds its ethical and dramatic examples in the operation of lighter, but not really less vital motives."[74]

---

70. William Dean Howells (1837–1920), American playwright and novelist.
71. Novelist, Henry James (1843–1916).
72. English novelists Samuel Richardson and Henry Fielding.
73. American novelist, Nathaniel Hawthorne (1804–1864).
74. This misquotation is from W. D. Howells, "Henry James, Jr.," *The Century Magazine* 25, no. 1 (November 1882): 28; see New, ed., *The Complete Novels*, 560 n. 14.

Such a flourish of trumpets, coming as it does from one of the leaders of the new school, is in itself of no little significance. It tells us at once what value the artist has attached to his work, where he has aimed, and by what standard he wishes to be judged. We propose to examine the claims of the writers who, they tell us, have raised fiction to such a pitch of artistic perfection.

The names of Mr. Henry James, junior, and Mr. W. D. Howells, naturally occur to us in considering the question. The author of "That Lass o' Lowrie's"[75] by her story "Through One Administration,"[76] and Mr. Crawfurd[77] by his "Dr. Claudius" and "Mr. Isaacs,"[78] may be considered to have enrolled themselves members of the new school of fiction. The work of the vast crowd of lesser disciples is to be met throughout the American literature of today, and is, in its own way, exceedingly instructive.

In an article published some time ago in the "XIXth Century,"[79] Mr. Ruskin complained that the persons of George Eliot's novels suggested nothing so much as the sweepings of a Pentonville omnibus.[80] What would he have said of a literature which, if the expression be allowed us, occupies itself so largely with the Pentonville omnibus of the soul?

Nothing is too trivial, too sordid, or too far-fetched to engage the attention of these "fine art" writers. "The new school finds its ethical and dramatic examples in the operation of lighter but not really less

75. Frances Eliza Hodgson Burnett's (1849–1924) novel, *That Lass o' Lowrie's* (1877).
76. Burnett's *Through One Administration* (1883).
77. Misspelling, which should read "Crawford," referring to American novelist Francis Marion Crawford (1854–1909).
78. Crawford's novels, *Mr. Isaacs: A Tale of Modern India* (1882), and *Dr. Claudius* (1883).
79. The journal is *The Nineteenth Century: A Monthly Review.*
80. The text that Levy is referring to is John Ruskin's "*Fiction–Fair and Foul: V.* The Two Servants," *The Nineteenth Century: A Monthly Review* 10, no. 56 (October 1881): 516–31. In the article, Ruskin says: "the characters are simply the sweepings-out of a Pentonville omnibus" (521).

vital motives,"[81] says Mr. Howells, who, no doubt, is proud of the fact that in his "Chance Acquaintance"[82] he has managed to fill a whole volume with the tepid and protracted flirtation of a commonplace young woman, and a worse than commonplace young man; – a flirtation which leads up to nothing, signifies nothing, which as far as we can see is utterly devoid of interest and instruction.

The method of the new school is no doubt the reaction from the obviousness of such a writer as Dickens, whose influence was at one time so largely felt in America; now each man would outdo his neighbour in subtlety; would prove that he is quite different to Peter Bell;[83] that a primrose by the river's brim[84] means so infinitely more than a primrose to his finer perception.

Perhaps the first note of the new music was struck when Mr. James produced his "Roderick Hudson."[85] It is undoubtedly a remarkable book, though few of its readers may be disposed to agree with a friend of ours who divided the world into people who had read it and people who had not.

In "Roderick Hudson" we are presented with a deep though less obvious truth, so interwoven with the story as to be identical with it – of course the true artistic method. The fine perception, the skilful wielding of language, the many qualities which have won for Mr. James his position as novelist, are all apparent in this book; but those other qualities which have made his subsequent work in so many respects a failure, are not wanting even here, in his greatest and most individual production. Some people are inclined to quarrel with him for the fragmentary nature of his stories, but whatever unity or completeness a work of art possesses, such lie deeper than

81. Howells, "Henry James," 28; again, Levy's quotation is incorrect.

82. Howells' *A Chance Acquaintance* (1873).

83. Refers to William Wordsworth's *Peter Bell: A Tale in Verse* (1819); see New, ed., *The Complete Novels*, 561 n. 19. See also John Hamilton Reynolds' (1796–1852) *Peter Bell: A Lyrical Ballad* (1819) and Percy Bysshe Shelley's *Peter Bell the Third* (1839).

84. "A primrose by the rivers brim" is a quotation from Wordsworth's *Peter Bell.*

85. James' novel, *Roderick Hudson* (1875).

its outward shape; what may fairly be complained of is that intense self-consciousness, that offensive attitude of critic and observer, above all that aggressive contemplation of the primrose which pervades his work. He never leaves us alone for an instant; he is forever labelling, explaining, writing; in vulgar phrase, he is too clever by half. And this perpetual cleverness defeats its own ends; it is wearisome and confusing for all its brilliancy. With the flash of gems in our eyes, and the smell of lamp-oil in our nostrils, it is impossible to give an undivided attention to the most important matter on hand. For a time, certainly, the intellect is stimulated, the interest awakened; but the emotions are rarely stirred. And with regard to such a production as a story, is not much, very much to be learned from the emotions. We devour, breathless, whole pages of that "old-fashioned" and "intolerable" writer – William Makepeace Thackeray – without pausing to trouble our minds about ethics or aesthetics. It is not till later perhaps that shape and meaning grow upon our senses; that truth flashes up at us from the wonderful pages. We must stand back from the large and crowded canvas ere we can fully realise the splendour of the composition, the skilful massing of light and shade; perhaps indeed we never realise it at all, and are only vaguely conscious that it is a great work of art, a fragment of the eternal truth that we are contemplating.

Might not a novel of Thackeray's and a story of Mr. James's be respectively compared to a painting of Rembrandt's[86] and a study of Mr. Alma Tadema's?[87]

Those who have read Mr. James's story of "Benvolio"[88] will remember with pleasure that clever little study in surface emotions. Benvolio is a "complex" young man who, according to his mood, is poet or man of the world. But he vibrates between two loves, each of which appeals to a different side of his nature. One of the heroines, discover-

86. Rembrandt (1606–1669), Dutch painter.

87. Lawrence Alma-Tadema (1836–1912), Dutch painter who lived and worked mostly in London.

88. James' *Benvolio* was published in 1875 (New, ed., *The Complete Novels*, 561 n. 22).

ing the state of affairs, succeeds in banishing her rival to distant climes, only to find herself completely deserted by Benvolio, for whom her charm had been the charm of difference – a relative not a positive attraction. Nothing could be more perfect of its kind than this little sketch, either as regards conception or treatment.

Our complex modern world is full of such fine problems, and Mr. James is the writer best fitted to interpret them. But is it of such stuff that a great literature is made?

In his attempts at larger novels the weakness, not of the writer, but of his method, is plainly shown. "I find," says Mr. Howells, "in the 'Portrait of a Lady'[89] an amount of analysis which I should call superabundance if it were not such good literature."[90] Did Thackeray superabundantly analyse Beatrix Esmond? Yet most of us feel that we know her better than we do Isabel Archer; and own to far greater intimacy with Colonel Esmond than with Ralph Touchett.[91] "The genius of Mr. James," goes on the authority before quoted, "is a metaphysical genius working to aesthetic results."[92]

Perhaps; but must not the greatest aesthetic as a matter of course embrace ethical results? This, Mr. James seems instinctively to have recognised in "Roderick Hudson," but the work by which he is best known, which has made him the centre of a crowd of disciples – his entire latter work – seems to be that of a very clever man exerting himself in the wrong direction. He is losing his sense of proportion; where he would be subtle he is often merely futile. Certainly he makes us see a great many things, but we should see them better if we could feel them as well. But if such things can be said of Mr. Henry James who is an artist, what can we say of his followers who have not all

89. James' novel, *The Portrait of a Lady* (1881).
90. Howells, "Henry James," 26; Levy's quotation is again inaccurate.
91. Beatrix Esmond and Colonel Henry Esmond are characters from Thackeray's *The History of Henry Esmond* (1852); Isabel Archer and Ralph Touchett are characters in James' *The Portrait of a Lady* (see New, ed., *The Complete Novels,* 561 n. 23).
92. Howells, "Henry James," 26 (misquotation).

this distinction? What is his futility, his triviality, his want of human red blood to theirs?

Of these followers Mr. Howells naturally claims our first attention; he enjoys not only an American but a European reputation, and perhaps his work should be classed rather as a development than an imitation of that of Mr. Henry James.

Mr. Howells is a person of considerable shrewdness and some humour, who has taken to writing novels; he believes moreover that there is one infallible recipe for novel-making, and that he and Mr. James and M. Daudet[93] have got hold of it.

No one can deny that up to a certain point he is highly realistic; that he is in any sense real is another matter. If we compare Henry James's books to paintings by Alma Tadema, so may we compare those of Howells to a photograph from life. There are all the familiar details; the table, the picture in its frame, the very orange lying cleft on the casual plate. We ourselves, to be sure, are a little self-conscious in our attitudes, a little stiffly posed; but then there were those uncomfortable head-rests, and the photographer made us put our hands on the silly ornamental columns he brought with him. We are like and yet strangely unlike ourselves. And the novels of Mr. Howells are just so many photographs where no artistic hand has grouped the figures, only posed them very stiffly before his lens. There seems to be quite a remarkable want of unity underlying his work; no doubt he is shrewd enough, funny enough at times, but he drives us out continually in that Pentonville omnibus of his which he, apparently, mistakes for an altogether different conveyance.

> "Greift nur hinein ins volle Menschenleben,
> Ein jeder lebt – nicht vielen ist's bekannt;
> Und wo's Ihr's packt da ist's interessant." – [94]

---

93. Alphonse Daudet.
94. From Johann Wolfgang von Goethe's *Faust* (New, ed., *The Complete Novels*, 561 n. 25).

says one who is greater than Mr. James and Mr. Howells put together. And Mr. Howells himself says with no little complacency, "Ah, poor real life which I love, can I make others share the delight I find in thy foolish, insipid face?"[95]

"To plunge into the full human life," is not for Mr. Howells, and truly the face which he shows us is foolish and insipid, though a good many people appear to find delight in it.

In the "Lady of the Aroostook,"[96] one of the longest of his novels, we are introduced to a monosyllabic young woman from the country who is wooed throughout the book by an irresolute young man; he has been a great flirt in his time, the author tells us. The course of true love runs sufficiently smoothly, and hero and heroine are duly married at the close of the story, by which time we know about as much of the latter as if she had in reality been our very silent fellow-passenger on board the Aroostook. The story has neither shape nor meaning; it is only very occasionally amusing; it is trivial and insipid besides violating all laws of artistic proportion; and the same remarks apply to "A Chance Acquaintance." Throughout the whole of the "Lady of the Aroostook," the heroine rarely says much more than yes, or no; but each monosyllable is generally followed by an elaborate statement of the varying shades of emotion it produces in the hero. This is no doubt a pleasing exhibition of subtlety and ingenuity on the part of the writer, but it might also strike some people as a trick, and a trick of the very cheapest.

In "A Foregone Conclusion"[97] a conception of some strength has been hopelessly spoiled by vulgarity of treatment. Mr. Howells has evidently given much thought to his Italian monk, who falls in love with the fair American; but he takes us too much into his workshop secrets; allows the smell of the lamp to pervade the whole production. The figures labelled Florida, Kitty, Lydia; the other figures of intolerable snobs labelled Terris and Staniford; – [98] no doubt they

95. This quotation is from Howells' *Their Wedding Journey* (1872).

96. Howells' *The Lady of the Aroostook* (1879).

97. Howells' *A Foregone Conclusion* (1875).

98. Florida is a character in *A Foregone Conclusion*; Kitty is a character in *A Chance*

are to be admired as the outcome of the orthodox system of novel writing, but we should be sorry to think that they would go down to posterity either in England or America as types of nineteenth-century young men and young women.

To many, these remarks may seem like the traditional breaking of a butterfly on a wheel. But the writers quoted have taken so high a stand, their admirers and disciples claim for them so high and important a position, that we are judging them as they and their followers would be judged. Regarded from another standpoint, Mr. James is a man of a very high order of ability, who has produced impressive work; and Mr. Howells is a person of shrewdness, with a good deal of literary knack. But what we wish to consider is the general tendency of their work, and we unhesitatingly pronounce that tendency a bad one.

In the first place, the moral standard of the new school is a low one. It is with the selfish record of selfish people that these writers chiefly occupy themselves. There is never a spark of ideality (Mr. James used to give us occasional flashes), the whole thing is of the earth, earthy. Take what is perhaps Mr. Howells' best work, "A Modern Instance";[99] can anything be less ennobling than that minute and skilful study of such a scamp and snob as Bartley Hubbard, such a woman of commonness as Marcia Gaylord?

And we protest against the artificiality, the self-consciousness, the *pose* of the novels of the new school. Are people in real life perpetually on the *qui vive* to observe the precise shade and meaning of one another's smiles, to attach precisely the right interpretation to one another's monosyllables? Some of us take a certain melancholy pleasure in reflecting that we live in a morbid and complex age; but do the most complex of us sit tense, weighing our neighbour's turn of head, noting the minute changes in his complexion? Is our every word and look fraught with deep though subtle

---

Acquaintance; Lydia and Staniford are characters in *The Lady of the Aroostook*. Levy possibly means "Ferris" instead of "Terris."

99. See *A Modern Instance* (1882).

meaning? Those who have read the "Lady of the Aroostook" will remember, no doubt, the consternation of its sub-hero Dunham when he observes Lydia to blush faintly on bowing to him at dinner. He concludes at once that she is in love with him, and proceeds to act on the conclusion.

> "Girls blush sometimes because they are alive,
> Half wishing they were dead to save the shame,"[100]

says Mrs. Browning, but apparently that well-poised being, the American girl, never blushes without due cause. We all know how, in the hands of a master, detail can be used to broaden, not confuse effect; but it is a dangerous tool in the hands of persons of less correct instincts. It is all very well not to overlook the primrose, but roses make a better bouquet after all.

"The new school finds its ethical and dramatic examples in the operation of lighter but not really less vital motives."[101] Among these half-hearted young men, these monosyllabic young women, these trivial ideal-less persons of the new fiction, are we ever shown the "operation of motives" "vital" as those which worked in the hearts of Maggie Tulliver,[102] of Lydgate,[103] of Colonel Esmond, even of old Mr. Osborne?[104] In the whole range of the fashionable novel-literature do we ever come across a group of persons acting on one another to such tragic end, pointing so awfully yet unobtrusively to the irony of fate, as those composed respectively of Amelia, George Osborne, Dobbin and Becky;[105] the Casaubons and the Lydgates?[106]

---

100. Taken from Browning's *Aurora Leigh* (1857).
101. Misquotation of Howells, "Henry James," 28.
102. Maggie Tulliver is a character in George Eliot's *Mill on the Floss* (1860).
103. Lydgate is a character in Eliot's *Middlemarch* (1871–1872).
104. Mr. Osborne is a character in Thackeray's *Vanity Fair.*
105. Characters in *Vanity Fair.*
106. Characters in *Middlemarch.*

The clever study of Marcia Gaylord is tragic enough for all its moral squalor and inartistic unreserve. But do we feel her tragedy as we feel that of Beatrix Esmond[107] with its awful inevitability, its great unpreached moral lesson? The men and women of Thackeray and George Eliot are neither for today, nor tomorrow; they are for all time. But it is not so with the people of the new novels. They are for us, who have just experienced that interesting little emotion, or tossed about with that pretty little passion.

For all their cosmopolitanism, it is an eminently provincial note which the new musicians have struck.

Shall we be allowed, without exciting ridicule, to say that what is wanting to these novels is a touch of the infinite? For all the fragmentary endings, they are so terribly finite. And in this finiteness lies the germ of decay. This is the heaviest charge we make against the new literature; it is a literature of decay.

In work of imaginative literature, when analysis supersedes narration; when the artist turns aside from the universal and simple to the particular and rococo; when he stands by us throughout to point out the mysteries of his work; then, indeed, however good in its way that work may be, it inevitably contains within itself the germs of decay.

In Mr. Howells' article we hear the death-knell of the modern novel.

"Will the reader be content to accept a novel which is an analytic study rather than a story?"[108] We answer emphatically, no. The first function of the novel is pleasurably to engage the attention. Its truths must be conveyed to us by means not only of the intellect but the emotions. There are certain finer ethical points which can be understood emotionally as they never could be understood intellectually.

The skilful manipulation of emotional and intellectual machinery, so that one shall help and perfect the other, is the highest triumph of the novelist's art.

---

107. Character in *The History of Henry Esmond.*

108. Howells, "Henry James," 28.

But perhaps, in spite of Mr. Howells, the novel is not dead or dying after all. Perhaps we are worthy of a better, fuller fiction than this self-conscious, half-hearted literature with its want of simplicity and moral greatness.

Perhaps after all we are not doomed to go down to posterity as skilful hands have depicted us in these small-beer chronicles of the soul.

The Ghetto at Florence (1886)

[From A Correspondent]

Florence, March 19, 1886

They are going to pull down the Ghetto at Florence; it is an old, old dismantled structure "springing seven stories high," staring at you with innumerable sashless windows, like the vacant eyes of the blind. It stands in the old market, where the picturesque busy life goes on buzzing and stirring very much as it did in the days when Tito Melema bought a cup of milk of poor Tessa with a kiss.[109] It is in the very heart of the town; from window, and archway and passage you obtain glimpses of the matchless architectural mass composed by the Duomo and Campanile – that many-tinted, many-faceted jewel of which Florence is but the rich and seemly setting.

Long ago, the Ghetto was a palace of the Medici family.[110] It was not till the 16th century that Cosimo I[111] made it over to the Jews, whom he had summoned to Florence to act as a check on the Italian moneylenders; we are left to guess at the extortions of these Christian usurers; we only know that 20 per cent was fixed as a moderate rate of interest for their Jewish successors!

109. Refers to Eliot's *Romola* (1862–1863).

110. Powerful Italian financial and political dynasty.

111. Cosimo I de' Medici (1519–1574), Duke of Florence, 1537–1569.

The Jews continued to dwell in the old Ghetto (and very huddled up they must have been, if their rate of multiplication was up to its usual average) until modern toleration set them free, and modern sanitary science declared their dwelling place unfit for human habitation. Then the great arched doorways, solid and satisfying in their strong curves, were boarded up; the very panes went from the windows; from top to bottom those crazy seven storeys were a squalid and dismantled ruin. They set up a turnstile at the back of the building, and on payment of half a lire the casual stranger could wander at will amid the endless passages and stairways, the dusky intricacies of Cosimo's palace, for which more changes were yet in store.

For by the end of Carnival, the poor old structure had undergone a complete transformation. The dingy walls were painted in gay stripes, Eastern rugs hung from the empty windows, coloured lanterns were swinging over the doorways, themselves draped and gilded out of all knowledge. Great posters announced the fact that the "Citta di Baghdad" was to be seen in the Ghetto. All through Carnival week those old courts and archways echoed to the mirth of the masquers, and now quieter folk have taken to drinking their evening coffee in the tricked-out Ghetto-Palace. There is nothing that need remind one of the cramped life that once thronged and huddled and swarmed here, that need call up unpleasant memories of the sordid, struggling, choked existence that went on wearily from generation to generation. It is true that the cells and arches are very close together, but they are hung charmingly with gay stuffs, and the shopmen, with their red caps and Tuscan faces, are more than picturesque. Actually there are real camels to be seen and real studio-models posing as Orientals in all the glory of turban and fez. Down below the walls are painted so gaily that you forget to look upwards at the gloomy storeys above, at the crowding, empty windows. But now and then you may find yourself strolling unawares down some tortuous passage out of sight of the lanterns, out of hearing of the band, away from the fuss and stir of a modern pleasure-place.

How dreary, how inexpressibly gloomy it is! Even the moonlight, that wonderful moonlight of an Italian spring, cannot penetrate into these courts and alleys, around which the tall, tall houses crowd so closely. The air strikes chill and damp; are those human faces, or the faces of ghosts, that peer so wistfully through the grated lower windows? Is it the sound of human footsteps, or the sound heard in a dream, that echoes on the close, irregular pavement, that startles one from the gloom of unexpected angles and archways?

It is only sentimentalists, like ourselves, that trouble themselves in this unnecessary fashion. There are a great many Jews here tonight, evidently quite undisturbed by "inherited memory." A sprightly, if unhandsome, son of Shem urges us, in correct cockney, to take shares in a lottery; another, with his wife on his arm, trips gaily from booth to booth; the repressed energy, the stored exuberance of centuries is venting itself with its wonted force. We ourselves, it is to be feared, are not very good Jews; is it by way of "judgment" that the throng of tribal ghosts haunts us so persistently tonight? That white-bearded old man peering round the corner, surely it was he that Mantegna chose for the model for his famous Circumcision?[112] ...

The Jews have ceased to dwell in the Ghetto, but they have by no means ceased to dwell in the city. They swarm in the quaint streets adjoining the old market, and in more important thoroughfares such names as Dante Levi stare at us in hybrid significance from the shopfronts.

But you do not here identify the Jew with the same ease and readiness as in England or Germany. There is no doubt, for instance, about the inhabitants of Petticoat Lane, or the Brühl at Leipzig, apart from all accident of locality. But sometimes, when a dark face peers at you from a doorway of the Mercato Vecchio, and a pair of shrewd, melancholy eyes meet with your own, you are puzzled at the equal suggestion of Jew and Florentine in their glance. Who knows but that,

112. Andrea Mantegna (1431–1506), Italian Renaissance painter. In the painting, "Adoration of the Magi," Levy's "white-bearded old man" can indeed be seen delivering the circumcision of Jesus.

long ago, those old and mystic races, the Etrurians and Semites, were kinsfolk, pasturing their flocks together in Asia Minor? But this is opening up a very big question, over which wiser heads than our own have puzzled often and in vain. Let us go back and take our farewell of the Ghetto, where the lights are still shining and the band still playing. Poor old Palace-Prison! This is positively your last appearance; you are very splendid, but it is only a funeral pomp, after all. The lamps flicker, the people stream out, the musicians play louder and louder, –

> "That when he dies he make a swan-like end,
> Fading in music."[113]

113. From Shakespeare's *The Merchant of Venice*, albeit reworded (New, ed., *The Complete Novels*, 562 n. 31).

The Jew in Fiction (1886)

It is curious, that, while the prominent position of the Jew is recognised as one of the characteristic features of English social life of the present day, so small a place should be allotted him in contemporary fiction.

In finance, in politics, in society; in every branch of art and science, the English Jew is to be found in a position of more or less distinction. It is only in the novel, with one notable exception, that his claims to consideration hare been almost entirely overlooked. Rebecca of York, with her hopeless love for the Gentile knight, and Isaac of York,[114] divided, like Shylock,[115] between his ducats and his daughter, remain today the typical Hebrews of fiction. Dickens, as might be expected, places himself on the crudely popular side, but tries to compensate for his having affixed the label "Jew" to one of his bad fairies by creating the good fairy Riah.[116] Thackeray has reproduced Jews in less romantic guise, as Mr. and Miss Moss of the sponging houses,[117] and today Mr. Baring-Gould (a clergyman of the Church

114. Characters in Walter Scott's *Ivanhoe: A Romance* (1819).

115. See the discussion on p. lv.

116. Riah is a character in Dickens' *Our Mutual Friend* (1865); on Dickens' own antisemitism and the difference between the crude antisemitic stereotyping in *Oliver Twist* (1838) and *Our Mutual Friend*, see Deborah Epstein Nord's "Dickens's 'Jewish Question': Pariah Capitalism and the Way Out," *Victorian Literature and Culture* 39 (2011): 27–45.

117. Characters in Thackeray's *Vanity Fair*.

of England) slavishly follows the old Jew-baiting traditions in his absurd portrait of Emanuel Lazarus in *Court Royal.*[118]

In *Daniel Deronda,* it is true, a sincere and respectful attempt was made to portray the features of modern Judaism. But which of us will not acknowledge with a sigh, that the noble spirit which conceived Mirah, Daniel and Ezra, was more royal than the king? It was, alas! no picture of Jewish contemporary life, that of the little group of enthusiasts, with their yearnings after the Holy Land and dreams of a separate nation. Nor can we derive much satisfaction from the superficial smartness of such sketches as that of Jacob Alexander Cohen and his family. As a novel treating of modern Jews, *Daniel Deronda* cannot be regarded as a success; although every Jew must be touched by, and feel grateful, for the spirit which breathes throughout the book; perhaps, even be spurred by its influence to nobler effort, and taught a lesson, sadly needed, to hold himself and his people in greater respect.

As for Lord Beaconsfield's grandiloquent attempts in this direction, is not *Coningsby* forgotten in *Codlingsbey* and which of us remembers the original of Raphael Mendoza?[119]

In that clever, vulgar, unpleasant novel *Mrs. Keith's Crime*[120] we are presented with several specimens of Jewish portraiture, which at least make some attempt at realism. Perhaps, however, no outspoken picture of Jewish vice could be so offensive as the author's condescending acknowledgement of Jewish virtue. "The Sardine," (as, with characteristic refinement, he is called throughout the book) is an impossibly slangy Jew of wealth and position, who spends his

---

118. Sabine Baring-Gould's (1834–1924) *Court Royal* (1886).

119. Here Levy refers to Benjamin Disraeli's novel, *Coningsby, or the New Generation* (1844), and its parodying by Thackeray in "Codlingsby," first published in *Punch* in 1847 (Bernstein, ed., *Reuben Sachs,* 177 n. 2–3). See also D. Shrewsberry, "Codlingsby," in *Thackeray's Complete Works: The Adventures of Philip* (Boston: Estes and Lauriat, 1883), 14–25. Bernstein's edition of *Reuben Sachs* includes "The Jew in Fiction," with commentary, in the appendices (175–8).

120. Lucy Lane Clifford's (1846–1929) novel, *Mrs. Keith's Crime* (1885); see Bernstein, ed., *Reuben Sachs,* 177 n. 4.

time in doing good to ungrateful Gentiles. The patronising reception of his kindness on the part of the extremely unpleasant heroine, is enough to fill with wrath the honest Semitic bosom. However, as a concession, no doubt, to modern feeling, the despised Sardine is allowed to be happy with a woman of his own race and is not, as we had expected, left forlorn at the last; a male and modern Rebecca of York. There is far more cleverness in the sketch of the elderly Jewess in the same book, with her indolence and persistence; her indifference and tenacity of purpose; a sketch which for once shows real insight into Jewish character, not mere observation of outward peculiarities.

But these and kindred efforts are, when all is said, of the slightest nature. There has been no serious attempt at serious treatment of the subject; at grappling in its entirety with the complex problem of Jewish life and Jewish character. The Jew, as we know him today, with his curious mingling of diametrically opposed qualities; his surprising virtues and no less surprising vices; leading his eager, intricate life; living, moving, and having his being both within and without the tribal limits; this deeply interesting product of our civilisation has been found worthy of none but the most superficial observation.

There is yet to be done for him, the comparison inevitably suggests itself, what M. Daudet has done for the inhabitants of Southern France. No picture of English 19th century life and manners can be considered complete without an adequate representation of the modern son of Shem.

While writers and readers of fiction complain that *tout èst dit*, producers and consumers, alike, sending forth an Athenian cry for something new, it is strange that a field at once so rich and so untrodden, should have been almost entirely overlooked.

We have, alas! no M. Daudet among us. His mingled brilliance and solidity; his wonderful blending of picturesqueness and fidelity, have no counterparts among our own contemporary novel-writers. It is in the throng of aspirants to fame that must be sought a writer able and willing to do justice to the Jewish question in its social and psychological aspects.

Jewish Humour (1886)

Every family, with its fair share of intelligence and fair share of good-fellowship, has its joke. You may be a brilliant wit outside the family circle, yet retain, all the while, an irritated consciousness that your most delicate conception of the comic, your very happiest turn of phrase, can be really appreciated by no one but your brother (whom you hate), or your sister, with whom you quarrelled years ago about the will, and to whom you have never spoken since. And even the dullest person, brought up in a healthy atmosphere of family humour, can contribute his share to the joke of his clan, if only by an appreciative chuckle or a sympathetic twinkle of the eye.

The analysis of his own family joke would be a hard task to set a man. To nicely weigh the mass of recollection, allusion, and mutual understanding which make up for him so delicious a whole; to pronounce it, in cold blood, intrinsically witty or not witty, humorous or not humorous; what employment could be more thoroughly fruitless and ungrateful? The task is as impossible as to give the full meaning of the subtle words *'hine* and *chutzpah*, so expressive as they are to those Jews who have used them from childhood.

We have, then, no little hesitation in dealing with the subject of the time-honoured Jewish Family Joke; in pronouncing on its merits or demerits; its relative or absolute value.

In general circles the mention of Jewish Humour is immediately followed by that of HEINE; nor is this a *non-sequitur*. For HEINE, in truth, has given perfect expression to the very spirit of Jewish

Humour; has cracked the communal joke, as it were, in the language of culture, for all to enjoy and understand.

The world laughs, and weeps and wonders; bows down and worships the brilliant exotic. We ourselves, perhaps, while admiring, as we cannot fail to admire, indulge in a little wistful, unreasonable regret, for the old cast clouts, the discarded garments of the dazzling creature; for the old allusions and gestures, the dear vulgar, mongrel words; the delicious, confidential quips and cranks which nobody but ourselves can understand.

It is no new story, that the spirit of a nation should find expression in the utterances of its men of genius; nor that in those utterances the local, the accidental, the particular, should be subordinated to the universal.

When all is said, let us then be grateful to the man who has proved so triumphantly the worth, who has brought out so successfully the peculiar and delicate quality of the tribal humour.

> Sonne, Monde und Sterne lachen;
> Und ich lache mit – und sterbe.

> Sun and moon and stars are laughing;
> I am laughing, too – and dying.[121]

These lines of HEINE, with which no doubt most of us are familiar, strike the keynote of his mood: "*Ich lache mit – und sterbe.*" The Poet stretched on his couch of pain; the nation whose shoulders are sore with the yoke of oppression; both can look up with rueful humorous eyes and crack their jests, as it were, in the face of Fortune. Heaven knows what would have become of them, people and poet alike, had it not been for this happy knack, or shall we say this tough persistence in joke-making under every conceivable circumstance; this blessed power of seeing the comic side of things, when a side by no means comic was insisting so forcibly

121. From "The Homecoming" in Heine's *Buch der Lieder*; see Hal Draper, ed., *The Complete Poems of Heinrich Heine: A Modern English Version* (Boston: Suhrkamp/Insel, 1982), 101.

on their notice. True humour, we are told, has its roots in pathos; there is pathos, and to spare, we think, in the laughter that comes from that Paris lodging, or which surges up to us through the barred gates of Ghettos.

But it must not be forgotten that this very power of defying Fate with a conceit, has its own disadvantages to contend with. There is a limit to human power of suffering no less than to human endurance; sensibilities grow blunted, and the finer feelings are lost. A tendency to "debase the moral currency" by turning everything into a joke, never to take oneself or one's neighbour quite *au sérieux*, is, perhaps, one of the less pleasing results of our long struggle for existence. What was at first reserve and pluck, bids fair to grow into callousness and cynicism. We sneer at a man; we whisper some apt saying in Jüdisch-Deutsch[122] about his personal appearance, even while we are helping him or receiving his help. *Apropos*, we are keen as women, on the subject of clothes and looks; the result no doubt of prolonged life in cities; indeed, its distinctly urban quality is one of the chief features of Jewish humour. The close and humorous observation of manners (we use the word in its widest sense); the irresistible, swift transition to the absurd, in the midst of everything that is most solemn; the absolute refusal to take life quite seriously, do we not recognize these qualities as common, more or less, to all bred and born in great cities?

If they are more marked in the Jew, let us remember how long it is since he gave up pasturing his flocks and "took (perforce) to trade"; he hardly has left, when all is said, a drop of bucolic blood in his veins. He has been huddled in crowded quarters of towns, forced into close and continual contact with his fellow-creatures; he has learned to watch men's faces; to read men's thoughts; to be always ready for his opportunity. If he could raise a laugh at his neighbour's expense when his neighbour's demeanour was such a matter of importance to him, who will grudge him the solace and the vengeance?

The humorous point of view from which we survey one another, *quâ* Jews and that from which we survey our neighbours *quâ* Gentiles,

122. Yiddish.

are, of course among the more local and characteristic features of the subject. It would be impertinent to dilate in this journal on what every Jew realises so thoroughly; if he does not, no amount of explanation will help him. To make the comic character of a play or novel a Jew is a sufficiently common device; as unsuccessful, it must be added, as it is common. Perhaps these Merry-Andrews[123] of fiction have their uses, and serve to rouse the laughter of the Gentile public; perhaps we have a comic side which we ourselves are incapable of perceiving, and yet we are by no means sparing of one another in this respect.

As far as we can judge we should say, that only a Jew perceives to the full the humour of another; but it is a humour so fine, so peculiar, so distinct in flavour, that we believe it impossible to impart its perception to anyone not born a Jew. The most hardened Agnostic deserter from the synagogue enjoys its pungency, where the zealous alien convert to Judaism tastes nothing but a little bitterness. In these days, indeed, of slackening bonds, of growing carelessness as to long-cherished traditions; when the old order is changing and giving place to new with startling rapidity it is, perhaps, our sense of humour as much as anything else, which keeps alive the family feeling of the Jewish race. The old words, the old customs, are disappearing, soon to be forgotten by all save the student of such matters. There is no shutting our eyes to this fact. The trappings and the suits of our humour must vanish with the rest; but that is no reason why what is essential of it should not remain to us a heritage of the ages too precious to be lightly lost; a defence and a weapon wrought for us long ago by hands that ceased not from their labour. If we leave off saying Shibboleth,[124] let us, at least, employ its equivalent in the purest University English. Not for all Aristophanes[125] can we yield up our national free-masonry of wit; our family joke, our Jewish Humour.

---

123. A term used to describe a clown.

124. In Judges 12:5–6 Ephraimites say "'*sibboleth*'" instead of "'*shibboleth*'"; this worked as a password as Ephraimites were not "able to pronounce it correctly" and could therefore be identified and slain "by the fords of the Jordan."

125. Ancient Greek playwright.

Middle-Class Jewish Women of Today (1886)

By A Jewess

Conservative in politics; conservative in religion; the Jew is no less conservative as regards his social life; and while in most cases outwardly conforming to the usages of Western civilisation, he is, in fact, more Oriental at heart than a casual observer might infer. For a long time, it may be said, the shadow of the harem has rested on our womankind; and if today we see it lifting, it is only in reluctant obedience to the force of circumstances, the complex conditions of our modern civilisation.

What, in fact, is the ordinary life of a Jewish middle-class woman? Carefully excluded, with almost Eastern jealousy, from everyday intercourse with men and youths of her own age, she is plunged all at once – a half-fledged, often half-chaperoned creature – into the "vortex" of a middle-class ballroom, and is there expected to find her own level. In the very face of statistics, of the unanswerable logic of facts, she is taught to look upon marriage as the only satisfactory termination to her career. Her parents are jealous of her healthy, objective activities, of the natural employment of her young faculties, of anything in short which diverts her attention from what should be the one end and aim of her existence! If, in spite of all the parental efforts she fail, from want of money, or want of attractions, in obtaining a husband, her lot is a desperately unenviable one. Following out the old traditions, the parental authority is strained to the utmost verge, and our community affords us many a half ludicrous, half pathetic spectacle of a hale woman of thirty making her way about the world in the very shortest and tightest of leading strings. It follows that in a society constructed on such a primitive basis, the position of single women, so rapidly improving in the general world, is a particularly unfortunate one. Jewish men have grown to look upon the women of their own tribe as solely designed for marrying or giving in marriage, and naturally enough, under the circumstances approach them with extreme caution. If a Jewess has social interests beyond the crude and transitory ones of flirtation, she must seek them, perforce, beyond the tribal limits. Within, frank and healthy intercourse between both sexes is almost impossible; the more delicate relations between men and women, the very flower and crown of civilisation, are not even understood. A mutual attitude of self-consciousness, bred of the deplorable state of things, is almost inevitable between Jews and Jewesses. Once the all-important business of marriage and settlement over and done with, they find that they have nothing left to say to one another; that the degree of pleasure afforded by mixed social intercourse, never very high, has sunk to zero; just as a person whose sole educational aims are cramming and pot-hunting, sits down blankly among his books when the degree is conferred and the fellowship won.

The inevitable result is that Jewish men and women of any width of culture, are driven to finding their friends of the other sex in the Gentile camp. That mixed marriages, comparatively frequent as they are, do not more readily accrue, must be set down either to the fact that, when all is said, our race instincts are strong; or to the less pleasing one that we are a wealthy nation and have not been educated to a high ideal of marriage.

Of course this state of things falls most hardly on the woman. As a matter of fact, so many of our men are absorbed in money-making, and are moreover such genuine Orientals at heart, that they scarcely feel the need of feminine society in its higher forms. Whereas the women, such of them as are beginning to be conscious of the yoke, are more readily adaptable, more eager to absorb the atmosphere around them; and by reason of their extra leisure, have in many cases outstripped their brothers in culture. Thus often, with greater social capabilities they have far less social opportunity. That this latter evil is common to all commercial communities, cannot be denied; and the same may be said of some other evils which have been pointed out in the course of this paper. But I maintain that in the Jewish community they flourish with more vigour, more pertinacity, over a more wide-spread area, with a deeper root than in any other English Society.

It must be frankly acknowledged, that for all anxiety to be to the fore on every occasion, the Jew is considerably behind the age in one very important respect. That a change is coming o'er the spirit of the communal dream cannot be denied; but it is coming very slowly and at the cost of much suffering to everyone concerned. The assertion even of comparative freedom on the part of a Jewess often means the severance of the closest ties, both of family and of race; its renunciation, a life-long personal bitterness. And the state of things is the more to be regretted, when we consider the potentialities of the women of our race. One of the most brilliant social figures of the century – the late Lady Waldegrave[126] may be claimed as a compatriot; and among distinguished women of today who are of Semitic origin we may mention that eminent journalist and writer on Schopenhauer, Miss Helen Zimmern;[127] that graceful poet and writer of *belles lettres*, Miss Mathilde Blind;[128] and that highly successful mathematical coach, herself the inventor of a mathematical instrument, Miss Marks[129] (now

126. Francis Elizabeth Anne Waldegrave (1821–1879), popular societal and political hostess; see Bernstein, ed., *Reuben Sachs*, 180 n. 1. Bernstein's edition includes "Middle-Class Jewish Women of Today" with accompanying footnotes (178–81).
127. Helen Zimmern (1846–1934), author and translator.
128. Mathilde Blind (1841–1896), popular author of poetry, fiction, and essays.
129. Phoebe Sarah Hertha Ayrton, née Marks (1854–1923); mathematician, suffrage campaigner, and first Anglo-Jewish woman at Cambridge's Girton College

the wife of Professor Ayrton).[130] Add to these an ever increasing roll of successful examination candidates, of writers in various branches of literature; examine the list of students at the high schools and female colleges, and we shall find good reason to hope for a better state of things.

But when all is said, to a thoughtful person thoughtfully surveying the feminine half of our society, the picture is depressing enough. On the one hand, he sees an ever-increasing minority of eager women beating themselves in vain against the solid masonry of our ancient fortifications, long grown obsolete and of no use save as obstructions; sometimes succeeding in scaling the wall and departing, never to return, to the world beyond. On the other, a crowd of half-educated, idealess, pampered creatures, absorbed in material enjoyments; passing into aimless spinsterhood, or entering on unideal marriages; whose highest desire in life is the possession (after a husband) of a sable cloak and at least one pair of diamond earrings. Looking on them, it is perhaps hard to realize the extent of our undeveloped social resources; of the wickedness of our wilful neglects of some of the most delicately-flavoured fruits which the gods can make to grow. I for one believe that our Conservatism with regard to women, is one of the most deeply rooted, the most enduring sentiments of the race; and one that will die harder than any other; for die it must in the face of modern thought, modern liberty and, above all, of modern economic pressure.

(see Bernstein, ed., *Reuben Sachs*, 180 n. 4). New speculated that "Miss Marks" might have been Constance Isabelle Marks (1860–1940), a mathematician (*The Complete Novels*, 562 n. 38).

130. William Edward Ayrton (1847–1908).

Jewish Children (1886)

By A Jewess

"I'll shwop!" said Jacob Alexander Cohen, as he held out the celebrated corkscrew-knife to Daniel Deronda. He spoke, we are told, in a voice "hoarse in its glibness, as if it had belonged to an aged commercial soul, fatigued with bargaining after many generations"; and was possessed of a *physique* which "supported a precocity that would have shattered a Gentile of his years." "The marvellous Jacob" in his red stockings and velveteen knickerbockers; Adelaide Rebekah with her "miniature crinoline and monumental features"; her fine name and Sabbath frock of braided amber; Eugenie Esther who "carries on her teething intelligently" and looks about her with such precocious interest;[131] these three little persons are drawn, it must be owned, with considerable shrewdness and humour, though with an absence of tenderness which we should hardly have expected from the creator of Tottie,[132] of Eppie,[133] of Tom and Maggie Tulliver.[134]

The rather laboured jocoseness, the straining after pompous epigram which characterise George Eliot's later manner seem singularly

131. "Jewish" characters from Eliot's *Daniel Deronda* (1876).
132. Character in Eliot's *Adam Bede* (1859).
133. Character in Eliot's *Silas Marner* (1861).
134. Characters from Eliot's *Mill on the Floss* (1860).

out of place in her description of the young Cohens.[135] She has caught, indeed, the humours; but has failed to catch the charms of Jewish childhood.

To expatiate on those charms in this journal would be nothing less than an impertinence. We Jewish men and women are in no danger of ignoring them; our danger lies rather in their too great appreciation. From the earliest times, the nursery has held a prominent, perhaps a too prominent, position in the Jewish household. A love of children is one of the most deeply-rooted instincts of our nature. Our marriages are so often mere matters of arrangement, that, though in many cases followed by affection, they are apt to make no overwhelming demands on our emotional resources. Domestic affection has always held a higher place with us than romantic passion; the love of Jewish lovers suggests comparison with that of the ancient Greeks; and even the conjugal feelings give way in strength and importance to the parental ones. Love of offspring might, indeed, be described as our master-passion, stronger than our love of money, than our love of success. Even Shylock[136] can divert some of his attention from his ducats to his daughter, and Rebekah is dearer to Isaac of York than all his hoarded store.[137]

And whereas the Greeks and Romans gloried in tales of filial piety, pointing with admiration to Aeneas with the weight of Anchises on his shoulders,[138] to Antigone as she leads the faltering steps of Oedipus,[139] the most touching and characteristic stories of the Hebrew Scriptures are those which turn on the affection of parents for their

135. See *Daniel Deronda.*

136. From Shakespeare's *The Merchant of Venice.*

137. Refers to Scott's *Ivanhoe: A Romance.*

138. Trojan son (Aeneas) and father (Anchises) in Greek/Roman mythology; in Virgil's *Aeneid,* Aeneas carries Anchises away from Troy, which is in flames (New, ed., *The Complete Novels,* 563 n. 42).

139. In Sophocles' *Oedipus at Colonus,* the blinded Oedipus has to be led by Antigone (New, ed., *The Complete Novels,* 563 n. 42).

children. Hagar;[140] Isaac;[141] David;[142] Jacob,[143] that most pathetic and most injudicious of fathers; these are only the most striking instances of a long list of devoted Biblical parents. And nowadays the Jewish father leads his bright-eyed Barmitzvah son to the reading-desk of the synagogue with even greater pride than the bridegroom led his bride

140. In the Genesis account, Hagar (Egyptian) is Sarah's maidservant; Sarah is unable to conceive so allows Abraham to take Hagar as a "concubine," who then bears a son, Ishmael (16:1–4). Eventually, however, Abraham acquiesces to Sarah's demand that they be banished (21:9–14).

141. Isaac "favoured Esau" over Jacob and intended to offer him "blessing"; however, Rebekah conspires with Jacob so that the blind and elderly Isaac mistakenly blesses her favourite, with Esau only realising on his return from hunting. Jacob had earlier acquired Esau's "'birthright'" in exchange for stew (Genesis 25:28–34, 27:1–34).

142. Following David's liaison with Bathsheba and subterfuge in arranging Uriah's death, he is informed by Nathan that although his "sin" has been "remitted," the child to be born from their adultery would "die" (2 Samuel 12:1–14). Accordingly, David begs "God for the boy," fasts, and spends "the night lying on the ground," but all to no avail (12:15–18). Later, when David's son, Amnon, rapes Tamar (13:14), Absalom, another of David's sons, outraged, has him killed and then flees (13:28–29, 34), leaving David grieving (13:31, 36, 39). Eventually, Absalom returns and leads a rebellion against David (15:10–13), who is forced to flee and again weeps in his grief at the betrayal (15:30). Absalom is finally defeated at the battle of "the forest of Ephraim" and when fleeing he becomes entangled in a tree. Joab, ignoring David's orders that his son be spared, drives "three darts" into the defenceless Absalom (18:6–16). On hearing the news, David bewails: "'My son Absalom! O my son, my son Absalom! If only I had died instead of you! O Absalom, my son, my son!'" (18:33).

143. In Genesis 37:3 it is revealed that "Israel [Jacob] loved Joseph best of all his sons, for he was the child of his old age; and he made him an ornamented tunic." Jealous and further infuriated by his dreams suggesting he would come to "'reign over'" the family (37:4–11), Joseph's brothers, despite Reuben's protestations, take his "ornamented tunic" and throw him into a "pit" (37:23–24). Regretting their actions, they then sell Joseph to "Midianite traders" (37:28) without Reuben's knowledge. The brothers agree on a story that Joseph was killed by a wild animal. On hearing the news, Jacob bewails: "'I will go down mourning to my son in Sheol'" (37:31–35). Jacob later learns that Joseph is still alive and now "'lord of all Egypt'" (45:1–10, 26). Thus, based on God's promise, father and son are reunited, Jacob avowing: "'Now I can die, having seen for myself that you are still alive'" (46:4, 29–30).

beneath the canopy; and the Jewish mother, her taste for diamonds notwithstanding, glories no less than her Roman predecessor in the human "jewels" with which she has adorned herself. Indeed, the child, his wants, his interests, his attractions, are, and ever have been, one of the most striking features of communal life; I, for one, should be among the last to deprecate the bestowal of the utmost care on the rising generation. But it must be owned that the pleasing communal domestic picture has a side by no means so attractive.

We can pass over with a smile and a sigh the funny exhibitions of vicarious vanity of which we are almost all guilty with regard to our children. Our deep-seated Oriental love of splendour might easily vent itself less innocently than in the plush costumes and dangling ringlets of our little Lionels and Stanleys. We can bear without wincing George Eliot's good humoured satire on Adelaide's frock and Jacob's stockings.[144] But a much more serious charge than a love of high-sounding names and fanciful garments must be brought against many Jewish parents.

The most insidious form of self-indulgence, all the more dangerous that it looks so uncommonly like self-sacrifice, the injudicious petting of children, has long been gaining ground in our community. The Jewish child, in point of fact, runs great danger, metaphorically speaking, of being killed with kindness.

It must not be forgotten that those very things which go to make up the peculiar and irresistible charm of young Israel constitute at the same time his danger. Such vivacity, such sense of fun, such sensibility and intelligence at so early an age, could only be the product of a very delicate and elaborate organism; a bit of mechanism that will not bear to be tampered with rashly. We scarcely needed Mr. Sully[145] and his psychology to tell us that mental precocity is by no means necessarily the forerunner of mental mediocrity, but it may nearly always be accepted as the sign of a highly developed nervous organisation.

144. See *Daniel Deronda*.

145. Psychologist, James Sully (1842–1923).

And the Jewish child, descendant of many city-bred ancestors as he is, is apt to be a very complicated little bundle of nerves indeed, to whom woe betide should he meet with unduly rough handling.

"Lilies that fester smell far worse than weeds."[146]

The curious extremes of character which are to be met with among us, often, in the case of members of the same family, testify to our immense possibilities for both good and evil. Am I overstating the case in saying (and I say it in all sadness) that there is scarcely a Jewish family which does not possess its black sheep; its member who is rarely mentioned, rarely if ever seen in the family circle, and whose very existence is often nothing but a subject of regret to his nearest kinsfolk? His tint is of course of varying degrees of blackness, and sometimes he himself is the positive society; merely the negative sufferer by his condition. But knave or nervous eccentric, his elimination from the fold is in every respect desirable. English society is beginning at last to give ear to the teachings of psychology and physiology and to recognize the importance of careful training in youth of human beings. The Jewish community, conservative as ever, absorbs very slowly the modern educational doctrine. Both parents and children suffer, as I pointed out, from the defects of their qualities. Inordinate parental pride and parental fondness are no doubt at the root of the over-feeding, over-dressing, over-indulgence generally, which work such havoc among the constitutions and characters of the rising generation. On the other hand, the acute perceptions and sensibilities of the child himself make him a terribly favourable subject for the self-consciousness, arrogance and other worse vices, which, in any case, would be the logical sequence of his injudicious treatment.

To direct the manifold energies of our little ones into the proper channels is a duty we owe not only to them, not only to ourselves, but to society generally, to the country to which is due so large a

146. From Shakespeare's Sonnet 94.

debt of justice and generosity. That the scientific teachings of the day are bound eventually to permeate even the close-grained stratum of Jewish conservatism, we have no manner of doubt. But the process is a slow one, involving the waste of much energy. The rate of mental and nervous diseases among Jews is deplorably high. That the causes of this melancholy fact are numerous and complicated I do not deny; we are suffering no doubt for the conditions of our past existence; conditions which only our abnormal toughness and vitality have enabled us to survive at all: the comparative smallness of our numbers, our centuries of city life.

It is only by the most careful training, mental, moral, physical, that we can hope to counteract the tendencies inherited through countless generations by our children. It is to Jewish parents that we must look for the future; on their care, intelligence and self-restraint rests our chief hope of improvement and even of survival as a race.

The Poetry of Christina Rossetti (1888)

A woman-poet of the first rank is among those things which the world has yet to produce. Even the broken, beautiful strains which float up from Lesbos, tell of a singer whose lyre had few strings; whose voice, exquisite as it must have been, but few notes.

Only twice, I think, has Mrs. Browning achieved excellence – in "Sonnets from the Portuguese"[147] and the "Great God Pan";[148] and when we have named Sappho and Mrs. Browning, who remains to be added to the list of poetesses with any claim to a place in the first class?

But if no woman has grown to the stature of a Dante,[149] a Homer, or a Shakespeare, it cannot be denied that, within the narrow limits imposed by her hitherto narrow range of vision, of emotion, of experience and opportunity, woman has produced work which will bear the severest test. The creator of "Come unto these Yellow Sands"[150] need not have been ashamed to acknowledge,

147. Barrett Browning's *Sonnets from the Portuguese* (1850).

148. See Barrett Browning's poems, "A Musical Instrument" and "The Dead Pan."

149. Italian philosopher and poet, Dante Alighieri (1265–1321).

150. From Shakespeare's *The Tempest*.

Γέσπερε, πάντα φέρεις, ὅσα φαίνολις ἐσκέδας ἀύως;[151]

nor he who sang "Ye banks and braes of bonnie Doon,"[152] to claim as his own the tragedy-lyric of "Auld Robin Gray."[153] If I may be allowed the paradox, there has been no excellent woman-poet, but much woman's poetry of excellence.

The name of Christina Rossetti stands high among the producers of such poetry. With unusual opportunities of culture, breathing from the first an atmosphere almost uniquely favourable to artistic production, she had never to contend with those obstacles which are apt to confront her sex at the outset of a literary career. On the other hand, steeped as she must have been in strong and peculiar influences, she ran the risk of losing her artistic individuality. These influences, indeed, have left their mark on her work; but it is always her own voice – no echo – her woman's voice, curiously sweet, fantastically sad, which floats up to us as we listen to her singing.

Miss Rossetti was born in London, in 1830, of Italian parents. As in the case of Dante Gabriel Rossetti,[154] her talent was a precocious one, and as early as 1847 she appears as the author of a book of poems, "Verses," dedicated to her mother, privately printed at the press of her grandfather, Mr. Pollidori, at 15, Park Villas East, Regent's Park.

This modest little volume, which may be seen by the curious in the Large Room of the British Museum, is introduced by a preface

151. Bernstein states that the translation is as follows: "Hesperus, you bring all things that lightgiving dawn has scattered," linking it to a similar line in Shakespeare's *All's Well that Ends Well*; see *The Romance of a Shop*, by Amy Levy (Peterborough: Broadview Editions, 2006), 204 n. 3. Bernstein's edition includes "The Poetry of Christina Rossetti," with accompanying footnotes, in the appendices (204–13). The line, however, is actually one of Sappho's fragments which was popular with poets at the time: "O Hesperus, bringing everything / the bright dawn scattered" (Sappho, *The Poetry of Sappho*, ed. and trans. Jim Powell (Oxford: Oxford University Press, 2019), 28).

152. Robert Burns' "Ye Banks and Braes o' Bonnie Doon."

153. "Auld Robin Grey" was written by poet, Lady Anne Lindsay (1750–1825).

154. Dante Gabriel Rossetti, brother of Christina Rossetti (1830–1894).

from the printer, who explains that the poems are printed by his own desire. As the work of so young a poet, they are, indeed, remarkable. Those qualities which stamp the work of her maturity – the quaint yet exquisite choice of words; the felicitous *naïveté,* more Italian than English; the delicate, unusual melody of the verse; the richness, almost to excess, of imagery – are all apparent in these first fruits of her muse. And not less apparent are the mysticism and the almost unrelieved melancholy which we associate with Christina Rossetti's better-known poetry. Indeed, there is here to be found that youthful exaggeration of sadness, that perverse assumption of the cypress, to which a half-complacent, half-mournful poet of our own time has alluded –

> "Our youth began with tears and sighs,
> With seeking what we could not find;
> Our verses were all threnodies ..."[155]

Miss Rossetti's verses, at this period, were all threnodies, more or less.

"The City of the Dead,"[156] the most important poem in the "Verses," contains many passages of great beauty, and testifies throughout to the strong imagination of the writer, no less than to her power over her instrument. A little poem, dated as far back as 1842, is interesting; it will, perhaps, be remembered by some that another woman-poet, a sweet singer, as undervalued in our day as she was overvalued in her own – Mrs. Hemans – chose[157] the same subject for her first poetic effort. Here are Miss Rossetti's lines: –

> "TO MY MOTHER.
> "Today's your natal day;
> Sweet flowers I bring;
> Mother, accept, I pray.
> My offering.

155. From Andrew Lang's poem, "Ballade of Middle Age."
156. Refers to Christina Rossetti's poem, "The Dead City."
157. Felicia Hemans.

"And may you happy live.
And long us bless;
Receiving, as you give,
Great happiness."[158]

In 1850, our poet, under the name of Ellen Alleyn, contributed several poems to the *Germ,* that wonderful little periodical whose career, as short-lived as it was glorious, is now a matter of history. Ellen Alleyn's verses have, with one exception, been found worthy a place in the latest edition of Christina Rossetti's poetry. "Repining,"[159] the longest, in some ways the most important, though distinctly the least *réussi* of them all, has never, I believe, been reprinted. Vague, mystic, melancholy, it contains passages stamped with the right stamp. I quote a few lines, which seem to me unmistakable, coming as they do from a poet of twenty: –

"What is this thing? Thus hurriedly
To pass into eternity;
To leave the earth so full of mirth;
To lose the profit of our birth;
To die and be no more; to cease.
Having numbness which is not peace."

The italics are my own.

It was not till fifteen years after the printing of the "Verses" that Miss Rossetti came before the public with a volume of poems. "Goblin Market, and other Poems," appeared in 1862, a dainty little book enriched by two beautiful designs from the pencil of her brother, Dante Gabriel Rossetti. This was followed, in 1866, by "The Prince's Progress, and other Poems," also with two designs from the same hand, and, in 1872, by "Sing Song," a charming book of rhymes for children; and, in 1881, by "A Pageant, and other Poems." Besides the little masque of the months, which gives its name to the book, this last volume contains

158. Rossetti's poem, "To My Mother."

159. This poem can be found in *New Poems by Christina Rossetti,* published in 1896 (Bernstein, ed., *The Romance of a Shop*, 207, n. 2).

many poems of considerable interest, including a series of Petrarchian sonnets, written from the point of view of an imaginary Laura.

"Had the great poetess of our own day," says Miss Rossetti, "been unhappy instead of happy, her circumstances would have invited her to bequeath us, in lieu of the Portuguese Sonnets, an inimitable *donna innominata,* drawn, not from fancy, but from feeling, and worthy to occupy a niche beside Beatrice and Laura."[160] Few of us, I think, would wish to have reversed the decree of Fate in this respect.

The list of Christina Rossetti's works includes, besides those mentioned, two volumes of prose tales, and several volumes of devotional pieces in both prose and verse. But it is with her poetry alone, and moreover with her best poetry, that I have to deal. This latter is undoubtedly contained in the two volumes of her maturity – "Goblin Market" and "The Prince's Progress." These, with but few additions or alterations, have been reprinted in one volume; and with this volume the general reader who wishes to make acquaintance with Christina Rossetti's poetry may content himself.

"Goblin Market," which occupies the first twenty pages of the book, is a whimsical fairy fancy, full of beauties, yet curiously unequal. Here and there, as in other productions of the poet, we are reminded of the magic notes which rang out for us in "Christabel" and "Kubla Khan;"[161] though, indeed, the sweet music of our minstrel, weird, exotic, vaguely fascinating as it is, tinkles faintly within sound of those mighty strains.

For "The Prince's Progress," a vaguely allegorical poem of some length, there is not much to be said as a work of sustained imagination; it contains, however, occasional felicities, and concludes with a passage of such rare beauty that I cannot do better than quote some of it here. The Prince, who has been variously tempted to linger unconscionably long on his journey to his betrothed, arrives at last at the palace to find the Princess dead – worn out by waiting. Her maidens reproach him –

160. The quotation is from Rossetti's *A Pageant and Other Poems* (1881).

161. Both poems were written by Samuel Taylor Coleridge (1772–1834); see Bernstein, ed., *The Romance of a Shop*, 208 n. 2.

"Too late for love, too late for joy,
  Too late, too late!
You loitered on the road too long,
  You trifled at the gate:
The enchanted dove upon her branch
  Died without a mate…
The enchanted princess in her tower
  Slept, died, behind the grate;
Her heart was starving all this while
  You made it wait.

* * * *

"Is she fair now as she lies?
  Once she was fair;
Meet queen for any kingly king,
  With gold-dust in her hair.
Now these are poppies in her locks,
  White poppies she must wear;
Must wear a veil to shroud her face.
  And the want graven there;
Or is the hunger fed at length,
  Cast off the care?

"We never saw her with a smile,
  Or with a frown;
Her bed seemed never soft to her,
  Though tossed of down;
She little heeded what she wore,
  Kirtle, or wreath, or gown;
We think her white brows often ached
  Beneath her crown….

"Her heart sat silent through the noise
  And concourse of the street;
There was no hurry in her hands,
  No hurry in her feet;
There was no bliss drew nigh to her
  That she might run to meet.

"You should have wept her yesterday,
Wasting upon her bed:
But wherefore should you weep today
That she is dead?"

But it is, perhaps, when she is least mystic, least involved – when she is simplest, most direct, most human, that Christina Rossetti is at her best.

"A Royal Princess," while retaining all the writer's indescribable charm of manner, glows throughout with genuine passion;

"Shows a heart within, blood-tinctured of a veined humanity."[162]

It is terribly appropriate reading for these days, the tale of the luxuriously-reared Princess whose castle is attacked by the starving mob. I quote, with reluctance – for no quotation can give an idea of the beauty of this poem – the last stanzas: –

"'Sit and roast there with your meat, sit and bake there with
your bread,
You who sat to see us starve,' one shrieking woman said;
'Sit on your throne and roast with your crown upon your head.'

"Nay, this thing will I do, while my mother tarrieth,
I will take my fine spun gold, but not to sew therewith,
I will take my gold and gems and rainbow fan and wreath;

"With a ransom in my lap, a king's ransom in my hand,
I will go down to this people, will stand face to face, will stand
Where they curse king, queen, and princess of this cursed land.

"They shall take all to buy them bread, take all I have to give;
I, if I perish, perish; they today shall eat and live;
I, if I perish, perish; that's the goal I half conceive."[163]

162. This quotation is from Barrett Browning's "Lady Geraldine's Courtship" (Bernstein, ed., *The Romance of a Shop*, 210 n. 1).

163. From Rossetti's "A Royal Princess."

In "Maude Clare" is again apparent the dramatic power which gives life to "A Royal Princess." This little poem is worthy to take a place in our ballad-literature, the traces of whose influence it so deeply shows. In a few vivid verses we are told how the stately Maude Clare followed her faithless lover and his bride to the church, overwhelming the one with reproaches, the other with taunts: –

"'Take my share of a fickle heart,
Mine of a paltry love:
Take it or leave it as you will,
I wash my hands thereof.'

"'And what you leave,' said Nell, 'I'll take;
And what you spurn, I'll wear;
For he's my lord for better and worse,
And him I love, Maude Clare.

"'Yea, though you're taller by the head,
More wise, and much more fair,
I'll love him till he loves me best,
Me best of all, Maude Clare.'"

Only a woman could have written this poem.

Almost perfect, in their way, are "The Hour and the Ghost," "The Ghost's Petition," and "Wife to Husband." Who that has read them can forget these lines (from the last), with their plaintive refrain? –

"Blank sea to sail upon,
Cold bed to sleep in:
Goodbye.
While you clasp, I must be gone
For all your weeping:
I must die.

"A kiss for one friend,
And a word for two:
Goodbye.

A lock that you must send,
A kindness you must do:
I must die.

"Not a word for you,
Not a lock or kiss:
Goodbye.
We, one, must part in two;
Verily death is this:
I must die."[164]

I should be disposed to place this group of poems – "A Royal Princess," "Maude Clare," "The Hour and the Ghost," "The Ghost's Petition," and "Wife to Husband" – very high in our literature. And of great excellence are Miss Rossetti's more purely lyric poems – for instance, the lines beginning, "When I am dead, my dearest,"[165] and those headed "A Birthday,"[166] both of which have been made familiar to us by their musical setting. Nor must it be forgotten that Miss Rossetti has been among the numerous writers of our day who have ventured frequently within the sonnet's scanty plot of ground. Many of her sonnets are good, but none, I think, of that supreme excellence which gives to such productions their *raison-d'être.*

There is a fatal fascination about sonnet-writing, to which too many of our poets have succumbed. The critic who objected to sonnets on the ground that they looked like bricks, was undoubtedly a crude person, but not altogether without his perceptions. Certain dramatic and descriptive qualities notwithstanding, it is as a lyric poet that Miss Rossetti must be classified; that is to say, if we are to occupy ourselves with terms and labels in the matter. Hers is, at best, a poetic personality difficult to grasp, difficult to classify. As with Shelley[167] and Coleridge,[168] she is at one moment intensely

164. From Rossetti's "Wife to Husband."
165. From Rossetti's "Song."
166. From Rossetti's "A Birthday."
167. Percy Bysshe Shelley.
168. See above footnote 161.

human, intensely personal; at another, she paddles away in her rainbow shell, and is lost to sight as she dips over the horizon-line of her halcyon sea.

A fervid human spirit; a passionate woman's heart; an imagination deep and tender; a fancy vivid and curious; is it to be wondered at that the poet in whom such qualities are met should elude the hard and fast measurements of the critic? Her muse personifies itself for us, an elfin sprite with iridescent wings, and eyes that startle us with their mournful human gaze.

I hesitate to pronounce what should seem to be meant for a verdict on Christina Rossetti's poetry, still less to indulge in prophecy as to its power of resisting the action of the waves of Time. If, indeed, the art be not always worthy of the artist; if the vessel, at times, obscure the flame within; if manner grow here and there to mannerism, *naïveté* to bathos, subtlety to thinness; it must be remembered how delicate, how fine, how unique is that art at its best. Christina Rossetti stands alone, as Dante Gabriel Rossetti stood alone. From the branches of a wondrous tree, transplanted by chance to our clime, we pluck the rare, exotic fruit, and the unfamiliar flavour is very sweet. It is not here the place for criticism of the author of "The House of Life."[169] But of Christina Rossetti let it be said that if she is not great, at least, artistically speaking, she is good.

169. Dante Gabriel Rossetti's *The House of Life.*

Women and Club Life (1888)

"Send your horse home and stop and dine here with me, Julia; I've asked Trixy Rattlecash and Emily Sheppard," says Mr. du Maurier's Miss Firebrace, as she reclines at ease in the luxurious club-chair.

"Can't, my dear girl; my sainted old father-in-law's just gone back to Yorkshire, and poor Bolly's all alone," replies Mrs. Bolingbroke Tompkins with a sigh of regret for the freedom of spinsterhood and the charms of club life.

It is not ten years since the appearance of this little bit of dialogue and its accompanying sketch in the pages of *Punch*,[170] and already the world has drifted into a stolid acceptance of the fact of feminine club life; has come to look on, without surprise or amusement, at the rapid growth of women's clubs, adapted to the various requirements of various classes.

Demand, say the makers of that mischievous pseudo-science, political economy, creates supply. What has hitherto been felt as a vague longing – the desire among women for a corporate life, for a wider human fellowship, a richer social opportunity – has assumed the definite shape of a practical demand, now that so many women of all ranks are controllers of their own resources.

---

170. The quotations are from a cartoon by du Maurier, "Female Clubs v. Matrimony," *Punch's Almanack for 1878* 74 (December 14, 1877); see Bernstein, ed. *The Romance of a Shop*, 213 n. 1; for a reprint of the cartoon see p. 214. Bernstein's edition includes "Women and Club Life," with commentary, in the appendices (213–20).

From the high and dry region of the residential neighbourhood the women come pouring down to those pleasant shores where the great stream of human life is dashing and flowing.

In classroom and lecture-theatre, office and art-school, college and clubhouse alike, woman is waking up to a sense of the hundred and one possibilities of social intercourse; possibilities which, save in exceptional instances, have hitherto for her been restricted to the narrowest of grooves.

The female club must be regarded as no isolated and ludicrous phenomenon, but as the natural outcome of the spirit of an age which demands excellence in work from women no less than from men, and as one of the many steps towards the attainment of that excellence.

As Miss Simcox points out, in a recent number of the *Nineteenth Century*,[171] no great performance in art or science can justly be expected from a class which is debarred from the inestimable advantages of a corporate social life.

To turn from the general to the particular: it is now my intention to enumerate and consider the most important of those ladies' clubs in London, which have followed so closely on the heels of Mr. du Maurier's little skit.

Of these, the Albemarle Club (founded in 1881) is, perhaps, the best known. Its members consist of ladies and men in about equal numbers, from whom an annual subscription of five guineas is exacted, the original entrance-fee of eight guineas having been suspended by the committee in 1884. In the large, conveniently-situated house in Albemarle Street, ladies can entertain their friends of both sexes, make appointments, or merely pass the time pleasantly in the perusal of periodical literature.

---

171. Refers to Edith Simcox's (1844–1901) article, "The Capacity of Women," *The Nineteenth Century: A Monthly Review* no. 127 (September 1887): 391–402 (Bernstein, ed., *The Romance of a Shop*, 214 n. 1; New, ed., *The Complete Novels*, 563 n. 46).

How many a valuable acquaintance has been improved, how many an important introduction obtained in that convenient neutral territory of club-land!

Here, at last, is a chance of seeing something of A or B or C apart from her sisters, her cousins, and her aunts – all excellent people, no doubt, but with whom we personally have nothing in common, and whose acquaintance we have no desire to cultivate. And here is a haven of refuge, where we can write our letters and read the news, undisturbed by the importunities of a family circle, which can never bring itself to regard feminine leisure and feminine solitude as things to be respected.

Of more recent date is the Alexandra Club, for ladies only, situated in Grosvenor Street, whose list of members, no less than that of the Albemarle, includes many names well known in society, and in artistic and political circles. For this club no lady is eligible "who has been, or would probably be, precluded from attending Her Majesty's Drawing Rooms"; a nice phrase, full of the sound and fury of exclusiveness, and signifying not so much after all.

There is an entrance-fee of three guineas, and an annual subscription of three and two guineas for town and country members respectively; and sleeping accommodation is available at moderate charges, including beds for ladies' maids.

Men may not be introduced to the club as visitors – a restriction which, in my opinion, places it at a disadvantage with the Albemarle.

It is a significant fact that, established as recently as 1884, the Alexandra already numbers about 600 members.

Not the least interesting of female clubs is the University Club for Ladies, which came into existence at the beginning of last year. For this are eligible as members the graduates of any University; registered medical practitioners of the United Kingdom; students or lecturers who have been in residence for at least three terms either at Newnham or Girton College, Cambridge, or at Somerville or Lady Margaret Hall, Oxford; undergraduates of any University who have passed the examination next after matriculation; and students who have passed the first professional examination of any medical corporation. It will be seen, therefore, that this is a club of workers; and the working woman not being apt to have much spare cash at her disposal, it has been organised on a more modest basis than either of those before alluded to. A guinea entrance-fee and a guinea annual subscription represent the expenses of membership; nor have the University ladies aspired, so far, to the dignity of a clubhouse, but have contented themselves with a small but daintily-furnished set of rooms on the upper floors of a house in New Bond Street. Simple meals at moderate charges can be obtained of the housekeeper; but if Cornelia Blimber[172] or the Princess Ida objects to the austerity of this scholar's fare, an arrangement has been entered into with the Grosvenor Restaurant opposite, by which more luxurious cates can be supplied to her on the shortest notice.

Here, amid Morris[173] papers and Chippendale chairs, old acquaintances are renewed, old gossip resuscitated, and any amount of "shop" of various descriptions discussed.

> "And where have all my playmates sped,
>   Whose ranks were once so serried?
> Why, some are wed, and some are dead,
>   And some are only buried.
> Frank Petre, then so full of fun,
>   Is now St. Blaise's prior;
> And Travers, the attorney's son,
>   Is member for the shire."[174]

The suburban high-school mistress, in town for a day's shopping or picture-seeing, exchanges here the discomfort of the pastrycook's or the costliness of the restaurant for the comforts of a quiet meal and a quiet read or chat in the cosy club precincts; the busy journalist

172. Character in Dickens' *Dombey and Son* (1848).
173. William Morris.
174. From Frederick Locker-Lampson's poem, "The Jester's Moral."

rests here from her labours of "private viewing," strengthening herself with tea and newspapers before setting out for fresh lands to conquer. The mingled sense of independence and *esprit de corps* which made college life at once so pleasant and so wholesome are not wanting here in the colder, more crowded regions of London club-land.

Differing somewhat in scope from the clubs described above is the Somerville Club,* in Oxford Street, which aims at combining the usual advantages of the club proper with those of the class or college; organising debates, lectures, and social evenings for the benefit of its members. These latter are drawn from all classes of society; the annual subscription is ten shillings. The original idea of its founders was to create a social centre for women to whom the ordinary social advantages are not easily accessible. Only women are eligible as members, but men may be introduced as visitors. Reading room, library, etc., are provided, as at other clubs, and refreshments can be obtained at very moderate charges.

The ice, then, may be considered to have been fairly broken, and the woman's club to have taken its place among our social institutions. There is, so far, no good reason to suppose that, intoxicated by the sweets of club liberty, ladies have been led away into any of those extravagances prophesied by Mr. du Maurier and other humourists.

The female club-lounger, the *flâneuse* of St. James's Street, latch-key in pocket and eye-glasses on nose, remains a creature of the imagination. The clubs mentioned are sober, business-like haunts enough, to which no dutiful wife or serious-minded maiden need feel ashamed of belonging. If the Alexandra, with its talk of Drawing Rooms, aims rather more at smartness than the rest, it is none the worse for that; nor are we to blame the "frivolous" woman for following in the wake of her professional sister.

---

* The original subscription to the Somerville Club (founded in 1878) was five shillings. The club dissolved itself at the end of last year, and has recently re-established itself on a slightly different basis. After June, 1888, an entrance-fee of ten shillings will be charged.

But it is to the professional woman, when all is said, that the club offers the most substantial advantages. What woman engaged in art, in literature, in science, has not felt the drawbacks of her isolated position? Apart from that intellectual solitude to which Miss Simcox alludes in the article before quoted, she has had to contend with every practical disadvantage.

She has had to fight her way unknown and single-handed; to compete with a guild of craftsmen all more or less known to one another, having easy access to one another, bound together by innumerable links of acquaintance and intercourse. It is all uphill work with her, unless she be somebody's sister, or somebody's wife, or unless she have the power and the means of setting in motion an elaborate social machinery to obtain what every average follower of his calling has come to regard as a right.

The number of professional women of all kinds has increased so greatly, and is still so greatly increasing, that, with a little more *esprit de corps*, women might do a great deal for themselves and for one another. A level platform of intercourse for members of the same craft, regardless of distinction of sex, may assuredly be looked forward to in no distant future; but at present I believe the fact of sex to have too great social insistence to render such an arrangement practicable, though such institutions as the Albemarle Club are steps in the right direction.

Not long ago, indeed, a motion was brought forward for the admission of women to the Savile Club. Its rejection must be a matter of regret to all women engaged in literature and education; but the fact that such a motion was brought forward and considered is of itself significant.

At this point we seem to hear the voice of some excellent Conservative upraised in protest. "You have dismissed Trixy Rattlecash and Julia Wildrake,"[175] it says, "but do you hold up anything so admirable after all? Is Cornelia Blimber elbowing her way into a man's club room

175. Characters in du Maurier's cartoon, "Female Clubs v. Matrimony."

such an edifying spectacle, when all is said? Is it such a beautiful thing that Mrs. Jellaby[176] should absent herself from home at all hours of the day, or the Princess Ida take to haunting the neighbourhood of Bond Street? Are we expected to rejoice over the fact that Blanche and Psyche can entertain Cyril and Florian[177] at a club dinner, or to sympathise with the selfishness of Penthesilea[178] in disregarding the social claims of her family?"

In reply, I can only say that I am considering things as they are, not as they might be. We are in England, not in Utopia; it is the nineteenth century, and not the Golden Age; the land is not flowing with milk and honey; those commodities can only be obtained by strenuous and competitive effort.

It is not for me to rejoice over, or to deplore, the complete and rapid change of the female position which has taken place in this country during the last few years. It is a phenomenon for our observation rather than an accident for our intervention; the result of complex and manifold circumstance over which none of us can be thought to have much control. The tide has set in and there is no stemming it.

It is not without regret that one sees the old order changing and giving place to new in this respect. The woman who owns no interests beyond the circle of home, who takes no thought for herself, who is content to follow where love and superior wisdom are leading – this ideal of feminine excellence is not, indeed, to be relinquished without a sigh.

But she is, alas! too expensive a luxury for our civilisation; we cannot afford her.

To ignore blindly this fact, to refuse obstinately to face it, only means the bringing down of sorrow and distress on the heads of everyone concerned.

A day has come when the most conservative among us must realise the necessity for women of leaving off weeping and taking to working, no less than man.

176. Character in Dickens' *Bleak House* (1853).

177. Characters in Tennyson's *The Princess.*

178. Figure of Greek mythology.

Now an unmixed diet of work is no more suited for Jill than it is for Jack; she must be left, moreover, to choose her own games, and play after her own fashion. A course of worsted-work and morning calls to a woman desirous of the peaceful amenities of club-land would be about as enlivening as the celebrated game of chevy-chase, in *Vice Versâ*,[179] to the young gentlemen of Dr. Grinstone's Academy.

There is no reason to suppose that because she is a member of a club a woman will develop the selfishness of her husband and brother; that, for instance, she will seek to emulate the young man in *Punch* who wondered why his family went to the expense of taking in the papers, considering he saw them all at his club![180]

Do we hear of unladylike excesses among the students of Girton or of Somerville Hall? Of the undue extravagance and evil habits of those hard-working and self-respecting bodies? And who does not remember the prophetic chorus of many Cassandras and Isaiahs[181] which greeted the establishment of lectures for women at Cambridge?

Let it be remembered that, while the old state of affairs was in many respects beautiful and satisfactory, it was the source of much and of increasing evil; adapted rather for the happiness of the chosen few than of the unchosen many. To its upholders in these days can only be attributed an unphilosophic disregard of the greatest happiness of the greatest number.

And yet, in the words of Clough's undergraduate: –

179. Thomas Anstey Guthrie's novel, *Vice Versâ: A Lesson to Fathers* (1882).
180. Refers to another *Punch* cartoon.
181. Prophetic figure of Greek mythology (Cassandra) and biblical prophet (Isaiah).

> "Often I find myself saying – old faith and doctrine abjuring,
> Into the crucible casting philosophies, facts, convictions –
> Were it not well that the stem should be naked of leaf and of tendril,
> Poverty-stricken, the barest, the dismallest stick of the garden,
> Flowerless, leafless, unlovely for ninety and nine long summers,
> So at the hundredth, at last, were bloom for one day at the summit,
> So but that fleeting flower were lovely as Lady Maria?"[182]

Often I find myself saying it, perhaps; but always to return, as the hero of the poem did, to the recollection that interchange of service is, after all, the law and condition of beauty.[183] Let us, then, remember that, while we lose much, we gain, perhaps more, by the new state of affairs.

---

182. From Arthur Hugh Clough's "The Bothie of Tober-Na-Vuolich: A Long-Vacation Pastoral."

183. New (*The Complete Novels*, 563 n. 54) identifies Levy's paraphrasing of Clough's poem here; see the lines from Clough that begin chapter seven of *The Romance of a Shop* (p. 57).

Readers at the British Museum (1889)

"For out of old fieldes, as men saithe,
Cometh al this new corne fro yere to yere,
And out of old bookes, in good faithe,
Cometh al this new science that men lere."

THE ASSEMBLY OF FOULES[184]

Those readers of *Atalanta* who have been to the British Museum will probably have obtained a momentary glimpse of the great Reading Room, with its book-lined walls, its radiating rows of seats, and its characteristic, suggestive scent of leather bindings.

Under the great dome – almost the largest in the world – they will have noticed a motley crowd of readers, in various stages of industry and idleness, absorbed in their books, bustling hither and thither with important faces, gossiping, lounging, wrapped in thought, or even, in some rare instances, fast asleep like the man in the picture.[185]

The great library of the Museum, which has recently been described as incomparably the best, and is, with the exception of the National Library, at Paris, the largest in the world, attracts to itself in ever-increasing numbers all sorts and conditions of men and women. Students as sharply contrasted as the dry-as-dust, paper-laden old scholar of our illustrations and the trim young person in the *pince-nez*,

184. From Geoffrey Chaucer's poem, *The Parlament of Foules*.

185. The original publication includes various images of readers.

jostle one another from the opening of the doors at 9 a.m., to those hours of the afternoon or evening when the lavender-white light of the electric lamps shines somewhat fitfully through the thick atmosphere.

The "Room" has indeed become a centre, a general workshop, where in these days of much reading, much writing, and competitive examinations, the great business of book-making, article-making, cramming, may be said to have their head-quarters, while it has not ceased to be the resort of the genuine student who loves knowledge for its own sake.

The library and the Reading Room, or rather a reading room, are as old as the Museum itself.

In the middle of the eighteenth century the trustees of Sir Hans Sloane,[186] an eminent Chelsea physician, offered, in accordance with his will, his valuable collection of curiosities, manuscripts, and books to the nation, at a price greatly below its actual value. This bequest suggested the notion of a National Museum. In 1753 the foundation charter of the British Museum was granted, and in 1759 the nucleus of our present world-famed collection was stowed away in Montague House, a mansion originally belonging to the Duke of Montague, situated where the Museum buildings now stand.

The library was from the first an important feature of the collection.

In the years which elapsed between the act of incorporation and the purchase of Montague House several valuable additions had been made to Sir Hans Sloane's treasure of books, MSS., including the Harleian and Cottonian MSS. and the library of another private collector, Major Edwards.[187]

But the most important addition of all was that of the Royal Library, presented in 1757 by George II[188] to the nation.

---

186. Hans Sloane (1660–1753), whose collections helped to found the British Museum.

187. Major Arthur Edwards (1680–1743); see Bernstein, ed., *The Romance of a Shop*, 222 n. 2. "Readers at the British Museum," with accompanying footnotes, is included in Bernstein's appendices (220–7).

188. George II (1683–1760), King of Great Britain and Ireland, 1727–1760.

This collection, brought together by the kings of England from Henry VIII[189] to William III,[190] included the libraries of Archbishop Cranmer[191] and of Isaac Casaubon,[192] the great scholar, and the Alexandrian Codex of the Bible. With the Royal Library passed also the privilege of being supplied with a copy of every publication entered at Stationers' Hall; a privilege which, retained to this day, gives to our National Library one of its most important and characteristic features.

Since this first sowing of the seed, the library has been enriched by gifts and purchases too numerous to mention; though a word must be said of the King's Library, presented (or sold) by George IV[193] to the Museum.

This collection, brought together by the agents of George III,[194] includes many books printed by Caxton,[195] and early editions of the classics. Its choiceness is partly owing to the fact that it was collected during the period of the suppression of the Jesuit houses, whose valuable libraries were, consequently, for sale.

Of rare value also is the Grenville Library, bequeathed in 1845 by Mr. Grenville,[196] one of the trustees of the Museum.

Among other treasures it contains a unique copy of a hitherto undiscovered edition of *The Canterbury Tales*,[197] printed in 1498 by Wynkyn de Worde;[198] a second edition (Caxton) of the same work; a first edition of Shakespeare's collected dramatic works; and the only

189. Henry VIII (1491–1547), King of England, 1509–1547.
190. William III, "William of Orange" (1650–1702); King of England, Scotland, and Ireland, 1689–1702.
191. Thomas Cranmer (1489–1556), Archbishop of Canterbury, 1533–1555.
192. Isaac Casaubon (1559–1614), classics scholar.
193. George IV (1762–1830), King of the United Kingdom of Great Britain and Ireland, 1820–1830.
194. George III (1738–1820), King of Great Britain and Ireland, 1760–1801; King of the United Kingdom of Great Britain and Ireland, 1801–1820.
195. William Caxton (1422–1491); introduced printing in England.
196. Thomas Grenville (1755–1846), statesperson and collector of books.
197. Geoffrey Chaucer's *The Canterbury Tales*.
198. Wynkyn de Worde was a German migrant who came to London to work with Caxton (Bernstein, ed., *The Romance of a Shop*, 223 n. 4).

known fragment of the New Testament in English, translated by Tyndale and Roy,[199] printed in 1525 at Cologne, when the translators had to interrupt the printing and flee for their lives. Besides its vast stores of MSS. and printed books of many periods and in many tongues, the Museum boasts a collection of newspapers dating from 1588 downwards; and one of books on vellum surpassing that of every other library with the exception of the Bibliothèque Nationale, including a first edition of the Bible known as the Mazarin Bible, printed in 1454.

A room was set apart for readers from the opening of the British Museum at Montague House in 1759.

It was a basement apartment, opening by glass doors on to a pleasant garden, and contained an oak table with chairs for twenty readers. A superintendent was appointed to answer questions and help the readers generally with their work, but these were few in number, and three years after the opening of the library to the public there is an entry to the effect that "no company coming to the Reading Room, Dr. Templeman [the superintendent] ventured to go away about two o'clock."

We hear later on however of this same Dr. Templeman, that, strolling in the garden of Montague House in office hours, he was met by a trustee of the Museum, who, indignant at this neglect of duty, called out to him, "Go back, sir!" Not long afterwards his resignation was sent in. In July, 1759, Gray,[200] the poet, writes from London to a friend: – "I am just settled in my new habitation in Southampton Row, and though a solitary and dispirited creature, not unquiet nor wholly unpleasant to myself. The Museum will be my chief amusement. I this day passed through the jaws of a Great Leviathan that lay in my way, into the presence of Dr. Templeman, Superintendent of the Reading Room, who congratulated himself on so much good company." Gray, himself, as he goes on to explain, made the fifth reader present.

199. William Tyndale (1494–1536), scholar of the Protestant Reformation, who, with the help of William Roy, translated into English the Pentateuch and New Testament (Bernstein, ed., *The Romance of a Shop*, 223 n. 5).

200. Thomas Gray (1716–1771); see Bernstein, ed., *The Romance of a Shop*, 224 n. 1.

But if the company was small, it was certainly select. Besides that of Gray, we find the names of Hume[201] among the earliest readers: Johnson[202] was admitted in 1761, and one cannot help regretting that the Reading Room of the present day was unknown to him.

In that large and crowded building, with its opportunities for gossip and lounging, the Doctor would have been in his element. Fleet Street, I firmly believe, would have been abandoned in favour of Bloomsbury, and those thundering sledge-hammers of common-sense would have echoed in the tall stone galleries, or sounded more faintly under the dome of the Reading Room itself.

Isaac Disraeli, father of Lord Beaconsfield,[203] was among the habitual readers at the end of the last century, and he records that there were never more than a dozen of them present.

The French Revolution brought about an increase in the number of readers, many of the refugees, some people of distinction among them, seeking consolation from books in the land of exile.

The names of Scott,[204] Sydney Smith,[205] Lamb[206] (recommended by Godwin),[207] and Hallam,[208] figure among the list of readers in the first years of the present century.

As time went on applications for admission to the library became more and more numerous; and the original arrangements for the accommodation of readers at Montague House were found quite inadequate.

One apartment after another was made use of as Reading Room, but it was not till 1857 that the present structure was completed.

---

201. Philosopher, David Hume (1711–1776).
202. Samuel Johnson.
203. Isaac Disraeli (1766–1848), father of Benjamin Disraeli.
204. Walter Scott.
205. Sydney Smith (1771–1845), author and cleric.
206. Charles Lamb.
207. William Godwin (1756–1836): philosopher and novelist who married foundational First-Wave feminist, Mary Wollstonecraft (1759–1797).
208. Arthur Henry Hallam (1811–1833), poet.

This we owe to the genius of Anthony Panizzi,[209] an Italian political exile, but a naturalized Englishman, and formerly superintendent of the Reading Room.

He planned and closely overlooked the carrying out of his scheme which has given us a library and Reading Room unparalleled for arrangement in the world.

The vast, circular apartment, whose aspect is no doubt familiar to many of my readers, can accommodate at the present day no less than 460 readers. The desks and tables are models of comfort and convenience; the lighting is by electric light; and so carefully is the temperature regulated by means of an elaborate ventilating apparatus, that an enthusiastic American lady once compared the atmosphere of the place in summer to that of a cool and shady dell.

Let the people who grumble at the closeness of the densely crowded apartment take this to heart, and bear in mind that the unwholesome condition of a former reading room was such as to give rise to a peculiar complaint, known at the time as museum megrims. But perhaps, as a writer in *Blackwood* points out,[210] the fact which most strikes us in connection with the Museum library is its wonderful accessibility. Any person above the age of twenty-one, who can induce one householder to vouch for his good behaviour, has the whole collection of books within his easy reach.

It is a mere matter of transcribing the name and press-mark of any volume from the catalogue, of taking your seat and waiting for the attendant to bring what you have ordered.

There is rarely, if ever, a long delay, and no limit is fixed to the number of books which a reader may demand.

209. Anthony Panizzi (1797–1879), the British Museum's Assistant Librarian, 1831–1837, and subsequently Principal Librarian, 1856–1866.

210. The source is R.K. Douglas, "The British Museum and the People Who Go There," *Blackwood's Edinburgh Magazine* 144, no. 874 (August 1888): 196–217 (see Bernstein, ed. *The Romance of a Shop*, 226 n. 1).

Not only the Reading Room, but the surrounding libraries, are models of arrangement, where millions of books are stowed in such a manner that any one of them may be obtained on the shortest notice.

A French professor told me that he found it on the whole a greater saving of time to come over and read in the Museum during his vacations than to remain in Paris, where the National Library, though larger than our own, and very valuable, and furnished moreover with a reading room, is not so easily accessible.

Perhaps, alas! it is this very accessibility which has brought about such frequent abuse of the privilege of reading at the library, where many people have no scruple in taking up the time of the officials, or crowding out genuine workers from the desks in pursuit of such futilities as answers to word-competitions, chess-problems, or mere novel-reading.

The lower shelves of the Reading Room are filled with books of reference, and these may be taken out by the reader at will, a chart of their positions being furnished. There is an extra room devoted to the consultation of newspapers, and an apartment known as the large room, where may be seen works too valuable to be carried into the Reading Room, or where, sometimes, by the kindness of the officials, readers under the age of twenty-one anticipate the privilege of their majority.

As for the readers who come and go in these various apartments, they include, as I have said, all sorts and conditions of men and women. To begin with, they might be roughly classified into *habitués* and occasional visitors. It is naturally the former class that comes most under observation, and the people composing it, various as they are, develop after a time certain qualities in common.

What are his marks? A premature baldness, a roundness in the shoulders, a slouching gait, an increasing tendency to short-sight, a growing disinclination for the use of the clothes-brush. These are the marks of the Reading Room *habitué*.

Rich and poor, old and young, competent and incompetent, the successes and failures of life and of literature may be met beneath the dome in indistinguishable fellowship.

To each and all, no doubt, the "Room" presents its attractions, for each and all has its uses. For some it is a workshop, for others a lounge; there are those who put it to the highest uses, while in, many cases it serves as a shelter, – a refuge, in more senses than one, for the destitute.

Bibliography

Texts by Amy Levy Cited

"A Ballad of Last Seeing." *The Cambridge Review: A Journal of University Life and Thought* 4, no. 95 (May 2, 1883): 337.

"A Ballad of Religion and Marriage" (1915). Circulated privately by Clement Shorter.

"A Cross Road Epitaph." *The Cambridge Review: A Journal of University Life and Thought* 4, no. 96 (May 9, 1883): 353.

A London Plane-Tree and Other Verse. London: T. Fisher Unwin, 1889.

"A Meadowshire Romance: In Five Chapters." *Lawn-Tennis* (August 18; August 25; September 1; September 8, 1886): 176–7; 186–8; 202–3; 214–5. Reprinted with permission of The Camellia Collections.

A Minor Poet and Other Verse. 1884; rpt. London: T. Fisher Unwin, 1891.

"A Slip of the Pen." *Temple Bar: A London Magazine for Town and Country Readers* 86, no. 344 (July 1889): 371–7.

"A Wall Flower." *The Woman's World* 2 (1889): 320.

"Addenbrooke." *Belgravia: A London Magazine* 68, no. 269 (March 1889): 24–34.

"After Heine." *The Cambridge Review: A Journal of University Life and Thought* 6, no. 136 (December 3, 1884): 123–4.

"After Heine." *The Cambridge Review: A Journal of University Life and Thought* 7, no. 169 (February 24, 1886): 237–8.

"Alma Mater." *The Cambridge Review: A Journal of University Life and Thought* 9, no. 203 (June 1, 1887): 362.

"Another Morning in Florence." *London Society: An Illustrated Magazine of Light and Amusing Literature for the Hours of Relaxation* 49, no. 292 (April 1886): 386–90.

"At Dawn." *The Woman's World* 3 (1890): 65.

"At Prato." *Time* 19, no. 43 (July 1888): 68–74.

"Between Two Stools." *Temple Bar: A London Magazine for Town and Country Readers* 69 (November 1883): 337–50.

"Captivity." *The Cambridge Review: A Journal of University Life and Thought* 7, no. 163 (December 9, 1885): 142–3.

"Cohen of Trinity." *The Gentleman's Magazine* 266, no. 1901 (May 1889): 417–24.

"Definitions." *Kind Words for Boys and Girls,* December 1, 1876, 51.

"Easter-Tide at Tunbridge Wells." *London Society: An Illustrated Magazine of Light and Amusing Literature for the Hours of Relaxation* 47, no. 281 (May 1885): 481–3.

"Eldorado at Islington." *The Woman's World* 2 (1889): 488–9.

"Epitaph." *The Cambridge Review: A Journal of University Life and Thought* 4, no. 96 (May 9, 1883): 353.

"Euphemia: A Sketch." *The Victoria Magazine* 36 (August-September 1880): 129–41, 199–203.

"From Grillparzer's Sappho." *The Cambridge Review: A Journal of University Life and Thought* 3, no. 59 (February 1, 1882): 141.

"From Heine." *The Cambridge Review: A Journal of University Life and Thought* 3, no. 67 (April 26, 1882): 270.

"Griselda." *Temple Bar: A London Magazine for Town and Country Readers* 84, no. 334 (September 1888): 65–96.

"Griselda." *The Evening Star* (October 27-November 17, 1888).

"Griselda." *The Living Age* 64, no. 2312 (October 20, 1888): 143–59.

"Imitation of Heine." *The Cambridge Review: A Journal of University Life and Thought* 3, no. 58 (December 7, 1881): 127

"In Holiday Humour." *London Society: An Illustrated Magazine of Light and Amusing Literature for the Hours of Relaxation* 46, no. 272 (August 1884): 177–84.

"In Retreat." *London Society: An Illustrated Magazine of Light and Amusing Literature for the Hours of Relaxation* 46, no. 273 (September 1884): 332–5.

"In Switzerland." *London Society: An Illustrated Magazine of Light and Amusing Literature for the Hours of Relaxation* 46, no. 271 (July 1884): 120.

"In the Black Forest." *London Society: An Illustrated Magazine of Light and Amusing Literature for the Hours of Relaxation* 46, no. 274 (October 1884): 392–4.

"James Thomson: A Minor Poet." *The Cambridge Review: A Journal of University Life and Thought* 4, no. 89 (February 21, 1883): 240–1; 4, no. 90 (February 28, 1883): 257–8.

"Jewish Children." *The Jewish Chronicle*, November 5, 1886, 8.

"Jewish Humour." *The Jewish Chronicle*, August 20, 1886, 9–10.

"Jewish Women and 'Women's Rights.'" *The Jewish Chronicle*, February 7, 1879, 5; February 28, 1879, 5.

"Junior Prize Essay." *Kind Words for Boys and Girls*, October 1, 1876, 292.

"Junior Prize Review: Aurora Leigh." *Kind Words for Boys and Girls*, October 1, 1875, 318.

"Last Words." *The University Pulpit: Supplement to The Cambridge Review: A Journal of University Life and Thought* 6, no. 141 (February 11, 1885): lxxi.

"Lohengrin." *The Academy* no. 724 (March 20, 1886): 201.

"London in July." *The Academy* no. 795 (July 30, 1887): 70.

"Lost and Won." *Lawn-Tennis* (August 4, 1886): 152–3. Reprinted with permission of The Camellia Collections.

"Mariana in the Ballroom." *London Society: An Illustrated Magazine of Light and Amusing Literature for the Hours of Relaxation* 45, "The Holiday Number for 1884" (1884): 76.

"Middle-Class Jewish Women of Today." *The Jewish Chronicle*, September 17, 1886, 7.

Miss Meredith. London: Hodder and Stoughton, 1889.

Miss Meredith. The British Weekly: A Journal of Social and Christian Progress (April 19-June 28, 1889).

"Mrs. Pierrepoint: A Sketch in Two Parts." *Temple Bar: A London Magazine for Town and Country Readers* 59 (June 1880): 226–36.

"Newnham College." Reprinted with permission of The Camellia Collections.

"Olga's Valentine." *London Society: An Illustrated Magazine of Light and Amusing Literature for the Hours of Relaxation* 45, no. 266 (February 1884): 152–7.

"Original Definitions: Heroism." *Kind Words for Boys and Girls*, December 1, 1875, 27.

"Out of the World." *London Society: An Illustrated Magazine of Light and Amusing Literature for the Hours of Relaxation* 49, no. 289 (January 1886): 53–6.

"Paul Heyse." *The Jewish Chronicle*, October 12, 1883, 4.

"Peace." *The Woman's World* 3 (1890): 7.

"Philosophy in the Ballroom." *London Society: An Illustrated Magazine of Light and Amusing Literature for the Hours of Relaxation* 48, no. 284 (August 1885): 175.

"Readers at the British Museum." *Atalanta* 2, no. 7 (April 1, 1889): 449–54.

Reuben Sachs: A Sketch. London: Macmillan and Co., 1888.

"Revenge." *London Society: An Illustrated Magazine of Light and Amusing Literature for the Hours of Relaxation* 47, no. 280 (April 1885): 389–99.

"Rondel." *Pall Mall Gazette*, February 24, 1888, 13.

"Run to Death." *The Victoria Magazine* 33 (May-October 1879): 248–50.

"Sokratics in the Strand." *The Cambridge Review: A Journal of University Life and Thought* 5, no. 113 (February 6, 1884): 163–4.

"Sonnet." In *Women's Voices: An Anthology of the Most Characteristic Poems by English, Scotch, and Irish Women*. Edited by Elizabeth Sharp, 348. London: Walter Scott, 1887.

"Sonnet" ("The Two Terrors"). In *Women's Voices: An Anthology of the Most Characteristic Poems by English, Scotch, and Irish Women.* Edited by Elizabeth Sharp, 349. London: Walter Scott, 1887.

"The Ballad of Ida Grey (A Story of Woman's Sacrifice): Part I." *The Pelican: A Quarterly Magazine Advocating the Social and Educational Progress of Woman* 2, no. 5 (January-April 1875): 20–1; "Part II." Reprinted with permission of The Camellia Collections.

"The Birch-Tree at Loeschwitz." *The Woman's World* 2 (1889): 429.

"The Diary of a Plain Girl." *London Society: An Illustrated Magazine of Light and Amusing Literature for the Hours of Relaxation* 44, no. 261 (September 1883): 295–304.

"The Dream." *The Cambridge Review: A Journal of University Life and Thought* 6, no. 130 (October 22, 1884): 29.

"The Ghetto at Florence." *The Jewish Chronicle*, March 26, 1886, 9.

"The Jew in Fiction." *The Jewish Chronicle*, June 4, 1886, 13.

"The New School of American Fiction." *Temple Bar: A London Magazine for Town and Country Readers* 70 (March 1884): 383–9.

"The Old House." *The Spectator: A Weekly Review of Politics, Literature, Theology, and Art* 62, no. 3173 (April 20, 1889): 543.

"The Poetry of Christina Rossetti." *The Woman's World* 1 (1888): 178–80.

"The Promise of Sleep." *The Woman's World* 3 (1890): 52.

"The Recent Telepathic Occurrence at the British Museum." *The Woman's World* 1 (1888): 31–2.

The Romance of a Shop. 1888; rpt. Boston: Cupples and Hurd, 1889.

"The Shepherd (From Goethe)." *The Cambridge Review: A Journal of University Life and Thought* 1, no. 26 (June 9, 1880): 158.

"The Sick Man in the Garden." *The Cambridge Review: A Journal of University Life and Thought* 3, no. 60 (February 8, 1882): 157.

The Unhappy Princess: An Extravaganza for Little People. London: Samuel French, 1888.

"The Village Garden." *The Spectator: A Weekly Review of Politics, Literature, Theology, and Art* 62, no. 3163 (February 9, 1889): 199.

"To Death." *The Cambridge Review: A Journal of University Life and Thought* 3, no. 60 (February 8, 1882): 157.

"To E." *London Society: An Illustrated Magazine of Light and Amusing Literature for the Hours of Relaxation* 49, no. 293 (May 1886): 447.

"To Sylvia." *The Cambridge Review: A Journal of University Life and Thought* 3, no. 65 (March 15, 1882): 289.

Translation of Heinrich Heine in Katie Magnus, *Jewish Portraits.* London: T. Fisher Unwin, 1888, 73.

Translation of J.B. Peres, *Historic and other doubts; or the non-existence of Napoleon proved.* Edited by Lily. London: E. W. Allen, 1885.

Translations of Jehudah Halevi in Katie Magnus, *Jewish Portraits.* London: T. Fisher Unwin, 1888, 15–6, 24–5, 30.

"Wise in Her Generation." *The Woman's World* 3 (1890): 20–3.

"Women and Club Life." *The Woman's World* 1 (1888): 364–7.

Xantippe and Other Verse. Cambridge: E. Johnson, 1881.

Other Works Cited

Alderman, Geoffrey. *Modern British Jewry*. Oxford: Clarendon Press, 1992.

Alexander, Christine, and Juliet McMaster, eds. *The Child Writer from Austen to Woolf*. Cambridge: Cambridge University Press, 2009.

Armstrong, Isobel, and Virginia Blain, eds. *Women Poetry, Late Romantic to Late Victorian: Gender and Genre, 1830–1900*. Basingstoke: Macmillan Press Ltd, 1999.

Arnold, Matthew. *Culture and Anarchy: An Essay in Social and Political Criticism*. London: Smith, Elder and Co., 1869.

______. *Lectures and Essays in Criticism*. Edited by R. H. Super. Ann Arbor: The University of Michigan Press, 1962.

Austin, Sarah. *Characteristics of Goethe: From the German of Falk, von Müller, &c.* Volume 1. Philadelphia: Lea & Blanchard, 1841.

Beckman, Linda Hunt. "Amy Levy." The Shalvi/Hyman Encyclopedia of Jewish Women (2021). Accessed August 27, 2021. https://jwa.org/encyclopedia/article/levy-amy.

______. *Amy Levy: Her Life and Letters*. Athens: Ohio University Press, 2000.

______. "Leaving 'the Tribal Duckpond': Amy Levy, Jewish Self-Hatred, and Jewish Identity." *Victorian Literature and Culture* 27, no. 1 (1999): 185–201.

Bernstein, Susan David. "Radical Readers at the British Museum: Eleanor Marx, Clementina Black, Amy Levy." *Nineteenth Century Gender Studies* 3, no. 2 (Summer 2007): no page numbers.

______, ed. *Reuben Sachs*. By Amy Levy. Peterborough: Broadview Editions, 2006.

______, ed. *The Romance of a Shop*. By Amy Levy. Peterborough: Broadview Editions, 2006.

Bristow, Joseph. "'All Out of Tune with this World's Instrument': the 'Minor' Poetry of Amy Levy." 4, no. 1 (1999): 76–103.

______, ed. *Cambridge Companion to Victorian Poetry*. Cambridge: Cambridge University Press, 2000.

______, ed. *The Fin-de-Siècle Poem: English Literary Culture and the 1890s*. Athens: Ohio UP, 2005.

Chase, Jefferson. *Inciting Laughter: The Development of Jewish Humor in 19th Century German Culture*. Berlin: De Gruyter, 1999.

Cheyette, Bryan. "From Apology to Revolt: Benjamin Farjeon, Amy Levy and the Post-Emancipation Anglo-Jewish Novel, 1880–1900." *Transactions of the Jewish Historical Society of England* 24 (1982–1986): 253–65.

______, and Nadia Valman, eds. *The Image of the Jew in European Liberal Culture, 1789–1914*. London: Vallentine Mitchell, 2004.

Cook, Roger, ed. *A Companion to the Works of Heinrich Heine*. Woodbridge: Camden House, 2002.

______. *By the Rivers of Babylon: Heinrich Heine's Late Songs and Reflections*. Detroit: Wayne State University Press, 1998.

Cooper, Gabriel. "Facing the East: Orientalism and Anti-Semitism in Heine's *Hebräische Melodien*." *Seminar: A Journal of Germanic Studies* 56, no. 1 (2020):

Danby, Frank. *Dr. Phillips: A Maida Vale Idyll*. London: Vizetelly, 1887.

Devine, Luke. "Exile and Redemption: Amy Levy's Association with Yehuda Halevi and the Transmission of the Sephardic Tradition of Hebrew Poetry." *Literature & Theology* 26, no. 2 (June 2012): 125–43.

______. *From Anglo-First-Wave towards American Second-Wave Jewish Feminism: Negotiating with Jewish Feminist Theology and its Communities in the Writing of Amy Levy*. Piscataway: Gorgias Press, 2010.

______. "Imagining Fin-de-Siècle Anglo-Jewish Minority Sub-Genres: Proto-Feminist Visions of Religious Reform in 'West End' London in Amy Levy's *Reuben Sachs* and Lily Montagu's *Naomi's Exodus*." *Melilah: Manchester Journal of Jewish Studies* 8, no. 1 (2013): 69–83.

______. "'I Sleep, but my Heart Waketh': Contiguity between Heinrich Heine's '*Imago*' of the Shulamite and Amy Levy's 'Borderland.'" *Association for Jewish Studies Review* 40, no. 2 (2017): 219–40.

______. "'The Ghetto at Florence': Reading Jewish Identity in Amy Levy's Early Poetry, 1880–86." *Prooftexts* 31, no. 1–2 (Winter/Spring 2011): 1–30.

Dobell, Bertram, ed. *The Poetical Works of James Thomson: The City of Dreadful Night*, Volume II. By James Thomson. London: Reeves and Turner, 1895.

Douglas, R.K. "The British Museum and the People Who Go There." *Blackwood's Edinburgh Magazine* 144, no. 874 (August 1888): 196–217.

Draper, Hal, ed. and trans. *The Complete Poems of Heinrich Heine: A Modern English Version*. Boston: Suhrkamp/Insel, 1982.

Dwor, Richa. *Jewish Feeling: Difference and Affect in Nineteenth-Century Jewish Women's Writing*. London: Bloomsbury, 2017.

______. "'Poor Old Palace-Prison!': Jewish Urban Memory in Amy Levy's 'The Ghetto at Florence' (1886)." *Partial Answers* 13, no. 1 (2015): 155–69.

______. "The Racial Romance of Amy Levy's *Reuben Sachs*." *English Literature in Transition, 1880–1920* 55, no. 4 (2012): 460–78.

Efron, John. *German Jewry and the Allure of the Sephardic*. Princeton: Princeton University Press, 2016.

Eliot, George. *Daniel Deronda*. Ware: Wordsworth Classics, 1996.

______. "German Wit: Heinrich Heine." *The Westminster Review* 137 (January 1856): 1–18.

Endelman, Todd. *The Jews of Britain 1656 to 2000*. Berkeley: University of California Press, 2002.

Engle, Sherry, and Susan Croft, eds. *Thousands of Noras: Short Plays by Women, 1875–1920*. Bloomington: iUniverse, 2015.

Fuchs, Anne, and Florian Krobb, eds. *Ghetto Writing: Traditional and Eastern Jewry in German-Jewish Literature from Heine to Hilsenrath*. Drawer: Camden House, 1999.

Galchinsky, Michael. *Grace Aguilar: Selected Writings*. Peterborough: Broadview, 2003.

______, ed. *The Origin of the Modern Jewish Woman Writer: Romance and Reform in Victorian England*. Detroit: Wayne State University Press, 1996.

Gallagher, David. *Metamorphosis: Transformations of the Body and the Influence of Ovid's Metamorphoses on German Literature of the Nineteenth and Twentieth* Centuries. New York: Rodopi, 2009.

Geiger, Abraham. *Divan des Castiliers Abu'l-Hassan Juda ha-Levi*. Breslau: Kern, 1851.

Gilman, Sander. *Jewish Self-Hatred and the Hidden Language of the Jews*. Baltimore: John Hopkins University Press, 1986.

______. *The Jew's Body*. New York: Routledge, 1991.

Goetschel, Willi. "Street, Life, and Other Signs: Heine in the Rue Laffitte." *City & Society* 21, no. 2 (2009): 230–44.

______. *The Discipline of Philosophy and the Invention of Modern Jewish Thought*. New York: Fordham University Press, 2015.

Goody, Alex. "Murder in Mile End: Amy Levy, Jewishness, and the City." *Victorian Literature and Culture* 34, no. 2 (2006): 461–79.

Gracombe, Sarah. "Converting Trilby: Du Maurier on Englishness, Jewishness and Culture." *Nineteenth-Century Literature* 58, no. 1 (June 2003): 75–108.

Lee-Hamilton, Eugene. *Sonnets of the Wingless Hours*. Chicago: Stone & Kimball, 1894.

Harrington, Emily. "'A Merciful Fury Sent to Save Me': Amy Levy's 'Xantippe' and Women's Conversations." *Victorian Studies* 62, no. 2 (2020): 188–93.

Heine, Heinrich. *Hebrew Melodies.* Translated by Stephen Mitchell and Jack Prelutsky. University Park: Pennsylvania State University Press, 2019.

______. *Ludwig Börne: A Memorial.* Edited and translated by Jeffrey Sammons. Woodbridge: Camden House, 2006.

______. *The Harz Journey and Selected Poems.* Edited and translated by Ritchie Robertson. London: Penguin Books, 2006.

Hermand, Jost, and Robert Holub, eds. *Heinrich Heine's Contested Identities: Politics, Religion, and Nationalism in Nineteenth-Century Germany.* New York: Peter Lang, 1999.

Hoffman, Christhard. "From Heinrich Heine to Isidore Kracauer: The Frankfurt Ghetto in German-Jewish Historical Culture and Historiography." *Jewish Culture and History* 10, no. 2–3 (2008): 45–64.

Howells, W. D. "Henry James, Jr." *The Century Magazine* 25, no. 1 (November 1882): 25–9.

Hoyt, J.K., and Anna Ward. *The Cyclopaedia of Practical Quotations.* New York: I.K. Funk and Co. Publishers, 1882.

Hughes, Linda. "Discoursing of Xantippe: Amy Levy, Classical Scholarship, and Print Culture." *Philological Quarterly* 88, no. 3 (2009): 259–81.

Hunt, Linda. "Amy Levy and the 'Jewish Novel': Representing Jewish Life in the Victorian Period." *Studies in the Novel* 26, no. 3 (Fall 1994): 1–16.

Ingoldsby, Thomas. *The Ingoldsby Legends or Myths and Marvels.* London: Richard Bentley & Son, 1879.

Jebb, R. C., ed. and trans. *Sophocles: The Ajax.* London: Rivingtons, c. 1880.

Joskowicz, Ari. "Heinrich Heine's Transparent Masks: Denominational Politics and the Poetics of Emancipation in Nineteenth-Century Germany and France." *German Studies Review* 34, no. 1 (2011): 69–88.

Jusova, Iveta. *The New Woman and the Empire.* Columbus: Ohio State University Press, 2005.

______, and Dan Reyes. "Edward Said, Reuben Sachs, and Victorian Zionism." *Social Text* 24, no. 2 (2006): 35–46.

Lask, Beth Zion. "Amy Levy." *Transactions of the Jewish Historical Society of England* 11 (1928): 168–89.

Leighton, Angela. "'Because Men Made the Laws': The Fallen Woman and the Woman Poet." *Victorian Poetry* 27, no. 2 (Summer 1989): 109–27.

Lennartz, Norbert. "Oscar Wilde's 'The Sphinx'–A Dramatic Monologue of the Dandy as a Young Man?" *Philological Quarterly* 83, no. 4 (Fall 2004): 415–29.

Levenson, Alan. "Invidious Distinctions: Hebraism and Hellenism in Heinrich Heine and Matthew Arnold." *Jewish Quarterly Review* 110, no. 1 (Winter 2020): 102–6.

Ludlow, Elizabeth. "Christina Rossetti, Amy Levy, and the Composition of Roundels in Late-Victorian Bloomsbury: Poetic Snapshots of Urban Subjects," *English Literature in Transition* 56, no. 1 (2013): 83–103.

Mather, R. H., ed. and trans. *The Prometheus Bound of Aeschylus*. Boston: John Allyn, 1883.

Maurier, George du. "Female Clubs v. Matrimony." *Punch's Almanack for 1878* 74 (December 14, 1877): no page number.

McDermott, Emily. *Euripides' Medea: The Incarnation of Disorder*. University Park: Pennsylvania State University Press, 1989.

Medd, Jodie, ed. *The Cambridge Companion to Lesbian Literature*. Cambridge: Cambridge University Press, 2015.

Melnyk, Julie, ed. *Women's Theology in Nineteenth-Century Britain: Transfiguring the Faith of Their Fathers*. New York: Garland Publishing, 1998.

Minsloff, Sarah. "Amy Levy and Identity Criticism: A Review of Recent Work." *Literature Compass* 4, no. 4 (2007): 1318–29.

Miron, Dan. *From Continuity to Contiguity: Toward a New Jewish Literary Thinking*. Stanford: Stanford University Press, 2010.

Murphy, Jessica. "'"[T]he World's a Beast, and I Hate It!"': *Naturalism in Amy Levy's* The Romance of a Shop." *Studies in American Naturalism* 15, no. 1 (Summer, 2020): 75–91.

New, Melvyn, ed. *The Complete Novels and Selected Writings of Amy Levy, 1861–1889*. Gainesville: University Press of Florida, 1993.

Nord, Deborah Epstein. "Dickens's 'Jewish Question': Pariah Capitalism and the Way Out." *Victorian Literature and Culture* 39 (2011): 27–45

______. "'Neither Pairs nor Odd': Female Community in Late Nineteenth-Century London." *Signs* 15, no. 4 (Summer, 1990): 733–54.

______. *Walking the Victorian Streets: Women, Representation, and the City*. Ithaca: Cornell University Press, 1995.

Perrey, Beate. *Schumann's Dichterliebe and Early Romantic Poetics: Fragmentation of Desire*. Cambridge: Cambridge University Press, 2002.

Peters, George. "'Jeder Reiche ist ein Judas Ischariot': Heinrich Heine and the Emancipation of the Jews." *Monatshefte* 104, no. 2 (2012): 209–31.

Petuchowski, Elizabeth, ed. *The Rabbi of Bacherach and Other Stories*. Princeton: Markus Wiener Publishers, 2014.

Pick, Daniel. *Svengali's Web: The Alien Enchanter in Modern Culture*. New Haven: Yale University Press, 2000.

Pines, Noam. "Life in the Valley: Figures of Dehumanization in Heinrich Heine's 'Prinzessin Sabbat.'" *Prooftexts* 33, no. 1 (2013): 25–47.

Prawer, S.S. *Heine's Jewish Comedy: A Study of His Portraits of Jews and Judaism*. Oxford: Clarendon Press, 1983.

Prell, Riv-Ellen. "The Dilemma of Women's Equality in the History of Reform Judaism." *Judaism* 30, no. 4 (Fall 1981): 418–26.

______. "The Vision of Woman in Classical Reform Judaism." *Journal of the American Academy of Religion* 50, no. 4 (Dec. 1982): 575–89.

Pullen, Christine. *The Woman Who Dared: A Biography of Amy Levy*. Kingston: Kingston University Press, 2010.

Radford, Ernest, ed. and trans. *Translations from Heine, and Other Verses*. Oxford: Oxford University Press, 1882.

Read, Donald. *The Age of Urban Democracy: England 1868–1914*. Abingdon: Routledge, 1994.

Robertson, John, ed. *Poems, Essays, and Fragments*. By James Thomson. London: A. & H. Bradlaugh Bonner, 1892.

Rochelson, Meri-Jane. "Jews, Gender and Genre in Late-Victorian England: Amy Levy's *Reuben Sachs*." *Women's Studies* 25 (1996): 311–28.

Roshwald, Mordecai. "Heinrich Heine: The Predicament of a Cultural Pluralist." *Modern Age* 53, no. 1 (Winter/Spring, 2011): 29–40.

Ruskin, John. "*Fiction–Fair and Foul*: V. The Two Servants." *The Nineteenth Century: A Monthly Review* 10, no. 56 (October 1881): 516–31.

______. *Mornings in Florence: Being Simple Studies of Christian Art, for English Travellers*, 6 Vols (Orpington: Grant Allen, 1875–1877).

______. *The Seven Lamps of Architecture*. New York: John Wiley, 1849.

Russo, Stephanie, and Lee O'Brien. "Sex, Sisters and Work: Mary Robinson's The Natural Daughter and Amy Levy's Romance of a Shop." *Women's Writing* 28, no. 1 (2021): 37–58.

Sammons, Jeffrey. "Heine's *Rabbi von Bacherach*: The Unresolved Tensions." *The German Quarterly* 37, no. 1 (April 1964): 26–38.

______. *Heinrich Heine: A Modern Biography*. Princeton: Princeton University Press, 1979.

Sappho. *The Poetry of Sappho*. Edited and translated by Jim Powell. Oxford: Oxford University Press, 2019.

Scheinberg, Cynthia. "Canonizing the Jew: Amy Levy's Challenge to Victorian Poetic Identity." *Victorian Studies* 39 (1996): 173–200.

______. "Recasting 'Sympathy and Judgement': Amy Levy, Women Poets, and the Victorian Dramatic Monologue." *Victorian Poetry* 35, no. 2 (Summer, 1997): 173–91.

______. *Women's Poetry and Religion in Victorian England: Jewish Identity and Christian Culture*. Cambridge: Cambridge University Press, 2002.

Sharot, Stephen. "Reform and Liberal Judaism in London: 1840–1940." *Jewish Social Studies* 41, no. 3/4 (Summer/Fall 1979): 211–28.

Simcox, Edith. "The Capacity of Women." *The Nineteenth Century: A Monthly Review* no. 127 (September 1887): 391–402.

Simonsen, Cecile Schroder. "A Spatial Expansion of a Pocket-Size Homeland: Heinrich Heine's Construction of Jewish Space." *Partial Answers* 14, no. 2 (2016): 303–21.

Skolnik, Jonathan. *Jewish Pasts, German Fictions: History, Memory, and Minority Culture in Germany, 1824–1955*. Stanford: Stanford University Press, 2014.

Sover, Arie. *Jewish Humor: An Outcome of Historical Experience, Survival and Wisdom*. Newcastle: Cambridge Scholars Publishing, 2021.

Stokes, John, ed. *Eleanor Marx (1855–1898): Life, Work, Contacts*. Aldershot: Ashgate, 2000.

Styler, Rebecca. *Literary Theology by Women Writers of the Nineteenth Century*. Farnham: Ashgate, 2010.

Swinburne, Algernon Charles. *Poems and Ballads*. London: John Camden Hotten, 1866.

Thackeray, William Makepeace. *Thackeray's Complete Works: The Adventures of Philip*. Boston: Estes and Lauriat, 1883.

Thomson, James. *The City of Dreadful Night and Other Poems*. London: Reeves and Turner, 1880.

Tonkin, Maggie, *et al.*, eds. *Changing the Victorian Subject*. Adelaide: University of Adelaide Press, 2014.

Tynan, Katherine. *Memories*. Edinburgh: The Edinburgh Press, 1924.

Umansky, Ellen. *Lily Montagu and the Advancement of Liberal Judaism: from Vision to Vocation*. New York: Edwin Mellen Press, 1983.

Vadillo, Ana Parejo. "Cosmopolitan Disturbances: Amy Levy in Dresden." *Forum for Modern Language Studies* 53, no. 3 (July 2017): 325–37.

______. "New Woman Poets and the Culture of the *Salon* at the *Fin de Siècle*." *Women: A Cultural Review* 10, no. 1 (1999): 340–46.

______. *Women Poets and Urban Aestheticism: Passengers of Modernity*. Basingstoke: Palgrave Macmillan, 2005.

Valman, Nadia, ed. *Jewish Women Writers in Britain*. Detroit: Wayne State University Press, 2014.

______. "Semitism and Criticism: Victorian Anglo-Jewish Literary History." *Victorian Literature and Culture* 27, no. 1 (1999): 235–48.

______. *The Jewess in Nineteenth-Century British Culture*. Cambridge: Cambridge University Press, 2007.

______, and Naomi Hetherington, eds. *Amy Levy: Critical Essays*. Athens: Ohio University Press, 2010.

Villalba-Lázaro, Marta. "Radicalizing the Myth: Amy Levy's Medea, the (Un)Assimilated Jewish Victorian Woman." *Women in Judaism: A Multidisciplinary Journal* 15, no. 2 (2018): 1–30.

Virdee, Satnam. "Socialist Antisemitism and its Discontents in England, 1884–98." *Patterns of Prejudice* 51, no. 3–4 (2017): 356–73.

Wallas, Ada. "The Poetry of Amy Levy." *The Academy*, August 12, 1899, 162–3.

Wanczyk, David. "Framing Gertrude: Photographic Narration and the Subjectivity of the Artist-Observer in Levy's *The Romance of a Shop*." *Victorian Literature and Culture* 43, no. 1 (2015): 131–48.

Weisman, Karen. "Playing with Figures: Amy Levy and the Forms of Cancellation." *Criticism* 43, no. 1 (Winter 2001): 59–79.

Whittington-Egan, Richard. "Amy Levy: A Tragic Victorian Novelist." *Contemporary Review* 280, no. 1632 (January 2002): 40–6.

Wilde, Oscar. "Amy Levy." *Woman's World* 3 (1890): 51–52.

Wilson, Cheryl. "Politicizing Dance in Late-Victorian Women's Poetry." *Victorian Poetry* 46, no. 2 (2008): 191–205.

The fonts used in this book are from the Arno family

The Library of the Jewish People